HOUSEHOLD ACCOUNTS AND DISBURSEMENT BOOKS OF ROBERT DUDLEY, EARL OF LEICESTER, 1558–1561, 1584–1586

HOUSEHOLD ACCOUNTS AND DISBURSEMENT BOOKS OF ROBERT DUDLEY, EARL OF LEICESTER, 1558–1561, 1584–1586

edited by

SIMON ADAMS

CAMDEN FIFTH SERIES
Volume 6

CAMBRIDGE
UNIVERSITY PRESS

FOR THE ROYAL HISTORICAL SOCIETY
University College London, Gower Street, London WC1E 6BT

Published by the Press Syndicate of the University of Cambridge
The Pitt Building, Trumpington Street, Cambridge CB2 1RP
40 West 20th Street, New York, NY 10011–4211, USA
10 Stamford Road, Oakleigh, Melbourne 3166, Australia

First published 1995

A catalogue record for this book is available from the British Library

Library of Congress cataloging in publication data applied for

ISBN 0 521 55156 0 hardback

SUBSCRIPTIONS. The serial publications of the Royal Historical Society, *Royal Historical Society Transactions* (ISSN 0080–4401), Camden Fifth Series (ISSN 0960–1163) volumes and volumes of the Guides and Handbooks (ISSN 0080–4398) may be purchased together on annual subscription. The 1995 subscription price (which includes postage but not VAT) is £35 (US$56 in the USA, Canada and Mexico) and includes Camden Fifth Series, volumes 5 and 6 (published in July and December) and Transactions Sixth Series, volume 5 (published in December). There is no volume in the Guides and Handbooks series in 1995. Japanese prices (including ASP delivery) are available from Kinokuniya Company Ltd, P.O. Box 55, Chitose, Tokyo 156, Japan. EU subscribers (outside the UK) who are not registered for VAT should add VAT at their country's rate. VAT registered subscribers should provide their VAT registration number.

Subscription orders, which must be accompanied by payment, may be sent to a bookseller, subscription agent or direct to the publisher: Cambridge University Press, The Edinburgh Building, Shaftesbury Road, Cambridge CB2 2RU, UK; or in the USA, Canada and Mexico: Cambridge University Press, 40 West 20th Street, New York, NY 10011–4211, USA. Copies of the publications for subscribers in the USA, Canada and Mexico are sent by air to New York to arrive with minimum delay.

SINGLE VOLUMES AND BACK VOLUMES. A list of Royal Historical Society volumes available from Cambridge University Press may be obtained from the Humanities Marketing Department at the address above.

Printed and bound in Great Britain by Butler & Tanner Ltd, Frome and London

CONTENTS

Acknowledgements   vii
Abbreviations   ix
Introduction   1

Part I.   Household Accounts and Disbursement Books   37
A.   The Account of William Chauncy, 1558–9 (Longleat,
    Dudley Papers XIV)   39
    Textual Notes   110
B.   The Account of Richard Ellis, 1559–61 (Longleat,
    Dudley Papers XV)   113
    Textual Notes   175
C.   Disbursement Book 1584–86 (Evelyn MS 258b)   177
    Textual Notes   365
D.   Disbursement Book 1585–87 (The Staunton Manuscript)   367
    Textual Notes   374
Appendix I.   Amy Dudley in 1559–60: the Identity of William
            Hyde   377
Appendix II.   Leicester's Departure for the Netherlands Sep-
            tember–December 1585   385

Part II.   Household Lists   397
A.   The Book of my Lords Servantts Wages and Boord Wages,
    1559–1561   399
    Textual Notes   418
B.   Bill for Livery [1559]   419
C.   Bill for Livery, 1560   422
D.   Bill for Badges [1567–8]   423
E.   Bill for Livery Cloth [c.1567–8]   426
F.   A Note of the Number which are to attend your Lordship
    in your Journey into the Low Countries [1585]   429
    Textual Notes   429
G.   The Names of your Excellency's Howsehold Servants, 21
    July [1587]   430
    Textual Notes   439
H.   Household Embarkation List, November 1587   440
    Textual Notes   447
I.   The Proceeding at the Earl of Leicester's Funeral
    [10 October 1588]   448
J.   The Funeral of the Earl of Leicester, 10 October 1588   450
    Textual Notes   459

Index of Servants	461
Glossary	489
General Index	491

ACKNOWLEDGEMENTS

The present volume has taken me six years to bring to press, and it rests on a further twenty years of research. Over that period I have incurred a great number of debts, only a few of which can be acknowledged here.

My primary debt is to the kindness of the owners or custodians of the documents published in this volume. Dudley Papers XIV and XV and the ancillary lists are edited with the permission of the Marquess of Bath, Longleat House, Warminster, Wiltshire. Permission to publish Evelyn MS 258b was first granted by the Evelyn Trustees and the Dean and Students of Christ Church, Oxford, and has since been confirmed by the Keeper of Manuscripts of the British Library, who has also given permission for the printing of the two Cotton Manuscripts. The Keeper of Western Manuscripts of the Bodleian Library, Oxford, has given permission for the printing of MS Ashmole 818, fo. 38; the Archivist to the College Of Arms the extract from Sir William Dethick's Book of Funerals; and the Folger Shakespeare Library, Washington D.C., the extracts from the Halliwell-Phillipps scrapbooks.

I should also like to thank the Marquess of Salisbury, the Marquess of Anglesey, the Viscount De L'Isle and Mr J.R. More-Molyneux for permission to consult and cite papers from their muniments, and the custodians and staffs of the numerous libraries, archives and record offices mentioned in the notes for the access I have been granted over the years. I should particularly like to record my thanks to Dr Kate Harris, Librarian and Archivist to the Marquess of Bath, Mr John Wing, Assistant Librarian of Christ Church, Mr Robert York, Archivist to the College of Arms, Mr G.M.D. Booth of the Warwickshire County Record Office and Mr W.H. Liversedge, Hon. Archivist to Abingdon Town Council, for their generosity with their time and assistance.

The transcription and editing of these manuscripts would not have been possible without the generous financial assistance of the British Academy, the Carnegie Trust for the Universities of Scotland, the Wolfson Trust, and the History Department of the University of Strathclyde.

On a more personal level, I owe a particular debt of gratitude to Dr Sally-Beth Maclean, Executive Editor of *Records of Early English Drama*, for her generosity in waiving any moral claim to the publishing of Evelyn MS 258b, which was her discovery. This work also owes much to the scholarly assistance of many people over many years. Some specific debts are acknowledged in the notes, but I should like to record here my thanks to Dr H.R. Woudhuysen of University College, London, and Mr A.J.A. Malkiewicz of Edinburgh University, who have shared without reserve the fruits of their extensive research into Leicester and the Dudleys. To Dr Blair Worden and Professor Michael Jones, the successive literary directors of the Royal Historical Society, I owe much, both for their encouragement and, in the case of Professor Jones, for his forbearance as well. Lastly, but by no means least, I should also like to use this occasion to thank Professor Patrick Collinson for his support; I trust he will enjoy the outcome.

Edinburgh
September 1995

ABBREVIATIONS

Abbreviations are normally short titles, but authors or editors have been used where confusion may otherwise result. References in calendars and other serial publications are to pages and not entries.

AGS	Archivo General de Simancas
E	Sección de Estado
AMAE	Archives du Ministère des Affaires Etrangères, Paris
CPA	Correspondence Politique, Angleterre
CPH	Correspondence Politique, Hollande
ARA	Algemeen Rijksarchief, The Hague
RvS	Raad van State
BIHR	Borthwick Institute of Historical Research, York
Bindoff	S.T. Bindoff (ed.), *The History of Parliament: The House of Commons 1509–1558* (1982)
BL	British Library
Add. MSS	Additional Manuscripts
Harl. MSS	Harleian Manuscripts
Black Book	T. Kemp (ed.), *The Black Book of Warwick* (Warwick [1889]).
Bodl.	Bodleian Library
MS Rawl.	Rawlinson Manuscripts
BN,	Bibliothèque Nationale, Paris
VCC	MSS Cinq Cents Colbert
BRL	Birmingham Reference Library
HH MSS	Lyttelton of Hagley Hall Papers
CA	College of Arms
CCC	Corpus Christi College, Cambridge
CKS	Centre for Kentish Studies
U1475	Manuscripts of Viscount De L'Isle (Penshurst Place)
CPR	*Calendar of the Patent Rolls*
CSPD	*Calendar of State Papers, Domestic Series*
CSPF	*Calendar of State Papers, Foreign Series, Elizabeth I*
CSPSc	*Calendar of State Papers relating to Scotland and Mary, Queen of Scots*
CSPSp	*Calendar of Letters and State Papers ... preserved*

	in the Archives of Simancas
Chambers	E.K. Chambers, *The Elizabethan Stage* (Oxford, 1923)
CUL	Cambridge University Library
DP	Longleat House, Dudley Papers
'Dudley Clientèle'	S. Adams, 'The Dudley Clientèle 1553–1563', in G.W. Bernard (ed.), *The Tudor Nobility* (1992), pp. 241–65.
E.H.R.	*English Historical Review*
EUL	Edinburgh University Library
H.-P. Coll.	Halliwell-Phillipps Collection
Evelyn MSS	Evelyn Papers, formerly at Christ Church, Oxford, now in the British Library
FSL	Folger Shakespeare Library, Washington D.C.
'Feria Dispatch'	M.J. Rodríguez-Salgado and S. Adams (edd.), 'The Dispatch of the Count of Feria to Philip II of 14 November 1558', *Camden Miscellany XXVIII* (Camden Soc. 4th ser., xxix, 1984), 302–43
HEHL,	Henry E. Huntington Library, Pasadena
EL	Ellesmere Papers
HA	Hastings Papers
Hamilton Papers	J. Bain (ed.), *The Hamilton Papers* (Edinburgh, 1890–2)
Hasler	P.W. Hasler (ed.), *The History of Parliament: The House of Commons 1558–1603* (1981)
Hatfield MSS	Manuscripts of the Marquess of Salisbury, Hatfield House
Hist MSS Comm	Historical Manuscripts Commission
'House of Commons'	S. Adams, 'The Dudley Clientele and the House of Commons 1559–1586, *Parliamentary History*, viii (1989), 216–39
ITL	Inner Temple Library
JRL	John Rylands Library, Manchester
King's Works	H.M. Colvin (ed.), *The History of the King's Works* (1965–82)
Leic. Corres.	J. Bruce (ed.), *Correspondence of Robert Dudley, Earl of Leycester* (Camden Soc., xxvii, 1844)
'Leic. Pap. I'	S. Adams, 'The Papers of Robert Dudley, Earl of Leicester. I. The Browne-Evelyn Collection', *Archives*, xx (1992), 63–85
'Leic. Pap. II'	*Ibid.*, 'II. The Atye-Cotton Collection', *Archives*, xx (1993), 131–44

'Leic. Pap. III'

Lettenhove

Lodge

Lords Journals
LPL
Machyn

NLW
'North Wales'

'Outbreak of the
Elizabethan Naval
War'

Paget Papers

Pepys MSS

PML
PRO
  C
  E
  LC4

  LR
  PROB/11

  REQ
  SC6

  SO
  SP
'Puritan Crusade'

Ibid., 'III. The Countess of Leicester's
Collection', *Archives*, xxii (April 1996), 1–26
J.M.B.C. Kervyn de Lettenhove (ed.),
*Relations Politiques des Pays-Bas et de l'Angleterre
sous le règne de Philippe II* (Brussels, 1882–1900)
E. Lodge (ed.), *Illustrations of British History*
(1791)
Journals of the House of Lords (1846)
Lambeth Palace Library
J.G. Nichols (ed.), *The Diary of Henry Machyn
... A.D.1550 to A.D. 1563* (Camden Soc., xlii,
1848)
National Library of Wales
S. Adams, 'The Gentry of North Wales and
the Earl of Leicester's Expedition to the
Netherlands, 1585–1586', *Welsh History
Review*, vii (1974), 129–47
S. Adams, 'The Outbreak of the Elizabethan
Naval War against the Spanish Empire', in
M.J. Rodríguez-Salgado and S. Adams
(edd.), *England, Spain and the Gran Armada
1585–1604* (Edinburgh, 1991), pp. 45–69
Manuscripts of the Marquess of Anglesey,
Plas Newydd, copied by the Staffordshire
RO
Pepys Manuscripts, Magdalene College,
Cambridge
Pierpoint Morgan Library, New York
Public Record Office
Chancery
Exchequer
Lord Chamberlain's Department: Statute
Staple Recognizances
Land Revenue Department
Prerogative Court of Canterbury:
Registers of Wills
Court of Requests
Special Collections:
Ministers' and Receivers' Accounts
Signet Office
State Papers
S. Adams, 'A Puritan Crusade? The
Composition of the Earl of Leicester's
Expedition to the Netherlands', in P.

	Hoftijzer (ed.), *The Dutch in Crisis, 1585–1588* (Leiden, 1988), pp. 7–34
RO	Record Office
SBTRO	Shakespeare's Birthplace Trust Record Office, Stratford-upon-Avon
Second Part of a Reg	A. Peel (ed.), *The Seconde Parte of Register* (Cambridge, 1915)
Sidney Papers	A. Collins (ed.), *Letters and Memorials of State … by Sir Henry Sidney* (1746)
STC	Short Title Catalogue
Teulet	A. Teulet (ed.), *Relations Politiques de la France avec l'Ecosse au xvi siècle* (Paris, 1862)
UCNW	University Collge of North Wales Library
V.C.H.	Victoria County History
Warrender Papers	A.I. Cameron (ed.), *The Warrender Papers* (Scottish History Society, 3rd ser., xviii-xix, 1931–2)
WCRO	Warwickshire County Record Office
CR1600/LH	Leicester's Hospital Deposit
'West Midlands'	S. Adams, ' "Because I am of that countrye & mynde to plant myself there", Robert Dudley, Earl of Leicester and the West Midlands' *Midland History*, xx (1995), 21–74
Wright	T. Wright (ed.), *Queen Elizabeth and her Times* (1838)
*	Signifies an entry in the 'Index of Servants'

ABBREVIATIONS OF MAJOR DUDLEY FAMILY DOCUMENTS

The following documents yield much miscellaneous information and will be referred to extensively. To avoid repeated manuscript references they will be cited in summary fashion. They are listed in chronological order.

The Duke of Northumberland's Household. A list of Northumberland's servants is included among the documents relating to the confiscation of his property by the Crown in 1553, PRO, LR 2/118.

The Duchess of Northumberland's Will. The registered copy is PRO, PROB 11/37 [PCC 26 More]/194-5v; an abbreviated and frequently inaccurate transcription is printed in *Sidney Papers*, i, 33-6.

The Duchess of Northumberland's Debts. The Hales Owen muniments in the Hagley Hall MSS in the BRL are an extremely valuable source for the Dudleys in the late 1550s. A schedule of the Duchess's debts is attached to HH MS 351613, an agreement of 20 November 1555 in which Leicester's brothers Lord Ambrose and Lord Henry assigned their interests in the Hales Owen estate to him, under the condition that he repay the Duchess's debts. MS 351621 contains a related schedule of annuities charged to the Hales Owen estate dated July 1560.

Funeral of Amy Dudley. The attendants at Amy Dudley's funeral in Oxford on 22 September 1560 can be found in CA, Arundel MS XXXV (The Booke of Burials of Nobilitie, 1559-1570), fos. 18-21, and Bodl., MS Dugdale T. 2, fo. 7 (printed in *The Gentleman's Magazine*, new ser. xxxiv (July-Dec. 1850), 123-5).

KGB. The 'Kenilworth Game Book', a list of deer in certain of the parks of Kenilworth, deceased either through hunting or natural causes between 1568 and 1578, now CKS, U1475/E93. This provides a valuable record of those who hunted at Kenilworth in those years and is discussed in 'West Midlands' where it is argued that it was kept by Anthony Dockwra*.

1582 Will. Longleat, DP Box III, art. 56, a will drawn up by Leicester on 30 January 1581/2 prior to his embarkation to escort the Duke of Anjou to Antwerp.

The Countess's Jointure. The indenture for the jointure of the Countess of Leicester (15 July 1585) is DP Box II, art. 15.

Funeral of the Lord of Denbigh. The funeral list of Leicester's son Robert, Baron of Denbigh (1 August 1584) is found in CA, Sir William Dethick's Book of Funerals of the Nobility 1586-1603, i, fo. 8.

Netherlands Lists. Lists of the gentlemen who accompanied

Leicester to the Netherlands in December 1585, discussed on pp. 22–3.

Netherlands guard. BL, Cotton MS Galba C VIII, fos. 96v-7, a list of Leicester's guard compiled by Henry Goodere, captain of the guard on 12 January 1586. It is divided into 'such as be ordinary servants in your house' (thirteen), 'your Excellency's old retainers' (twelve), and 'those preferred by others' (twenty-four).

Sidney Funeral. The list of attendants at Sir Philip Sidney's funeral (17 February 1587) is printed in J.A. van Dorsten *et al.* (edd.), *Sir Philip Sidney: 1586 and the Creation of a Legend* (Leiden, 1986), pp. 52–6.

1587 Will. Leicester's last will, drawn up at Middelburg in July and August 1587. The original is WCRO, CR1600/LH4, the registered copy PRO, PROB 11/73 [PCC 1 Leicester]/2–4. There are several other notarised contemporary copies, and it is printed reasonably accurately in *Sidney Papers*, i, 70–5. The problems of the dating and the copies are discussed in 'Leic. Pap. III', 3.

Brevis Abstract. The *Brevis Abstract et Collectio Redd et revenue ... Robt. Comit. Leicester* is a summary rental of Leicester's estates c. 1588. It survives in two copies, CKS, U1475/E90 (imperfect) and DP III, fos. 69–79v. Discussed in 'Leic. Pap. III', 13.

GVE. The General View of the Evidences, a posthumous (c. 1588–89) schedule of Leicester's muniments of title and other major evidences, of which two copies survive, DP XX and CKS, U1475/E91. Discussed in 'Leic. Pap. III', 12–3.

Leicester's Debts. These are included in the notarised copy of his probate inventory, BL, Harl. Roll D 35.

Sir Robert Dudley Case. The surviving depositions of the witnesses in the Star Chamber case arising from the Countess of Leicester's contesting of Sir Robert Dudley's claim of legitimacy in 1604–5 are found in DP Boxes VI-VIII and CKS, U1475/L2/1–4.

INTRODUCTION

The four documents published in Part I of this volume comprise, as far as is known, the surviving household accounts of Robert Dudley, Earl of Leicester (1532–88).[1] The earlier in date are two full household accounts, the first covering the period 20 December 1558 to 20 December 1559, and the second the period 22 December 1559 to 30 April 1561. They are presently Volumes XIV and XV of the Dudley Papers in the Marquess of Bath's collection of manuscripts at Longleat House. The third document is a large fragment of what is best described as a wardrobe disbursement book. The earliest surviving leaf is headed 10 and 17 April 1584, but the fragment thereafter runs consecutively from 2 October 1584 to 13 December 1585 and concludes with two sets of entries covering 21–31 March and 26 May–30 June 1586. It was discovered among the Evelyn Papers in 1986 and given the catalogue number MS 258b. The Evelyn Papers were then deposited in the library of Christ Church, Oxford, but in the spring of 1995 the collection as a whole was sold to the British Library, where it is presently being re-catalogued.[2] The fourth document is what appears to have been another wardrobe disbursement book, covering the period 11 December 1585 to 8 April 1587. This volume was destroyed in 1879 in the Birmingham Reference Library fire, but prior to this disaster two sets of transcriptions had been made of a number of entries from the pages covering December 1585 and the early months of 1586.[3]

Household accounts of the nobility and greater gentry survive in considerable quantity from the fourteenth century onwards, and a number have been published in various forms.[4] Although Evelyn MS

---

[1] For the sake of convenience he will be referred to throughout as Leicester, although he was not created Earl of Leicester until 29 Sept. 1564.

[2] Information from the Department of Manuscripts suggests that the cataloguing will not be completed before the end of 1996, and that Additional MS numbers will not be assigned till then. The eventual catalogue will, however, include cross-references to the Christ Church Evelyn Papers catalogue numbers, which perforce are those employed here.

[3] These are, it should be admitted, the only ones known to me, but no others have been detected by the WCRO, the SBTRO or the BRL, the obvious repositories for any antiquarian notes of local provenance.

[4] See in general K. Mertes, *The English Noble Household 1250–1600* (Oxford, 1988), esp. Appendix A, 'A List of Household Records, c.1250–1600', pp. 194–215. The Elizabethan section is not the strongest part of this list, however, for it omits not only Leicester's accounts but also those of Sir Henry Sidney and the Earls of Essex and Hertford. This work has now been superseded for the medieval period by C.M. Woolgar (ed.), *Household Accounts from Medieval England* (British Academy Studies in Social and Economic History, xvii-xviii, Oxford, 1992–3), but the catalogue of accounts published here (ii, 691–726) ends at 1500.

258b was discovered only recently, the existence of the two Longleat volumes has been public knowledge since the 1870s, and both sets of transcriptions from the fourth volume are in print. Yet such is the potential importance of the united corpus of Leicester's accounts for Elizabethan history that the present edition needs little justification. Not only do the accounts provide a mass of biographical information, but they also make possible the close analysis of the composition of Leicester's household, a subject of considerable wider interest. To assist in the identification of the personnel of the household, the accounts have been supplemented by the surviving lists of the household (Part II), and by a biographical index of the servants referred to. These will be discussed in further detail below.

Of even greater interest perhaps is the almost unique insight into the daily life and routines of the Elizabethan Court that these accounts provide. However large its overall quantity, Elizabethan household and other personal documentation has survived, until the nineteenth century at least, largely by accident.[5] If some Privy Councillors and courtiers – Sir William Petre or Sir Henry Sidney, for example – have left extensive household documentation, others, and among them the most important (Sir Francis Walsingham and Sir Christopher Hatton, for example), have left practically no personal material at all. Despite the vast scale of his surviving papers, only two of Lord Burghley's household account books are extant, one for 1554–57 and the other for 1575–77.[6] Leicester – ironically enough, given his reputation as the most mysterious of the greater Elizabethans – has in fact left more household documentation than the great majority of his peers, although its scale has been concealed by the radical dispersal of his papers. Together with these accounts, we also have eleven volumes of household inventories – the largest number for any Elizabethan – and several miscellaneous accounts.[7] His nearest rival among the greater courtiers is the 2nd Earl of Essex, five of whose accounts survive.[8] In the absence of comparable material from his colleagues, it can be argued that as a source for the Court Leicester's accounts are possibly second only in importance to the Treasurer of the Chamber's account books.[9]

[5] Cf. Woolgar's comments on the survival of medieval household accounts, *Household Accounts*, i, 5–7.

[6] The earlier Burghley account is BL, Lansdowne MS 118; the later (which has been badly damaged) Hatfield MS 226. See the discussion in C. Read, 'Lord Burghley's Household Accounts', *Economic History Review*, 2nd ser. ix (1956), 343–8. There are also some summary accounts.

[7] Listed in 'Leic. Pap. III', Appendices I–IV.

[8] They are now found in Vols. II, III and V of the Devereux Papers at Longleat House. These reached Longleat (coincidentally) by the same means as Leicester's papers.

[9] E.g. BL, Harl. MS 1641, the account book of Sir Thomas Heneage for 1585–86, to which reference is made in the notes. The accounts rendered by the Treasurer to the Exchequer (PRO, E 351/541–3) are only summaries. Officers and servants of the Crown

THE DOCUMENTS: PROVENANCE

Since these documents do not form part of a single family collection, some account of their provenance is necessary, though this need only be a summary one.[10] The ultimate provenance of all four volumes was Leicester's central household archive, which was probably located in Leicester House (Essex House after 1593). There is some evidence that his papers as a whole were consolidated, examined and possibly sorted after his death in 1588 in order to facilitate the settlement of his estate.[11] The two accounts now at Longleat were among that section of his papers retained by his widow (Lettice, Countess of Leicester and dowager Countess of Essex) either at Essex House or at the manor house of Drayton Bassett (Staffs.), which became her own home in the mid-1590s.[12] On the Countess's death in 1634 her estate and possessions descended to her grandson, the 3rd Earl of Essex, and then to his sister Frances, Duchess of Somerset. On the Duchess's death in 1674 the Leicester papers (among others) came into the possession of her executor, her grand-daughter's husband, Thomas Thynne (later 1st Viscount Weymouth), either during the subsequent sale and destruction of Essex House or during Thynne's own residence at Drayton Bassett in the late 1670s. Thynne inherited the Longleat estate in 1682 and moved there from Drayton Bassett fairly soon thereafter. The various papers he had accumulated he probably brought with him at this stage.

The two account books were discovered by Canon J.E. Jackson during his sorting of the muniments at Longleat House in 1863–64. His searches also brought to light the second of the two surviving letters by Lady Amy Dudley (Amy Robsart), and this discovery inspired him to trace all material relating to her in the Longleat collection. In 1878 he published an article about her in which he included relevant extracts from the accounts.[13] Further brief summaries of the accounts can also be found in the recent Historical Manuscripts Commission calendar of the Dudley Papers.[14]

and departments of the Court are capitalised to distinguish them from possible equivalents in Leicester's household.

[10] For a fuller discussion and more extensive references, see 'Leic. Pap. I–III'.

[11] For Leicester House, see below, p. 26. The settlement of Leicester's estate is discussed in 'Leic. Pap. III'. There was also an 'evidence house' at Kenilworth Castle. In the case he brought against her in Chancery in 1590 (PRO, C21/ElizI/D/5/2, see below, p. 29), Sir Robert Dudley (Leicester's illegitimate son, see n. 393 to the texts) accused the Countess of Leicester *inter alia* of having papers removed from it after Leicester's death (presumably to be transported to Leicester House).

[12] These papers are the subject of 'Leic. Pap. III'.

[13] 'Amye Robsart', *Wiltshire Archaeological and Natural History Magazine*, xvii (1878), 47–93, see 84–5.

[14] Hist MSS Comm, *Calendar of the Manuscripts of the Marquess of Bath. V. Talbot, Dudley and Devereux Papers 1533–1659* (1980), 136–8, 148–51.

The two fragments require a more extensive discussion. The volumes from which they come were both part of a substantial portion of the Leicester House archive that came into the possession of Leicester's former household officer (Sir) Richard Browne* after 1588.[15] About the time of Leicester's death Browne entered the Queen's service as a Clerk of the Board of Green Cloth, and as an officer of the Household obtained a long lease of Sayes Court, near Deptford, part of the manor of Greenwich. In 1652–3 Sayes Court became the residence of John Evelyn, who had married Browne's great-granddaughter. The quite extensive 'Browne Papers' Evelyn incorporated in his own library, which he transported to the Evelyn family house at Wotton (Surrey) when he moved there in 1694. In 1950 the Evelyn Papers at Wotton were deposited in Christ Church Library. At that stage the 1584–86 disbursement book had not been identified or catalogued and it was filed among the uncatalogued Evelyn Papers until 1986 when it was discovered by Dr Sally-Beth MacLean, the Executive Editor of *Records of Early English Drama* (REED).[16]

The 1585–87 disbursement book was one of a number of manuscripts (the full extent is unknown) removed from the library at Wotton by William Upcott between 1813 and 1818. It is entered in Upcott's published library catalogue of 1836, together with two other volumes of Leicester's accounts, a household account for 1570–71 and a provisioning account for 1585–86, both also of undoubted Wotton provenance.[17] The 1585–87 book and the 1570–71 account were lots 53 and 54 in the auction of Upcott's manuscripts in 1846, and were purchased in the first instance by the bookseller Thomas Rodd.[18] Shortly thereafter they were obtained by William Staunton (1765–1848) of Longbridge (Wars.) and added to his extensive collection of manuscripts relating to the history of Warwickshire. The collection was inherited by his son Joseph, from whom it was purchased by Birmingham Corporation (partly through public subscription) in 1875 to initiate a local historical collection to supplement the recently-founded Shakespeare Memorial Library in the Free Reference Library. On 11 January 1879 the Reference Library was destroyed by a fire started accidentally by a workman who was

---

[15] For a full discussion of this collection and biographical notes on Browne, see 'Leic. Pap. I'. * indicates an entry in the Index of Servants.

[16] See her article, 'Leicester and the Evelyns: New Evidence for the Continental Tour of Leicester's Men', *Review of English Studies*, new ser. xxxix (1988), 487–93. I have since examined the uncatalogued Evelyn Papers myself and found no further Leicester material apart from one or two pages from a household inventory. Any other unidentified or mis-catalogued Leicester material will undoubtedly come to light during the BL's cataloguing.

[17] *Original Letters, Manuscripts and State Papers ... Collected by William Upcott* (1836), p. 30.

[18] *Catalogue of the Collection of Manuscripts and Autograph Letters formed by the Late William Upcott Esq.* (Leigh, Sotheby at Evans, 22 June 1846). The annotated copy in the BL (Pressmark 824 K. 10/2) gives the purchasers.

attempting to thaw a frozen gas pipe, and only a few volumes from its various collections were saved.[19] As well as the two accounts, the Staunton Collection contained at least three further Leicester manuscripts. One was the provisioning account for 1585–6 listed in Upcott's 1836 catalogue. Since it does not appear in the 1846 sale catalogue, Staunton presumably purchased it directly from Upcott. The other two were a 1588 revision of the Kenilworth inventory of 1584 and a copy of the Statutes of the Order of St Michael. These do not appear to have been in Upcott's collection.[20]

Both sets of transcriptions from the 1585–87 disbursement book were made before the sale of the Staunton Collection. The larger of the two was the work of the Revd Edward Hadarezer Knowles (c.1820–c.1900), who included it as illustrative material in *The Castle of Kenilworth, A Hand-book for Visitors*.[21] This is a work of some scholarship, but a slightly mysterious one, for it is quite unlike anything else Knowles published, and his reasons for writing it are unknown. Knowles spent most of his life in Cumberland, where he was a master at St Bees School in the 1850s and 1860s, and then Principal from 1871 until his retirement in 1894. In the interval (1866–71) he lived in Kenilworth, and this presumably was the period in which *The Castle of Kenilworth* was written.[22] His papers appear to have been destroyed at the time of his death, and if he made any further transcriptions from this book or any of the other manuscripts in the Staunton Collection they have not survived.

Seven entries from the book were also transcribed by the celebrated and controversial Shakespearean expert J.O. Halliwell-Phillipps (1820–89). They are of greater interest than their number would suggest, for Halliwell-Phillipps is the one Victorian scholar who is known to have worked on the manuscripts at Longbridge House, and his own vast collection of papers, notes and transcriptions, now in the Folger

[19] The circumstances of the fire are reported in detail in *The Times*, 13–15 January 1879. For other sources, see 'Leic. Pap. I', 77. The completeness of the destruction was attributed to the tardy arrival of the fire engine (though this was disputed) and frozen water mains.

[20] The former is discussed below, pp. 6–7. The latter is described as a manuscript codex of the Statutes of the Order of St Michael on vellum, autographed by Leicester on 25 Jan. 1565/6. This was the day after he was invested with the order; the statutes were probably presented to him on that occasion. The volume can be found in several early nineteenth- century sale catalogues, see 'Leic. Pap. I', 82.

[21] (Warwick, 1872), Postscript II, pp. 46–50.

[22] Knowles introduced the extracts with the note (p. 46) 'I am enabled by the kindness of Mr. Staunton of Longbridge, to give my readers a few extracts from the Book of Expences of the Earl of Leicester, in 1585–6, beginning after his arrival at Flushing.' Mr Staunton was presumably Joseph. I am extremely grateful to Mr G.M.D. Booth of the WCRO, Mr Kenneth Mount, secretary of the Cumbria Branch of the Historical Association, and my former student Mr John Rule, now of Wadham College, for their generous assistance in tracing what is known of Knowles's life and career.

Shakespeare Library and Edinburgh University Library, is an obvious possible source for further material from the Staunton Collection. Unfortunately, what evidence we can uncover of his researches is inconclusive.

In a note on the Coventry city records in his *Outlines of the Life of Shakespeare*, Halliwell-Phillipps refers to the recent destruction of the Staunton Collection, and then comments:

> In many former years, through the kind liberality of its possessor John Staunton, Esq. of Longbridge House ..., every possible facility was given me for consulting those treasures, and I have at least the consolation of believing that they included no fact of interest, bearing on the history of the poet's life, that could have eluded my researches.[23]

This would imply extensive periods of research at Longbridge, but his correspondence contains only one letter from William Staunton, and none from his son. The letter is dated 27 July 1847 and in it Staunton responds to a request to see the 'Guildbook of Knolle' with an invitation to visit Longbridge House 'any day when you might find yourself in our neighbourhood'.[24] According to the very detailed diary kept by his wife, Henrietta, Halliwell-Phillipps was then in Warwickshire, for he had gone to Warwick on 17 July to attend a meeting of the Archaeological Association. On the 24th she came out to join him and they visited and toured in the county until 2 August. In September he paid another visit to Warwickshire, this time on his own, and spent the last fortnight of the month in Stratford upon Avon and Warwick. If he took up Staunton's invitation then, it was probably on the latter occasion, for his wife, who recorded their visit to Leicester's Hospital and her husband's examination of the Black Book of Warwick in July, makes no reference to going to Longbridge House.[25]

It is possible that he had been there before, but the tone of Staunton's letter implies the opposite, and therefore any further research must have been undertaken in the 1850s. In 1854 Halliwell-Phillipps published a transcription of the 1588 revision of the 1584 Kenilworth inventory in the collection *Ancient Inventories*. He supplied no provenance for it, apart from a general note that some of the documents in the collection

---

[23] This quotation is taken from the 1st edition (Brighton, 1881), p. 101; however it is also found without amendment or addition in the much expanded 7th edition (1887), ii, 290. The 'poet' is, of course, Shakespeare, and the Coventry records the famous collection that Staunton bought from Thomas Sharp. All the sources I have consulted (see 'Leic Pap.I', 77) give the younger Staunton's christian name as Joseph.

[24] EUL, H.-P. Coll., L.O.A. 55, fo. 14. The Knowle Guild-Book was one of the few Staunton MSS to survive the fire.

[25] EUL, H.-P. Coll, MS 327 [Diary of Henrietta Halliwell-Phillipps, vol. I, 1836–56], see pp. 298–301, 307.

were copied from manuscripts 'inaccessible to the general public'.[26] It would be reasonable to assume that he employed the Staunton manuscript, but a late eighteenth-century copy of this inventory is also to be found in the Bodleian Library.[27] This volume contains numerous antiquarian notes initialled 'R.S.T.', and since Halliwell-Phillipps refers to the notes of R.S.T. 'attached to a transcript of the original MS', it is probable that this was the version he copied, though he apparently knew of the original at Longbridge.[28]

His transcriptions from the 1585–87 book survive today in the form of slips pasted in two scrapbooks, one devoted to noble theatrical companies and the other to the actor William Kemp*, which are part of the large series of scrapbooks now in the Folger.[29] There they were discovered by Professor R.C. Bald, who published them in 1943.[30] The scrapbooks were compiled in the latter part of Halliwell-Phillipps' life from earlier notes and transcriptions, but clearly over a period of years. He noted in the margin of one that the entries from Leicester's account had been copied 'many years ago' and that the Staunton Collection had since been destroyed by fire.[31] In a further note he recorded that according to the account Leicester was in Bath and Bristol in April 1587, which suggests that he had at least surveyed the volume in its entirety.[32] His original notes cannot be traced, and it is possible that they too were victims of the Birmingham Reference Library fire.[33] All

[26] *Ancient Inventories ... illustrative of the Domestic Manners of the English in the Sixteenth and Seventeenth Centuries* (1854). The Kenilworth inventory is found on pp. 115–54.

[27] Bodl. MS Malone 5. Since Edmund Malone died in 1812 and his collection was deposited in the Bodleian in 1821, roughly when Staunton began collecting in earnest, it is probable that this copy was made before Staunton obtained the original.

[28] *Ancient Inventories*, pp. 157–9. See also 'Leic. Pap. III', Append. III, n. 142.

[29] FSL, MS Wb 160 [Kemp] and Wb 200 [Noble Companies]. The entries are found on Wb 160, p. 1, and Wb 200, pp. 70–1 and 78 (pp. 24–85 of this volume are devoted to Leicester's company).

[30] 'Leicester's Men in the Low Countries', *Rev. English Studies*, xix (1943), 395–7. He appears to have published all the Halliwell-Phillipps extracts, my own examination of the scrap-books has not discovered any others, and I was unable to locate one of the entries he prints, see p. 374 below.

[31] FSL, MS Wb 160, p. 1.

[32] FSL, MS Wb 200, p. 78. He may have done so in the hope of finding evidence for Shakespeare's purported service in the Netherlands expedition.

[33] Not only has my admittedly rapid and selective examination of the vast number of notebooks in the Halliwell-Phillips' Collections in Washington and Edinburgh proved unsuccessful, but so has what I assume to be the more exhaustive search by R.W. Ingram, the editor of *Records of Early English Drama: Coventry* (Toronto and Manchester, 1981), see p. lxviii, n. 36. The report on the Birmingham fire in *The Times* for 14 January (p. 10) includes a collection of Shakespearean notes given to the library by Halliwell-Phillipps among the casualties. Although the marginal note referred to in n. 31 above was clearly written after 1879, there is no evidence that the other scrapbook entries were. This is perhaps the most convincing explanation for the absence of all but a few notes of

we can say is that he appears to have had the opportunity to make more extensive transcriptions. On the other hand, it will also be observed that all the scrapbook entries relate to individual actors or to Leicester's company. These were Halliwell-Phillipps' main interest in the 1850s and 1860s, and it is therefore quite possible that these entries were the only ones he considered relevant to his purposes and that they were the extent of his notes from the book.

THE DOCUMENTS: PHYSICAL DESCRIPTION

The four volumes are examples of the two conventional types of sixteenth-century household account: the basic day-book (usually of expenditure) and the version presented for auditing.[34] The latter, while normally derived from a day-book, usually involved a re-casting of the entries into various categories of expenditure and/or income. The day-book maintained a nominal chronological sequence of entries; the audited version, which was more concerned with categories of expenditure than chronology, generally kept to the sequence, but within the categories.[35]

The two Longleat accounts are versions presented for audit. Both were written by a clerk or scrivener and both contain marginalia by the auditors (discussed below). Dudley Papers XIV retains its original vellum binding, although it was placed in a slip cover when the Dudley Papers were bound in the 1890s.[36] The pages measure $12\frac{1}{2}'' \times 8\frac{1}{2}''$ and are watermarked with a hand and star. Dudley Papers XV also retains its vellum binding, but it has been rebound rather than placed in a slip cover. Its pages measure $13\frac{1}{2}'' \times 8\frac{1}{2}''$, but there is no obvious watermark. There are numerous blank leaves in both volumes, especially towards the end. Both also contain extensive pencil marginalia by Canon Jackson, and notes by him have also been tipped in; these relate in the main to Amy Dudley. A poulterer's bill has been pasted into the end of Dudley Papers XIV and two capper's bills and a shoemaker's bill in Dudley XV. These were undoubtedly abstracted from the main series of Leicester's bills at Longleat, presumably by Jackson. In the case of

[34] See the discussion in Mertes, *Noble Household*, pp. 79–86.

[35] As a result entries relating to a specific episode are scattered among several different categories; two good examples are those relating to Leicester's visit to his wife in March 1559 and her visit to London several weeks later. See the discussion in Appendix I.

[36] The twenty volumes of the Dudley Papers were bound in red leather or placed in uniform slip covers. Further loose papers were filed in eight boxes. However, the Dudley Papers do not exhaust the Leicester papers at Longleat; a large number are also to be found in the general collection of estate muniments. These are referred to here as 'Longleat MS'. See 'Leic. Pap. III' for a fuller discussion.

the three bills pasted in Dudley XV, this was probably because they contain references to Amy Dudley, though this does not apply to the poulterer's bill.[37] The foliation in both volumes is modern.

The two Evelyn accounts, by contrast, are day-books. The only known physical description of the 1585–87 book is that supplied by the Upcott catalogues which describe it as a volume of 333 pages, half-bound in russia by Hering (presumably when in Upcott's possession).[38] Whatever binding the 1584–86 volume had has completely disappeared, leaving only fragments of the threads. What survive are five gatherings, although the first (presumably covering the period April to October 1584) has suffered from damp and only its outer sheet remains. There was at least one further gathering at the beginning, and possibly one at the end. The pages measure $11\frac{3}{4}'' \times 7\frac{13}{16}''$, but there is no foliation. When the book began is obviously unknown, but if this volume was roughly the size of the 1585–87 book, then about two-thirds have survived, and assuming that there were no major gaps in the entries, a date of late 1583 or early 1584 can be suggested.

The two books present a number of technical problems, and they are best discussed jointly. The entries in the 1584–86 book are written uniformily and neatly, which suggests that they were written up at some remove from the dates concerned. But they are also written in three distinct hands.[39] The first (Hand A) runs from the beginning of the surviving fragment to half-way down the page headed 4 June 1585; this is a neat secretary hand, the spelling is reasonable and the chronology relatively accurate. The second hand (Hand B) runs from that point to the end of the page headed 12 June 1585. A third hand (Hand C) begins on the page headed 14 June 1585 and runs to the end of the page headed 5 July 1585. The page headed 6 July 1585 is written by Hand B as is the first half of the next (headed 7 July), but then Hand C resumes. Hand C is a dramatic contrast to Hand A; it is crabbed, the spelling is phonetic and primitive, the entries more formulaic and heavily abbreviated, and the chronology almost useless. It runs to half-way down the page headed 13 December 1585 and concludes with an entry relating to Leicester's departure from Flushing for Middelburg. The heading is a good example of the chronological vagaries of this hand, for Leicester actually left Flushing for Middelburg on the 11th.[40]

---

[37] The bills are printed below, see pp. 108, 173–5. It will be noted that the poulterer's bill covers the period January 1560–April 1561 and has no connection to this account. There is no obvious reason why it should have been pasted into the volume.

[38] The descriptions in the 1836 and 1846 catalogues are practically identical, the sale catalogue may simply have reproduced the relevant entries of the earlier one.

[39] The change of hands is noted in the text.

[40] See Appendix II. These vagaries are the main reason why Appendix II has been necessary.

This entry is followed immediately by one referring to his visit to Amsterdam on 21 March 1586, without any gap or other indication of a change of date. There follows a section covering the period 21–31 March 1586 (but including entries to 14 April), and then a section beginning with the heading 26 May 1586 (again without any indication of a change) and ending in the middle of the page under the heading 30 June 1586. The gathering also ends here, and the contents of the possible further gathering mentioned above can only be speculated upon. These last two sections are written in the same hand, but its relationship to Hand C is not straightforward. It is a more open hand, but the style of penmanship is very similar, as is the general formula of the entries. Vagaries of spelling are not a reliable guide to Elizabethan hands, but here again there are similarities (in particular the penchant for the use of the letter k) and no dramatic or obvious differences. On balance we can assume that these sections were also written by Hand C, though possibly in more haste and more loosely than his previous section.

For the 1585–87 book we are largely dependent upon the transcriptions, although we also have the descriptions from Upcott's catalogues which state that it began on 11 December 1585 and ended on 8 April 1587. Halliwell-Phillips noted that it concluded with references to Leicester's visit to Bath and Bristol, which occurred between 5 and 16 April 1587.[41] Knowles's transcriptions run from 11 December 1585 to 3 February 1586. The last entry Halliwell-Phillipps copied is dated 6 May 1586, but since his notes are purely of individual entries they are of no further use here. Knowles, however, does indicate what appear to be page headings as well as entries, and these suggest a day book similar in format to the 1584–86 book. Although Knowles has clearly included only a selection of the entries under each page heading, given Upcott's description there is no reason to doubt that his first heading – 11 December 1585 – was the initial one of the book.[42] This in turn suggests the obvious relationship between the two books: the first was taken up to Leicester's arrival in Flushing, and the second began at that point.[43] However, before we accept this hypothesis, the initial intention to draw up a sum total in the middle of the page headed 3 December 1585 should be noted.[44] This may reflect a decision to end the account then,

[41] Leicester spent 5 to 14 April in Bath taking the waters, and then visited Bristol on 15–16 April. There is a detailed account of his visit to Bristol in Bristol RO, MS 04026(12) [Chamberlains' Accts, Audit Book, 1587–92], pp. 29–30. Presumably 8 April was a page heading and the page contained entries for later dates as is the case in the 1584–86 book.
[42] The implication of Knowles's introduction (quoted in n. 22 above) is that his extracts are taken from the beginning of the volume.
[43] This is suggested by MacLean (487–8), though her knowledge of the 1585–87 account is derived from Bald's edition of Halliwell-Phillipps' notes. Dr MacLean informs me that she was not aware of Knowles's extracts at the time, nor presumably was Bald.
[44] See p. 340 below.

which was later reversed and the account continued until Leicester's arrival in Flushing.

The hand or hands of the 1585–87 book are obviously unknown, and we have only the phrasing of the individual entries to go on. For the phrasing we are, in turn, completely dependent on Knowles's and Halliwell-Phillipps' transcriptions, but they appear to be reasonably literal and neither extensively abbreviated nor modernised.[45] The differences between the formula of these entries and those by Hand C are obvious, in particular the writing out of the sum involved at the end of most of the entries, and, furthermore, the compiler of this book begins to refer to Leicester as your Excellency from 17 December, while Hand C in the 1586 sections never does. Nor does the formula of the entries suggest a resumption by Hand A. The compiler can thus be designated Hand D. However, Hand C was clearly a member of the Netherlands household for he must have written up his final entries after the arrival in Flushing. The retention of this book in the Netherlands household during 1586 helps to explain the March and May-June sections. Although we have only a few entries after February from the second book, none of them overlap these sections. Moreover, there is a possible clue in the entry on the departure of Leicester's players for Denmark in the 1584–86 book under the heading 31 May 1586.[46] Given Halliwell-Phillipps' interest in the players, had this also been entered in the 1585–87 book, it would be reasonable to have expected him to have noted it. The fact that he did not suggests that these sections were missing in the 1585–87 book, and therefore that the reason they were added to the previous book was because Hand D and his book were not available at the time. The abrupt changes of date would not have mattered, because the entries in both books would have been re-ordered when the final accounts were prepared for auditing.

The transcriptions we possess from the 1585–87 book give us no idea of the marginalia in the volume. The earlier book, however, contains much less than the two Longleat volumes. The most immediately interesting are a number of notes by Leicester himself, which suggests that he at least had examined it at some point. Given that the last of these is found on the page headed 6 December 1585, it is possible that his examination occurred before the 1586 entries were drawn up.[47] Otherwise there are a few pointing hands and two series of letters, a

---

[45] There may be some minor emendations to specific entries, e.g. the introduction of dates in brackets from the headings, but there is no radical transformation apparent, with the exception of the entry for 2 Jan. 1586, where Knowles seems to have run two entries together, see p. 371. He has also misread a few names (corrected in the notes).

[46] See p. 353.

[47] See p. 343. The two Longleat volumes, by contrast, contain no obvious Leicester marginalia.

lower case a and a capital B, many of the latter against entries in which
Richard Browne is mentioned. However, in the lower left hand of
every page there is a note 'pvs', possibly a version of p*erus*[ed?], and
an initial (possibly a more abbreviated 'perused') after the final sum on
the page. It is difficult to determine whether these books had in fact
been used to prepare a version for auditing. The 1585–86 provisioning
account does appear to have been examined, but the fact that Leicester's
own perusal of the 1584–86 book was limited to the 1584–5 section
may be significant.[48] The demands of his Netherlands governor-generalship in 1586–87, the crisis over Mary, Queen of Scots, on his return
in 1586, and then that over the Armada after his final return in 1587
would appear to have allowed him little time to attend to his personal
affairs. His secretary, Arthur Atye*, later informed Lord Burghley that
on the eve of his death Leicester was intending a major survey of his
finances at the end of 1588.[49] It is possible, therefore, that the auditing
of these books was still outstanding at the time of his death, which may
account for their survival.

THE DOCUMENTS: CONTENT AND CONTEXT

The two Longleat books are full household accounts, which include
both receipts and expenditures. Yet although similar in overall format,
there are some significant distinctions between them. The earlier
account (Dudley Papers XIV) was kept by William Chancy*, who
appears to have left Leicester's household after 1559.[50] It can be
described as a complete account in that it contains evidence of the final
examination and audit, either in March 1560 or March 1561, and also
appears to contain the full receipts and expenditures for the period of

[48] The description of the provisioning account in Upcott's 1836 catalogue reads 'Book
of such provision sent out of England by Richard Browne for the use of the Earl of
Leicester, 10 October 1585 ending 18 June 1586. Signatures of Gabriel Harvey and
William Gorges.* Folio half-bound in Russia.' The reference to the signatures of Harvey
and Gorge implies that they audited the account. 'Gabriel Harvey' may be a wishful
extrapolation from a signature G. Harvey, which is more likely to have been that of
George Harvey*.
[49] BL, Lansdowne MS 61, fos. 206–7, Atye to Burghley, 9 Dec. 1589 (printed in H.
Ellis, *Original Letters Illustrative of British History* (3rd Ser., 1846), iv, 75–9).
[50] As is noted in the entry in the Index of Servants, Chancy received livery in 1567,
but no further reference to him in the household after 1559 can be traced.

account.[51] The only item obviously missing from the receipts is the rent of the Robsart estate in Norfolk.[52] There are, however, two categories of expenditure that need further discussion – servants' wages and kitchen provisions – but they are best approached in the context of another feature of this account. As noted above the account contains extensive marginalia, which are found in both the right- and the left-hand margins. The right-hand marginalia are essentially auditor's notes and references to bills, many in the clear Chancery hand of Leicester's auditor William Kynyat*.[53] The left-hand margin, however, contains page references to another book, undoubtedly a day-book.[54] This day-book began when the main account itself began in December 1558, but ended on 30 September 1559, when there was at least an initial drawing up of the main account.[55] Thereafter, however, the main account was extended to December 1559 (a full year), though apparently without the benefit of a day-book, for the chronology of the entries of this section is much more explicit.

Servants' wages will be discussed in further detail in the next section, but it should noted that there are only three references to the payment

[51] The note on the examination of this account is not dated, see pp. 107–8. The Ellis account (DP XV) contains references to the expenses of an audit in March 1561 in which Thomas Blount* took part, see p. 148. It could not have been for the Ellis account itself, for it ran until 30 April. The Chancy account is a more likely candidate, but Blount did not sign the examination. The Ellis account does not refer to an earlier audit, though the purchase of paper and ink and a case for the Watton books in March 1560 (see p. 135) may be relevant. The March 1561 audit may have been concerned with the 'Book of Servants Wages' (Part II: Document A, discussed on pp. 20–1 below) which both terminated on Lady Day 1561 and was signed by Blount, but it also includes payments in early April. The audit is, however, referred to in John Guy the capper's bill, from which Part II: Document C is extracted, which suggests that it was at least used to settle some accounts.

[52] The Robsart estate (the manors of Syderstone, Bircham Newton and Great Newton near King's Lynn) was inherited by Leicester and his wife on the death of Lady Elizabeth Robsart in the spring of 1557, see 'Dudley Clientèle', pp. 249–51. (There I assumed that Lady Elizabeth died in the winter of 1557–8; however since I wrote it I have discovered at Longleat an assignment to Leicester and his wife of chattels from the estate by John Appleyard* administrator of the late Lady Elizabeth dated 27 June 1557 (MS 3188).) Rents from the Robsart estate for Michaelmas 1560 can be found in the Ellis account (see p. 116). The earlier rents may have been included in one of the lump sum receipts in the Chancy account, or alternatively they may have been paid directly to Amy Dudley herself (who of course was dead by Michaelmas 1560).

[53] These have not been reproduced here, see p. 36. However, reference is made to such bills as survive.

[54] These have been reproduced, see p. 36. Canon Jackson surmised from these page references that this account had been extracted or copied from another, see p. 39, n. 1. It is more likely that the page references are to a day-book.

[55] See p. 101. It will noted that no further page references are encountered after 30 September. See also the comment in n. 182 to the texts on the possible omission of some items of expenditure after that date.

of wages in this account: rewards given to thirteen servants at Easter 1559, wages paid to twenty-six at Midsummer and board-wages and expenses for the royal progress paid to a few servants in September.[56] The section on 'Diet' in the account is composed almost entirely of references to sweetmeats, 'banquetting stuff' and drink. Basic provisions for the kitchen would appear to have been included in lump sum payments to the cooks and acater ('cater' in the account) in the section 'Payments made by William Chancy not before mentioned', which implies they were not included in the day-book.[57] In the September-December 1559 section they appear to be included in further lump sum payments to the cooks and to Richard Horden*, who may have been appointed clerk of the kitchen by then.[58] Thus although Chancy may ultimately have funded the kitchen, he may not have been responsible for the details of kitchen expenditure.

The second Longleat account (Dudley Papers XV) was kept by Richard Ellis*, who still held a post in Leicester's household in the late 1560s, but may have ceased to be a financial officer after 1561, for there is evidence that Leicester was dissatisfied with this account.[59] Unlike the Chancy account this is incomplete, for there is no evidence of a final examination and audit, and, while the receipts appear to be complete, the expenditures come to an end practically in mid-entry and no sums or totals have been computed.[60] The marginalia include references to bills by Kynyat and other auditor's notes similar to those in the Chancy account, but these are found only in the first section of the expenditure.[61] There are no references to a day-book, although there is one to a clerk of the kitchen's book, kept by Richard Jinks*, who appears to have succeeded Horden in that office in the summer of 1560.[62] Servants' wages are not included, but Ellis compiled a separate 'Book of Servants Wages' covering the period Midsummer 1559–Lady Day 1561. Whether the total from this book would ultimately have been entered in the main account is, obviously, unknown.[63] The period

[56] See pp. 56, 74–5, 81–3.

[57] See p. 101.

[58] See p. 106.

[59] See BL, Add. MS 35308, fo. 205, Henry Killigrew to Sir Nicholas Throckmorton, 28 Sept. 1561. In discussing the journey to France of John Marbury*, Killegrew referred to 'his brother Ellis (who was then and still is in disgrace about his account to my lord)'.

[60] See p. 173. DP III (a volume of miscellaneous papers) contains what appear to be drafts of sections of this account and a number of pages of sums which are probably related to it.

[61] See p. 118, textual note F.

[62] See p. 176. There are also references to lump sum payments to Jinks, Horden and the acaters on p. 130.

[63] Part II: Document A. For the evidence that it was compiled by Ellis, see the introduction to the document on p. 399. See also the two entries deleted in the main account (pp. 131–2) and noted as entered in the Book of Servants Wages.

of Ellis's account, one year and four months, is even more eccentric than that of the Chancy account. Although it clearly began at the termination of Chancy's account, the date of conclusion is more ambiguous. One would expect the quarter day (Lady Day 1561) to be of significance (as it clearly is in the Book of Servants Wages), but the account continues to the end of April. Possibly more important was the fact that Leicester received his first substantial grant of landed estates from the Queen on 1 March 1561. This could be expected to have strengthened his financial position considerably and to have made possible the settlement of a number of debts and outstanding claims.[64]

Despite the various omissions and qualifications noted here, we can still be reasonably confident that these volumes present a more or less accurate account of the state of Leicester's finances during the years in question. This is obviously not the case with the two Evelyn books, which are no less similar in both form and content. They are concerned solely with expenditure and contain no reference to receipts. Most of the items of expenditure – personal expenses, alms, rewards, occasional purchases, travelling expenses, odd building costs, and a few wages – are casual and correspond to the 'Foreign Charges' and related sections of the earlier accounts. The identities of the accountants pose something of a challenge.[65] We can only discuss Hands A, C and D, for the limited number of pages written by Hand B make any conclusion almost impossible. Hand A makes several references to 'myself', once in the company of Mr Sandes* and Mr. Lloyd* (21 April 1584), and twice in the company of 'Pitchford'* and 'Stephen' [Johnson]* (7 and 13 May 1585).[66] Hand C refers regularly to my 'fellows' Pitchford and Mearaday [Richard Meredith]* during the autumn of 1585, and occasionally to 'my fellow Ambrose' [Waller]* and 'my fellow Stephen [Johnson].[67] Both A and C account for payments for messes for servants on a fortnightly basis, but while A describes them simply as your lordship's servants, C describes them as servants of the wardrobe. The surviving entries for D are less helpful. They include only one reference to 'I' (2 January 1586) and none to 'my fellows'.

[64] *CPR, 1560–63*, 189–191. This consisted of a number of the duke of Northumberland's lesser properties, most of which were sold or otherwise disposed of in the following years, see 'West Midlands', 30. On the other hand, no reference this grant can be found in the Ellis account.

[65] Had the accountant of the 1585–87 book been identified in an introduction to the volume it is probable that either Upcott or Knowles would have referred to him; Upcott noted the accountants of the other Leicester accounts he possessed, probably from their introductions. It is possible that, since they were only day-books, it was not considered necessary to provide formal introductions to this or the 1584–86 book.

[66] See pp. 179, 249, 251. As is noted in the Index of Servants there were possibly two household servants William and Robert alternately named Pitchford or Pitchfork.

[67] E.g. pp. 302–3.

The similarity of the contents of the two books suggests that Hands A, C and D were servants of roughly similar rank and office, and more likely to have been drawn from the yeomen rather than the obviously gentlemen servants.[68] Hand C clearly appears to have been one of the servants of the wardrobe, and we may assume A to have been so too. It is for this reason that these accounts have been described above as wardrobe disbursement books. The identities of the servants of the wardrobe are supplied both by the disbursement books and by the two lists of the household in the Netherlands in 1587[69] There are a number of names common to both the lists and the books, and thus a possible identification may be made by extrapolating from the names missing during the periods of the various accountants. On this basis a strong candidate for Hand A is Ralph More*, who is mentioned in the sections by Hands C and D but not in that by A.[70] Moreover, there is a reference to him (23 October 1585) in the section by Hand C in the company of Stephen and Pitchford similar to the earlier references to 'myself' in their company in the section by Hand A. Hand C is more difficult because most of the obvious wardrobe servants mentioned by Hand A are also mentioned by him. He was from his penmanship and spelling a less educated man than Hand A. A possible candidate is Rutherick Lewis*, who may have been a Welshman, and who served in Leicester's guard in the Netherlands in 1586 (and therefore would have been available in March and May).[71] Hand D may have been Thomas Ardern*, a gentleman servant, who was clerk comptroller of the Netherlands household in 1587; he is referred to in Hand A's section, but not in C's.

I have suggested elsewhere that the survival of the two Longleat accounts may be related to the fact that this collection also contains Leicester's surviving correspondence and a number of bills and other miscellanea from the same period (1559–61), and that they may all have been the contents of a single box or chest.[72] The Evelyn Papers are known to have contained at least four of Leicester's household accounts, the two disbursement books, Richard Browne's provisioning account for 1585–6, and an account for 1570–71. The last is described in the Upcott catalogues as 'Declaration of all sums of money received by

---

[68] This is a subjective assessment, and to some extent it is contradicted by the suggestion below that Hand D was Thomas Ardern. However, as will be clear from the entries in the Index of Servants, a number of the established household servants fall into the large grey area between yeomen and gentlemen.

[69] The Netherlands household lists are Part II: Documents G and H.

[70] For references to More by Hands C and D, see below pp. 324, 367.

[71] His Welsh origins are suggested by the lease in the lordship of Chirk, referred to in the entry in the Index of Servants. Hand C's phonetic spellings suggest that he had a strong regional accent.

[72] See 'Leic. Pap. III'.

Robert Christmas to the use of the Earl of Leicester, 20 February 1569 [i.e. 1569/70] to 30 December 1571. 403 pp. folio bound in russia by Hering'.[73] Although this description suggests it was solely an account of receipts, its size implies a full account similar to the Longleat volumes.[74] It is possible that there had been more at Sayes Court in the seventeenth century. Evelyn informed Sir Joseph Williamson early in the 1660s that many of the papers there had been destroyed during the Civil War.[75] In his library catalogue Evelyn refers to several Leicester accounts, but not in sufficient detail to make precise identification possible, and there is evidence to suggest that he discarded items that he considered uninteresting.[76]

Given the fragmentary nature of the survivals, we can only speculate as to the full range of Leicester papers that Sir Richard Browne possessed. He had been a leading, if not the leading, officer of Leicester's household between 1566 and 1588 and the household archive at Leicester House may have been in his keeping. However, whether his retention of Leicester's papers was anything more than accidental is unclear. The Countess of Leicester appears to have been primarily concerned with the muniments of title and other items directly relevant to the settling of her husband's estate. Some of the papers Browne retained may have been those in which he had a personal interest, the provisioning account for example, for he was still settling accounts arising from the Netherlands expedition in the 1590s.[77] Whether the same applied to the two disbursement books is not obvious, though the 'B' marginalia in the 1584–86 book may be of significance.

Only a rough and conjectural outline can thus be given of the accounts as a series. References in the Chancy and Ellis accounts indicate that there had been an earlier one, kept by William Grice*,

[73] Robert Christmas (d. 1584), MP, was a central figure in Leicester's household between 1565 and the late 1570s. He received livery and a badge in 1567 (for references to the documents in Part II, see p. 31 below), and in 1571 was described as Leicester's treasurer (*Black Book*, p. 36).

[74] There is a note that this volume also included outpayments in an article on the Staunton Collection in the *Birmingham Weekly Post* of 18 Dec. 1886. See the volume of cuttings on the Staunton Collection kept in the manuscripts department of the BRL, p. 46. This was one of a series of articles that attempted to reconstruct the catalogue of the collection.

[75] PRO, SP45/20/282 (Williamson's notes on the State Papers), 'a great part of them have perished by time & the distraction of the warres & being left in England by Sir R. Browne during the Rebellion many had been abused to the meanest uses &c.' I discovered this after writing 'Leic. Pap. I' and it suggests that my conclusion (p. 85) that most of the Browne Leicester papers had survived should be revised.

[76] 'Leic. Pap. I', 78–80.

[77] A number of papers relating to these settlements were filed at Christ Church prior to 1995 in Evelyn Papers, Sir Richard Browne Miscellaneous Boxes, Box IV.

which came to an end in December 1558.[78] Of the succeeding accounts
we have only a single-page 'Estimate' of an account of Richard Browne's
for receipts totalling £1,507 16s 7d between 29 August 1566 and 26
January 1570, and expenditures totalling £1,748 14s 10d between 10
July 1566 and 27 January 1570. This refers to 'divers books of receipt'
and 'sundry books of his payments', the latter of which were for 'my
lord's diet and payment of his lordship's servants' wages as also for
sundry emporcions and provisions by him made for the use of the said
Earl'.[79] It is reasonable to assume that these books were the central
household accounts for the later 1560s. As noted above, the Longleat
collection includes a series of bills, the great majority from the period
1559 to mid-1566, immediately prior to the beginning of this account.[80]
It is tempting to see what survives as the remains of the contents of
two chests, one for the pre-1566 period and the other for the post. This
would imply that the household account books for the period 1561–66
were originally among those papers that ultimately reached Longleat,
while the account books and bills of the period after 1566 were at Sayes
Court. What lends weight to this theory is the fact that Leicester's
correspondence for the later 1560s came into Browne's possession.[81]

The 'Browne account' of 1566–70 was clearly succeeded by the
'Christmas account' of 1570–71. Thereafter we have no evidence of the
accounting process until we reach the disbursement books of the mid-
1580s; in fact little household or central financial material of any
description has survived for the 1570s and early 1580s.[82] What the
fragments do suggest is an erratic series of accounting periods. Although
superficially they appear to follow one- or two-year periods, in fact
change-over of officers or other extraneous factors may have been

[78] See below, p. 39, n. 3.
[79] Evelyn MS 16, art. 3.
[80] The bills at Longleat are filed in DP, Box V. Those relevant to the Chancy and Ellis
accounts are referred to in the notes. There are some exceptions to the statement made
above, in particular the two bills for badges and livery of 1567–8 (Part II: Documents D
and E), and a series of wardrobe warrants for the period 1565–67 (fos. 300–438). A large
number of the bills were settled in the early months of 1566 when Leicester was
negotiating a substantial exchange of lands with the Queen, which was finally granted
on 29 June 1566 (*CPR, 1563–66*, 457–66). There may have been a connection between
this grant and the commencing of the Browne account two months later, similar to that
suggested above between the 1 March 1561 grant and the conclusion of the Ellis account.
[81] See 'Leic. Pap. I', 68–72, 85. Most of the correspondence Evelyn gave to Samuel
Pepys and is now found in Pepys MSS 2502–3 (Letters of State, Vols. I-II).
[82] The only accounts of the 1570s extant are an account of cloth supplied to William
Whittle and Maynard the hosier in 1571–74 (Longleat, DP XII), and the account of
Leicester's factor in Spain for 1576–79 (Evelyn MS 257). However, a number of household
inventories of the early 1580s have survived, see 'Leic. Pap. III', Appendices III-IV.
Leicester's correspondence for the 1570s and 1580s survives in quantity (see 'Leic. Pap.
II'), but the fate of the household archive is unknown.

more important. When the Grice account began is unknown, and it is no clearer why the Chancy account began in December 1558. This was originally to end on 30 September 1559 but was extended to a full year. The possible reasons why Ellis's account ended in April 1561 have already been discussed. The commencement of the Browne account may have been related to the exchange with the Crown in the summer of 1566. If the suggestion made above that the 1584–86 disbursement book began in December 1583 is correct then a two-year period appears to have been employed (although with several accountants), but whether the termination in December 1585 was caused solely by the Netherlands expedition or would have happened ordinarily at the end of 1585 we cannot say. Nor is there any obvious reason why the 1585–87 disbursement book ended in April 1587, unless, of course, the accountant had simply reached the last page.

THE HOUSEHOLD LISTS

Not the least important aspect of these accounts is the information they provide about the structure and composition of Leicester's household. At an early stage in the editing it became clear that, if this volume was to serve as a serious work of reference, a biographical index of servants should be included. However, this then posed the problem that in many cases the identifications were based on manuscript lists of the household to which the reader would not have easy access. The further decision was therefore taken to supplement the accounts with such lists of the household as survive. Ten lists are printed in Part II. The term 'household list' is in fact used extremely loosely, for none of these documents are chequerrolls or conventional quarterly, semi-annual or annual wage lists.[83] They are a heterogeneous collection, but they are also the only surviving sources for the personnel of Leicester's household other than the casual.

Although textual descriptions accompany the lists themselves, some introductory comment is necessary. The lists fall into three categories.

---

[83] For check or chequerrolles, see Mertes, *Noble Household*, p. 90. It might be noted that Elizabethan practice appears to have varied. A single wage-list of the household of the 3rd Earl of Huntingdon for the half-year ending Michaelmas 1564 survives in HEH, HA, Financial Box I. Sir William Petre employed quarterly wage-lists (see F.G. Emmison, *Tudor Secretary: Sir William Petre at Court and Home* (1961), pp. 151–4), as did Cecil in 1554–5 (BL, Lansdowne MS 118, fos. 42v-44), while the 9th Earl of Northumberland employed annual check-rolls (see G.R. Batho (ed.), *The Household Papers of Henry Percy, Ninth Earl of Northumberland (1564–1632)* (Camden Soc. 3rd Ser., xciii, 1962), 148). Overall, relatively few chequerrolles have survived, see the comments on fifteenth-century chequerrolles in Woolgar, i, 35, and K.B. McFarlane, *The Nobility of Later Medieval England* (Oxford, 1973), pp. 109–13.

The first group (Documents A-E) are a 'Book of Servants Wages' of 1561 and lists extracted from four bills for the supply of livery in 1559, 1560 and 1567, all of which are found among the Longleat Dudley Papers. The Book of Servants Wages (A) is the nearest equivalent to a chequerroll of the lists included here. As noted above this was compiled by Richard Ellis in conjunction with his main account, but unlike the latter it has been examined and audited. The terminal date of the period of account (Lady Day 1561) is close to that of the main account, but the date of commencement (Midsummer 1559) is clearly related to the payment of wages on Midsummer 1559 entered in the Chancy account.[84] Twenty-seven gentleman servants and sixty-three yeomen servants (exclusive of laundresses and the kitchen boys) are entered in the Book of Servants Wages.[85] The payments to the gentlemen are casual and rarely dated, but thirty-nine of the yeoman servants are entered as in receipt of wages. The others either have incomplete entries or received casual payments. Of the thirty-nine waged servants, twenty-nine were paid to Lady Day 1561. Seventeen of these were paid from Midsummer 1559; four for longer periods (one, George Gyles, from Michaelmas 1558 and three from Lady Day 1559); and eight for shorter periods. The final ten waged servants were paid for periods ending before Lady Day 1561. The entry in the Chancy account includes the names of twenty-six servants paid wages at Midsummer 1559, half of whom (thirteen) are among those paid by Ellis to Lady Day 1561, and most of the other half found among those paid for shorter periods or casually.

It would be reasonable to assume that those found both at Midsummer 1559 and Lady Day 1561 represent the permanent core of the household. Those paid at Midsummer 1559 but then for shorter periods than Lady Day 1561 may be assumed to have left Leicester's service in the meantime, while those found at Lady Day 1561 and not at Midsummer 1559 had entered it since. There would thus appear to be a distinct turnover of servants but such a conclusion rests on the assumption that the 1561 Book is complete and includes all outstanding claims from present or former servants. Nor can we be sure how complete the Midsummer 1559 payments were, for we have no information about the earlier payment of servants apart from the entry for the rewards paid to sixteen servants at Easter, though whether these were genuine rewards and supplementary to wages or interim payments of wages is no clearer. The Ellis account includes an entry to rewards at Easter 1560, but without giving names and at the much lower rate

[84] See p. 14 above.
[85] The division between the gentlemen and the yeomen appears to be between Mr [Richard] Hilliard* and George Gyles*, see p. 403.

of 6s.[86] It is also clear from the Book of Servants Wages that many received interim payments not obviously entered in the main account.[87] However, the very fact that the Book of Servants Wages includes a number of payments for the period prior to Midsummer 1559 suggests that it did settle all known outstanding claims and therefore can be regarded as inclusive.[88]

The lists from the bills for livery (B, C, D and E) pose a similar problems of inclusiveness. Document B lists seventeen gentlemen and seventeen or twenty yeomen in receipt of coats and twenty gentlemen and twenty-six or twenty-nine yeomen in receipt of hose.[89] The names are sufficiently similar to those paid wages in Midsummer 1559 to suggest that these liveries were granted in that year. There is also some contemporary evidence to suggest that liveries were bestowed in particular on those servants in attendance on the royal progresses, and therefore we may assume that the men named in Document B attended Leicester on the 1559 progress.[90] Document C lists nineteen servants, clearly yeomen, to whom caps were delivered on 4 April 1560. This would appear to be a supplementary provision, for the two cappers bills pasted into the Ellis account (which date from 1560–61) include caps for thirty-two and fifteen servants, and the Chancy account includes an entry for thirty-five caps supplied in 1559.[91]

The two later lists for badges and livery cloth (D and E) pose further difficulties, not least because we have no ancillary household documentation for the period in question (1567–68) to serve as a comparison.[92] It would appear that some 140 men received badges and 196 livery cloth. Once again there is no definite evidence that this was an inclusive rather than a supplementary grant, but the scale suggests that it was inclusive. Given that the household in 1559–61 appears to have numbered between thirty-five and fifty, the jump to over 150 appears to be a fairly dramatic increase in size, though, given Leicester's promotion to the peerage in the meantime, this might be expected.

---

[86] See p. 155.

[87] See, for example, the entry for Richard Flamock* on p. 412.

[88] Nevertheless, some caution should be employed in reaching any precise conclusions about numbers on the evidence of this book. Hugh Jones*, for example, who received wages only for the year Midsummer 1559–Midsummer 1560 (p. 406), was apparently still in the household in 1567.

[89] Each list refers to three further un-named yeoman servants in receipt of liveries.

[90] In his letter to Throckmorton on John Marbury of 28 Sept. 1561 (see n. 59 above) Henry Killigrew referred to Marbury 'being denied his coat because he was not bent to follow the progress'. See also the reference on p. 74 to the supply of liveries for the progress of 1559.

[91] See pp. 98, 174.

[92] All that survives is the series of wardrobe warrants for 1565–67 (see n. 80 above); these two bills may well have been filed with them.

However, the award of badges and liveries on this scale raises certain technical issues. Under the 'Great Statute' of Liveries of 1504 (19 Henry VII, c. 14), which formed the basis of all later Tudor regulation of retaining, granting of badges and liveries was restricted to manual servants, officers and legal counsel, unless under royal licence.[93] Leicester had received a licence to retain one hundred men on 3 August 1565.[94] Practically nothing is known about his employment of this licence, apart from the fact that twelve members of his guard in 1586 were described as 'your excellency's old retainers'.[95] Nevertheless, it is reasonable to assume that the licenced retainers made up at least some proportion of those awarded badges and liveries in 1567, and therefore that the household itself may not expanded as greatly as the overall numbers suggest. A number of those liveried were artisans or tradesmen, and these men may have been among those retained under the licence, for this practice featured in some of the indictments for illicit retaining in the reign of Henry VII.[96]

The second group (Documents F-H) are three lists of the household at the time of the Netherlands expedition, the first immediately prior to Leicester's departure in 1585, and the latter two during the second phase of his governor-generalship in 1587. They are the only lists to give the structure of the household, which is the reason for the inclusion of Document F, which does not otherwise identify the members. However, the composition of the Netherlands household raises its own technical issues. In an appendix to *Leicester's Triumph* Sir Roy Strong and the late Professor J.A. van Dorsten compiled a table of the members of 'Leicester's train' on his arrival in the Netherlands in December 1585.[97] The use of term 'train' was possibly unfortunate for it obscures the distinction between the two bodies that comprised it. One was the

[93] See the discussions in 'Puritan Crusade', pp. 21–22, and Adams 'The English Military Clientele 1542–1618', in C. Giry-Deloison and R. Mettam (edd.), *Patronages et Clientélismes 1550–1750* (Lille, 1995), pp. 220–1, and the literature cited there.

[94] *CPR, 1563–66*, 206. This was one of fifteen licences to retain granted by Elizabeth between her accession and 1571, either to Privy Councillors, peers or officers of the Crown (listed in BL, Lansdowne MS 14, fo. 1v). One hundred men was the highest number licensed, and together with Leicester, the Duke of Norfolk, the Earls of Sussex, Shrewsbury and Pembroke, and Lord Clinton received licences of this size. Precisely why they were granted is unclear, though in some cases they may have been related to offices.

[95] See Netherlands Guard in Abbreviations of Major Dudley Family Documents above. The list of 'Leicester's train' in 1585 now Bodl. MS Eng. Hist. C 272, pp. 82–7 (see n. 103 below) identifies forty-five men in the train as retainers but how much weight should be placed on it is unclear.

[96] For examples, see A. Cameron, 'The Giving of Livery and Retaining in Henry VII's Reign', *Renaissance and Modern Studies*, xviii (1974), 26–7, and for the admittedly notorious case of Lord Abergavenny, J.P. Cooper, 'Retaining in Tudor England' in *Land Men and Beliefs* (ed. by G.E. Aylmer and J.S. Morrill, 1983), p. 83.

[97] (Leiden and Oxford, 1964), see Appendix III, pp. 108–134.

household proper and the second those gentlemen and noblemen whom, together with their retinues, Leicester summoned to accompany him in September 1585. These retinues were mustered at the Hague on 10 January 1586 and were then formed into companies to constitute the 1,000 cavalry of the English contingent as provided for under the treaties of Nonsuch.[98] The distinction between the household proper and the 'train' is made clear in Document F, which lists the household, a total of ninety-nine men (inclusive of under-servants), and the lords and gentlemen of the train and their servants (to a total of seventy-two) separately.

Strong and van Dorsten compiled their appendix from five sources: two billeting lists from Leiden and the Hague in early 1586,[99] a list of the retinues at the Hague muster of January 1586,[100] a list of the 'train' sent by the Spanish ambassador in Paris, Don Bernadino de Mendoza, to Philip II,[101] and what they described as 'the list drawn up by Henry Goodyer first half of January 1585'. The last is in fact two separate documents, a list of Leicester's guard in early 1586 and a list of the household dated 21 July 1587, which is printed here as Document G.[102] The 'Spanish list' is very similar to two other manuscript lists, which Strong and van Dorsten overlooked.[103] All three are long lists of gentlemen and retinues, with the number of horses included, and in the 'Spanish list' ships as well. They would appear to be versions of embarkation or early muster lists from 1585.[104] These lists, together with the 10 January 1586 muster list, are invaluable sources for Leicester's wider clientele, but they have not been printed here for they are not of direct relevance to the accounts. The two 1587 household lists (G and H) were both compiled for specific purposes, the earlier (21 July) for the administration of the oath of loyalty, and the later (November), given the date and the attention it pays to under-servants, probably as an embarkation list for Leicester's final return to England. Both have

---

[98] For the summoning of these men see Appendix II, and for a further discussion, 'North Wales', 137–9, and 'Puritan Crusade', pp. 17–24.

[99] The Leiden list came from a local source, the Hague list is BL, Cotton MS Vespasian C XIV, fos. 321–28.

[100] PRO, SP84/6/79ff, printed in E.M. Tenison, *Elizabethan England* (14 vols., Leamington Spa, 1933–61), vi, 45–7.

[101] AGS, Estado K 1564, fo. 4, entitled 'El sequito del Conde de Lestre', it was enclosed in Mendoza's despatch of 29 Dec./8 Jan. 1585/6, and is printed in *CSPSp, 1580–6*, 554–6.

[102] For the list of the guard, see Netherlands Guard in Abbreviations of Major Dudley Family Documents.

[103] Bodl., MS Rawlinson B 146, fo. 235–v; MS Eng. Hist. C 272, pp. 82–7. The latter was originally a Gurney manuscript and is calendared among them in Hist MSS Comm, *XIIth Report, Pt. 9* (1891), 146.

[104] Discussed in 'Puritan Crusade', pp. 17–18.

been printed here in their entirety, despite the fact that much space is taken up by Leicester's guard. This is not simply for the sake of completeness, but also because the guard was composed in part of Leicester's ordinary servants.[105] There is, however, one very important difference between the two lists. Excluding the guard and the bargemen (and in the November list the under-servants as well), the July household consisted of 167 men, but the November only 95. The significance of these figures will be discussed in the next section.[106]

The last group (Documents I and J) are lists of the attendants at Leicester's funeral in October 1588. Document I gives the order of the procession, including the identities of a number of the chief mourners and attendants. Document J is composed of two separate lists of those given mourning blacks, the first being a list of the principal mourners and attendants including household officers, and the second the full list of the blacks granted (gowns for esquires and above, and cloaks for the rest). The latter appears to have been the earlier of the two for it contains a number of people (the Earl of Warwick, for example) who did not in the event take part in the funeral procession. Document I may have been a revised version of the first part of Document J.[107] Like the 1567–68 livery lists these contain both personnel of the household and a much larger body of servants, followers and friends. Some household officers and offices are noted but the overall structure of the household is not.

THE STRUCTURE OF THE HOUSEHOLD

Some introductory comment on the structure of the household is also necessary. With the exception of the two 1567–68 bills for badges and liveries (D and E), the dates of the household lists correspond relatively closely to the dates of the accounts. The reason, especially for the earlier lists, which were part of the accounting process for the Ellis account, is not entirely coincidental. As noted above, there is little surviving household material for the 1570s and early 1580s, and as a

---

[105] See the comments on the Netherlands Guard in Abbreviations of Major Dudley Family Documents above.

[106] The names counted in the July list are those on fos. 98–99v (pp. 430–5), the sum tallies with the totals computed on each folio. Those counted in the November list are found after the middle of fo. 212 (p. 442) and exclude the bargemen. Owing to the difficulty of identifying under-servants precisely, the sum is approximate, but the magnitude of the difference is clear enough.

[107] Also found in the earlier but not the later are the Lord Admiral (Howard of Effingham) and the Lord Chancellor (Hatton). The earlier list includes twenty-one knights and ten esquires, the later only twenty knights and ten esquires.

result we are presented with a detailed picture of the household at two dramatically different stages. In 1559–61 Leicester was a rising and controversial figure at Court. In 1584–86 he was at the height of his eminence. The earlier period was only four years removed from the date of his release from the Tower, and while a household had been formed (or re-formed) it was still a growing one. The Chancy account opens almost on the day of the grant of the house at Kew which was to be his residence, when not at Court, during the early 1560s. Where he had lived previously is unclear, though the account suggests it may have been either at Christchurch or his uncle Sir Andrew Dudley's house in Westminster.[108]

The household lists discussed above suggest that the household at this stage numbered between thirty-five and fifty, but neither they nor the accounts reveal much about its structure, although there are passing references to a chamber and a wardrobe. Offices are hardly ever mentioned, and the main distinction is the conventional one between the gentlemen and the yeomen servants. Chancy, Ellis and even Richard Browne in 1570 identify themselves simply as servants.[109] Yet, whatever their precise functions, the central figures and officers are reasonably easy to identify. Many of them had previously been in the service of the Duke of Northumberland and we have some fragmentary evidence of their association with Leicester during Mary's reign.[110] The household was resolutely masculine in composition, the only female occupation being that of laundress, a characteristic of the contemporary household to which Kate Mertes has drawn attention. Amy Dudley's one known female attendant, Mrs Picto, accompanied her and figures only peripherally in these accounts.[111]

Although the 1567 livery lists reveal the numerical expansion of the personnel, they do not help with the question of structure or offices. By 1565 Kew had been sold, and Leicester appears to have been using Durham House as his London residence.[112] He had been granted

---

[108] See nn. 28 and 267 to the texts.

[109] See the introductions to the Chancy and Ellis accounts, pp. 39, 113, and for Browne, Evelyn MS 16, art. 3.

[110] See 'Dudley Clientèle', esp. pp. 243–7.

[111] Mertes, *Noble Household*, pp. 57–8. There was one later exception, the keeper of the napery at Kenilworth Castle in the 1580s was a woman, Anne King*. For Mrs Picto see n. 161 to the texts.

[112] The GVE (fo. 59) notes the sale of Kew to Francis Pope (see n. 173 to the texts), but the date is not given. It ultimately came into the possession of Thomas Gardiner, a Teller of the Exchequer, who surrendered it to the Queen in 1574 (V.C.H. *Surrey*, iii, 483). The evidence for Leicester's residence at Durham House is supplied by bills and wardrobe warrants dated 1565–8, Longleat, DP Box V, fos. 215, 263, 300, 438. The house was used for the accommodation of ambassadors and courtiers throughout Elizabeth's reign (*King's Works*, iv, 76).

Kenilworth Castle in 1563, but prior to 1568 had visited it only during the 1566 progress.[113] Thereafter, however, the number of his houses expanded considerably. In January 1570 he purchased Paget Place near St Clement Danes from the 3rd Lord Paget, which then became Leicester House and his principal residence.[114] In 1576–77 he leased Wanstead House in Essex from the 2nd Lord Rich and purchased it in 1578.[115] From 1570 onwards he visited Kenilworth on a more or less annual basis, and during the 1580s he made use of three other country houses as well: Grafton House in Northamptonshire, Benington in Hertfordshire and Langley in Oxfordshire.[116]

The number of residences alone makes the household of 1584 a more complex body than it had been in the early 1560s. Kenilworth Castle, which also served as the administrative centre for his west midland estates, had its own permanent, if skeleton, staff of officers and keepers. The Kenilworth inventories reveal that the Kenilworth staff were also responsible for the contents of Grafton, but both Grafton and Langley may have been assigned to gentlemen servants, who appear to have acted as keepers.[117] A more difficult question is posed by the household at Leicester House, Wanstead House and the Court. Elizabeth's preference for regular removes between the main Thames-side palaces (Whitehall, St James's, Greenwich and Richmond) made a major central London residence essential for the greater court figures. Similarly a 'suburban' residence near to one of the outlying palaces was an undoubted convenience. The proximity of Kew to Richmond is obvious enough, and this was shared (it might be noted) by Cecil's first house at Wimbledon and later by Walsingham's house at Barn Elms.[118] Whatever Leicester's motives were in purchasing Wanstead House, its proximity to Greenwich – which emerges clearly from the 1584–86 disbursement book – was undoubtedly a consideration. Kenilworth Castle, regardless of its symbolic or political importance, was, like

---

[113] For Leicester's visits to Kenilworth, see 'West Midlands', 33–4.

[114] PRO, C54/818/32 (30 Jan. 1569/70).

[115] Essex RO, D/DCw [Child Deposit, Wanstead Estate]/T3C/3 (lease, 15 April 1577); T3C/5 and 7 (bargain and sale, 10 Feb. 1577/8). Leicester may have been using it as a residence before the spring of 1577.

[116] He was granted the stewardship of the honour of Grafton on 4 Dec. 1571 (*CPR, 1569–72*, 478), and several further leases thereafter. This grant is overlooked in the account of Grafton in *King's Works*, iv, 94–5. Benington was a Devereux manor and part of the jointure lands of the Countess as Countess of Essex (V.C.H. *Hertfordshire*, iii, 75). For Langley see n. 391 to the texts.

[117] For the Kenilworth staff, see 'West Midlands', 41–2; for the keepers of Grafton and Langley, see nn. 584, 587 to the texts and Edmund Carey*.

[118] The attraction of residences near Richmond for Tudor courtiers is also noted in V.C.H. *Surrey*, iii, 482.

Burghley House, too remote to be used for anything other than occasional recreational visits.

All the surviving evidence suggests that Leicester House and Wanstead functioned as a unit and that there was a single central household, although the Wanstead estate had its own staff and there was possibly a skeleton one for the house itself. Out of this central household those members who attended Leicester at Court were drawn, but given the amount of river-traffic referred to in all the accounts there was a considerable coming and going between the houses and the Court. The same applied to furniture and personal possessions, for the accounts also reveal that whatever chambers were assigned at Court were furnished privately. Only during the progresses or at the removes to the more peripheral palaces (Windsor Castle or Hampton Court) was it necessary to find nearby lodgings for servants. An example can be found in the reference in the Chancy account to the expenses of lodgings for servants at Greenwich during the summer of 1559, for the distance from Kew made it obviously too inconvenient for Leicester to base his servants there.[119]

A further complexity is introduced by the Netherlands household, about whose structure we have the most detailed information. As it was intended to be a permanent establishment, not just a temporary one for a brief campaign, the best comparison would be with the household of one of the vice-regal officers, the Lord Deputy of Ireland or the Lord President of the North. However, the evidence for its size poses some problems. The 1585 list (Document F) gives seventy-five men (exclusive of under-servants), the July 1587 list (G) 167, and the November 1587 list (H) ninety-five (also exclusive of under-servants). Assuming that (as suggested above) the November 1587 list was an embarkation list for Leicester's final departure from the Netherlands, one explanation for the difference between it and the July list might be that part of the household had already been sent home. This would make the 1587 household much greater than the 1586 one, but it may also have been the case that further household servants arrived after Leicester himself landed in 1585 and thus the 1586 household was ultimately larger than Document F would imply. An alternative explanation is that G, which was used to administer the oath of loyalty, was based on a list of the central household in England and that only the eighty-three men who swore the oath actually went to the Netherlands; thus the Netherlands household throughout was in the region of seventy-five to one hundred, as is implied by F and H.

The importance of this question lies in the relationship between the Netherlands household and the central household. It is clear from a

[119] See p. 75 below.

number of sources that several of Leicester's leading officers (Thomas Dudley*, Alexander Neville*, or Mr Sandys) remained in England in 1586, and we should also expect sufficient servants to provide for the Countess.[120] If the structure of the Netherlands household is compared to that suggested for the household of an earl by Richard Braithwait in the early seventeenth century, it can be seen to follow it quite closely, although in some offices the numbers are greater.[121] Thus the Netherlands household should be seen as the core of the central household, with many of the staff probably holding offices identical to the ones they held at home. If we further assume the Netherlands household to have numbered upwards of one hundred, then the central household would have been upwards of 150.[122]

The 1584–6 disbursement book, like the earlier accounts, reveals little about the household's structure apart from the general references to the kitchen and its related departments, an outer (utter) chamber, as well as a chamber and a wardrobe. The Countess of Leicester's immediate attendants, many of whom would have been women, appear only peripherally in the book, possibly because she financed her own chamber out of her own income as dowager Countess of Essex.[123] The difficulty of assigning specific offices to individuals encountered in the earlier household also remains, with the exception of those included in the Netherlands lists. The funeral lists refer to the conventional household offices of steward, comptroller, treasurer and auditor, and identify five 'officers of household', but without naming the offices. Charles Wednester* is clearly identified elsewhere as the auditor, Richard Browne was probably the steward, William Gorge the comptroller and Edward Boughton* the treasurer, but the offices held by Alexander Neville, William Garnett*, George Harvey or Mr Sandys, to cite some important examples, are unclear.

The funeral lists include a large contingent of servants from the central household, but the numbers are swelled by the Kenilworth staff and the west midlands tenants and officers, as well as kindred and gentlemen of the wider affinity. The last raise one of the basic difficulties posed by the noble household, and indeed by the royal Household as well, the distinction between waged servants 'in ordinary' and the

[120] For Thomas Dudley, see his letter to Leicester of 11 Feb. 1586 from Leicester House, *Leic. Corres.*, 111–14.

[121] Braithwait's outline of an earl's household is printed in Batho, xxii. There are nine secretaries listed in the July 1587 Netherlands household where Braithwait only recommends one, but obviously special circumstances applied.

[122] Batho notes that Braithwait's household for an earl would number over one hundred. An interesting point of comparison is the reference to the fifty-eight servants who accompanied Leicester on his tour to Kenilworth in August 1585 on p. 301.

[123] Leicester left bequests to Bridget Fettiplace and Lettice Barrett, the Countess's maids, in his 1582 will. For Lettice Barrett, see also also n. 436 to the texts.

extraordinary or casual.[124] Since gentlemen made up a large number of the extraordinary servants, many of the gentlemen attendants at the funeral may formerly have been part of the household – though they can often be identified only by casual references.[125]

On the other hand, many of the gentlemen servants found in both the accounts and the lists achieved some prominence, and a considerable number became Members of Parliament. Their biographical details are therefore reasonably accessible, though their association with Leicester may not have been appreciated heretofore. The yeomen servants present a greater challenge. Often they are only names in various household documents. A trawl through wills occasionally yields some further incidental information but often not enough to justify the effort involved.[126] However, the later litigation over Leicester's estate, in particular the Chancery case between his illegitimate son, Sir Robert Dudley, and the Countess over Kenilworth in 1590, and the notorious Star Chamber case over Sir Robert Dudley's legitimacy in 1604–5, has provided some invaluable ancillary sources. In both these cases a number of Leicester's former servants (and in 1604–5 friends as well) were cited as witnesses and required in their depositions to supply both personal details and the nature of their relationship to Leicester. The 1590 case involved solely the officers and tenants of Kenilworth, but a considerable number of Leicester's former household servants were cited in the Star Chamber case. Only a few of the depositions have survived, unfortunately, but the information they supply is unique.[127]

Returning to the vexed question of size, some comparisons cannot be evaded. The evidence presented here suggests a household of between thirty-five and fifty in 1559–61, between fifty and one hundred in 1567, and between one hundred and 150 in 1584–5. This is roughly

---

[124] Leicester, for example, left a general bequest of a year's wages in his 1582 will to his servants 'that are in ordinary & receave wages'. For the Household and the Court, see Adams, 'Eliza Enthroned? the Court and its Politics', in C. Haigh (ed.), *The Reign of Elizabeth I* (1985), pp. 59–60.

[125] Extraordinary servants were not solely gentlemen, they also included some 'professional' yeoman servants as well. Huntsmen are a good example, see the Book of Servants Wages, pp. 407–8, 412.

[126] The wills, for example, of Thomas Blount and Anthony Dockwra* (PRO, PROB11/51/51v, 11/69/461), two of his leading servants, contain no reference of their relationship to him, while that of John Dudley* (PROB 11/63/117v-8) does. In his 1582 will Leicester left gifts to several named servants as well as the general bequest of a year's wages. In his 1587 will he noted his intention of adding for his servants a 'bill under my hand what I will have done for them', but no trace of this document can be found.

[127] The depositions in the Kenilworth case (referred to above, n. 11) are found in PRO, C21/ElizI/D/5/2; the case is discussed in 'West Midlands' 50. The 1604–5 Star Chamber case depositions are discussed in Abbreviated Documents above. Both the Longleat and the Penshurst collections contain lists of the deponents, fifty-six for the Countess and ninety for Sir Robert Dudley. Relevant surviving depositions are referred to in the notes.

similar to the size of the households of his peers. Sir William Cecil had a household of between twenty-five and thirty-five in the 1550s, and one of over one hundred after becoming a baron.[128] Sir William Petre (then Secretary of State) had one of sixty in 1554; the Duchess of Suffolk one of eighty in 1560–62; the Earl of Huntingdon one of sixty-eight (fifty- seven yeomen and eleven gentlemen) in 1564; Lord North ninety-four (seventy yeomen and twenty-four gentlemen) in 1578, though only seventy- five in 1582; and the 7th Earl of Northumberland in 1568 and the 4th Earl of Derby in 1587–90 between 120 and 150.[129] In Leicester's case the expansion of his household can be linked to his rank and status. In 1559–61 his rank was distinctly ambiguous, he was a commoner at law and possessed a minimal landed estate, yet he was also a senior officer of the Household and could to some extent claim to be a member of the nobility. However, if not overly large for his status, his household was probably pushing the limits of his means. His peerage and the expansion of his estate would justify the expansion of his household by 1567; by 1584–5, if somewhat more generously staffed than the ideal that Braithwait suggests for an earl, it was not extravagant for his eminence.

THE *APPARATUS CRITICUS*

The justification for publishing these documents is less their possible use as another example of the noble household economy than their potential contribution to the study of the reign of Elizabethan I, and it is this concern that has shaped the critical apparatus. The apparatus is admittedly extensive, but the range of subjects referred to in the documents demands it. At the most basic level there is the simple issue of Leicester's movements and those of the Court. Here the relationship of these accounts to the surviving registers of the Privy Council should be noted. The first volume of the Elizabethan registers covers only 22

[128] The lower figure for Cecil's household is given in C. Read, *Mr. Secretary Cecil and Queen Elizabeth* (New York, 1955), p. 87, and the higher in R.C. Barnett, *Place, Profit and Power: a study of the servants of William Cecil, Elizabethan statesman* (Chapel Hill, N.C., 1969), p. 9. My own examination of the wage lists for 1554–5 in BL, Lansdowne MS 118, fos. 42v-44, suggests that there was a core of about twenty liveried and waged servants and an overall household of some thirty odd. Owing to limited sources, it is not easy to be precise about Burghley's later household, but see Barnett for the expansion and Batho, xxiii. G.R. Morrison, 'The land, family and domestic following of William Cecil, Lord Burghley, c. 1550–1598' (Unpub. Oxford University, D.Phil. thesis, 1990), is more concerned with wider patronage than the household.

[129] These totals are drawn from Batho, xxii-iii; Emmison, p. 154, for Petre; the 1564 wage list (see n. 83 above) for Huntingdon; and BL Stowe MS 774 (Household Accounts, 1576–89), pt. i, fos. 2v-3, pt. ii, fo. 2, for North.

November 1558 to 12 May 1559 and then resumes in May 1562. The register for the period June 1582 to 19 February 1586 has been missing since the early seventeenth century. Therefore these accounts supply information about the movements of the Court which is invaluable. The Netherlands expedition, by contrast, is less of a problem for there is a detailed contemporary diary together with numerous other reliable sources against which Leicester's movements as reported in the dis- bursement books can be checked.

The second broad area of concern is that of episodes of significance, the Lambeth Conference of December 1584, for example, to which possible reference is made. There are, however, two topics, the entries relating to Amy Dudley found in the two Longleat accounts and the circumstances of Leicester's departure for the Netherlands in 1585, that demand a more extensive discussion than can be effectively supplied in the notes. These have been relegated to the two appendices to Part I.

The last broad area is persons other than household servants. Because these accounts take us to the heart of the political nation, references to persons are extensive. To keep the notes manageable, cross-referencing has been kept to a minimum and full references will be found only in the general index. However, because some cross-referencing is unavoidable the notes have been numbered consecutively across the four texts at the risk of taking them into the upper hundreds. It has also been decided to restrict references to those persons who appear in the accounts. Therefore those who are found only in the 1567–68 livery lists or the funeral lists are, with a few exceptions, not identified. A further problem arises from the decision to provide a separate Index of Servants, for the placing of men who might at one stage have been servants, but who were not in 1584–86 (Sir Edward Dyer, for example), is not straight-forward. The Index of Servants therefore is limited to persons who appear in the accounts as such; all others will be identified in the notes to the texts. Clergymen, who might have been chaplains at some point, raise similar difficulties and, for the sake of covenience, the identification of all clerics is made in the notes to the texts rather than the Index of Servants.

The biographical information supplied both in the notes and the Index of Servants has been reduced as much a possible to a standard formula: 1) basic biographical details, including membership of the House of Commons (indicated MP), 2) references to the lists in Part II, 3) any other immediately relevant evidence of association with Leices- ter.[130] For Members of Parliament, more extensive biographical infor-

---

[130] Reference to the documents in Part II is made in the following manner: [A] BSW, [B] livery 1559, [C] livery 1560, [D] badge 1567, [E] livery 1567 [G and H] Netherlands household 1587, [I and J] funeral. References to rank or office are also noted.

mation should be sought in the relevant volumes of Bindoff and Hasler.[131] As well as *The History of Parliament* and references to the various Dudley documents listed in the Abbreviations, the following sources have also been used silently: F.F. Foster, *The Politics of Stability: A Portrait of the Rulers of Elizabethan London* (1977) for office-holders of the City of London; G.M. Bell, *A Handlist of British Diplomatic Representatives 1509–1688* (1990), for diplomatic postings; and J. and S.A. Venn, *Alumni Cantabrigiensis* (Cambridge, 1922–7), and J. Foster, *Alumni Oxoniensis* (Oxford, 1891–2), for university and clerical careers.

The dating employed throughout is that of the Julian calendar, including the period of Leicester's lieutenant-generalship in the Netherlands. Where necessary the first quarter is indicated by a divided annual date. As noted above, although he did not receive his earldom until 29 September 1564, for the sake of convenience Lord Robert Dudley is referred to throughout as Leicester. Offices under the Crown and departments of the Court or royal Household are capitalised to distinguish them from possible equivalents in Leicester's household. A. Prockter and R. Taylor, *The A to Z of Elizabethan London* (Lympne Castle, 1979) has been employed for London topography; Chambers, iv, Appendix A, 'A Court Calendar' for removes of the Court; and Dr John James's 'A Journal of my Lord of Leycesters Actions at his first being in Holland 1585' (BL, Add. MS 48014, fos. 149–64v) for Leicester's movements in the Netherlands.[132] A glossary of some of the more obscure foodstuffs, saddlery and other terms has been supplied.

Finally, in view of their importance, some comment should be made about two specific documentary sources employed here. The first is really a class of document, the reports of foreign resident ambassadors, possibly the most widely-used source for the court politics of this period.[133] At the accession of Elizabeth, Philip II was represented by his councillor Gómez Suárez de Figueroa, Count of Feria, who remained in England until May 1559.[134] Feria was succeeded by Alvaro de La Quadra, Bishop of Aquila, who served as resident ambassador until he died of the plague in October 1563. The French resident ambassador had been withdrawn on the outbreak of war in 1557, and the permanent French embassy was not reinstated until May 1559. The new resident, Gilles de Noailles, Abbé de l'Isle, was the brother of the previous

---

[131] The spelling of surnames in the notes follows that employed in Bindoff and Hasler.

[132] For James, see n. 465 to the texts. Reference will also be made to a second (anonymous) diary in French covering December 1585–February 1586 in CA, Vincent MS 216, pp. 15–22.

[133] This discussion is limited to the resident ambassadors, comments on the extraordinary embassies will be found in the notes.

[134] The account here of the Spanish embassy is derived from that in the 'Feria Dispatch', where full reference to the scholarly literature is made.

residents and had served as acting ambassador himself in 1556. Noailles was replaced at the beginning of February 1560 by Michel de Seurre, whose embassy lasted until February 1562. The Spanish diplomatic correspondence survives in great quantity and has been published in three separate documentary collections. Unfortunately none of these is complete and the reliability of the transcriptions varies.[135] For ease of reference the *Calendar of State Papers, Spanish* will be cited here in the first instance, and the other collections or the originals only when the documents are omitted or mis-transcribed.[136] A certain amount of Noailles' correspondence survives, and a selection has been published.[137] Seurre's correspondence has disappeared almost entirely.[138].

In 1584 the situation was almost the reverse. The dismissal of Don Bernardino de Mendoza in January 1584 terminated the resident Spanish embassy for the remainder of the reign. Mendoza's knowledge of English affairs as ambassador in Paris in 1584–5 was derived from the reports of spies and agents.[139] The French embassy was therefore the only permanent one; the ambassador, Michel de Castelnau, Sieur de Mauvissière, had been in post since 1575. Castelnau was due for replacement in 1585, and returned to France in September, after his successor Guillaume de l'Aubépine, Baron de Châteauneuf, had finally arrived in the previous month.[140] Unfortunately, Castelnau's correspondence for 1584–5 is scattered and fragmentary.[141] There was,

---

[135] 'Feria Dispatch', esp. 304. The 1558–63 section of *CSPSp 1558–67* is little more than a translation of the first volume in the Spanish series *Correspondencia de Felipe II con sus Embajadores en la Corte de Inglaterra 1558 á 1584* (Colección de Documentos Inéditos para la Historia de España [CODOIN], lxxxvii, Madrid, 1886), supplemented by transcriptions made at Simancas by J.A. Froude. The CODOIN series is limited to correspondence between the ambassador and the King. Lettenhove included such correspondence in his collection as he considered relevant to Anglo-Netherlands relations. There is a substantial overlap with *CSPSp*, but also numerous omissions and the addition of correspondence with the Netherlands government. The relevant *legajos* in the AGS, E 812–3, contain much unpublished material.

[136] In the 'Feria Dispatch' all the various versions of the documents are cited, but this has not been considered necessary here.

[137] They are found in the Noailles collection, AMAE, CPA, IX-XX: XIII, XIV and XX are the relevant volumes. Some have been transcribed for the PRO (PRO31/3/24), and a selection has been published in Teulet, i, 318–400.

[138] A fragment from one of his despatches is referred to in n. 282 to the texts.

[139] Discussed in Adams, 'Outbreak of the Elizabethan Naval War', p. 50.

[140] The best introduction to Castelnau's embassy is provided by John Bossy in *Giordano Bruno and the Embassy Affair* (1991). His announced study of the embassy itself is eagerly awaited.

[141] The present location of both Castelnau's own papers and contemporary copies poses a number of technical problems, see the discussion in Teulet, i, xxvi-vii. Employed here are the volume of in-letters for 1584–5, BN VCC 470, and the selections of correspondence published in Teulet, iii, 249–330, and in the eccentric but useful F.H. Egerton, *The Life of Thomas Egerton, Lord Chancellor of England* (Paris, 18[28]), pp. 189–206.

however, also a resident agent of the States of Holland and Zeeland, Joachim Ortel (1542–90), who had been in post since 1583, and who was joined in the summer of 1584 by an agent for the States of Brabant, Jacques de Gryse.[142] Their reports to the States-General survive, but are not in print.[143] In the summer of 1585 they were joined by the commissioners sent to negotiate the treaty of assistance, who have left *inter alia* a detailed report of their negotiations.[144]

It is interesting to compare the information provided by the accounts with the diplomatic despatches. As will be quickly seen Leicester enjoyed very close social contact with the French embassy in 1559, but only peripheral reference is made to him in the Noailles despatches. By contrast, his contact with the Spanish embassy, as revealed in the accounts at any rate, was minimal. Therefore the comments on him in the Spanish despatches, which have been used extensively as sources, must be treated with some caution.[145] He enjoyed quite friendly social relations with Castelnau, although the political implications are still not entirely clear.[146] L'Aubépine was another case, although here only a few months passed before Leicester departed for the Netherlands. There is fragmentary evidence of Leicester's social relations with Ortel, but Ortel's despatches, in common with other Dutch diplomatic correspondence of the period, tend to the strictly businesslike and contain little of the wider political reporting found in the Spanish.[147]

The second source is the anonymous history or collection of notes found in BL, Add. MS 48023, which has attracted considerable interest in recent years.[148] This begins with the circumstances of the fall of the Duke of Somerset in 1549, covers the first years of Elizabeth's reign in

---

[142] For Ortel's appointment, see *CSPF, 1583–4*, 43.

[143] ARA, Eerste Afdeling, Regeringsarchieven 90A-B. Some extracts can be found in the relevant chapters of J.L. Motley, *History of the United Netherlands*.

[144] ARA, Eerste Afdeling, Regeringsarchieven 101B (Staten Generaal 8299).

[145] Examples will be found in the notes. However, it might be noted that there is some support here for Spanish claims that Leicester was 'French' in allegiance.

[146] Apart from the evidence found here, see also Bossy, *Bruno*. It should be noted, though, that by 1584 the relationship was nearly ten years old and had to some degree been affected by the complex intrigues surrounding the Anjou marriage. As Bossy suggests, one gets the sense that Castelnau was very discreet about his social relationships in his despatches.

[147] The Collectie Ortel, in ARA, Eerste Afdeling, is a disappointment, consisting mainly of his papers as a military commissioner for Orange in the 1570s. Few of his diplomatic papers survive, *lias* 50 includes an undated account of expenses, with a few references to Leicester.

[148] The 'history' is found on fos. 350–69v. It was first brought to my attention over a decade ago by Dr G.W. Bernard and Ms Pam Wright; I am extremely to Dr Bernard for his generosity in supplying me with a copy of his transcription of the document, which has saved me a great deal of work. The history is used extensively in N.L. Jones, *The Birth of the Elizabethan Age* (Oxford, 1993).

some detail, and ends in the autumn of 1562. The provenance and authorship of this document is a vexed and complex subject, and all that can be said here is that if it is now part of a collection formed by Robert Beale, it was previously in the possession of Thomas Norton.[149] The 'author' was a protestant layman of quite outspoken opinions, which included a deep suspicion of the Dudleys and Leicester in particular. He does provide some very valuable information and some refreshing comment, but his reliability as a source cannot be taken for granted.[150] He will be used here only when directly relevant, and referred to simply as BL, Add. MS 48023.

EDITORIAL METHOD

The editing of the documents has been undertaken in accord with current Camden Society practice and the guidelines suggested in R.F. Hunnisett, *Editing Records for Publication* (British Records Association, 1977). The documents are printed in their entirety, with the exception of the extracts from the four bills for livery in Part II, where the remainder of the bill is not relevant. The bills pasted in Dudley Papers XIV and XV have been included.[151] Evelyn MS 258b and the Staunton Manuscript have been treated as separate documents, despite the chronological overlap. The basic text for the Staunton Manuscript is the Knowles transcription, with the entries transcribed by Halliwell-Phillipps added and identified. Capitalisation has been modernised, abbreviations extended silently, elisions separated (thannunication) and broken words joined (a nother). Possessives have presented some difficulty, for in many cases it is clear that a contemporary form of possessive has been employed, and the somewhat rough and ready system of modernising the possessive of words ending in a consonant and leaving those ending in a vowel in their contemporary form has been adopted. Otherwise, the modernisation of spelling has been limited

---

[149] A collection 'on the rivalry between the Dukes of Northumberland and Somerset' which can only be be this work was among the papers of Norton's that were seized by the Privy Council after his death, see M.A.R. Graves, *Thomas Norton the Parliament Man* (Oxford, 1994), p. 147. Patrick Collinson has noted the preservation of Norton's papers among Beale's, see 'Puritans, Men of Business and Parliaments', in *Elizabethan Essays* (1994), p. 77, but the whole subject needs further examination.

[150] The author, together with 'Mr Dannet', was at Hampton Court when Leicester returned to Court after his wife's death (see n. 280 to the texts), but he states 'And for my self I knewe him not, for I never sawe him before', which suggests that he did not have much contact with the Court.

[151] Owing to a considerable overlap between the two capper's bills, only part of the second is printed.

to i and j, and u and v, despite the temptation to standardise the spelling of proper names and places. Abbreviations of weights and measures have been left in their contemporary form.

The nature of the texts themselves has also been of influence. As these are not literary texts, only minimal modernisation of punctuation has been necessary, and as much of the original form of the document as possible has been retained. On the other hand the numerous variants of accountants' jargon or abbreviations have been standardised (e.g. *summa paginae* or 'by your lordship's commandment') and dd has been extended to delivered, and neays to necessaries. Where necessary dropped particles have been supplied. Given that they are in print, the Knowles and Halliwell-Phillips transcriptions from the Staunton Manuscript have been copied without amendment. The present foliation of Dudley Papers XIV and XV has been followed, including the omission of the blank leaves. Evelyn MS 258b has not yet been foliated, and therefore only recto or verso have been indicated. However, since each page has a separate heading, comparison with the original should present no difficulty. The Staunton Manuscript obviously possesses no foliation and the pagination of *The Castle of Kenilworth* is not of much relevance to a reconstruction of the original. Therefore only the location of the Halliwell-Phillipps extracts has been noted.

Asterisks (*) after names indicate entries in the Index of Servants and are usually limited to the initial appearance in the texts; full references to individuals will be found in the general index. Round brackets have been limited to their use in the original, square brackets have been employed for editorial interventions, and angle brackets to introduce marginalia into the text. With the exception of one or two references in the notes, J.E. Jackson's marginalia and notes in Dudley Papers XIV and XV have been omitted as they simply draw attention to references to Amy Dudley. It has also been decided to omit most of the accountants' marginalia in these volumes as well, as they would clutter the text to no purpose. However the page references to the day-book in Dudley Papers XIV have been included, for they are of considerable assistance in establishing the chronology of the entries. In Evelyn MS 258b it has been considered unnecessary to include the 'pvs' annotation which is found on every page, but Leicester's marginalia, which are both interesting and important, and the initials a and B have been retained. No marginalia survives from the Staunton Manuscript. Any specific treatment of the household lists is described in the notes to those texts. Textual notes to Part I, Items A, B, C and D, and Part II, Items F, G, H and J, are grouped at the end of the individual item.

PART I

HOUSEHOLD ACCOUNTS AND
DISBURSEMENT BOOKS

A. THE ACCOUNT OF WILLIAM CHANCY
1558–9
(LONGLEAT, DUDLEY PAPERS XIV)

[Cover]

Anno Primo Regie Elizabeth.
Compotus William Chancy Servient' Domini Robarti Duddeley prenobilis Ordinis Garterij Militis Magistri Equorum domine nostrae Reginae tam de omnibus et singulis denariorum sive de dicto domino receptis quia de allocationibus et solucionibus eoreandem factis inter xx diem mensis Decembris anno superdicto et ultimum diem mensis Decembris tunc proximo sequit' prout in libro sequent' plenibus continentur.[1]

[fo. 1]
Money receivid by the hondes of me William Chansye to the use of the right honourable the Lord Robert Duddeley, Master of the Quenes Majesties Horsis begynnynge the xxth of December anno primo Regine Elizabeth and ending the xxth of December then next folowing for one hole yeare.[2]

Imprimis receivid of William Grice the xxth of December}	lxiijli.
Item of him the xxiiijth of December}	xlli.
Item of him the xxvijth of December}	Clvli.[3]
Item of Mr Thomas Blunt the iiijth of February}	xxxli.[4]
Item Platt of Iremonger Lane at divers tymes takin uppon Interest}	[Cljli. *deleted*] VIIJCljli.
Item of Mr Aleworthe the xvth of Aprill}	Cli.[5]
Item of Master Forteskewe xvjth of Aprill}	iiij**vjli. xiijs. iiijd.[6]
Item of Master Anthony Foster* the ijde dey of May}	CCCli.

---

[1] There is a pencilled note on the flyleaf by J.E. Jackson that the marginal references to pagination suggest that this volume had been extracted or copied from another one.

[2] The title on the cover gives a different terminal date (ultimum diem mensis Decembris), but 20 December is also the one employed by the auditors, see p. 107 below.

[3] These receipts were presumably Grice's cash in hand on the closing of his account. Other references to Grice's account can be found on pp. 121, 123 below.

[4] This was a loan, for the repayment, see p. 50 below.

[5] Richard Aylesworth, see p. 107 below.

[6] Later references to Henry Fortescue (pp. 59, 130) and the christening of his son (p. 47) suggest that this was Henry Fortescue (1515–76), Esquire of the Body from 1559, rather than his better-known cousin (Sir) John Fortescue (1533–1607), MP, Master of the Wardrobe from 1559.

Item of my Lord of Northefolke the ijde of May}   lli.[7]
Item of Rivett marchaunt of London}   CCli.[8]
Item of Mr Apleyerd the vijth of May}   Cli.
Item of Mr Bartie marchant the ijd of June}   Clxvli. vs. vjd.[9]
Item receivid of your lordship at Grenwich the xth of July}   lli.
Item receivid of Edward Carye* the xvij of July}   xlli.
Item receivid of William Huggans* at divers tymes in August}   Cxli.
Item receivid of my Lord Admirall in August}   xlixli. vjs. viijd.[10]
Item receivid of Edward Huggans marchant of London in
September}   li.[11]
Item receivid of Mrs Palmer uppon Pope the vintener's bill}
ªin Decemberª   Cli.[12]
Sum of the hole receits}   MMVCxlli. vs. vjd.
                                                          [*signed*] Wm. Chancy

[fo.2]
<1 pagina>

Forin expinses and chargs with rewards
Imprimys gyvin in almes xx Decembris}   vjd.
For the charges of the buriall of your lordship's boye}   xiiijs. viijd.
Gyvin to Gowre* for his charges riding in to Lincolne
shire to my ladye}   xxs.[13]
Item peid for hier of certeyne haknes for my ladye by
Mr Blunt's command}   lxjs.

---

[7] In November 1558 the 4th Duke of Norfolk married Margaret Audley (1540?-1564), the widow of Leicester's brother Lord Henry Dudley, who had been killed at St Quentin in September 1557 (N. Williams, *Thomas Howard, Fourth Duke of Norfolk* (1964), pp. 34–5). See also n. 28 below.

[8] (Sir) Thomas Revett (d. 1582), mercer. For the repayment of this loan, see p. 118 below.

[9] Francis Bartie (d. 1611), naturalised Flemish merchant, later salt monopolist and conspirator with Ridolphi (E. Hughes, 'The English Monopoly of Salt in the years 1563–71', *E.H.R.*, xl (1925), 337–40; M.B. Donald, *Elizabethan Monopolies: The History of the Company of Mineral and Battery Works 1568–1604* (Edinburgh, 1961), pp. 54–7). The Duchess of Northumberland owed him £133 6s 8d at her death, Leicester repaid a debt of £719 in late 1560 (see p. 125 below), and a bill for commodities supplied between 1559 and 1566 can be found in DP Box V, fo. 7.

[10] Edward Fiennes, Lord Clinton (1512–1585), 1st Earl of Lincoln in 1572. His second wife was Northumberland's niece and he enjoyed close relations with the Dudleys. This payment was probably made when the court was at his house at West Horsley during the progress, see p. 80 below. For Leicester's attendance at his funeral in 1585, see n. 474 below.

[11] Edward Huggins or Hogan, mercer and common councillor (1565–93), brother to William Huggins* and Sir Thomas Gresham's factor.

[12] For Mrs Palmer, also see pp. 72, 106 below. Probably the wife of the goldsmith Simon Palmer and mother of the more prominent goldsmith Andrew Palmer (c.1544–1599), MP.

[13] Lady Amy Dudley. See Appendix I.

To Jamys Thompson* for the lyverye of your lordship's
horsys lying at Envild mensis November per bill}   xxxs. vjd.[14]
Item gyvin in reward to Mr Umpton's man bringing ij does
per Blunt}   xijs. viijd.[15]
For a ladder and certeyne tenterhokes for your lordship's
chamber deliveryd to Johnes*}   xxd.
<2 pagina>
Item for vj drinking glassys bowght by Hannce*}   viijs. viijd.
Item for his botehier then}   iiijd.
To Powell* for a glasse to putt in quinces}   vjd.
Gyvin in reward to the woodberers}   xijd.
Item for cariage of [your] lordship's stuff from
Somersett house to Whithall mensis December}   xvjd.[16]
Item for a lace for your lordship's keyes}   viijd.
Item for my chargs taking possession of the house}   ijs.[17]
Item gyvin in reward to Mr Cobham's servant comying to
your lordship of messages}   xijd.[18]
Item in reward to the shomaker}   xijd.
<3 pagina>
Item to Mr Foskewes man for his reward bringing conservid
quinsys}   iijs. iiijd.
Item to Mr Spynulas servant bringing a bores speare}   xxs.[19]
Item to Thomas Johnes* for his botehier at sundry tymes
going into London about your lordship's affeires}   ijs. vjd.
                    Pagina} ixli. iijs. iiijd.

[fo. 2v]

Forin charges
Item to John Forest* for his charges ryding to Mr

[14] Enfield. See Appendix I.
[15] Edward Unton (1534-82) of Wadley, Berks., MP. Second husband of Anne (Seymour),
widow of Leicester's elder brother John, Earl of Warwick (d. 1554). For references to her
and to their son Sir Henry, see pp. 67, 213-4 below.
[16] The court removed from Somerset House to Westminster on 22-3 December 1558.
[17] Kew, see n. 21 below.
[18] It is not clear whether he is the same man as the Cobham* identified as a servant
on p. 105.
[19] Benedict Spinola (c.1528-1579/80), the leading Genoese merchant in London. In
1572 Leicester described him to Walsingham as 'my dear friend and the best Italian I
know in England', see G.D. Ramsay, 'The Undoing of the Italian Mercantile Colony in
Sixteenth Century London', N.B. Harte and K.S. Ponting (edd.), *Textile History and
Economic History* (Manchester, 1963), pp. 41-3. Some correspondence and a large bill
covering 1562-66 (DP Box V, fos. 146-50v) survive. See also p. 161 below.

Hides to my ladye}   iijs. iiijd.[20]

Item for bromes for the chamber}   ijd.

Item peid unto Mr Gryse for your lordship's lettres
patents of your house at Kewe}   xiiijli. xijs. viijd.[21]

Item for mending certeine stoles & tables}   viijd.

Item peid to Gower for his charges riding to my ladye over
and besides the xxs. which ys before wrytten per bill}   xxvjs. viijd.

Item gyvin in reward for bringing a rinlett of reynisse wyne}   vs.

Item for a locke for the pantry dore}   ijs.

For botehier to Eglinbye* being sent for Whittill}   viijd.[22]

<4 pagina>

Item to my Ladye Butler's man bringing a lampre pie}   ijs. vjd.[23]

Item for ribon for keyes}   iiijd.

Item to the launders for wasshing your lordship lying at
Somersett Place}   xixs.

Item in reward to Mrs Clarentius's servant bringing
a crymson bedd embrodryd}   xls.[24]

Item for dressing Black Cordall your lordship's gelding}   ijs.

Item to Mr Johnes servant of Lynne for
bringyng wildfoule}   js. iiijd.[25]

Item to the Mr of the Rolls' servant for bringing the
blacke gelding}   xs.[26]

Item to Sir John York's man for bringing a suger lofe}   iijs. iiijd.[27]

---

[20] William Hyde of Throcking, see Appendix I.

[21] The letters patent for the house known as 'the capital messuage of Kew' are dated 29 Dec. 1558 (*CPR, 1558–60*, 60), see also Introduction, p. 25, and V.C.H., *Surrey*, iii, 482–3. This was Elizabeth's first grant to him.

[22] William Whittle or Whittell, Leicester's favourite tailor, see the frequent references below. Numerous bills for 1562–6 survive (DP Box V, fos. 44–86) and he and Maynard the hosier (see n. 255 below) were the main recipients of the cloth supplied in the 1571–4 account (DP XII). He may be the William Widnell, merchant taylor, listed by Foster (p. 167) as a common councillor 1574–8.

[23] Possibly Silvestra Butler, who was arrested for complicity in the Dudley Plot (D.M. Loades, *Two Tudor Conspiracies* (Cambridge, 1965), pp. 229, 234). Mrs Butler the elder and the younger attended Amy Dudley's funeral; she may have been related to Leicester's servant Anthony Butler*.

[24] Susan White (d. 1567), known as Mrs Clarentius following her marriage to Thomas Tonge, Clarenceux King of Arms (1534–6). A long-standing member of Queen Mary's household and a Gentlewoman of her Privy Chamber, she went into exile with the Countess of Feria in the summer of 1559 and died in Spain. The Duchess of Northumberland left her a gift in her will.

[25] The proximity of the Robsart estate (see Introduction, p. 13) to King's Lynn gave Leicester a close association with the town. He had attempted to hold it for Lady Jane in 1553 and became its high steward in 1572.

[26] Sir William Cordell (1522?–1581), MP. Cordell had numerous business dealings with John Dudley*.

[27] Sir John York (d. 1569), MP. York was close to Northumberland and his family: his

Item to Eglamby for cariege of a trunke from
Christchurche to Somersett Plaice}   iiijd.[28]
Item for i quire browne paper and one of white}   vjd.
To the hosier's servant in reward}   iiijd.
        Pagina} xxli. xvs. xd.

[fo. 3]

                 Yet forin charges
<5 pagina rewards gyvin for New Years giftes>
Item in reward to Sir Ambros Caves servant}   iijs. iiijd.[29]
Item to the Spanishe teyler}[b]   xs.[30]
To Doctor Howell for a New Years gift}   vjli. iijs. iiijd./xx pistolls[31]
Item to the Surveyor's of the Works servant}   ijs.[32]
To Mrs Ashelyes servant}   iijs. iiijd.[33]
Item to your lordship's hondes to give in reward}   xls.
Item to Jamys shomaker's servant}   xijd.[34]
Item to Pope the draper's servant}   iijs. iiijd.
Item to my Lord Hastings' servant}   vs.[35]

wife was a witness of the Duchess's will, and he lent money to the Duchess, Lord
Ambrose Dudley in 1557 (PRO, C54/548/12), and Leicester in 1560 (see p. 100 below).
For Leicester's later relations with his sons, see n. 691 below.

[28] Christchurch or Cree Church was the common name for the former Augustinian
priory of the Holy Trinity adjoining St Katherine Cree, obtained at the dissolution by
Thomas, Lord Audley, and converted into his London residence. It was inherited in 1556
by his daughter Margaret, wife to Lord Henry Dudley and then the Duke of Norfolk
(see n. 7 above), who rebuilt it. It was thereafter known as Duke Place (see Williams,
Norfolk, p. 35). It is clear from the numerous references in this account (see pp. 46, 61, 94
below) and in bills that Leicester used it as a London residence during the later 1550s.
In 'Dudley Clientèle' (p. 252) it is incorrectly located as 'by St Bartholomew the Grand'.

[29] Sir Ambrose Cave (1503-58), Chancellor of the Duchy of Lancaster, MP. For his
membership of Elizabeth's household in 1558, see 'Feria Dispatch' n. 34. In May 1559
he and Leicester were appointed joint lords lieutenant of Warwickshire.

[30] See also pp. 87, 89 below. He may be John Anthonio (p. 121), for whom a warrant
(29 Dec. 1565) and a bill (Antony the tailor) survive in DP Box V, fos. 274, 300.

[31] The frequent references to the use of foreign coin in both this and the Ellis account
reveal the extent to which it was preferred to the debased English coinage.

[32] Lawrence Bradshaw (from 1547 to 1560), see *King's Works*, iii, 55-9.

[33] Katherine Astley (d.1565), the central figure in Elizabeth's household from the mid-
1540s, and Chief Gentlewoman of the Privy Chamber after the accession.

[34] James Crokeham, see p. 122 below. A bill of his (n.d.) is pasted into the Ellis Account,
see pp. 174-5 below.

[35] References to Lord Hastings in this and the first half of the Ellis account cannot be
assumed to be to Henry, Lord Hastings (c.1536-95), 3rd Earl of Huntingdon from 23
June 1560, for his uncle Edward, Lord Hastings of Loughborough (1519-72), Master of
the Horse and then Lord Chamberlain to Mary, was on good terms with Leicester (see
DP I, fo. 16, Loughborough to Leicester, ? May 1559). By 1559 Henry Hastings was the
husband of Leicester's sister Katherine (whose letter to her brother of 5 May 1559 (DP

Item to your lordship's cutler for a rapier
and dager gyvin to your lordship}   xxxvijs./vj pistulls
To Lewes's wyfe for reward}   vjs. ijd.
To the childerne of the kychin}   vs.
Item to Mr Ildersam's servant}   vs.
Item to my Lady Clerk's servant}   ijs.
Item to your lordship's hand to give in regard [*sic*]
for bringing a wrought shirt}   xviijs. vjd./ iij pistulls
Item to Mr Litchefild for New Yers gift by your
lordship's commandment}   xlixs. iiijd.[36]
Item to your lordship's owne honds which you sent
to Marshall* your servant being sick}   xls.
Item to your lordship which you gave to Holland*}   iijs. iiijd.
Item peid for a table & tristill at Kewe}   xs.
Item for tothepyks per Hannce}   iijs. iiijd.
Item to a power woman of Hatfild bringing aples}   iijs. iiijd.
Item for my botehier to London}   iijd.
Item gyvin to the Gard for New Years gift
by the honds of Turner}   xxvs. iiijd.
Item to Mrs Yong part of peyment dewe unto her for
her annuite}   lijs. iiijd.[37]
Item peyd to Mr Gower for parcill charges of my
lady's comyng out of Lincoln as appearythe uppon

I, fo. 14) was clearly written as his wife), but the date of their marriage poses problems.
Some form of marriage took place in May 1553 (Hist MSS Comm, *VIIth Report* (1879),
608), but it was not a full one, for while the Duchess of Northumberland refers to her
daughter as Katherine Hastings in her will, she also notes a condition 'if it so chance
that my Lord Hastings do refuse her or she him', which would imply that she was still
under the age of consent (12). Her date of birth, in common with most of Northumberland's
thirteen children, is not easy to establish, and in her case the difficulties are compounded
by the fact that he had two daughters christened Katherine. The Dudley pedigrees (see
'West Midlands', 27) agree that Katherine Hastings was the elder of the two and that
the younger was his fifth and last daughter who died as a child, but two state that
Katherine Hastings was his third daughter and one his fourth. One pedigree (CA,
Muniment Room, Roll 13/1) possibly states that the younger died aged 7 (the section is
damaged), but it was certainly before the Duchess herself died for of her daughters only
Katherine Hastings and Mary Sidney were alive then. Katherine Hastings' funeral
monument in Chelsea Old Church states that she died aged 72 in 1620, but a date of
birth of 1548 is clearly too late, for Katherine, Duchess of Suffolk, christened one of the
two in 1545 (see n. 320 below). However, if this birthdate is assigned to Katherine
Hastings, it is difficult to fit in a younger sister who died aged 7 before 1555. On the
other hand, if it was the younger, Katherine Hastings could have been born no earlier
than 1543 if she was less than 12 at the beginning of 1555. Either date, though, would
make her no older than 16 in 1559.

[36] Probably Thomas Lichfield (d. 1586), Groom of the Privy Chamber from 1559, MP.

[37] Not included among the Duchess of Northumberland's servants or bequests or in
the schedule of Hales Owen annuitants in BRL, HH MS 351621.

a bill befor mentionyd}   xxvjs. viijd.

Pagina} xxiijli. xixs. xjd.

[fo.3v]

Yet forin charges

<6 pagina>

Item in reward to Mr Hides servante bringing partriges}   vjs. iiijd.

Item to Jamys the shomaker uppon a bill}   lxs.

Item in reward for the Quenes New Yers gift}   j gilt cuppe xxxviijs.

Item for ij brusshis iiijs. iiijd., for ij quilt cappes
iijs., for ij penne knyves xvjd., for a whetstone vjd., in
toto per bill} <G. Jyles>   ixs. ijd.

'Item to Mr Gryse for certeyne perles xli.ᶜ quia post

Item to Eglmbye for bringing your lordship a
New Years gyft}   vjs. iiijd.

Item to Maddy's man bringing red wine}   ijs.

<7 pagina>

Item to Johnes for botehier to London}   viijd.

Item for my botehier to London}   ixd.

Item for linkes}   iiijd.

Item for iij pottpaines for the buttry}   iiijs.

Item to Mr Cordall's servant bring[ing] fesants}   iijs. iiijd.

Item to Mr Gryse to give in reward among your
lordship's embroderers}   xxs.

Item to Plumber Mr Thesaurer's servant for mony
which your lordship borowyd by Roberts*}   xixs.³⁸

Item to Daggs minstrall at the Tower}   xijd.

Item to the porters and warders of the Tower}   xs.

Item the same daye for almes}   [xijd. *deleted*]

Item in reward emong Smythes the embroderear's servants
your lordship being present}   xs.

Item the same dey in almes}   xijd.

Item for i*dd.* tynne plattes}   iiijs. vjd.

For my botehier to London & back to Westminster}   viijd.

Item for bedstaves}   xijd.

Item to Edward Roberts for botehier being sent for
John Lawnyson goldsmith}   [xijd. *deleted*] iiijd.³⁹

---

³⁸ Sir Thomas Parry (1515–60), Treasurer of the Household from Jan. 1559, MP. For
repayments, see p. 120 below.

³⁹ John Lonison (1523–1582), Master of the Mint in 1572 (Donald, *Elizabethan Monopolies*,
pp. 47–53). A bill of c.1560–1 (DP Bx V, fos 38–41) survives and he may be the Mr
Lanyson given livery in 1567. See also pp. 88, 119, 124 below.

Pagina} ixli. xviijs. vd. [xvijs. vd. *deleted*]

[fo. 4]

Yet forin charges

Item in reward to Whittell's servants your lordship being in his shoppes}	vjs. viijd.

<8 pagina>

Item for our dyners the same deye your lordship dyning with Mr Harrington}	xiijs. iiijd.[40]
Item to Oswald* for botehier being sent to the Tower to make ready your lordship's lodging ther & backe ageine}	vjd.[41]
Item for cariage your lordship's stuff from Whitehall to the Tower}	viijd.
Johnes for botehier being sent from the Tower to Mr Brideman for bear}	xijd.
Item for the charges of your lordship's patent to Mr Cotton's man}	liiijs. iiijd.[42]
Item to Holland for horsemeat in Seint Johnes Streat}	xviijd.
Item to George Jyles for botehier being sent for a gildsmythe}	viijd.
Item for thread bought by him}	ijd.
For urinalls bought by him at sundry tymes}	xiiijd.
Item sent unto Edmund being syke}	xs.
Item to Forest for his charges of horsemeat & his owne your lordship being at Christ Church}	xijd.
Item peid for links going from Christ Church to Whitehall & backe ageyne}	xijd.
Item to Johnes for the cariage of a steall saddle to my Lord of Bedford[43] from Sir William Pykering[44]}	vjd.

---

[40] John Harington (1517–82), of Stepney and Cheshunt, MP, see also 'Feria Dispatch', n. 31. In December 1560 Harington, Sir Henry Sidney and John Tamworth were sureties for Leicester's loan from William Byrde, see n. 200 below. This dinner was probably the occasion for the gaming referred to on p. 99 below.

[41] The Queen removed to the Tower prior to the Coronation on 12 January 1559.

[42] Probably that as Master of the Horse, dated 11 Jan. 1559 (*CPR, 1558–60*, 61).

[43] Francis, 2nd Earl of Bedford (1527–1585). Extensive evidence of their friendship survives. For Leicester's involvement with his funeral in 1585, see nn. 578, 618 below.

[44] Sir William Pickering (1516/7–1575), MP, follower of Northumberland and a central figure in Wyatt's Rebellion. He was employed in 1558 on an embassy to Germany and did not return to England until 4 May 1559, see 'Feria Dispatch', n. 343, and *CSPSp, 1558–67*, 67. For Pickering and Leicester, see also n. 93 below. On 9 Sept. 1559 (as calendared in *CSPSp*, 96) La Quadra reported rumours that Pickering had challenged Bedford to a duel and that Leicester was his second. Bedford is an error by the editor, the original (AGS, E 812, fo. 114) gives the Earl of Arundel. See also nn. 140, 151 below.

Item to my Lord Clinton's horse keaper for i horse lent}   vs.
Item to Mr Robster's* servant for bringing a hawke}   vs.
Item for candells bought by Morrys}   ijs.
Item to Mr Apleyerd's servant bringing your
lordship a hawke}   vjs. viijd.
Item gyvin to Mr Butler* at his departing in to the
country after the coronation by your lordship's commandment}   xls.
Pagina} vijli. xjs. ijd.

[fo. 4v]

Yet forin charges and rewards

<9 pagina>
Item to Oswald for cariage of certeine stuff from the
Tower & for other mony laid out by him}   xxd.
Item to Mr Bewe* for paper by him bought at sundry tymes} ijs. iiijd.
Item to Eglmby for botehier going about
your lordship's busines}   viijd.
Item to the launder by Morrys}   xijd.
Item to Henry Johnes for his botehier going in to London}   xd.
<oi pagina [sic]>
Item to George Jyles for his lyke botehier}   iiijd.
Item for the making of Brandon's obligation per Gryse}   ijs. vjd.[45]
Item for lights bought at sundry tymes}   xvjd.
Item gyvin to Mr Gower by your lordship at his going home}   xls.
Item gyvin to the nurse and mydwife at the christening
of Mr Foskewes child}   xxijs. vjd.[46]
Item gyvin unto your lordship the same tyme}   xlvjs. ijd.
Item for the charges of the warrant for the making
of your lordship's armor}   vjs. viijd.[47]
Item for horsemeat & other charges your lordship being
at Wolwich with my Lord Amirall}   vs.
Item to Eglamby for his botehier to Grenwich being sent
with your lordship's warrant for your armor}   ijs.

---

[45] See also pp. 50, 121 below. Possibly Robert Brandon, goldsmith and chamberlain of London (1583–91), see p. 224 n. 473 below.

[46] Probably Dudley (d. 1604), MP, son of Henry Fortescue, see n. 6 above.

[47] To the armourer at Greenwich, see the next entry but one. It would appear from further entries below (esp. pp. 81–2) that this armour was not ready until August. A Greenwich armour of Leicester's survives in the Tower Armouries, but it is dated c. 1575 (A. Young, *Tudor and Jacobean Tournaments* (1987), p. 66). Although Leicester has been identified as one of the challengers in the Coronation tournament on 16–17 January by some sources (e.g. Williams, *Norfolk*, p. 39), this would appear to be an error, for he is not found in the tournament records, CA, Tournament Portfolio, it. 4a–f.

Item for the cariage of beare by water to Kewe} ijs. viijd.
Item for my botehier to London} iiijd.
Item gyvin by Slifild* for a reward for a horse and
foteclothe which your lordship borowyd to the Parliament} xijd.[48]
Item to John Forest for necessaries for the stable} xxd.
Pagina} vjli. xviijs. viijd.

[fo. 5]

Yet forin charges and rewards

<11 pagina>
Item for rybon for your lordship's keyes} vjd.
Item to Mr Hides servant careng your lordship's letters
to his master} vs.
Item to Sermaunt* for his botehier going about your
lordship's affeires to London} viijd.
Item to a boy bringing your lordship's spaniells out
of Barkshire} vs.
Item to Morrys* for the launders} ijs. vjd.
Item to hym for candell} viijd.
Item for aples} iiijd.
Item peid by Curssing* for watching the stable stuff at [the]
Coronation} iiijs.[49]
For rybon for your lordship's tablett} xijd.
Item for a pair of Garnesey hose} vs.
Item for lace and sylke by Powell} iiijd.
Item to Powell for the making clen of the Coronation stuff} xxvs.
<12 pagina>
Item for candells bought by Morrys Edwardes} viijd.
Item for parfumes} iiijd.
Item to Holland for botehier being sent to London about
your lordship's affeires} xd.
Item to Morrys Edwardes for candells} viijd.
Item for my botehier to London} iiijd.
Item for perfumes to burne} xvjd.
Item to Morrys Edwardes for wasshing} iiijs. xd.
Item in reward to Mr Hides servant bring[ing] partrigs} iijs. iiijd.
Item gyvin almes by Slyford} ijd.
Item to Parker for cariage of j brace wardens out of
Northefolke} ijs. iiijd.
Pagina} lxiiijs. xd.

---

[48] The opening of Parliament took place on 23 January.
[49] The Coronation was held on 15 January.

[fo. 5v]

Forin charges & rewards

<13 pagina>

Item to my Lord of Darbyes servant for bringing your lordship j brace of puffins}	xs.[50]
Item to Forrest riding to Kewe about your lordship's affeires}	xijd.
Item to Morrys Edwards for candell}	xvjd.
Item to Forest for necessaries for [the] stable}	xxd.
Item for paper}	iiijd.
Item for the carriag of dy beafe [sic] from Gryse}	viijd.
Item for tothe pikes}	xviijd.
Item for browne paper}	ijd.
Item to Morrys Edwards for wasshing}	vjs. viijd.
Item to Mr Brudnell for drawing of armes} <Bricknell>	xxxviijs.[51]
Item for the exchange of certeine French crownes which I peid to George Mr Thesaurer's servant}	xxd.
Item peid George Mr Thresaures servant xl Frenche crownes which your lordship outhe him}	xijli. xiijs. iiijd.
Item for my boteheir to London and backe ageyne about your lordship's affeires}	viijd.
Item gyvin to Holland being syke by your lordship's commandyment}	vjs. viijd.
Item delivered to your lordship in gould which you gave to Mr Knowles*}	xxs.[52]
Item to Lewes for a hargabus with the appurtenances}	xxxviijs.
Item to my Lord of Darbyes servant bringing your lordship puffins}	vs.
Item to Johins for his chargys riding to Mr Hides to my ladye}	iijs. iiijd.
Item to Gryffin* the under cooke for hose and shoys for himselfe}	viijs. viijd.

Pagina} xixli. xviijs. viijd.

---

[50] Edward Stanley, 3rd Earl (1509–1572), with whom considerable correspondence survives in DP I-II.

[51] See also p. 61 below

[52] Numerous references to members of the family of Sir Francis Knollys (1512–96), Vice-Chamberlain (and after 1570 Treasurer) of the Household, will be found in these accounts. Leicester and Sir Francis appear to have been on good terms since the reign of Edward VI, and the connection was an established one long before Leicester's marriage to Lettice Knollys (21 September 1578). BL, Add. MS 48023, fo. 363v, records the death of one of Sir Francis's children named Dudley Warwick in June 1562.

[fo. 6]

Yet forrin charges & rewards

Item to Father Parker by your lordship's commandment}	xxxs.
Item to Eglmby being sent to Grenwich to the armerers for his botehier}	ijs. vjd.
Item to Bewe for paper bought by him at sundry tymes}	ijs.
Item for wardons and aples}	xijd.

<15 pagina>

Item to Morrys Edwardes for candells}	viijd.
Item for a lynke bringing monny from Platt}	viijd.
Item for my dyner that deye being about the receit of monnye}	viijd.
Item peid to Mr Thomas Blunt for so mouche monny of him borrowid}	xxxli.
Item peid to Brandon the goldsmith for so muche monny by him peyd for your lordship}	iiij^{xx}xli.
Item to Bird the marchant dewe unto him uppon a bill of your lordship}	Cxxxli.[53]
Item to Peyntell of Stretford of the Bowe for the matter towching Philpott}	xiijli. vjs. viijd.[54]
Item deliverid to your lordship's hond vj French crownes which yow gave to the armorers of Grenwich}	xxxviijs.
Item to Sir George Blunt[55] to be gyvin to the norse and mydwife for the christening of my Lady Jobson's[56]	

[53] William Byrde or Burd (1527–86), mercer and collector of the petty custom of London, see M.B. Donald, *Elizabethan Copper. The History of the Company of Mines Royal* (1955), pp. 63–6, and G.D. Ramsay, *The City of London in International Politics at the Accession of Elizabeth Tudor* (Manchester, 1975), pp. 154–6. Leicester had borrowed from him since December 1556 (PRO, C54/533/20, 'Dudley Clientèle', p. 250); he may have been his largest single creditor in the 1550s and early 1560s. See also below, pp. 113, 117–8, 241 and Byrde's bill for 1564–66, DP Box V, fo. 246.

[54] Presumably a reference to the case brought by Edward Philpot against Leicester in the Court of Requests in the spring of 1556 (PRO, REQ 1/10/42v, 48v). The subject is not stated but it was probably the wardship of Thomas Philpot, a lunatic, which had been granted to Leicester on 17 April 1553 (*CPR, Edward VI*, v, 137).

[55] Sir George Blount (1513–81), of Kinlet (Salop.), MP. He was an established member of the older Dudley connection, a cousin of the Duchess of Northumberland and an executor of her will, see 'West Midlands', 40. George Blount* was probably his son.

[56] Lady Elizabeth Jobson, daughter of Northumberland's mother Elizabeth by her second marriage to Arthur Plantagenet, Viscount Lisle, and married to Sir Francis Jobson (1509–1573), MP. Jobson was an overseer of the Duchess's will, in which Lady Jobson was left a gown; for his relations with Leicester, see 'Dudley Clientèle', pp. 242–7, 255–7. Jobson's sons had a long association with Leicester's household. Edward and John received livery in 1567, served in the Netherlands in 1586, and were bannerol-bearers at Leicester's funeral; John was also a bannerol-bearer at the Lord of Denbigh's funeral. A third brother, Thomas, is included as a bannerol-bearer in the first funeral list.

childe}   xxs.

To my Lord of Hunsdon for a hauke bought at the
Queen's price}   xxxs.[57]
\<16 pagina\>

Item for [a] urinall}   xvjd.
Item for iij*ll.* candell by Morrys}   xijd.
To him for his botehier to the Pole for reignishe wine}   viijd.
Item to Read the capper in full peyment of suche monny
as your lordship ought him in your father's deis}   xls.
\<ould det Read\>

Pagina} CClxxjli. xvs. ijd.

[fo. 6v]

Yet forin charges & rewards

Item gyvin to a joyner by your lordship's commandment
per Slyfild}   xijd.
Item for my botehier going in your lordship's affeires}   viijd.
Item to Lewes the crosbow maker for ij daggs gyvin to
my Lord of Darby}   xlivs.
Item for tothe picks vj*d.* and for milk bought by
George at sundry tymes}   xd.
\<17 pagina\>

Item for my dynner at London being about your lordship's
affeires in provision of fustian}   viijd.
Item for my botehier}   iiijd.
Item gyvin to your lordship which you gave unto Tindall}   xs.
Item for a torche xvj*d.* and for candell xvj*d.* bought
by Morrys Edwards}   ijs. viijd.
Item peid to the shipwright by your lordship's
commandment for·making your barge}   xli.
Item to a joyner for certeine sealing about the seid
barge}   xxs.
Item to Morrys Edwards for wasshing}   xs.
\<18 pagina\>

Item gyvin in reward to Mr Purveis man bringing sucking
rabetts and other presents}   vs.
Item peid to Mr Whithead for mony laid out by him for

---

[57] Henry Carey (1526–96), created Baron of Hunsdon on 13 January, Lord Chamberlain
from July 1585. His son Edmund* was later in Leicester's service; for the christening of
his son Robert, see p. 166 below.

the coppy of your lordship's restituytion}   vjs. viijd.[58]
Item to a joyner for taking downe certeine stuff at
Christchurche}   iiijd.
Item for the cariag of the said stuff to
your lordship's house}   xd.
Item for cariage of bedds from Mr Thamworth to Seint
Jamys}   xijd.[59]
Item for a lace for your lordship's pomander}   viijd.
Item to Partrige* for his botehier being sent to Whittill
for my Lord of Pembrokes gowne}   vjd.[60]
                    Pagina} xvli. vjs. ijd.

[fo. 7]

                    Yet forin charges & reward
Item peid to Morrys for candell}   xvjd.
<19 pagina>
Item to him for botehier being sent for wine}   iiijd.
Item for russhes with the cariage to Seint Jamys}   iiijs. iiijd.[61]
Item for cariage of stuff from your lordship's
house to Seint Jamys}   viijd.
Item for tenterhokes and a hammer}   xijd.
Item in reward for bringing a wodcocke pie unto
your lordship}   iijs. iiijd.
Item to Morrys Edwards for candell}   xvjd.
Item for beare fett by Johnes at divers tymes}   vjs.
Item for perfumes for the chamber}   iiijd.
Item for tothe pikes bought by Johnes}   iijs. iiijd.
<02 pagina [sic]>

[58] The act repealing the attainders of Leicester and Lord Ambrose Dudley and restoring
them and their sisters Mary and Katherine in blood (4&5 Philip and Mary, c. 12, not c.
15 as stated in G.R. Elton, *The Parliament of England 1559–1581* (Cambridge, 1986), pp.
304, 385) was passed in the first session of the 1558 Parliament.

[59] John Tamworth (c.1524–69), Groom of the Privy Chamber and Keeper of the Privy
Purse from 10 January 1559, MP. Tamworth was one of Leicester's sureties for the
December 1560 loan from William Byrde (see n. 200 below), and his deputy as Constable
of Windsor Castle from 1562 (see the accounts for the honour of Windsor Castle, PRO,
SC6/ElizI/136 *et seq.*)

[60] William Herbert, 1st Earl (c.1506–1570). It is possible that Pembroke had been a
protector of Leicester's during Mary's reign. Leicester was an overseer of his will and
an assistant mourner at his funeral.

[61] Although the council sat at Westminster throughout February 1559, entries on this
and the following pages suggest that the Court removed to St James's Palace. This is not
mentioned in Chambers, but would appear to be confirmed by the references to St
James's Park in the Count of Feria's despatch of 19 March (*CSPSp, 1558–67*, 37).

Item for jll. gunpowder bought by Saule*} xiiijd.
Item for more powder bought} xviijd.
Item for a lace for the key of a gunne} xjd.
Item to Sall for his botehier to Grenwich being sent by your lordship for the armyrer to Grenwich} xxd.
Item for wheat for fesants} vjd.
Item peid unto Mrs Coudry for mony dewe unto her uppon your lordship's bill} vjli. xs.[62]
Item in reward to Mr Thesaurer's servant bringing the blacke curtall} xs.
Item for cariage of stuffe from Seant Jamys} viijd.
Item peid to Partrige for monny leid out by him about your lordship's barge by a bill} xlvs. vjd.
Item for rybon lace bought by Slifild for your pomander & keys} ijs.
Item to Cary for his botehier being sent about your lordship's affeires} vjd.
Item to Thomas Sadler for such stuff provydid of him as appearith bi bill} xvjli. ijs. vjd.[63]
                Pagina} xxvjli. xviijs. xjd.

[fo. 7v]

Yett forrin chargs & rewards

<21 pagina>
Item to Sir George Blunte for so muche gold deliveryd to one of your lordship's servants} xls.
Item to Mr Bridges servante bringing bakemeats & cheasis} iijs. iiijd.
Item to William Cooke* your lordship's reward} xls.
Item to John Fawkner your lordship's reward} xxs.
Item to Morrys Edwards for the laundrye} xs.
Item to him for candell} xvjd.
Item for cariage [of] stuff from Seint Jamys} xijd.
Item to the joyner for setting uppe and takinge downe the same at Seint Jamys} xijd.
Item for the cariage of ihh. wine gyvin your lordship by Spynula} vjd.
Item to Mr Jerningham's servant bringing a blacke

[62] Mrs Katherine Cowdrye (shepster), her bill for shirts 1561–6 is DP Box V, fos 166–7. She may be the wife of the 'Mr Cowltry shepster' referred to on p. 119 below.
[63] Possibly Thomas Holloway the saddler, see p. 123 below.

hound}   vjs. viijd.[64]

Item for a glasse of rose water}   ijs. viijd.

Item for Mr Blunt's man's chargs out of Worcestershire
bringing the purple bed embrodryd}   vjs. viijd.

Item givyn to [the] clocke maker by Mr Blunte for
mending the clocke}   xijd.

Item for Mr Blunt's horsehier when he rode to my lady
in the Christmas}   vjs. viijd.

Item for a lace for your lordship's pomander}   ixd.

<22 pagina>

Item to Morrys Edwardes for candell}   xvjd.

Item deliveryd to your lordship's owne handes in a
purse of silver and goulde}   xxvjli. xiijs. iiijd.

Item to Mr Glasier* by your lordship's commandment
riding into Northfolke}   liijs. iiijd.

Item peid for the fees of a supena which Mr Glasier
had with him ageinst Elis}   ijs. viiijd.[65]

Item deliveryd to Edmund for his charges riding with
Mr Glasier}   xiijs. iiijd.

For my botehier to Southwarke and [back?]
ageyne}   viijd.

                    Pagina} xxxvijli. vjs. iiid.

[fo. 8]

                    Yet forin charges and rewards

Item for vj linkes [torches *deleted*] at vj*d*. the pec}   iijs.

Item for John Frencheman's* dynner while he trymid uppe
your lordship's new lodging}   vjd.

Item peid for a peir of virginalls by your lordship's
commandment}   Cs.

Item to my Lord of Darb[y's] servant for a
hawke}   xixs.

Item to the gardner of White hall by your lordship's
commandment per Gyles}   ijs.

[64] Probably Sir Henry Jerningham (1509/10–1572), MP, Mary's last Master of the Horse.

[65] This entry refers to the case of Dudley v. Hugh Ellis over the manor of Hemsby (Norf.), heard in Chancery in November 1559 (PRO, C78/17/10). Northumberland had obtained the manor for Leicester; it had been lost on Leicester's attainder, but had been restored by Mary in 1557 (see 'Dudley Clientèle', pp. 249–510). Ellis, brother of Leicester's servant Richard* and a former servant of Northumberland's, claimed that the Duke had also given him certain rights to the manor. Further references to this case can be found on pp. 58, 71 below.

Item to one of the hunters that brought your
lordship a hare}   xijd.
Item to the clockemaker by your lordship's
commandment}   iijs. iiijd.
<23 pagina>
Item to Mr Bagnoules man bringing your lordship a
hobbye}   vjs. viijd.[66]
Item to Morrys Edwardes for candell}   ijs.
Item for jdd. torchis}   xijs.
Item to Morrys Edwardes for candell}   vjd.
To him for the carrag of j rintlet reignishe wine
from your house}   vjd.
Item to Johns by your lordship's commandment
for my ladye}   lxvjs. viijd.
Item peid by Mr Hiham* for dressing of your
lordship's sword}   xlviijd.
Item sent to Ralfe Aldersey* uppon your lordship's
commandment beyng sick}   xs.
Item to Morrys Edwards for the launders}   xs.
Item peid to Mr Hogans for monny by him laid
out about your lodging at St. Jamys}   iiijs.
Item peid to Mr. Hogans for cariage of your
lordship's tents from Hoynsdon}   iiijs.[67]
<24 pagina>
Item to the colebearer for bringing coles to your
lordship's chamber}   vjd.
Item peid for the cariag of hanging to my Lady Sidny's
chamber at St. Jamys}   vjd.[68]
                    Pagina} xijli. vijs. viijd.

[fo. 8v]

[66] Both the Bagnall brothers, Sir Nicholas (c. 1510–c.1590) and Sir Ralph (1508–80),
were MPs in the Parliament of 1559. They are leading examples of the reforming of the
older Dudley clientele under Leicester, see 'Dudley Clientèle', pp. 246–7, 256. See also
p. 99 below.
[67] Hunsdon in Herts. See Appendix I.
[68] Leicester's sister Mary (d. 1586), Sir Henry Sidney's wife, who was one of the
extraordinary Gentlewomen of the Privy Chamber. Sidney, who had been in Ireland
since 1556, was presently acting as Lord Justice in the absence of the Lord Deputy, the
Earl of Sussex, and did not return to England until the autumn of 1559. Mary Sidney
had returned in September 1558 (marginal note in CKS, U1475/A26/5, Sidney's clerk
of the kitchen's account, Aug. 1558–Mar. 1559). She was the eldest of Northumberland's
daughters.

Yet forin charges &c.

Item for iij hedstalls and patrells with j peir of stroppe lethers}	vijs.
Item to Henry Fawkner in reward uppon your lordship's commandment}	xls.
Item to Oswald for certeyne necessaries by him bowght uppon his bill}	iijs. ijd.
Item peid to Jamys Thompson and George Cooke* for your lordship's reward at Ester} xxs.}	
To Morrys Edward x*s.*, Edward Roberts x*s.*, Griffin Lloyd* x*s.*, Griffin Clun* x*s.*, John Sermant x*s.*, Henry Johns* x*s.*, Robert Holland x*s.*, Davy Powell* x*s.*, John Powell x*s.*, George Giles x*s.*, Thomas Brabroke* x*s.*, John Forest x*s.*: in toto as appeareth by your lordship's booke mad at Easter} vjli.}	{vijli. xs.
To Edmund uppon your lordship's commandment by Hogans} xs.}	
Item gyvin unto your lordship's players}	xxs.[69]
Item to the shomaker in reward}	ijs.
Item to the teler's man for setting on of buttons}	vjd.
Item to the Spanishe hosier's servant in reward}	xs.
Item to Sir John Souchis man for bringing hounds}	vjs. viijd.[70]
Item to my Lord of Darbyes servant for bringing your lordship a shurte}	vjs. iiijd.
Item to the joyners bringing home of beddes out of Southewarke}	viijd.
Item for ribond for the keys}	viijd.
<25 pagina>	
Item to the hackny man for the hier of a horse for Glaiser in Northfolk}	xs.
Item to my Lord of Hundisdon's visition}	xijs. viijd.[71]
Item for ij basketts for tente pynnes}	xvjd.

Pagina} xiijli. xjs. [iiijd. *deleted*]

[fo. 9]

---

[69] The earliest reference to Leicester's players, see S.-B. MacLean, 'The Politics of Patronage: Dramatic Records in Robert Dudley's Household Books', *Shakespeare Quarterly*, xliv (1993), 177–8. See also that to Laurens on p. 63 below.

[70] Sir John Zouche (d. 1585), of Ansty, Wilts., MP. He wrote to Leicester on 12 Aug. [1559] (Longleat MS 8692), referring to himself as a kinsman; he may have been in Northumberland's household.

[71] See the reference to Burkhard on p. 58 below.

Yet forin charges

To the woodbearer* for his wages}	vjs. viijd.
Item to Morrys Edwards for candell}	xvjd.
Item to the wyne porters for cellarage of wine at your lordship's house}	viijd.
Item for a rundlet for wine}	xijd.
Item to Johnis for bear}	vjd.
Item to Mrs Clarentius's man for bringing the moyle per Cursson}	vjs. viijd.
Item for ij boxis of tothe piks}	xiiijd.
Item for cloves & perfumes}	iiijd.
Item to the watermen by your lordship's command that rowid the Quene to Chelsey}	xijs. viijd.
Item for lace for the keys by Slifild}	viijd.
Item for Slifildes botehier going to my Lady Sidneye for your lordship's durkys [door keys?]}	viijd.
<26 pagina>	
Item for ij hacknys for Mr Glasiar's men riding in to Northfolk}	xxs.
Item to Morrys Edwards for candell}	viijd.
Item gyvin to the enterlude pleyers by the handes of Mr Blunt}	lxs.
Item for browne paper}	ijd.
Item to the carre men for carriag of the tents to the fild}	viijd.
Item to Morrys Edwards for candell}	viijd.
Item to Slifild for his botehier when he went to Newma[rket?]}	viijd.
Item for a paper boke bought for your lordship by Hogans}	vs.
Item for urinalls bought by Johnes}	viijd.
Item for perfumes}	ijd.
Item peid to George Mr Thresaurer's servant which your lordship borowyd of him}	xijli. xiijs. iiijd.
Item to Mr Cobham's servant for vij peir of [Frenche crowns *deleted*] perfumyd gloves at vjs. iiijd. the peir}	xliiijs. iiijd.

Pagina} xxli. xviijs. ixd.

[fo. 9v]

Yett forin charges & rewards

Item gyvin to the watermen that rewyd the barge when your lordship see her first}	viijs.

Item to Mr Charles Howard's servant bringing your
lordship a great horse}   xs.[72]

Item for Symons Dud' that set upp the tents in Covin
Gardin}   ijs. xd.[73]

Item for paper}   vjd.

<27 pagina>

Item to the virginall maker for tryming the virginalls
per Slyfild}   xxd.

Item for virginall wiar}   xiiijd.

Item to Burkard the vesition in reward}   xxxviijs.

<my Lord Hunsedon's visition>

Item for ij carres for the carriage of the tents from
the Covin Garden to Sct Jamys Parke}   viijd.

Item necessaries for the same tents, viz points, neadills
& packe thread}   vjd.

Item to Sir John Alies servant for bringing the jenet
deliveryd to Slifild by your lordship's commandment}   xxxviijs.[74]

Item gyvin in reward by the hondes of Hogans to the nurse
and midwife of my Lady Knevett's child}   xxs.[75]

Item for our botehier at the same tyme}   vjd.

Item for a paper boke bought by Mr Bewe}   vjd.

Item for ij paper books for your lordship}   ijs. iiijd.

Item for j pint rose water to make perfumes}   xiiijd.

Item to Mr Glasier for matters of l[aw?] with
Elys as appearithe by his bills}   xxiijs. vjd.

<28 pagina>

Item for iiij*ll.* candell to Morris Edward}   xvjd.

                    Pagina} vijli. xs. viijd.

[fo. 10]

Yet forin charges & rewards
Item to my Lord of Lynnys servant that brought your

---

[72] The future 2nd Lord Howard of Effingham (1536–1624), MP, Lord Chamberlain 1583–85, and then Lord Admiral.

[73] Covent Garden. The purpose is unclear, as is the date, but given the proximity to Easter (26 March), the subsequent reference to moving the tents to St James's Park, and later entries to a banquet in the tents (see pp. 61, 94 and nn. 87, 168 below), this may be related to the Morris games held by Queen's Household in St James's Park on 21 March (see Machyn, 191).

[74] Probably Sir John Leigh (1502–66), on whose curious career see E.H. Harbison, 'French Intrigue at the Court of Queen Mary', *American Historical Review* xlv (1940), 542–5. He wrote to Leicester from Antwerp on 5 April 1560 (DP I, fo. 127).

[75] Probably the wife of Sir Henry Knyvet (c.1537–98), MP.

lordship a counterpoint of crymson sattin embrodryd}   xls.[76]

Item for balls for your lordship at Kewe}   xijd.

Item to my Lord of Darby's servant that brought the waterspaniell per Saull}   ijs.

Item peid for the locke of your lordship's lute}   viijs.

Item peid to Cragg* for his botehier and dynner being sent from Grenwich to the sergeant peinter}   xvjd.

Item gyvin in almes your lordship ryding to Grenwich}   iiijd.

Item for horse ferrage to Lambethe when your lordship rode to Grenwich}   ixd.

Item for dressing the sword which Mr Godryke gave your lordship}   iiijs. vjd.[77]

Item to my Lord Marques's man that brough[t] the nightingall}   vjs. iiijd.[78]

Item for a case for a cristall cuppe}   ijs.

Item for a peir of gloves}   xd.

Item delivered unto your lordship to putt into your lordship's purse xxiij Frenche crownes when your lordship went to Grenwich}   vijli. vs. viijd.

<29 pagina>

Item to Partrige for tallowe & other necessaries for your lordship's barge}   xiijs. xd.

Item to the skynner for making Mr Foskewes obligation of Cli.}   xijd.[79]

Item for corne for the fesants}   ijd.

Item for my fellowes dyners your lordship dyning at Arundells}   xijs. vjd.[80]

Item gyvin in reward to the nurse and mydwyf of my Lady Cheakes child}   xxvjs. viijd.[81]

Item gyvin to Aspeley* by your lordship's owne commandment}   xxs.

---

[76] Matthew Stewart, Earl of Lennox (1516–71), in exile in England since 1545, see Adams, 'The Release of Lord Darnley and the Failure of the Amity', M. Lynch (ed.), *Mary Stewart: Queen in Three Kingdoms* (Oxford, 1988), pp. 129–31.

[77] Richard Goodrich (c.1508–62), Attorney of the Court of Wards, MP.

[78] William Parr, Marquess of Northampton (1513–1571), rather than William Paulet, Marquess of Winchester (c.1483–1572), who was normally referred to as my Lord Treasurer.

[79] Possibly related to the money received from him on 16 April, see p. 39 above.

[80] A tavern near St Lawrence Pountney, which featured in the Earl of Surrey's riot in 1543, the Wyatt Rebellion and the Dudley Plot. See Read, *Mr. Secretary Cecil*, p. 108, and 'Dudley Clientèle', p. 253 (where it is incorrectly located in Eastcheap).

[81] Mary or Margaret (Hill), widow of Sir John Cheke (d. 1557) and married c.1558 to Henry Macwilliam (c.1532–86), Gentleman Pensioner and MP. See also the reference to young Mr Macwilliam on p. 210 below.

Item for our dyners your lordship dyning with my
Lord of Westmorland}   xiijs.[82]
          Pagina} xiiijli. xixs. xjd. [xvli. iijd. *deleted*]

[fo. 10v]

Yet forin charges & rewards

Item to the laundres for wasshing your lordship's
sheats from Christmas to our Lady Deye}   xxs.
Item to Partrige for the watermen's wages as
appeareth by his bill}   xxxixs. vijd.
Item to Morrys Edwards for candell}   ijs.
Item for browne paper}   iiijd.
Item for beare fett for your lordship at sundry
tymes in Westminster}   xs.
Item to the gardeners at Mr Sicell's}   ijs.[83]
Item to one for helpe dressing your lordship's horsys ther}   vjd.
<30 pagina>
Item for horse fearrage at Lambethe & Kewe}   xxd.
Item to Mr Hogans for Ralfe Alderseye}   xs.
Item for a case for the nest of bowls wrought with
antyke}   iijs.
Item to the bargemen from Kewe}   xijs.
Item to a jogler at Ware}   iijs. iiijd.[84]
Item to the blind harper ther}   iijs. iiijd.
Item to putt in your lordship's purse ij ould angells,
ij dy soferans & iij Frenche crownes}   lixs.
Item deliveryd to my ladye ther by your lordship's
commandment}   Cs.
Item to Mr Blunt my Lord Ambroses servant by
your lordship's commandment}   xls.[85]
Item in reward for bringing venison to Mr Hides}   ijs.
<31 pagina>
Item to Mr Barker for full peyment of xxxij*li.*
x*s.* which your lordship ought as appearith by his bills}   xijli. xs.[86]

---

[82] Henry Neville, 5th Earl (1524/5–1564), whose politics in the previous reign have
been the subject of some dispute, see J. Loach, *Parliament and the Crown in the Reign of Mary
Tudor* (Oxford, 1986), pp. 19, 119–22. Evidence of a friendship with Leicester can be
found in his letters of 4 Aug. 1559 and 20 Jan. 1560 (DP I, fos. 59, 100).

[83] Probably Wimbledon, given the proximity to Kew, rather than Cecil's house at
Cannon Row. Cecil did not purchase Theobalds until 1564.

[84] For this visit to his wife at Mr Hyde's, see Appendix I.

[85] His brother (c. 1528–1590), created Earl of Warwick at Christmas 1561.

[86] Probably Francis Barker, shepster, see also pp. 87, 119, 129 below. DP Box V, fos.
97, 141–5, are bills of his for 30 April 1561 and 1564–66.

Item for matting your lordship's chamber at Cort}   vs.
Item in reward for bringing hereof from Eltham}   ijs.
Item in reward to Mr Burknall's servante that drew
your lordship's petigre}   vjli. vjs. viijd.

             Pagina} xxxiiijli. xijs. vd.

[fo. 11]

           Yet forin charges and rewards
Item to Morrys Edwards for ijll. candell}   viijd.
Item for Hughe Johns for bothier sent to Whittell for
your lordship's cote}   viijd.
Item for browne paper}   vjd.
Item for urinalls}   iiijd.
Item for perfumes}   ijd.
Item for milke}   ijd.
Item for bowes for your lordship's chamber}   iiijd.
Item to Mr Tamworthes man that brought the bucke
from Waltham}
                                vs.
Item peid to Mr Hampden for your part of the
supper made unto the Quene in the parke
at Seint Jamys}   vijli. xviijs. ijd.[87]
Item for mending the locke of the wardrop doore}   viijd.
Item for corne for the fesants}   viijd.
<32 pagina>
Item for reward [iij littell *deleted*] to my Lord
of Penbrokes servant bringing your lordship
a hatt}   iijs. iiijd.
Item to Mr Gower for his chargs ryding to my ladye} ixs.
Item to Morrys Edwards for the launder}   xs.
Item to Cragge going with your lordship's lettres
to Waltham Parke for a bucke for your lordship}   ijs.
Item to the grome of the stable which keapithe your
lordship's great horse}   xs.
Item to the yeomen of the barges at ij severall tymes, viz
for rowing the Quenes highnes at one tyme and your
lordship at another tyme}   xxvs. vjd.
Item to a vitteling wyfe by Christchurch for Edmunds,
Burd and Frances coming from St Quintans}   liiijs.[88]

[87] See n. 73 above.

[88] This is the first of several references in this account to the campaign of 1557, in which Leicester and his brothers (Lord Henry being killed in action) served in the English contingent in Philip II's army. Pembroke commanded the English contingent and Leicester was the Master of the Ordnance. This entry is also evidence of Leicester's residence at Christchurch in 1557–8 (see n. 28 above).

Item for a case for your lordship's garter bought
by Empson*}   ijs. vjd.[89]
Item for a horn brushe bough[t] by him}   xvjd.
                    Pagina} xiiijli. vs.

[fo. 11v]

                    Yett forin charges & rewards
Item for mending your lordship's girdell}   ijd.
<33 pagina>
Item for a wrest for your lordship's virginall}   vjd.
Item for mylke}   ijd.
Item for candell}   viijd.
Item to Sir Jamys Stampes servant for bakemeat which
he brought}   xxd.[90]
Item to the shomaker's servant in reward}   vjd.
Item to Jamys shomaker as appeareth by his bill by your
lordship's commandment}   ixli.
Item to Johns for bear at sundry tymes}   xxijd.
Item for bowys for your lordship's chamber}   ijd.
Item to John Sermant, Gr[iffith] Clonne, Flowerdew*
and Lloyd for ther bord wages at iiij severall
tymes either of them iiij meales at vjd. a meale}   viijs.
Item in reward to a poer woman that brought
your lordship queiles}   vs.
Item for wild tansye by Empson*}   vjd.
Item for milke fett by him}   ijd.
Item to Johns riding to my ladye}   vs.
Item gyvin to Cragge the foteman by your lordship's
commandment}   xxs.
Item peid for the Signet for your lordship's warrant
to the Wardrope for your lordship's robes}   xs.
<34 pagina>
Item for your lordship's servants' dyner when your
lordship dynyd at my Lord of Pembrokes}   xijs.[91]
Item peid to Cooke the parfumer for certen gild
buttons sett uppon a peir of gloves which your

[89] Leicester was elected a Knight of the Garter on 23 April (Machyn, 196), further
references to Garter robes and insignia can be found on pp. 65, 89 below. For his
installation, see pp. 66–8 below.

[90] Of Wallingford. His connection with Leicester (see also p. 157 below) is otherwise
unknown, except that he commanded a company in the St Quentin campaign.

[91] This was probably on 25 April, when Pembroke gave a dinner for the Queen at
Baynard's Castle (Machyn, 196).

lordship gave to the Quenes majestie}   xviijs. iiijd.[92]
Item peid for our diners when your lordship
dyned with my Lord Ambrose}   xvjs. viijd.
Item sent unto Mr Beynton by your lordship's
commandment}   xls.
Item to Eglmby for iiij meales being about
your lordship's affeires}   ijs.
Item to Lesam's* doughter bringing your lordship erbes}   ijs.
                          Pagina} xvjli. vs. iiijd.

[fo. 12]

                    Yet forin charges & rewards
Item for an erthin jugge bought by Empson}   vjd.
Item for wild tansy and dasye rotes}   ijd.
Item for mylke}   ijd.
Item for a case for the silver tonne}   xvjd.
Item for bringing herons from Eltham}   ijs.
Item peid to Powell for monny laid out for certeyne
necessaries for the wardroppe}   vjs. viijd.
Item for our suppers when your lordship supid
at Sir William Pykering's}   xs.[93]
Item for boteheir being about your busines}   viijd.
<35 pagina>
Item to the smythe at Grenwich for x plate lockes}   Cs.
Item to the trumpeter by your lordship's command}   xxs.
Item to Partrige for his servise donne as well
to the Quenes majestie as to your lordship
at severall tymes}   xxxvjs. vjd.
Item to Mr Kempes man that brought your lordship
a spanniell xs. and for a lyan for the seid
spaniell xijd.}   xjs.
Item to Laurens one of your lordship's pleyers by
your lordship's commandment}   xls.

---

[92] Feria's despatch of 18 April contains the earliest surviving comment on Dudley's intimacy with the Queen and reports gossip that his wife 'está muy mala de un pecho' and that Elizabeth was only waiting for her to die in order to marry him (AGS, E 812, fo. 28).

[93] Pickering House was at St Mary Axe near Christchurch. As noted in n. 44 above Pickering did not arrive in England until 4 May. Feria's report of gossip that Dudley had gone hunting at Windsor out of jealousy to Pickering (10 May, CSPSp, 1558-67, 67) is contradicted by the evidence of his movements here, though it is possible Windsor was an error for Eltham, see n. 176 below. Leicester gave Pickering at least two books during the 1560s, but only one item of correspondence survives (DP II, fo. 94, Pickering to Leicester, 4 May 1572).

Item for a peir of knyves for your lordship}	xijd.
Item for cariag of bedsteads from London to Kewe by water}	ijs. viijd.
Item for our diners at London your lordship dyning with the Mr of the Rowells}	xs.
Item for carriag of bedding and hangings to Mr Skott's of Camberwell}	ijs. vjd.[94]
Item to Partrige the waterman for service done unto your lordship at iiij severall times as appearithe by his bill}	xlviijs.
Item to Mr Glasiar for certeine of your lordship's affeires in the lawe}	vjs. viijd.
Item peid to Mr Hogans for monye laid out by him as appearithe by your lordship's bill}	vjs.
Item to Cutbert Musgrave* by your lordship's honds}	lxjs. viijd.

Pagina} xviijli. vijs. vjd.

[fo. 12v]

Forin charges & rewards

Item to the armerers at Grenwich by your lordship's commandment per Sall}	xs.
Item to my Lady Throgmorton's servant bringing your lordship a bucke}	vjs. viijd.[95]
<36 pagina>	
Item to my Lord of Northefolk's man bringing your lordship a hound}	vs.
Item gyvin to a woman that brought your lordship pescoddes}	vs.
Item to the gardner at White hall by your lordship's commandment}	iijs. vjd.
Item for a haspe for the coffer}	viijd.
Item for tansy, erbis etc.}	vjd.
Item for mending of ij girdills}	iiijd.
Item for a case for the dyall}	vjd.
Item for strewing herbis for your chamber per Johns}	xviijd.

[94] The family of Amy Dudley's mother, Lady Elizabeth Robsart (d. 1557, see n. 52 to the Introduction). The bedding was sent there in preparation for her visit, see below pp. 65, 68, 71, 102–3 and Appendix I.

[95] Probably Anne, Sir Nicholas Throckmorton's wife. She was clearly on good terms with Leicester for Throckmorton used her as an intermediary in 1561–2 (See BL Add. MS 35830, fo. 195, Anne Throckmorton to Leicester, 30 Aug. 1561, and MS 35831, fo. 22, Cecil to Throckmorton, 24 Mar. 1562). Throckmorton himself had departed on his embassy to France on 3 May, and did not return until October.

Item for browne paper}	vjd.
Item for mending your lordship's girdill}	ijd.
Item for candell by Morrys Edwards}	ijs. iiijd.
Item for a cage for queyles}	[*blank*]
Item gyvin in reward to Mr Pykering's servant that brought your lordship the horse}	xxs.
Item to the Clerke of the Signett for your lordship's warrant for the mantill and the hode with xxd. for the wryting}	viijs. iiijd.
Item to William Sall for powder and other necessaries by him bought as appeareth by his bill}	vijs. iiijd.
Item in almes coming from Sir William Pykering's}	vjd.
Item for the hier of xij horse when my lady came from Mr Hides to London}	lxs.[96]
Item to Sir Ambrose Caves servant for bringing freshe sturgion}	iijs. iiijd.
Item for ribon for your lordship's keys}	xijd.
Item for erbes and bowes for your lordship's chamber}	vjd.
Item for tanyse}	iijd.
Item for mylke}	ijd.

Pagina} vjli. xviijs. jd.

[fo. 13]

Yet forin charges and reward

Item for mending your lordship's stonebowes}	iijs. iiijd.
Item peid to Cooke the perfumer by your lordship's commandment}	vjli. xijs. iiijd.
Item for meat for the queiles}	xd.
Item peid to Partrige the bargeman for service done by him at severall tymes as appearithe by bill}	ls.
Item peid to Mr Hogans for ij boes for your lordship}	xvs.
<38 pagina>	
Item to Mr Gresham's servant for bringing gould canvas to your lordship}	vs.[97]

---

[96] For her visit see Appendix I. Assuming the entries are in reasonable chronological sequence, the date would appear to be the middle of May.

[97] Sir Thomas Gresham (c. 1519–79), who returned from a financial mission to the Low Countries in April. Numerous further references here and elsewhere reveal a close relationship that began in the reign of Edward VI. Gresham also had family and business ties to a number of Leicester's servants of Norfolk background, including Richard Ellis, William Huggins, and John Marbury (see DP I, fo. 155, Gresham to Leicester, 18 Aug. 1560).

Item to the skryvener for making of obligation for
monny borowyd}   xxiijs. iiijd.

Item peid for wrytings mad betwene Foster and
Detersall for CCC*li*.}   xxs.[98]

Item to Jemynie the Frencheman for an instrment of
astronymye}   xli.[99]

Item in reward to Sir Peter Carowes servant for
bringing a white curtall}   vjs. viijd.[100]

Item for our suppers your lordship supping at
Mr Dannett's}   xiijs. iiijd.[101]

Item for our dyners your lordship going to Tower
Wharfe to receave the ambassador}   xxiiijs. viijd.

Item for our dyners your lordship dyning with
the Frenche ambassadors}   xxijs. vjd.[102]

Item for your servants' botehier your lordship
going to fetch the Frenche to Cort}   iijs. iiijd.

Item to Partrige for service done at divers tymes}   xxxiijs. vjd.

<39 pagina>

Item to Powell of the wardrope necessaries by him
bought per bill}   xiijs. xd.

Item to Cragge to provide him girdel and shois
ageinst your lordship's going to Windsor}   vjs. viijd.[103]

Item to Kenningham by your lordship's commandment
at his going into Flanders}   vjli. xiijs. iiijd.

Item in reward to Whittell's men}   vs.

---

[98] This was probably the £300 received from Foster on 2 May, see p. 39 above. The £310 paid to Foster in the autumn of 1560 may be the repayment of this loan, but see n. 247 below.

[99] See also the reference to 'Gemyny of the Blacke Fryers', p. 138 below. Thomas Gemini (d. 1562), a Netherlander, founded an engraving works in the Blackfriars in the reign of Edward VI and is celebrated as the earliest maker of navigational instruments in London, see E.G.R. Taylor, *The Haven-Finding Art* (1956), p. 196, and D.W. Waters, *The Art of Navigation in Elizabethan and Early Stuart Times* (1958), p. 145. Photographs of an astrolabe made by Gemini in 1552 and engraved with Northumberland's and Edward VI's arms can be found in Waters, plates xxvii–viii.

[100] Sir Peter Carew (c.1510–75), MP. No other evidence of close relations survives, but Carew's cousins and ultimate heirs, Sir Peter Carew the younger and Sir George (1555–1629), the future Earl of Totnes, were in Leicester and Warwick's service, see the reference in LPL, MS 618, fo. 13, Sir G. Carew to Leicester, ? Dec. 1587.

[101] Probably Thomas Dannet the elder (d. 1569), but see the comments on BL, Add MS 48023 in the Introduction, p. 35.

[102] The French embassy to ratify the Treaty of Cateau-Cambrésis arrived at Tower Wharf on 23 May and went to Court on the 24th (Machyn, 197–9). They returned to France on the 28th leaving behind the new resident ambassador, Gilles de Noailles, and the hostages for the return of Calais. The embassy had been expected earlier, see DP I, fo. 18, Pembroke to Leicester, 18 May.

[103] For the Garter installation, see pp. 67–8 below.

Item for balls for your lordship in the pley
at Westminster}   xviijd.[104]

Pagina} xxxvli. xvs. iijd.

[fo. 13v]

Yet forin charges and rewards
Item in reward to my Lady of Warwick's servant
bringing a bucke}   xs.[105]
Item for a quicell bought for Na[n?] by Cursson}   ijs. vjd.
Item to Morryse Edwarde for courd}   ijs.
Item for carriag of red wine from your house to the
Cort with the cask}   ixd.
Item to Sir John Souches servant that brought your
lordship a cast of hauks}   xviijs. vjd.
Item for our dyners your lordship dyning with my
Lord Ambros and vjd. for almes} <Junij>   xvs.
Item to Nicholas for meat for the queyles}   xxd.
Item to Mr Hogans for MM billetts xxs. and one
lode coles xvijs. leid at Kewe}   xxxvijs.
Item for his botehier to Kewe and backe ageyne}   iiijs.
Item for his charges ther}   xijd.
Item to him for pease bought}   xviijd.
Item peid to Powell for making iijdd. napkins}   vs.
<40 pagina>
Item for Caries botehier to Kewe}   xxd.
ᵈItem peid to Cursson for horsemeat at Branford
and Windsor with xs. gyvin in reward to the Dean
of Glosester's servant bringing a stonid horse
per bill}   xiijli. xviijs. viijd.[106]
Item for your servants' charges ther of bordwages}   xxviijs. vjd.
Item for lodging ther peid by Vanse and Powell}   xs.
Item for your lordship's offering ther}   ijs.
Item to the herolds ther for ther fee at your
lordship's instalment}   xxxvijli. vs. iiijd.

---

[104] Presumably at one of the two tennis courts at Whitehall, which feature regularly
below. At Westminster on 27 May Leicester issued a commission to Thomas Keys to
deputise for him in the regulation of the export of horses from Kent (BL, Stowe MS
856, fos. 34v–5).

[105] Anne (Seymour, d. 1588), widow of John, Earl of Warwick, and now wife of Sir
Edward Unton, see n. 15 above. Her jointure lands from the marriage to Warwick
included the manor of Langley (Oxon.), which later came into Leicester's possession, see
n. 391 below.

[106] The installation took place on 6 June (Machyn, 200).

Pagin} lviijli. vs. jd.

[fo. 14]

Yet forin chargs & reward

Item in reward to the servants of the house whear your lordship ley at Windsor}	xixs.

<41 pagina>

Item to the keaper of the Litel Parke at Windsor per Carye}	vjs. iiijd.
Item to a power woman that exhibit[ed] a bill to your lordship per Gryse}	ijs.
Item to Vanse and Powell ther charges being at ij deis at Windsor before your lordship's comyng thither}	xs.
Item for hacknys to Windsor}	viijli. viijs. iiijd.[d]
Item to one that brought yow chearys per Carye}	ijs. vjd.
Item to your lordship's pleyers for ther charges at Thisselworthe that night they pleyd before your lordship at Kewe}	iiijs.[107]
Item to Mr Peckesall's servant that brought your lordship a hound}	vs.
Item to Langham* for ij deys bord and wages attending uppon my lady at Christchurch your lordship being at Windsor}	iijs. vjd.[108]
Item for cherys bought by Johns}	xijd.
Item for ij penne knyves bought by your lordship's commandment per George}	xvjd.
Item to the keper of Seint Jamis Parke for a bucke gyvin to Mr Knevet per Hogans}	xs.[109]
Item to Thomas Johns and his fellows for ther dyners weyting uppon my lady from Christchurche to Camberwell}	iijs. viijd.
Item to my Lord of Rutland's servant that brought the bey gelding}	xs.[110]

[107] Iselworth. Just before or just after the journey to Windsor, Leicester wrote from Westminster to the Earl of Shrewsbury asking for liberty for the players to tour in Yorkshire (LPL MS 3196, fo. 29, dated only June 1559). For further references to the tour of the players in 1559–60, see MacLean, 'Politics of Patronage', 178–9. She dates the letter to Shrewsbury 10 June.

[108] See Appendix I. On 6 June La Quadra reported that Amy Dudley's health had improved but that she was taking care about what she ate (Lettenhove, i, 536). It is not clear if he knew where she was.

[109] Probably Sir Henry Knyvet, see n. 75 above.

[110] Henry Manners, 2nd Earl (1526–1563), an ally of Northumberland's, who also served in the St Quentin campaign. He sent Leicester a dog in 1560 (DP I, fo. 146, to Leicester, 4 June 1560).

Item to Mr Blunt for hawksmeat xxj*d*., for a hauks
bagge ij*s*., for a hauks glove viij*d*., in toto}   iiijs. vd.
     Pagina} xijli. xjs. jd.

[fo. 14v]

    Yet forin charges and reward
Item for a skarfe for your lordship bought by Empson}   ixs.
Item to Robert of Cornewall*, Thomas Davies* and the
Frencheman for ther charges by the space of iij wekes
at Kewe attending the stuffe ther and for carrage of
the same from thense to London}   lvs.
Item to the huntsmen to by [*sic*] Hanse}   xs.
Item to the surgion for letting your lordship's blodd}   xs.[111]
<43 pagina>
Item in reward to one that brought your lordship
lard from the ambassadors}   xs.
Item for hier of vessell to Kewe}   vjs. viijd.
Item to my Lady Cotton's servant that brought
your lordship pewetts}   xxs.
Item delyveryd to Cooke of Seint Martins uppon
a reckning}   iiijli.
Item peid for bowes for your lordship}   xxxiiijs.
Item for graving your lordship's seale with the garter}   xxxs.
Item for tothe piks}   iiijs. viijd.
Item to George Cooke by your lordship's commandment
going into the countrye}   xxs.
Item to Henry Cooke for parcell of annuytie dew unto him}   xxs.[112]
Item to Morys Edwards for candells   ijs.
Item to Mr Harrington's servant that brought
your lordship a cast of hawks}   xixs.
Item for charges of botehier your lordship going
to the Ould Swanne wher you dynid with the French
ambassador}   vs. viijd.[113]
Item for our dyners the same dey}   xxvijs.
    Pagina} xviijli. iijs.

---

[111] Both Katherine Hastings' and Pembroke's letters of 5 and 18 May (DP I, fos. 14, 18) refer to Leicester suffering from an illness, which they described variously as a fit and a quartain ague.

[112] The Duchess of Northumberland bequeathed to her servant Richard Cook an annuity of 5 marks a year. A pension of 26s 8d to Henry Cooke was charged against the Hales Owen estate in 1560, see BRL, HH MS 351621.

[113] The Old Swan Inn near London Bridge.

[fo. 15]

Yet forin charges and reward

Item to Nycholas for queyles meat}	xxd.
<44 pagina>	
Item for a peir of virginalls}	Cs.
Item to Joyse your lordship's mother's meyd for monny dewe unto her uppon a bill signed by your lordship and your brothers}	Cxs.[114]
Item to Mr Strange for certeine muske deliveryd to Cooke of St. Martyns}	lxxiijs. iiijd.
Item to Partrige for service done at divers tymes with x crownes gyvin unto him for reward when your lordship wonne the wager of my Lord of Penbrok comyng from Kewe as appeareth bi bill}	viijli. xvijs. xd.
Item to Mr Blunt for hawks meat}	ijs.
Item to Oswald for bowes and flowers for the chamber per bill}	ixs. xd.
Item to a power woman that named her self your lordship's father's nurse by your lordship's commandment}	ijs. viijd.
Item to Ward's widow the skynner for an ould dett dew unto her as appeareth by her bill}	xxxvs.
Item to Allin the crosbow maker for ij crosbowes at xxvs. the pece}	ls.
Item to your pleyers by your lordship's commandment}	iiijli.
Item to Ashpeley for his botehier to Grenwich careing the virginall}	ijs.
<45 pagina>	
Item to Flowerdewe for hawks meat and other necessaries per bill}	vs.
Item to the keaper of the tennys cort for balls and erbes at sundry tymes for your lordship's chamber}	vjs. viijd.
Item to Mr Willowby your lordship's chaplin by your lordship's command}	xls.[115]

[114] Joyce Prelly. In her will the Duchess acknowledged she owed her £4 and added a further £4 to it. The 'bill' was a consequence of the agreement of November 1555 over Hales Owen, see Abbreviations: the Duchess of Northumberland's debts.

[115] Thomas Willoughby, a former chaplain of Northumberland's, proposed by Lord Ambrose as Archdeacon of Canterbury or Dean of Lincoln (DP I, fo. 70, to Leicester, 17 Aug. 1559). In February 1561 he was presented by Thomas Blount to the vicarage of St Mary's, Kidderminster (Hereford and Worcester RO, Index to Presentations, Diocese of Worcester, 1526–1602). He was presumably the Thomas Willoughby (d. 1581) the Edwardian canon of Canterbury and Frankfurt exile, who was restored to his canonry

Item for cariag of stuff from White hall to your
house per Powell}   iijs. iiijd.

        Pagina} xxxiiijli. xixs. iiijd.

[fo. 15v]

        Yett forin charges and reward
Item to Mr Glasier for monny leid out by him to the
Clerks of the Rolls for coppys of certein matters
betwene your lordship and Ellys}   xiijs. iiijd.
Item for my botehier to Grenwich bringing your
lordship's sparver}   xijd.
Item to Edward Roberts, Hugh Johnes, William Cooke
Thomas Davis, Holland for ther charges ij deys before
at Grenwich for hanging your lordship's lodging
& making of lodging ther}   xvs. ijd.[116]
Item to Morryce for carriage of certene stuff from
Whithall to Grenwich}   xd.
Item to Morrice Edwards for candell}   viijd.
<46 pagina>
Item for Morice Edwards' botehier from London
to Grenwich}   iiijd.
Item for my botehier to London being sent to
my Lord Keaper}   xijd.[117]
Item for my supper that night}   vjd.
Item for my botehier from London to Grenwich}   viijd.
Item for my botehier to London being sent
thither about the dispatch of my ladye}   viijd.[118]
Item for a peir of hose for my ladies boye}   xs.
Item to Eglmby for certene bordwages dew unto
him after your lordship's coming from St. Quintyns
by your lordship's command}   xls.
Item for a trunke saddell with the appurtenances
for carriag of my ladyes apparell}   xxs.
Item for my botehier then}   viijd.
Item my botehier and iij of my fellowes that
nyght to Grenwich}   xijd.
        Pagina} Cvs. xd.

---

in September 1560 and promoted Dean of Rochester in 1574 (C.H. Garrett, *The Marian Exiles* (Cambridge, 1966 ed.), p. 338).

[116] The Court removed to Greenwich on 21 June 1559. See also the reference on p. 75 below to the payment of lodgings for servants at Greenwich for four weeks.

[117] Sir Nicholas Bacon, probably over the dispute with Hugh Ellis, see n. 65 above.

[118] See Appendix I.

[fo. 16]

Yet forrin charges and rewards

Item for my bordwages for iij deis then being
about your lordship's affeirs}   iijs.

\<47 pagina\>

Item to Randall Johns for his bord wages being
about lyke affeires}   xijd.

Item for my botehier being sent to London by
your lordship to Palmer's wyfe}   viijd.

Item to the watermen that caried your lordship
to London with my Lord Chamberlain and backe
ageine to Grenwich when your lordship huntyd
in St Jamis Parke}   xijs.[119]

Item for ij boxis of tothe piks}   xijd.

Item in reward to my Lord of North' servant
that brought your lordship a hound}   iijs. iiijd.[120]

Item to one of the kichin bringing your lordship
eggs in to the cellar for your lordship's breakfast}   iijs. iiijd.

Item to Cary and Hogans for ther botehier
to London and backe attending your lordship
to St Jamys}   iiijs.

Item to Dunkin* for his botehier being sent
to Whittill with your taffita night gowne}   iiijd.

Item to one of the yeamen for his bothier
and backe being sent for saddells to
Sir William Pykering}   xxd.

Item for iiij staves which your lordship brock}   vjs. viijd.[121]

Item for bote hier for me and my fellowes
to Tower Wharfe when your lordship went to dinner
to the French ambassador}   vjs.

Item for our dyners in London}   xiiijs. viijd.

Item for our botehier from Wolwich}   viijd.[122]

Item to Mr Vaughan's servant that brought
your lordship a hound}   vs.[123]

[119] William, 1st Lord Howard of Effingham (d. 1573).

[120] Probably North[folk], but possibly Northumberland.

[121] Leicester was present at Greenwich on 2 July when the London militia exercised before the Queen. The exercise was followed by a tilt, and a second tilt was held on the 11th (Young, p. 201; Machyn, 202–3). Given the sequence of the subsequent entries, this probably refers to the earlier tilt.

[122] On 3 July the Queen went to Woolwich to launch the *Elizabeth Jonas* (Machyn, 203).

[123] Probably Cuthbert Vaughan (d. 1563) MP, the former Wyatt rebel and now officer of the Berwick garrison. It is clear from his correspondence as Comptroller at Le Havre in 1562–3 that he knew Leicester well.

Item for botehier to London when your lordship
suppid with Mr Gresham}   vs. viijd.
                        Pagina} lxixs.

[fo. 16v]

                    Yet forrin charges and rewards
Item for our suppers when your lordship suppid
with Mr Gresham}   xviijs. vjd.
Item peid for the fees of a Privye Seall
sent ageinst my Lord of Comberland}   viijs. iiijd.[124]
Item for my botehier to London about your
lordship's affeires}   xijd.
Item for my botehire from Grenwich to London}   viijd.
Item for my charges ther Frideye and Satterdeye}   xxd.
<49 pagina>
Item to Mr Glasier for drawing the boke
of Watton per bill}   xxs.[125]

[124] Henry Clifford, 2nd Earl (1517–70). Writs of Privy Seal were the normal process by which appearances before the Court of Requests were ordered. The dispute between Leicester and Cumberland concerned jewels and other property originally belonging to Leicester's uncle Sir Andrew Dudley (c.1507–22 Nov. 1559), who had been bethrothed to Cumberland's daughter Margaret in 1553. The marriage collapsed after the fall of the Dudleys, but Cumberland had retained Dudley's property. The writ was delivered to Cumberland in August, who claimed that the property in question had been forfeited to the Crown on Dudley's attainder and had been granted to him by Queen Mary. He proposed that the dispute be settled by arbitration (DP I, fo. 66, George Lamplaugh to Leicester, 13 Aug.). The case was ultimately heard by the Court of Requests in the winter of 1561–2 and Leicester was granted all of Sir Andrew Dudley's forfeited estate by letters patent in April 1562 (*CPR, 1560–3*, 239). After November 1559 (see n. 192 below) he was acting as both overseer and beneficiary of his uncle's will, but it is not clear what his role was in the summer. Andrew Dudley's will is printed in *Sidney Papers*, i, p. 30; references to the case can be found in L.M. Hill (ed.), *The Ancient State, Authoritie and Proceedings of the Court of Requests by Sir Julius Caesar* (Cambridge, 1975), pp. 184–5, and there is a brief account in R.W. Hoyle (ed.), 'Letters of the Cliffords, lords Clifford and earls of Cumberland. c.1500–c.1565', *Camden Miscellany XXXI* (Camden Soc.. 4th ser., xliv, 1992), 20–1. Cumberland does not appear to have harboured any resentment for he gave Leicester his proxy in the Parliament of 1566, but the case is a good (if minor) example of the political difficulties posed by the restoration of the Dudleys discussed in 'Dudley Clientèle', pp. 253–7.

[125] This entry refers to the survey of the site of the priory of Watton (Yorks., East Riding) undertaken later in the month (DP I, fo. 44, John Yerwerth* to Leicester, 19 July). Watton had belonged to Northumberland, and was ultimately granted to Leicester on 23 Jan. 1560 ('Dudley Clientèle', p. 254, n. 108). It was the only landed property he obtained from the Queen between the grant of Kew and that of 1 March 1561 (see Introduction, p. 15), which included several other estates in the East Riding. Some contemporary pedigrees traced the Dudley descent from a Saxon Lord Sutton of Holderness, and the creation of an estate to support a claim to the lordship of Holderness may have inspired this interest in the East Riding (see 'West Midlands', 30). On 19 June

Item for my botehier to London about the lyverys}	xijd.[126]
Item for my supper that night}	viijd.
Item to Thomas Davys for his charges lying at Kewe about eyring of the stuffe and for the cariag of certeine stuff to Grenwich}	xs.
To Erasmus's meyd for bringing your lordship a sallett per Carye}	vs.
Item to the stopper of the tennys cort by your lordship's commandment}	xijd.
Item to one that brought your lordship a bucke}	iijs. iiijd.
Item to Langham for hawksmeat &c. per bill}	viijs. iiijd.
Item to Flowerdewe for hawksmeat}	vijs. xjd.
Item to Morrys Edwards for candell}	iiijs. xd.
Item for ij pair of blacke stockings bought for the foteman}	viijs.
Item to John Audwine* for halfe year's wages dewe at Midsommer}	xxvjs. viijd.
Item to Mr Blunt for his charges for killing of a bucke}	xviijd.

Pagina} vjli. viijs. vd.

[fo. 17]

Yet forrin charges & rewards

<50 pagina wages dewe at Midsommer>

Davye Powell xs.	H[ugh] Johnes xs.
John Powell xs.	William Barker* xs.
Robert Holland xs.	William Burn* xs.
Ralfe Alderseye xs.	Edmond Nicolls* xs.
Breybrok xs.	

Griffin Lloyd xs.
Jamys Thompson xs.
George Cooke xs.
William Cooke xs.
Morrys Edward xs.
Thomas Davies xs.
Robert Dunkin xs.
Edward Roberts xs.

La Quadra reported that the Queen had given Leicester £12,000 'ayuda de costa' (CSPSp, 1558–67, p. 77, AGS E 812, fo. 63). No such sum appears in this account, although the description does, with some exaggeration, fit the export licence for wool granted him in April 1560, see p. 116, n. 215 below.

[126] This may be a reference to preparation of liveries for the progress, see p. 21 above.

Hugh Bristowe* xs.
Forest & Ralfe* xxs.
Partridge xs.
Cragge and Ned fotemen xxs.
George Gyles xs.
John Empson xs.   {xijli. xs.
Item to Forest by your lordship's command
to by him hose}   vjs. viijd.
Item for my botehier from Grenwich to London
and backe ageine}   viijd.
Item for your lordship's mens botehier when
you dyned with the Frenchemen}   ijs. viijd.[127]
Item for our dyners the same deye}   xxs.
Item to Mr Sperte* your lordship's servant
for a gelding which your lordship bough[t] of
him at Seant Quintyns}   iiijli. xiijs. iiijd.
Item to Partrige for service donne at divers
tymes as appearith by his bills}   iiijli. vs. xjd.
Item to Nicolson for making heye &c. per bill}   ljs.
<heymaking at Kewe>
                    Pagina} xxvli. xs. iijd.

[fo. 17v]

                    Yet charges of [*deleted*] & rewards
To Mrs Laundres for her quarter's wages dewe at mydsommer
last} <51 pagina wasshinge>   xxs.
Item for your menes lodgings the Quenes highnes
lying at Grenwich by the space of iiij weaks}   lxxvjs. viijd.
                                                        per Holland
Item to William Browne, William Ba[r]ker and Edmund
gromes of the stable for ther burdwages vij deis
either of them viij[d.] per diem}   xiiijs.
Item for your lordship's horsemeat at Dartford
on Mondey night}   xiijs. xd.[128]
Item to Edmund Robarts for v of your lordship's
servants that night}   ijs. vjd.
Item for lodging ther that night}   xxd.
Item for your lordship's servants at Rochester

---

[127] Probably the hostages (or pledges) for Calais, who are identified in Teulet, i, 323. References to individuals will be found below.

[128] The beginning of the progress into Kent. The Court spent Monday 17 July at Dartford (Machyn, 204).

on Tuysdey night supper}   xijs.[129]

Item for i parr new gerthers for John Trumpett*}   xd.

Item to Cragge for monny leid out by him for
your lordship uppon the weye}   xijd.

Item for your lordship's servants' suppers at
Rochester on Thursday night having part of
your allowans from Cort}   viijs. viijd.[130]

Item for our diners the Quenes majestie being
at Gillingham}   ixs. vjd.[131]

Item horsehier at Rochester}   ijs. iiijd.

Item for our suppers at Rochester}   viijs. ixd.

Item in reward to the boyes of the kychin
at Cobham per Holland}   ijs.

Item for our suppers at Rochester Tuysday night}   xs.[132]

<52 pagina>

Item to Henry Johnes vs., George Gyles iijs. vjd.,
John Empson iijs. vjd., Dunkin iijs. vjd., John
Allin* iijs. vjd. and Thomas Davies iijs. vjd.,
in toto for ther burdwages from Tuysdey night
till Saturdey morning the Quene lying at Cobham}   xxijs. vjd.

           Pagina} xli. vjs. iijd.

[fo. 18]

        Yet forin Charges, burdwages & rewards

Item to a grome of the stable for fetching Grey
Riche from Ware Parke}   iiijs. viijd.

Item to Bridges the teyler for the cariage of
your lordship's tente from London to Otford}   lxxvijs. viijd.[133]

Item to the iij gromes of the stable for ther
burdwages for vij deis ending the xxiiijth of July}   xiiijs.

Item gyvin to Powell of the wardrobe being
syke at London}   vjs. ijd.

Item to Christopher mylloner for iij peir of gilt
spurs for your lordship}   xxviijs.[134]

Item to the drum* and fyef* to pei their charges

[129] 18 July. The Queen went to Cobham Hall on that day, where she remained until Saturday the 22nd, see the entries below.

[130] Probably Thursday the 20th.

[131] The Queen was at Gillingham on Sunday and Monday 23–4 July.

[132] Probably the 25th, given the earlier entry.

[133] The Court was at Otford on 26–28 July.

[134] Christopher Carcano, milliner, see also, pp. 86, 103, 119 below, and his bill for 1557–May 1559 (DP Box V, fo. 4).

at Otford}	xxd.
Item for pears bought for your lordship}	iiijd.
Item for carriag [of] ij bucks from Otford to London to Mr Chelsham and Mr Gresham}	vjs. viiijd.[135]
Item to Wodd* for carriag of the velvett saddell from London to Grenwich and backe ageine}	xviijd.
Item for a luer for the marlynes}	xvjd.
Item for a grey negge bought for your lordship in Smythefild}	lxjs. viijd.
Item for a white negg bought ther}	xxxiiijs. viijd.
Item for iijll. wex lightes spent at Otford}	iijs.

<53 pagina>

Item to William Kynyat for the particulars of Watton}	xiiijs.
Item for lemans bought}	iijs. iiijd.
Item to Mr George Blunt* for hauks bells per billam}	xijd.
Item to Cutbert of the stable for an ambling black negge}	iiijli. xiijs. iiijd.[136]
Item to Jo[h]n Empson to provid[e] certen necessaries for your chamber}	xs.
Item to Henry Johnis to peie the cart cariage}	vjs. ijd.

Pagina} xviijli. viijs. ijd.

[fo. 18v]

Yet forrin charges &c.

Item to George Martyn* for his dinner and others your lordship's servants when the Quenes majestie dyned at Sir Persivall Hart's}	iiijs. iiijd.[137]
Item to Langham for hauksmeat viijd. and for ij meales ij removing deies}	xxd.
Item to Breybroke for monny leid out by him per bill}	viijs. ijd.
Item to thre gromes of the stable for vij deis ending the last of July}	xijs.
Item to Bristoo for monny leid out by him per bill}	vs. viijd.
Item to the drum and fiefs for ther lodging at Sevenoke}	iijs.
Item to John Trumpet for the carriag j tonne wine from St Katerins to the Savoy gyvin by the Frenchmen}	ijs.
Item peid to Potkins for the lodging of dyvers	

---

[135] William Chelsham, mercer and common councillor (1558–71), see also pp. 87, 98, 109, 123, 134 below and his bills for 1558–9 and 1562–6 (DP Box V, fos. 5–6, 158–65).

[136] Possibly Cuthbert Johnston, who was a Groom of the Stables in 1552 (BL, Stowe MS 571, fo. 37v-8). Only partial lists of the Stables staff survive for Elizabeth's reign.

[137] Lullingstone (Kent), probably on 29 or 30 July. Sir Percival Hart (d.1580), MP, was a Sewer to the Queen and Knight Harbinger.

your lordship's servants from the xxjth of July
to the second of August}   xviijs. viijd.
<54 pagina>
Item peid to George Martin for his burwages at Otford}   vs.
Item to Owin* for burwages} <burdwages>   xijd.
Item for your lordship's horsemeat at Eltham}   xd.[138]
Item to Cursson for horsemeat at Otford}   vjli. iijs. iiijd.
Item for tethe pykes}   xviijd.
Item for wex lights}   vs.
Item to the grosser's man that served out the bankett}   xijd.
Item peid for the carriage of the same stuff
from London}   iijs. iiijd.
ᶜItem for the charges of your lordship's supper at Eltham
the iijde deye of August besides Cs. dewe to Underwood's
wife for foule as appearethe by a bill of Chawod's}ᵉ
                          Pagina} ixli. xviijs. ijd.

[fo. 19]

Yet charges of burwages & reward
Item for your lordship's mennes dynears being at
London with my Lord Ambrose}   vs. vjd.[139]
Item peid to Flowerdew and Langham for hauksmeat
per bill}   ixs. vjd.
Item to John Trumpet for iiij meales at Eltham,
Croidon and Nonesuche}   ijs.[140]
<55 pagina>
Item to the ambassadour of Swetheland's servant
for bringing your lordship ij gr[eat?] horses}   xxxvijs.[141]

[138] According to the entries that follow this and those on pp. 95–6 below, Leicester was at Eltham on 2 and 3 August. The Court remained at Eltham until the 5th, when it removed to Nonsuch (Machyn, 206). It is not clear whether the supper referred to in these entries was a private one or a banquet.

[139] Given this supper early in August it is curious that in three letters written later in the month (DP I, fos. 64, 68, 70; 9, 15, 17 Aug.), Ambrose Dudley complained about not hearing from his brother.

[140] The Court removed to Nonsuch via Croydon, where the Queen spent the night of the 5th/6th. Leicester wrote to Francis Yaxley from Croydon, 'this Saturday in August' (PRO, SP 12/6/76), i.e. the 5th. The court remained at Nonsuch, which then belonged to the Lord Steward, the 12th Earl of Arundel (1511–80), between the 6th and the 10th. Arundel's entertainment of the Queen, particularly at a banquet on the 6th, was outstandingly lavish (see Machyn, 206). BL, Add. MS 48023 (fo. 357) attacks Arundel for initiating the extravagant entertainment that became a feature of Elizabethan progesses. A month later La Quadra reported that this banquet was to have been the scene of a plot to murder Elizabeth and Leicester (CSPSp, 1558–67, 95–6, 7 Sept.).

[141] An embassy sent by Gustavus Vasa to propose the marriage of his son, the future Eric XIV, to Elizabeth arrived in mid-July and left in mid-August CSPF, 1558–9, 404, 483, 501).

Item to the fletcher for shaftes by your
lordship's commandment per bill}   xiijs. iiijd.
Item to the iij gromes of the stable for ther
burdwags ending the vijth of August per vij dies}   xiiijs.
Item to George Martin for v meales viz Eltham,
Croydon and Nonesuche}   ijs. vjd.
Item to Wood the waterman for carriage of certeyne
stuff from Eltham to Kew}   vjs. ijd.
Item for neyles and tenter hokes sent to Kewe}   viijd.
Item for matts sent to Kewe}   iijs. iiijd.
Item for carriag of certeyne [sic] from
London to Kewe by water}   iijs. iiijd.
Item to the minstrell at Kewe}   xxd.
Item for carriag of the crimison fild bedd and
the tisshewe from London to Kewe by water}   ijs.
Item for carriage of the provisions[?] for your
lordship's dyner at Kewe by water}   xs.
Item to the upholster's man for setting uppe the beddes}   xijd.
Item for rose water at Kewe}   viijd.
<56 pagina>
Item to a certen woman to make cleane the house and
vessell at Kewe}   xviijd.
Item to one that mattid the chamber at Kewe for
ij deyes}   xviijd.
Item for erbes to tryme the house at Kewe per Hogans}   vs.
                    Pagina} Cxixs. viijd.

[fo. 19v]

                 Yet forin charges & reward
Item to Angila Marion's man for presenting your lordship
with ij stound horsys}   xxs.[142]
Item for the burdwages of iij gromes of the stable
ending the xiiijth of August}   xiiijs.
Item to George Cooke for monny dewe unto him
per bill}   vs. ixd.
Item to the boy for spaniell meat}   iijs. iiijd.
Item to him for i parr shois}   xijd.
Item to Yexlyes man that gave your lordship

---

[142] Angelo Maryano, see p. 126 below.

viij partriges}	vs.[143]
Item to the keaper of Bushy Parke at Hampton Cort in reward}	vs.[144]
Item to the keaper of the Great Park of Hampton for his reward for a bucke which your lordship gave to the porters}	vjs. iiijd.
Item to Sall for monny leyd out by him per bill}	vijs.
Item gyvin to Cragge being sent by night to London for the barge}	xxd.
Item for one of your lordship's yeomen botehier being sent to London for your caparison}	iijs. xd.

<57 pagina>

Item to Higham for a case of knyves}	vjs.
Item to Gryffith Lloid for his botehier from Hantoncort to London}	iiijs. iiijd.
Item gyvin amonge your lordship's fotemen [ther *deleted*] for ther lodging and tryming at Horsely the Quenes majestie being ther}	ijs. vjd.[145]
Item for your lordship's men's suppers that night at Guildeford}	vjs. ijd.
Item to a pore woman that seid your lordship was her gossippe at Horslye}	vjs. iiijd.
Item to the yeomen of Lord Clinton's stable in reward}	vjs. iiijd.
Item to the boye for doggs meat}	jjs.

Pagina} Cvjs. vijd.

[fo. 20]

Yet forin charges &tc.

Item for ij*dd.* rabond points for your caparison ageynst the running at Horselye}	xijd.[146]
Item to a power man for a hawking pole}	iiijd.
Item gyvin to pore men for the cariag of your	

[143] Francis Yaxley (c.1528–1565), Clerk of the Signet to 1559, MP. He was arrested in the spring of 1562 for intriguing with La Quadra and the Countess of Lennox and his papers seized. These are now distributed among the State Papers. The letter from Leicester of 5 Aug. (see n. 140 above) was a response to this gift.

[144] The Court removed to Hampton Court on 10 August and returned to Whitehall on 28 September. In his letter of 15 Aug. (DP I, fo. 68) Ambrose Dudley appears to have expected that the progress was continuing to Windsor.

[145] The Queen visited Clinton's house at West Horsley between 17 and 23 August.

[146] On 22 August Noailles reported that Leicester and others practised running at ring ('courre la bague') before the Queen at Horsley (AMAE, CPA XIII, fo. 305, not mentioned in Young). The entries to paying off servants and sending household stuff to Kew on the following pages suggest that the progress was regarded as concluded.

lordship's armor at sundry tymes from your chamber to the place whear your lordship armid you}	xviijd.
Item gyvin in almes at sundry times by Higham}	xd.
Item to Cursson for meat of a tyrd horse going to Horselye}	ijs.
Item for lodging and other charge of your lordship's servants at Guildford}	vs.
Item peid to Carie for a negge which your lordship gave unto Ralfe Hunte}	xls.
Item to Henry Fawkner in reward xls. and for his horsemeat whiles he attendyd at Hantoncort}	ls.
<58 pagina>	
Item to the boy for spaniells meat}	ijs.
Item for a gunne deliveryd to Henry Fawkner}	xvjs.
Item for flaske and touche box}	ijs. viijd.
Item for gunpowder for hem}	iijs. iiijd.
Item to Partrige for servise donn at Hamptoncort per bill}	Cvijs. vjd.
Item to the iij gromes of the stable for xiiij deis burdwages ending the xxviijth of August}	xxviijs.
Item for meat for the spaniells}	iijs.
Item for a hose clothe and lyning for the boy that keapithe the spaniell}	iiijs. viijd.
Item to William Smithe* for horse meat and burdwages per bill}	xxviijs. ixd.

Pagina} xiiijli. xvjs. vijd.

[fo. 20v]

Yet forin charges and rewards

Item for our dyners at Grenwich your lordship being their to sey your armor}	vs. iiijd.
Item for your lordship's horsemeat ther}	vjs. iiijd.
Item for a lure for the marlyn}	xvjd.
Item for making of the boy's coote and hose per Flowerdewe}	vjs. viijd.
Item to Mr Darsye* for his horsemeat for xxviii deis at xd. the deye}	xxiiijs.
Item to John Muleteer* for his bordwages being in progresse begyning the xvij of July and ending the xxviijth of August inclus}	xxviijs.
Item to Mr Streat's servant bringing a bucke from Otlandes}	vs.
<59 pagina>	
Item to Owin for his horsemeat in progresse per bill}	xxvs.

To Thomas Davies for monny dew to him
per bill}   xvijs. iijd.
Item to the tente men for cariage of the tents per
bill}   viijli. vjs. ijd.
Item to Ralfe the huntsman as apperith by ij
severall bills per Blunt}   liijs. vjd.
Item to George Cooke per bill}   xxiijs. vjd.
Item to Jamys Thomson for his charges per bill}   xxvijs.
Item to Robart Holland for his charge in progresse
per bill}   xxvs.
Item to Henry Johns per bill}   vijs. ijd.
Item to Robert Duncking for his chargis in progres}   xxxvs.
Item to Edward Roberts for his charges
ᶠper billᶠ}   lvijs. viijd.
Item to Breybroke for lyke allowans by his bill}   xxs.
Item for cariag of your tentes to London}   ijs.
                    Pagina} xxvjli. xvs. xjd.

[fo. 21]

                    Yet forin charges & rewards
Item to Mr. High[a]m for his horsemete xxx deis at
x*d*. the day per bill}   xxvs.
Item to John Forest for like charges as apperith
by his bill}   liijs. iiijd.
Item for a hose clothe for Cragge the foteman}   viijs.
Item for v*ll*. wax lights sent to Hampton Cort}   vs.
<60 pagina>
Item for a sesterne for your lordship's chamber
at the Cort}   xxviijs. vjd.
Item for the carriag of a close stole, the sesterne
and other things from London to Hamptoncort}   iijs. iiijd.
Item to George Blunt for hauks meat iij weaks at
xiiij*d*. the weake iij*s*. vj*d*. and for his supper
attend[ing] your lordship a huntinge vj*d*., in toto}   iiijs.
Item for horsemeat and shoing at Nonesuche
your lordship being ther}   xxijd.
Item for spaniell meat}   ijs.
Item for iij gromes of the stables burwages ending the
iiijth of September}   xiiijs.
Item among the armyrers at Grenwich}   xxs.
Item for strewing erbis at Kewe ageinst your lordship's
comyng thither}   xxd.
Item for carriage of wine and accats from London

to Kewe}	ijs. iiijd.
Item for stone juggs sent to Kewe}	xiiijd.
Item for horsebread at Kewe}	xijd.
Item for a peir snuffers[?] and a chopping knyfe}	xiiijd.

<61 pagina>

Item gyvin in reward to Sir Nichollas Poynes that presentyd the mares [sic]}	xxxs. xd.[147]
Item to the watermen for bringing certeyne stuff from London to Hampton}	ijs. viijd.

Pagina} xli. vs. xd.

[fo. 21v]

Yet forin charges & rewards

Item to the drome and fief to bear ther charges whiles thei ley syke at Kingiston}	xiijs. iiijd.
Item to Bristo for his horsmeat xxx deis at xd. the deye}	xxvs.
Item peid to Forest the hunt[sman] for a ronne at Kingston to put his hond}	xxd.
Item to iij gromes of the stable for ther burdwages for xxj deis ending the xxvth of September either of them viijd. by the deye}	xlijs.
Item to John Audwine for his charges in progres for himselfe, his horse and hauks}	lxvjs. viijd.
Item to William Cooke by your lordship's commandment at his departing from your service}	xxs.
Item to the embroderers in reward being your cote and hatt embrodrid with silver}	iijs. vjd.

<62 pagina>

Item for a great hawks bagge bought at the Cort gate}	xijs. iiijd.
Item for russhis at Somersett House}	viijd.
Item for your lordship's lights at Somersett House viz quarners, torches & white Lights}	vs. vijd.
Item to George Blunt for hauksmeat}	ijs. vjd.
Item for the cariag of hanging and other stuff from London to Kewe}	iijs. iiijd.
Item for cariage of stuff from Whitehall to the wardrope}	xd.
Item to one in earnest for certin steals for [sic]	

---

[147] Sir Nicholas Poyntz (1528–85), MP. According to a letter he wrote to Leicester, which may have accompanied the mares (DP I, fo. 77, undated but endorsed August 1559), he had just left the Court. For their later relations see 'West Midlands', 48.

your lordship}	iijs.
Item to Mr Norrys's boy when your lordship sent him aweye}	vjs. iiijd.[148]
Item to your lordship's faukner that was Sir Henry Leis man to by a gunne}	xxs.[149]

Pagina} xjli. vjs. ixd.

[fo. 22]

Yet forin charges & rewards

Item for jdd. par coples and a lyne for your spaniell}	iijs.
Item for torches at Westminster}	iijs.
Item for my fellowes dyner and myne your lordship dyning with the Marques de Trant}	vjs. vjd.[150]

<63 pagina>

Item to the godwyfe of the Lyon at Kingiston for spaniell meat}	xjs.
Item to the Frenchman for to by floures to macke a nosegeye by your lordship's commandment}	ijs. vjd.
Item to Mr Darcye for ij yerds dy velvet for his lyvery cote by your lordship's commandment}	xxxijs.
Item to John Faukener for a great haukes bagge}	xs.
Item for my fellowes dyner and min[e] your lordship dyning at Sir John York's}	ixs. vjd.
Item to Mr Norrys's boy by your lordship's command being sent to your lordship with a letter}	iijs. iiijd.
Item to Ralfe the hunt[sman] for part of peyment of a more sum sins the last of August}	xs. xd.
Item to Forest for parte of peyment of a more some for spannells meat since the last of August}	vs.
Item to my Lord of Arundell's servant rowing your lordship from Arundell Plase per Hogans}	vjs. iiijd.[151]

[148] Probably (Sir) Henry, the future Lord Norris of Rycote (1525–1601), MP. His wife Margery was the chief mourner at Amy Dudley's funeral, see n. 260 below.

[149] Sir Henry Lee (1530/1–1611), MP, Keeper of Woodstock Palace from 1570 and Master of the Armory from 1580. He was a deponent in the Sir Robert Dudley case, but his deposition has not survived. Further references to him can be found below.

[150] Gaston de Foix, Marquis de Trans, one of the French hostages. Possibly the M de Foix who sent Leicester 'garnitures d'oyseaux' from London on 5 Aug. (DP I, fo. 161). The day-book reference suggests that this took place at the end of September. He and Leicester appear to have been on quite friendly terms, see the conversation on the Queen's marriage reported by La Quadra to the Bishop of Arras on 12 Nov. (Lettenhove, ii, 87), and further references to dining on p. 164 below.

[151] This visit presumably took place at the end of September; it is difficult to reconcile with La Quadra's contemporary reports of intrigues against Leicester by Arundel and others (see n. 140 above and CSPSp, 1558–67, 107 (29 Oct.)).

Item to other botes bringing your men from thense}   ijs.
Item for a henne which the spanell killid}   vijd.
<64 pagina>
Item to the watermen that fett the sorell gelding
that swam over the water at Cheswyke}   xijd.

Pagina} Cvjs. vijd.

[fo. 22v]

Yett forin charges & rewards

Item for botehier for your lordship's servants
from Lambeth to White hall}   viijd.
Item to the yeoman of Sir Henry Sidney's horsys
that brought your lordship a bey hobbye}   xijs. iiijd.
Item for cariag of your lordship's buttry and
kychin stuff from Westminster to Grenwich and
backe ageyne}   ijs. viijd.
Item to Mrs Osunis for bredd & bear the same tyme}   xijs. iiijd.[152]
Item for horsemeat ther}   vs. vjd.
Item to my Lord of Arundell's bargemen bringing
your lordship from Arundell House to White hall}   xijs. viijd.
Item to Thomas Davies for candell and other
things as apperithe by his bill}   xvijs. viijd.
Item for your meanys dyners when your lordship
dyned with Sir William Daunsell}   vjs.[153]

Pagina} lxixs. xd.

[g]Forin charges & rewards}   VCxxixli. iiijs. ixd.
Ould peyments of detts}   CCCixli. xiijs. iiijd.
Peyments uppon your lordship's
commandment & for your lordship's
pursse}   iiij[xx]xvjli. vjs. iiijd.
Sum of the hole forin charges,
peyments and rewards}   IXCxxxvli. iiijs. vd.[g]

---

[152] See also p. 96 below and the later references on pp. 190, 322, 327 to the annuity
for Mother Ossinus, presumably the same woman. She would appear to have been the
keeper of a lodging house at Greenwich.
[153] Sir William Damsell or Dansell (1521–1582), Receiver-General of the Court of Wards
from 1550.

[fo. 23]

Charges of apparell & goldsmithes work

In primys ij small cheynes for a cappe weying
iij *qt. oz.* at lv*s.* [the] *oz.*, xlj*s.* iij*d.* & for
the fation ix*s.* iiij*d.*, in toto}   liijs. iiijd.

To Hanse Franke for perle in part of peyment
of a more some as apperith by his bill}[h]   xli.[154]

Item peid to Read the capper uppon his bill}   vjli.

To Christopher milloner for certeyne stuff as
appearithe by his bill of partic[ulars]
Mensis Decembris}   xxxli. xxd.

Item for ij Spanishe skynnes to make your
lordship's jerkin trymyd with sylver lace}   xxijs.

Item to the goldsmythe for sundry jewells
bough of Hanse Francke for New Year's gifts
xxv*li.*, for perles x*li.*, for enamyling a
cheyne iij*s.* iiij*d.*, in the hole by your
lordship's commandment} <29 Decembre>   xxxvli. xiijs. iiijd.

Item for lace for gold buttons}   vjd.

Item to Mr Gryse for certen perle}   xli.

Item to him for more perle}   iiijli.

Item for a peir of Gernesey hose for your lordship}   iijs. iiijd.

Item for sweate bagges with pendants per Powell}   viijs. viijd.

Item for a loking glasse bought by Mr Gryse}   xijs.

Item to Hanse the goldsmith for certene
perles in part of peyment of a more some}   xli.

Item for ij peir of knitt hose for your lordship}   iiijs. viijd.

Item for ij peir of knit hose}   vs. iiijd.

Pagina} Cxjli. iiijs. xd.   Apparell} xlviijli. viijs. ijd.
                             Gou[l]dsmithes} lxijli. xvjs. viijd.

[fo. 23v]

Yet charges of aparell &c.

Item for ij*dd.* yellowe silke poynts}   xxijd.

Item for lace for your buskens}   vjd.

Item for iij yerds of white fustian to lyne
your lordship's doblett trymyd with gould lace}   ijs. iiijd.

Item to the myloner for points and lace bough by
Edward Robarts}   xxd.

---

[154] Hans Frank, goldsmith, see pp. 90, 117 below. He should be distinguished from Leicester's servant Hans or Hance.

Item to Mr Holborne for a peir of white knitt silke hose}	liijs. iiijd.[155]
Item for a peir of hose bought for my lady by Thomas Johnes}	iijs.
To Mrs Barker in parte of peyment of more monny dew for shirtes &c.}	xli.
Item peid to Smythe the merser for viij yerds of russett sattin for your lordship's doblett and hose trymed sylver}	iiijli. xs.[156]
Item to the Spanishe teyler for the making of girkins trymmyd with silver lace and for the making of ij sattin doubletts per bill}	lvijs.
To Mrs Holborne for a peir of silke knitt hose russett}	liijs. iiijd.
Item for vj yerds of gild canvas at iiijs. vjd. the yerd}	xxviijs.
Item peid to Chelsam for x yerds dy of taffita sarsenet at xs. the yerd to make a quilt of}	Cvs.
Item peid to Smythe the mercer for vj yerds i qtr. of velvet at xviijs. the yerd and iiij yerds to the Spanishe teiler for your lordship's doblet and hose & ij yerd qtr. for the garding of my lady's cloke}	Cxijs. vjd.
Item for dy yard blewe velvet at xvijs. deliveryd to the embroderer for your lordship's armes}	viijs. vjd.
Item for xxviij yerds fustian at xd. the yerd to lyne the quilte}	xxiijs. iiijd.
Pagina} xxxvijli. ijd.	Apparell} xxxvijli. ijd.
	Gouldsmythes} nil

[fo. 24]

Charges of aparell &c.

Item peid to Allin the skynner for xiiij skynnes of blacke jenitts delivered to George Gyles}	xvli.[157]
Item to Smythe the mercer for xxviij yerds of crymson Spanish taffi[ta] at viijs. the yerd	

[155] William Holborne, haberdasher, see pp. 122, 139, 142, 146, 158 below.

[156] Ambrose Smith, mercer, see also pp. 123, 177 below. Several references to him can be found in G.D. Ramsay (ed.), *John Isham Mercer and Merchant Adventurer* (Northamptonshire Rec. Soc., xxi, 1962).

[157] Thomas Allen, skinner, see p. 123 below and his bill for 1559–60, DP Box V, fo. 8.

to make curtens for your lordship's fild bedd}   ixli. xvjs.
Item to the seid Smythe for xxvj yerds crymson
damaske at xiijs. iiijd. the yerd to make
curtynes for your great bedd embroderyd}   xvijli. vjs. viijd.
Item for a peir of gilt sporres vjs. viijd.,
for cupers for your cappe iiijd., in toto}   vijs.
Item for your lordship's deske coveryd with
velvett & the lock &c.}   xls.
Item to my Lord of Penbrokes servant for the
making of your lordship's canvas doblett}   xjs. ijd.
To Mrs Jermayne for mony dew to her which
Mr Blunt was bound for}   ixli.[158]
Item peid to the mercer for viij yerds of
grograne deliveryd to Whittell to make your
lordship a gowne}   iiijli. xvjs.
Item peid to John Gouldsmithe upon a
reckning} <Lanyson>   lli. vjs. viijd.
ᶦItem peid to him for a butt of renis wyne}   Cxiijs. iiijd.ᶦ
Item peid to Whittill the teyler by your
lordship's commandment per bill}   ixli. xs. viijd.
Item peid to Allen the skynner uppon his
bill of xxxli. the sum of}   xxli.
Item for ijdd. ribon points}   xviijd.
Item to John Gye the capper uppon his bill}   viijli.[159]
Item for j yerd cotton for your lordship's
buskins}   viijd.
Pagina} Cxlvjli. xvjs. iiijd.   Apparell} iiijˣˣxvjli. ixs. viijd.
                                        Gouldsmithes}   lli. vjs. viijd.

[fo. 24v]

Aparell and gouldsmith's worke
Item for a salt gyvin to Mr Knevett's child at the
christening weying viij oz. dy at vjs. viijd. the oz.}   lvijs. vijd.
Item for a taffita hatt stitched for your lordship}   vijs. vjd.
Item for a salt which your lordship sent to my
Lady Cheakes childe at the christening}   Cs.
Item to the myloner for a cappe and a fether

---

[158] Probably the wife of German Cyall, London agent for the Bonvisi; she was the daughter of Sir John Gresham the elder (Ramsay, *City of London*, p. 157).

[159] There are numerous references below and in the Ellis account to Guy, described alternately as a capper and a haberdasher. One of his bills is pasted into the Ellis account, see pp. 173–4 below, and Document C of Part II (see p. 422 below) is extracted from another.

for your lordship}	xvs.
Item to the milloner for ij*dd.* crymson riband points}	ijs.
Item iij litell chines to tryme a cappe whereof	
ij wear deliveryd to Christopher milloner}	vjli. xviijs.
Item for ij ells of crymson taffita sarsenet	
to lyne your doblett & hose of crimson sattin	
weltyd with velvett}	xxiiijs.
Item for vj*dd.* ribon points deliveryd to Empson}	iijs. vjd.
Item for i yeard dy Spanishe ribon to hange	
your lordship's George bye}	xijd.[160]
Item for a gilt salt for your lordship's awne table}	xxxixs.
Item for a lace for your lordship's George}	xijd.
Item for sylke points}	vjd.
Item to the Spanishe teyler for making of vj peir	
velvett hose as apperith by his bill}	xvjli. vjs. viijd.
Item peid to Evererd for a George and a cheyne	
set with dyamons}	lxxli.
Item to Gwyllam for a Spanishe chene for	
your lordship}	ixli.
Item to Mrs Holborne for a peir of crymson	
knitt hose}	lxvjs. viijd.
Item for a pece of ribon to hang your lordship's	
George bye}	iiijs. iiijd.

Pagina} Cxviijli. vjs. viijd.   Apparell} xxvli. ixs. viijd.

Gouldsmyth} iiij^{xx}xijli. xvijs.

[fo. 25]

Yet charges of aparell &c.

Item to Mrs Holborne for a peir of russett knitt	
stoocks liij*s.* iiij*d.* and for lengthening of a	
peir whit sylke hose iiij*s.*} <36 pagina>	lvijs. iiijd.
Item to Mrs Holborne for iiij peir of Spanish	
gloves for your lordship}	ijs. viijd.
Item for j*dd.* white silke points}	viijd.
Item peid to Lucas the skynner as appearithe	
by his bill}	xliiijli. xiijs. iiijd.
Item to Smythe the mercer in parte of peyment	
of a more sum}	Cxxli.

---

[160] These entries refer to the 'lesser George', which could be worn on either a chain or a ribbon (E. Ashmole, *The Institution ... of the ... Order of the Garter* (1672, rep. 1971), pp. 226–7).

Item to Thomas Johns to by a hoode for my ladye}	xxxvjs.
Item peid to Gilbert the gouldsmithe for vj*dd.* gould buttons of the Spanishe fation and for one litel cheyne deliveryd to Mr Forest for my ladye's use}	xxxli.
Item to Reignold the teiler by your lordship's commandment in part of peyment of a more sum}	xxli.

<37 pagina>

Item peid to White for a Spanishe lether jerkin gardyd with velvet}	lxxjs.
Item peid for vj*dd.* ribond points and a pece of Spanishe lace}	iijs. iiijd.
Item peid to the Spanishe teylor for making your lordship iij peir of Spanish hose viz white, russett & yellowe}	ixli.
Item for a peir of white knitt hose for your lordship ix crownes}	lvijs.
Item to the miloner for a velvett night cappe vj*s.*, for points and ribond lace ij*s.*, in toto}	viijs.
Item to Hanse the goldsmithe in full peyment of all suche monny as your lordship ought him before the xxjth of May}	xvjli. vijs. xjd.
To Mrs Victoe for lynen clothe bought for my ladye}	ljs.[161]
Pagina} CCLiiijli. viijs. iijd.	Apparell} CCviijli iiijd.
Gouldsmith} xlvjli. vijs. xjd.

[fo. 25v]

Yett charges of aparell and goldsmith

Item peid to Denham the goldsmith as appearithe by his bill}	iiijxxli.[162]
Item to Deryke the goldsmith in full peyment of all such mony dew to him the xxijth Maij}	xvjli. xjs. ixd.[163]

[161] *Sic* or Picto, see p. 102 below. She is the 'Picto who doth dearlie love her' mentioned in Thomas Blount's report to Leicester on the death of his wife, 11 Sept. 1560 (Pepys MS 2503, pp. 705–6). Her name was mistranscribed in the first printing of this correspondence as 'Pinto' (Richard, Lord Braybrooke, *The Diary of Samuel Pepys F.S.A.* (1848), i, 385), which has been repeated in most modern accounts.

[162] William Denham, goldsmith and common councillor (1576–7), see also p. 121 below and his bills for 1560 and 1561–6, DP Box V, fos. 26, 92–5.

[163] Derek Anthony, goldsmith and engraver at the Tower mint (C.E. Challis, *The Tudor Coinage* (Manchester, 1978), pp. 34–6). DP Box V, fo. 96, is a bill of his dated 20 May 1561.

Item to Bowes for a hatt which your lordship
bought of him}   viijs.
Item to Ballett the goldsmithe for ij litell
white cuppes}   <36 pagina>   lxxvijs. ixd.
Item to my Lady Clerke for ij knitt peticotts
of silke for your lordship}   vijli.
Item peid to Hanse the hosier for making your
lordship a peir of crimson velvet hose with
stuff to the same}   <42 pagina>   lxs.
Item to the Spanishe teyler for making your
lordship iij dobletts weltyd with velvet and
on[e] of gould canvas}   ixli. vs. iiijd.
Item for ij ells fine holland for to make my
lady ruffes}   <46 pagina>   xijs.
Item for ij ells dy qtr. of russett taffita
to make my lady a gowne at xiijs. iiijd.
the ell}   <48 pagina>   xxxvs.
Item for xlviij enamylid rings whereof your
lordship had iij and I had one for a ring of
myne which your lordship gave to my Lord Marques}   xxvjs. viijd.
Item for tynsell sarsenett for to lyne your
lordship a peir of carnat hose}   xvijs.
Item to Diryke the goldsmithe for part of a
more sum dewe for a garter of perle}   xxli.
Item for a peir of knitt hose for your
lordship}   liijs. iiijd.
Item for ij peir of knitt hose for your
lordship}   xs.
Pagina} Cxlvijli. xvjd. xd.   Apparell} xxvijli. vijs. iiijd.
                              Gouldsmith}   Cxxli. ixs. vjd.

[fo. 26]

                  Yet charges of apare[*tear*]
Item peid to Mrs Holborne for a peir of knitt
hose}   <60 pagina>   liijs. iiijd.
Item for the making of ij newe velvett bagges}   ixs.
Item for a new velvet bagge}   xiiijs.
Item to the myloner for ij new cappes for
your lordship}   xxiiijs.
Item for ij peir Garnesey hose for your lordship}   ixs.
Item to Mrs Holborne for a peir of black knitt
silke hose}   liijs. iiijd.
Item for a yerd and qtr. kersey for your

lordship's blacke botehose}   <62 pagina>   vjs.
Item ij peir of hose sent to my ladye by Sir
Richard Vernies servant}   viijs.[164]
Item from [sic] trymyng vjdd. egletts sett
uppon your lordship's cote embroderyd}   vijs. viijd.
Pagina} ixli. iiijs. iiijd.   Apparell} ixli. iiijs. iiijd.
                                                      Gouldsmith}   nil

Sum total of the apparell and
Gouldsmithes worke}   VIIJCxxiiijli. xvijs. vd.
Apparell}   IIIJCljli. xixs. viijd.
Goldsmith}   IIJClxxijli. xvijs. ixd.

[fo. 26v *blank*]
[fo. 27]

Diett

Imprimis for beare provided for your lordship
at Somerset Howse}   xxijd.
Item for beare bought at Westminster}   <2 pagina>   xijd.
Item for renish wyne fet from the Styllyard
by Mr Blunt's man}   ijs.
Item for thre boxes of codynoick mens December}   iiijs.
Item for beare fet by Jones at sundry tymes
whyles the Quenes majestie laye at Whithall}   ijs. iijd.
Item for smale beare per Johnes}   <6 pagina>   xijd.
Item for oranges per Huddleston}   <7 pagina>   vjs. viijd.
Item for our dyners your lordship dyning
with the Levetenant of the Tower}   xiiijs. vijd.[165]
Item for vj boxes of codynoke gyvin unto my
Lady Clinton}   vjs. viijd.[166]
Item for oranges bought at sundry tymes
for your lordship}   xijd.
Item for smale beare fett at sundry tymes
by Johnes}   xiiijd.
Item for aples bought at sundry tymes for the

[164] Sir Richard Verney (d. 1567/9) of Compton Verney (Wars.), deputy for Leicester as
lieutenant of Warwickshire, see 'West Midlands', 44. For his association with Amy Dudley
see Appendix I.
    [165] Sir Edward Warner (1511–65), MP, Lieutenant of the Tower 1552–3, involved in
Wyatt's Rebellion, and restored to office in November 1558. The occasion was probably
the remove to the Tower on 12 January, see n. 41 above.
    [166] Elizabeth (Fitzgerald), the 'fair Geraldine' (1528?–1590), Gentlewoman of the Privy
Chamber, see 'Feria Dispatch', 329–30, n. 8.

porpontynes}   <01 pagina>   xiiijd.[167]
Item peid for our dyners your lordship
dyning with Mr Foskewe christening his child}   xxijs.
Item for suckett iij*dd*.}   vjs.
Item for orenges & lemans}   iiijd.
Item for cumsetts}   iijs. iiijd.
Item for bear fett from Westminster at sundry
tymes}   xvjd.
Item for iij boxes of codymake}   iijs. vjd.
Item for a pound & comsetts} [*sic*]   xijd.
Item for *jdd*. greane suckett}   xxd.
Item for aples}   iiijd.
Item for *jdd*. suckett}   <12 pagina>   xxd.
Item for iij boxys of codymacke}   iijs. vjd.
Item for dy *ll*. cumsetts xij*d*., j*ll*. of almond
cumsetts xviij*d*., biskett &c. viij*d*.,
for peares and apples viij*d*., dy *ll*. almond vj*d*.,
in toto}   iiijs. iiijd.

Pagina} iiijli. xijs. vd.

[fo. 27v]

Diett

Item for j*ll*. suckett xx*d*., for aples ij*d*., for
marmylade ij*s*., for suckett xx*d*., for orenges
xviij*d*., in toto}   vijs.
Item to Hogans for a pom[e]granat}   <13 pagina>   ijs.
Item for ij*ll*. round cumsetts iiij*s*., for a
baskett & carig xviij*d*., for oranges and lemans
ij*s*. vj*d*., in toto}   viijs.
Item for ij boxis of cumsetts which your lordship
gave to my Lord of Darbye}   vjs. ijd.
Item for suckett}   xxd.
Item for aples}   iiijd.
Item for cumsetts and other sweat meats gyvin to my
Lord of Darbye}   iiijs.
Item for wardons}   iiijd.
Item to Henry Johnes for beare fett for your
lordship at divers tymes}   vjs.
Item for ij*ll*. almonds bought by William Smythe}   ijs. xd.
<16 pagina>
Item for wardens to rost}   xijd.

---

[167] Porcupines, presumably those in the Tower menagerie.

Item for orenges}	xijd.
Item for beare fett by your lordship at sundry tymes by Henry Johnes}	vijs.
<17–23 paginae>	
Item for our dyners whiles the stuff was taking downe at Christchurch}	xxd.
Item for our dyners tryming uppe the lodging at Seint Jamys}	iijs.
Item for a box of cumsetts}	iiijs.
Item peid for wardens}	xiiijd.
Item for aples}	ijd.
Item for orenges}	xiiijd.
Item for ij*ll.* cumsetts}	iiijs.
Item for oranges bought}	iiijs.
Item to John Gouldsmithe for j butt of reignish wine per bill}	Cxiijs. iiijd.
Item for bear fett by Johnis at sundry tymes}	vijs.
Pagina} ixli. vjs. xd.	

[fo. 28]

Diett

<25–32 paginae>	
Item for ij*ll.* cumsetts for your lordship}	iiijs.
Item for lemons}	xvjd.
Item for aples}	iiijd.
Item for aples}	ijd.
Item for oranges and lemens}	xvjd.
Item for the banketing stuff preparid at the Quenes highnes being at your lordship's tents within the Parke}	vjli. xiiijs.[168]
Item for oranges}	viijd.
Item for xg. of reynishe wine at xxd. the *gall.*, xvjs. viijd., for the runlett and carriage of the same xviijd.}	xviijs. ijd.
Item for lemans bought by Johnis}	viijd.
Item for spises bought by the cookes when your lordship rode to my ladyes}	xxijs.[169]
Item for drinke at Waltham}	xiiijd.
Item for your lordship's supper that night at Ware}	xxxiiijs. viijd.

[168] Probably during the Morris games held in St James's Park on 21 March, see p. 58, n. 73 above.
[169] See Appendix I.

Item for horsemeat, shoing and other
charges their}   lviijs. viijd.
Item for your lordship's breakfast at Ware}   xxxvs.
Item for your lordship's men's charges iiij
meales at Buntingford}   iiijli. ijs. xd.
Item for horsemeat ther all that tym with
vj*bz*. otys conveid to Mr Hides}   iiijli. vs. ijd.
Item for all our suppers at Waltham}   xxvijs. vjd.
Item for horsemeat ther x*s*. viij*d*. & for
horsehier your lordship being in the jornye
lij*s*. viij*d*., in toto}   lxiijs. iiijd.
Item for my fellowes diner and myne when
your lordship dyned at Sir Morrys Dennys's}   xijs. iiijd.[170]
Item for my botehier the same dey about
your lordship's busynes}   xvjd.
                    Pagina} xxixli. iiijs. viijd.

[fo. 28v]

                              Diet
<34, 26, 40, 42, 54, 60 paginae>
Item peid to Maddye for reynishe wine at
sundry tymes as apperithe by his bill}   vijli. vijs. vijd.
Item for small bear for your lordship}   ijd.
Item for sage ale for your lordship}   vjd.
Item for mylke}   ijd.
Item for v*dd*. queyll bought by your lordship's
commandment signified unto me by Hogans}   ls.
Item for fine bread sent to Kewe}   ijs.
Item for certeine provision made at Kewe
as apperithe by a bill of Jenkins}   iiijli. xvijs. xd.
Item to Halys wyfe for lyke provisions ther}   xxxixs. vd.[171]
Item for iiij*dd*. queiles bought by the trumpeter}   xxiiijs.
Item the chargis of your lordship's dyner the
Frenche men dyning with your lordship with
xxxj*s*. viij*d*. for banketing stuff}   iiijli. ijs. xd.
Item the charges of your lordship's supper at
Eltham the second of August as apperith by

---

[170] Sir Maurice Denys (1516–1563), treasurer of Calais 1550–3 and treasurer at Le Havre
1562–3, MP.

[171] The wife of John Hales of Kew, see p. 131 below. He was presumably the John
Hales who was granted the ferry between Kew and Brentford by Henry VIII in 1536
(V.C.H., *Surrey*, iii, 485).

a bill of the particulars}	ixli. xviijd.
Item for reynishe wine sent thither for the same supper}	vs. viijd.
Item for the charges of your lordship's supper at Eltham iij August besides Cs. dew to Underwood's wyfe for foule as apperithe by a bill of accat}	Cxvijs. xd.
Item for freshe sturgeon bought the same tyme by Ellice}	xs.
Item for reignishe wine the same tyme with the cariage}	vs. xd.
Item for dy c mult spent your lordship being at Kewe [Nonsuch deleted]}	iiijs.
Item for peares and nuts bought by Horden}	vjd.
Item for a runlett of renishe wine sent to Hamptoncort}	xs. xd.
Item for reignishe wine sent to Kewe ageinst your lordship comying thither}	ijs.
Item for lemans ther}	xijd.
Pagina} xxxixli. iijs. vijd.	

[fo. 29]

Diet

<62–64 pagina>

Item for reynishe wine spent at your lordship's supper at Somersett House}	vs. iiijd.
Item for bread and bear ther}	viijs.
Item pomegranettes}	xvjd.
Item for reignishe wine sent by your lordship's commandment to Wimbleton}	vjs. iiijd.
Item for reynishe wine sent to Grenwich your lordship dyning with Osunis}	vs. iiijd.
ʲItem to [blank] for carriage of your lordship's buttry and kichin stuff}ʲ	
Pagina} xxvjs. iiijd.	
Sum of the hole peyment of the dyett}	iiijˣˣiijli. xiijs. xd.

[fo. 29v blank]
[fo. 30]

Necessary Provisions

<1–9 paginae>

ᵏImprimis to Mrs Myliner by the hand of Powell for lv ells holland and divers particulars per bill}	xlvjs. iiijd.ᵏ

To Mrs Myller for xxv ells iiij *qtr.* [*sic*]
holland at xx*d.* the ell xliij*s.*, for xxx ells
iij *qtr.* dy at xviij*d.* the ell xlvj*s.* iiij*d.*,
for xvij ell canvas at xj*d.* the ell xv*s.* vij*d.*,
xxvj ells holland at xiiij*d.* the ell xlij*s.*,
vj ells brod canvas at iij*s.* the ell xviij*s.*,
for xij ells brode canvas at ij*s.* viij*d.* the ell
xxxij*s.*, in toto}   ixli. xvijs.
Item for xj ells iij *qtr.* holland at iij*s.* iiij*d.*
the ell xxxix*s.* ij*d.*, for xvj ells *qtr.* holland at
vj*s.* ij*d.* the ell C*s.* ij*d.*, for ij peces holland cont lx
ells ad ij*s.* iiij*d.* the ell vij*li.* xxj*d.*, in toto per bill}   xiiijli. xiiijd.
For making the seid stuff as apears by the bill viz
ij pair fine shetts, iij*dd.* napkins, vj coberd
clothes, vj table clothes, iiij pair pallet
shetts, iij trussing sheats, ix canvas rubbers}   xvs. iiijd.
Item for the frame of cheres}   lxs.
Item for j*dd.* of tynne plates}   vs.
Item for a baskett for the buttrye}   viijd.
Item peid for the square table and for i peir
trestills for the long burd at the Cort}   xiijs. iiijd.
Item for lute strings by Hans}   iijs.
Item for ij*ll.* wex lights}   ijs.
ᴵItem beare fett at sundryeᴵ
Item for iiij flagons of tynne stonding in ij
gardevians}   lxvjs. viijd.
Item for a gimlet and other necessaries bought
for the buttry}   xxjd.
                    Pagina} xxxijli. vs. xjd.

[fo. 30v]

                        Necessary Provisions
<16-54 paginae>
Item for a parfuming panne}   iiijs.
Item for a frying panne}   xxd.
Item for a gredyearne}   ijs. xd.
Item peid to the smithe for a locke for the
close stole and for mending the table}   ijs.
Item for a cace of knyves bought by Mr Blunt}   vs.
Item to the joyner for ij walnot tre bedds}   lxxvjs. viijd.
Item peid for ij fild beddes sent to Kewe}   lxxiijs. iiijd.
Item for vj candelstiks sent to Kewe}   xijs.
Item for v candell plates sent to Kewe at

ij*s*. vj*d*. the pece}	xijs. vjd.
Item for j*dd*. grene cusshins sent to Kewe}	ixs.
Item for stone jugges}	iiijs. iiijd.
Item for urinalls ij*s*., for cord for beddes ij*s*. vj*d*., for viij staff torchis viij*s*., j*dd*. dy quarners iij*s*. vj*d*., x*ll*. white lyghts ij*s*., in toto sent to Kewe}	xvijs. vjd.
Item sent to the joyner of Charing Crosse for stuff delivered to your lordship's chamber per bill}	viijli. xiijs. iiijd.
Item to the Quenes glasear for certeine glasse at Kewe as apperith bi hys bill}	lxiijs.
Item to the upholster for the spervers of gold and for making the fild bed of redd gardyd with velvett and for lyning to them bothe}	xliiijs. ijd.
Item for iij garnishe pewter vessell}	Cxijs. ixd.
Item for a square table with a fram}	xiijs. iiijd.
Pagina} xxxjli. vijs. vd.	
Sum totalis of necessary provision}	lxiijli. xiijs. iiijd.

[fo. 31]

Charges of liverye

<13, 15, 32, 61 paginae>

To Chelsam for ij yards of velvet for the Cornishe man's cote}	xxxijs.
Item Gosling draper in parte of peyment of a further some as apperithe by obligation}	xxli.[172]
Item peid to Pope the draper uppon a reckoning per bill}	lli.[173]
Item for a peir of hosin for Dering}	xxs.
Item to Guye the Capper for xxxv velvet cappes gyvin by your lordship to your servants at x*s*. the cappe}	xvijli. xs.
Item for iiij clothe cappes with ther bonds and fethers xxvj*s*. viij*d*.}	xxvjs. viijd.
[*total of last two entries*]	{xviijli. xvjs. viijd.
Sum Totalis}	iiij^{xx}xjli. viijs. viijd.

---

[172] Robert Gosling, draper, see p. 121 below and his bill for 1559–60, DP Box V, fo. 2.

[173] Francis Pope, merchant taylor and common councillor (1559–61), see also p. 121 below. Possibly the purchaser of Kew, see Introduction, p. 25.

[fo. 31v *blank*]
[fo. 32]

Pleying monnye

\<2 pagina\>
Imprimis to Roberts for your lordship being
in pley mensis December}   xxs.
\<3 pagina\>
Item peid to Sir Raffe Bagnoll for monye which
your lordship ought hym}   iiijli.[174]
Item gyvin to your lordship for Mr Tamworth
for money lost at pley which your lordship
dyd borrowe of him}   vijs. vjd.
\<6 pagina\>
Item delyveryd to your [*sic*] at Mr
Harrington's howse which yow lost at pleye}   lxs.
\<20 pagina\>
Item deliveryd to your lordship at pleye being
in your gallery with my Lord Admirall
and others}   xijli. xiijs. iiijd.
                                                                 xl crownes
\<26 pagina\>
Item to your lordship by the hands of Slyfield
when your lordship pleyed at cards with Mr Fowler}   xs.[175]
\<31 pagina\>
To Mr Hide which he lent your lordship at pley
at his owne house}   xls.
Item deliveryd to your lordship at Mr Hides at
sundry times viz by my hands xxs., by Hogans xixs.,
and by Mr Aldersham xxviijs.}   lxvijs.
ᵐItem peid to Mr Barker for full peyment of his
bill which your lordship ought him}ᵐ
\<32 pagina\>
Item to your lordship's honds the viijth of
Aprill pleying in your chamber with my Lord
of Northefolke, the Erle of Sussex & others xx
crownes and the dey that your lordship went to

---

[174] For Bagnall see n. 66 above. Thanks to his old friend Edward Underhill, uncle of
Leicester's servant Thomas Underhill*, Bagnall enjoys immortality as a dicer, see J. G.
Nichols (ed.), *Narratives of the Days of the Reformation* (Camden Soc., lxxvii, 1859), 158.
[175] Probably John Fowler (1520?-75?), Groom of the Privy Chamber, MP.

Eltham other xx crownes}   xijli. xiijs. iiijd.[176]
<34 pagina>
Item to your lordship which yow sent to my
Lord Chamberleyne by Mr Perne xl crownes}   xijli. xiijs. iiijd.[177]
<37 pagina>
Item to my Lord of Hartford for mony which
your lordship lost at dise by your
lordship's command}   xlli.[178]
<48 pagina>
Item deliveryd unto your lordship by Hogans
in Mr Comptrouler's chamber to pley at the tables}   xs.[179]
                    Pagina} iiij[xx]xijli. xiiijs. vjd.

[fo. 32v]

Pleying Monnye

<52 pagina>
Item deliveryd to your lordship at Cobham being at
dyse with my Lord of Sussex and others}   vjli. iijs. iiijd.[180]
<63 pagina>
Item to Mr Thomas Warcoppe[181] for money borrowyd of
him by your lordship at the Duke of Swetheland's}   vjli. iijs. iiijd.[182]

---

[176] Thomas Radcliffe, 3rd Earl (c.1525–83), Lord Deputy of Ireland from 1556 until he returned to England after the accession. He went back to Dublin in July 1559 and but then returned again in January 1560. The date of the visit to Eltham is unclear, but given the references to Eltham on pp. 61, 63, it was possibly in late April or early May.

[177] For Mr Perne, see also p. 124 below. Robert Jones refers to him in his letter to Sir Nicholas Throckmorton of 30 Nov. 1560 (see n. 285 below), 'Mr Perne is nothing so brag as he hath been of late'. The contexts of the references would suggest he was a gentleman servant, but he does not appear in the lists of the household. He is most likely to have been Christopher Perne (b.c. 1530), MP.

[178] Edward Seymour (1539–1621), the recently restored earl.

[179] Sir Edward Rogers (c.1498/1500–1568), MP, Comptroller of the Household, Jan. 1559–68.

[180] During the progress, probably just before Sussex departed for Ireland; his instructions are dated 16 July.

[181] Probably Thomas Warcop (d. 1589), Gentleman Pensioner and (from 1568) governor of Carlisle, MP. He was associated with John and Thomas Dudley*, and with Simon Musgrave (see n. 302 below), with whom he petitioned Leicester for the farm of the customs of Hull and Beverley (DP III, fo. 86, n.d.). There are further references to him below, and he may have had a chamber at Wanstead House in 1588.

[182] John, Duke of Finland (1537–92), the future John III. His embassy had been announced in July 1559, but he did not arrive in England until early in October, having been expected for some time (see Paget Papers V, fo. 3, Leicester to Sir Henry Paget, 13 Sept. 1559). Leicester and the Earl of Oxford met him at Colchester and escorted him to London, where he arrived on 5 October (Machyn, 214, AMAE, CPA XIII, fo. 325v, Noailles to Francis II, 6 Oct.). Leicester also entertained him at Court on the 19th (Machyn, 215). He stayed in England until April 1560, and numerous further references

<64 pagina>
Item delivered to Cary to putt in
your lordship's purse}   iiijli. vjs. viijd.
              Pagina} xvjli. xiijs. iiijd.
Sum totalis of the pleying monnye}   Cixli. vijs. xd.

"Forin charges and rewards}   IXCxxxvli. xiiijd.
Chargis of aparell & gouldsmithes worke}   VIIJCxxiiijli. xvjs. vd.
Diet}   iiij^{xx}iijli. xiijs. xd.
Necessary provisions}   lxiijli. xiijs. iiijd.
Charges of lyverye}   iiij^{xx}xjli. viijs. viijd.
Pleying mony}   Cixli. vijs. xd."
Sum totalis alloc' huius libri solut' per William Chansye incipient xx
Decembris anno primo Reginae Elizabeth et finient ultimo Septembris
tunc proximo sequit' prout in in [sic] dicto libro cont'} MMCviijli. xvd.

[fo. 33]

      Peyments made by William Chansye not before mentioned.
In primys to William Cooke at severall tymes
from the xxth of December unto the xix of
February next folowing as appearithe by
his particulers bill [sic]}   xxjli. xiijs. vjd.
Item peid for the charges of your lordship's
kychin from the xixth of February unto
the last of Marche with mony peid unto the
butcher of Westminster}   xxvli. xijs. iiijd.
Item more peid to the butcher of Westminster
for certin accats bought of him from the
xxvth of Marche to the xxiijth of May xijli.,
and to him in part of peyment of a more sum
from the xxiijth of May to the xvjth of
June xli., in toto}   xxijli.
Item peid unto Jamys Tompsons the cater
for certeine accates by him provided from
the iiijth of Marche unto the [blank] of
November ut patens [?] per billas}   Cixli. xiijs. xd.
Item to the lynnen draper for certen
drapery per bill}   xxxjli. xiijs. xd.
Item peid to Singleton Sir Henry Sidneis

to him will be found below. It might be noted that this entry would appear to fall outside
the initial period of the account; the absence of expenses arising from the journey to
Colchester is curious.

servant in part of peyment of the arrerages
deu unto him for his annuite by the hands
of Mr Thomas Blunte}   xls.[183]

Item peid to Cooke the parfumier in parte
of peyment of a more sum per bill}   iiijli. xviijs. iiijd.

Item peid to Sir George Blunt's joyner
for his charges out of Worcestershire and
hom ageyne}   xlvjs. viijd.

Item allowed to Platt the broker for his
fee of brokage vj*li*. and for the makyng of
obligation for M*li*. takin uppon interest
xx*s*., in toto}   vijli.

          Pagina} CCxxvjli. xvijs. vjd.

[fo 33v]
Item peid to Eglmby for my ladyes charges from
Mr Hides to Camberwell}   xli.

Item peid to the launders by the hands of Morice
Edwardes}   xxvjs. viijd.

Item to Smythe the embrodrer per bill}   iiijli. viijs. xd.

Item to Evered the gouldsmithe by my
lord's commandment}   xxvjli.

Item peid to Empson for certeyne necessaries by
him bought as apperyth by his bill}   xijli. vjs. viijd.

Item peid to Grene the coffermaker in parte
of peyment of a more sum}   vjli. xiijs. iiijd.[184]

Item deliveryd for my ladyes charges
riding in to Suffolke with xl pistolas
deliveryd to Hogans to putt in hir
ladyshippes purse & xx*s*. to Mrs Pycto and
the rest to Mr T. Blount}   xxvjli. xiijs. iiijd.[185]

Item to your lordship's cutler dwelling in
Sct Nicholas Lane}   xli.

Item to the Frenche gardner* at Kewe}   xxs.

Item to Hales wyfe of Kewe for certen
accates and other necessaries as apperithe

---

[183] Thomas Singleton, a former servant of the duchess of Northumberland, who was
left an annuity of 4 marks in her will. He is included in the list of Hales Owen annuitants,
BRL, HH MS 351621. See also p. 128 below.

[184] John Green, coffermaker, see p. 122 below and his bills for 1559 and 1562–6, DP
Bx V, fos. 11, 24.

[185] See n. 161 above and Appendix I. For Hogans, see also p. 133 below and Appendix
I.

by her bill}   [vjli. iijs. vijd. *deleted*] iiijli.
Item to Ledshin the skynner in preste}   xxxli.
Item to my lady at Mr Scott's}   lxjs. viijd.
Item to Christopher mylloner at your
lordship's commandment}   xxli.
                    Pagina} Clvli. xs. vjd.
Sum totalis of the prest paid uppon
billes}   CCCiiij^{xx}ijli. vijs. xjd.

Sum of the hole peyments and prestyd monye made by William
Chansye ending the last of September conteynid within this booke}
                                    MMIIIJCiiij^{xx}xli. ixs. ijd.
Item peid more by him uppon a newe receyte begyning the first of
October and ending the xx December iiij^{xx}xviij*li*. xij*s*. xj*d. ob.*, in toto}
                                    MMVCiiij^{xx}ixli. ijs. jd. ob.

[fo. 34]

                    1559 Forin Expenses and Rewards°
<x November>
Imprimis peid to Eaton* the clarke of the
stable for so muche monye laid out by him
viz for a horse drench[er?] ij*s*., for malt
for the same horse iij*s*. ij*d*., in reward
to one that brought your lordship a greyhound
v*s*., and for nayles occupied in the stable xj*d*.}   xs. iiijd.
                                                            per bill

Item peid to John Allin for his horse meate in the
progres viz for xxx daies after the rate of x*d*. per
diem xxv*s*., and for so much monye laid out by him
more during the same tyme x*s*. iiij*d*., in toto}   xxxvs. iiijd.
                                                            per bill

Item in r[eward] to my Lord Scroop's man bringing
partridges per T.D.}   ijs. vjd.[186]
<xij [November]>
Item for the cariage of your lordship's armor

---

[186] Henry, Lord Scroop of Bolton (1534-92), Warden of the West March from 1563.
He gave Leicester his proxy in the Parliaments of 1571, 1572, 1581 and 1584. T.D. is
Thomas Dudley.

from Grenewich to London by water per Beaumont}	ijs.[187]
Item in reward to one at Grenewich that presentid your lordship a nose gaye}	xijd.

\<xiiij [November]\>

Item for the caryage of your lordship's armor from Whithall to Grenewich by water per Thomas Duddeley}	ijs.
Item in reward to one that brought your lordship a barrell of capers}	ijs. vjd.
Item in r[eward] to James shomaker's man per Thomas Duddeley}	xxd.
Item for the caryage of stooles from Kew to Whithall by water}	xvjd.
Item in r[eward] to Sir Henry Percyes man that broght your lordship a grey nagge}	xijs. viijd.[188]
Item peid for xxiiij of your lordship's men's dyners in London your lordship being at dyner with the French}	xiijs. viijd.[189]

\<xvj [November]\>

Item peid to Leonard the Frenchman for one pair of racks and v broches weying fower hundreth lacking ij*li*. accompting vj score per the hundred at ij*d. ob. qd.* le pound}	iiijli. xs.
	per bill

Sum huius paginae} viijli. xvs.

[fo. 34v]

Item to Wood the waterman for service doon by him ut pag' per bill sign'}	viijs.

\<xvij Novembris\>

Item peid to Eaton of the stable for necessaryes provided for the stable per bill sign'}	xiiijs. vjd.

[187] For the tournament held at Whitehall on 5 November, in which Leicester was a challenger with Hunsdon and judged the winner. See Young, p. 201, Machyn, 216–7, AMAE, CPA XIII, fo. 337, and CA, Tournament Portfolio, it. 5. The now well-known drawing of a tournament in which Leicester is identified by his arms has been assigned either to this or to the tournaments in April 1560 (see Young, pp. 126–7). However, if the tentative identification of the Earl of Sussex as one of the other jousters is correct, it was the later occasion, for Sussex was in Ireland in November 1559. For the April 1560 tournaments, see n. 268 below.

[188] (c.1532–85), MP, 8th Earl of Northumberland from 1572.

[189] Probably the hostages.

Item peid to the purveyor of the Quenes
majesties buttery for one tun of beare sent
to Kew xxxiijs. iiijd., and for the caskes
iijs. iiijd. To him more for one hogeshead
of beare spent at Eltham in June last viijs.
iiijd. And to Benbolt for ij hogsheads of
beare sent to Kew in May last xvijs., in toto}   lxijs.
                                                         per bill

<xxiiij [November]>
Item peid to Glaser the buttler for candells
and other necessaries provyded by him for
the butterye ut pag' per bill sign'}   xxijs. vd. ob.
Item in allmes to one that was one of your
lordship's soldyers at St Q[uentin] by
your commandment signiffyed unto me by Higham}   xs.
<xxvj [November]>
Item paid to Cobham* your lordship's man for
so moche monye lent by him to your lordship
at Cobham Hall in the progres tyme}   xxs.
Item peid for ij bushells of barly sent to
Kew for the pigions}   iiijs.
Item peid to Robert Duncking for so moche monye
laid out by him sythens the begynnyng of
August unto November last}   xiiijs. ijd.
                                     per bill

Item peid for torches and lincks for your
lordship cummyng from my Lord Ambrose to
the Court}   iiijs. viijd.
Item peid to the laundres for wasshing the
naperie from the xxj of Julie inclus unto
the xxj of November inclus after the rate
of vjs. viijd. per mensem}   xxvjs. viijd.
                                     per bill

          Suma Paginae} ixli. vjs. vd. ob.

[fo. 35]
Item peid to Mr Glaser for monye laid out
by him about your lordship's affeirs in the lawe}   viijs.
Item paid to George Blound for hawks meate
and other thinges ut pag' per bill sign'}   xxjs.
<Dec[ember] xviij>
Item for a lace for your lordship's George}   iijs.

Item for ij doss of crimson sylke rebond points}   iijs.
<xx [December]>
Item for a looking glas sent to my ladie by Mr
Forster}   vjs. viijd.[190]
Item for ijꝑ. of blew sowing sylke sent to
my ladie by Mr Forster}   iiijs.
Item peid to James Thomesone for monie due
to him ut pag' per bill sign'}   xxviijs. iiijd.
                           Sumam huius} lxxvs.
Totalis of forin expenses and rewards}   xxjli. xvjs. vd.

[fo. 35v *blank*]
[fo. 36]

                    Goldsmythes worke and apparell
Imprimis paid to Stocke of Chepesyde for perle
and sylver parle delyverid by him to Smyth the
embroderer to make the cote which your lordship
rode in the same daie the Prince of Fineland came in
and allso for to imbroder a pair of bss' of black vellet}   xxxli.[191]
Item peid to Mrs Pallmer for a pair of women's
sleves of purle gold delyverid to your
lordship's owne handes}   xli. xs.
Item peid to Tempest your lordship's hossier
by your owne commandment}   ixli. xiijs.
                           Sumam huius} lli. iiis.

                              Dyet
<x November>
Item delyverid to Mr Horden for provisions to be
made for the kichen}   xli.
<xxv [November]>
Item to George Coke for like provisions}   liijs. iiijd.
<xx December>
Item for a pottell of mallmesye fet by
Hugh Jones to your lordship's chamber}   xvjd.
                           Sumam huius} xijli. xiiijs. viijd.

[fo. 36v]

[190] See Appendix I.
[191] See n. 182 above, presumabiy 5 October.

Prests

<x Novembris>

Item peid to the cutler in Abchurch Lane by your
lordship's commandment signiffied unto me by Wm. Hougans}   Cs.

M[emoran]dum the rest per Ellis

<x, xx Novembris>

Item prest to the gromes of the stable, viz William
Bowrne, Stevins, Lytle John and Patricke, for
theyr borde wages}   iiijli. xvijs.

rest per Ellis

Item prest to Briscoe for the charge of a
lettre of administracion}   xxvs. iiijd.[192]

<M[emoran]dum to Brystow to answer the same>

Item prest to Awdewin}   vjs. viijd.

rest per Ellis

Item in prest to Hance your lordship's hossier
when he was in hand with your lordship's hose
which Coke embroderid}   xixs.

Item prest to Rafe Hunt}   viijs. viijd.

rest ut supra

Item prest to Thomas Forest* the huntsman}   xxijs. ijd.

rest ut supra

Sumam huius} xiijli. xviijs. xd.

Summa Totalis huis solucionibus}   iiij^{xx}xviijli. xijs. xjd. ob.
Forin expenses & rewards}   xxjli. xvjs. vd.
Gouldsmythes worke}   lli. iijs.
Dyett}   xijli. xiiijs. viijd.
Prests}   xiijli. xviijs. xd. ob.

[fo. 37]

RECEIVED of the which some by the hands of the seid William
Chansye at sundry tymes of diverse men as in the beginning of this
booke doth pleynly appeare}   MMVCxlli. vs. vjd.
AND SOO ther restythe dew unto the seid William Chansey uppon
this accompt}   xlviijli. xvjs. vijd. ob.
This Accompt ys dewlye tryed & examynid by us appointyd by your
lordship for the same ending the xxth of December anno secundo regni
Elizabeth.

---

[192] For the will of Sir Andrew Dudley (d. 22 November), see n. 124 above. Leicester's
bond to the Dean and Chapter of Canterbury for administration of the will (25 Nov.
1559) is DP Box IV, art. 68; although only nominated an overseer, he appears to have
acted as executor. Hugh Briscoe or Bristoe* had been a servant of Dudley's.

[*signed*]
John Duddeley*
R. Horden
William Kynyatt

[fo. 38]^p

Pultre Warys servyd to the ryght honourabyll Lorde Robbett Dudlay frome the xxth day of January in the seconde yere to the last day of Aprell of the therde of ower soferrant Lady Elsabett by the grace of God Quene of England, France & Ireland etc.[193]

Fyrst in January and Febrowary	viijli. xviijs. jd. ob.
Item in Aprell	vjli. iijs. iiijd.
Item in Maye	xxvijli. xs. jd.
Item in June	xxxiijli. vijs. viijd.
Item in July	xxli. ijs. vjd.
Item to the bankett at Kewe	xxjli. xs. xd.[194]
Item in September	xixli. xjs. vd.
Item in November	xxiijli. viijs. xd.
Item in Desember	xxxvli. xvs. viijd.
Item in January	xxixli. xs. xjd.
Item in Febrowary	xvjli. iiijs. ixd.
Item in Marche	xijli. xvjd.
Item in Aprell	xvijli. xvs. ijd.

Sum} CClxxijli. vjd. ob.

Were off resavyd} viij^xxxvijli. xjs. iiijd.
So Reste unpayd} iiij^xxxiiijli. ixs. ijd. ob.

[fo. 38v *blank*]
[fo. 40]^q

Memorandum that sence the taking of this accownte upon further serche to understand yf the sayd William Chansey were dewly to be charged further then in this accownte upon his othe and under his hand he dyd charge him self, yt hath cum to our knowlege thatt the sayd Chansey by vertew of the Quenes majesties warrantt receyved in the standing Wardropp in the accownte of Sir William Walgrave knyght the some of fyftie pounds or there abowts wherwith he hathe not charged himself in this accownte which some is dew to your lordship for certaine sadylls sold to the Quene parcell of your lordship's fees at the tyme of the Coronacion upon which recypte the sayd Chansey

---

[193] The bill is anonymous. It may be from the poulterer Robert Shaw, see p. 122 below, but the payments do not tally.

[194] See pp. 141–2 below.

remaynethe in debett xxiij*s*. iiij*d*. *ob*. and not in superplusage as in thys accownte is declared.[195]

[fo. 40v *blank*]
[fo. 39]
Memorandum that sence the takin of this accounte upon searche to understand yf the sayd Chansye were further to be charged then in this accownte he dyd uppon his othe and under his hand charge himself, yt hathe appeared unto us and is com to our knowledge that the sayd Wylliam Chansye by vertew of the Quenes majesties warrantt receyved in the standing Wardroppe in the account of Sir Wylliam Walgrave knight the some of fyftie pownds or there abouts dew to your lordship for certaine sadylls sold to the Quene parcell of your lordship's fees at the tyme of the Coronacion upon which recete the sayd Chansye remaynethe in debett xxiij*s*. iiij*d*. *ob*. and not in superplusage as in this accounte is declared.

[fo. 39v *blank*]
[fo. 41]

William Chansye
Memorandum that William Chansey in the fyrst yere of the Quene's Majestie receyved of Mr Byrde the som of CC*li*. upon my lord's lettre wherof as he sayth C*li*. was payde to Mr Warley mercer & 1*li*. to Mr Chelsham.
<He allegethe Cl*li*. was payd as appearethe by a statute cancelled delivered to my lord's hands at Westminster>[196]
Item more for liij*s*. iiij*d*. a payre of whyte sylke netherstocks which he receyved of Mr Edmond Hugins & delivered the same againe for that they were nott lyked & he is to be charged therwith}   liij*s*. iiij*d*.
<Memorandum William Chansye confesseth to pay to [Wylliam *deleted*] Edmond Huggans>

[195] Presumably an error for Sir Edward Waldegrave, Master of the Wardrobe from 1553. Waldegrave appears to have remained in office until Lady Day 1559, for the letters patent appointing his successor, John Fortescue, are dated 22 July 1559 (*CPR, 1558–60*, 90), though with effect from Lady Day. Why this memorandum is repeated is not clear.
[196] John Warley, mercer of Cheapside. This entry was added to the Ellis account, see p. 134 below. The debt may have originated with the Duchess of Northumberland (who acknowledged one of £79 2s 8d in her will, though only £20 on the schedule of debts). On 17 July 1557 Leicester entered into a recognizance by statute staple for a debt of £450 7s 6d to Margaret Warley, widow, *et al*. This appears to have been paid off in instalments and the bond finally cancelled on 5 March 1559, which is presumably what Chancy is referring to. See DP Box III, art. 67, PRO, LC4/188/370, and a reference to the release in GVE, fo. 52. It would appear that Warley himself died between 1555 and 1557 and that the later transactions were conducted with his widow and executors.

Item remember that Guye the capper doth confesse butt xv*li*. to be receyved of William Chansye of the some of xxvj*li*. xvj*s*. viij*d*.
<Chansy askethe allowance of xxix*li*. payd to Guy the capper.>
Item Ledsham doth confess butt xx*li*. of xxx*li*. wherof Chansy asketh allowance} xli.
<wherof he confesseth to all} xvli.>
Also to charge William Chansy for my lord's fee in the Excheker for one yere orells di.[197]

A note to charge Rychard Ellis

Fyrst to charge him with lv*li*. borowed in my lord's name of William Warensby upon the harralds' bill which is to be showed}	lvli.
Item to charge him with v*li*. borowed of Banyster merchantt}	vli.
Item to charge him with xl*li*. borowed of Sir Thomas Gresham}	xlli.
Item to charge him with a C*li*. which he borowed of Mr Thomas Bluntt merchant}	Cli.[198]

TEXTUAL NOTES

page

40   a-a. *interlined*

43   b. *In this and several other entries on this folio the last word is followed by what appears to be* nts. *If not a flourish, it may be a reference to New Years' gifts.*

45   c-c. *deleted*

67   d-d. <Windsor at the Installation>

78   e-e. *Entry deleted and moved to fo. 28v.*

82   f-f. *interlined*

85   g-g. *The order of the totals has been slightly rearranged.*

86   h. *William Kynyat's references to bills in the right hand margin begin at this entry.*

88   i-i. *deleted and moved to fo 27v.*

96   j-j. *deleted*

96   k-k. *deleted*

97   l-l. *deleted*

99   m-m. *deleted*

101   n-n. *The order of the totals has been slightly rearranged.*

[197] Presumably as Master of the Horse.

[198] Thomas Blount, collector of the tunnage and poundage of London in 1561. See also pp. 115, 120 below.

103   o. *The text of this section of the account is in a different hand to the previous section. Marginal references to pages cease, but dates are supplied.*

108   p. *Pasted in, see p. 8 above.*

108   q. Sic. *There is no obvious explanation for the misfoliation. Both copies of the memorandum are in the same hand.*

B. THE ACCOUNT OF RICHARD ELLIS
1559–1561
(LONGLEAT, DUDLEY PAPERS XV)

[fo. 1 *blank*]¹⁹⁹

[fo. 2]

THE ACCOMPTE of all suche somes of monneye as I Richard Elles do charge myself to have receavid of sondrye persones to your lordship's use as well in monney borroughed and taken upp by exchange as also for your lordship's rennts and other deapts due as hereafter appearethe from the xxijth day of December in the second yeare of the raigne of our souveraigne lady Quene Elizabethe unto the last daye of Aprell in the thirde yeare of our said soveraigne lady, Viz}

Receaved of William Byrde mercer in monneye
borroughed at sondrye tymes for the payment of
dyvers persons}   MMMDCCCCxxxli. xs. vd.

Receavid more of the said William Byrde in
monneye taken upp by exchange the vij day
of Maye anno secondo dominae Reginae for the
losse of xij*li*. x*s*.}   VCli.

Receavid more of the same in monney taken upp by
exchange the xvjth daye of December anno predicto
for vj monethes endyng the xvj daye of June}   MMli.²⁰⁰

Receavid in monneye borroughed of John Chapman
grocer for the payment of sondry persons}   MCCCCxli. xviijs. iijd.

Receavid more of ᵃthe said John Chapmanᵃ
Thomas Aldersaye merchant for payment of sondrye
persons}   Miiijˣˣxiijli. vs.²⁰¹
                                      [iiijs. iiijd. *deleted*]

Receavid in monneye borroughed of Thomas Ryvet

---

¹⁹⁹ Apart from a description of the volume by J.E. Jackson, the only inscription on the cover is the word 'Pyerson'. This may indicate that the text was the work of the scrivener Thomas Pyerson or Person (common councillor 1558–9).

²⁰⁰ For Byrde, see n. 53 above. On 20 December Leicester bound himself to repay Byrde £1,630 by 16 June 1561. Recognizances dated 30 December by Sir Henry Sidney, John Harington and John Tamworth as sureties for this bond are enrolled in PRO, C54/584/5. The making of the bond was probably the occasion for the dinner at Byrde's on 22 December, referred on p. 165 below. As will be seen on p. 118 below, Leicester also repaid Byrde a total of £3,726 within the period of account.

²⁰¹ Thomas Aldersey (d.1599), haberdasher and common councillor 1571–99, MP. See also p. 194, n. 408 below.

mercer for the payment of sondrye persons}
Receavid more of the said Thomas Ryvet in
money taken upp by exchange the xvth daye
of Maye anno secondo dominae Reginae to be
repaid agayne in July following by the losse
of xij*li.* xiiij*s.* iiij*d.*}

DCCli.[202]

VCli.

[*signed*] Rychard Ellys

[fo. 2v]
Receavid of William Sheldon esquier in monney
borroughed of him for the payment of dyvers
persons}
Receaved of Mr Lyttleton by too severall bounds
and eyther of them conteyning one thousand marks
one due in October anno secondo dominae Regine
and the other in February nexte
followinge, summa}
Receavid of William Crompton mercer in monney
taken upp for one yeare's daye [*sic*] of
payment endyng in February anno quarto
dominae Reginae}

DCCClli.[203]

MCCCxxxiijli. vjs. viijd.[204]

DCCvjli. xiijs. iiijd.

Memorandum that dyvers persons standethe bounde unto the said
William Crompton to paye in February anno superdicto eight hundreth
pounds.
Receavid of Thomas Smythe customer in monney

---

[202] See n. 8 above.
[203] William Sheldon (1500–73) of Beoley, Worcs., MP, deputy to Leicester as lord-
lieutenant of Worcestershire 1559–60. For their relations see 'West Midlands', 44. A
reference to making the bond for this loan in May 1560 is found on p. 138.
[204] (Sir) John Lyttelton (1519–90) of Frankley, Worcs., MP. These payments were the
consequence of a dispute arising from the sale of the lands of the former monastery of
Hales Owen. This estate had belonged the Duchess of Northumberland, who left it to
Ambrose Dudley, with various interests assigned to her other surviving children. In a
remarkable family compact in November 1555, Leicester's brothers gave him their
interests (see Abbreviations: the Duchess of Northumberland's debts). He sold the estate
to Thomas Blount and George Tookey on 27 March 1558, and they in turn sold it to
Lyttelton on 20 October 1558. The sale to Lyttelton included (apparently by oversight)
lands assigned to an annuity the Duchess left Katherine, Lady Hastings, and to recover
them Leicester brought suit against Lyttelton in Chancery in 1560. Arbitration by the
Lord Keeper resulted in Lyttelton buying out her interest for 2,000 marks. The settlement
(dated 31 July 1560) is enrolled in PRO, C54/578/17, 21. All that survives of the case files
is Lyttelton's badly worn answer (C3/50/120), but BRL, HH MS 351621 (a fresh
conveyance to Lyttelton by Blount and Tookey, 26 July 1560) recites the history of the
dispute. See also 'Dudley Clientèle', pp. 250–1, and 'West Midlands', 30.

borroughed}   CCCxxiijli.[205]
Receivid in monney borroughed of William
Hide gentleman ᵇxiij die February anno
secondoᵇ}   Cxxxiijli. vjs. viijd.
Receavid in monney borroughed of Thomas Blunt
customer ᶜxiij die February anno secondoᶜ}   CCCCli.
Receavid of Thomas Egerton gentleman of monney
borroughed xxvj January anno predictoᵈ}   Cli.[206]
Receavid of Nycholas Culverwell and the Company
in money borroughed in July anno secundo
Dominae Reginae}   CCiiijxxli.[207]
Receavid of Mr Alfford of the Exchequer in
monney borroughed of him xx February
anno predicto}   Cli.[208]
Receavid of Sir John Yorke in monney borroughed}   CCCli.
Receavid in monney borroughed of John Gressham
mercer ultimo October anno predicto}   CCli.[209]
[*signed*] Rychard Ellys

[fo. 3]
Receavid in monney borroughed of Mr Alderman
Roo xxiiij Decembris anno tercio}   CCli.[210]
Receavid in monney borroughed of Mr Standley
of the Mynte ultimo Decembris}   Cli.[211]
Receavid in monney borroughed of John Marshe
ultimo December}   Cli.[212]
Receavid in monney borroughed of [William *deleted*]
Ph[ilip]e Gunter in June anno secondo}   xxxli.[213]
Receavid in monney borroughed of William Marbury

---

[205] Thomas Smythe (1522–91), MP, the notorious Customer Smythe. Smythe later became Leicester's deputy in the administration of the Sweet Wines Farm, see his account for 1578–80 (BL, Harl. MS 167, fos. 135–7) and A.L. Merson (ed.), *The Third Book of Remembrance of Southampton, 1514–1602* (Southampton Records Series, viii, 1965), 72–5. He claimed a debt of £3,235 from Leicester's estate. Smythe was also a close associate of John and Thomas Dudley; the reference to the 'great love and friendship that hath been between us' attributed to Leicester's will in the entry on Smythe in Hasler comes, in fact, from John Dudley's.

[206] Thomas Egerton (1521–90/7), mercer, MP.

[207] The Company of the Staple, see p. 116, n. 215 below.

[208] Roger Alford (c.1530–80), Teller of the Exchequer 1556–62, MP.

[209] John Gresham the younger, mercer and common councillor 1560–76.

[210] (Sir) Thomas Rowe, merchant taylor and lord mayor 1568–9.

[211] Thomas Stanley (1512–71), Under-Treasurer of the Tower mint.

[212] John Marshe (1516–79), mercer and governor of the Merchant Adventurers, MP.

[213] Philip Gunter, skinner and alderman.

gentleman secondo Aprilis anno tertio^d}   Cli.[214]

Monney receavid for your lordship's lycence and for rennts as also
otherwyse due unto your lordship, viz:
Receavid of Nycholas Culverwell and the Company
for the satisfacion of the first three thousands
poundes due unto your lordship for your lycence
by the agrement of your lordship and
them, suma}   MMDCCCCxxxiijli. vjs. viijd.[215]
Received more of the said Nicholas Culverwell
and [the] Companny by vj severall bounds payable
in May anno tercio Reginae Elizabeth}   MMMli.
Receavid of James Bigott* gentleman the xijth
daye of Maye in the second yeare of the Quene
for one hole yeares rennt of the mannor of
Hemesby endid at the feast of St. Mighell
the Archangell anno [predicto *deleted*]}   xliijli. vs. xjd. ob.[216]
Received more of the said James the xxiiijth
of November anno predicto for the half yeares
rennt of the mannor of Hemesby due at the
Annunciacion of our Lady anno secondo
xxij*li.* iij*s.*, which by the fall of the money
made but the summa of}   xvli. vs. iijd.[217]
[*signed*] Rychard Ellys

[fo. 3v]
Receavid more of the forsaid James Bigott
the xxiiijth daye of November anno predicto
for rennt corne due unto the manor of Siderstearne
viz. for Cxv coome of malte and rye at iiij*s.*
the coomeb, summa}   xxiijli.[218]
Receavid of John Marbury the xijth of November
anno predicto in parte of payment of the half
yeares rennt of the mannor of Hemesby due at

<hr>

[214] Probably the lawyer and MP (1524–81). He may have been related to Leicester's
servant John Marbury*.

[215] A licence for the export of 1000 sarplers of wool, granted on 12 April 1560 (*CPR,
1558–60*, 321), see also p. 157 below. The importance of this grant for his finances needs
no emphasis. According to BL, Add. MS 48023 (fo. 353v) it was greatly resented by the
Staplers.

[216] See n. 65 above and p. 157 below.

[217] I.e. the reminting of the debased silver coinage initiated by the proclamation of 27
September 1560.

[218] The principal Robsart manor, see Introduction, p. 13, and Appendix I.

Mighelmas anno tercio [*sic*] dominae Reginae}   xli.
Received of Thomas Hungatt gentleman the vj daye
of May anno secondo dominae Reginae for the halffe
yeares rennt of the mannor of Watton dwe at the
feast of the Anuntiacion of our Lady anno predicto}   xxijli.[219]
Receavid of Mr Alfforde of the Excheaquer
for your lordship's fee dwe at Mighelmas}   lxvjli. xiijs. iiijd.[220]
Receavid of Sir Henry Sydney the vj day of
Marche anno secondo}   xxli.[221]
Receavid for monney won by your lordship at
tennys in my Lorde of Sussex's side}   xijli. vjs. viijd.[222]
Receavid of John Empson your lordship's servant}   xls.
Received of Dwe the goldsmithe for ij smale
booles of sylver waing xj *oz.* iij *qtr.*, iiij*s.*
viijd. the *oz.*, summa}   liiijs. xd.
Receavid of Franke for one hoggeshead of redd
wynne sold to hym in August anno predicto}   ls.
Receavid for monney won by your lordship of
my Lord Admirall at Grenewich the xxviijth
daye of June l pistollets which amounteth to}   xvli. viijs. iiijd.[223]
Receavid of Sir Harry Sydney knight the xijth
day of Marche anno tercio regni Reginae dwe
unto your lordship for armor}   CCxljli. vs.
[*signed*] Rychard Ellys

[fo. 4]
Received of John Empson your lordship's servant
the iiijth daye of Aprill anno tercio dominae

[219] Hungate was the sitting tenant of Watton (see n. 125 above), he is mentioned in DP I, fo. 44, Yerwerth's report on the survey of Watton, 19 July 1559.
[220] As Master of the Horse.
[221] Sidney had returned from Ireland in the previous autumn (see n. 68 above). He was appointed Lord President of the Council in the Marches of Wales c. April 1560 (see P. Williams, *The Council in the Marches of Wales under Elizabeth I* (Cardiff, 1956), pp. 251–2), and departed for Ludlow on 12 June 1560 (Machyn, 238).
[222] Sussex had obtained leave from Ireland in January 1560 and did not return to Dublin until June. He came back to England again in January 1561. According to the entry on p. 153 below, this match took place in March 1560. The supper Leicester had with Sussex in the same month (see p. 170 below) may have followed it. The sporting companionship revealed in this account and the friendly correspondence cited below suggests that their future enmity had not yet begun.
[223] After the Queen's return to Whitehall on 28 September 1559 (see n. 144 above) the Court remained at Whitehall or Westminster throughout the winter. On 14 May 1560 it removed to Greenwich and was there until 29 July when the progress began (Machyn, 234, 241).

Reginae}   Cli.
[*signed*] Rychard Ellys
Receavid of Mr Birde}   CCli. <Per Chancye>ᵉ
Item more receavid of the same} CCCli. <for the losse of MMD*li*. to
                                                         Culverwell>
Item more receavid of the same}   xijli. xs. <for the losse of exchange
                                                         of D*li*.>
Item more receavid of him}   vli. xs. <for the loss of part of the
                                                         former exchange>
Item more receavid of him}   xxijli. vs. xd. ob.
for a peece of fyne lynen cloth containing xxx elles iij *qtr*.ᵉ
[*signed*] Rychard Ellyse

[fo. 4v *blank*]

[fo. 5]
THE ACCOMPTE of all suche somes of monney as I Richard Elles
have paid unto dyvers persons for your lordship's use as heareafter
maye appeare particularly from the xxijth daye of December in the
second yeare of the raigne of our soveraigne ladye Quene Elizabeth
unto the last daie of Aprell in the thirde yere of her highness's raigne,
viz:ᶠ
PAID unto William Byrd mercer by severall bounds
amounting unto the some of}   MMMVIJCxxvjli. xiijs. iiijd.²²⁴
Paid unto John Chapman grocer at sondry payments
the some of}   MCCCiiijˣˣli.
Paid to Thomas Aldersaye merchant at sondry
payments the some of}   DCCxlviijli.
Paid unto Thomas Ryvet mercer at sondry payments
the some of}   DCCCClxxixli. vijs. viijd.²²⁵
Paid unto Nycholas Culverwell and the Company
the some of}   CCxlli.
Paid unto William Sheldon esquier}   DCCClli.
Paid to Richard Pecock mercer the xxiijth day
of December anno secundo dominae Reginae Cx*li*.,
the xiijth daye of Aprell following VC*li*., and
the last day of February anno predicto CCClxxviij*li*.

---

²²⁴ This and many of the subsequent entries are the repayments of loans found in the
previous section or in the Chancy account.
²²⁵ Revett was repaid in part by the first instalment of 1000 marks that Leicester
received from John Lyttelton following the Hales Owen settlement (n. 204 above). The
assignment to Revett by Leicester, 8 Aug. 1560, is BRL, HH MS 35622, and the receipt
by Revett, 6 Nov. 1560, MS 35628. William Byrde (who was Revett's brother-in-law)
collected the money from Lyttelton (MS 351624).

ijs. vjd., summa}   Mxviijli. ijs. vjd.[226]

Paid unto Francis Barker lynin draper the
xxiijth of December anno predicto 1*li.*, the xth
daye of June followinge lx*li.*, and the xijth
daye of February anno tercio dominae Reginae
x*li.*, summa}   Clxxli.

Item paid unto Thomas Cooke perffumer the
xxiiijth daye of December xx*li.*, the xth daye
of January xij*li.*, the xijth day of June xx*li.*,
and the thirde of July xx*li.*}   lxxijli.

Item paid unto Thomas Smithe customer the
xvjth daye of December anno tercio Reginae}   CCCxxiijli.

[fo. 5v]

Paid unto Mr Cowltrye shepster the xxiiijth daie
of December anno secundo dominae Reginae xxli.,
the xth daye of January xl*li.*, the
[*blank*] day of Aprell [x*li. deleted*],
the xxixth daye of June followinge lx*li.*,
the [*blank*] of September x*li.* and the ixth of
December xx*li.*}   Cxlli. [x *deleted*]

Item paid unto Christopher Calcarne the xxxth of
January anno secundo dominae Reginae}   lxli.

Item paid unto James Stocke gooldfyner at
sondry payments for certayne obligacions}   CCixli.

Item paid unto William Dawe lynnyn draper the
xxxth of January anno secundo dominae Reginae}   xli.[227]

Item paid unto [*blank*] Robotham of the Roobes
for the discharge of certayne obligacions
whearin Lanyson gooldsmith and other stoode
bownd for the payment of CCCC*li.*}   CCCCli.[228]

Item paid unto Ph[ilip]e Gunter the [*blank*] daye
of February in the second yeare of the Quene}   Cli.

Item paid unto Thomas Nicholson the elder mercer
the xvjth daye of Marche anno predicto for monney
receavid by William Chancy}   CCli.

Item paid unto William Leonard mercer the
xvjth of March anno predicto}   Cli.[229]

[226] Of Cheap. DP Box V, fo. 268, is his bill for 1567–8, and most of the wardrobe warrants for 1565–7 (fos. 300ff, see Introduction, n. 80) are addressed to him.

[227] See also DP Box V, fos. 29–32, his bills for 1560–4 and 1566.

[228] Robert Robotham (1522?–71), Yeoman of the Robes by 1549, MP. For Lonison, see n. 39 above.

[229] Common councillor 1560–73.

Item paid unto George [*blank*] Mr Threaserer's
man for money borroughed by your lordship being
one hundrethe and fortye crownes at vj*s*. iiij*d*.
the crowne and for lx Englishe crownes borroughed
in October anno [*blank*], summa}   lixli. vjs. viijd.
Item paid unto Richard Poynter draper the xth
daye of June for the dyscharge of bounds in [*sic*]
whearin John Whight alderman and John Ellyot
mercer stoode bownd for the payment thereof}   CCli.²³⁰

[fo. 6]
Paid unto Thomas Egerton gentleman the xth day of
June anno secundo for the payment of a hundreth
pound borroughed of him}   Cli.
Paid unto Richard Tattershall the xvjth daye
of Maye for the discharge of a bund whearin
Anthony Forster stoode bownd unto him}   CCCxlvli.
Item paid unto Thomas Blunt customer at severall
payments, viz the vijth of Maye CC*li*. and the xth
daye of June C*li*.}   CCCli.
Paid unto my Lord Hastings at severall payments,
viz the vijth of Maye anno secundo CC*li*. and
the vijth of June anno predicto CC*li*.}   CCCCli.²³¹
Item paid unto Mr Barbor* your lordship's man
the xiijth daie of Aprell x*li*. and the xvth
daye of August following x*li*.}   xxli.
Item paid to Mr Allford of the Exchequer the vij
daye of June for monney borroughed of him}   Cli.
Item paid unto Davye Smithe embroderer at severall
payments, viz the xiijth of Aprell CClx*li*. and the
[*blank*] day of November Clx*li*., summa}   CCCCxxli.²³²
Paid unto Mrs Smithe silkewoman the xiijth daye
of Aprell anno secundo Reginae}   CCCCxxxli.
Item paid unto John Walton silkman at severall
payments, viz the xxth daye of May lxxxiiij*li*.
vij*s*. vj*d*. and the xiiijth of November CCxvij*li*.
xviij*s*. j*d*. *ob*., summa}   CCCijli. vs. vijd. ob.
Item paid unto William Marbury gentleman the
viijth daye of June anno predicto for money of

²³⁰ Common councillor 1558–61.
²³¹ Probably Henry, for in May 1559 (DP I, fo. 14) Leicester's sister Katherine
complained to him about his failure to pay her husband money that he owed him.
²³² David Smith, the Queen's embroiderer, DP Box V, fos. 14–16, 98–101, are his bills
for 1559, 1560, 1561, and 1561–6

him borroughed}	Cli.
Item paid unto William Denham gooldsmith the	
xiiijth day of May l*li*., the xth day of June	
followinge C*li*. and the xvijth of December	
CC*li*.}	CCClli.
Paid unto Branden gooldsmith the xth of June}	lxxxjli. xs.
[fo. 6v]	
Paid unto Harry Allycock the xth of June}	xixli.
Item paid unto William Whittle taillor at	
severall payments, viz the xth of June lxx*li*.,	
the xxij day of June x*li*., and the xvijth	
of December xl*li*.}	Cxxli.
Item paid unto John Anthonio taillor	
the xth day of June anno secundo	
Reginae Elizabeth}	xxviijli.
Item paid unto William Ledsham skynner at	
severall payments, viz the xth of June xxx*li*.	
and the xiijth daye of Aprell viij*li*.}	xxxviijli.
Paid unto Robert Gosling draper at severall	
payments, viz the xviijth of January anno	
secundo dominae Reginae by a bound xxviij*li*.,	
the xiijth daye of Aprell following x*li*.,	
and the xth daye of June anno predicto xxx*li*.}	lxviijli.
To Raynold Cartor tallir at severall payments	
for the dyscharge of monney due in Grise's	
tyme the summ of}	xxli. vs. viijd.[233]
Paid unto John Guye habberdassher at severall	
payments, viz the xiijth of Aprell x*li*. and the	
xth daie of June xx*li*.}	xxxli.
Paid unto John Maria cutteler at severall	
payments, viz the xiiijth day of February	
anno secundo dominae Reginae x*li*. vij*s*.	
iiij*d*. and the xvth daie of June anno	
predicto x*li*.}	xxli. vijs. iiijd.
Paid unto Francis Pope draper at severall	
payments, viz the xth of June anno predicto	
lx*li*. and the vijth daie of February anno	
tercio regni Reginae CCC*li*., summa}	CCClxli.
Paid unto William Cure sadler the xth daye	
of June anno secundo dominae Reginae}	xxxli.[234]

[233] DP Box V, fos. 109, 127 are the bills of Francis Carter, linen draper, for 1561-2.
[234] DP Box V. fos. 87-91, 109-15, 172, are the bills of Thomas Cure, the Queen's saddler, for 1561-2, 1562-3, and 1563-4.

[fo. 7]

Paid unto James Crokeham shomaker at
sondry payments with xij*li.* vij*s.*
for my Lord Ambrose, suma}   lxij*li.* vij*s.*

Paid unto Rowland Fryse shomaker the xth daye
of June anno predicto}   xl*i.*[235]

Item paid unto John Greene cofermaker at several
payments, viz the vijth of June anno predicto lx*s.*,
the xvth of December x*li.* and the xiiijth daye of
March anno tercio dominae Reginae vij*li.* xx*d.*, summa}   xxl*i.* xx*d.*

To William Holborne habberdassher in parte of
deapt due unto him}   xxiij*li.* xix*s.* ij*d.*

Item paid unto Edney the taillor the xvth daye
of June anno secundo dominae Reginae}   xl*i.*[236]

Item paid unto William Hide gentleman the
xviijth daye of June anno predicto}   xxxiij*li.* vj*s.* viij*d.*

Paid unto Mrs Wilkinson the ixth daie of
June for monney due unto her}   iiij^{xx}xvj*li.* ix*s.*[237]

Item paid unto Mr Appliard for monney dwe
unto him by your lordship sum}   C*li.*

Paid unto Robert Shawe the powlter at
severall payments, viz in March and Aprell
by the handes of Richard the Cator* and by
myself the sum of viij*li.* xvj*s.* iiij*d.*,
the xth daye of June anno secundo
xxxiiij*li.* xij*d.*, and the ixth of October
lv*li.*, the xth of August xx*li.*, the vijth
daie of February anno tercio dominae
Reginae lx*li.*, summa}   Clxxvij*li.* xvij*s.* iiij*d.*[238]

Item paid unto Thomas Lodge alderman for
a horsse bought of him and geavin to the
Emperoures embassador, sum}   xxl*i.*[239]

[235] DP Box V, fos. 169–71, is his bill for 1563–6.

[236] William Edney. This payment is recorded in a bill of his, which was discovered by Jackson at Longleat in 1863. Attached to it was a letter from Amy Dudley from Cumnor (24 Aug. [1560]), see Introduction, p. 3. The bill and the letter (DP IV, fos. 3–4, 7) are printed in 'Amye Robsart', 85–8, 66.

[237] DP Box V, fos. 27–8, is a bill dated 18 November 1559 from 'Wilkinson' for gold and silver lace supplied in 1558–9.

[238] See n. 193 above.

[239] (Sir) Thomas Lodge, grocer and lord mayor 1562–3. The Imperial ambassador was George, Count Helffenstein (1518–1571), who had been sent to England at the beginning of the reign and left in May 1560 (see n. 342 below). He was joined in the summer of 1559 by the Archduke Charles's chamberlain Caspar, Baron Brüner, who departed at the beginning of 1560. A number of their despatches are printed in V. Klarwill, *Queen Elizabeth and some Foreigners* (1928). In this account Helffenstein is anglicised to Elverston.

To Thomas Allayne skynner the viijth day of
June anno predicto}   lxli.

[fo. 7v]
To Ambrose Smith and Horewood mercers at
several payments, viz the xvjth daye of June
anno predicto xxxix*li.*, and more paid to them the
said monethe l*li.* and the xiiijth daye of
November Cxxij*li.* xvij*s.*, summa}   CCxjli. xvijs.
To William Chelsham mercer the xxixth of
June anno secondo for wares bought in
Gryses time}   Clli.
Paid unto Steaphin Rowley paynter for woorke don
as may appere by severall billes}   xxiijli. vijs.
To Harry Lylly mercer the xxth daye of June for
silks bought in Chancy's tyme}   xli. iiijd.
Item paid unto John Duddley gentleman for money
by him dysbursed [*added*] for a cheyne geven
by my lord to the Vydames man and others as
apperethe by the byll upon the fyll}   xixli. xviijs. xd.[240]
To Richard Aylesworthe the xxvijth daie of
February for the dyscharge of a band
whearin John Duddley and William Kynnyat
gentlemen stoode bownd, suma}   xvjli.
Paid unto Thomas Holloway sadler at
severall payments, viz the xxth daye of
June anno secondo xx*li.* and the xth
daye of August anno predicto xxxij*li.*
x*s.*, summa}   lijli. xs.[241]
To Thomas Doughty bytmaker the xxth daye of
June anno superdicto}   xli.[242]
To my Lady Sidney at severall payments by your
lordship's commandment}   lxvli.
To the Companny of the Sherers for money at
Bourdeux disbursed by them for iij tonne of
wyne bought theare and for the freight and
other chargs of the same wyne and paid to
Wilson my Lord Admyrales servant ᵍfor the

---

[240] François d'Ailly, Vidame of Amiens, who arrived in April 1560 as one of the
substitutes for the original French hostages (*CSPF, 1559–60*, 518). See also p. 138 below.
[241] DP Box V, fos. 35–7, 134–40, are his bills for 1560–62 and 1562–66.
[242] The Queen's bitmaker, DP Box V, fos. 33, 128–33, are his bills for 1560–2 and
1562–6.

said charges and weyne^g}   xviijli. vs.[243]
Paid unto Richard Butter mercer the xxiijth of
February anno secundo Reginae for wares
bought of him for redy monney as appeareth
by the bills of parceles}   xijli. vs. ijd.

[fo. 8]
To Mr Pearne the xth daye of August by
your lordship's commandement}   xxli.
To [*blank*] Almery the botcher at severall
payments the xiijth daye of February anno
secundo dominae Reginae x*li*., the xiiijth of
June following x*li*. and the xxvijth of
March anno tercio predictae Reginae x*li*., summa}   xxxli.
Paid for powltrye wares bought in
Grationes Street by William Chauncy, summa}   vli. viijs. vjd.
To Thomas Duddley for monney receavid by
him of Mr Byrde}   Cli.
To Gwyllam Tyan silkewever for monney dwe
unto him}   xiijli. vjs.
To James Mondaye sylkewever for monney dwe
unto him for wurk}   xxli.
To Roger Young upholster in full payment of
a bill and paid by Mr Thomas Blunt}   xiiijli. xvjs. viijd.
To Everard gooldsmith the xth of August
Clviij*li*. vj*s*. viij*d*. and the xiiijth of
September followinge xxvj*li*., suma}   Ciiij^{xx}iiijli. vjs. viijd.
To John Empson your lordship's servant for
sondry somes of monney delyvered unto him
as by severall accompts thearof may appere}   VIIJClxxxli. vjs. ijd.
To Peter Robinson cooffermaker the ixth
daye of June anno secondo at severall
payments for the hole deapte}   vli. ixs. iiijd.
To Androo Weston joyner uppon severall
billes as maye appeare}   xvijli. ijd.[244]
To John Lanyson gooldsmithe at severall
paymentes, viz the xth daye of August anno
secundo vij*li*. xv*s*., the xijth of December
lx*s*., and vijth of February anno tercio

<hr/>

[243] The Shearmens' Company? However, this had merged with the Fullers to form the
Clothworkers' Company in 1528 (Ramsay, *City of London*, p. 43). All the London livery
companies had the liberty to import wine.

[244] DP Box V, fos. 263–7, is his bill for 1566–8, which includes work done at Kenilworth.
See also p. 148 below.

dominae Reginae xviij*li*. x*s*.}   xxixli. vs.

[fo. 8v]
To Richard Barnes mercer at severall
payments, viz the viijth of June xiiij*li*.
xj*s*. viij*d*. and the ixth of July followinge
xxxvij*s*.}   xvjli. viijs. viijd.[245]
To John Lacye mercer the xiiij of June
anno secundo xxij*li*. xiiij*s*. ij*d*. and
the xxth of July anno predicto v*li*. iij*s*.
iiij*d*., summa}   xxvijli. xvijs. vjd.[246]
To Arthur Higham the xxvijth daye of July
in monney delyverid him by your
lordship's commandment}   xxli.
To Anthonny Forster the xvjth of September
Cxl*li*. and paid unto him the xxvth daie
of October Clxx*li*., summa}   CCCxli.[247]
To Jasper the joyner uppon his billes}   xjli. xs. vjd.
Paid unto Garter, Clarentius and other of
the herrauldes for theare paynes abought
my ladies funerales at Oxfurth}   lvjli. xvjs. viijd.[248]
Paid unto my Lorde of Hunnesdon by your
lordship's commandment the thirde daie
of November anno secondo dominae Reginae
to be repaid agayne the last of Marche
anno tercio dominae Reginae}   CCli.
Paid unto Charles Hodgkynes and [*blank*]
Slead mercers for silks bought of them}   xxxli. xiiijs. xd.
Item paid unto Richard Whetell stapler
the xxiijth daye October for the redeamyng of
a dyamonnd of my ladies}   xxvli. vjs. viijd.
Paid unto Francis Barthewe stranger for
monney due unto him by your lordship for
the which Anthonny Forster stoode bownd}   VIJCxixli.
Paid unto Anthonny Butteler the xvj daye

[245] (d.1598) common councillor 1558–71. Probably the Barnes the mercer at Leicester's
funeral. He claimed a debt of £140 for silk from Leicester's estate.
[246] Common councillor 1558–83. Possibly the John Lacye at Leicester's funeral.
[247] These may have been repayments of the loan from Forster in May 1559, see p. 66
above, but the proximity to Amy Dudley's death seems more than coincidental. They
are not for the funeral expenses, which are entered separately below, but they may have
been for the expenses of winding up her household. See Appendix I.
[248] The heralds' expenses are found in CA, Arundel MS XXXV, fo. 21 (see Abbreviations: Amy Dudley's Funeral). Sir Gilbert Dethick was Garter King of Arms (1550–84),
and William Harvey, Clarenceux King of Arms (1557–66).

of November for the discharge of a
bounde in the which Thomas Blunt
esquier stoode bounde unto the said
Anthonny Butteler}   Cli.

[fo. 9]
Paid unto dyvers strangers for hawkes
bought for your lordship}   xxxixli.
Paid unto Angelo Maryano the xth daye
off December for horsses bought for
your lordship}   iiij^{xx}xli.
Paid unto Mr Brightman and others for
great seales and pryvy seales as may
appeare by the billes}   [blank]
Paid unto Arthur Auwdley guylder uppon
sondry billes for wurke don by hym for
your lordship}   xviijli. vijs.
Paid unto William Hoode smithe for wurke
don by him as may appeare in the billes}   xli.
Paid unto John Gabbed for spers}   xliiijs. iiijd.
Item paid unto [blank] Handford
habberdassher the xxvijth daie of December}   xli.[249]
Paid unto Adam Bland skynner the first daye
of December 1560}   lxxxijli. vjs. viijd.
Paid unto Richard Buckley butcher the
vijth daye of February anno tercio regni
Reginae as more plainly may appeare by
the clerke of the kytchin's booke the some of}   xli.
Paid unto Roberte Cooke herrauld the xxijth
daye of December by your lordship's commandement}   xli.[250]
Paid unto Dwes the gooldsmith the vijth
day of February for a guylte bolle with
a cover waing xvij oz. qtr. do. at xs. le
oz., summa}   viijli. xiijs. ixd.
Item more paid unto the same for a whight
bolle waing xvij oz. qtr. at vjs. viijd.
le oz.}   vli. xvs.
Item paid unto Anthony Elspyt gooldsmith

---

[249] DP Box V, fos. 176–7, is the bill of Richard Handull, haberdasher, for 1566.

[250] Robert Cooke (d. 1593), Blancherose Pursuivant January 1562, Chester Herald
February 1562, Clarenceux King of Arms from 1567. His office in 1560 is unclear. Henry
Machyn (275) greeted his appointment in 1562 with scorn, on the grounds that he was
inexperienced and that it was solely Leicester's work. See 'West Midlands', 27–8, for a
discussion of Cooke's relations with Leicester and his Dudley pedigrees.

the xijth daye of May anno secundo dominae
Regine for the sylver knobbes of the bedd
waing xxxij *oz. do. qtr.* at viijs. le *oz.*, summa}   xiijli. xijd.

[fo. 9v]
Paid unto [*blank*] Kettlewood gooldsmith
the secund daye of June anno predicto for one
douzen [*blank*] of goold wreathed buttones
waing one *oz.* one *qtr.* viij graynes at lvs.
le *oz.*, and for the fasshion being wrought
in hast xxxs.}   iiijli. xixs. ixd.
Paid unto Harryson gooldsmith for one
dousen of goold buttones of the ragged
staffe waing one *oz.* di at lvs. the *oz.*,
sum iiij*li.* ijs. vjd., and for the
fasshion at xvjd. the button, suma xxiiijs.}   vli. vjs. vjd.²⁵¹
Paid unto [*blank*] Parteridge gooldsmithe
for a smale chayne being made after the
Frenche fasshion wainge one *oz.* one peny
waight *d.* at lvs. the *oz.*, suma lixs., and
for the fashion xviijs., sum}   lxxvijs.
Paid unto [*blank*] Gilbart gooldsmith for
a chayne wainge one *oz. d.* lackyng a penny
waight at lvs. le *oz.* suma lxxixs. xd., and
for the fasshion xxs., in toto}   iiijli. xixs. xd.
Item paid unto the same for a chayne
bought by your lordship's commandment
waing v *ozes.* and odd waight at lvs.
the *oz.* with the fashion}   xvjli.
Paid unto Arthur gooldsmithe at sundry tymes
as well in monney as by sylver to him
delyverid as maye appeare by the accompte
thereof}   xxxli. xvs. iijd.
Paid unto Jacob gooldsmithe that made
the knobbes for the chaier waing vij
oz. at viijs. le *oz.*, suma}   lvjs.
Paid unto Augustyne Beane gooldsmithe
for pearles that werr delyverid to Davy
Smithe embroderer as may appeare by a

---

²⁵¹ Probably John Harryson, goldsmith, common councillor 1558–71, and alderman in
1574. It was reported in 1562 that Leicester and Warwick had formally re-adopted the
Bear and Ragged Staff device ('West Midlands', 31), but it would appear that he was
using it casually before then.

bill of the said Davy of the receipt
of them}   xjli. vjs. viijd.

[fo. 10]
Item paid unto the said Augustyne Beane
and others for pearles delyverid unto
the said Davy Smithe as appeareth by
his billes for the receipt thereof, suma}   xiijli. xvjs. ijd.
Paid unto William Boddy the vth day of
Marche anno secundo Reginae for v yerds
and a half of clothe of goold at xxvjs.
viijd. the yerd}   vijli. vjs. viijd.
Paid unto Thomas Shingleton the xjth
daye of June anno predicto for arrerages
of his anuity going oute of the mannor
of Halesowen by your lordship's commandment
ʰliijs. iiijd. per annumʰ}   vijli. vjs. viijd.
Paid unto Mr Thomas Duddley for his
annuitie goinge oute of the mannor of
Watton}   vjli. xiijs. iiijd.
Paid unto William Hugganes for his
annuitie goinge oute of the said mannor
of Watton}   vjli. xiijs. iiijd.²⁵²
Paid unto [blank] Smithe fletcher
uppon his billes for deapte due unto him}   vli. xs.
Paid unto Mr Hugganes for the charges
of a prevy seale for the Deane of Chestre
at your lordship's commandment}   lxxvjs. ijd.²⁵³
Paid unto John Sonett stranger the xiiijth
daye of July anno secundo dominae
Reginae for ij rapieres bought of him
with the furnyture}   xijli.
Paid to Mr Curson for a horsse bought
by him for your lordship}   xli.
Paid unto a cutteler of Bruxeles for the
hiltes of ij rapiers with the furnitures}   vijli.
Paid unto Ferdinando Sola stranger the
last daye of Marche for one payer of
silke hoose bought by William Chancy

---

²⁵² For Singleton's annuity, see n. 183 above. The Duchess of Northumberland left
Dudley an annuity of £5 a year out of Hales Owen, but it does not appear on the
schedule in BRL, HH MS 351621. The origin of Huggins's annuity is unknown.

²⁵³ Richard Walker, Dean of Chester 1558–67. The purpose of the Privy Seal is unclear,
though it may have been related to dispute with Cumberland, see n. 124 above.

and for pearles bought of him, in toto}   vijli. xs.

[fo. 10v]
Paid unto Thomas Wasshington, Mary Hill
and others for shepstrye wurke don by
them as appeareth by their severall
billes of the parcelles, summa}   ljli. vjs.
Paid unto Francis Barker lynin draper
for vij ellies di of fyne lynin
clothe bought by him for your
lordship at xvjs. the elie, in toto}   vjli.
Paid unto Richard Whight of the Quenes
Prevy Bakehousse for bread}   xxxvijs. viijd.
Paid unto Robert Wright baker at severall
payments, viz the viijth daye of Marche
anno secondo regni Reginae xxxs., the xiijth
of Aprell following xlviijs., the xxiiijth
of December anno predicto lxs., the vth
daye of January anno tercio dominae Reginae
vjli. vijs., the iiijth daye of June anno
secundo at Grenewich ljs. vjd., and the
vjth of Aprell anno tercio xli., summa}   xxvli. xvjs. vjd.
Paid unto Hawnsse the hoosier uppon a
bill for wurk as appeareth by the same
bill lxxs. xd. and paid unto his hoste
for borde wagies and bedding and for his
wagies being behind xlixs. iiijd., summa}   vli. xixs. xd.
Paid unto Deathike my Lord of Penbrookes
hossier for wurke don by him as maye
appeare by his severall billes}   xxxijli. iijs. vijd.
Paid unto Roger Tempeste for his
wurkmanshipp as also for hoosen
bought for Dearynng* and others as by
his severall billes of the parceles
more at large appearethe}   xli. iiijs. viijd.[254]
Paid unto Maynard your lordship's hossier
for woorkmanshipp don by him as appearethe by
his severalle billes of the parceles}   viijli. xijs.[255]

[254] DP Box V, fos. 116–9, is the bill of William Tempest, hosier, for 1561–4.
[255] Although a tradesman, he does to some extent fall into the category of servant, for he received livery in 1567, and is referred to as 'my lord's man' in DP IV, fo. 18, Anthony Foster to Richard Pecock, 14 Jan. 1567. DP Box V, fos. 152–7, is his bill for 1562–6, and he and William Whittle (see n. 22 above) were the main recipients of the cloth deliveries recorded in the account of 1571–74 (DP XII).

To Henry Foskewe gentleman and [*blank*]
Maddy uppon a bound whearin Thomas Blunt
esquier stode bound for one Cli. wheareof paid}   lli.

[fo. 11]
Paid unto Francis Dixson jerkin maker for
wurkmanshippe as appeareth by his billes}   viijli. xviijd.
Paid unto John Foxe hossier uppon his
severall billes as maye appeare by them}   lixs. xd.
Paid unto [*blank*] Booreman hossier for
wurkmanshippe as may appeare by his billes}   [*blank*]
Paid unto [*blank*] Forman Yeoman Purvayor
for beare provided by him for your
lordship as appeareth by his severall
bills, summa}   xijli. xjs. vijd.
Paid unto Richard Horden at sondry tymes
from the xxijth of December anno secundo
regni Reginae unto the xvjth daie of June
anno predicto at severall payments}   xxxiiijli.
Paid unto Richard Flammocke cator* at
severall payments from the xvijth daie
of January anno secundo dominae Reginae
unto the xxijth daye of May followinge, suma}   lvjli. xixs. xjd.
Paid unto James Tompson cator from the
xxvth daie of Maye anno predicto unto the
xxvjth daye of June anno predicto}   xjli. ixs. iiijd.
Paid unto Richard Jyncks clerke of the
kytchen and to William Woodman* cater
from the xvijth daye of July unto the
last daie of Aprell in the thirde yeare
of the Quenes majesties raigne}   Cvjli. xjs. vijd.[256]
Paid unto William Hugganes gentleman
for sondry charges at Kewe and also
to other as by dyvers sondry billes
appearethe amounting to}   xlijli. xvijs. xd.
ᶦItem more paid unto the said Mr
Hugganes upon a bill for money by him
laid oute of Kewe as appearethe by his bill}   xlijs. xd.ᶦ
<Allocat' in summa predicta>

[256] The kitchen expenses are discussed in the Introduction, p. 14.

[fo. 11v]

Paid unto Thomas Eaton your lordship's servant for monney laid oute in reparacions at Kewe & for other necessaryes as appeareth by his billes}	xxli. ixs.
Paid unto dyvars carpenters for woork don at Kewe by your lordship's commandment and agrement with the said woorkmen, summa}	vjli. xiijs. iiijd.
Item for tymber provided for the same reparacions with the carrage there}	xls.
Paid unto John Hales of Kewe for a reste of monney dwe unto him in William Chaunceyes tyme as the bill appeareth}	vjli. iiijs. jd.

ʲPaid unto Mr Thomas Duddley, John Hales and
others for dyvers other charges abought the
banket as by the billes of parcels may appeare, summa}ʲ
<vacat'>

Paid unto Richard Robinson powlter by a bill of Hordenes hand xxijs. viijd., paid unto him uppon a bill of Junkes' hand as by the same appearethe xxxjs. iiijd., payd unto the same uppon a bill of Richard Hordenes as by the same appeareth lxijs. iiijd.}	vli. xvjs. iiijd.
ᵏPaid unto Thomas Watson* armorer the xviijth daye of Marche anno tercio Reginae uppon his billes examined before Mr Blunt and others}	viijli. xvjs.
Item more paid unto the said Thomas for wurke don by him at Kewe as appeareth by a bill and paid unto him by Mr Thomas Blunt}	xvjs. xd.ᵏ

<entred amongst the servants> ²⁵⁷

Paid unto George Halle armorer at sondry tymes for wurkmanshippe as appearethe by the bill of particulars, sum}	vli.
Paid unto Henry Popeley casemaker uppon his billes as appeareth by the particulars}	lxvjs.
Paid unto William Curward smithe for certayne wurke don by him as appeareth by the particulars}	xxiiijs. viijd.

[fo. 12]

ˡPaid unto Petro* my lord's musicion for lute strings and other things for his lute}	xxxs. ijd.ˡ

²⁵⁷ See the Book of Servants Wages, p. 411 below.

\<entred amongst the servants\>[258]

Paid for charges of the lawe against
Lyttleton and penninge of certayne writings
as doth appeare by a bill of the parcelles}   lxvijs. iiijd.[259]

Paid unto William Haynes fyshemonger}   xxxviijs.

Paid for the chargies of suying oute
a pattente}   iiijli. iijs. iiijd.

Paid unto Bagnoll grocer uppon his billes
for grocery wares hadd of him}   vijli. ijd.

Paid unto Pawle Neyle tallowe chaundeler uppon
a bill for candeles of lxs.}   xxs.

Paid unto John Argill matter for certayne
peeces of mattes and wurkemanshippe}   lxxvs. iiijd.

Paid unto Francis myllyoner for wares as
by the bill of particulars}   xxvijs. iiijd.

Paid for a parryes head with other furnyture
for the chieff mourner at my ladies buryall
as appeareth by a bill}   ls. ijd.[260]

Paid unto Petre Borne myllynor for wares
bought of him for your lordship as appeareth
by the bill of parceles, summa}   iiijli. xvjd.

Paid unto John Titbatche armorer that bargayned
for the some of vli. to make cleane certayne
gonnes in parte of payment}   ls.

Paid unto Humffraye Mott spurryer for ij paier
of spurres the one paier of xvijs. and the other
of xiijs., summa}   xxxs.

[fo. 12v]

Paid the xxiiijth daye of December in the third
yeare of the Quenes majesties raygne unto dyvers
prysonne howsses by your lordship's commandment}   xijli. viijs.

Paid unto Mr Thomas Blunt esquier for monney
layde oute by him by your lordship's
commandment as appearethe by a byll thereof
appearethe [sic], suma}   vjli. vs. iiijd.

Paid unto Mr Carye for monney by him
laid oute for your lordship}   xli. xvs. ijd.

Paid unto [blank] Deathike gooldsmithe by

---

[258] Ibid., p. 401.

[259] For the Hales Owen case, see n. 204 above.

[260] The chief mourner was Sir Henry Norris's wife Margery. Rank in the county was the probable reason, for her relations with Amy Dudley are otherwise unknown.

xltie *oz.* of sylver delyverid unto him at
iij*s.* x*d.* the *oz.* for your lordship's
standishe}   ixli. xiijs. iiijd.
Paid for rennyshe wyne, muscadell and
malvesy fett by the rynlett and in
other measures at sondry tymes for your
lordship as maye appeare by the
particulers}   xiiijli. xvjs. ijd. ob.
Paid unto Gregory Pryncell gooldsmithe
for the wurkmanshipp of a seale lx*s.* and
for sylver for the same seale ix*s.,* summa}   lxixs.
Paid unto the ferryman of Lambethe for the
ferryage of your lordship's horsses at
sondry tymes as appeareth by his billes}   viijs. xjd.
Paid unto Albon Austray ferryman of Grenewiche
uppon ij severall bills}   xjs. ijd.
Paid unto Thomas Whiteley keper of the tennys
courte at Whitehall uppon iiij severall billes
as may appeare}   viijli. xs. vjd.
Paid unto the keper of the tennys courte in
Southwarke whan your lordship plaied against
the Duke of Swethen, suma}   ixs.[261]
Item paid unto Rauffe Taillior bearebruer
for ij hoggesheads of beare with caske as
by a bill appeareth}   xxs.

[fo. 13]
Paid unto John Stedman glasior for wurk don by
him}   xjs. vjd.
Item paid unto Henry Starkey glasior for wurke
don by him}   vijs. vjd.
Item paid for apparell for my lady and for the
charges of Huggenes her man lying in London
for the same as maye appeare by a bill, suma}   lxs. vjd.[262]
Item paid unto Mr Alderman Heughet the xijth
daie of March anno tercio Reginae}   CCli.[263]

---

[261] John, Duke of Finland, see n. 182 above, and pp. 163–4 for other references in 1560. This entry appears to be out of sequence for he left England in April 1560 (see n. 337 below).

[262] Apart from her funeral expenses this is the sole reference to Amy Dudley in this account. Like the entry to the Duke of Finland above it is out of chronological sequence and cannot be dated. Huggenes was probably the servant referred to on p. 102 above (see n. 185), he was clearly not William Huggins*. He is not mentioned in Edney's bill (n. 236 above).

[263] Sir William Hewet, clothworker and lord mayor 1559–60.

ᵐItem paid unto Warley['s] executors by the
handes of William Chancy}   Clli.
Item paid unto William Chelsham mercer per Chancy}   lli.
Item paid for the interest of MMVC*li.* to
Culverwell and the Companny}   CCCli.
Item paid for the losse of VC*li.* taken upp by
exchaunge of Mr Birde}   xijli. xs.
Item for the losse of parte of the same monney
to paye Mr Sheldon esquier}   vli. xs.
Item paid more to Mr Birde for one peece of
fyne lynin clothe conteyning xxx elies and iij
qtrs. at xiiij*s.* vj*d.* the elie}   xxijli. vs. xd. ob.ᵐ

[fo. 13v *blank*]
[fo. 14]
PAYMENTS unto dyvers personns for extraordynary charges from the
xxijth daye of December in the second yeare of the raigne of our
soveraigne Quene Elizabethe unto the last of Aprell in the thirde yeare
of hir Highnes's raigne as followethe, viz in

December Anno Secundo

Paid for a coverlet for the gromes of the chamber}   ixs. vjd.
Item for ij woollen blanquetts for them}   xjs. iijd.
Item delyvered unto Mr Bewe for paper and
other necessaries for your lordship}   xs.
Item for ij emptye rynletts}   iijs. viijd.
Item for a skynne of parchement and a letherne
bagg for monney}   xijd.
Item paid for ij netherstocks bought by William
Chancy in his tyme and paid for by me}   vli.

January

Paid the second daie of January for a paire of
perfumed gloves}   xxxviijs.
Item paid for ij skynnes unto William Whittle
taillior}   xvjs.
Item paid unto a pore man that was stayed by
your lordship's commandment for the suspicion
of a murder for his charges and recompence after
he hadd cleared himself}   xs.
Item for payntyng of your lordship's barge & beare}   vs.
Item for a coole basket lyned with leather}   ijs. iiijd.
Item for one realme of browne paper}   xxiijd.
Item for one case of knyves}   viijs.

Item for one payer of black stocks bought in Abchurch Lane} <xxvijth of January>	ls.

[fo. 14v]

February Anno Secundo Regni Reginae

Paid the first daie of February unto Henry Johanes, Empson and Allayne for muskadell}	ijs.
Item paid for iij quire of paper}	xviijd.
Item paid for the wasshing of your lordship's aparel}	xijd.
Item for ix paier of younge house doves at xiiijd. the paier, suma}	xs. vjd.
Item paid unto John Marbury for paper}	xijd.
Item for one hundreth of oringes}	xvjd.
Item to Wanton the appoticary for bisket bread}	viijs.
Item for one paier of yellowe stocks the xxth daye of February the breeches made by Dedicke}	lijs.
Item for one joyle and ij rounds of sturgeon whan the French embassador and the pledges dyned with your lordship}	xvjs. viijd.[264]

Marche Anno Predicto

Paid for iiij torches at xijd. the torch}	iiijs.
Item paid for a case to put in Watton books}	iiijs.[265]
Item paid for the setting upp of a bathinge tubb at Hawnces howse and for faggots spennt theare}	xxijd.[266]
Item paid for ij tapnetts of figgs}	ijs. viijd.
Item for ij quyer of paper, ynnke and pyn dust}	xxd.
Item for ij flasks with the furnyture the xiijth day of March to a Spanyerd}	xxs.

---

[264] This would appear to be the dinner on 8 February to which Leicester invited all the ambassadors, and which La Quadra refused to attend. See Lettenhove, ii, 228, La Quadra to Feria, 12 Feb. 1560, for his reasons. Noailles expected both La Quadra and Helffenstein to be there, AMAE, CPA XIV, fo. 162v, Noailles to the Cardinal of Lorraine, 8 Feb.

[265] Presumably estate books of Watton Priory following the grant in January (n. 125 above).

[266] This may be the Hawnce's house near the orchard at Whitehall where Leicester's former mistress Lady Sheffield lived in the late 1570s, see her deposition in the Sir Robert Dudley case, CKS, U1475/L2/2, fo. 12. The orchard itself was not created till 1561 (*King's Works*, iv, 316), but the house probably faced King Street just below the Holbein Gate. Whether it belonged to one of the Hawnces or Hanses mentioned in these accounts is unclear.

Item paid for the carryage of ij chests unto
your lordship's house in Tothill Streete}   vjd.[267]

Item paid for the dyning [*sic*] of a paier of hoos
unto Empson}   xijd.

Item for the carryage of stuff to the Court
from London by a carr man}   viijd.

Item for oysters bought and sennt unto Islington
for your lordship}   xvjd.

Item delyvered to Mr Hordeyne for russhes}   ijs. ijd.

Item for one groose of rybbon poynts of sondry
coollers}   xvs.

Item paid for ix gallones of mylk the xvjth daye
of Marche}   iijs. ixd.

[fo. 15]

Item for beare and faggots}   xd.
Item for viij roose cakes}   ijs. vjd.
Item for a pynnt of oyle of rooses}   ijs. viijd.
Item for malvesey and butter to Empson}   vjd.
Item for a payer of Jernesey hoose to Empson}   vs. iiijd.
Item paid for a paier of silke garters}   xviijd.
Item for one dousen of rybbon poynts}   xiiijd.
Item for one quart of roose water}   ijs.
Item for vj roose cakes}   xijd.
Item for a bottle of roose water}   xxd.
Item for a glasse for your lordship's water}   xd.
Item for v roose cakes}   xijd.
Item for iij quyer of paper}   xviijd.
Item delyverid to Empson for paper}   vjd.

Item paid for the coverynng of a payer of your
lordship's vyrginales}   xxxijs.

Item for the mending of your lordship's jewell
boxe}   vjd.

Item for one paier of black neytherstocks of
black silke made by Dedicke}   <xijth Marche>   xlviijs.

Item for one other paier of black nether stocks
made by Deadick, price}   <xxvijth of Marche>   ls.

[267] Formerly Sir Andrew Dudley's house. In his will (see n. 124 above) Dudley left it to
Lord Ambrose, Sir Henry Sidney and Sir Francis Jobson jointly, so there appears to
have been some form of further settlement.

Aprell Anno Secundo

Paid unto Thomas Harlam* the first daye of Aprell
for russhes}   ijs. viijd.

Item for bringing your lordship's armor to the
armory in Tothill Streete}   ijs.[268]

Item delyverid unto Thomas Forrest beinge sent
to Waltham Forrest in your lordship's busynes
for his expenses}   vjs. viijd.

Item paid for leimones and orings}   xd.

Item for the making of iij seates for iij chaiers}   xxs.

Item one dousen of skynnes for the coveryng
of the same chaiers}   xiijs.

Item paid for bysket bread to Edward the appoticary}   iiijs.

Item paid unto John Pyckman bowyer for iij bowes
for your lordship}   xvjs.

[fo. 15v]

Item paid for iiij *yds.* of yellowe kerseye at
iiij*s.* iiij*d.* the yerd for Richard Yngle and
William Sedgrave by your lordship's commandment}   xiijs. iiijd.

Item for the carriage of your lordship's
armor to Grenewich}   iijs. iiijd.

Item paid unto Mr Darcy for monney by him
dysbursed for iij staves broken by your
lordship at Grenewiche}   vs.

Item paid unto Mr Tamwurthe for monney by him
dysbursed to your lordship's bargemen}   xs.

Item paid for lemons}   vijd.

Item for one dousen of rybbon poynts}   xiiijd.

Item for the mending of the fote of your

---

[268] This entry and several following refer to the transport of Leicester's armour from Greenwich to Whitehall for a tournament and then its return. There is also a further entry on p. 153 below to the mending of his armour when he 'shuld have run' at Whitehall dated late in March. Relating them to what is otherwise known of the tournaments in the spring of 1560 poses some difficulties. Three are recorded (Young, p. 201): one at Shrovetide (26 February), and then 21 and 28 April. The latter two are described by Machyn (pp. 231, 233), who includes Leicester among the participants on the 28th. The score cheques assigned to these dates in CA, Tournament Portfolio, arts. 6–7, do not list Leicester among the participants on the 21st and state that Sussex ran in his place on the 28th. The entry below to broken staves suggests that he certainly ran on one occasion, and the 28th would appear to be the most obvious. The entry on p. 153 implies that he failed to participate on one occasion owing to broken armour; this would appear to be the one when Sussex took his place. This may have been on the 21st, alternatively his armour may have broken during course of the tournament of 28th and he only participated in part of it. Neither the dates in this account nor those assigned to the score cheques can be relied on absolutely.

lordship's harneyes and bringing the same from Westmester to Grennewiche}	iijs.
Item paid unto Thomas Forrest for lyens and collers for your lordship's hounds}	ijs. vjd.
Item paid unto Gemyny of the Blacke Fryers for compasses}	xxxs.
Item for a looking glasse bought by George Giles}	xls.
Item for ij yerdes of Englishe rybbon bought for your lordship by Mr Carye}	ijs.
Item for buttered beare for your lordship}	viijd.
Item paid to John the stopper by your lordship's commandment for iij *yds.* of cotten rybbon}	iijs.
Item horssemeat at Grenewich whan the Quenes majestie rode to Detford}	viijs.[269]
Item for one paier silke hoosen bought at William Holbornes the xiiijth daye of Aprell}	lxs.

[fo. 16]

May Anno Secundo

Paid for bringinge of rennishe wyne brought oute of Barbycan to my Lord Hastings the first daye of Maye}	xijd.
Item paid unto the Vidames man for the dressing of a horsse and the monneye delyvered unto Ph[ilip]e* the Frenche cooke}	vjs. iiijd.
Item delyverid unto Thomas Davies being sennt to Grennewich as harbinger}	xs.[270]
Item paid unto William Whittle taillior for iiij skynnes for your lordship}	xxxvijs.
Item paid for a trompet bought for John Trompetter}	ls.
Item paid unto the skryvenner in Bowe Lane for the drawing and writing of certayne bonnds betwixt your lordship and William Sheldon esquier [Byrd mercer *deleted*]}	vjs. ijd.[271]
Item to Branden skryvener for the drawing and	

---

[269] Machyn (p. 232) refers to the Queen's visit to Deptford to see the ships c. 24 April. The entries on pp. 154, 164 below (the latter dated 13 April) would appear to refer to this occasion as well.

[270] For the remove on the 14th. Leicester and Pembroke wrote to Archbishop Parker in favour of an Esquire of the Stables from Greenwich on the 16th, CCC, Parker MS 114a, fo. 219. He and Parry probably sent their good wishes to Cecil on 3 June from there as well (PRO, SP12/12/84).

[271] For the loan on p. 114 above.

writing of the bonnds betwixt your lordship and Lyonell Ducket}	vjs. ijd.[272]
Item paid for an empty rynlet for my Lady Sydney}	xijd.
Item for the carriage of a rynlet with wyne to Whitehalle}	viijd.
Item paid for lemones bought for your lordship by Partridge waterman}	xvjd.
Item paid for a case to putt in your lordship's vessell}	xvs.
Item paid for iiij lonnge bottles of pewtre}	xlvjs. viijd.
Item for xij newe knyves for the case}	vjs.
Item paid to Isacke Burges racket maker in parte of payment of a dousen of rackets at iiij*li.* the dousen}	xls.
Item for iiij dousen of rybbon poynts}	vs. iiijd.
Item for a pound of pynneapple compffets}	xiiijd.
Item for one pound of synamond compffets}	xiiijd.
Item for one quarter of clove compffets and of so muche ginger compffets}	xiiijd.
Item for one pound of banqueting bread}	xiiijd.
Item for an empty rynlet cont[aining] vj gall[on]s}	xd.
Item for the convayinge of lettres to Andwerpe}	iiijd.[273]

[fo. 16v]

Item for one paier of silke hoose the vth daye of May bought at William Holbornes}	lxs.
Item one other paier of neyther stocks for growgrayne breeches made by Dethick with turned fringe}	ls.

June Anno Secundo

Item paid unto Robert Holland being sennt in your lordship's busynes for his expences}	xviijs. vjd.
Item paid for a quart of roose water}	ijs.
Item paid for a *pp.* of straburyes and the pott}	ijs. ijd.
Item paid for viij baskets of cheryes at iij*s.*	

[272] (Sir) Lionel Duckett (d.1587), mercer, common councillor from 1558, alderman from 1564, and lord mayor 1572–3. The subject of this bond is unclear, for no loan from Duckett is recorded in this account.

[273] Either to George Gilpin (see n. 323 below) or to Sir Thomas Gresham who was on a financial mission in the Netherlands between the spring and autumn of 1560.

iiij*d*. the basket}	xxvjs. viijd.
Item paid for a vyolannt for Elles Stempe*}	xxs.
Item paid to Thomas Forrest for lyenes and collers}	vs.
Item paid for a perfummyng pan}	ijs. viijd.
Item paid for the carryinge oute of brycke of the gardeyne at Kewe by the space of vij daies}	iiijs. viijd.
Item for one pottle of roose water}	iijs. iiijd.
Item for a busshell of hempseed for the quayles}	xviijd.
Item paid to Richard Jinkes for the rest of the monney by him laid furthe for quayles}	iijs. iiijd.
Item for a loking glasse}	xxvjs. viijd.
For one other glasse bought the xxvijth daye of June}	xijs.
Item to a porewoman bringing bowes and flowers}	iijs. iiijd.
Item for one round and joyle of sturgeon whan the Duke of Holkest dyned with your lordship}	xiiijs.[274]

[fo. 17]

July Anno Predicto

Item for iij quyre of paper the first of July}	xvd.
Item paid to Archicrage going in your lordship's busynes for his expences}	ijs. viijd.
Item paid unto Richard Elles glover}	vjs.
For half a pound of red waxe}	viijd.
Item paid for one paier of Spannyshe gloves for your lordship}	xd.
Item for ij busshelles of hempsseed}	vjs. vd.
Item for bringing the same to Lyon Kay}	vjd.[275]
Item delyverid unto Thomas Forrest for lyenes and collers}	ijs. iiijd.
Item for bowes and flowers bought by Ph[ilip]e Wattye*}	ijs. viijd.
Item paid unto Maynard the hossier for one	

[274] Adolph, Duke of Holstein-Gottorp (1526–86). Holstein visited England in March and stayed until 28 June. The later entry to gambling (p. 168 below) dated 24 June was probably to this occasion, the day of Holstein's election to the Order of the Garter. His visit may have been connected to the raising of German troops for use in Scotland, but he was also suspected of harbouring ambitions to marry Elizabeth. Further references to dining with him in April and May can be found on pp. 156, 167 below.

[275] Lyon Quay just below the Bridge.

nayle [*sic*] of black velvet}   xijd.
Item paid unto William Kettle draper for vij
yerds iij *qts.* of yellowe kersay at iiij*s.* ij*d.*
the yerd}   xxxijs. iijd.
To Rauffe Lockeye for a quyver of joyners
wurke for your lordship}   ixs.
Item paid for iij dousen of yron haulted knyves
for the banquet at Kewe}   xxiijs.[276]
Item paid unto Mrs Mundaye for rooses and
other flowers for your lordship's chamber
by the space of xxvij daies at vj*d.* the day}   xiijs. vjd.[277]
For salt petre bought by Ph[ilip]e Wattye for
your lordship}   xijd.
Item for ij*ll.* of shuger at xvj*d.* the *ll.*}   ijs. viijd.
Item for one pound of pepper}   ijs. viijd.
For one pound of dates}   vd.
For ij*ll.* of smale reasones}   viijd.

---

[276] The best date for this banquet, to which a number of entries below as well as the poulterer's bill on p. 108 above refer, would be 30 July–3 August, when the Court was at Richmond on the initial stage of the progress. It will be seen below that this account is far less informative about the progress than the Chancy account is about that of 1559. There are also serious *lacunae* in other major sources for the whole of the latter half of 1560, which have hindered reconstruction of the circumstances of Amy Dudley's death. The Queen invited La Quadra to join the progress, but he claimed to be unequipped to do so (Lettenhove, ii, 324, to the Bishop of Arras, 13 Aug.). Moreover, apart from his well-known letter on Amy Dudley's death from Windsor on 11 September, few of his despatches survive for the period August–December. Similarly there are very few letters for this period by Cecil, who rejoined the Court in mid-July after the conclusion of the treaty in Scotland. The decision on the progress may have been delayed by the treaty (news of which reached the Court c. 11 July when it was relayed by Leicester both to Sussex (BL, Cotton MS Caligula B IX, fo. 132), and, apparently, to Arundel (DP I, fo. 151, Arundel to Leic., 20 July)), as well as the expected arrival of Eric XIV of Sweden (reported as imminent by Leicester to Sir Henry Paget on 30 June, Paget Papers V, fo. 1). On 19 July Sir William Petre informed Cecil that the Queen intended to begin a progress towards Portsmouth on the 29th (*CSPSc, 1547–63*, 451, according to La Quadra, the fleet was assembled at Portsmouth, Lettenhove,ii, 523, 12 Aug.). She left Greenwich then, dined at Lambeth and proceeded to Richmond, where she spent five days before going to Oatlands on 4 August and Sutton Place on the 5th (Machyn, 241). Leicester wrote to William Sheldon from Richmond on the 1st (DP I, fo. 4).

[277] This and the following entries are to the expenses of Leicester's men at Greenwich from mid-May to the end of July. John Trompet may be Leicester's trumpeter John Richards*. Apart from various dinners in London, Leicester appears to have been there himself throughout June and early July; his letters to Paget and Sussex (see the previous note) were both from Greenwich. However, in mid-June Leicester proposed to visit his brother-in-law, now 3rd Earl of Huntingdon, at Ashby de La Zouche in the near future, possibly for the 2nd Earl's funeral which took place on 14 July (DP I, fo. 147, Huntingdon to Leic., 30 June). This visit was obviously cancelled, but Leicester's movements in late July cannot be established. He may have gone on to Kew ahead of the progress, which may account for the reference below to his abode there.

Item paid unto Mrs Monday for vj bedds at
Grenewiche for your lordship's gentlemen and
yeomen by the space of a xj weeks}   lxvjs.

[fo. 17v]
Item paid for dyvers of your lordship's servants
beds at Grennewiche at John Trompet's house by the
space of xj weeks}   xjs.
Item for one vyrkin of sturgeon conteyning one
joyle and iij rounds provided for the banquet
at Kewe}   xxxs.
Item for vj glasses and a basket bought by
your lordship in the Powltry}   xxs. vjd.
Item for vij glasses and a basket to put
them in against the banquet at Kewe}   xviijs.
Item for the charges of wynne sennt unto Kewe
by Frannke against the banquet}   vjs. viijd.
Item for one busshell of hempseed bowght by
William Juncks for the quayles}   xviijd.
Item paid for a paier of silke hoose the xxixth
daie of July bought at William Holbornes of
blacke, price}   liijs. iiijd.

[fo. 18]

                    August Anno Secundo Reginae
Item paid for filberts, walnutts, peares and
other frutes as well for the provision against
the banquet at Kewe as also at sondry tymes
duryng the tyme of your lordship's aboode and my
Lady Sydney's}   xs.[278]
Item for the carryage of a bedd from Mr Byrd's
housse to my Lord Ambroses house}   vjd.[279]
Item one payer of yellowe silke hoose bought
at William Holbornes the xiiijth of August}   ixs.

---

[278] The Court removed from Sutton Place to Farnham on 6 August, where Leicester
informed the Countess of Sussex that 'advertysements of a great princes coming [Eric
XIV] very shortly causeth her [the Queen] to make that outward almost a posting
journey rather then a progress' (L. Howard (ed.), *A Collection of Letters* (1753), pp. 210–11).
He went on to relate that his sister Mary Sidney was 'lacking six or seven weeks to be
delyvered of a child' [her daughter Elizabeth, born on 10 October]. Since Sidney was
then in Wales, she may have taken up residence at Kew for her lying in.
[279] Ambrose Dudley's house was in Holborne.

September Anno Predicto

Item paid unto Thomas Forrest at Hampton Courte for lyenes and collers}	vjs.[280]
Item paid for maylinge corde for the clothe that was sennt unto Oxffurthe}	xviijd.[281]
Item paid unto the carryers that carryed the said packs to Oxfforthe}	xls.
To Griffith Clunne for his charges with the said packs}	xjs. viijd.
For iij elies of canvas to put the spices in}	ijs.
Item for ij quyer of paper}	viijd.
For a pound of red waxe}	viijd.
For a pynnt of ynnke}	viijd.
For a pound of pynnedust}	viijd.
For iiij *oz.* of fyne black sowing silke delyverid unto the shepsters that wrought uppon your lordship's wurke at iijs. iiijd. le *oz.*}	xiijs. iiijd.[282]
Item for a pursse of black leather}	vijs.
For lemonnes and orínges}	iiijd.

[fo. 18v]

Item for ij kylderkynes of ale that werr sennt unto Kewe and the vessells and also for ij standes of ale with the vesselles, suma}	xiijs. iiijd.
Item for the carriage of the same at iiij sondry tymes at xxd. every tyme}	vjs. viijd.
Item paid for the exchange of one hundreth pound of whight monney into goold which was sennt to Oxffurth for the chargs of the buryall}	xvjs. viijd.
Item for vj bedstaves and ij lonng brusshes	

---

[280] The Queen left Farnham on 8 August and went to Portsmouth, Southampton, Winchester, Basing and then Windsor, which she reached on 30 August–1 September. The Court remained at Windsor until the end of September when it removed to Hampton Court. There is no record of Leicester's movements after 6 August until he wrote to Sussex from Windsor on 7 September, commenting on the Queen's enthusiastic hunting (BL, Cotton MS Titus B XIII, fo. 17). Two days later came the news of his wife's death and he retired to Kew. According to BL, Add. MS 48023, fo. 353, he did not return to Court (then at Hampton Court) until the Tuesday after Michaelmas Day (1 October). The references to his abode at Kew may also refer to this period.

[281] For Amy Dudley's funeral.

[282] Leicester's mourning is mentioned both in a fragment of a despatch from Michel de Seurre to the Cardinal of Lorraine of 24 September (L. Paris (ed.), *Négotiations, Lettres et Pièces diverses … tirées du Portefeuille de … Evêque de Limoges* (Paris, 1841), p. 542), and in BL, Add. MS 48023, fo. 353, which notes that it continued until Easter 1561 and considers it to have been completely hypocritical.

bought by Harry Johanes}   xvjd.
Item for ij pennknyves for your lordship}   xijd.

October Anno Secundo Regni Reginae

Item paid for a paier of shoes for Best at
Hampton Court by your lordship's commandment}   ijs.
Item paid unto Thomas Harlam for his expenses being
sennt to Kewe for your lordship's plate}   xd.
Item paid for ij leatherne guyrdels for your lordship}   vjs.
Item for the provender of your lordship's
horsses at Bosomes In and at the Maydens Head
when your lordship dyned at the Mayor's feast}   xvs. iiijd.[283]
Item paid to Davy Powell for monney by him
laid oute for faggots occupied abought your
lordship's busynes as by a bill apeareth}   iiijs. iiijd.

[fo. 19]

Item paid for the losse of ij hundreth nyne
and twenty cruceadows receavid of Sir John Yorke
with other monney as parcell of the money
borroughed of him and receavid after the rate
of vjs. xd. the pece and coulde not be paid
oute for above vjs. iijd. the peec}   vli. xiiijs. vjd.
Item for ij paier of neytherstocks bought of
Fredynando}   vli. xs.

November Anno Predicto

Item paid unto Christopher myllyoner for vij
glasses of sweete water}   xiiijs.
Item for ij quyer of Frankford paper}   ijs.
Item paid for corde occupied abought the trussinge
of the bedds that werr sennt to Kewe}   iijs.
Item for a bottle of roose water}   xxd.
Item for basketts bought by Godffray*}   xs.
Item paid unto Sturman for your lordship's beare's
meate at London and in the progresse}   xiiijs.

---

[283] The Lord Mayor's Banquet was held on 29 October (see p. 165 below). The new lord mayor was (Sir) William Chester, MP. Bosom's Inn was at St Lawrence, Cheapside, and the Maiden Head in the Steelyard.

Bedding at Hampton Courte in the Progresse tyme[284]

Item for iiij bedds by the space of vij weeks at xij*d.* the week for the gentlemen and viij*d.* for yeomen}	xjs. viijd.
Item for vj bedds theare by the space of vij weeks certeyne of the yeomen} [*sic*]	vs.
Item for iij bedds by the space of vij weeks for the yeomen}	xs.
Item for Edward Wullemes* bedd by the space of vij weeks at vj*d.* the weeke}	iijs. vjd.

[fo. 19v]

Item for Ph[ilip]e Wattyes bedd theare by the space of vij weeks at vj*d.* the week}	iijs. vjd.
Item for Thomas Harlam's bedd by the said tyme at viij*d.* the week}	iiijs. viijd.
Item for James Acones* bedd by the said tyme}	ijs. iiijd.
Item for xx sparres of vyir for the wardrobe with the carriage of them}	xs. iiijd.
Item for faggotts occupied in the wardrobe whan the stuff came from Kewe}	viijd.
Item paid for iij of your lordship's yeomen's suppers that werr appointed to kepe the wardrobe}	xvjd.
Item for iiij torches to Empson}	iiijs.
Item delyverid unto Thomas Davies for his expenses being sennt to Eltham before the Quenes majesties comming theather}	iiijs.

Banqueting stuff against the Banquet at Elthame[285]

Item for a brick of marmalade}	ijs. iiijd.
Item for a marchepayne}	xs.

[284] The Court removed from Hampton Court to Whitehall in mid-November. The seven weeks referred to here are probably October and the first weeks of November. It is curious that while these expenses and those for Greenwich in June and July are entered here, there are none for the progress in August. Only a few vague references can be found in the Book of Servants Wages (e.g. the entry for Ralph Aldersey, pp. 408–9 below).

[285] The Queen visited Greenwich and Eltham for a few days in late November, and the banquet appears to have been held on the 27th. Throckmorton's secretary Robert Jones, who had been sent to warn her about a possible marriage to Leicester, reported that he had his first interview at Greenwich in the evening of Wednesday the 27th after she had returned from hunting and dining at Eltham (BL, Add. MS 35830, fo. 66, 30 Nov.). A fragment of a letter from Sir Humphrey Radcliffe to Sussex refers to Leicester's great banquet for the Queen at Eltham being on Wednesday (BL, Cotton MS Titus B XIII, fo. 28).

Item for dyvers other kynds of banqueting stuff
as may appeare by a bill of the parcels}   iiijli.
Item more for a boxe of collingale}   xvjd.
Item for ij*ll.* of quinces}   vs.
Item for ij torches when your lordship supped
with the Emperoures embassadores}   ijs.[286]
For iiij torches whan your lordship wennt to my
Lord Ambrose in his sicknes}   iiijs.
Item delyverid to Empson for torches}   ijs.
Item delyverid unto Archicrag for his expences
being sennt unto Eltham in your lordship's message}   ijs. vjd.
Item paid unto George Lovel's wiffe of Kewe for
suche stuff as was occupied of hers at the banquet
theare}   xviijd.
Item for the charge of Ph[ilip]e Wattie and
Thomas Harlam in the barge coming with your
lordship's stuff}   xijd.
"Item for my charges at Kewe and divers others of
your lordship's men}   xijs."

[fo. 20]
Item paid for ij paier of black silke [*sic*]
bought at William Holbornes the xxvij of November
at liij*s.* iiij*d.* the paier}   vli. vjs. viijd.
Item one paier of neytherstocks of russet
For a paier of velvet breaches pulled oute with
clothe of sylver}   liijs. iiijd.[287]

December Anno Tercio Dominae Reginae
Item for banqueting stuff bought whan the
Scottishe embassador dyned with your lordship
at Whitehall}   xiiijs. vjd.[288]

[286] There was no Imperial ambassador in England in November 1560, see n. 239
above. The entry has either been misplaced from November or December 1559 or
'Emperoures' is a mistake for Scottish, see below.
[287] Machyn (p. 245) recorded 'a grett fray' at the Court between Leicester's servants
and 'Harbard's men' on 30 November, but no record of it can be found in this account.
[288] William Maitland of Lethington and the Earls of Morton and Glencairn had arrived
in early November to propose the marriage of the Earl of Arran to Elizabeth. Elizabeth
finally gave them a negative answer on 8 December, and they left a week or so later.
According to Jones (to Throckmorton, 30 Nov., see n. 285 above), the Scots held a dinner
for the Council on 26 November (Leicester being with them) and then they were dined
at the Earl of Pembroke's on the 28th and at the Earl of Bedford's on another occasion.
The entry on p. 165 below probably refers to the dinner on the 26th. This entry would
appear to be to one of the series of reciprocation, presumably in early December.

Item for a glasse of roose water}	xd.
For ij men helping George Cooke in the kytchen}	ijs.
Item for one case of knyves typped with sylver}	vijs.
Item paid unto Mr Doctor Nevison for his paynes cominge to the Courte to take recognizance of your lordship and others viij French crownes, suma}	xlviijs.[289]
For rose water to William Cooke}	vjd.
Paid unto the sryvenner that drewe the bonnd between your lordship and Thomas Rivett mercer} <Thomas Holme>	iijs. iiijd. ob.[290]
Item paid unto Mrs Dane for the hemminge of ix dousen of napkynes}	ixs. vjd.
Paid unto William Holborne habberdassher for a paier of swete gloves}	xxxjs.
Item paid unto Christopher mylloner for roose water at severall tymes}	iijs. vjd.
Item for iiij douzen of rybbon poynts}	vs. iiijd.
Item for a warmmynge pann}	iiijs.
Item for a hatt bought for your lordship and the monney disbursed by Mr Sawle}	xs.
Item for banqueting stuff bought against Christmas}	xxxs.
Item paid unto Best habberdassher for a payer of swete gloves}	xxiiijs.
Item delyverid unto Richard Fawconer* for his charges beinge sennt to Walthame Forrest}	xxd.

[fo. 20v]

Item delyverid unto Glasiour's boye John Allayne and others for apples, peares and other fruites bought by them at sondry tymes}	vjs. viijd.

January Anno Tercio Reginae

°Paid for a coole baskett lyned with leather}	ijs. iiijd.
Item for a realme of browne paper}	ijs. ijd.°
Item paid unto Lewes for mending your lordship's dagg}	xxs.
Item for the bringing of a counter to your lordship's chamber}	vs.

Assuming the singular is not a slip, the reference is probably to Maitland, who knew Leicester from his previous embassies in 1559-60 (see DP I, fo. 164, Arran to Leicester, 28 Sept. 1560).

[289] Probably those for the loan with William Byrde, see n. 200 above.

[290] This bond does not correspond to the dates of his loans from Revett entered on pp. 113-4 above.

February Anno Predicto

For iij quarters of a pound of peaches of Jenoway [Genoa] at vj*s*. viij*d*. the pound}	vs.
For viij *oz*. of plomes of Jenoway at x*s*. the pound}	vs.
Item for a buckler for your lordship}	iiijli.
For ij*ll*. iij *qtr*. of Jenowaies at vj*s*. viij*d*. the *ll*.}	xviijs. iiijd.
For one pound di of plomes of Jenoway at x*s*. the pound, suma}	xvs.

[fo. 21]

Item delyverid to Mr Yorke for a wryte against Heughe Elles}	xvs.[291]
Item for mending your lordship's clocke}	xijs.

March Anno Tercio Reginae

Paid for faggots occupied at Androwe Westones howse joyner in the tyme of Mr Blunt's being theare for the audyt}	viijs. xd.[292]
Item for beare theare at sondry tymes}	xvjd.
Item for viij quyer of paper occupied theare}	iijs. iiijd.
Item for ynnke occupied theare}	xd.
Item for quylles and pennes}	iiijd.
For one quyer of royall paper}	xvd.
Item for a standishe}	ijs. viijd.
Item for one paier of neytherstocks of whight}	lxs.

April Anno Predicto

Item delyverid unto Thomas Harlame for russhes against Ester}	iijs.
Item paid unto a stranger for ij payer of netherstocks for your lordship}	vli. vs.
Item geavin in earnest to Mondaye for silke for a paier of whight hose for your lordship}	xs.
Item paid for [a] scabberd bought for your lordship by Mr Kynnyat in October last}	iiijs.
Item one paier of neytherstocks of crymson for old velvet breeches, cost}	lxs.
Item for a paier of other crymson hoose and mending of other hoose at severall tymes as appearethe by the bill}	vli. xvjs. viijd.

---

[291] Probably related to the 1559 case over Hemsby, see n. 65.

[292] The audit is discussed in the Introduction, n. 51. For Weston see n. 244 above,

[fo. 21v *blank*]
fo. 22.

Anno Secundo Reginae Elizabethae
REWARDES geavin unto dyvers officers within the Quenes majesties
Housshold by your lordship's appoyntment at New Years Tyde anno
predicto.

To the Celler in reward}	liijs. iiijd.
To the Butterye in reward}	xls.
To the Pantrye in reward}	xls.
To the servants of the said offices}	xvs.
To the Spicery in reward}	xxvjs. viijd.
To the Prevy Kytchen in reward}	xls.
To the Lordes Kitchen in reward}	xls.
To the Quenes Side Hall place}	xls.
To the children of all sides}	xxxiijs. iiijd.
To the turnebroches of all sides}	viijs. iiijd.
To the porters and scowrers of all sides}	iijs. vjd.
To the Powltrye and Scaulding House}	xls.
To the Boyling Housse}	xs.
To the servants theare}	xijd.
To the Scullarye}	xls.
To the servants in reward}	iijs. iiijd.
To the Woodyerd in reward}	xls.
To their servants}	iijs. iiijd.
To the Pitcherhousse in reward}	vs.
To their servants in reward}	xijd.
To the Pastrye in reward}	xxs.
To thear servants in reward}	ijs. vjd.
To the Larders in reward}	xxvjs. viijd.
To their servants}	iijs. iiijd.
To the Chaundry in reward}	vjs. viijd.
To the Conffecyonary in reward}	vjs. viijd.
To the servants theare}	xijd.
To the Wasserye in reward}	vs.
To the Accatrye in reward}	xiijs. iiijd.
To the porters in reward}	xls.
To their servants}	iijs. iiijd.
To the carte takers in reward}	xxs.
To their servants}	ijs.
To the Harbingers in reward}	xls.
To the Ewery in reward}	xxvjs. viijd.
To their servants in reward}	ijs. vjd.

[fo. 22v]

To the Prevy Bakehousse in reward}	xxs.
To the armers in reward}	vjs. viijd.
To the swepers of the housse}	vjd.
To the yeomen of the Counting House}	xs.
To the Great Bakehousse in reward}	xxs.

The Chamber

The Wardrobe in reward}	xls.
To their servants in reward}	ijs. vjd.
To the groomes of the Chamber}	xxvjs. viijd.
To the pages of the Chamber}	xls.
To the vyolantes in reward}	lxjs. viijd.
To the shagbuttes in reward}	xls.
To the flutes in reward}	liijs. iiijd.
To the bagpipes in reward}	xxs.
To Blynd Moore in reward}	xs.
To the trompetts in reward}	lxjs. viijd.
To the drompe and phiphe}	xxvjs. viijd.
To the herrauldes in reward}	lxjs. viijd.
To the hobboyes in reward}	xxs.

[fo. 23]

REWARDES geavin unto sondry persons by your lordship's appointment from the xxijth daie of December in the second yeare of the Quenes majesties raigne unto the last daye of Aprell in the thirde yeare of her highnes's raigne as hereafter doth appeare, viz in}

December Anno Secundo Reginae

IN REWARD unto William Whittles servants the xxvth daie of December}	xijs. viijd.
To Sir Moryce Barkleyes man presenting your lordship with a doo}	vjs. iiijd.[293]

January Anno Predicto

IN REWARD the first of January to William Whittles servants}	xijs. viijd.
To George Woodhousse* in reward the monney dysbursed by Mr Hide}	xxs.
To Mr Huttones man presenting your lordship a	

---

[293] Sir Maurice Berkeley (c.1512–81) of Bruton, Som., MP.

hawke the money dysbursed by Mr Hide}   xxs.[294]
To Mr Cutteller* your lordship's man in reward
the monney dysbursed by Mr Duddley}   xxxvijs. viijd.
To the armorer of Grenewiche bringing your lordship's
privy coote to be assaied}   vjs.[295]
To my Lord Riches man presenting oysters}   ijs.[296]
To my Lord Mayor's man presenting a galmon of bakon}   iijs. iiijd.[297]
To my Lady Throgmorton's man for presenting your
lordship with a doo}   vjs. iiijd.[298]
To one of Wyndsor Forrest presenting your lordship
with a hynde}   xs.[299]
To Barnes of Waltham Forrest presenting your
lordship with a hinde}   vjs. iiijd.

[fo. 23v]
To Hannsse your lordship's man in his sicknes
by your lordship's commandment}   xxs.
To Sir William Petres man presentinge to your
lordship a pedegree}   xxs.[300]
To my Lady Dudleis man presenting your lordship
with a cheese}   ijs. vjd.[301]
To Mr Musgraves man presenting a horsse to
your lordship}   xls.[302]

---

[294] Probably John Hutton (d.1591) of Dry Drayton, Cambs, MP. Leicester described his servant Robert Hutton* in 1562 as 'the younger brother of John Hutton of Cambridgeshire', FSL, MS Xc 34, to Throckmorton, 20 April 1562 (a transcription of this letter is calendared in *CSPF, 1561-2*, 617). There is a further reference to Hutton on p. 225 below.

[295] A coat of mail to be worn under ordinary clothing. This entry would suggest that Leicester was taking seriously the various rumours of plots against him in the winter of 1559-60.

[296] Richard, 1st Lord Rich (c.1496-1567), for his son and grandson see n. 347 below.

[297] William Hewet, see n. 263 above.

[298] Probably Sir Nicholas Throckmorton's wife, see n. 95 above.

[299] Leicester had been appointed Lieutenant of Windsor Castle on 24 November 1559 (*CPR, 1558-9*, 324), after the Marian Constable, Sir Francis Englefield, had gone into exile. Englefield was later dismissed and Leicester appointed Constable on 23 February 1562 (*CPR, 1560-3*, 310).

[300] Sir William Petre (1506/7-72), Privy Councillor and former Secretary of State, MP. See also Emmison, *Tudor Secretary*. His son, Sir John Petre, is referred to on pp. 339, 343-4 below.

[301] Probably Katherine (Bridges), wife of Edward Sutton, 4th Lord Dudley (d.1586). See 'West Midlands', 29, 31, 39, for his relations with Leicester.

[302] (Sir) Simon Musgrave (d.1597) of Eden Hall, Cumb., MP. Musgrave was a former servant of Northumberland's, for his relations with Leicester see 'Dudley Clientèle', p. 113, and 'House of Commons', 227. Musgrave acknowledged a letter from Leicester on 6 March (DP, I, fo. 118). The Musgraves were related by marriage to the Yanwith Dudleys (see John Dudley*) and thus part of a wider Cumbrian connection, which included Thomas Warcop and Thomas Aglionby.

To one that kept one of the Quenes majesties
jennetts}   vjs. iiijd.
To Mr Walgrave, captain, at his departing towards
Berwick by your lordship's command}   vli.[303]

February Anno Secundo

To my Lord Mayor's man presenting old peares}   ijs. vjd.
To a poore woman presenting your lordship
with a carnacion gilliflower the xvjth daie}   ijs.
To Archicrage in reward by your lordship's
commandment}   xviijd.
To Robotham bokebynder presenting your lordship
with bookes the xxth daie of February}   xls.[304]
To my Lord Riches man presenting oysters}   ijs.
To Poweles daughter presenting peares}   ijs. vjd.
To the Herraulds of Armes in reward whan
your lordship and my Lord of Hunesden were calling}   xls.
To the trompetres the same tyme}   xxs.
To Mr Young's man presenting a rynlet of
renish wynne}   vjs. iiijd.
To Griffith Clunne by your lordship's commandment
whan he was hurte}   xxs.

[fo. 24]
To Mr Cooper presenting a wheat eare of goold the
xxiiijth of February}   xijs. viijd.
To Barnes' man of Waltham forest presenting woodcocks
and partridges}   xxd.

March Anno Secundo Regni Reginae

[303] Presumably the same man whose child was christened in May, see p. 166 below.
He was probably John Walgrave, who in 1551 had been a man at arms in the Duke of
Somerset's retinue (BL, Egerton MS 2815), and later served at Le Havre.

[304] There is also a reference to the £6 4s 'which my Lord did will me to pay to Randall
Tyler a bookbynder for Italian books delyvered at Christchurche in the iiij year of Q.
Mary [1556–7]' in an undated bill, DP Box V, fo. 3. The two references are of some
importance to H.M. Nixon's study of the bindings of Leicester's books, see his essay
'Elizabethan Gold-Tooled Bindings', in D.E. Rhodes (ed.), *Essays in Honour of Victor
Scholderer* (Mainz, 1970), pp. 219–70, esp. 226–9. Nixon has divided the bindings into four
classes and dated the first two, the 'cartouche' and the 'frame' bindings, c. 1558 and c.
1560. These would fit the dates of the two references quite neatly, except that none of
the surviving books in cartouche bindings are Italian, while a number of those in frame
bindings are.

To Mr Basshes man presenting beef and neates toungs}   xs.[305]
To my Lord Riches man presenting oysters}   ijs.
To my Lord Admyrales man in reward the vijth
daie of Marche}   xs.
To Gyttenes* presenting a seale and puffens}   ijs.
To your lordship's cater taking the dogg oute
of the water}   iiijd.
To Mr Sheldones man in reward coming with message unto
your lordship}   ijs.[306]
To an Itallian captain presenting your lordship
with a swerd the xth of March}   vjli. iijs. iiijd.
To my Lord Riches man presenting oysters}   xxd.
To Sir Gyles Pooles man presenting your lordship
with lamprie pies}   xijs. iiijd.[307]
To Anthonny the fidler in reward}   xijd.
To dyvers poore folkes in almes the xvijth
daie of Marche}   xvjd.
To Mr Westwoodes man in reward the xviijth of March}   vjs. iiijd.
To poore folks the same daie in almes}   ijs. ijd.
To one that brought the monney won at tennys
in my Lord of Sussex's side}   xxiiijs. viijd.
To my Lord Riches man presenting oysters}   ijs.
To Hales' wiffe of Kewe the xviiith daie of
Marche in reward}   vjs. iiijd.

[fo. 24v]
To dyvers carpenters at Kewe with whome your
lordship bargayned for certayne wurke to be don
theare in reward to them}   vs.
To the woman that keapith Master Bakon's house at Kewe}   xijd.
To my Lord of Hunsden's man presenting your lordship
with carpes}   xs.
To the armorer of Grenewiche whan your lordship
shuld have runn at Whit hale for the bringing of your
armor and mending your head peec being broken}   xs.[308]
To Mr Gryce for monney by hym dysbursed by your

---

[305] Edward Bashe (c.1507–87), Surveyor of Naval Victuals, MP. See also the entry to dining with Bashe on 10 February 1561 on p. 166.
[306] Probably over mustering of soldiers in Worcestershire
[307] Sir Giles Poole (1517–89) of Sapperton, Gloucs., MP. Poole served at St Quentin; in the 1570s he assisted Leicester in the Berkeley law suit (see 'West Midlands', 47–8) and hunted regularly at Kenilworth. His son, Sir Henry, is referred to on p. 216, n. 461 below.
[308] See n. 268 above.

lordship's command}	vs.
To a stopper at Whitehall the monney dysbursed by Mr Darcy}	xijd.
To a poore old man in almes}	ijs.
To the keper of the lyones in reward}	iijs. iiijd.
To the wurkmen of the Mynt}	vs.
To a trompeter at the Tower}	iijs. iiijd.
To iij pore women at the iij Cranes in almes}	vjd.[309]
To certayne laberers wurking uppon a bridg by Heughe Brystos housse}	xijd.
To Harry Johannes in reward by your lordship's commandment for a paier of hoose}	xijs. viijd.
To Mr Creek your lordship's chaplayne in reward}	xls.[310]
To a marker at the tennys court at Whighthall the xxvth daie of Marche}	xijd.
To my Lord of Arundel's man presenting a redd deare}	xijs. iiijd.
To my Lord Admyrales man presenting your lordship with a doo}	xijs. iiijd.
To Whittles servants in reward the last daie of Marche}	xijs. iiijd.

[fo. 25]

April Anno Secundo Regni Reginae

In reward unto Mr Basshes man presenting beef and neetes toungs}	vs.
To a pore woman presenting aples}	vs.
To Mr Cobham for monney by [him] disbursed to the poore at Detfford}	xijd.[311]
To my Lord Admyrales bargemen by Partrege at your lordship's commandment}	vs.
To my Lord Riches man presenting oysters}	ijs.
To Mr Barley's man presenting venison}	xs.
To one that presented ij rackets}	xs.
To ij stoppers in the tennys courte at Whight halle the second daie of Aprell}	xs.[312]

[309] Three Cranes Wharf near the Vintry.

[310] Alexander Craik (d. 1564), an émigré Scot, who had been a chaplain of Northumberland's and a Marian exile. He was nominated Bishop of Kildare in May 1560 and died in Ireland. See also 'Dudley Clientèle', p. 255.

[311] See n. 269 above.

[312] On 9 April La Quadra complained that the Queen had failed to attend an important meeting on the previous day on the ground that she was indisposed, but in fact had gone to watch Leicester playing tennis (Lettenhove, ii, p. 304, to the Bishop of Arras).

To Mr Marshall in reward by your lordship's commandment accompaninge an Italian captaine to Windsor}	xxs.
To a pore woman presenting your lordship with a nosegaye at the Privy Chamber dore}	iijs. iiijd.
To Barnes presenting a hobby}	xs.
To a stopper at the tennys courte the vj daie of Aprell}	ijs.
To Mr Barley's man presenting ij phesaunts}	vs.
To Robert Sympsome Sir William Stanley's man by your lordship's commandement}	xxs.
To a pore woman presenting leamons and oringes in reward}	iijs. iiijd.
To the Marques of Elverstones man in reward by your lordship's commandment the monney delyverid to Mr Granado}	lxjs. viijd.[313]
To sondry of your lordship's yeomen in reward by your lordship's commandment}	vjs.[314]
To my Lord of Bedford's man presenting aples}	iijs. iiijd.
To Mr Petre Vanes sone presenting pigeons}	iijs. iiijd.
To one presenting your lordship with stonebowes}	xs.
To a pore woman in reward}	iiijd.
To Mrs Arundeles man for presenting swete water}	ijs. vjd.[315]
To my Lord of Westmerland's [man?] presentinge your lordship with a cast of leoneetts}	lxiiijs.

[fo. 25v]

To Thomas Langham* by your lordship's commandment when he was prysonner}	xls.
To Mr Thomas Duddley for monney by him dysbursed for a hawke}	xixs.
To a stopper at the tennys courte the xjth daie of Aprell}	xijd.
To Sir William Sentloyes man presenting a lampree}	vjs. viijd.[316]
To Mr Nichasius Clerke of the Sighnet for a	

---

[313] Count Helffenstein, see n. 239 above. Mr Granado was Bernardine Grenado, the nephew of Sir Jacques Grenado; both were Flemings and Equerries of the Stables by 1552 (BL, Stowe MS 571, fo. 37v). Sir Jacques was a favourite of the Duchess of Lorraine and was killed in a famous riding accident on 4 May 1557. Leicester sent Bernardine Grenado to buy horses in the Netherlands in the summer of 1559, a mission that was believed by the Spanish authorities to be a cover for reviving diplomatic contact with the Duchess. There are numerous references to this mission in *CSPF, 1559–60*; see also DP I, fos. 50, 72, Grenado to Leicester, 27 July, 23 Aug. 1559.

[314] Presumably at Easter (14 April) as in 1559.

[315] Presumably Mrs Arundel the tavern-owner, see n. 80 above.

[316] Sir William St Loe (c.1518–1565), Captain of the Guard from 1559, MP.

Prevy Seale}	lxijs. iiijd.[317]
To Mr Hide in monney to be distributed unto the poore}	xls.
To Mr Knolles' man for monney by hym dysbursed for pidgeons}	xxd.
To the children of the Chappell in reward the xiiijth daie of Aprell}	xijs. iiijd.[318]
To Poweles daughter for presenting peares}	ijs.
To Swan of the Garde presenting a calf}	xjs. viijd.
To one presenting a redd deare the xiiijth daye of Aprell being Ester day}	vjs. iiijd.
To a stopper viz Fletcher at the tennys courte at Whight Halle}	iijs. iiijd.
To certayne waterman [*sic*] in reward whan your lordship dyned at the Duke of Holkest's}	ijs.
To my Lord Hastings' man presentinge your lordship with a greyhound}	xxs.[319]
To an olde man sometyme your lordship's father's porter uppon a supplicacion delyverid}	xixs.
To Mr Tamwurthe for monney by him dysbursed to your lordship's bargemen}	xs.
To a porewoman in almes}	xxd.
To Mr Duddley for money by him geavin in almes the xxvth of Aprell}	xviijd.
To Mr Hugganes for a crane presented and the reward to him delyverid}	xiijs. iiijd.
To Mr John Dudley for money by him dysbursed in almes the xxvijth of Aprell}	xijd.
To the gardynner of Chelsey for flowers by him presented}	iijs. iiijd.

[fo. 26]

To the Captain of the Gardes man presenting a lampree pye}	ijs.
To the children of the Chappell the xxixth daye of Aprell in reward by your lordship's commandment}	vjs. iiijd.
To Henry Johanes your lordship's man beinge hurt to him in reward}	xls.

[317] Nichasius Yetswert (d. c. 1587), Secretary for the French Tongue.
[318] The Chapel Royal.
[319] Both Hastings and his father, the 2nd Earl of Huntingdon, wrote to Leicester on 9 April (DP I, fos. 133, 135) to support a suit of William Stokes (see n. 352 below).

May Anno Secundo Regni Reginae

To my Lord of Hunesdenes man for presenting your lordship with a doo the vjth of May}	vjs. iiijd.
To Poweles daughter presentinge aples}	xijd.
To Mr Hordeynes man presenting aples}	ijs. vjd.
To the Duches of Suffolkes man presenting rennyshe wyne}	xixs.[320]
To a fawlconner presenting a hawke}	xijs. viijd.
To Sir James Stompes man presenting your lordship with lampres and bakon}	ijs. vjd.
To Ph[ilip]e Wattie in reward}	xijd.
To a stopper at the tennys courte the xijth daie of May}	ijs.
To my Lord Maior's man presenting a singing blackburd}	vjs. ijd.
To Mr Bigottes man in reward for bringing upp of Hemmesbye rennt}	xxs.
To John Burnell Mr Lewces servant in reward}	xls.[321]
To the keper of the gardeyne at Whight halle in reward for strawing erbes}	viijd.
To the gromes of the stable in reward by your lordship's commandment by Mr Barbor}	xijd.
To a poore woman in almes the monney dysbursed by Mr Gylmer* the xvjth of May}	iijs. iiijd.

[fo. 26v]

To my Lord Cobhames man presentinge a connger and a brett in reward}	vjs. ijd.
To Mr Holcrofte Sir William Ciceles servant for bringing the Privy Seale for your lordship's lycence}	xxs.[322]

June Anno Secundo Reginae

To [blank] Demhames men goldsmithe in reward by your lordship's commandment}	xxs.
To my Lady Carooes man presenting cheese}	ijs. vjd.

[320] Katherine (Willoughby), dowager Duchess of Suffolk (1519–80). She had been a friend of the Duchess of Northumberland and god-mother to one of her daughters (see n. 35 above and S.J. Gunn, *Charles Brandon, Duke of Suffolk 1484–1545* (Oxford, 1988), p. 198). Two of her letters to Leicester in 1559–60 survive (DP I, fos. 90, 125), the latter (March 1560), petitioning for mercy for Lord Wentworth, the former governor of Calais.

[321] (Sir) Thomas Lucy (1532–1600) of Charlecote, Wars., MP. Lucy attended Leicester's funeral, for their relations, see 'West Midlands', 44, and p. 295 below. Only one letter from Lucy survives, dated only 8 April (DP I, fo. 95), but since it refers to sending Burnell (who was an archer), it can be assigned to 1560 on the basis of this entry.

[322] Thomas Holcroft (d.1591), MP. The licence was probably the wool export licence, see n. 215 above.

To Poweles daughter presenting straberyes and creame in reward}	vs.
To Sir John York's scolemaster of his children in reward the viijth of June}	lxxiiijs.
To Thomas Davies in reward by your lordship's commandment being sicke}	xxs.
To the gardyner of Chelsey for roses}	iijs. iiijd.
To Ferne my Lord Marques's man presenting your lordship with a crosebowe}	vjs. ijd.
To the cookes of the Quenes majesties Houshold for bringing in the with} [sic]	ls.
To the post of Andwerpe for the bringing of letters and silke hoose from George Gylpin}	iijs. iiijd.[323]
To a pore man in reward the monney dysbursed by Mr Gylmer}	iijs. iiijd.
To Mr Holbornes servant the habberdasher for his botehier and paynes in cominge to Grenewich with glasses to your lordship}	xijd.
To Barnes' man of Waltham Forrest presentinge ij lyve hares}	ijs.

[fo. 27]

July Anno Predicto

To the under keper of Eltham Parke the monney dysbursed by Mr Power*}	ijs.
To Archicrage your lordship's foteman in reward the vijth of July by your lordship's commandment vij pistoles}	xliijs. ijd.
To the cookes of the Prevy Kytchen at Grennewich dysbursed by Mr Gylmer whan your lordship supped theare}	vjs. viijd.
To the keper of the kytchen dore}	vjd.
To Mr Buttler for a caste of tasselles presented unto your lordship}	xls.
To Christopher Hilliard for presenting your lordship with ij mares and ij coltes}	xls.[324]

[323] George Gilpin (1514–1602), secretary to the Merchant Adventurers. Fragments of an extensive correspondence survive, largely concerned with Netherlands news, though not this letter. The series begins with a letter of 6 March 1559 (DP I, fo.11), the earliest to Leicester extant; according to a later one (fo. 31, 15 July 1559) the correspondence was begun at Leicester's request. The silk hose was probably for the Queen and may have been sent by Gresham, see Gresham to Leicester, 18 Aug. (DP I, fo. 155).

[324] Christopher Hilliard (c.1523–1602) of Winestead, Yorks., MP.

To Mr Younge for money disbursed by him to John
Fletcher by your lordship's commandment}   xijs. viijd.
To Dearynng my Lord Lumleyes man presenting your
lordship with ij buckes against the Mercers' Feast
[Drapers Haule *deleted*]}   xijs. iiijd.[325]
To the keper's wiffe of Grenewiche for the keaping of
a fawne}   xs.

Auguste Anno Secundo Dominae Reginae
To my Lord Hastings' man presentinge your lordship
at Richemond with a redd deare baked}   vjs. iiijd.[326]
To Sir Percyvale Lyes man presenting your lordship
at Richmound with a redd deare baked}   vjs. iiijd.

[fo. 27v]

September Anno Secundo Regni Reginae
To Jennings William Whittles servant for his
botehier and paynes cominge to Kewe to take
measure of your lordship}   iijs. iiijd.
To Clarentius and other the herraulds for theare
paynes takinge at my ladies buryall in reward to them}   vli.
To one that sewed to have bin your lordship's
foteman to him in reward}   xixs.
To him that presented Mr Chitwood's armor to your
lordshipe in reward}   xixs.[327]

October Anno Predicto
To Sir Rauff Egertones man for presenting your
lordship with cheeses}   vs.[328]

November Anno Predicto
To Archicragge in his sicknes by your lordship's
commandment in reward and the monney sennt unto
him by Parteridge}   xixs.

---

[325] The Mercers' Feast was held on 22 July, see p. 165 below. John, 6th Lord Lumley
(1533/4–1609), was Arundel's son-in-law, and lived with him at Nonsuch Palace (see n.
140 above). Frequent references to Lumley and Nonsuch will be found in the 1584–6
disbursement book.
[326] This was probably Lord Hastings of Loughborough (see n. 35 above), for Henry,
Lord Hastings, had succeeded his father as Earl of Huntingdon on 23 June.
[327] Richard Chetwoode (d. Jan. 1560), MP, formerly a Gentleman of the Privy Chamber
to Edward VI. Leicester was an executor of his will.
[328] Sir Ralf Egerton of Wrinehall, Staffs. He attended Leicester's funeral.

To [*blank*] Barnes' man presenting wildfowle}   ijs.
To the gardyner of Hampton Courte}   iijs. iiijd.
To Everard the gooldsmithe for his paynes
takinge in cominge to Grenewich to see a juell for
your lordship}   xviijs.

[fo. 28]

December Anno Tercio Regni Reginae

To [*blank*] man in reward by your lordship's commandment}   xls.
To iij pore women in almes the monney dysbursed by
John Awdwyne}   xijd.
To my Lord Windsores man in reward}   xxs.[329]
To Sir Anthony Cookes man for the presenting
your lordship with a doo whan yow dyned at Mr Byrd's}   xijs.[330]
To Maynard the hossier's servantes in reward the
xxvth daie of December}   xs.
To John Trompeter in reward the xxvth of December}   xiijs. iiijd.
To Richard Evan drompe plaior in reward
the said daie}   xs.
To John Johnson the phiphe in reward the said daye}   xs.
To Mr Cutteler your lordship's man in reward by
your lordship's commandment}   lxvjs. viijd.

January Anno Predicto

To John Trompeter for tothe pickeres and playing
[*before* deleted] over New Yeres Daye}   xxs.
To Richard Evan drompe playor the same daie in reward}   vs.
To John Johnson phiphe the same day}   vs.
To the Frencheman that kept the Quenes majesties
mulets in consideracion of his goods lost by the
casualty of fyer}   vjli. xiijs. iiijd.[331]

[fo. 28v]

[329] Edward, 3rd Lord Windsor (1532–75). There was a distant family connection created by Edmund Dudley's first marriage to Anne, sister of the 1st Lord Windsor. The 3rd baron served at St Quentin and later went into semi-exile in Venice.

[330] Sir Anthony Cooke (c.1505–76) of Gidea Hall, Essex, MP. The dinner with Byrde took place on 22 December, see p. 165 below and n. 200 above.

[331] These may have been the mules that Leicester purchased for the Queen through Throckmorton in 1559, see DP I, fo. 58, Throckmorton to Leicester, 2 Aug. 1559.

February Anno Tercio Dominae Reginae

To Mr George Woodhousse the vjth daie of February in reward}	xls.
To [*blank*] man in reward by your lordship's commandment}	xxs.
To Henry Mannesfeald in reward at his going to Barwik}	vjli.
To Archicrage at his goinge in to Fraunce by your lordship's commandment}	lxxijs.[332]
To a pore woman presenting your lordship with ij carnacion gilliflowers}	ijs.

March Anno Predicto
[*blank*]
April Anno Predicto

To Benedic Spynolas man the iiijth daye of Aprell presenting banqueting stuff}	xxxs.

[fo. 29]

Monney paid unto Mr Thomas Duddley for sondry rewards geavin by him at your commandment as by the bills of the particulars appeareth and heare after rehearsed, viz}

To iij women presenting your lordship with orinjes and flowers}	xvs.
To the Sergeant of the Buckhounds for lyenes and collers presented to your lordship}	xxiiijs. viijd.
To Sir William Woodhouses man}	vjs. viijd.[333]
To the Vycount Harryford's man}	xijs. iiijd.[334]
To Mrs Coo presenting a wheat yeare of goold}	[xijs. *deleted*] xxs.
To a poore man presenting peares}	iijs. iiijd.
To Lovell keper of Rychemond Gardeyne}	iijs. iiijd.
To Edmund Mr Threasorer's man presentinge leamons}	xijs. iiijd.
To your lordship's launder presenting a galmon of bakon}	vjs. iiijd.
To my Lord Admyrales man presenting venyson}	ijs. vjd.
To one presenting one dousen and a half of pidgeons}	vjs. iiijd.
To Mr Vaughanes Mr [*sic*] presenting woodcocks}	xijd.
To my Lord Maior's man presenting peares}	ijs. vjd.

---

[332] This entry would appear to be misplaced. On 22 January Throckmorton wrote angrily to Cecil to complain about Archie Craig's arrival in France on the 20th, ostensibly on personal business; Throckmorton believed he was on a political errand, though it is not clear what this was. See PRO, SP 70/22/119, calendared in *CSPF, 1560– 61*, 512.

[333] Sir William Woodhouse (1517–64) of Hickling, Norf., MP.

[334] Walter Devereux (1539–76), 2nd Viscount Hereford, 1st Earl of Essex in 1572. In 1562 he married Lettice Knollys, the future Countess of Leicester.

To the Gromeporter's man presentinge of byrds}   xijd.
To my Lord Hastings' man presentinge heromies and
shovelles}   vjs. iiijd.
To Mr Bower Master of the children of the Chappell}   xixs.
To younge Mr Zouche in reward}   xijs. viijd.
To a pore man unto whome your lordship
promesed a gowne}   vjs. iiijd.
To the keper of Hervord Gayoll}   xxs.[335]

[fo. 29v *blank*]
fo. 30. <Anno Tertio Regni Reginae>
REWARDES geavin unto dyvers officers within the Quenes majesties
Howsehold against New Yeares tyde in the third yeare of her Highnes's
raigne by your lordship's appointment}
IN REWARD to the Celler}   liijs. iiijd.
To the Butterye in reward}   xls.
To the Pantery in reward}   xls.
To the servants of the said offices}   xvs.
To the Spicery in reward}   xxvjs. viijd.
To their servants}   vjs. viijd.
To the Privy Kytchen in reward}   xls.
To the Lordes Kytchen}   xls.
To the Quenes Side Halle place}   xls.
To the children of all sides}   xxxiijs. iiijd.
To the turnbroches of all sides}   xxs.
To the porters and scowrers of all sides}   iijs. vjd.
To the Powltery and Scaulding House}   xls.
To their servants}   xijd.
To the Boyling House in reward}   xxs.
To their servants}   xijd.
To the Scullery in reward}   xls.
To their servants}   iijs. iiijd.
To the Woodyerde in reward}   liijs. iiijd.
To their servants}   vs.
To the Pitcherhousse in reward}   vjs. viijd.
To their servants in reward}   xijd.
To the Pastrye in reward}   xls.
To theyr servants in reward}   ijs. vjd.
To the Larders in reward}   xxxiijs. iiijd.
To their servants in reward}   iijs. iiijd.
To the Confecionary in reward}   vjs. viijd.
To their servants in reward}   xijd.

[335] Hertford Gaol?

To the Chaundrye in reward}	xxxs.
To their servants in reward}	ijs.
To the Wasserye in reward}	vs.

[fo. 30v]

To the Accatrye in reward}	xxvjs. viijd.
To the Porters in reward}	xls.
To ther servants in reward}	vjs. viijd.
To the cartt takers in reward}	xxs.
To ther servants in reward}	ijs.
To the Herbingers in reward}	xls.
To the Ewery in reward}	xxvjs. viijd.
To their servants in reward}	ijs. vjd.
To the Privye Bakehouse}	xxs.
To their servants in reward}	xijd.
To the Great Bakehousse}	xxs.
To the armers in reward}	vjs. viijd.
To the yeomen of the Countinghouse}	xs.
To the sweeper of the housse}	vjd.

The Chamber

To the officers of the Wardrobe}	xls.
To their servants in reward}	vs.
To the gromes of the Chamber}	xxvjs. viijd.
To the pages of the Chamber}	xls.
To the vyolaunts}	lxjs. viijd.
To the shagbuttes in reward}	xls.
To the flutes in reward}	liijs. iiijd.
To the bagpipes in reward}	xxs.
To Blynd Moore in reward}	xs.
To the drompe and phiph in reward}	xxvjs. viijd.
To the hobboyes in reward}	xxs.
To the herrauldes in reward}	lxjs. viijd.
To the trompettres in reward}	[*blank*]

[fo. 31]

Paymennts for dynners and suppers at sondry tymes whan your lordship hath dyned and supped in the Cytty and at other places as hereafter appearethe:

Paid for your lordship's mennes dynners the xth day of January 1559 whan your lordship dyned at the Duke of Fyneland's and they at the Beare at Bridge foote}   xxiiijs.

Paid for their dynners the viijth daye of February whan your lordship dyned at the Duke of Fyneland's and

they at the Beare at Bridge foote, sum}   xviijs.
Paid for their dynners the ixth of February whan
your lordship dyned at the Marques de Traunces}   xiiijs.
Item paid for their dynners the xijth of February
whan your lordship dyned at the Frenche embassador's}   xvs. vjd.[336]
Item paid for your lordship's gentlemen's and yeomen's
dynners whan your lordship dyned at the Tower the xth
daye of Marche}   xxijs. ijd.
Item paid for ther dynners the xvijth of Marche
your lordship dyning with the Marques de Traynes and
they at the Salutacion of our Lady in Tower
Streete, summa}   xxxiijs. vjd.
Item paid for their dynners the xxiiijth of
Marche your lordship dyning with the Emperoures
embassador}   xxiijs. vjd.
Item paid the xviijth daie of February anno
predicto for their dynners whan your lordship
dyned with [sic] at the Lord Mayor's with the
Duke off Fyneland, summa}   [xlijs. deleted]
                                                                           xvjs.

Item paid for their dynners the vj daye of Aprell
your lordship with the Emperoures embassador}   xlijs.
Item paid for their dynners the xvijth day of
Aprell whan your lordship dyned with the Duke of
Fyneland at Grenewich}   xs. iiijd.[337]

[fo. 31v]
Item paid for their dynners the xijth of Aprell
at the Quenes majestie being at Detfford and they
at Grenewiche}   xxiijs.
Item paid for their dynners the xxixth daye of
Aprell your lordship at my Lord Windsores}   xijs.
Item for their dynners the thirde day of May
your lordship at the Countye of Russyes}   xxxviijs.[338]
<per Yerwerth* sol'>
Item for their dynners when your lordship was in
Holborne with my Lord Ambroose in his sicknes}   xijs.
Item paid for their dynners your lordship

---

[336] This may have been a farewell dinner, for Gilles de Noailles was formally replaced
as ambassador by Michel de Seurre on 15 February (*CSPF, 1559–60*, 378).

[337] This must have been a farewell dinner, for the Duke left London on 11 April 1560
(Machyn, 230).

[338] Louis de Luxembourg, Count of Rouci, who replaced one of the original French
hostages on 5 April (*CSPF, 1559–60*, 502).

dyninge with the Earle of Northumberland}   xvs.[339]
Item paid for their dynners the vth day of May
whan your lordship dyned at Mr Stuckeleis and
they in Lombard Streete}   xxijs.[340]
Item for their dynners the xvth of Maye your
lordship at the Lord Maior's}   xviijs.[341]
Item paid for their dynners the ixth day of June
your lordship with the County of Elverston}   xvijs.[342]
Item paid for their dynners the xxjth daie of June
whan your lordship dyned at my Lady Sidney's at Ratcleef}   viijs.
Item paid for their dynners the xth day of July
and your lordship at the Frenche pledges}   xijs.
Item paid for their dynners the xvjth day of July
whan your lordship dyned with Mr Alderman Offelay} xvs.[343]
Item paid for their suppers the xviijth day of July
when your lordship dyned at my Lord of Pennbrokes} xvjs.
Item paid for their suppers the xxijth daye of July
whan your lordship dyned at the Mercers' Feast}   xxjs. vjd.

[fo. 32]
Item paid for your lordship's menes dynners the
xxixth daye of October whan your lordship dyned
at the Mayer's Feast}   xxiiijs.
Item paid for their dynners whan your lordship
dyned at [the] Scottishe embassadors'}   xvijs.
Item paid for your lordship's menes dynners the
xxijth daye of December whan your lordship dyned
at Mr Bird's}   xxs.
Item paid for their dynners whan your lordship
dyned in Powles churche yerd with Sir John Mason, summa}   ixs.[344]
Item paid for their dynners the ixth daye of
February whan your lordship dyned at the

[339] Thomas Percy, 7th Earl (1528–72).

[340] Thomas Stuckley, the later notorious catholic exile, killed in Morocco in 1578. He served at St Quentin, Le Havre and (briefly) under Henry Sidney in Ireland in 1566.

[341] William Hewet, see n. 263 above.

[342] This is must be an error for May, for Gresham reported Helffenstein's departure from Antwerp to Brussels on 29 May, see *CSPF, 1560–61*, 89.

[343] Probably Hugh Offley, leatherseller and alderman, rather than his brother Sir Thomas, merchant taylor and lord mayor 1556–7.

[344] Sir John Mason (1503–66), Treasurer of the Chamber, MP. His wife, Lady Elizabeth Isley, was a relation of the Duchess of Northumberland. He recommended Leicester to Oxford University as his successor as Chancellor in December 1564 (Bodl., University Archives, Convocation Register KK9, fo. 6–v).

Lord Mayor's}   xvijs.[345]
Item paid for their dynners the xth daie of
February whan your lordship dyned at Mr Basshes}   xxiijs.
Item paid for ther dynners whan your lordship
dyned at the Tower}   xviijs.[346]

[fo 32v *blank*]
[fo. 33]
THE charges of christening of soundry children as hereafter appearethe.
Memorandum delyverid to Mr Hugganes the second
day of January anno secondo Reginae for the
christening of Mr Riches child, viz vj pistolets}   xxxvijs.[347]
Item delyverid unto Mr Hugganes the viijth daye of
February for the christening of Sir Thomas
Chamberlayn's child, vj French Crownes}   xxxviijs.[348]
Item delyverid unto Mr Cary the xvijth daye of
March for the christening of [*blank*] a sylver
salt guylt wainge xj *oz*. di *qt*. at viijs. le oz.,
sum iiij*li*. viijs. viij*d*., and in monney delyverid
to him for the same christeninge the some of
lvjs. viij*d*., in toto}   vijli. vs. iiijd.
Item delyverid unto Mr Higham the xxjth of May
in the second yeare of the Quenes majesties
raigne for the christening of Mr Walgraves
child, viz a sylver salte guylt wainge x *oz*.
iij *qtres*. which cost iiij*li*., and in monney for
his charges xxs., in toto}   vli.
Item more delyverid unto Mr Hugganes the
xxiiijth daie of July for the christening
of [*blank*], the some of}   lxs.
Item delyverid unto Sir Henry Sidney knight for
the christening of my Lord of Hunesdones child
the some of one hundreth crownes at vjs. iiijd.

---

[345] This dinner took place after Leicester, Cecil and various councillors had heard
James Pilkington, the newly elected Bishop of Durham, preach at Paul's Cross, see
Machyn, 248.
[346] This may have been have been the Garter feast, which was held on 18 February
1561, see Machyn, 250.
[347] The future 2nd Lord Rich (1537–81), from whom Leicester purchased Wanstead
House in 1578, see Introduction, p. 26. His child was Robert, 3rd Lord Rich (1559/60–
1619) and later 1st Earl of Warwick, who was an assistant mourner at Leicester's funeral.
[348] Sir Thomas Chamberlain (1504–80), MP, ambassador in Spain 1560–1. According
to Machyn (p. 216) the christening of Chamberlain's son took place on 27 October 1559,
the other godfather being the Duke of Finland. He has been identified as John
Chamberlain (c.1560–1617), MP.

the crowne}   xxxli.[349]

Item delyverid unto Mr Thomas Duddley the xxvth
daye of November for the christeninge of Mr
Richemound's childe}   lxs.

Item delyverid unto Mr Gylmer the iij daie of
January anno tercio regni Reginae for the
christeninge of the gardeyner's child of Chelsey}   xxvjs. viijd.

[fo. 33v]
Item delyverid unto Mr Dearynng for the christening
of Mr Fermer's child the vjth day of January anno
predicto}   lijs.

Item delyverid unto your lordship in February anno
predicto at the christeninge of Mr Anslowes child}   xxxs.[350]

[fo. 34]
Monney delyverid unto your lordship at sondry tymes for your owne
pursse as well by myself as by others:

Memorandum delyverid unto your lordship the xxth
daye of January in the second yeare of the Quenes
majesties raigne xxtie pistollets at vj*s*. ij*d*.
the pistollet}   vjli. iijs. iiijd.

Item more delyverid unto your lordship the
xxiiijth daye of January xviij pist[ollets]
& ij Frenche crownes}   vjli. iijs. viijd.

Item the xxvth daie of February by the handes
of John Merbury l pistollets}   xvli. viijs. iiijd.

Item the second daye of Aprell anno predicto
l angeles at x*s*. vj*d*. the angell}   xxvjli. vijs. jd.

Item the xijth daye of Maye delyverid
unto your lordship lx pistollets}   xviijli. xs.

Item the xxiiijth daie of May delyverid unto
your lordship by the handes of William Hugganes
in angels and other goold, suma}   vli. xs. xd.

Item the said xxiiijth daie to your lordship
at the Duke of Holkest's xxiiij pist[ollets]
and vj French crownes, suma}   ixli. vjs.

Item the xxvjth daie by the handes of Mr

[349] Robert Carey (1560–1639), later 1st Earl of Monmouth. Leicester and Sidney are
identified as his godfathers in Hunsdon's notes on his children's nativities, but his date of
birth is not given. Carey was coy about his relationship to Leicester in his autobiographical
memoir, see F.H. Mares (ed.), *The Memoirs of Robert Carey* (Oxford, 1972), pp. 5, 90–1.

[350] Richard Onslow (1527/8–71), MP. The child was probably his heir Robert, who
pre-deceased him. Onslow left a gift to Leicester in his will.

Arundell xxtie French Crownes}   vjli. vjs. viijd.
Item to your lordship the xxviijth of May
one hundreth and too pistolletts going to
Waltham Forest, summa}   xxxjli. ixs.[351]
Item to your lordship the xxiiijth daie
of June whan your lordship plaid at cardes
with Mr Stooks x pistolletts and xiiijs.
viijd. in other money}   lxxvjs. iiijd.[352]
Item the said xxiiijth daye of June for so
muche lost by your lordship to the Duke of
Holkest xx pistolletts, suma}   vjli. iijs. iiijd.

[fo. 34v]
Item more to your lordship the foresaid xxiiijth
daye of June to the handes of my Lord Wyndser
for your lordship, sum xxtie pistolletts}   vjli. iijs. iiijd.
Item to your lordship the xxixth daie of June
xv pistolletts and v French crownes}   vjli. iiijs. ijd.
Item more delyverid unto your lordship the
same daye by Mr Comptroller lxj pistolletts}   xviijli. xvjs. ijd.
Item more the same daye to my Lord of
Penbrok for your lordship l pistolletts}   xvli. viijs. iiijd.
Item the same daye by the handes of Georg
Gyles the some of}   vjs. viijd.
Item the vth daie of July to your lordship
by the handes of Thomas Cornewalles receaved
for monney borroughed of hym, viz xxtie French
crownes & xxtie pistolletts}   xijli. xs.[353]
Item the vijth daie of July delyverid to
your lordship in my Lord Chamberlaynes
chamber Clx pistolletts}   xlixli. vjs. viijd.
Item the xixth daye of July xxtie pistolletts
for so muche monney borroughed of Thomas
Cornewalles}   vjli. iijs. iiijd.
Item delyverid unto your lordship the vijth
daye of November by the handes of Sir Harry
Sidney xviij crownes at vjs. a pece, sum}   vli. viijs.
Item to your lordship the same daye by

---

[351] No other reference to this trip can be found in this account.

[352] Possibly William Stokes (b. 1525) elder brother of Adrian (c.1532–85), MP, for whom Hastings and his father had written in April (see n. 319 above).

[353] Probably Thomas Cornwallis, Gentleman Pensioner 1560, not Sir Thomas (1518/9–1604), MP.

Fowke Grevell xltie crownes}	xiiijli. xjs. viijd.[354]
Item to your lordship the xxth of December	
xxtie pistollets at vs. xd. the pece}	vli. xvjs. viijd.
Item to your lordship the xxijth of December	
at Mr Bird's house xxtie crownes}	vjli.
Item delyverid unto your lordship the	
xxiiijth day of December xxtie pistollets}	vli. xvjs. viijd.

[fo. 35]

Item to your lordship the xxixth of December	
xxtie pistollets at vs. xd. the pece, suma}	vli. xvjs. viijd.
Item the last daye of December by the handes	
of Mr Appliard xxxtie French crownes at vjs.	
the crowne, suma}	ixli.
Item to your lordship the first of January	
xxtie pistollets, suma}	vli. xvjs. viijd.
The second daie of January by the handes of	
John Yerwurth xxtie pistollets}	vli. xvjs. viijd.
The same daye in monney lennt to Mr Riche	
by your lordship's commandment}	xxvs. iiijd.
The viijth daie of January in monney lennt	
to Mr Tamwurth by your lordship's commandment}	vli. xs.
The xiijth daie of January delyverid unto your	
lordship xx pistollets by the handes of	
Mr Tamwurth, suma}	vli. xvjs. viijd.
Item delyverid unto Sir George Howard for	
your lordship which he gave unto one of the	
Privy Chamber the sum of}	iijs. iiijd.[355]
Item to your lordship by Heytherley* of the	
roobes vj crownes and iiij pistollets, suma}	lixs. iiijd.
To Mr Cary in monney to him delivered to	
paye my Lord Marques xxtie crownes}	vjli.
Summa Totalis}	[blank]

[fo. 35v blank]

[fo. 36]

Monney paid for botehier at sondry tymes for the carriage of wyne
and otherwise as appeareth particularly:

Item the xxiiijth daie of December in the second
yeare of the raigne of the Quene for bringing one

---

[354] (Sir) Fulke Greville (1536?-1606) of Beauchamps Court, Wars. See 'West Midlands',
44, for his relations with Leicester. He attended his funeral.
[355] Sir George Howard (d. c. 1580), Master of the Armoury.

rynlett of wyne to the Court at Whight hall}   xijd.
Item to the xxvjth daie of the same moneth for the
carryage of a rynlett of wyne to the Court}   xijd.
Item for the fetching a paier of garters by water}   viijd.
Item for the fetching a flaggon with rhennish wyne}   viijd.
Item for botehier fetching a flaggon of wyne the
xvijth of December}   viijd.
Item for the fetting a rynlet of wyne by water the
xxviijth daie of December to the Court at Whight
halle}   xijd.
Item for botehier the last of December fetting ij
flaggons of wyne}   viijd.
Item for wyne fett by water the vth of January}   viijd.
Item for wyne fett by water the vjth day of January
one rynlet}   xijd.
For wyne fet the viijth of January}   viijd.
For wyne fet the xviijth of January}   xijd.
Item for wyne fett the same [sic]}   viijd.
Item for wyne fett the xxiiijth of January}   viijd.
The first daie of February}   viijd.
The vith of February a rynlet}   xijd.
The viijth daie of February one rynlet}   xijd.
Item the xxijth daie of February a rynlet}   xijd.
Item the xxiijth daie of February a rynlet}   xijd.
The same daie for Mr Duddley's botehier}   xijd.
Item for a pair of garters fett by water for
your lordship}   xijd.
Item for iij whiryes for bringing your lordship's
men to the Duke of Fyneland's}   xijd.

[fo. 36v]
Item for wyne fett by water the first day of
Marche one rynlet}   xijd.
Item for wyne fett by water the iiijth daye of
March in flaggons}   viijd.
Item the viijth of March for wyne fett}   viijd.
Item to Mr Duddley for monney by him dysbursed to
watermen whan your lordship supped in Cannon Rowe
with my Lord of Sussex}   iijs. xd.
To Mr Cary for his botehier being sennt by
your lordship to London}   xijd.
Item the ixth of March for monney delivered to John
Frennchman for botehier}   xijd.
Item wyne fett the xjth of March}   viijd.

Item the xvijth of March for one rynlet fett by
water to the Court}   xijd.
For wyne fett the xviijth of March}   viijd.
Item the same daie for botehier for wyne}   viijd.
Item the xxtie of March}   viijd.
Item for ij whiryes for certayne of your lordship's
yeomen from Westminster to London}   viijd.
Item the xxiijth of March for a whirry for certayne
of your lordship's men}   iiijd.
Item the xxvjth of March for ij whirryes carrying
certayne of your men to Grenewich and agayne to
Whitehale}   iiijs.
Item paid unto John Parterige for monney by your
lordship's commandment to be geavin unto my
Lord Admyrales watermen}   vs.
Item to Mr Duddley the xixth daie of Aprill for
his botehier}   xijd.
Item the same daie to Mr Cary}   viijd.
Item to Thomas Harlame being sennt for Mr Byrd
and Mr Ryvet to come unto your lordship}   viijd.

[fo. 37]
Item for botehier for one being sennt for Davy
Smith embroderer to come unto your lordship}   viijd.
Item for Archicragges botehier beinge sent
for rackets to London}   viijd.
Item the xxvijth of March for a rynlet of wyne
fett by water}   xijd.
Item the xxviijth of March for a flaggon of wyne
fet by water}   viijd.
Item the xxixth of March for wyne fett}   viijd.
Item for muskadell fett by water}   viijd.
For redd wyne fett by water}   viijd.
Item for a rynlet of rennysh wyne that was brought
to Grenewich the xxvijth daie of Aprell}   [iijs. vjd. ob. *deleted*]
                                                                                             xxd.
For claret wyne fet by water to Grenewich}   xiiijd.
The vjth daie of May for ij wheryes to Powles for
certayne of your lordship's men}   viijd.
To Raphe Smithe the Quenes majesties bargeman
for the hier of a barge from Grenewich to
Blackewalle}   xiijs. iiijd.
To Knowles your lordship's man for his botehier
being sennt in your lordship's busynes}   xijd.

Item to Thomas Braybroke the vth daye of July being
sennt for a bowe to London for your lordship}   xijd.

Item to James Acone being sennt to London for bread}   xijd.

Item to Griffithe Lloyde being sennt for biskets and
carrawaies to London}   xijd.

To Archicrage bringing a fawne from Grenewiche to
Westminster}   xvjd.

To Thomas Harlame for his botehier from London to
Grenewich with a bedsteed}   xviijd.

To Oswoold the xxiiijth daie of June being sennt
to London from Grenewich in your lordship's busyness}   xijd.

[fo. 37v]

Item for the carriage of beddes and stooles to
Grenewiche}   ijs. vjd.

Item to William Cure sadler for his botehier being
sent by your lordship in busynes}   xijd.

Item for botehier to one being sennt for russet
satten to London}   xd.

Item paid unto Richard Hillyard beinge sent unto the
Deane of Powles from Greenwich with letters}   ijs.[356]

Item for the carriage of glasiores stuff & the cooks
to Grenewich}   ijs. viijd.

Item for the carriage of oysters and other stuff to
Grenewich by water}   viijd.

Item for botehier to London with letters of your
lordship's}   xxd.

Item for the carriage of stuffe to Grenewich the xvijth
daie of December}   ijs. viijd.

Item for the carriage of banqueting stuff to Eltham
at the Quenes being theare and the wherry man wayting
and carriag of certayne stuff agayne}   iijs. iiijd.

Item to James Acon for his botehier being sennt in
your lordship's busynes}   xijd.

To Mr Thomas Duddley for his botehier fetching
your lordship's armor by water to Grenewiche}   ijs. vjd.

Item paid to Richard Jinks for his botehier being
sennt to Mr York's with a sholder of venison}   xijd.

Item for botehier with letters to Sir Ambrose Cave
at sondry tymes from your lordship}   vijs.[357]

Item for the carriage of vij peeces of tappestry

---

[356] Alexander Nowell (c.1507–1602).
[357] Probably relating to Warwickshire lieutenancy business.

and other stuff from Kewe by Child the waterman}   xxd.
Item to him for the carriage of other stuff to
Westminster from Kewe}   xxd.

[fo. 38]
Item for the bringing of a vessell of seck from Kewe
by water}   iiijs.
Item for the bringing of a cheste by water from Kewe}   ijs.
Item paid for the hier of a westermen barge that
your lordship's apparell and other stuff
from Kewe} [*sic*]   xvs.
Item paid unto Buckland of Kingston for the carriage
of certayne stuff from Kewe at ij severall tymes}   xijs.
Item for the hier of a barge from Kewe for myself,
Richard Jinks and other bringing certayne of the
fynest stuff with us}   xiijs. iiijd.
PGoing for your lordship's stuff and our chargesP

[fo. 38v *blank*]
[fo. 39]q
Delyvered to my Lord Robert Dudley sens the last day in Marche.
Item a sylver band for a hatt}   xvjs.
Item a velvett cap the 16 of Apryll}   xjs.
Item ij velvett night cappes the 23 of May}   xiijs. iiijd.
Item a velvet hatt ymbrothered with gold
for my ladie}   iijli. vjs. viijd.
Item ij velvet cappes fringed with blacke
sylke & sylver & sypres bandes edged with sylver}   xxxijs.
Item ij velvet night cappes scytched frenged the
11 of June}   xiijs. iiijd.
Item for rybbynnyng iiijxx & viii
payer of agletts for a gowene}   vijs. iiijd.
Item a velvet hat of fyne velvet & lynd with taffety}   xvs.
Item a band of damaske sylver}   xxvjs. viijd.
Item for a herons topper sett in a button of sylver}   vjs. viijd.
Item vj cloth cappes & vj copper sylver bandes and
vj white fethers}   xls.
Item for makyng a chrymissin velvet cap for Sir Henry
Sydney's son & a band of copper sylver & a fether &
trymyng it with buttons}   vijs. vjd.358
Item for cuttyng out and makyng his hatt ymbrothered
with sylver & for felt lynyng & underturfes to ytt}   vs.

358 Philip, for Robert was not born until 1563.

Item for velvet for a garter band ymbrothered}   xvjd.
Item a sylver band & a large whyte fether for
Whyttell the taylor}   ixs.
Item for rybbynyng xij payer of agletts with poyents}   xvjd.
Item vj whyte toppes to sett his herons in}   viijs.
Item a cap band of sylver & a whyte fether for Mr
Deryng}   ixs.
Item a velvet cap with a copper sylver band & a white
fether for his foteman the 10 of October}   xiiijs. vjd.

[fo. 39v]
Item a velvet cappe for Mr Oweyng}   xs.
Item a velvet cap for Mr Deryng}   xs.
Item a yalowe fether, a red, a white & a russet at
iiijs. a pece}   xvjs.
Item a velvet cap for my lord with a band of damaske
gold & pearle}   xxvijs. vijd.
Item a sevel set all black}   xiijs. iiijd.
Item ij velvet cappes & one night cappe}   xxxs. viijd.
Item a sypres band for my lordes cap}   xd.
The some ys: xxli. xs. vjd.
And for the rest of xxxij velvet cappes with xxxij
sylver bandes & xxxij white feathers as appeareth
by another bill}   viijli. iijs. iiijd.[359]

[fo. 40]ʳ
[fo. 40v]
Item for the rest of xv velvet cappes with xv sylver
bandes & xv white fethers delivered to your lordship's
men at Hampton Court at xvjs. viijd. a pec whereof I
resseaved xs. for a pec}   vli.
Item for the rest of xv velvet cappes for your lordship's
yeomen with xv copper sylver bandes & xv whyte fethers
at xiijs. iiijd. a pec wherof I have resseaved xs. a
pec}   ijli. xs.
[endorsed] Guye the capper's byll for xxvjli. xijs. viijd.

[fo. 41 blank]
[fo. 41v] <James Shomaker's byll>ˢ

[359] Cf. the entry for thirty-five caps in the Chancy account, p. 98 above.

Item for my Lord Robart

Item i payre of whyte boskyns}	xiiijs.
Item i payre of blacke boskyns}	xiiijs.
Item ij payre of black velvet shous}	xiiijs.
Item ij payre jeloe velvet shous}	xiiijs.
Item ij payre of cremson velvet shous}	xvjs.
Item ij payre of whyt velvet shous}	xiiijs.
Item iij payre of rosed velvet shous}	xxjs.
Item i payre of black velvet shous doblesolde}	vijs.
Item iij payre of velvet moyles}	xxjs.
Item ij payre of boneventer bouts lynd wyth velvet}	xxiiijs.
Item i payre of black boskyns}	xiiijs.
Item i payre of whyte boskyns}	xiiijs.
Item ij payre of boneventer boutes}	xviijs.
Item i payre of whyt boskyns}	xijs.
Item j payre of freselether boskyns}	xijs.
Item j payre of bouts wythe gylted bouckels lynd wythe velvet}	xviijs.
Item j payre of Spanyshe bouts ferde}	xxs.
Item j payre of velvet slypers and one payre of velvyt moyles}	xiiijs.
Item ij payre of quarterd shous eged wythe velvet}	iijs.
Item j payre of armynge shous}	vjs.

Somme: xiiijli. xjs.

fo. 42.

Item for my lady

Item x payre of velvet shous}	iijli.
Item iiij payre of doblesolde shous for the foutman}	iijs. vjd.
Item ij payre of pompes for your foutmane}	xxs.
Item j payre of bouts for Dereynge}	vijs.

Somme: iijli. xijs. ijd.

[fo. 42v]

[*endorsed*] James Shomaker's byll for xviijli. iijs. ijd.
Let parties make answer before the examynation.

TEXTUAL NOTES

page
113   a-a. *deleted*
115   b-b. *interlined*

115	c-c. *deleted*
115	d-d. *dates in these entries interlined*
118	e-e. *For the sake of clarity the order of these entries has been slightly rearranged, the marginalia are in the left-hand margin*
118	f. *This section (to the end of fo. 13) has headings of entries in William Kynyat's hand in the left-hand margin and notes of evidence of payment in the right-hand margin.*
123	g-g. *interlined*
128	h-h. *interlined*
130	i-i. *deleted*
131	j-j. *deleted*
131	k-k. *deleted*
131	l-l. *deleted*
134	m-m. *added*
146	n-n. *added in a different hand*
147	o-o. *deleted*
173	p-p. *deleted*
173	q. *pasted in*
174	r. *copy of previous bill [omitted] with additional entries on fo. 40v.*
174	s. *pasted in*

C. DISBURSEMENT BOOK 1584-6
(EVELYN MS 258b)

[recto]

xth of April [1584]

Gyven the same day by your lordship's commandment to a poor woman of Leighton}	xijd.[360]
Gyven in reward the xjth of Apryll by your lordship's commandment to one Seager a <u>gardineir</u>} <painter>[a]	xls.[361]
Gyven in reward the same day by your lordship's commandment to a poore woman that sueth for her sonnes pardon}	vs.
Gyven in reward the same day by your lordship's commandment to Hugh the mercer servant to Mr Ambrose Smyth}	xs.[362]
Gyven in reward the xijth of Aprill by your lordship's commandment to Bedwill* your lordship's cowper at Leicester House}	xs.[363]
Paid the same day by your lordship's commandment to a stranger that came with Goodyneir [*sic*] to Leicester House for a looking glasse of cristall}	ls.
To Mr Aytie* the same day which he gave in reward by your lordship's commandment to Garret* your lordship's footeman when he was sent to Maidestone}	vjs.
Gyven in reward the xiijth of Aprill by your lordship's commandment to the gardneir's wieff at Wansted}	ijs.
Gyven the same day [*tear*][b]	

[360] On 9 April Leicester wrote to Thomas Egerton, the Solicitor-General, from Wanstead House (HEHL, EL MS 1879), where he was presumably on the 10th as well. The Court was at Whitehall until the end of April when it removed to Greenwich. For Wanstead see Introduction, p. 26.

[361] (Sir) William Segar (d.1633), Portcullis Pursuivant, later Garter King of Arms. He served as a herald in the Netherlands in 1585-6 and was recommended by Leicester as Somerset Herald in 1588 (Hist MSS Comm, *Bath MSS*, v (1980), 89). See also p. 255 below. These payments may be for one of the 'Segar type' portraits, which would appear to be c. 1584-5, see R.C. Strong, *Tudor and Jacobean Portraits* (1969), i, 196.

[362] Probably the mercer Ambrose Smith mentioned in the Chancy and Ellis accounts, see n. 156 above.

[363] For Leicester House, see Introduction, p. 26, and C.L. Kingsford, 'Essex House, formerly Leicester House and Exeter Inn', *Archaeologia*, xxiii (1924), 1-52.

Gyven in reward the xvth of Aprill by your
lordship's commandment to Mr Anthony Dowcray* at his
going downe to Kenilworth}   xli.
Gyven in reward the same tyme by your lordship's
commandment to Thomas Underhill* your lordship's servant}   xxxs.
Gyven in reward the same day by your lordship's
commandment to a poore woman of Stepney}   vs.
Delivered to John Keane* your lordship's servant
the xvijth of Aprill by your lordship's commandment
to pay for haulf a tonne of Orlience and white wyne
a[t] Courte}   viijli.
Summa Paginae: xxvli. xixs. vjd.

[verso]

xvijth of April [1584]
Gyven in reward the same day by your lordship's
commandment to Thomas King* your lordship's
servant the bruer}   xxxs.
Gyven in reward the same day by your lordship's
commandment to Ned Wilperforce* at Wansted}   xxs.
Gyven in reward the same day by your lordship's
commandment to the blackamore}   vs.[364]
Your lordship loste in play the same day at Wansted}   ls.
Delivered the xviijth of Aprill by your lordship's
commandment to Lovell* your lordship's servant to
fetche tymber out of Kent}   xls.
Gyven in reward the same day by your lordship's
commandment to the musicions who came from
London to Wansted}   iiili.
Paid the same day by your lordship's commandment
to fower gardneirs which made and sett a knott in
the garden at Wansted}   xjs. viijd.
Gyven in reward the same day by your lordship's
commandment to one Lane* a keper at Wansted}   vs.
Paid the same day for botehire for Stephin* from
Ratlief to the Court}   xijd.
Gyven in reward the xixth of Aprill by your
lordship's commandment to Harrys the shomaker}   vs.
Paid for the two messes of meat for your lordship's

---

[364] He does not reappear in this account, but the Leicester House inventory used after
March 1583 records a mattress given to the blackamore (DP VI, fo. 16v). Cf. Ralegh's
blackamore, p. 210 below.

servants for a fortnight from the vth of Aprill
untyll the xixth of the same moneth}   lvjs. viijd.
Gyven in reward the same day by your lordship's
commandment to a poor woman of Stepney}   ijs.
[*tear*]^{c} ... for Step[hen] ... [fr]om
[W]hitha[ll] to Leicester House and back
againe going for buttons}   vjd.
Paid for botehire for Mr Sandes*, Mr Lloyd*
and myself from Leicester House to Barnelmes the
xxjth of Aprill}   xxd.^{365}
Gyven in reward the same day by your lordship's
commandment to Mr Secretary Walsingham's cooke}   xs.
To Mr Ardern* the same day which he gave in reward
by your lordship's commandment to Chapman the keper
of Hampton Courte Park}   xs.
To Mr Blunt* the xxijth of Aprill which he gave
in reward by your lordship's commandment to Mr
Marwood my Lord of Bedford's surgion}   xxs.
        Summa Paginae: xvjli. viijs. vjd.

[recto]

        second of October [1584]^{366}
To Mr Richard Knowlls* the same day which he gave
in reward by your lordship's commandment to Mr Davyson's
men presenting a caste of fawkons to your lordship}   xls.^{367}
To Mr Thomas Dudley the iijth of October which
your lordship gave in reward to yong Addams* for
making the dyall in the garden at Leicester House}   xls.
To him more which he gave in reward by your
lordship's commandment to the armourers at
Winchester House the second of October}   xxxs.

---

^{365} Sir Francis Walsingham's house, see the following entry.

^{366} The intervening folios have disappeared, presumably through destruction by damp.
May and June 1584 saw Leicester's tour to Kenilworth, Shrewsbury, Denbigh, Chester
and Buxton, the most extensive he made. A reference to it will be found on p. 245 below.
On 19 July his son, Robert, Baron of Denbigh (b. 6 June 1581), died at Wanstead, see
Abbreviations: Funeral of the Lord of Denbigh.

^{367} William Davison (1541–1608), Secretary of State 1586–7, MP. His wife was a daughter
of Lady Elizabeth Isley, Sir John Mason's wife, and thus related to the Duchess of
Northumberland (see n. 344 above); Leicester addressed him as cousin. He was ambassador in Scotland between April and September 1584, and then in the Netherlands from
20 October to June 1585, and 3 September 1585 until Leicester's arrival (his last embassy
is discussed in Appendix II). His papers survive in quantity, the bulk of them now
distributed among the State Papers (see 'Leic. Pap. II', 138).

Payd to William Smyth's* wieff the lander at
Leicester House the iijth of October by your
lordship's commandment as appereth by her bill}   vjli. ixs. vd.

Paid for the two messes of meate for your
lordship's servants for a fortnight from the
xxth of September untill the iiijth of October}   lvjs. viijd.

Given to a poore woman at Knightesbridge the
vth of October as your lordship came from London}   vjd.[368]

To Richard Pepper* your lordship's footeman
the same day for his charges when your lordship
sent him to Grays to my Lady Shandoys}   xviiijd.[369]

Gyven by your lordship's commandment the same
day to poore Irisshemen}   vjd.

To Robert Pitcheford* the same day which he paid
for iiij paire of dry perfumed gloves for your
lordship at iijs. iiijd. a paire}   [tear]d

[tear] paid for two paire of large gloves lyned
with [...]amell perfumed and trymed with black
silke and goulde}   xxiiijs.

To Cooke your lordship's habberdassher the same
day for vj black silke nightcaps at vjs. a pece
which were geven to my Lord of Shrewsbery at Otelands}   xxxvjs.[370]

To him more the vjth of October for two thick
nightcaps for your lordship at vjs. a pece}   xiijs.

Gyven in reward the same day by your lordship's
commandment to a poor woman, a suetor which
came oute of Devonshere}   xs.

Summa Paginae: xixli. xiiijs. xjd.

[368] The 1580s saw a major reduction in the scale of the royal progresses and the Court
spent the summer of 1584 at Greenwich, Richmond, Nonsuch and, from 7 August,
Oatlands. Leicester appears to have been at Leicester House during first days of October
(see next page) and returned to Court on the 6th.

[369] Rotherfield Greys (Oxon.), Sir Francis Knollys' house. Lady Chandos was Dorothy
Bray (d.1605), who married Edward 2nd Lord Chandos (1522–74) and then (Sir) William
Knollys (1545–1632), Sir Francis's 2nd son, MP. Knollys was a trustee for Leicester's
jointure for the Countess (15 July 1584), governor of Ostend in 1586 and a mourner at
both Sidney's and Leicester's funerals. Lady Chandos had a chamber at Leicester House.

[370] George Talbot, 6th Earl (1522–90). He had come to Court on 15 September to be
relieved as guardian of Mary, Queen of Scots, and was publicly greeted by Leicester on
his arrival at Oatlands, see Hist MSS Comm, *Calendar of the Manuscripts of ... the Duke of
Rutland*, i (1888), 169. An extensive correspondence between Leicester and Shrewsbury
survives, and Leicester acted as his deputy as Earl Marshal.

[verso]

vjth of October [1584]

Gyven in reward the same day by your lordship's
commandment to Mr Gifford's footeman}   vs.[371]
To Smull* [tear] oteman the same day which he
gave [tear] ore at Hamersmyth when your lordship
came from London}   xijd.
Gyven in reward the vth of October by your lordship's
commandment to my Lady Dorathy at Leicester House}   xxli.[372]
Gyven in reward the vjth of October by your
lordship's commandment to Becham*}   iijs. iiijd.
Gyven in reward the same day by your lordship's
commandment to my Lord of Arrundell's man for
presenting a cowple of houndes to your lordship}   xxxs.[373]
Gyven by your lordship's commandment the same
day to the poore betwene Otelands and London}   vijd.
To Stephen Johnson your lordship's servant the
same day for his botehire from Otelands to London
with your lordship's apparell}   vjs.
Given the same day by your lordship's commandment
to two poore women betwene London and Otelands}   ijs.
Paid the same day for thre glasses for your
lordship's chamber}   xviijd.
Paid the same day for ix cartes to carry your
lordship's [tear] Otelands to Hampton Courte}   xjs. iijd.[374]
To vj of your lordship's servants [tear] their
dynners wayting on your lordship's stuff by the way}   iijs.
Payd the same day for corde for your lordship's bed}   viijd.
Given in reward the vijth of October by your
lordship's commandment to Walter* your lordship's
servant carring letters to Kenelworth}   vjs. viijd.
[Gyven] in reward the same day by your lordship's

---

[371] Probably (Sir) George Gifford (1552–1613), Gentleman Pensioner, MP. He was
married to Lady Chandos' daughter Eleanor.

[372] Given that Dorothy Knollys is referred to throughout as Lady Chandos, Lady
Dorothy is presumably the Countess of Leicester's daughter Dorothy Devereux, who had
married Sir Thomas Perrot (see n. 478 below) in 1583. Leicester was particularly fond of
her and proposed in his 1582 will that she and Philip Sidney should marry. There was a
portrait of her in the Leicester House collection.

[373] Philip Howard, 1st Earl (1557–95), the Duke of Norfolk's son by his first wife,
daughter of the former Earl (see n. 140 above). Norfolk had named Leicester one of the
trustees for his lands in 1570 (Williams, Norfolk, p. 121), but Arundel's political alienation
led to antagonism by the mid-1580s.

[374] The Court removed to Hampton Court between 6 and 10 October.

commandment to [*tear*]len's man at Otelands for
carring an [*tear*] to Wanstead}   vs.
Gyven in reward the same day by your lordship's
commandment to Goodrowse* the surient}   xli.
           Summa Paginae: xxxiijli. xvjs.

[recto]

                    vijth of October [1584]
Your lordship loste in play at Syon the same day at night}   xs.
To Harry Stringer the same day which he laide oute for
fishe their}   xijd.[375]
Gyven in reward viijth of October by your lordship's
commandment to my Lady Huntington's footeman}   xs.[376]
Given in reward the ixth of October by your lordship's
commandment to Mr Gyles Tracy* at his goyng into the country} vli.
Gyven in reward the xth of October by your lordship's
commandment to Mr Grene's* man for presenting a dossin
and haulf of partridges to your lordship}   vs.
Given in reward the same day by your lordship's
commandment to [*blank*] Hall* your
lordship's servant}   xls.
To Roger Gillions* your lordship's bargeman for
carring my lady[377] from Leicester House to Putney and
back ageyne the xijth of September xij*s*., for
carring your lordship from Lambeth to Leicester House
the third of October ix*s*., for carring the imbassador[378]
from Leicester House to Ivy Bridge the iiijth of
October ix*s*., and for carring your lordship from
Leicester House to my Lord of Bedford's the vth of
October ix*s*., so in all}   xxxixs.

---

[375] Identified on pp. 211, 344 below as the Queen's footman, but the frequent references
to him here suggest that he was a former servant of Leicester's.

[376] His sister Katherine, see n. 35 above. They had met at Leicester on 18 June on his
return from his tour.

[377] Lettice, Countess of Leicester. There are regular but peripheral references to her
throughout this book, which make it difficult to follow her movements with any precision,
though she was clearly residing at either Leicester House or Wanstead. As noted in the
Introduction (p. 28), this was probably because she financed her own chamber out of
her revenues as dowager Countess of Essex. One effect of her marriage to Leicester was
to solidify his relations with her numerous brothers and sisters, who appear here regularly,
but no less striking is the paternal concern he showed for her children by Essex.

[378] Michel de Castelnau, Seigneur de Mauvissière, see Introduction, pp. 33–4. Castelnau
was lodged at Salisbury Court (Bossy, *Bruno*, p. 10), Ivy Bridge Lane was next to Bedford
House, and Leicester House was between them.

To Richard Gardneir* for his bord wages for iij daies
being sent before to mak reddy your lordship's chamber
at Hampton Courte and for a labourer to help him}   iiijs. ijd.
Gyven in reward the xijth of October by your
lordship's commandment to George Weale at his
goyng to Porchemouth}   xs.[379]
Gyven in reward the same day by your lordship's
commandment to the keper of Kempton Park when you
sent Gwyn* thither to make a shute for your
lordship's hounds}   iijs. iiijd.
To Gawen* the groome the same day for his botehire
from Hampton Courte to Leicester House being sent
thither with partridges}   ijs.
To Richard* your lordship's spaniell keper for keping
v cowple of your lordship's spaniells from the first
of September till the xxixth of the same month
at xd. per diem}   xxiijs. iiijd.

              Summa Paginae: xijli. vijs. xd.

[verso]

                 xiijth of October [1584]
To Richard Gardneir the same day for his botehire
from Hampton Courte to Leicester House being sent
thither with partridges}   xviijd.
To Smolkin the footeman for his charges goyng
and comyng being sent to Lees the vijth of October}   vs.
Gyven in reward the same day by your lordship's
commandment to Luck the foole for presenting a
basket of aples to your lordship}   vjs. viijd.
Gyven in reward the same day by your lordship's
commandment to Robyn my Lord Lumley's foole}   xs.[380]
To Mr Brooke* the same day which he gave in
reward by your lordship's commandment to my

---

[379] On 10 October the Privy Council decided in principle on intervention in the
Netherlands and advised that a parliament be summoned. The writs for elections are
dated the 12th, and on that day Leicester wrote a number of letters asking for nominations
of MPs, see 'House of Commons', 217–9. The absence of any reference to messengers
here, with the possible exception of this entry, suggests that Leicester probably sent his
letters by the pursuivants carrying the writs. The entry under 1 November (see p. 191)
probably refers to the answer from Portsmouth.
[380] Lumley inherited Nonsuch Palace on the Earl of Arundel's death (see n. 325 above)
and continued to reside there, although the Queen used it regularly. He attended the
Lord of Denbigh's funeral and gave Leicester his proxy for the Parliament of 1584.

Lord Chamberlaines man for presenting a spaniell bitche to your lordship}	vjs.[381]
To Fardenandoe* for his quarter's waiges due at Michaelmas last at x*li.* per annum}	ls.
To Gyllam's wief* your lordship's lander for her quarter's waiges due at Mighelmas laste at x*li.* a yere}	ls.
To Jesper that mends instruments the same day for his quarter's waiges due at Mighelmas laste at xl*s.* a yere}	xs.
Gyven in reward the xiiijth of October by your lordship's commandment to Thomas Bedwell your lordship's servant} <a>	v*li.*
Paid to Mr Dudley the same day for a case for two dagges of your lordship}	vs.
Gyven in reward the same day by your lordship's commandment to the keper of the gatehouse at Westminster for presenting grapes to your lordship}	iijs. iiijd.
Paid the same day for a realme of writing paper for your lordship}	vs. vjd.
Gyven in reward the same day to Thomas Dawlton* your lordship's footeman}	xxs.
Gyven in reward the same day by your lordship's commandment to one Harry Barker* a cooke at Leicester House}	xs.
Gyven in reward the xvijth of October by your lordship's commandment to one Pallavesynes man for presenting dryde peaches to your lordship}	ijs. vjd.[382]

Summa Paginae: xiiijli. vs. vjd.

[recto]

xvijth of October [1584]

Gyven in reward the same day by your lordship's commandment to a larck ketcher at Twickenham}	ijs. vjd.
Gyven in reward the same day by your lordship's	

[381] Charles, Lord Howard of Effingham (see n. 72 above) was Lord Chamberlain between 1 January 1584 and 8 July 1585 when he was appointed Lord Admiral (see n. 567 below). Despite the scandal created by the revelation of Leicester's affair with his sister, Douglas, Lady Sheffield, they remained on very friendly terms and Leicester appointed him an overseer of his 1587 will. He was expected to attend Leicester's funeral.

[382] Sir Horation Palavicino (c.1540–1600), see L. Stone, *An Elizabethan: Sir Horatio Palavicino* (Oxford, 1956). Palavicino's relations with Leicester were closer than Professor Stone allows.

commandment to the keper of St James's Park for
opening the gate for your lordship paid by
Smoulkin the footeman}   ijs.
Gyven to a poore woman at Twicknam the same day}   iijd.
Gyven in reward the same day by your lordship's
commandment to Mr Pallevesynes man for bringing
dride peaches to the Quenes majestie at Hampton Corte}   xxs.
Paid the same day for a dossin of handkerchiefs
for your lordship}   xviijs.
Paid for the two messes of meate for your lordship's
servants for a fortnight from the iiijth of October
untill the xviijth of the same month}   lvjs. viijd.
Paid the same day for a dossin of towelles for
your lordship}   xxixs.
Paid to Roger Gillions and Merrick* your lordship's
watermen for carring your lordship at sondry
tymes in your lordship's barge as appereth
by their bill}   iiijli. vijs.
To Richard Pepper your lordship's footeman
the same day which he gave to the spitle at
Knightesbridge}   vjd.
Gyven in reward the same day by your lordship's
commandment to Chapman keper of Hampton Courte Park
for opening a gate for your lordship}   vs.
Gyven in reward the same day by your lordship's
commandment to Moulkin the footeman when he went to Greys}   vs.
To Mr Sandes the same day which he gave in reward
by your lordship's commandment to Mr Knevettes man
at Whithall vs. and to the gardneir their ijs. vjd.}   vijs. vjd.[383]
Gyven in reward the xixth of October by your
lordship's commandment to a merchant's servant for
bringing letters oute of Flaunders}   ijs. vjd.
Gyven in reward the same day by your lordship's
commandment to Mr Stanhoppes boy for presenting
spaniells to your lordship}   xiijs. iiijd.[384]
       Summa Paginae: xijli. ixs. iijd.

[verso]

[383] Probably Thomas Knyvett (1545–1622), Groom of the Privy Chamber, MP.
[384] Sir Thomas Stanhope (c.1540–96) of Shelford, Notts., MP, see the the entry on p.
191 below.

xixth of October [1584]

Gyven in reward the same day by your lordship's
commandment to Sir Christopher Hatton's kocheman
carring your lordship from Syon to Colbrook}   vjs. viijd.[385]

Gyven the same day by your lordship's commandment
to the poore at Henlye}   ijs.

Paid the same night for your lordship's men's
charges at Henlie}   xxvijs. jd.

Paid for iij sumptermen's suppers at Kingston
the night before your lordship tooke jorney}   xviijd.

Paid more at Colbrook for their dynners and thre of
your lordship's yeomen that went wyth them}   iijs.

Paid more at Dorchester for the sumptermen's baite
with iij of your lordship's yeomen}   iijs.

Paid the xxth of October for the dinners of xxiiijth
of your lordship's gentilmen and yeomen at Oxeford}   xxjs. vjd.[386]

Gyven the same day to the poore betwene Graies
and Woodstock}   xviijd.

Gyven in reward the same day by your lordship's
commandment to my Lord Dudleis musicians at Woodstock}   xxs.[387]

Paid at Woodstock for the charge of your lordship's
servants for iij meales in the towne as
appereth by a bill}   iijli. ixs. xd.

Gyven in reward the xxijth of October by your
lordship's commandment to the kepers of Woodstock Parke}   xls.

Gyven in reward more the same day by your
lordship's commandment to the servants of the
house at Sir Harry Leis}   xls.[388]

Delivered the same daie by your lordship's
commandment to yong Docwraie* to be geven to
Sir Henrie Leas man for bringing a doe to your lordship}   xs.

Gyven in reward the same daie by your lordship's
commandment to Mr Bluntes footeman for carring a

---

[385] Hatton was then Vice-Chamberlain and Captain of the Guard. Despite the rivalry that is often claimed for them, Hatton and Leicester were on very friendly personal terms. Leicester appointed him an overseer of both his surviving wills, and he was sent blacks for Leicester's funeral. This entry marks the beginning of a journey referred to on p. 196 below as 'when your lordship rode to Langley'. The purpose, the subsequent entries make clear, was to see his illegitimate son. If the dating is accurate he left the Court at Hampton Court on the 19th.

[386] Unlike his subsequent journey in January 1585, see pp. 212–3 below, he does not appear to have visited the University.

[387] Edmund, 4th Lord Dudley, see n. 301 above.

[388] Lee (see n. 149 above) was the keeper of Woodstock Palace, where he generally resided.

letter to London} vs.

Gyven in reward the same daie by your lordship's
commandment to Mr Harman's* servants when your
lordship dyned their} vs.

To Smoulkyn the footeman the same daie which he
gave to the poore at Woodstock} vjd.

Paid to Cole* and Black your lordship's servants
the xxiijth of October for their charges in
comying after your lordship to Woodstock} vjs. vjd.

   Summa Paginae: xiijli. iiis. jd.

[recto]

   xxiijth of October [1584]

Gyven in reward the same daie by your lordship's
commandment to Mr Giles Tracie being sent poste
from Whitney to the Courte} xls.[389]

Paid to a carrier the same daie for carring a
doe to the Courte} xs.

Gyven in reward the same daie by your lordship's
commandment to Humfrey* your lordship's footeman
for carring letters from Whitney to London} vs.

Delivered the same daie by your lordship's
commandment to Mr Blunte imprest to defray charges
for your lordship's horsses} xli.

To Rutherick Lewes* the same daie for the charges
of iiij sumptermen and iiij yeomen when they came
before from Woodstock to Whitney} iijs.

To Stephen the same daie which he gave in reward
to Mr Aysshfield's[390] man for fetching your lordship's

[389] On 24 October Leicester wrote a number of letters from Whitney circulating copies of the Bond of Association: one to Lord Chandos is now Bodl., MS Clarendon I, fos. 13-4, and a copy of another to an unnamed peer is Bodl., MS Rawl. C 358, fo. 38. The main Bond was signed by the Privy Council on 19 October, presumably just before Leicester left the Court (see n. 385), and Burghley and Walsingham were discussing the circulation of copies on the 19th and 20th (PRO, SP 12/173/85,6). Whether Leicester's role in circulating the Bond had been arranged before he left is unclear. See, in general, D. Cressy, 'Binding the Nation: the Bonds of Association, 1584 and 1696', in D.G. Guth and J.W. McKenna (edd.), *Tudor Rule and Revolution: Essays for G.R. Elton from his American Friends* (Cambridge, 1982), pp. 220-1, and P. Collinson, 'The Monarchical Republic of Elizabeth I', in *Elizabethan Essays*, pp. 48-9.

[390] Humphrey Ashfield of Heythrop, Oxon. He attended Leicester's funeral and claimed £124 from his estate 'for money laid out at Langley'. See also the reference to his son John, p. 214 n. 455 below.

bootes from Whitney to Langlei}   ijs.[391]
Gyven in reward the same daie by your lordship's
commandment to certene men that fetcht in the
woodlace in the forrest of Wychewood}   xs.
To Smolkin the footeman the same daie which
he [sic] by your lordship's commandment
to the poore at Whitney towen's ende}   vjd.
Gyven in reward the xxiiijth of October by your
lordship's commandment to Doctor Dallapere at Whitney}   vli.[392]
Gyven in reward the same daie by your lordship's
commandment to Mr Canellae, Mr Robert Dudleis
scholemaster, at Whitney}   iijli.[393]
Delivered to Mr Dowckrey the same daie by your
lordship's commandment to geve to Thorneton
for bringing two does from Woodstock to Whitney}   xs.
Gyven in reward the same daie by your lordship's
commandment to Brampton* your lordship's servant
when he was sent from Whitney to Wylton}   xls.
Gyven in reward the same daie by your lordship's
commandment to yong Mr Clynton}   xls.[394]

[391] In 1584 Leicester held two manors in western Oxfordshire, Whitney and Langley
(near Leafield), and the keepership of the Forest of Wychwood under a complex series
of tenures. Langley had been held in conjunction with the keeperships of Wychwood
Forest and Cornbury House and Park since the previous century. All had been obtained
by Northumberland, who assigned Cornbury to his wife's jointure and a life interest in
Langley and the keepership of Wychwood to the Countess of Warwick's (see n. 105
above). Elizabeth granted Leicester the fee simple of Langley in January 1581 (CPR, 1580–
2, 27, GVE, fo. 23v), and the Countess of Warwick's interests in Langley and Wychwood
were assigned to him after she was declared a lunatic in 1582 (Longleat MS 3283). He
received a separate lease of Whitney from the Queen in 1583 (GVE, fo. 46v). His right
to Cornbury, which owing to Northumberland's attainder had reverted to the Crown on
the Duchess's death, is not clear, but he made use of Cornbury House (where he died in
1588), as well as the house at Langley. See, in general, V.J. Watney, *Cornbury and the Forest
of Wychwood* (1910), pp. 68–74, and *King's Works*, iv, 160–1; the discussion in 'West
Midlands', 34, is abbreviated.
[392] John Delabere, principal of Gloucester Hall 1581–93, see also the entry on p. 216
below, which suggests that he was the host of Leicester's son. An introduction to
Leicester's relations with Delabere and many of the other Oxford figures mentioned
below can be found in P. Williams, 'State, Church and University', in J.K. McConica
(ed.), *The History of the University of Oxford, III: The Collegiate University* (Oxford, 1986), 423–9.
[393] (Sir) Robert Dudley (1574–1649), his illegitimate son by Douglas Sheffield. The
implication here is that Robert Dudley was then living either in Oxford or Whitney.
This is a slight mystery, for he is generally believed to have been living at Offington in
Sussex, see n. 499 below. A greater mystery is how and when he came into Leicester's
custody given that several years earlier Douglas Sheffield had adamantly refused to
surrender custody.
[394] Probably Thomas Clinton (1568–1619), later 3rd Earl of Lincoln, MP. Clinton was
a student at Oxford at this point.

Gyven in reward the same daie by your lordship's
commandment to the servants of the house at Bryses}   xxs.[395]
Gyven in reward the same day by your lordship's
commandment to the nurce at Bryses}   xxs.
                    Summa Paginae: xxviijli. vjd.

[verso]

                    xxiiiith of October [1584]
Gyven in reward the same daie by your lordship's
commandment to Mr Robert Dudley}   xs.
Gyven in reward the same day by your lordship's
commandment to Allen* your lordship's servant at Whitney}   xxs.
Delivered the same daie by your lordship's
commandment to one Yates to geve to the poore of Whitney}   xxs.
Gyven in reward the same daie by your lordship's
commandment to the clerck of the towne of Whitney}   iijs. iiijd.
Gyven in reward the same daie by your lordship's
commandment to the singers of Whitney}   vjs. viijd.
Delivered the same daie by your lordship's
commandment to Mr Bostock to geve to the
poore at Abington}   xxs.[396]
Gyven in reward the same daie by your lordship's
commandment to the musycions at Abington}   vs.
To Mr Sandes the same daie which he gave in reward
by your lordship's commandment to Mr Bryses man
for bringing victuells to Abington}   vs.
Gyven to the poore at Burford bridge the same daie
by your lordship's commandment}   xijd.
Your lordship loste in plaie at Greys the same day}   iiili.
To Richard Pepper the footeman the same day which
he gave by your lordship's commandment to a
fisher at Whitney}   xijd.
Gyven more by your lordship's commandment to a
poore man at Whitney}   vjd.
To Rutherick Lewes the same daie for the charges
of a dynner and supper at Abington and a dynner

---

[395] Mr Bryse may have been Robert Dudley's host, but see n. 392 above.

[396] Leicester had been high steward of Abingdon since 1566. The borough chamberlain's accounts for the year Michaelmas 1583–Michaelmas 1584 (Berkshire RO, A/AFAc 2 (1582–88), fo. 21) record a gift of sack to Leicester at Mr Read's. The draft chamberlain's accounts (Abingdon Town Council, Chamberlains Accounts, II, fos. 21v, 25) record this and one earlier in the year. Neither record any visits by him in the year 1584–5. Mr Bostock was probably Lancelot Bostock (c.1533–88), Gentleman Pensioner, MP.

at Henley for vj of your lordship's servants
being sent before}   xs. ixd.
Paid for Mr Clinton's and Mr Deverox's horsemeate
for fower nights when they came to Woodstock
to your lordship}   xiijs.[397]
Paid more the same day for the charges of your
lordship's servants being xxx in nomber for
Satterday night and Sonday breakfast at Henlye
as appereth by a bill}   xxxijs. iiijd.
        Summa Paginae: xli. viijs. vijd.

[recto]

        xxiiiith [*sic*] of October [1584]
Paid more the same daie for the dynners of the
sumptermen at Colbrooke and iij of your lordship's
yeomen and for the sumptermen's suppers at Kingston}   iiijs. vjd.
Gyven in reward the xxvth of October by your
lordship's commandment to Mr Knolles's men at Greys}   xxs.
To Richard Pepper the same day which he gave
to the poore betwene Greys and the Courte}   xijd.
To Robert Pitcheford the same daie which he paid
for wasshing your lordship's lynnen in the iorney}   xijd.
To Watt her majesty's page of the Chamber the xxvjth
of October for him to deliver to Mother Ossynus
for her haulf yeres annuytie due at Mighelmas last}   <a>   vli.[398]
Gyven in reward the same daie by your lordship's
commandment to one that brought letters
from Sir Franceis Drake}   ijs. vjd.[399]
Gyven in reward the same daie by your lordship's
commandment to a carrier for bringing of thre does
from the forrest of Whichewood}   xiijs. iiijd.
To Giles Homerstone* the same day for keping your
lordship's hounds for three weekes at iij*d*. a day}   iiijs. vjd.
To Fardenandoe your lordship's servant the
xxviijth of October which he laide oute for

[397] For Clinton see n. 394 above. Mr Devereux was probably Walter, the Countess's
younger son (d. 1591), who matriculated at Christ Church in 1584. Howard of Effingham
praised 'your son Mr Devereux' during the Armada campaign (BL, Cotton MS Otho E
IX, fo. 210, corrected from Pepys MS 2876, pp. 315–6, to Leicester, 6 June 1588).
[398] See n. 152 above.
[399] Possibly concerning the Moluccas, later the West Indies, Voyage. Leicester was
one of the adventurers, as listed by Burghley on 24 November, see Adams, 'Outbreak of
the Elizabethan Naval War', p. 54.

certene charges for Walter Ridgeway* your
lordship's boy as appereth by two billes}   <a>   xlvijs. vjd.
Gyven in reward the same daie by your lordship's
commandment to Mr Bellingham's man for presenting
of a hawke}   xs.
To Mr Sandys the xxixth of October which he paid
to a waterman for carring of a hinde that came
from Whitney from Braynford to Hampton Cort}   iijs.
Delivered to Mr Sutton* the same daie by your
lordship's commandment to pay for certene writings}   xxs.[400]
To Gawen the groome the same daie for his botehire
being sent for your lordship's barge}   xijd.
To Richard Hessey your lordship's spaniell keper
for keping v cowple of your lordship's spaniells
for one moneth ended the xxvjth of October at jd.
a pece per diem}   xxiijs. iiijd.
Paid more for keping of three cowple of your
lordship's spaniells that came from Sir
Thomas Stanhopp}   vs. vjd.
Gyven to the poore the last of October by your
lordship's commandment}   xijd.
                    Summa Paginae: xijli. xviijs. ijd.

[verso]

                 first of November [1584]
Gyven in reward the same daie by your lordship's
commandment to Jonas my Lord Chamberlaynes paige at
his goyng into France}   ls.[401]
Gyven in reward the same daie by your lordship's
commandment to one that brought letters from
Porcemouth to your lordship}   vjs. viijd.
Gyven in reward the same day by your lordship's
commandment to Sir Thomas Tressam's man for

---

[400] Leicester wrote to the borough of Maldon on the parliamentary election from
Leicester House on 30 October (Essex RO, D/B3/3/422)

[401] He probably took the letter Leicester wrote to Jean Hotman* on 2 November from
Hampton Court (HEHL, MS HM 21714), asking him to hire a gardener for him in
France. In a subsequent letter (29 Nov., n. 418 below) Leicester expressed his good
opinion of the bearer and 'assured accompt' of the letter's safe arrival. On the gardener
and the correspondence with Hotman as a whole, see n. 467 below and the entry for
Hotman in the Index of Servants.

presenting a brace of does to your lordship}	xiijs. iiijd.[402]
Your lordship loste in plaie the same daie at my Lord of Warwick's chamber}	xxs.
Paid for the two messes of meate for your lordship's servants for a fortnight from the xviijth of October until the first of November} <a>	lvjs. viijd.
To Smolkyn which he gave to the poore by your lordship's commandment at Nettlebed and Greys}	xviijd.
To him more the iiijth of November which he paid to a poore woman at Hampton Ferry}	vjd.
Gyven in reward the vth of November by your lordship's commandment to Sir Franceis Carowes man for presenting fatt conneis to your lordship at Nonesiche}	xs.[403]
Gyven in reward the same day by your lordship's commandment to Humfrey footeman ᵉfor comyng from Leicester House to Nonesychᵉ}	iijs. iiijd.
Gyven the same day by your lordship's commandment to thre poore women}	vjd.
Paid the same day by your lordship's commandment to William Bennett* for a bay horrse}	xxli.
Gyven in reward the vjth of November by your lordship's commandment to Mr Oxenbridges* man for presenting a hawke to your lordship}	xls.
Gyven in reward the same day by your lordship's commandment to Humfrey the footeman}	ijs. vjd.
Your lordship loste in play the same day to Mr Drake}	vli.[404]
To Mr Sandes the vijth of November which he gave in reward by your lordship's commandment to Thomas Hilton a suetor of Lancashere}	iijli. vjs. viiijd.
Gyven in reward the same day by your lordship's commandment to Garrett your lordship's footman}	iiili. vjs. viiid.

Summa Paginae: xljli. xviijs. iiijd.

---

[402] (1545–1605) of Rushton (Northants.), arrested and imprisoned for aiding Edmund Campion and recusancy in 1581, see M.E. Finch, *The Wealth of Five Northamptonshire Families 1540–1640* (Northamptonshire Record Soc., xix, 1956), 76–8. Leicester appears to have been instrumental in reducing his imprisonment to house arrest, see BL, Add. MS 39828 [Tresham Papers], fo 93, Tresham to Leicester, 1 Oct. 1583.

[403] (1530–1611) of Beddington, Surr., MP.

[404] Richard Drake (1535–1603), Equerry of the Stables by 1576 and Groom of the Privy Chamber 1584, MP. Drake was Sir Francis's cousin, and had been in Leicester's service in the 1560s. He received livery in 1567 and was described as a servant of Leicester's by Archbishop Young of York in his will (BIHR, Archiepiscopal Register R.I. 30 [1561–76], fo. 57, 25 June 1568).

[recto]

viijth of November [1584]

Your lordship loste in play the same day at Leicester House}	iiili.
To Richard Pepper the same day which he gave to the poore by your lordship's commandment}	ixd.
To Mr Blunt the which he gave in reward by your lordship's commandment to the keper of Nonsyche Park the vjth of November}	xs.
To him more which he gave to the keper's man their by your lordship's commandment}	xijd.
To him more the viijth of November for the charges of fower koche horsses and vij geldings and fower of your lordship's servants at Lambeth the vjth and viijth of November}	xxixs. iiijd.
Delivered to Sir Richard Knightley the xth of November by your lordship's commandment for Mr King of Tossetor}	vli.[405]
Gyven in reward the same daie by your lordship's commandment to Awdrian* your lordship's gardneir at his goyng to Langley}	xxxs.
Your lordship loste in play the same day}	xs.
Given in reward the xjth of November by your lordship's commandment to the Frenche gardneir at Nonsyche}	xxs.[406]
Gyven in reward the same daie by your lordship's commandment to Gittens the keper of the wardrop at Nonesuche}	xs.
Gyven in reward the xijth of November by your lordship's commandment to the keper's sonne of Mortlack Parke}	vjs. viijd.
Gyven in reward the same day by your lordship's commandment to a mayde at Puttney}	vs.
To Stephen Johnson your lordship's servant the same daie for botehire betwene Putney and London}	ijs.

[405] Sir Richard Knightley (1533–1615) of Fawsley, Northants., MP. The entry refers to Leicester's contribution to the subscription for a lectureship at Towcester for Andrew King, a member of the Northamptonshire classis, that Knightley had organised. See PRO, SP 12/150/150, Knightley to Leicester, 17 Oct. 1581, and W.J. Shiels, *The Puritans in the Diocese of Peterborough 1558–1610* (Northamptonshire Record Soc., xxx, 1979), 26–8. Further contributions by Leicester are entered on pp. 243–4, 302, 327 below.

[406] Probably Lumley's gardener, as Leicester was in the process of hiring one, see n. 401 above.

To Owen Jones* your lordship's servant the same
daie which he gave in reward by your lordship's
commandment to the keper of Putnei Park}   vs.
Payd the same day for a carte from Hampton Cort
to Nonesuche from Nonesuche to Putneie and
from Putney to London}   iijs. ixd.[407]
Gyven in reward the same day by your lordship's
commandment to the servants of Mr Alderseis
howse at Putney}   xxs.[408]

Summa Paginae: xvli. xiijs. vjd.

[verso]

xvth of November [1584]

Payd to Stephen Johnson the same day which
he paid for two girdells for your lordship
as appereth by his bill}   iijli. xijs. viijd.
To Mr Sandes the same day which he gave
in reward by your lordship's commandment to
the keper of St James's Park}   iijs. iiijd.
To him more the same daie which he paid
for Mr Dudleis boatehire from Hampton
Court to London}   vs.
To him more which he paid for ix cartes
from Hampton Court to London to St James's}   xviijs.
To Roger Gillyons the same day for carring your
lordship at sondrie tymes in your lordship's
barge as appereth by his bill}   iiijli. xs. iiijd.
Paid for the two messes of meate for your
lordship's servants for a fortnight from
the firste of November untill the xvth
of the same month}   <a>   lvjs. viijd.
To Gawen the groome the same day for goyng
from Hampton Courte to London for your lordship's barge}   vjd.
Gyven in reward the same daie by your lordship's
commandment to Humfrey the footeman for goyng
to Oxeford}   vs.
Gyven in reward the same day by your lordship's

---

[407] See also the subsequent entries. The Court removed from Hampton Court to St
James's on 12 November, and Leicester was noted as being in attendance on the Queen's
arrival by the German visitor Leopold von Wedel (Klarwill, p. 328). He signed the Privy
Council's letter on Barnaby Benison on 14 November, see n. 446 below.
[408] Presumably Thomas Aldersey, see n. 201 above.

commandment to Mr William Bridges man for presenting a hound}	xs.
Gyven in reward the same daie by your lordship's commandment to Parry Sir Thomas Hennedges man for presenting bottelles of wyne to your lordship}	vs.[409]
Gyven in reward the same day by your lordship's commandment to Robert Holland at his goyng in to the countrey}	xxs.
To Mr Thomas Dudley the xvjth of November which he gave in reward by your lordship's commandment to Sir Jerome Bowes's man presenting of a rayne deere}	xxxs.[410]
To him more the same daie which he gave in reward by your lordship's commandment to my Lord Lumleis man for presenting of seedes to your lordship}	xs.
Gyven in reward the same day by your lordship's commandment to Mr Brookes man being sent to hawk the phesant in Warwickshere}	xxs.
Gyven in reward the same day by your lordship's commandment to your lordship's spaniell keper being sent with Mr Brookes man}	xs.

Summa Paginae: xvijli. xvjs. vjd.

[recto]

xvijth of November [1584]

Gyven in reward the same daie by your lordship's commandment to Mr Seelies man for presenting a boare to your lordship}	vjs. viijd.[411]
To Robert Pitcheford the same daie which he gave to the poore by your lordship's commandment}	vjd.
Delivered to Mr Nevyle* the same daie by your lordship's commandment} <a>	xli.
Paid to Sheppard the same day for two paire of long gloves for your lordship}	xvijs.
Paid more for fower dowble silke nightcaps for your lordship the xviijth of November}	xxvjs. viijd.
To Mr Blount the same day which he gave to the	

[409] Sir Thomas Heneage (1532–95), Treasurer of the Chamber, MP. See n. 695 below for his mission to the Netherlands in 1586.

[410] Sir Jerome Bowes (d.1616), MP, who had been ambassador in Russia between July 1583 and September 1584.

[411] Possibly Thomas Seale, a servant of Leicester's in 1573, see Hasler, *sub* Ferrars, George.

poore betwene St. James's and the Tiltyard}   ijs.[412]
Gyven to the poore by your lordship's commandment
betwene Leicester House and Charing Crosse}   xijd.
Gyven in reward the xxth of November by your
lordship's commandment to the cookes of the
Sterchamber when your lordship paste throwe the
kitchen their}   vs.[413]
To Rudderick Lewes which he paid for two torches
to light your lordship to Leicester House the
xviijth of November}   ijs.
To Mr Sandys the xviijth of November which he
gave in reward by your lordship's commandment to two
of Mr Knevettes men at Whithall}   vs.
Delivered to your lordship the same day in
your lordship's pursse to geve to the poore},   iijs.
Your lordship loste in play at Wansted the same night}   vs.
Delivered to Mr Bapteste the same day which he
delivered to your lordship at Wansted}   xxs.[414]
Delivered more to your lordship at Wansted the
xxjth of November to geve to the poore}   vs.
To Mr Blunt the same day which he gave to the
fisherman at Wanstedd}   vs.
Payd to viij of your lordship's yeomen for their
dynners and suppers for two daies attending on
your lordship's stuff at the remove from Hampton
Courte to St James's as appereth by a bill}   ixs. vjd.

        Summa Paginae: xvli. xiijs. iiijd.

[verso]

        xxvth of November [1584]
To Mr Blunt the same daie by your lordship's
commandment in full payment of his bill for
horssecharges when your lordship rode to Langley

[412] En route to the Accession Day tournament (17 November), over which Leicester presided, see Klarwill, 330–2. See also the reference on p. 203 below.

[413] The Star Chamber had its own kitchens and the Council dined there when it sat in Star Chamber. See, for some examples, A.L. Simon, *The Star Chamber Dinner Accounts* (Food and Wine Society, 1959).

[414] Probably Giovanni Baptista Castiglioni (d.c.1589), Groom of the Privy Chamber, 1559–1589, and Elizabeth's former Italian tutor. His son, (Sir) Francis Castilion (1561–1638), MP, served in the Netherlands in 1586 and was a member of the Netherlands household in 1587. Francis Castilion may be the 'young Mr Baptist' on p. 196 below (n. 658) and the Francis Baptist at Leicester's funeral.

as appereth by his bill}   vjli. iiijs. viijd.
To him more for the charges of your lordship's
horsses and fower servants at Braynford the
xth of October for one night}   xs.
To him more which he paid the xijth of October
for the charges of viij horses and your lordship's
servants at Braynford}   xs.
Given in reward the same day by your lordship's
commandment to Mr Secretory Walsingham's man for
presenting a stagges headd to your lordship}   vs.
To Mr Gorge* the same day which he gave in
reward by your lordship's commandment to the
nurce and mydwief at the christening of Mr Richard
Knolles' childe}   xls.
Given in reward the same day by your lordship's
commandment to Sir Pierce a Lees man for
presenting a stagg}   xxs.[415]
To Mr Blunt the same day which he gave to
a poore woman}   xijd.
To Roger Gillions for carring your lordship
and my lady in your lordship's barge from
the xvijth of November till the xxiijth of the
same moneth as appeareth by his bill}   xljs.
To Mathew* the groome the same daie for his
charges being sent by Mr Sandes from Hampton
Courte to Graies and to Whitney}   ijs. xjd.
To him more the same day for his charges being
sent to Windsor about your lordship's busynes}   ijs.[416]
Gyven in reward the same day by your lordship's
commandment to a poore woman at St James's}   vs.
Gyven in reward the same day by your lordship's
commandment to my Lord Stafford's man for bringing
your lordship letters and a proxcei}   xs.[417]
Gyven in reward the xxvjth of November by your
lordship's commandment to Awdryan at his goyng

---

[415] Sir Piers Leigh of Lyme (Ches.). Leicester wrote to him on 19 November thanking him for sending a hind and a hound (JRL, Leigh of Lyme Correspondence, folder 1). The month in the date of the letter is obscured, but the letter does raise queries about the accuracy of the entries here.

[416] As Constable of Windsor Castle (see n. 299).

[417] Edward, 13th Lord Stafford (1536–1603). The proxy was recorded on 27 November. Leicester was Lord Steward for the parliament and in attendance at the opening on 23–4 November where he presided over the swearing in of the MPs (Wright, ii, 243). He was absent for the rest of November and on 1 and 2 December (attendances and other Lords business are taken from *Lords Journals*, ii (1581–1614), 61–108).

downe to Kenelworth}   xls.
Summa Paginae: xvli. xjs. vijd.

[recto]

xxvjth of November [1584]

Your lordship loste in play the same day at St James's}   xxxs.
To Mr Sandes which he paid the xxvth of November
for two torches for your lordship}   ijs.
Gyven in reward the xxvjth of November by your
lordship's commandment to James Iresshe of the larder}   xs.
Delivered to Mr Wigges* the same day by your
lordship's commandment for certeyne charges of
your lordship}   vli.
Gyven in reward the same day by your lordship's
commandment to Mr Dudley* your lordship's paige}   xxs.
To Harry Griffin* the xxvijth of November which
he paid for sprattes for your lordship}   vjd.
Paid for the two messes for your lordship's servants
from the xvth of November untill the xxixth
of the same month}   lvjs. viijd.
Given in reward the same day by your lordship's
commandment to my Lord Chamberlain's man for
presenting a doe to your lordship}   vjs. viijd.
Your lordship loste in play to Mr Leake the
xxixth of November at St James's}   iiili.[418]
Your lordship loste more in play the laste of
November at Leicester House}   xxs.
Your lordship loste more in plaie the second of
December at Leicester House}   xxxs.
To Mr Edmond Stafford* your lordship's servant
the iiith of December which your lordship gave
in reward to Cuttye Musgrave*}   iiili.
Delivered to Mr Dudley the same day by your
lordship's commandment to geve to my Lord of
Abergaineis man for bringing his proxcie}   xs.[419]
Payd to Mrs Cruxstone the iiijth of December
by your lordship's commandment for two dowblettes

[418] (Sir) Francis Leak (c.1542–1626), of Sutton Scarsdale, Derbys., MP. In 1605 he recalled that he 'was much bound in dutie' to Leicester (Lodge, iii, 166). On 29 November Leicester wrote to Hotman from the Court (AMAE, CPH, II, fo. 159).

[419] Henry Neville, 6th Lord Abergavenny (d.1587). Although this entry would imply that it was received on 3 or 4 December, the proxy was recorded on 27 November.

for my lady}   xxijli.[420]
Gyven in reward the vth of December by your
lordship's commandment to my Lord Mordentes
man for presenting a gelte buck to your lordship}   xs.[421]
To Roger Gyllions the vjth of December for
carring your lordship at sondrie tymes in your
lordship's barge as appeareth by his bill}   liiijs.
Summa Paginae: xlvli. ixs. xd.

[verso]

vjth of December [1584]
To Mr Sandes the same daie which he gave in
reward by your lordship's commandment to Sir
Henrie Nevilles man for presenting phesaunts
to your lordship}   ijs. vjd.[422]
To Richard Meredyth* the same daie which he gave
in reward by your lordship's commandment to Sir
Jerome Bowes's man for presenting a liefe sables [sic]
and the head of a stag to your lordship}   xxs.
Given in reward the vijth of December by your
lordship's commandment to the wyddowe King*
of Killingworth}   xls.
To Mr Dudley your lordship's paige the same day
which he gave by your lordship's commandment at
the chapple for your lordship's offring}   xijd.
To Owen Jones and Birche your lordship's
servants the viijth of December by your
lordship's commandment which they paid for a
hogshedd of white wine for your lordship}   iiijli. vjs. viijd.
Gyven the same day by your lordship's
commandment to the man where the wyne dyd stand}   vs.
Paid to Mr Parr the imbroderer the same day
for thre stomagers for your lordship at xviijs. a pece}   liiijs.
To him more the same daie for haulf a yearde

---

[420] Probably the same woman as the widow Croxton on p. 207 below, possibly related
to Leicester's cook Paul Croxton*.

[421] Lewis, 3rd Lord Mordaunt (1538–1601), MP. Although there is a reference in his
entry in Hasler to his 'near friendship' with Leicester, no evidence of this survives apart
from land sales to him in 1564 and 1574 (Longleat MSS 476–7).

[422] Sir Henry Neville (1520–93) of Billingbere, Berks., MP. Although Neville appears to
have been suspicious of Leicester at the beginning of the reign, Leicester appointed him
keeper of several of the parks of Windsor in 1563 and lieutenant of Windsor Castle in
1576 (PRO, SC6/ElizI/148).

and haulf a quarter of skarlett to lyne the
stomagers at xl*s.* the yeard}   xxvs.
Gyven in reward the ixth of December by your
lordship's commandment to one Mr Mathew a
Skottisshe preacher}   xxli.[423]
Your lordship loste in play the same day at Leicester House}   xxli.
To Mr Blunt the same day which he gave in reward
by your lordship's commandment to Leonard and Peter
the gardneirs at Whithall}   xs.
Your lordship loste in plaie at Leicester House
the ixth of December}   xls.
To Mr Sandes the same daie which he gave in reward
by your lordship's commandment to the Quenes
watermen for carring your lordship from Arrondell
House to Leicester House}   xs.
To him more which he delivered to your lordship
at the Parlyment House}   ijs.[424]
Your lordship loste at plaie at Wansted the
xjth of December}   xjs.

                    Summa Paginae: xlvli. vijs. ijd.

[recto]

                        xjth of December [1584]
Delivered to your lordship to geve to the poore
in small money from the first of December to the
xijth of the same month}   viijs.
To John Kellie* the same day which he gave to a
poore man in Fletestrete by your lordship's commandment}   vjd.
To him more the same daie which he gave to
the Spittle House}   vjd.
Gyven in reward the xijth of December by your
lordship's commandment to Savadges man for finding
of a hare for your lordship}   xijd.
Given in reward the same daie by your lordship's
commandment to Mr Ackton* your lordship's servant
at his goying in to the countrie}   iiili. vjs. viijd.
To Stephen Johnson the xiijth of December which
he paid for two girdelles and two paire of hangers
for your lordship trymed with gould lace for two

[423] He is not mentioned in G. Donaldson, 'Scottish Presbyterian Exiles in England
1584–8', in *Scottish Church History* (Edinburgh, 1985), pp. 178–90.
[424] Leicester attended the Lords on 4–6, 9–10, 14–5, 19 and 21 December.

shortswords of your lordship's}   iiili. xiijs. ijd.
To him more the same daie for divers necessaries for
your lordship as appereth by his bill}   ixs. xd.
To Roger Gillions and Merrick for carring your
lordship and my lady from the iiijth of December
to the xijth of the same moneth as appereth
by their bill}   xlixs.
To Owen Jones the same daie which he paid for
iij bottells of Warwickshere water}   ijs. ixd.[425]
Paid for the two messes of meate for your
lordship's servants from the xxixth of November
untill the xiijth of December}   lvjs. viijd.
Delivered to Gramer* of Killingworth for
your lordship's spaniell keper for keping of v
cowple of spaniells for a month from the xxvjth
of October till the xxiijth of November
at jd. a pece}   xxiijs. iiijd.
Gyven in reward the xiiijth of December by your
lordship's commandment to Thomas Sherman of
Chesshere a suetor to your lordship}   xxs.
To Mr Blunt the same daie which he gave in reward
by your lordship's commandment to Mr Trencher's man
for presenting two geldinges to your lordship}   xls.[426]
                Summa Paginae: xvijli. xjs. vd.

[verso]

                xvth of December [1584]
Gyven in reward the same daie by your lordship's
commandment to Gramer of Kenelworth for bringing up
phesaunts to your lordship}   xiijs. iiijd.
Gyven in reward the same daie by your lordship's
commandment to the keper of the dore at the
Parlyment House}   vs.
Gyven in reward the same daie by your lordship's
commandment to another olde man theire the same tyme}   ijs.
Paid the same daie by your lordship's commandment
to Robert More* in part payment for a new koche}   vjli. xiijs. iiijd.
To Mr Thomas Dudley the same daie which he gave
in reward by your lordship's commandment to Mr

---

[425] See also the references in nn. 577, 595 below, probably from the well at King's
Newnham.
[426] It is possible that the name is Trench rather than Trencher.

Tavernor* goyng into Kent}   <a>   liijs. iiijd.

To Roger Gillyons and Merrick for carring your
lordship at sondrie tymes in your lordship's
barge as appereth by their bill}   xxvjs.

To Lewes the yeoman usher the xvjth of December
which he paid for a shorte sworde blade which
was bought in Westminster for your lordship}   xiijs. iiijd.

To him more the same day which he paid for two
torches when your lordship came from the
Bishop of Canterburyes}   ijs. iiijd.[427]

Your lordship loste in play the same day at
Leicester House}   xli.

To Mr Aytie the same day which he gave in reward
by your lordship's commandment to Doctor Underhilles
man for bringing up one Long a sedicious papest
from Oxeford} <Q.a>   xls.[428]

Gyven in reward the xvijth of December by your
lordship's commandment to Mr Hynde* your lordship's
servant goyng into the countrie with
your lordship's hawkes}   iijli. vjs. viijd.

Gyven in reward the same daie by your lordship's
commandment to Mr Fetherstone parsone of
Hampton in Arden at his goying in to the countrie}   xls.[429]

Your lordship loste in play the xixth of December
at Saynt James's}   iijli.

             Summa Paginae: xxxijli. xvs. iiijd.

[recto]

xixth of December [1584]

Given in reward by your lordship's commandment
to the keper of St James's Park when your
lordship came from Chelsey}   ijs.

To Mr Greene which he gave in reward by your

[427] This entry suggests that 16 December was the date of the 'Lambeth Conference', which Leicester called to an end 'as it grew late' (*Seconde Parte of a Reg.*, i, 283).

[428] John Underhill (d.1592), a former chaplain, rector of Lincoln College from 1577, following a disputed election in which Leicester played a controversial role (see Williams, 'State, Church and University, 425–9), and Bishop of Oxford 1589–92.

[429] Leonard Featherstone, a member of the Warwickshire classis. He is also identified as vicar of Hampton in Arden in J.C. Adams, *Hampton in Arden. A Warwickshire Village* (Birmingham. n.d.), p. 52, but in the 1586 survey of the ministry in Warwickshire (*Seconde Parte of a Reg.*, ii, 174), which describes him as 'no allowed preacher, but dilligent in his cure and honest' he is identified as vicar of Long Itchington. Both were manors of Leicester's.

lordship's commandment to Mr Butler's nurce
at Waltone at the Justice Seate}
    xs.[430]

To Mr Blunt the xx[ij]'th of December which he gave
in reward to the Quenes watermen for carryng
your lordship over the water that day her
Majestie removed to Grenewich}
    xs.[431]

To Steven Johnson the same day for his botehire
from Grenewich to Leicester House with your
lordship's apparell}
    xviijd.

Payd for xj cartes to carry your lordship's stuff
from St James's to Grenewich the same day}
    viijs. jd.

To William Thomas* the same daie for his botehire
from London to Grenewich and for bordwaiges
for iij meales goying before to make reddie
the lodging [house *deleted*]}
    ijs. vjd.

Gyven in reward the same daie by your lordship's
commandment to Brampton at his goyng into the
countrie at Christmas}
    xls.

Gyven in reward the same daie by your lordship's
commandment to one Mr Carldon whose boy plaide on
the lute before your lordship}
    xxs.

Gyven in reward the same day by your lordship's
commandment to one that dyd let your lordship
in at the friers' gate}
    xijd.

Paid to xij of your lordship's yeomen for their
dynners the xvijth of November attending in the
Tiltyeard at Westminster}
    vjs.

To Steven Johnson which he gave to two poore folk
at the Parlyment House the xviijth of December}
    vjd.[432]

Paid for a looking glasse for your lordship
the xixth of December}
    iijs.

Paid more the same daie for haulf a dossin of

---

[430] This is one of several occasions in 1584–5 when Leicester is found presiding over the Waltham Forest court (see p. 242 below, and BL, Harl. MS 6993, fo. 70, and *CSPF, 1585–6*, 331, to Burghley, 8 July 1584 and 29 Jan. 1586). He does not appear to have held the keepership of Waltham, but on 25 November 1585 he was appointed Chief Justice in Eyre of the Forests south of the Trent (PRO, C66/1271). This office had held by the Earl of Sussex until his death in October 1583, and Leicester may have been acting in a temporary capacity in the interval. (Sir) Philip Butler (d.1592) of Watton Woodhall, Herts., MP, was married to Sir Francis Knollys' daughter Catherine, served in the Netherlands 1586, and was a supporter of the pall at Leicester's funeral. He is referred to frequently below.

[431] The Court removed to Greenwich just before Christmas where it remained until February.

[432] The Lords did not sit on the 18th.

course towells for your lordship}	vs. vjd.
Paid for two realme of coarse paper for your lordship}	vs. iiijd.

Summa Paginae: vli. xvs. vd.

[verso]

xxth of December [1584]

Paid the same daie for a realme of writing paper for your lordship}	vs. vjd.
Paid to a matlaier at Leicester House the same daie by your lordship's commandment in full payment of his bill} <a>	iijli.
Your lordship loste in plaie the same day at Leicester House}	xls.
Gyven in reward the xxijth of December by your lordship's commandment to Mr Cotten's man of the Wardrop}	xs.
Gyven in reward the same daie by your lordship's commandment to Mr Gabriell Bleekes man for presenting two swannes and a lamprie pye to your lordship}	vs.[433]
Gyven in reward the xxijth of December by your lordship's commandment to young Dockray at his goying into the countrie}	xxs.
Paid to John Savage the mattmaker the same daie in full dischardge off all reckonings as appereth by his bill} <a>	iiijli. xiiijs. xd.
Paid to the joyner at Leicester House the same day for vj joyned stooles}	ixs.
Gyven to a poore woman at Ratlief the same daie by your lordship's commandment}	vs.
Gyven in reward the same [day *omitted*] by your lordship's commandment to one Gifford a precher at Wansted}	vli.[434]
Given in reward the same daie by your lordship's commandment to Tobye Mathew* your lordship's servant at his goying into the country}	iijli. vjs. viijd.

[433] Gabriel Blike (c.1520–92) of Massington, Herefs. and Churcham, Glos., MP. Blike was a central, if shadowy, figure in Leicester's Gloucestershire connection throughout the 1570s and 80s, see 'West Midlands', 45, 'House of Commons', 221, and further references below. He attended Leicester's funeral.

[434] Probably George Gifford (d.1620), the suspended vicar of St Peter's and All Saints', Maldon, and an active member of the classical movement. He served as a chaplain in the Netherlands, see p. 368, n. 719 below.

Paid to Gramer of Killingworth the xxiiijth of
December for bringing a brace of does}   xs.
Paid to Thomas Underhilles man the same day by
your lordship's commandment for bringing two
carpettes from Killingworth}   xs.
Delivered to your lordship to put in your
lordship's pursse at Wansted for the poore the
xxijth of December}   vs.
To Roger Gillions for carring your lordship ix
sondri tymes in your lordship's barge from the
xvijth of December untill the xxiiijth
of the same month as appereth by his bill}   iiijli. ijs.
              Summa Paginae: xxvjli. iijs.

[recto]

              xxvijth of December [1584]
Payd for the two messes of meate for your lordship's
servants for a fortnight from the xiijth of December
untill the xxvijth of the same month}   lvjs. viijd.
Paid for the carredge of a new bedstede from
London to Grenewich for your lordship}   xijd.
To Richard Gardneir which he laid oute for iiij
dossin of larcks that he carried to Leicester
House and for caring a brace of does by water
to Leicester House the first of November}   iijs. viijd.
To him more for his bordwaiges for iij daies being
sent to St James's to make reddy your lordship's
lodgings}   iijs.
Paid to the fletcher that makes your lordship's
white staves the xxviijth of December by your
lordship's commandment}   xs.[435]
Delivered to Careles* the same day by
your lordship's commandment}   xls.
Gyven in reward the xxviijth of December by your
lordship's commandment to Mrs Barrett's man for
presenting preserved quinches to your lordship}   xs.[436]

[435] Presumably the wands carried by Household officers. Leopold von Wedel observed
his presence with the other Household officers carrying their staves at a banquet at
Hampton Court on 27 December (Klarwill, p. 335). The absence of any reference to
Hampton Court here suggests that it may be an error for Greenwich.

[436] Probably Mrs Lettice Barrett, the Countess's maid, to whom Leicester left £100 in
his 1582 will, and the Mrs Lettice at his funeral. There is a further reference to her on
p. 306 below.

To Harry Cater the same daie which he gave in
reward by your lordship's commandment to my Lord
Amyralles man for delivering cranes}   xs.
To Mr Franceis Knolles the same daie which he
gave in reward to the nurce and mydwief at the
christening of one Mr Bluntes child at Windsor}   xls.[437]
To Stephen Johnson the same daie which he paid
for vj dossin and iij buttons weying a oz. di
and iij peny wight at lvs. the oz.}   iiijli. xs. ixd.
To him more which he paid for fashioning of
the same buttons}   xviijs.
To him more the same daie for his botehire from
Grenewich to London and backe ageyne goying for
a shortgowen furred with sables to shewe the skinner}   ijs.
Gyven in reward the same daie by your lordship's
commandment to the Quenes plaiers at Leicester House}   xli.
To Fardenandoe which he gave in reward by your
lordship's commandment to George the sweper}   ijs. vjd.
Given in reward the xxixth of December by your
lordship's commandment to Mr Tavernower at his
goying into Warwickshere}   <a>   vli.
                Summa Paginae: xxixli. vijs. vijd.

[verso]

                    xxxth of December [1584]
Gyven in reward the same day by your lordship's
commandment to Mother Ossynus at Grenewich}   xxxs.
To Bakehowse* your lordship's servant the same
day which he paid for making xx bowes}   ls.
To ix of your lordship's yeomen for their bordwaiges
and botehire being sent before from St James's
to Grenewich with your lordship's stuff}   ixs.
Paid for two torches to light your lordship
the same night when your lordship was in London at

[437] (Sir) Francis Knollys the younger (1550–1648), MP. He commanded the *Galleon Leicester* on the West Indies Voyage, was captain of Leicester's guard in the Netherlands in 1587, and had a chamber at Leicester House. He is more likely than his father to have been the Sir Francis Knollys among the knights at Leicester's funeral. The identity of Mr Blunt is unclear.

the Scottisshe imbassador's}	ijs.[438]
Your lordship loste in plaie at Grenewich the xxixth of December}	xls.
Gyven in reward the first of January by your lordship's commandment to one Burton that made cleane two carpetts for your lordship}	xxs.
Gyven in reward the same day by your lordship's commandment to Ned Wilperforce being New Yeres Day}	xls.
Gyven in reward by your lordship's commandment to vj poore folkes at Towerhill the laste of December}	vjd.
Gyven in reward the same day by your lordship's commandment to Mr Secretory Walsingham's kocheman for carring your lordship to Leicester House}	vs.
Gyven in reward the same day by your lordship's commandment to the wyddowe Croxson at Grenewich}	xxs.[439]
To Mr Bapteste the firste of January which he gave in reward by your lordship's commandment to the extraordinary paiges}	xxxs.[440]
Gyven in reward the same day by your lordship's commandment to William Worteley being New Yeres Day}	xls.
Gyven in reward the second of January by your lordship's commandment to Thomas King your lordship's servant at Wanstead}	xxs.
Gyven in reward the same day by your lordship's commandment to [blank] wief for presenting two fighting to your lordship} <wherefore>[g]	xs.
Gyven in reward the same day by your lordship's commandment to Gillam's wief the gardneir at [Leicester House deleted] Wansted}	vs.

Summa Paginae: vjli. xviijd.

---

[438] Patrick, Master of Gray (d. 1611), later 6th Lord Gray, James VI's current favourite. His embassy in England (October 1584–January 1585) was possibly the most controversial episode of his notorious career. Sent to plead for Mary, he was won over by Leicester, Walsingham and Philip Sidney to support the English interest. Some of his subsequent correspondence with Leicester is printed in T. Thomson (ed.), *Letters and papers relating to Patrick, Master of Gray* (Bannatyne Club, xlviii, 1835).

[439] Leicester wrote to Davison from Greenwich on 31 December (PRO, SP83/23/art. 97).

[440] Presumably the Queen's pages. If Leicester continued to give New Year's presents to the personnel of the Household generally, as he did in 1560 and 1561, these must have been entered in another account.

[recto]

iijth of January [1585]

Given in reward the same day to Gramer of Killingworth for bringing two dossin of phesaunts from thence to your lordship}	iijs. iiijd.
Delivered more to him to geve to your lordship's spaniell keper for keping v cowple of spaniells from the xxiiith of November till the xxjth of December at jd. a dog a day}	xxiijs. iiijd.
Gyven in reward the iijth of January by your lordship's commandment to the servants of the Juell House when your lordship went throwe their}	xs.
To Warner the same day for carring your lordship from Grenewich to Blackwall and back ageyne}	viijs.
Gyven in reward the firste of January by your lordship's commandment to Harrys your lordship's shomaker}	xs.
Gyven in reward the iiijth of January by your lordship's commandment to a woman that presentid buttons to your lordship at Grenewich}	xs.
Gyven by your lordship's commandment the same day to the poore betwene Wansted and London}	xviijd.
Delivered to Danyel Downell* your lordship's new footeman the same day to geve to your lordship in Wansted Heath}	xxxs.
Your lordship loste in plaie the same daie at nighte at Leicester House}	vli.
To Harry Cater the same day for his charges being sent to my Lord Amyrall's for cranes}	vijs.
Gyven in reward the same day by your lordship's commandment to one that brought hangings to Leicester House}	vs.
Paid to a porter that carried your lordship's bed from the upholsters to St James's}	xiiijd.
Gyven to the poore at Towerhill the vth of January by your lordship's commandment}	vjd.
To Warner for carring your lordship from Grenewich to Blackwall the iiijth of January}	viijs.
Paid for botehire for myself, Pitcheford and Stephen from Leicester House to Grenewich the vjth of January}	xviijd.

Summa Paginae: xli. xixs. iiijd.

[recto]

vjth of January [1585]

Gyven in reward the same day by your lordship's
commandment to Mr Bleekes man for carring
letters to my Lord Deputy of Ireland} xxs.[441]
To Fardenandoe the same day for his quarter's
waiges due at Christmas last at x*li*. per annum} ls.
To Gillam's wief your lordship's lander for hir
quarter's waiges due at Christmas laste at x*li*. per annum} ls.
Given in reward by your lordship's commandment
to Roger Gillions and the rest of the watermen
at two sondry tymes the xxvjth of December and
the first of January which your lordship gave
them to drinck} xvs.
To Ambrose Waller* which he paid for hawks' hoods,
bells, peppering and tryming of iiij cast and
haulf of hawks of your lordship} xvs. viijd.
To Roger Gillions more which your lordship gave
him for his New Yeres gifte the first of January} xs.
To him more for carring your lordship in your
lordship's barge at vij sondry tymes as appereth
by his bill} iiijli. iiijs.
To Owen Jones which he paid the vth of January
for a torche for your lordship at Towerhill
and for two bottells to put wyne in} xviijd.
To Richard Pepper your lordship's footeman
which he gave by your lordship's commandment to
the Spitle in Kentisshestrete the vjth of January} vjd.[442]
To Mr Bentall* for his botehire from Grenewich
to Leicester House the xxviijth of December
being sent to my lady} ijs. viijd.
To Stephen Johnson for his botehire on twelve
yeve at night from Leicester House to
Grenewich and back ageyne being sent for dyvers
necessaries for your lordship} vs.
Gyven in reward the vjth of January by your
lordship's commandment to Mr Sackford a cup

[441] Sir John Perrot (c.1528/9–92), MP, Lord Deputy 1584–88. Perrot's letters to Leicester for this period are copied in his letterbook (Bodl., MS Perrot 1), but none from Leicester have survived. Perrot's letter of 17 February 1585 (fo. 64) acknowledges receipt of one from Leicester of 4 January. Bleke was probably Gabriel, see n. 433 above, who had served in Ireland in the early 1550s and may have retained some Irish interests.
[442] The Old Kent Road.

with xx*li*. for presenting the Quenes New Yeres gefte}   xxli.[443]
Gyven in reward the same day by your lordship's
commandment to Mr Rawles blackamoore}   xxs.[444]
Gyven in reward the same day by your lordship's
commandment to the locksmith of the armory for
making forks to fishe withall}   vs.
                Summa Paginae: xxxiijli. xixs. iiijd.

[recto]

vijth of January [1585]

Gyven in reward the same day by your lordship's
commandment to yong Mr Marckwilliams at the Courte}   xls.[445]
To Roger Gillions for carring your lordship from
Leicester House to Grenewich and back to Tower
Wharf the vth of January}   xijs.
To him more for caring your lordship from
Leicester House to Parris Garden steres the
vjth of January}   ixs.
To him more for carring your lordship from
Grenewich to Leicester House the vijth of January}   xijs.
Paid to Haunce Corpreo the same day for a paire of
braceletts garnished with dyamonds and rubies
uppon jett and elke's hooff}   xviijli.
To Mr Dudley which he gave in reward by your
lordship's commandment to one that went
for Mr Goldinggam*}   xs.
Gyven in reward the same day by your lordship's
commandment to Beneston the preacher at Leicester House}   ls.[446]
Your lordship loste in plaie the same day at night

[443] Henry Seckford, Groom of the Privy Chamber 1559–1603, Keeper of the Privy Purse from 1570.

[444] At the beginning of 1585 Walter Ralegh, an Esquire of the Body since 1581, was about to achieve some prominence at Court, and preparing the voyage to Virginia. Although one of Leicester's principal 'backbiters' in 1586–7, he had looked to him for patronage in the early 1580s. Presumably his blackamore was not the same man as the blackamore mentioned above, see n. 364.

[445] Probably Henry (d. 1599), son of Henry Macwilliam, the Gentleman Pensioner, see n. 81 above.

[446] Probably Barnaby Benison, preacher of London, imprisoned by Bishop Aylmer in 1584, who in turn was probably the Barnabas Benison, who matriculated at Trinity College (Cant.) in 1566 and was ordained a deacon in 1568. On 14 November 1584 the Privy Council, Leicester among them, ordered Aylmer to free him. Leicester may have been anonymous Councillor to whom he petitioned in 1580. See *Seconde Parte of a Reg*, i, 246–7. There are also possible references to him on pp. 234, 307 below.

at Leicester House}   xli.
Given in reward the same day by your lordship's
commandment to Harry Griffyn}   vli.
To Buck* your lordship's servant which he paid
for two botes to carry two truncks and hampers
with bottells from Grenewich to Leicester House}   iijs.
To him more the same day for the dynners for
himself, John Keame, Mathew Woodward and John
Nettleton* your lordship's servants attending
on the stuffe}   ijs.
Gyven in reward the same day (viijth of January)
by your lordship's commandment to Danyell Downell
the new footeman being sent from Colbrook to
Mr Babbington's}   vs.[447]
Gyven in reward the same day by your lordship's
commandment to my Lord Shandoes' musycians at Colbrook}   xs.[448]
Paid the same day for the charges of your lordship's
dynner at Colbrook}   iiili. xijs. vjd.
Delivered to Mr Blunt the same day at Colbrooke
imprest for horsemeate}   xli.
                    Summa Paginae: liiijli. vs. vjd.

[verso]

                        viijth of January [1585]
Gyven in reward the same day by your lordship's
commandment to the servants of the house at Colbrooke
where your lordship dyned}   xs.
Gyven in reward the same day by your lordship's
commandment to Ned Stone and Stringer
the Quenes footemen}   iiijli.
Paid for the supper and breakefaste for the iij
sumptermen and v of your lordship's men the
vjth and viijth of January}   ixs. iiijd.
Your lordship loste a[t] dice the same day
at night at Greys}   xxxs.
Gyven in reward the ixth of January by your
lordship's commandment to Mother Blackoll at

---

[447] Probably Philip Babbington, who served in the Netherlands in 1586. This entry
marks the beginning of Leicester's second visit to his son during the period of this
account, it probably began on 8 January. Parliament had been prorogued on 21
December until 4 February.
[448] Gyles Bridges, 3rd Lord Chandos (1548–94). He was an assistant mourner at
Leicester's funeral.

212 HOUSEHOLD ACCOUNTS OF ROBERT DUDLEY

Greis for presenting two capons to your lordship}   xxs.
Gyven in reward the same day by your lordship's
commandment to the servants of the house at Greys}   xxs.
Gyven to the poore at Greys the same day}   xijd.
Gyven in reward the same day by your lordship's
commandment to Smulkin for comyng from London to Oxeford} vs.
Delivered to your lordship the same day which
your lordship gave to the poore between
Colbrooke and Oxeford}   iiis.
Gyven in reward the xth of January by your
lordship's commandment to Dannyell Downell the
footeman being sente from Oxeford to London}   vs.
Gyven in reward the same day by your lordship's
commandment to the servants of the house at
the Dean's of Christ Churge in Oxeford}   xxs.[449]
Paid for the two messes of meate for your
lordship's servants for a fortnight from the
xxvijth of December untill the xth of January}   lvjs. viijd.
Gyven in reward the xjth of January by your
lordship's commandment to the servants of the
house at Mr Doctor Humfrey's}   xxs.[450]
Gyven in reward the same day by your lordship's
commandment to Mr Doctor Dellapere}   vli.
Gyven in reward the same day by your lordship's
commandment to the musycians at Oxeford}   xxs.
Summa Paginae: xlviijli. xs.

[recto]

xjth of January [1585]
To Mr Aytie the same day which he gave in reward
by your lordship's commandment to Synneor Gentyle
at Oxeford}   vli.[451]

[449] William James (d. 1617), a former chaplain, Archdeacon of Coventry 1577–84, Dean of Christ Church from 1584, vice-chancellor of Oxford 1589 and Bishop of Durham 1606–17. Leicester employed him in the Netherlands in 1586 and he is said to have attended Leicester on his deathbed. The expenses of Leicester's visit are recorded in Christ Church, Treasurer's Book xii.b.27, fos. 33–5, and it is also discussed in F.S. Boas, *University Drama in the Tudor Age* (Oxford, 1914), p. 192, where it is suggested that Leicester was accompanied by Sir Philip Sidney and the 2nd Earl of Pembroke. For a possible connection to the revival of Oxford University Press, see n. 488 below.

[450] Lawrence Humphrey (1527–1590), president of Magdalen College, vice-chancellor of Oxford at Leicester's nomination 1567–76.

[451] Alberico Gentili (1551–1608), appointed Regis Professor of Civil Law by Leicester in 1580. Atye may have been a personal friend, for evidence of correspondence between them survives (see PRO, SP12/147/43, Gentili to Atye, 27 Jan. 1581).

To hym more the same day which he gave in reward
by your lordship's commandment to the bedells at Oxeford}   iijli.
Gyven in reward the same day by your lordship's
commandment to yong Mr Clynton at Oxeford}   iijli.
Payd for the footeman's charges at Oxeford from
Satterday night till Monday morning}   xviijs. iijd.
Paid more for the charges of my Lord of
Comberland's fawckneir and my Lord Thomas
Howard's at Oxeford from Satterday night till
Monday morning}   xjs.[452]
Gyven in reward the same day by your lordship's
commandment to the singers at Sir Harry Ley's}   xs.
Your lordship loste in play at dice at Sir Harry
Ley's at Woodstock the same day at night}   lli.
Payd by your lordship's commandment to Mr
Arrundell which your lordship loste in play at
Leicester House}   xli.[453]
Given in reward the xijth of January by your
lordship's commandment to yong Dowcray at Sir Harry Leis}   xxs.
Your lordship loste in play to Mr Drake the same day}   ls.
Gyven in reward the same day by your lordship's
commandment to the servants of the house at
Sir Harry Leis}   xls.
Gyven in reward the xiijth of January by your
lordship's commandment to the singers at Mr
Umpton's at two sondry tymes}   xvs.[454]
To Smulkin which he gave by your lordship's
commandment to divers poore folks betwene
Oxeford and Woodstock}   xxjd.
To Richard Pepper which he gave by your
lordship's commandment to sondrie poore folks
betwene Colbrooke and Oxeford}   iijs.
Paid to a woman at Woodstock for wasshing
your lordship's lynnen}   xviijd.
Delivered to Mr Blunt the xiiijth of January by
your lordship's commandment at Bruern Mr Umpton's

---

[452] Lord Thomas Howard (1561–1626), the future Earl of Suffolk, was Norfolk's second
son. George, 3rd Earl of Cumberland (1558–1605), was married to Bedford's daughter
Margaret, who is referred to on p. 315 below.

[453] Probably John Arundel, who served in the Netherlands in 1586, and claimed a debt
of £1050 from Leicester's estate.

[454] (Sir) Henry Unton (1558–96), MP, son of Edward (see above n. 15), and the future
ambassador. He served in the Netherlands in 1586, but is usually described as a follower
of Hatton's.

imprest for horsemeat}   xli.
Gyven in reward the same day by your lordship's
commandment to Ned Wilperforce}   xxs.
                    Summa Paginae: iiii^{xx}xli. ixs. vjd.

[verso]

                    xiiijth of January [1585]
Gyven in reward the same day by your lordship's
commandment to the musycians at Mr Umpton's}   xs.
Gyven in reward the same daie by your lordship's
commandment to the servants of the house at Mr Umpton's}   xxs.
To Ned Wilperforce the same daie which he gave
to the poore at Langley by your lordship's commandment}   xijd.
Gyven in reward the same day by your lordship's
commandment to olde Cutty Musgrave* at Mr Umpton's}   iijli.
Gyven in reward the xvth of January by your
lordship's commandment to Sir Henry Leis man for
bringing two hindes to Whitney to your lordship}   xxs.
Gyven in reward the same day by your lordship's
commandment to Humfrey your lordship's footeman
when he carried letters from Wytney to London}   vjs. viijd.
Gyven in reward the same day by your lordship's
commandment to one that was sent from Witney
to Alesbery with a letter to Mr John Aysshfeld}   vs.[455]
To Mr John Tracye* the same day which he gave
in reward by your lordship's commandment to Mr
Harrington's sone at Mynster}   xs.[456]
To Mr Dockray the same day which he gave in reward
to a keper of Langley}   vjs. viijd.
Gyven in reward the same day by your lordship's
commandment to one that went from Witney to
Mr Warnford's}   vs.
Gyven in reward the xvjth of January by your
lordship's commandment to Mr Fynes' men for

---

[455] Son of Humphrey Ashfield (see n. 390 above). He served in the Netherlands in
1586, see Hasler *sub* Thomas Peniston.

[456] Sir John Harington (1540–1613) of Combe Abbey, Wars., MP. He served in the
Netherlands in 1586, and was an assistant mourner at both Sidney's and Leicester's
funerals. In 1588–89 he was keeper of Kenilworth Castle for Warwick. There are several
further references to him below.

presenting a fatt oxe and other things at Whitney}   xiijs. iiijd.[457]
Gyven in reward the same day by your lordship's
commandment to my Lord Shandoes' man for presenting
divers kinde of fowle to your lordship}   xs.
Gyven in reward the same day by your lordship's
commandment to Mr Umpton's man for presenting
divers sorts of fowle, ij fatt wethers and other things}   xs.
Gyven in reward the same day by your lordship's
commandment to Mr Yates and one of his neighbours
for presenting two turkies and other things}   xs.[458]

Summa Paginae: ixli. vijs. viijd.

[recto]

xvth of January [1585]

Your lordship loste in play with Mr Drake the
same day at Witney}   vijli. xs.
Gyven in reward the xvjth of January by your
lordship's commandment to Mr Anthony Dockray
at his goyng from Witney to Kenelworth}   iijli.
Gyven in reward the same tyme by your lordship's
commandment to Awdryan the gardneir at his goyng
to Kenelworth}   xxs.
Delivered to your lordship at Witney the same
day to put in your lordship's purrse for the poore}   vs.
Gyven in reward the same daie by your lordship's
commandment to Danyell Downell the footeman at his
goyng from Witney to London}   ijs.
To Mr Dockray the same day which he gave to one
of Sir Harry Ley's men for bringing a fatt doe to Witney}   xvjd.
Gyven in reward the xvijth of January by your
lordship's commandment to Mr Brook's man the fawckneir}   xls.
Gyven in reward the same day by your lordship's
commandment to Mr Tippin's man for presenting a
fatt oxe and wethers to your lordship at Witney}   xs.[459]
Gyven in reward the same day by your lordship's
commandment to Smulkyn the footeman}   xs.
Paid to a landerer at Witney}   xijd.

[457] Richard Fiennes (1555–1613) of Broughton Castle, Oxon., MP, later Lord Saye and Sele. He obtained Leicester's support for his claim to the barony of Saye and Sele, see Hist MSS Comm., *Bath MSS*, v, 91, Leicester to Shrewsbury, 30 May 1588, and *Calendar of the Manscripts of the ... Marquis of Salisbury*, iii (1889), 529, 670.
[458] Possibly William Yates, who attended Leicester's funeral.
[459] Possibly George Tipping, who served in the Netherlands in 1586.

To Thomas Dawlton which he gave to a dum man at Mr Umpton's}	iijd.
Paid to Mr Doctor Dellapere the same day for v horsehire and their meate for Mr Robert Dudley when he came from Oxeford to Witney}	liijs. viijd.[460]
Gyven in reward the same day by your lordship's commandment to the servants of the house at Mr Brises at Witney}	xls.
Gyven in reward the same daie by your lordship's commandment to the nurce that kepes Mr Brises childe}	xs.
Gyven in reward the same day by your lordship's commandment to a pursuyvant that came with letters to Witney to your lordship}	xxs.

Summa Paginae: xxjli. iijs. iijd.

[verso]

xvijth of January [1585]

Gyven in reward the same day by your lordship's commandment to Mr Pooles man for presenting a fawkon to your lordship at Witney which Mr John Aysshfield had}	xls.[461]
Delivered to Mr Bowghton* the same day which your lordship gave to the poore of Witney}	xxxs.
Gyven in reward the same day by your lordship's commandment to the musycians at Witney}	xxs.
Paid to Mrs Brise of Witney the same day by your lordship's commandment for your lordship's charges their from Wensday supper till Sonday after dynner as appereth by billes made by Mr Ardern}	xxiijli. vjs. ijd.
Gyven in reward the xviijth of January by your lordship's commandment to the musycians at Abington at Mr Reades}	xs.[462]
Gyven in reward the same day by your lordship's commandment to a pursyvaunt at Mr Reades}	xs.
Gyven in reward the same day by your lordship's commandment to one that brought letters from Leicester House to Abbington to your lordship}	iijs. iiijd.
Gyven in reward the same day by your lordship's	

[460] See the discussion of Robert Dudley's residence in nn. 392–3.

[461] Probably (Sir) Henry Poole (1541–1616) of Sapperton Glos., MP, rather than his father Sir Giles (see n. 307 above). Poole attended Leicester's funeral.

[462] See n. 396 above.

commandment to the servants of the house at Mr Read's}   xxs.
Sent to Oxeford the same day by your lordship's
commandment by [*blank*] to be geven to the
nurce and mydwief at the christening of
Mr Buttell's childe}   xls.
Gyven in reward the same day by your lordship's
commandment to the singers at Mr Reades}   xs.
Gyven in reward the same day by your lordship's
commandment to my Lord Thomas Howard's man the
fawckneir}   xls.
Gyven by your lordship's commandment the same day
to the poore at Dorchester and to a poore smyth
at New Elme}   ijs.
Paid the same day by your lordship's commandment
for the charges of my Lord of Comberland's, my
Lord Thomas Howard's and Sir Thomas Sissell's
fawckneirs for themselves and their horsses
from Oxeford to Henly for viij daies as appereth
by their bill}   vli. ixs. iiijd.[463]
To Ned Wilperforce the xixth of January which he
gave to an olde man that gathered setts at Greys}   xs.
                  Summa Paginae: xlli. xs. xd.

[recto]

                  xixth of January [1585]
To Fenner* the same day which he gave in reward
by your lordship's commandment to the keper of
New Elme Parke}   xs.
To Richard Pepper which he gave by your lordship's
commandment to a poore woman at Abbington}   xijd.
Gyven in reward the same day by your lordship's
commandment to Richard Pepper at his goyng from
Greys to Porcemouth}   xs.
Gyven in reward the same day by your lordship's
commandment to the servants of the house at Greys}   xxs.
Gyven by your lordship's commandment to the poore at Greys}   ijs.
Gyven in reward the same day by your lordship's
commandment to my Lord Compton's man}   xs.[464]

---

[463] Sir Thomas Cecil (1542–1623), MP, Burghley's son. There is evidence, including
several further references here, that he and Leicester were on quite friendly terms. He
was appointed captain of the Brill in 1585.
[464] Henry, 1st Lord Compton (1538–89) of Compton Wynyates, Wars., MP.

Gyven in reward the same day by your lordship's
commandment to Mother Blackoll at Greys}   xxs.
To Mr Blunt the same day which he gave in reward
by your lordship's commandment to the yeoman of
the horsse at Greys}   xs.
Your lordship loste in play at Greys the xviijth
of January}   xxxs.
Delivered to Mr Blount the xixth of January by
your lordship's commandment imprest for horsemeate}   xli.
Gyven in reward the same day by your lordship's
commandment to the spittlehouses at Hamersmyth
and Knightbridg}   ijs.
Delivered to your lordship at Abbington to geve
to the poore}   ijs.
Delivered to your lordship which your lordship
loste in plaie the same day at night at
Leicester House}   <a>   xxli.
Gyven in reward the xxth of January by your
lordship's commandment to my Lord of
Comberland's fawckneir}   xxs.
Gyven in reward the same day by your lordship's
commandment to Sir Thomas Sessell's fawckneir}   xxs.
Gyven in reward the same day by your lordship's
commandment to Ezard* your lordship's bonesetter}   iijli.
Gyven in reward the same day by your lordship's
commandment to Mr Doctor James}   vjli. xiijs. iiijd.[465]
            Summa Paginae: xlvijli. xs. iiijd.

[verso]

            xxth of January [1585]
Payd to Mr Grene your lordship's gentilman usher
the same day by your lordship's commandment which he
laid oute for the charges of your lordship's men
and the sumptermen when your lordship rode into
Oxefordshere as appereth by his bill}   xijli. xiiijs. iijd.
Delivered to Mr Toplieff the xxjth of January by

[465] This and subsequent references to Dr James are probably not to the Dean of Christ
Church (see n. 449 above), but to Dr John James (d. 1601), physician and Keeper of the
State Papers 1581–1601, MP. Leicester appears to have been one of his patients and may
have obtained his appointment as Keeper. He attended Leicester in the Netherlands in
1586, where he kept the diary employed below (see Introduction, p. 32), and also attended
Leicester's funeral.

your lordship's commandment to pay for certene bookes}   vli.[466]
Gyven the same day to the poore by your lordship's
commandment between London and Grenewich}   ixd.
To Homerstone the same day by your lordship's
commandment which he laide oute for certene charges
about your lordship's bowes as appereth by his bill}   ixs. ijd.
Paid to Ambrose Waller the same day for a haggerd
fawkon which your lordship gave to olde Mr Davers*
your lordship's servant at Witney}   iiijli.
To Mr Blunt the same day by your lordship's
commandment in full payment of a bill of xxxij*li*.
v*s*. for the charges of your lordship's horsses from
the Courte into Oxefordshire and back ageyne as
appereth by his bill}   xlvs.
Gyven in reward the xxijth of January by your
lordship's commandment to Mr Brookes man at his
goyng into the country}   xxs.
Gyven in reward the xxiijth of January by your
lordship's commandment to the keper of the
gatehouse at Westminster for bringing vyneslippes
to your lordship}   ijs. vjd.
To Roger Gillions for carring your lordship in
your lordship's barge at iiij sondry tymes from
the xxth of January till the xxiiijth of the same
month as appeareth by his bill}   xlviijs.
Gyven in reward the same day by your lordship's
commandment to your lordship's fawckneir that
Mr Umpton preferred to your lordship at his
goyng into the country}   xxs.
Payd for the two messes of meate for your lordship's
servants for a fortnight from the xth of January
till the xxiiijth of the same month}   <a>   lvjs. viijd.
Gyven in reward the xxvth of January by your
lordship's commandment to Ned Wilperforce at
his goyng into the country}   xls.
Gyven in reward the same day by your lordship's
commandment to Thomas Dawlton your lordship's
footman at his goyng into Fraunce}   xls.
      Summa Paginae: xxxvli. xvjs. iiijd.

---

[466] Richard Topcliffe (1531–1604), MP. Topcliffe was a deponent in the Sir Robert
Dudley case, but his deposition has not survived. He later referred to his relations with
Leicester and Warwick as being 'never for that lucre which was the lure to many
followers' (Lodge, iii, 428–9).

[recto]

xxvth of January [1585]

To Warner the same day for carring your lordship from Grenewich to Blackwall and backe agayne}	viijs.
Delivered to Mr Ardern the xxvjth of January by your lordship's commandment at his going into Fraunce for the charges of a Frenche gardneir and a Frenche cooke to be sent into England and for Croxson* tarrying their}	xxli.[467]
Gyven in reward the same day by your lordship's commandment to Mr Ardern for his charges at his goyng into France with the Erle of Darby}	vli.
To Mr Edward Barker* the same day which he gave in reward by your lordship's commandment to Mr Morgan my Lady Lincolnes man when he brought the blacks}	xls.[468]
To Mr Blunt the same day which he gave in reward by your lordship's commandment to the grome of the stable that keipt the horsse which my Lord Amyrall gave your lordship at his death}	xs.
To him more which he gave in reward by your lordship's commandment to Sir Thomas Sissell's man for presenting a pyde nag to your lordship}	xxs.
Gyven in reward the xxviijth of January by your lordship's commandment to Jeronomye the Quenes musycian}	vli.
Gyven in reward the same day by your lordship's commandment to my Lord Shandoes' man for presenting x lampry pies to your lordship}	xs.

To Richard Pepper the xxiixth of January which
he gave by your lordship's commandment to the spitle

---

[467] Thomas Ardern accompanied the Earl of Derby (see n. 494 below) on his embassy to France at the end of January. Whether Ardern had any political errand is not clear, but his domestic tasks as outlined here are confirmed by two letters from Leicester to Jean Hotman from the Court on 23 and 24 January (FSL, MS Vb 282, and AMAE, CPH, II, fo. 249). Hotman and Ardern were to arrange for Leicester's kitchen boy Paul Croxton to be trained by 'some good principall cook in Parris', and to hire a French cook and a gardener. Leicester had first asked Hotman to look for a gardener in November (see n. 401 above), but when the man reached Wanstead c. 19 February (see p. 225) he was found unsatisfactory and he returned to France in April (see pp. 240–1). The cook, Pierre or Pierrot Moreau*, on the other hand, was a great success. Having sent Hotman detailed instructions for Croxton's supervision in Paris, Leicester decided in April 1585 that the political situation in France was too dangerous and recalled him, see AMAE, CPH, IV, fo. 47, Leicester to Hotman, 10 Apr. 1585.

[468] The Earl of Lincoln (n. 10 above) died on 16 January 1585, for his funeral see p. 224 below. For the Countess of Lincoln, see n. 166 above.

in Kent Streete xij*d*. and to a poore man at St
George's Church vj*d*.}   xviijd.
Paid to John Keame the same day by your lordship's
commandment which he laide out for bottells of wyne,
carridge of your lordship's drinck and for other
chargs from the xiiijth of August till the vth of
January as appereth by his billes}   iijli. vs. ixd.
To Mr Thomas Dudley the xxxth of January which he
gave in reward by your lordship's commandment to
Mr Jacobes man of the glashouse for presenting
glasses to your lordship at Leicester House}   xs.
           Summa Paginae: xxxviijli. vs. iijd.

[verso]

                    xxxth of January [1585]
Your lordship loste in play the same day at Wansted}   iiijli. xs.
Gyven in reward the same day by your lordship's
commandment to Mother Perkins at Wansted}   xs.
Gyven by your lordship's commandment to the
gardneir's boy at Wanstedd}   vjd.
Delivered to your lordship which your lordship gave
to the poore betwene Blackwall and Wansted}   iiijs. vjd.
Delivered to Mr Richard Browne the laste of January
by your lordship's commandment to pay worckmen's
waiges at Wanstead}   <a>   lli.
To him more the same day which he gave in reward
by your lordship's commandment to the baker and
the gardneir at Wansted}   <B>   xvs.
To Roger Gillions for carring your lordship v
sondry tymes in your lordship's barge from the
xxvjth of January till the last day of the same
month as appeareth by his bill}   iijli. xijd.
Your lordship lost in play at dice the firste
of February at Wansted to Sir Thomas Sessell,
Mr Warcope and Mr Drake}   <a>   xxxli.[469]
Given in reward the second of February by your
lordship's commandment to Garland* for his
charges in bringing a horsse to your lordship}   xxxs.
Your lordship lost in plaie at dice the same day
at night at Wansted}   <a>   xli.
Gyven in reward the iijth of February by your

[469] Probably Thomas Warcop, see n. 181 above.

lordship's commandment to Mr Bedwill your
lordship's servant at Wansted}   vli.
Gyven in reward the same daie by your lordship's
commandment to Addams that killes the
woodecoks at Wansted}   vjs. viijd.
Gyven in reward the same tyme by your lordship's
commandment to his sonne}   iijs. iiijd.
To Mr Blunt which he paid to Warner for carrying
your lordship the first and second of February
in a barge betwene Grenewich and Blackwall}   xvjs.
              Summa Paginae: Cvjli. xvijs.

[recto]

            iijth of February [1585]
To him more which he gave in reward by your
lordship's commandment amongest the waterman to
drinck the same tyme}   ijs. vjd.
Gyven in reward the vth of February by your
lordship's commandment to yong Robert Alexander}   xls.[470]
Gyven in reward the same day by your lordship's
commandment to Underhill of the Wardrop
at Grenewich}   xiijs. iiijd.[471]
Gyven in reward the same time by your lordship's
commandment to Underhill's man}   vjs. viijd.
Payd to xj of your lordship's yeomen the same day
for their botehire at two sondry tymes betwene
Grenewich and London and for their suppers as
appereth by their bill}   xxs. ijd.
Payd the same day for x cartes to carry your
lordship's stuff from Grenewich to Somerset
House being v myles with money geven to the
carters to drinck}   xs.[472]
To Roger Gillions for carring your lordship

---

[470] (Sir) Robert Alexander was the son of Alexander Zinzan, an Albanian Rider of the
Stables in the 1550s and 1560s. He was a member of the Stables staff by 1576 and by
1588–9 an Equerry and Rider (PRO, E101/107/33, Stables wage list 31 Elizabeth).
However, his sons were named Henry and Sigismund (see Young, p. 69), and the
reference may be to Alexander himself. See also n. 551 below for his journey to Scotland
to deliver a gift of horses to James VI.
[471] Hugh Underhill (c.1520–1593), the father of Leicester's servant Thomas Underhill*
see J.H. Morrison, *The Underhills of Warwickshire* (Cambridge, 1932), pp. 62–4.
[472] The Court removed from Greenwich to Somerset House c. 4 February, which
coincided with the opening of the new session of parliament. Leicester attended the
Lords on 7–9, 15–18, 20 and 22–3 February.

in your lordship's barge from the iijth of
February till the vjth of the same month as
appereth by his bill}   xlijs.
Paid for the two messes of meate for your
lordship's servants for a fortnight from
the xxiiijth of January untill the vijth
of February}   lvjs. viijs.
To Mr Bapteste which he paid to one John Varnham
of Westminster gardneir for bringing xxviij
loades of turffes from Tuthill to Leicester House
in May laste at xijd. a loade}   xxviijs.
To William Thomas the same day which he delivered
to your lordship for your lordship's offring at
Somersethouse}   xijd.
To Mr Grene which he gave in reward the iijth of
February by your lordship's commandment amongest the
maryners at Wansted}   xs.
Paid for a realme of writing paper for your lordship}   vs. vjd.
Paid to Stephen Johnson the same day which he paid
for a girdell and hangers of velvyt trymed with
blacke silke and gould lace xxvs. viijd. and for
poynts, botehose, socks, spurres, rybben and other
necessaries bought for your lordship at sondry tymes
as appereth by his bill}   <a>   vli. ixs. vjd.
            Summa Paginae: xvijli. vs. iiijd.

[verso]

            vijth of February [1585]
Paid to your lordship's spaniell keeper for keping
v cowple of your lordship's spaniells for v wekes
from the xxjth of December and ending the xxvjth
of January at xd. a day}   xxixs. ijd.
To Mathew the groome for his charges for himself
and his horsse the xviijth of January being sent
by night from Greys to London for freshe koche
horsses to mete your lordship by the way}   ijs.
Gyven in reward the viijth of February by your
lordship's commandment to Homerstone Sir Phillip
Butler's keper for presenting a doe to your
lordship at Somersethouse}   xs.
Paid for rybben to hang a key of your lordship's
at Somersethouse}   vjd.
To Richard Gardneir for his bordwaiges for iij

daies goying before to Somersethouse to make
reddy your lordship's lodging}   iijs.
To Harry Myllington* for his bordwages for one
day goying before to Leicester House with two
loade of your lordship's stuff}   xijd.
Gyven in reward the xth of February by your
lordship's commandment to the chamberlaynes
man of London for presenting a gowne cloth
to your lordship}   xs.[473]
Gyven in reward the same day by your lordship's
commandment to Dowger the keper at Windsor for
presenting woodecoks to your lordship which
your lordship sent to the Queen's majestie}   xs.
Delivered to your lordship the same day which
your lordship dyd offer at Windsor}   vjs.[474]
Delivered more to your lordship the xjth of
February which your lordship did offer their}   xijd.
Gyven in reward the same daie by your lordship's
commandment to the servants of the house at Mr
Frenches at Windsor}   xs.
To Danyell the footeman the same day which he
gave by your lordship's commandment to a poore man}   xijd.
To Richard Pepper the same day which he gave by
your lordship's commandment to the spitle at Colbrooke}   vjd.
Delivered to your lordship which your lordship
gave to the poore betwene London and Wyndsor goying
and comyng}   vs.

            Summa Paginae: iiijli. ixs. ijd.

[recto]

            xjth of February [1585]
To Mr Grene the same day which he paid for the
suppers for certene of your lordship's men and the
sumptermen and others at Windsor}   xiijs. iiijd.
To Robert Gwyn the same day which he paid
for a staff with a pyke in ytt for your lordship}   vs.
To Roger Gillions for carring your lordship in

---

[473] The goldsmith Robert Brandon, see also n. 45 above.
[474] The journey to Windsor was to attend the Earl of Lincoln's funeral (CA, Dethick Book of Funerals, i, fo. 15. The day is not given, presumably it was the 11th). Burghley was also among the mourners and both he and Leicester were absent from the Lords on 10–11 February.

your lordship's barge viij daies from the vijth
of February till the xiiijth of the same month
as appeareth by his bill}   iijli. xs.
Paid to Shepperde a habberdassher the xiiijth of
February for thre paire of wassht gloves for
your lordship}   ixs.
Gyven in reward the same day by your lordship's
commandment to one that did cut your lordship's
cornes*}   xs.
To Edward Roberts my Lord of Warwick's man which
he gave to the poore by your lordship's commandment}   xijd.
To Mr Blunt the xvjth of February which he gave
in reward by your lordship's commandment to Sir
John Harrington's man for presenting a pyde horsse
to your lordship}   xls.
To John Keame your lordship's servant the same day
which he paid for a hogshed of comyock white wyne
for your lordship the price}   iijli.
To Charells Dudley your lordship's servant which he
gave in reward by your lordship's commandment to Mr
John Hutten's man for presenting fowle to
your lordship}   vjs. viijd.
To Roger Gillions for carring your lordship in the
barge the xvth and xvjth of February as appeareth
by his bill}   xvijs.
Gyven in reward the xixth of February by your
lordship's commandment to Wagstaff* your lordship's
servant at Wansted}   xls.
Gyven in reward the same day by your lordship's
commandment to the new French gardneir}   iijli.[475]
Gyven in reward the xxth of February by your
lordship's commandment to your lordship's baker
at Wansted}   xxs.
Given in reward the same day by your lordship's
commandment to old Browne of Wansted}   vs.
                    Summa Paginae: xvijli. xvijs.

[verso]

                    xxth of February [1585]
Gyven in reward the same day by your lordship's
commandment to Harry Day* the fisherman your

[475] See n. 467 above.

lordship's servant}	vs.
To Mr Ffluydd the same day which he payd for a paire of boots for the Frenche gardneir}	vijs.
To Mr Herdsome the xixth of February which your lordship borrowed of him and which your lordship loste in play}	xlli.[476]
Gyven in reward the xxth of February by your lordship's commandment to Mr Gyles Tracye}	xls.
To Mr Blunte the same day which he gave in reward by your lordship's commandment to one Cure a carver}	xxs.
To him more which he gave in reward by your lordship's commandment to my Lord of Warwick's footeman}	vs.
To Mr Baptiste the xxjth of February which he gave in reward by your lordship's commandment to the Frenche imbassador's man for bringing a bottell of white wyne to your lordship}	ijs.[477]
To Fardenando the same day which he paid to Jelp's wief that mends your lordship's instruments for his quarter waiges due at Christmas laste}	xs.
Paid for two messes of meat for your lordship's servants from the vijth of February untill the xxjth of the same month}	lvjs. viijd.
To Roger Gillions for carring your lordship in your lordship's barge from the xviijth of February till the xxijth of the same month as appereth by his bill}	xxxviijs.
To Smolkin the xxijth of February which he gave to the almes house at Stratford Bowe}	vjd.
Your lordship lost in play at dyce the xxvth of February at Wanstedd} <a>	xxxli.
Your lordship loste more at dice their the xxvjth of February} <a>	xxli.
To Smolkin the same day which he gave in reward by your lordship's commandment to the nurce of Sir Thomas Parrett's childe}	xs.[478]

Summa Paginae: iiij^{xx}xixli. xiiijs. ijd.

---

[476] A Mr Herdson attended the Lord of Denbigh's funeral, but no further information about him has been forthcoming.

[477] Castelnau, his despatches for January and February 1585 cannot be traced.

[478] Sir Thomas Perrot (1553–94), MP. Son of Sir John (n. 441) and husband of Dorothy Devereux (n. 372). He was a witness to the Countess's jointure (15 July 1584), served in the Netherlands in 1586 and attended Sidney's funeral.

[recto]

xxvijth of February [1585]

Payd the same day to one Empsone in Strond for
roomes for your lordship's pantry and kitchin stuff
during the tyme her majesty lay at Somersethouse}   xs.[479]

Paid the same day for xj cartes to carry your
lordship's stuff from Somersethouse to Grenewich
with money geven the carters to drinck}   ixs. vjd.[480]

Paid to two of your lordship's servants for their
bordwages for a day and haulph goyng before to
Grenewich with your lordship's stuff iijs. and
for mending your lordship's curten roddes iiijd.}   iijs. iiijd.

Gyven in reward the xxviijth of February by your
lordship's commandment to White a gardneir for
presenting philbud trees and pinck seedes to
your lordship}   xxs.

Gyven in reward the same day by your lordship's
commandment to an Irisshe gardneir for bringing
your lordship seedes to Greenwiche}   xs.

Delivered to Mr Bedwell your lordship's servant
the same day by your lordship's commandment to
buy poales, osiars and other provicion about
Wansted}   xli.

To Mr Barker the first of Marche which he paid
by your lordship's commandment to Mr Secretories
man that took paines about your lordship's busyness
for Lane and Lea}   xxs.[481]

Delivered to Giles Browne* your lordship's fawckneir
the second of Marche by your lordship's commandment
to pay for a caste of fore fawkons for your lordship}   xiiijli.

Given in reward more to him the same tyme to pay
for his charges}   xls.

Gyven in reward the same day by your lordship's
commandment to one that cutteth your lordship's cornes}   vs.

Paid the thirde of March for viij lynen nightcaps
for your lordship}   xxxijs.

---

[479] Given the proximity of Leicester House to Somerset House, it is difficult to understand why it was necessary for Leicester to move his kitchen and pantry equipment, unless they were being provided for the Queen's use.

[480] The Court removed to Greenwich between 23 and 26 February.

[481] The subject of this business is unclear. On 1 March Burghley wrote to Walsingham that Leicester had relayed the Queen's wish that the Lords adjourn for a few days so that Commons could hasten the subsidy (PRO, SP 12/177/1).

Paid the same day by your lordship's commandment
to Robert Moore of Ipswych your lordship's servant
in full payment for a coche}   lli.
             Summa Paginae: lxxxjli. ixs. xd.

[verso]

                    iiith of March [1585]
Paid to Mr Marten* which your lordship had of him
and loste in play the xxvjth of February at Leicester
House}   xli.
Gyven in reward the iiijth of Marche by your
lordship's commandment to Tobye Mathew your
lordship's servaunt at his goyng into
the country}   iiili. vjs. viijd.
Your lordship loste in play at Leicester House
to Sir Fraunceis Drake and Mr Gifford the
iijth of Marche}   xli.[482]
Gyven by your lordship's command to pay for your
lordship's standing at the execution of Doctor Parry}   xs.[483]
To Mr Grene which he paid for iij torches that
night your lordship was with the Skotteshe imbassador}   iijs.[484]
To Roger Gillions for carring your lordship in
your lordship's barge from the xxvth of February
to the iijth of March as appereth by his bill}   iijli. xjs.
To him more for carring your lordship the iiijth
of March from the L[?] House to the Parlyment
House and back to the Parris Garden Steres}   ixs.[485]
Gyven by your lordship's commandment to the poore
betwene London and Grenewich}   xijd.
To Robert* your lordship's trompeter the same day

[482] The future West Indies Voyage was then in abeyance. Mr Gifford was probably
George Gifford, see n. 371 above.

[483] Dr William Parry was executed in Palace Yard, Westminster, on 2 March 1585.

[484] Sir Lewis Bellenden, the Justice Clerk, see also p. 231 below. He received his
instructions on 16 February and was in England during March and April. Some
correspondence to him from James VI survives, EUL, Laing MS I, arts. 10–12. His
embassy is discussed in M. Lee, *John Maitland of Thirlestane and the foundation of the Stewart
despotism in Scotland* (Princeton, 1959), pp. 65–6. Leicester later referred to him as 'my
friend', *Warrender Papers*, i, 188, to John Maitland of Thirlestane, 28 July 1585.

[485] Leicester attended the Lords on 1, 4, 10–11, 13, 15, 18–9, 22–3, 27 and 29 March,
when the parliament was prorogued. On the 4th Burghley informed Walsingham (PRO,
SP12/177/10) that Leicester and some other Councillors were meeting at his house (Cecil
House on the Strand near the Savoy) in the afternoon to discuss how to publicise Parry's
execution. 'L House' may be an abbreviation for 'Lord Treasurer's House'.

which he paid for a new trompett}   iiijli.
To Warner for carring your lordship in his barge
the vth and vjth of Marche from Greenwich to
Blackwall and from thence to Greenwich}   xvjs.
Delivered to your lordship's owne hands the vjth
of Marche which your lordship gave to fishermen
and others at Wansted}   xls.
Gyven in reward the same day by your lordship's
commandment to Harry Lovell your lordship's servant}   xxs.
Paid for a stone pott with a cover the same day}   xd.
Paid for the two messes of meate for your lordship's
servants for a fortnight from the xxjth of February
till the vijth of Marche}   lvjs. viijd.
         Summa Paginae: xxxviijli. xiiijs. ijd.

[recto]

         viijth of March [1585]
Delivered to Mr Holland your lordship's chaplin
the same day by your lordship's commandment to
be geven amongeste all the prisonnes about London}   xli.[486]
Gyven in reward the same day by your lordship's
commandment to your lordship's matlayer at his
goyng to Killingworth}   xxs.
Gyven in reward the same day by your lordship's
commandment to Mr Robert Fulford* when he lay sick
at London}   iijli.
To Mr Grene which he gave by your lordship's
commandment to the Queen's watermen for carring
your lordship in my Lord Chamberlain's barge
from Parris Garden Steres to the Savoy the
vijth of Marche}   xxs.[487]

[486] Dr Thomas Holland (d. 1612), fellow of Balliol, Regius Professor of Divinity 1589–1612. Holland served Leicester as a chaplain in the Netherlands in 1587 (see Netherlands Household 1587), and possibly in 1586 as well. He also attended his funeral.

[487] This visit to the Savoy was probably related to the important Council meeting held at Cecil House on the 8th. On the 6th Walsingham had learned from Derby and Sir Edward Stafford in Paris that Henry III had rejected a Dutch request to intervene (Bodl., MS Tanner 79, fo. 234– 7, Derby and Stafford to Walsingham, 3 March). On the 8th the Council reviewed the Netherlands situation and decided to go ahead alone. Only a fragment of one of the memoranda survives, but in numerous copies, see, e.g. BL, Sloane MS 326, fo. 88–93, and Harl. MS 168, fos. 102–5. Leicester wrote a quick note to Davison later in the day to let him know (PRO, SP83/1/126), and Walsingham sent him a full account on the 9th (BL, Harl. MS 285, fos. 123–4). Walsingham and Leicester saw the Dutch agents in the morning of the 11th and then at Greenwich on the 12th, see

To Mr Nevile the xth of Marche which he gave in
reward by your lordship's commandment to one Mr
John Case of Oxford for presenting a booke to
your lordship}   vli.[488]
To Mr Ffluyd your lordship's secretory the same
day which he gave in reward by your lordship's
commandment to one Trappes at his goyng into Wailes}   vli.
Paid the same day for a pounde of waxe}   xd.
Paid for a realme of writing paper and a realme
of course paper for your lordship}   viijs.
To Mr Nevyle which he gave the viijth of Marche
to a poore man at the Blackfriers}   vjd.
To him more which he paid for the carridge of
damaske from Leicester House to the Courte both
by land and water}   ijs. vjd.
Gyven in reward the xjth of Marche by your
lordship's commandment to a woodcok ketcher
at Wansted}   vjs. viijd.
Gyven by your lordship's commandment to a boy
at Milende Grene for opening of a gate}   vjd.
Gyven in reward the same day by your lordship's
commandment to Elizabeth Sutten one of your
lordship's almes wemen}   xs.[489]
Paid the same day by your lordship's commandment
to Rutherick Lewes for his charges lying in Strande
in keping of a prisonner}   iijli. vs.

    Summa Paginae: xxixli. xiiijs. ijd.

ARA, Eerste Afdeeling, Regeringsarchieven, lias I-90B, Ortel and Gryse to the States-General, 14/24 March.

[488] John Case (c.1540–1599), the Oxford philosopher. This entry is of some significance for Case dedicated two books to Leicester, STC 4762 *Summa veterum interpretum in universam dialecticam Aristotelis* (licenced in August 1584), and STC 4759 *Speculum moralium questionum in universam ethicen Aristotelis* (1585). The latter was the first work published by the revived Oxford University Press, which had been refounded following a petition to Leicester in 1584. Case's dedication is dated 'Nonis Martii 1585' (the 7th) and thanks Leicester for his patronage of the press. This may have been agreed when he visited the University in January, for a committee to supervise the press had been set up in December 1584, although the Crown did not give final permission until 1586. The chronology is easier if the reference is to Case's earlier book, but, assuming Case meant 1585 and not 1585/6 in his dedication, the coincidence is intriguing, however tight the timing. It is possible that this was a manuscript produced in advance of going to press. See S. Gibson and D.M. Rogers, 'The Earl of Leicester and printing at Oxford', *Bodleian Library Record*, xxviii (1949), 240–5, and C.B. Schmitt, *John Case and Aristotelianism in Renaissance England* (Kingston, Ont., 1983), pp. 86–7.

[489] Possibly one of the residents of his hospital at Warwick.

[verso]

xiijth of Marche [1585]

To Roger Gyllions for carring your lordship at
sondrie tymes in your lordship's barge from the
viijth of Marche till the xiijth of the month
as appeareth by his bill}   iijli. xijs. iiijd.

Gyven in reward the same day by your lordship's
commandment to Mr Bentall at his goyng to Mr
Westes house}   xls.[490]

To Stephen Johnson the same day for two paire
of gilt spurres and two paire of velvet lethers
& for botehire as appeareth by his bill}   xviijs. xd.

Paid to v of your lordship's yeomen for their
botehire and dynners at the remove from Somerset
House to Greenwich}   iiijs. ijd.

To Harry Stringer the same day which he paid
for viij staves for the Quenes footemen at
xiijs. ijd. ob. qu. a pece}   vli. vjs. vjd.[491]

Paid to a xj of your lordship's yeomen for
their botehier from Grenewich to London and
back ageyne and for ther suppers wayting on
your lordship at Tower Hill when you went to
the Skottishe imbassador}   xs. iiijd.[492]

To Stephen Johnson the xvijth of Marche for a
girdell and hangers for a shorte sworde and
for a grose of pointes as appeareth by his bill}   xlvijs. iiijd.

Gyven the same day to the poore [hose deleted]
at Croydon}   xiid.

To Mr Bentall the same day which he gave in
reward by your lordship's commandment to
William Worteley}   xs.

To William Thomas the xixth of Marche which he
paid for iiij stone pottes to put violetts in}   iijs. iiid.

Gyven in reward the same day by your lordship's
commandment to Powell the foole}   xs.

---

[490] (Sir) Thomas West (c.1530–1602) of Offington (Sus.), MP and later the 11th Lord
De La Warre. Not only was there was an established connection with the Wests through
the Duchess of Northumberland's mother, but West was also married to Sir Francis
Knollys's daughter Anne. He served in the Netherlands in 1586 and attended Leicester's
funeral. This entry may be the first reference to Robert Dudley's residence at Offington,
see n. 499 below.

[491] The Queen's footmen came under the authority of the Master of the Horse.

[492] Bellenden, see n. 484.

Paid for the carring of a basket of violetts
from Blackwall to Wansted}   xijd.
Gyven to the spittle at Milende Grene}   vjd.
Gyven in reward the xxth of Marche to a boye
for presenting a nosegay to your lordship}   xijd.
                    Summa Paginae: xvjli. vjs. iijd.

[recto]

                        xxth of Marche [1585]
Delivered to your lordship owne hands in small
money to geve to the poore the same day}   ijs.
Gyven the same day by your lordship's commandment
to a gardneir for seedes for your lordship}   iijs. iiijd.
Gyven in reward the same day by your lordship's
commandment to Mondaies wief for presenting chickens}   vjs. viijd.
Gyven in reward the same day by your lordship's
commandment to Grey's men of Wisbidge for
presenting fowle}   iijs. iiijd.
Gyven in reward the same day by your lordship's
commandment to Blackesley* at his going from
Wansted to Kenelworth}   xxs.
Paid for horsemeate at Blackwall the same day}   ijs.
Gyven in reward the same day by your lordship's
commandment to Mr Dockrey at his goyng from
Wansted to Kenelworth}   vli.
To him more the same day which he paid to
certene worckmen about the pondes at Wansted}   xlvijs. vjd.
To Warner for carring your lordship betwene
Grenewich and Blackwall iij sondry daies as
appeareth by his bill}   xxiiijs.
Paid to Richard Hessey your spaniell keper
for his bordwaiges for two months lying a
hawking at Kenelworth, Grafton and
other places}   <a>   xxxvijs. iiijd.
To Roger Gillyons for carring your lordship
in your lordship's barge the xiiijth of Marche
till the xxth of the same month as appeareth
by his bill}   xlijs.
Gyven in reward the same day by your lordship's
commandment to Carelesse your lordship's servant}   xls.
Gyven in reward the same day by your lordship's
commandment to Mr Hearles man for presenting a

dog to your lordship}   xxs.[493]
Paid to one Shepparde for parfumyng of a paire of
gloves for your lordship}   iijs.
                          Summa Paginae: xvijli. xjs. ijd.

[verso]

                          xxith of Marche [1585]
To Mr Ffluyd which he gave in reward to my Lord of
Darby's man for bringing letters to your lordship
from his lord}   xxs.[494]
Paid for the two messes of meate for your lordship's
servants for a fortnight from the vijth of March
till the xxjth of the same month}   <a>   lvjs. viijd.
To Mr Ffluyd which he gave to a poore boy by
your lordship's commandment}   vjd.
To Robert Pitcheford the xxiiijth of March for
his botehire from Leicester House to Grenewich}   xviijd.
Gyven in reward the same day by your lordship's
commandment to the man that cut your lordship's cornes}   xs.
Gyven in reward the same day by your lordship's
commandment to Rutherick Lewes your lordship's servant}   xls.
Gyven to the spittle at Mylende Grene}   vjd.
Delivered to my Lady Stafford the xxvth of Marche
by your lordship's commandment}   vli.[495]
To Homerstone the same day which he paid for a
lyne and coller}   xviijd.
Gyven in reward the xxvjth of March by your lordship's
commandment to the baker at Wansted}   xxs.
Gyven in reward the same day by your lordship's
commandment to Thomas King your lordship's servant}   xs.
Gyven in reward to the gardneir at Wansted the same day}.   xs.
Gyven in reward to the baylie at Wansted the same day}   xs.
Gyven in reward to olde Browne at Wansted the same day}   vjs.
Gyven in reward to Harry the fisher at Wansted the

---

[493] William Herle (d. 1588/9) MP. The earliest item of an extensive correspondence
dates from 1561.

[494] Henry Stanley, 4th Earl of Derby (1531-93), then on his return from France. These
letters have not survived. Leicester had worked hard over the past five years to win
Derby's loyalty and friendship.

[495] Probably Lady Dorothy Stafford (d. 1603), Gentlewoman of the Privy Chamber
1559-1603, Mistress of the Robes. There is evidence an old friendship but it was strained
after her son Sir Edward Stafford (the ambassador in Paris) married Douglas Sheffield
(Sir Robert Dudley's mother) in 1579.

same day by your lordship's commandment}   vs.
To my Lord Chamberleynes bargeman for carring your
lordship from Greenwich to Blackwall the xxvth of Marche} xs.

Summa Paginae: xvli. xxd.

[recto]

xxvjth of Marche [1585]

Payd for botehire for certene of your lordship's
men from Grenewich to Blackwall}   viijd.
To Mr Candisshe which he lent your lordship at
Wansted}   xs.[496]
To my Lord Chamberlaines bargeman for carringe of
your lordship from Blackwall to Grenewich the
xxvjth of March}   xs. viijd.
Gyven in reward the same daie by your lordship's
commandment to Humfrey your lordship's footeman} vs.
Payd to Henry Phillit joyner the same day by your
lordship's commandment for worcke done at Wansted
as appeareth by his bill} <a>   viijli. vijs. vjd.
To Mr Dennys* which he gave to a poore woman at
the Corte the xxvth of Marche}   ijs. vjd.
Gyven in reward the same day by your lordship's
commandment to Sheffild that kepes Grenewich orchard} xs.
To Richard Pepper which he gave to a poore man} vjd.
Gyven in reward the same day by your lordship's
commandment to Garrett that was your lordship's
footeman}   xxs.
Gyven in reward the xxviijth of Marche by your
lordship's commandment to Mr Benason the precher
at Leicester House}   xxli.
Paid to Mr Holland which your lordship gave to
release a prisonner oute of the gatehouse at
Westminster}   xxs.
Delivered to your lordship which your lordship
gave to the Frenche cooke* at Leicester House}   iijli.
Paid the xxixth of March to Mr Gresleis man
by your lordship's commandment for charges in
bringing upp two greate horsses oute of
Staffordshere}   lvijs. viijd.

---

[496] Probably Richard Cavendish (d. c.1601), MP. An established follower (see 'House of Commons', 228), he served in the Netherlands in 1586, see the numerous references to Mr Candyse below.

Gyven in reward the same day by your lordship's
commandment to Allen your lordship's servant at
his goyng from London to Langley}   xls.
Paid to Mr Nevile the same day by your lordship's
commandment which he paid for certene apparell for
Croxson iij*li*. vij*s*. vij*d*., for two painted chestes
bound with iron at xxx*s*. a pece, iiij*li*., and for
fower courte cupbords at ix*s*. a pece,
xxxvj*s*. in all}   <a>   viij*li*. iiij*s*. viij*d*.
            Summa Paginae: xlviij*li*. ix*s*. ij*d*.

[verso]

                  xxxth of Marche [1585]
Paid for the carridge of your lordship's pantry
stuff from Grenewich to Lambeth and back ageyne
by land when the Queen's majestie was their}   xx*d*.[497]
To Roger Gillions for carring your lordship in
your lordship's barge from the xxjth of March
till the xxxth of the same month as appeareth
by his bill}   iij*li*. xvij*s*.
To Mr Blunt the xxxjth of Marche which he gave
in reward to my Lord of Darby's man for
presenting a dun horsse}   iij*li*.
To William Thomas which he gave in reward by
your lordship's commandment to Mr Hunnyces man
for gathering of violetts for your lordship}   ij*s*. iiij*d*.[498]
Paid for a basket to put violetts in}   vij*d*.
Paid to Edyth Eryth a poore woman that
followes the Courte for bowes and flowers for
your lordship's chamber at Corte from May last
till the xxxjth of March 1585}   xxiiij*s*. ix*d*.
Given in reward the same day by your lordship's
commandment to Mr Gabriell Blekes man for
bringing letters and writinges to your lordship}   xx*s*.
Gyven in reward the firste of Aprill by your
lordship's commandment to Vendra his man for
bringing iij gamons of bakon to Wansted}   ij*s*. iiij*d*.

---

[497] The Queen visited Lambeth Palace between 28 and 30 March, see also p. 238
below.
[498] William Hunnis (c.1530–97), Gentleman of the Chapel Royal and Master of the
Children. For his relations with Leicester see S.W. May, 'William Hunnis and the 1577
Paradise of Dainty Devices', *Studies in Bibliography*, xxviii (1975), 74–5.

Sent to Owen Jones your lordship's servant to
Mr Westes house the same day by your lordship's
commandment}   xls.[499]
Gyven in reward the same day by your lordship's
commandment to a poore woman at my Lord of
Oxeford's house}   ijs. vjd.[500]
Gyven in reward the same day by your lordship's
commandment to a poore man that came to your
lordship from Mr Dyer}   iijs. iiijd.[501]
Gyven in reward the same day by your lordship's
commandment to one Mr Harryson at Wansted}   <a>   vli.
Your lordship loste in plaie the same day at Wansted}   xxs.
Gyven in reward the second of Aprill by your
lordship's commandment to William foole at his
goyng from Wansted to my Lord of Essex}   xls.[502]
               Summa Paginae: xixli. xvijs. vijd.[h]

[recto]

Second of Aprill [1585]

To Mr Blount the same day which he gave in reward
by your lordship's commandment to Careles your
lordship's servant}   xxs.
Given in reward the same day to my Lord Lumleis
cooke for bringing gamons of bakon, trowts and
cockells from Nonesyche}   xs.
Delivered into your lordship's pockett for the

---

[499] As noted in his entry in the Index of Servants, the evidence of this book confirms Owen Jones's later claims that Leicester had placed him with his son at Offington when Robert Dudley was about ten years old (see his deposition in 1604, CKS, U1475/L2/2, it. 2). However, the book is equally clear that in late 1584–early 1585 Robert Dudley was living at Oxford or Whitney and therefore he did not move to Offington until the spring of 1585.

[500] Edward de Vere, 17th Earl of Oxford (1550–1604). Whatever their political antagonisms in recent years, Leicester was presently negotiating the purchase of Cranbrook from Oxford, see p. 264, n. 548 below.

[501] (Sir) Edward Dyer (1543–1607), MP. Although Dyer's close association with Leicester began in the late 1560s, there is no positive evidence for the claim that he had been Leicester's secretary then. He does not appear in the 1567 livery lists. He was a deponent in the Sir Robert Dudley Case, but his deposition, which might have clarified their relationship, has, unfortunately, not survived. Cf. R.M. Sargent, *At the Court of Queen Elizabeth: the Life and Lyrics of Sir Edward Dyer* (1935), p. 18, 'his position with Leicester appears to have been that of a confidential agent or gentleman secretary', and n. 534 below on Sir John Wolley.

[502] This is the earliest reference in this book to the 2nd Earl of Essex. They become more frequent in 1586, when he was general of the horse in the Netherlands.

poore at your goyng to Wansted}　　　　　　　　　　ijs.

To Richard Pepper the iijth of Aprill which he
gave by your lordship's commandment at Wansted
amongest the kepers}　　　　　　　　　　　　　　xs.

Given in reward the iiijth of Aprill by your
lordship's commandment to Mr Bedwell your
lordship's servant at Wansted}　　　　　　　　　vli.

To Mr Cave* the same day which he gave to a
poore woman that delivered a supplication to
your lordship at Wansted}　　　　　　　　iijs. iiijd.

Paid for the two messes of meate for your
lordship's servants for a fortnight from the
xxjth of Marche till the iiijth of Aprill}　　lvjs. viijd.

Paid to William Horsenaile* the keper the same
day by your lordship's commandment in part
payment of his waiges}　　<a>　　　　　　　vjli.

To Raphe Batty* for the charges of your
lordship's dynner at Wansted the first
of Aprill}　　　　　　　　　　　　　　xxs. vjd.

Gyven in reward to Sir Harry Leis man the
iiijth of Aprill for presenting a bucke to
your lordship}　　　　　　　　　　　　　　xs.

Paid to Moother Ossynous the vth of Aprill for
her haulf yeres annuytie due at Our Lady Day
laste paste at xli. per annum}　　　　　　　　vli.

Paid for my botehire from Grenewich to Leicester
House when your lordship sent me to Mr Dyer}　　xijd.

Gyven in reward the vjth of Aprill to Sir Thomas
Hennedges gardneir at Copthall}　　　　　　　xs.

Paid to John Devicks Sir Thomas Hennedges man the
same day by your lordship's commandment for certene
wynes which he brought for your lordship beyond sea}　vjli.[503]

Gyven in reward more to him the same tyme by your
lordship's commandment}　　　　　　　　　　xxs.

Summa Paginae: xxxli. iiis. vjd.[i]

[verso]

vjth of Aprill [1585]

Gyven in reward the same day by your lordship's
commandment to Richard Pepper your lordship's footeman}　vs.

To Stephen Johnson which he gave to my Lord

[503] John de Vic, see also p. 273 below.

Chamberlein's bargeman for carring your lordship
from Grenewich to the shipp at Detford}   vs.[504]

Sent to Mr Robert Dudley the viijth of Aprill by
your lordship's commandment}   xxs.

Gyven in reward to Mr Robert Dudleis footeman the
same day by your lordship's commandment}   vs

Paid for the hire of vj horsses for the mewsycians
from London to Wansted the vjth of Aprill}   xijs

Your lordship loste in plaie at Wansted the vijth
of Aprill}   xiijli. xs.

Delivered to your lordship in small money to geve
to the poore when your lordship went to Sir
Thomas Hennedges}   ijs.

Delivered to Ambrose Waller the viijth of Aprill
which he delivered to your lordship to geve to the
new gardneir at Wansted}   xls.

Delivered to Mr Bedwell your lordship's servant the
same day by your lordship's commandment imprest
for wourk at Wansted}   <a>   xxli.

To Warner the waterman for carring your lordship
at iiij sondrie tymes in his barge as appeareth by
his bill}   xxiiijs.

Gyven in reward the ixth of April by your
lordship's commandment to Savadges man the keper
for bringing a hynde to your lordship}   ijs.

Gyven in reward the same day by your lordship's
commandment to a poore man of Ham that Speake*
brought to your lordship}   ijs.

To Smolkyn the footeman for his charges being
sent to Tybbolles the xxixth of March and being
sent to Batty's house}   ijs. vjd.

To Stephen Johnson for his botehire the xxviij,
xxix and xxxth of Marche goyng about your
lordship's busynes when her majestie lay
at Lambeth}   ijs. iiijd.

Paid to Raphe Chilmeade* groome of the stable for
horsemeate for iiij horsses for one night at his
retorne from Mr Robert Dudley out of Sussex the
xxth of February}   vs.

Summa Paginae: xxxixli. xvjs. xd.[j]

---

[504] Presumably the *Galleon Leicester*, see also p. 252 below.

[recto]

ixth of Aprill [1585]

To Roger Gillions for carring your lordship in your lordship's barge from the xxxjth of Marche till the vijth of Aprill as appeareth by his bill}	xxvjs.
To Spyke your lordship's servant the same day which he gave by your lordship's commandment to a man of Ilford}	xxxs.
Gyven in reward the same day by your lordship's commandment to Ruddrick Lewes your lordship's servant}	vli.
Gyven in reward the same day by your lordship's commandment to Mistress Trentham}	xli.[505]
Delivered to Mr Richard Browne the xth of Aprill by your lordship's commandment towards the payment of wourkemen at Wansted} \<a B>	xxli.
Gyven in reward the same day by your lordship's commandment to Ramsey* your lordship's servant at Wansted}	xs.
Gyven in reward the same day by your lordship's commandment to Humfrey Cole your lordship's servant at his goyng to Kenelworth}	xls.
Delivered to your lordship the same day which your lordship gave to the gardneir of Wansted to buy hearbes to sett}	xxs.
Delivered more to your lordship which your lordship gave to the warner at Wansted the same day}	vjs.
Gyven more by your lordship to the fisherman at Wansted the same day}	vs.
Gyven in reward the same day by your lordship to olde Browne at Wansted}	vs.
Gyven by your lordship the same day amongest the wourkmen at Wansted}	iiijs. vjs.
Paid for your lordship's offring on Easter Day at the Corte}	xijd.
Delivered to Mr Ffluyd the xijth of Aprill by your lordship's commandment to geve to the Frenche	

---

[505] Probably Jane, the wife of Thomas Trentham (1538–87) of Rocester, Staffs., MP. Trentham may have been the Thomas Trenton who received a badge in 1567, his son Francis served in the Netherlands in 1586.

gardneir at his goyng into Fraunce}   iijli.[506]

Paid to Batty for the charges of your lordship's
supper at Wansted the vijth of Aprill}   xxiijs. ixd.

To Mr Nevill the xijth of Aprill which he gave
in reward by your lordship's commandment to the
kepers of Bridewell}   xs.

Your lordship loste in plaie at Wansted the xiijth
of Aprill}   xs.

Summa Paginae: xlvijli. xjs. iijd.

[verso]

xvth of Aprill [1585]

Gyven in reward the same day by your lordship's
commandment to Mr Tavernor at his goyng into
Worcestershere}   <a>   liijs. iiijd.

Gyven in reward the same day by your lordship's
commandment to a boy that brought letters from
my Lady Shrewsbery}   iijs. iiijd.[507]

Gyven in reward the same day by your lordship's
commandment to Mr Wrothes man for bringing a
crane to Wansted}   vs.[508]

Paid for botehire for certene of your lordship's
men from Grenewich to Blackwall the xiiijth of Aprill}   vjd.

To Mr Ffluydd the xvth of Aprill which he gave
in reward by your lordship's commandment to the
gardneirs at Wansted}   iijs. iiijd.

To Giles Homerstone the same day which he paid
for my Lord of Pembrook's man's horsemeate at Wansted}   ijs.[509]

To him more the same day which he gave to one
that carried a ladder into the forrest with

---

[506] See n. 467 above. On 10 April Leicester wrote to Hotman from the Court to say
that he was sending the gardener home, as 'he hath very little or no skill in that
profession, neither do I find him apt to conceive and to be instructed in the same'
(AMAE, CPH, IV, fo. 47).

[507] This letter has not survived, but it was probably related to the report of the
commission the Queen had appointed to adjudicate the financial settlement following
the Countess's separation from the Earl, which was revealed to Shrewsbury on 24 April,
see D.N. Durant, *Bess of Hardwick: Portrait of an Elizabethan Dynast* (1977), pp. 136–8.
Leicester may have informed her of the decision, see his letters to the Lord Chancellor,
30 April and 1 May (BL, Lansdowne MS 44, fos. 36–v, 38).

[508] Possibly (Sir) Robert Wroth (1539–1606), MP, but Robert Wrote* is more likely.

[509] Henry, 2nd Earl of Pembroke (c. 1538–1601). Leicester played a large role in
arranging his marriage to Sidney's daughter Mary in 1577 and left gifts to both of them
in his 1582 will.

your lordship} xijd.
To Mr Ffluyd which he gave to a waterman at
Blackwall for setting a forme for your lordship
to treade on the xiijth of Aprill} vjd.
Paid to a potmaker for vj dossin and haulf of
sparrowe pottes and for iij dossin of stare pottes
and for one hondrethe of gilleflowre pottes} xxiiijs.
Delivered to your lordship the same day which
your lordship put in your pocket to geve
away at Wansted} xls.
Gyven in reward the xvjth of Aprill by your
lordship's commandment to Pearowe* the Frenche cooke} xls.
Gyven in reward the same day by your lordship's
commandment to Mr Dowcrayes man at his goyng to
Kenelworth} xijs.
Gyven in reward the same day by your lordship's
commandment to a poore man that brought letters from
Mr Bowghton to your lordship} iijs. iiijd.
Gyven in reward the same day by your lordship's
commandment to my Lord of Penbrookes man for
presenting a brayche to your lordship at Wansted} xls.
Delivered to your lordship the same day which
your lordship put in your lordship's pockett
iiij Englishe crownes at Wansted} xxs.
To a waterman the same day for carring your
lordship from [Grenewich *deleted*] Blackwall
to Grenewich} xijd.
   Summa Paginae: xijli. ixs. iiijd.

[recto]

    xviijth of Aprill [1585]
Gyven in reward the same day by your lordship's
commandment to Mr Quarles's man for presenting
phesaunts at Wansted} vjs. viijd.[510]
Gyven in reward the same day by your lordship's
commandment to Mr Byrd's man for presenting
orenges and lemons to your lordship at Wansted} iijs. iiijd.[511]

[510] James Quarles (d. 1599), purveyor. Quarles was the victualler of the 1587 Netherlands campaign, succeeded Edward Bashe (n. 305 above) as Surveyor of Naval Victuals, and became a Clerk Comptroller of the Green Cloth in 1592–3. He attended Leicester's funeral.
[511] Probably William Byrde (n. 53 above), see Bodl., MS Tanner 79, fo. 207, Byrde to Leicester, 6 Sept. 1583, for evidence of their recent association.

Paid for the two messes of meate for your
lordship's servants for a fortnight from the
iiijth of Aprill untill the xviijth of the
same month}   lvjs. viijd.

Gyven in reward the xixth of Aprill by your
lordship's commandment to Sir Thomas Sherlowes
man for presenting hearbes at Wansted}   xxs.[512]

Delivered to Lovell your lordship's servant the
same day by your lordship's commandment to pay
for falling of trees and cutting them for palles
in Buckinghamshere}   xls.

Paid to Jeanneken Kitssen the same day for xvj
ells of cloth at vijs. the ell for iij wastcotes
for your lordship}   vli. xijs.

Paid more to him the same day for a dossin of
towells for your lordship}   xviijs.

Gyven by your lordship's commandment to a joyner
for presenting qualles to your lordship at Wansted}   xs.

Gyven by your lordship's commandment to a poore
man betwene Wansted and Waltham}   vjd.

Gyven in reward the same day by your lordship's
commandment to Mr Barker's man for presenting a
booke to your lordship at Waltam}   iijs. iiijd.

Paid to a poore man for carring necessarie thinges
from Wansted to Waltam and back ageyne to Wansted
the xxvth of Aprill}   ijs.

Gyven to a poore man at Waltam the same day by your
lordship's commandment}   vjd.

To Richard Gardneir the same day which he paid for
artichocks that he bought for your lordship}   iiijs.

To him more which he paid for carridge of a trunck
from Grenewich to Blackwall}   iiijd.

To Cooke your lordship's habberdasher the same day
for two knitt silke nightcaps which was geven to my
Lord of Darbye bought the xjth of December}   xiijs. iiijd.

To him more for a velvyt nightcap for your lordship
bought the xxth of November}   viijs.

       Summa Paginae: xiiijli. xviijs. viijd.

---

[512] Sir Thomas Shirley the elder (1542–1612), of Wiston, Suss., MP. Shirley served in
the Netherlands in 1586, became Treasurer at War in the Netherlands 1587–97, and
attended Leicester's funeral.

[verso]

xxth of Aprill [1585]

To him more for two silke nightcaps for your lordship bought the xxijth of December}	xiijs. iiijd.
To him more for a velvyt nightcap for your lordship bought the xxxth of January}	viijs.
To him more for a large silke nightcap lyned with unshorne velvyt for your lordship bought the xxvth of February}	xijs.
To him more for another silke nightcap bought for your lordship the same tyme}	vjs. viijd.
To him more for two silke nightcaps for your lordship bought this xxth of Aprill}	xiijs. iiijd.
Delivered to your lordship to put in your pocket for the poore which your lordship gave away betwene Waltam and London}	ijs.
To Pitcheford the xxjth of Aprill which he gave by your lordship's commandment to the spitle at Newington}	xijd.
Gyven in reward the same day by your lordship's commandment to the Quenes majesties pleyers at Leicester House}	vli.
To Mr Martyn the same day which he gave in reward by your lordship's commandment to the nurce and mydwief at the christening of Mr Farmer's childe}	xls.[513]
To Stephen Johnson the same day which he paid for the carridge of a trunck from Leicester House to Grenewich by water}	ijs.
To Warner for carring your lordship from the Courte to Blackwall and back ageyne the xth of Aprill}	viijs.
To him more for carring your lordship from Grenewich to Blackwall the xixth of Aprill}	viijs.
To Roger Gillions the xxjth of Aprill for carring your lordship from the Three Cranes to Leicester House}	ixs.
To him more for carring your lordship from Leicester House to Grenewich the xxijth of Aprill}	xijs.
Gyven amongest the watermen to drinck the same tyme}	vs.
Delivered to Sir Richard Knightley the xxiijth of Aprill by your lordship's commandment which your	

[513] (Sir) George Farmer (d.1612) of Easton Neston, Northants. He served in the Netherlands in 1586, àttended Sidney's funeral and claimed a debt of £106 from Leicester's estate. See also p. 301 below.

lordship sent to Mr King of Tosseter}   vli.[514]
Paid the Glode the cutler the same day by your
lordship's commandment in full payment for trymyng
of rapiers and daggers for your lordship as
appeareth by his bill}   xvli. xjs. xd.
       Summa Paginae: xxxijli. xijs. ijd.

[recto]

       xxiiijth of Aprill [1585]
Delivered to Sir Phillyp Sidney the same day by
your lordship's commandment to be geven to Mr
Capteyne Williams at his goyng beyond the seas}   xxvli.[515]
Delivered to Charells* your lordship's awdytor
the same day to be delivered to Mr Bedwell for
wourks at Wansted}   <a>   xvli.
Gyven in reward the same day by your lordship's
commandment to my Lord Presydent's man of Wailes for
presenting a hanger to your lordship}   xs.[516]
To Mr Tracie the same day which he paid for your
lordship's offring}   xijd.
Delivered to Mathew the groome the same day for his
botehire at sondrie tymes being sent about your
lordship's busynes}   xijd.
Gyven in reward the xxvth of Aprill by your

[514] See n. 405 above. On the 24th Leicester wrote to Davison referring him to a letter
from the Queen for instructions, 'myself coming short to the same, having been two or
three days at my house at Wanstead' (BL, Harl. MS 285, fo. 127, presumably from the
Court). The Queen's letter does not appear to have survived, but it is also referred to in
Walsingham to Davison, 22 April, *CSPF, 1584–5*, 423–4.

[515] (Sir) Roger Williams (d.1595), who went to see the King of Navarre, see *CSPF, 1584–
5*, 448, Walsingham to Philippe de Mornay, 1 May. During April Leicester had made
several offers, with the Queen's approval, of military assistance to Henry III against the
house of Guise, see Castelnau's despatches of 4/14 April, 16/26 April, 24 April/4 May
(Egerton, pp. 201–4), and Henry III to Castelnau, 7/17 April, BN, VCC 470, fos. 113–4.
Leicester wanted Henry to take action against the publishers of *Leicester's Commonwealth*,
but he also feared, as he wrote to Hotman on 5 June, that 'you will see a horyble
massacre' in France (AMAE, CPH, II, fo. 160). On 1/11 May Castelnau reported that
together with the mission of Sir Arthur Champernown to Navarre 'il y va encores deulx
ou trois captaines, de ceulx qui ont eu charge aulx guerres de Flandres, pour voir ce que
lad. Royne pourra fere pour luy [Navarre]' (Egerton, p. 204). It is possible that Williams
carried an offer from Leicester of assistance to Navarre. Simultaneously Navarre sent
Jacques de Pardilhan, Sieur de Ségur, to England (BN, VCC 401, fo. 77, Navarre to
Leicester, 28 April/8 May). This is also the first reference to Sir Philip Sidney in this
book.

[516] Sir Henry Sidney.

lordship's commandment to one Hughsesse wief of
Wotton under Hedge}   liijs. iiijd.[517]
To Mr Brooke the same day for certene rewards
geven by him to sondrie persons by your
lordship's commandment in your lordship's
iorney to Buxtons the laste sommer as
appeareth by his bill}   iiijli. iijs. iiijd.[518]
Delivered to Owen Jones your lordship's servant
the xxvjth of Aprill by your lordship's
commandment which was for Mr Robertes
scholemaister}   xls.
Delivered more to him the same tyme for his
charges and to pay the launderer for washing
Mr Robert}   xxxs.
Delivered to Savadge the keper the same day by
your lordship's commandment to geve to the marriadge
of Mr Scoward's servants}   xxs.
Gyven in reward the same day by your lordship's
commandment to Luck the foole of Wickham for
presenting a chese to your lordship}   xs.
Gyven in reward the same day by your lordship's
commandment to my Lady Dorathy's nurce at Wansted}   vs.
Geven to the spitle house at Mileend the same day}   viijd.
Gyven in reward the same day by your lordship's
commandment to Sir Walter Rawlis man for presenting
oyesters to your lordship}   xs.
Gyven in reward the xxvijth of Aprill by your
lordship's commandment to Cooke my Lord of
Warwick's man for presenting a bird to your lordship}   xxs.
To Roger Gillions for carring your lordship from
Grenewich to Leicester House the xxvth of Aprill}   xijs.
Gyven amongest the watermen to drinck the same tyme}   iijs. iiijd.
To him more for carring your lordship from
Blackwall to Grenewich the xxvjth of Aprill}   xijs.
              Summa Paginae: lxli. xjs. viijd.

[verso]

[517] Wotton-under-Edge (Gloucs.), one of the manors obtained by Leicester and Warwick
after they revived the 'Great Berkeley Law-Suit' in 1572–3, see 'West Midlands', 26, 34,
47–8.
[518] His tour in May–July 1584, see n. 366 above.

xxvijth of Aprill [1585]

To him more the same day for carring your lordship
from Grenewich to Leicester House and back ageyne} xijs.

To Merrick your lordship's waterman for carring
your lordship from the Parlyment House to Lambeth} xijd.

Your lordship loste at play at Croydon at the
tabling house the xxixth of Aprill} xli.[519]

To Mr Grene the same day which he gave in reward
by your lordship's commandment to the woman at
Bennington where your lordship fed fishe} vs.[520]

Delivered to your lordship the same day to put
in your lordship's pocket when your lordship went
a fishing to Benington} ixs.

To Fardinandoe for his quarter's waiges from
Christmas till Our Lady Day last at x*li.* per annum} ls.

Gyven in reward the same day by your lordship's
commandment to Harry the fisherman when your
lordship sent for him to come to Croydon} xs.

Gyven in reward the xxxth of Aprill by your
lordship's commandment to a poore woman of Colsell
that sues for land at Denbigh} xxs.[521]

Paid for ij cartes that carried your lordship's
stuff from Grenewich to Croydon the
xxviijth of Aprill} iijs. vjd.

Gyven in reward the xxxth of Aprill by your
lordship's commandment to Lane the keper of
Windsor Forrest} xs.

[519] The Court removed to Croydon for a brief visit at the beginning of May. The entries here suggest between 28 April and 3 May. The reference to the tabling house is explained by a postscript to Castelnau's despatch of 1/11 May. He reported that he hoped to see Leicester 'd'icy à deulx jours, en une assemblée qui ce fet jeudy, à sept mil de ceste ville, pour veoir quelques exercices et plésirs, entre aultres de voir courir une cantité de chevaulx, selon le coustume de ce Royaulme, avec grand pris pour ceulx qui sont les plus vistes et des gaigeures de grandes sommes d'argent' (Egerton, p. 205). There is no other occasion in May 1585 that fits this description, but, assuming this version is accurate, it is difficult to reconcile the days and the date.

[520] For Benington see Introduction, p. 26. Given the dates of the race meeting at Croydon, the best date for this fishing trip is 28 April. On the 27th Leicester wrote to Lord Chief Justice Wray from Leicester House (Puttick and Simpson Catalogue, 29 July 1861, lot 814, present location unknown); according to the entries on this page he was with the Court at Croydon on the 29th and 30th; and he wrote to the Earl of Shrewsbury from the Court on 30 April and 1 May (Hist MSS Comm, *Bath MSS*, v, 55–6, 69 (misdated to 1586)). See also the entry to bringing trout from Benington to Croydon on the next page.

[521] Leicester had held the lordship of Denbigh since 1563. Colsell is presumably Colshill, Wars., the home of his friend and follower George Digby, see n. 732 below.

To Mr Blunt which he gave in reward by your
lordship's commandment to Mr Denys man for
presenting a rone horsse to your lordship}   xxs.
Delivered to Mr Weste at Croydon the same day
by your lordship's commandment}   xli.
Paid the second of May by your lordship's
commandment to the poste of Westchester for his
charges from Chester to Croydon}   iiijli. vjs. viijd.
Gyven in reward the same day by your lordship's
commandment to Gittens my Lord Lumleis man that
kepes the wardrop}   xs.
Gyven in reward the same day by your lordship's
commandment to Gillam my Lord Lumleis gardneir
at Nonesyche}   xs.
Gyven in reward the same day by your lordship's
commandment to Mrs Notes man for presenting grene
geese, a pyg and a gamon of bakon to your lordship
at Croydon}   ijs. vjd.

Summa Paginae: xxxijli. ixs. viijd.

[recto]

second of May [1585]

Gyven in reward the same day by your lordship's
commandment to the woman that kepes the Bisshop's
house at Croydon for presenting rosewater and
apples to your lordship}   xs.[522]
To Batty which he gave to one for bringing trowtes
from Benington to Croydon}   vjd.
Paid for thre cartes at the remove from Croydon to
Grenewich the third of May}   iijs. vjd.
Paid for your lordship's botehire from [Fulham to
deleted] Barne Elmes to Fulham the second of May}   ijs.
Paid more to two botes from Westminster to Leicester
House the same day}   xviijd.
To Mr Cave the same day which he gave to a poore
man at Croydon churche}   ijs.
Geven to the almes house at Knightsbridge the same
day by your lordship's commandment}   xijd.
Gyven in reward the same day by your lordship's
commandment to the keper of St James's Park}   iijs. iiijd.
Paid for the two messes of meate for your lordship's

---

[522] The Archbishop of Canterbury's house.

servants for a fortnight from the xviijth of Aprill
untill the second of May}   lvjs. viijd.
Gyven in reward the same day by your lordship's
commandment to Bright the keper of Whithall}   vs.
Gyven to a poore man betwene Knightes Bridge and
Fulham the iijth of May}   ixd.
Paid for botehire for your lordship and your
lordship's men from Fullam to Barnelmes the same day}   ijs.
Paid for your lordship's dynner at the ordinary at
Croydon the same day}   xiijs.
Paid for the thre footemen's dynner at Croydon
the same day}   xviijd.
Gyven in reward the same day by your lordship's
commandment to Humfrey the footeman at Grenewich}   vs.
Gyven in reward the iiijth of May by your lordship's
commandment to Thomas the gardneir at Wansted}   xxs.
Gyven to a man that solde mackrells at Blackwall
the same day}   ijs.
Geven to thre poore women at Wansted the same day
by your lordship's commandment}   vjd.
Gyven in reward the same day by your lordship's
commandment to Mr Quarlus's man for presenting two
lyve phesants to your lordship}   iijs. iiijd.

Summa Paginae: vjli. xiijs. vijd.

[verso]

iiijth of May [1585]

To Stephen Johnson the same day which he paid for
ix dossin of gilte buttens for bootes at iiijs.
a dossin}   xxxvjs.
To him more for a dossin yeards of black silke rybben
for your lordship's Jersey hose at at [sic]
vd. the yeard}   vs.
To Warner the same day for carring your lordship
from Grenewich to Blackwall in his owne barge}   viijs.
To Fardenandoe which he gave by your lordship's
commandment to a boy that came poste to Croydon}   xijd.
To Gillam's wief your lordship's lander for her
quarter's waiges from Christmas tyll Our Lady Day
laste at xli. per annum}   ls.
Gyven in reward the vth of May by your lordship's
commandment to your lordship's pleyers at
Leicester House}   vli.

To Warner the same day for carring your lordship from Grenwich to Leicester House in my Lord Chamberleyn's barge}	xijs.
Gyven in reward the same day by your lordship's commandment to William Kympe* one of the pleyers}	xs.
Paid the vjth of May by your lordship's commandment to Mr Holmes's man for the carridge of wyne from Porcemouth to London}	xls.[523]
Paid for botehire for myself and Pitcheford from Grenewich to Leicester House}	xviijd.
Payd for a dossin of new towells for your lordship the same day}	xvijs.
Paid for iij realme of writing paper for your lordship}	xvjs. viijd.
Paid more for two realme of cource paper for your lordship}	vs.
To Mr Thomas Dudley which he gave in reward by your lordship's commandment to my Lady Dacres man for presenting a aggett cup with a cover garnished with gould}	xls.[524]
To him more which he gave in reward by your lordship's commandment to Alderman Martyn's man for presenting a Muskovye saddell with the furnyture of that countrie}	xs.[525]
Gyven in reward the vijth of May by your lordship's commandment to Giles Homerstone at his goyng into the countrie}	xs.
To John Keame the same day which he gave in reward by your lordship's commandment to the Frenche imbassadour's man}	xs.
Paid for a inck bottell the same day}	xd.
Paid for botehire for myself, Pitcheford and Stephen from Whithall to Grenewich}	xijd.
Delivered to William Sparke* the viijth of May by	

[523] Thomas Holmes, searcher of Southampton. He had some involvement in the administration of Leicester's farm of the customs on sweet wines, see BL, Cotton MS Otho E VIII, fo. 55, Holmes to Atye, 5 Jan. [1581?].

[524] Anne (Sackville), wife of Gregory Fiennes, Lord Dacre 'of the South' (1539–94), and possibly a member of the Privy Chamber.

[525] (Sir) Richard Martin (1534–1617), goldsmith. Martyn was appointed warden of the mint in 1572, became an alderman in 1578, governor of the Russia Company by 1584 and later lord mayor, see Donald, *Elizabethan Monopolies*, pp. 43–7, and T.S. Willian, *The Early History of the Russia Company 1553–1603* (Manchester, 1956), p. 209. He supplied commodities for sale by the Barbary Company (see Evelyn MS 155) and claimed a debt of £2500 from Leicester's estate. See also the numerous references below.

your lordship's commandment to be imploid for the
suyts in lawe for your lordship}   xxvli.
                    Summa Paginae: xliijli. xiiijs.

[recto]

                        viijth of May [1585]
Delivered to Mr Richard Browne the same day by
your lordship's commandment towards the payment
of the wourks at Wansted}   <B>   lxvjli. xiijs. iiijd.
Paid the same day to George Anders slater by your
lordship's commandment for X*M*. of slate at ix*s*.
the thowsand iiij*li*. x*s*. and for a liter with
them to Bowe x*s*.}   vli.
Gyven in reward the same day by your lordship's
commandment to Thomas Dawlton the footeman at his
goyng into Ireland}   xls.
To Smolkin the same day which he gave to the poore
betwene Wansted and Grenewich}   iiijd.
To Warner the same day for carring your lordship from
Grenewich to Blackwall and back ageyne}   viijs.
To Mr Grene which he gave in reward by your lordship's
commandment to Mr Secretories cook the iijth of May}   xs.
Gyven in reward by your lordship's commandment to
Lanes man one of the kepers of Windsor Forrest for
wayting at Croydon}   xs.
To Mr Mompersons the ixth of May which he gave in
reward by your lordship's commandment to Mr Varnam's
man for presenting a horsse to the Queen's majestie}   xxs.[526]
Gyven in reward the same day by your lordship's
commandment to Mr Leakes man for staying a letter of
your lordship}   vs.
Gyven in reward the same day by your lordship's
commandment to Sir Thomas Leighton's man for
presenting two paire of knitt stocks to your lordship}   vs.[527]
Gyven in reward the same day by your lordship's

---

[526] Richard Mompesson (d.1627), of Salisbury, MP, identified as an Esquire of the
Stables by 1574 in Hasler, but not found in the Stables lists of 1576 or 1589. Mr Varnham
was possibly John Farnham (1515–87), Gentleman Pensioner, MP.

[527] Sir Thomas Leighton (1535–1611), MP, Governor of Guernsey from 1570 and married
to Sir Francis Knollys' daughter Elizabeth. Leighton had been a follower of Leicester's
since the Le Havre expedition of 1562–3; he was a deponent in the Sir Robert Dudley
case, but his deposition has not survived. In April he had been sent on a special embassy
to Henry III, and the stocks may have been a present from France.

commandment to Raphe Hyde* your lordship's servant
at his goyng to Canterbury}   xxs.
Paid the xjth of May for a bote that carried certene
of your lordship's gentilmen from Grenewich to
Leicester House wayting on your lordship}   xviijd.
To Warner for wayting with his barge on your
lordship at Grenewich the xth of May}   vs.
To him more for carring your lordship from Grenewich
to Leicester House the xjth of May}   xs. viijd.
To Roger Gillions for carring your lordship at
sondrie tymes in your lordship's barge from the
xxixth of Aprill untill the xjth of May as appeareth
by his bill}   iijli. ixs.
To him more the xijth of May for carring your
lordship from Leicester House to Starchamber and
from thence to Grenewich}   xijs.

Summa Paginae: lxxxli. xlixs. xd.

iiij^{xx}ijli. ixs. xd.^k

[verso]

xijth of May [1585]

Paid for botehire for certene of your lordship's men
from Starchamber to Grenewich}   ijs.
To Warner the xiijth of May for carring your lordship
from Grenewich to Ratlief}   xs. viijd.
Gyven in reward to Mr Ayties man for bringing xl*li.* to
Mr Alderman Martin's house}   vs.
Gyven in reward the same day by your lordship's
commandment to Mr Brook's man [for deleted] at
his goyng into Ireland for hawks}   vli.
Paid for botehier for myself, Stephen & Pitchford
from Grenewich to Ratlief}   ixd.
Gyven in reward the same day to the servants of the
house at Mr Alderman Martin's}   xls.
To Daniell footeman the same day which he gave to a
poore man for a staff}   vjd.
To Richard Buck the same day which he gave to a
blinde man}   vjd.
To Mr Ffluyd which he gave to a poore man by Hackney}   vjd.
Gyven in reward the same day by your lordship's
commandment to the musycions at Alderman Martin's}   xls.
Delivered to Humfrey Cole your lordship's servant
the same day to pay for the carridge of iron, lead

and deale bords from London to Abbington}	ls.
To Mr Blunt the same day which he gave in reward to Alderman Martyn's sonne for an oration}	xs.
To Savadge the same day which he gave in reward to Ramson's* men the keper for bringing a buck to Wansted}	vjs. viijd.
Delivered to your lordship's own hands the xiiijth of May at Wansted}	xls.
Gyven in reward the same day by your lordship's commandment to the Frenche cooke at Wansted}	xxs.
To Mr Cave which he gave in reward to Mr Christopher's man for presenting a samon to your lordship}	vjs. viijd.
To Warner the same day for carring your lordship from Blackwall to Grenewich viijs. with ijs. vjd. to the watermen to drink}	xs. vjd.

Summa Paginae: xvijli. iijs. viijd.
xvijli. iijs. ixd.[1]

[recto]

xiiijth of May [1585]

To Sir Christopher Hatton's bargeman the same day in reward for wayting for your lordship}	xs.
Gyven in reward the same day by your lordship's commandment to Mr Wroth's two men for bringing a brace of bucks to the Courte}	xiijs. iiijd.
Gyven in reward the same day by your lordship's commandment to Mr Weston's man for bringing a dossin of partridges and phesaunts to your lordship}	xs.[528]
Gyven in reward the xvth of May by your lordship's commandment to one that did cutt your lordship's cornes}	xs.
To Raphe Batty for the charges of your lordship's supper at Wansted the xiijth of May}	vjs. viijd.
Gyven in reward the same day by your lordship's commandment to Raphe Battye at Grenewich}	xs.
Payd for a fustyan bagg for to carry your lordship's lynnen in the xvth of May}	xs.
To Mr Bapteste the same day which he paid for artichocks for your lordship at Detford}	vjd.
Your lordship loste at dice in the shippe at Wolledge	

---

[528] Richard Weston (1564–1613) of Sutton Place, Surr., MP. He served in the Netherlands in 1586 and named a chamber at Sutton Place after Leicester.

the same day}   iiijli.[529]
Gyven to the spitle and other poore in Kentisshe
Streete the same daie}   xvijd.
Gyven by your lordship's commandment to Sir
Christopher Hatton's kocheman for wayting on your
lordship from Grenewich to Wollege}   vs.
Gyven in reward the same day by your lordship's
commandment to my Lord Talbott's kocheman for
carring your lordship from Wolledge to Parisshe
Garden Steres}   vjs.[530]
Gyven by your lordship's commandment the same daie
to Garrett the footeman's hostis in Kentishe Streete}   vs.
Payd for your lordship's botehire from Parishe
Garden Steres to Leicester House the same day}   xviijd.
To Mr Grene the same day which he paid for iiij
canary byrdes for your lordship}   xijs.
Paid the xvjth of May for milke for your lordship}   vs.
Paid the same day for carring of the bathing tube
betwene Leicester House and Grenewich and back ageyne}   iijs.

Summa Paginae: ixli. viijs. ixd.

ixli. ixs. ijd.[m]

[verso]

xvjth of May [1585]

Gyven in reward the same day by your lordship's
commandment to the cowper}   ijs.
Given in reward the same day to Humfrey your
lordship's footeman}   vs.
Given in reward by your lordship's commandment to
the smythies at Detford}   ijs.
Paid for the two messes of meate for your lordship's
servants for a fortnight from the second of May till
the xvjth of the same month}   <a>   lvjs. viijd.
Gyven in reward the xvijth of May by your lordship's
commandment to Tarleton the pleyer}   xls.[531]
Gyven in reward the xviijth of May by

---

[529] Probably the *Galleon Leicester*, it may have been fitting out in preparation for what became the West Indies Voyage, see Adams, 'Outbreak of the Elizabethan Naval War', pp. 56–7.

[530] Gilbert, Lord Talbot (1552–1616), later 7th Earl of Shrewsbury.

[531] Richard Tarlton (d. 1588) was a member of the Lord Chamberlain's men 1570–1583 and then the Queen's men (see M.C. Bradbrook, *The Rise of the Common Player* (1962), pp. 162–7). There is no evidence of a direct connection to Leicester.

your lordship's commandment to Mr Heigham at
his goyng into Wailes}   iijli. vjs. viijd.
To Roger Gillions for carring your lordship from
Grenewich to Detford and back ageyne and from
thence to Wolledge the xvth of May}   xijs.
To him more for carring your lordship from
Leicester House to Grenewich the xvjth of May}   xijs.
To him more for carring your lordship from
Parisshe Garden to Leicester House and back
ageyne the xviijth of May}   ixs.
Gyven to the White Lyon in Sowthwourk the same day}   xijd.
Gyven to the spitle in Kentisshestreete and
other poor folk their the same day}   xvjd.
Gyven in reward the xixth of May by your lordship's
commandment to Richard Pepper your lordship's footeman
at his goyng into Ireland}   xls.
Gyven in reward the same day by your lordship's
commandment to one Law my Lord of Buckhurstes man}   xs.[532]
Gyven in reward the same day by your lordship's
commandment to my Lord of Warwick's kocheman for
carring your lordship from Grenewich to Paris Garden Steres}   vs.
Gyven the same day to two labourers and a poore
man at Paris Garden Steres}   viijd.
Gyven in reward the xxth of May by your lordship's
commandment to Mr Bryces man for bringing of a buck}   xs.
To Mr Blunt the same day which he paid for a pyde
horsse for your lordship}   xli.

Summa Paginae: xxiijli. vijs. iiijd.
xxiijli. xiijs. iiijd.ⁿ

[recto]

xxth of May [1585]

To Mr Richard Browne the same day which he gave
in reward by your lordship's commandment to the
nurce and mydwief at the christening of Mr
Leighton's childe}   <B>   xls.[533]
To him more which he gave to a poore man at Wansted
that had his house burnte}   <B>   ijs.

---

[532] Thomas Sackville, 1st Lord Buckhurst (1535/6–1608), MP.

[533] Given the reference to Lady Leighton's nurse on p. 256 below, probably Sir Thomas
(n. 527), who had two children, though his nephew Thomas Leighton (1554?–1613), MP,
who served in the Netherlands in 1586, is also possible.

Paid the same day at Milende for artichocks for
your lordship}   iijs.
Gyven the same day to the spitle and the poore at Myleende}   xijd.
Gyven in reward the same day to a man of my
Lord Talbott's that brought a birde to Wansted}   xs.
Gyven in reward the xxjth of May to the mayor's man
of Chichester for presenting conger, cockells and
other fishe}   xxs.
Gyven in reward to Mr Wolleis man for bringing a lettre
to Wansted}   vs.[534]
To Mr Haydon* which he gave to labourers in the way
betwene Wansted and London}   xijd.
Gyven in reward the xxijth of May by your lordship's
commandment to Sir Phillip Sidneis man for bringing a
letter from Courte to Leicester House}   ijs.
Gyven in reward the same day by your lordship's
commandment to Mr Marckhum's man for presenting a
hinde}   xxs.[535]
Gyven in reward the xxiijth of May by your lordship's
commandment to my Lord Treasourer's man for
presenting a bucke}   xs.
Gyven in reward the same day by your lordship's
commandment to your lordship's players at their
goyng into the countrie}   xls.
To Mr Giles Tracye the same day which he gave in reward
by your lordship's commandment to Sir Phillip Sidneis
page for bringing a message to Leicester House}   xxs.
To Roger Gillions for wayting and carring your
lordship in your lordship's barge the xixth, xxth
and xxiijth of Maie as appeareth by his bill}   xxxiijs.
To Steven Johnson the same day which he paid for a
grose of pointes for your lordship xiiijs. and
for thre paire of gilte spurres for your lordship xvs.}   xxixs.
Gyven in reward the xxiiijth of May by your
lordship's commandment to Seger the picture drawer}   vli.
Gyven in reward the same day to Mr Dockrey's man
for bringing letters from Killingworth to your lordship}   xxs.
                    Summa Paginae: xvijli. xvjs.

---

[534] (Sir) John Wolley (d. 1596), Secretary for the Latin Tongue from 1568, MP. Wolley
had chambers in Durham House in 1565 (DP Box V, fo. 215) and received livery in 1567;
he is more likely than Edward Dyer (see n. 501 above) to have been Leicester's secretary
in the mid-1560s.
[535] Probably Thomas Markham (1523–1607), Gentleman Pensioner, MP.

[verso]

xxiijth of May [1585]

Gyven in reward the same daie by your lordship's
commandment to the warner of Wanstead for bringing a
brace of grehoundes to Grenewich}   vs.

Gyven in reward the same daie by your lordship's
commandment to Mr Vernames man for presenting a
caste of falkons to your lordship}   xxs.[536]

Gyven in reward the same daie to my Lady Leighton's
nurce at Grenewich}   xs.

To Robert Pitchford the same daie which he paid for a
bushell of pese for your lordship}   ixs. viijd.

Gyven in reward the xxvjth of May to one of your
lordship's seamen that presented a mape at Leicester
House}   xls.

Paid to Warner the same day for carring your lordship
from Grenewich to Ratlief and from Blackwall to
Grenewich and from thence to London all in a day}   xvijs. iiijd.

To Roger Gillions for carring your lordship from
Leicester House to Grenewich the xxiiijth of May}   xijs.

To him for carring your lordship from Grenewich
to Leicester House and back ageyne the xxvth of May}   xijs.

Gyven amongest the watermen to drincke the same tyme}   iijs. iiijd.

To him more for carring your lordship from
Grenewich to Leicester House the xxixth of May}   xijs.

To him more for carring your lordship from Lyon
Key to Grenewich xxxth of May}   xijs.[537]

Paid to Robert Dowding for carring your lordship
from Leicester House in Iremongers' barge the
xxxth of May}   viijs.

Gyven in reward the same daie by your lordship's
commandment to Owen Jones that waites on
Mr Robert Dudley}   xxs.

Paid for the two messes of meate for your lordship's

[536] Probably John Farnham (n. 526), though it might be a form of Vernon.
[537] Leicester wrote to Dom António, the Portuguese pretender, inviting him to come to England, from the Court on 24 May (printed in P. Durand-Lapie, 'Un Roi détroné réfugié en France: Dom Antoine Ier de Portugal (1580–1595)', *Revue d'histoire diplomatique*, xviii (1904), 640). A delegation from the borough of Warwick finally obtained an interview at 'Leicester Garden' on the 28th and recorded that he was 'greatly occupied in matters of state & came seldome abroad' (*Black Book*, pp. 357–8). He signed the Council's licence for Castelnau to depart from England on 31 May (BN, VCC 470, fo. 95), and wrote to the governor of Sluys from Greenwich on 1 June (PRO, SP104/162/128–9).

servants for a fortnight from the xvjth of May
untill the xxxjth of the same month}   <a>   lvjs. viijd.
Payd to Thomas Harrys your lordship's shomaker the
xxxth of May by your lordship's commandment in full
payment of all recknings as appeareth by his bill}   xxxiijli. xixs.
Summa Paginae: xlvli. xviis.°

[recto]

xxxjth of May [1585]

Gyven by your lordship's commandment to Temple* of
Killingworth for bringing a fatt bucke to Grenewich
the xxixth of May}   xxs.
To Mr Grene the same daie which he gave by your
lordship's commandment to one that brought a buck
from Dutton Park}   xs.
To Mr Ardern which he gave in reward by your lordship's
commandment to one that brought v phesants to your
lordship the xxixth of May}   vs.
Gyven in reward the laste of May to two souldiars that
came oute of Flanders}   xls.
Gyven in reward the same daie by your lordship's
commandment to a carrier that brought two firkins
of oyesters from Colchester to Leicester House}   xiijs. iiijd.
Paid to Peter Dannyell* for the charges of your
lordship's dynner at Wansted the firste of June}   xjs. iiijd.
To Mr Grene the same day which he gave in reward
to John Kellye for presenting two grehounds to
your lordship}   vs.
To Griffyn Williams* the second of June which he
gave in reward to Mr Bulles man for presenting
artichokes to your lordship}   ijs. vjd.
Gyven in reward by your lordship's commandment
to Danniell the footeman when your lordship
sent him to Mr Gabriell Bleekes the same day}   vjs. viijd.
To Richard Gardneir the same daie for artichocks
which he bought for your lordship at severall tymes}   iiijs.
To him more for haulf a busshell of peacekoddes
which he carried to Wansted the xxvjth of Maye}   iijs. iiijd.
To Bartlett the paige the same day which your
lordship borrowed of him towards a pursse in
the Privie Chamber}   xs.
To Warner the same daie for carring your lordship
in his barge from Grenewich to Blackwall and

back ageyne}   viijs.
To Mrs Barker the iijth of June for ruffes
for a xj shirtes that my lady bought for
your lordship}   vjli. xiijs. iiijd.
Gyven in reward the iiijth of June by your
lordship's commandment to a keper of St
James's Parke for bringing a bucke to Leicester House}   xs.
Gyven to the poore at the spitle house at
Milende the same daie}   xijd.
Gyven to two poore folks at Stretford Bowe}   iijd.

Summa Paginae: xiiijli. iijs. ixd.[P]

[verso]

iiijth of June [1585]

Gyven in reward the same day to Walker Mr Vise
Chamberleines man for carring a lettre to Wansted}   vs.[538]
Gyven in reward the same daie by your lordship's
commandment to Cheslakes* sonne of Windsor for
bringing a young hinde to Wansted}   xs.
Your lordship loste at plaie at Wansted my Lord of
Comberland and my Lord of Darby being their the
same day at night}   xli.
To Mr Blunt the vth of June which he delivered to
your lordship in the walkes at Wansted which your
lordship gave away}   <a>   vli.
Delivered the same daie by your lordship's
commandment to Mr Richard Browne and Charells
Wednester the awdytor at Wansted}   <B>   Cli.
To Roger Gillions for carring your lordship in
your lordship's barge from the third of June till
the vjth of the same month as appeareth by his bill}   xliiijs.[539]
[*Hand B begins here*]
Paid to Robert Gwyn the which he gave by your
lordship's commandment to Manninges of Grenewich
for a buck the vjth of June 1585}   xxs.
Paid to Mr Hayden the which he gave by your
lordship's commandment to a smith at Stratford Langthorne}   xxs.

[538] Hatton.

[539] He must have returned to Greenwich on the 5th, for he wrote to Sir Amyas Paulet from the Court then, apologising for his 'great and continual business' (BL, Lansdowne MS 45, fo. 73). He also wrote to Hotman 'in haste', apologising for the failure of an earlier letter and money to reach him, praising the new French cook and reporting the departure of the gardener (AMAE, CPH, II, fo. 160).

Paid for your lordship's offering at Grenewich
the vjth of June 1585}   xijd.[540]
Geven to a poore man that caried roses from Grenewich
to Wansteed the vjth of June 1585}   ixd.
Paid to Mathewe Woodward for his boathyer from
White Hall to Grenewich when he brought 7 peeces of
hangings the 7 of June 1585}   ijs.
Paid to him more for his chardge divers tymes by
water from Grenewich to London and from Grenewich
to Wansteed}   xxd.
Given by your lordship's commandment to one Robert
Grene that presented a booke to your lordship
at Wanstead viij Junij}   vli.[541]
            Summa Paginae: Cxxvli. iiijs. vd.[q]

[recto]

                    viijth of June 1585
Geven by your commandment to Mr Poles man for
presenting a hobbie to dave [sic] larks at Wansteed}   vs.
To Charles Wednester your lordship's auditor the
same day to be paid by him, Richard Browne and
Thomas Bedwell paid over in full paye for the
building chardges att Wansteed due till Saturdaye
last thirttie eight poundes}   <B>   xxxviijli.
<all paid but the glasyer>[r]
Paid to the musiciones for vj horses from London
to Wansted viijth of June 1585}   xijs.
Delivered to my ladie the viijth of June when she
plaid with my Lord of Darbie att cardes}   xxli.
Paid to Richard Warner for caryng your lordship
from Grenewich to Blackwall the vjth of June 1585
on his owne bardge}   viijs.
Paid to him more for caryng your lordship from
Blackwall to Grenewich the viijth of June}   viijs.
Paid to Roger Julian for fetching your lordship
at Blackwall and carryng your lordship to
Grenewich the viijth of June}   xijs.

[540] On the 6th Walsingham informed Edward Wotton (see n. 545 below) that he had
just discussed his recent despatch from Scotland with Leicester (*Hamilton Papers*, ii, 648).
[541] STC 12299 *Planetomachia*. On the 8th Joachim Ortel sent Leicester his copy of the
Speculo delle Navigationi (*The Mariner's Mirror*, published in the Netherlands in 1584), see BL,
Cotton MS Galba C VIII, fo. 78, Ortel to Leicester, 8 June.

Paid to him more for caryng your lordship from Grenewich to Leycester House and back againe to Grenewich the ixth of June}	xijs.
Geven by your lordship's commandment to the watermen to drinck that day}	ijs. vjd.
Geven to Mr Robert Dudleies boye when he fetched a horse at Courte the ixth of June 1585}	ijs. vjd.

Summa Paginae: lxjli. ijs.ˢ

[verso]

9th of June 1585

Geven by your lordship's commandment to Robert Moore which made your lordship's cotche}	xxs.
Geven by your lordship's commandment to one that brought a litle begell from Lawrence Oldames of Warrwick the 9th of June 1585}	xxs.
Paid to Roger Julians for carying your lordship from Grenewich to Leycester House the xjth June 1585}	xijs.⁵⁴²
Paid to him more for carying your lordship from Leycester House to Grenewich xijth of June 1585}	xijs.
Paid to Robert Gwin by your lordship's commandment for ij cases of pistolles and theire furniture xj Junij 1585}	iijli.
Paid to him more for mending of the damask case of pistolles}	vjs.
Paid to him more for a stone bowe lath & a string}	vs.
Paid to him more for 3 dosen of crosbowe arrowes}	xvs.
Paid to him more for a newe rack}	xxs.
Paid to him more for a litle gaffle bowe}	xxs.
Paid for haulfe a dosen of arrowes to the same}	ijs. vjd.
Paid for trymming of a newe crossbowe and making of a newe feace for it and a newe case and stringes for the same}	vjs. vjd.
Paid to him more for three stringes for 3 old bowes and a dosen of arrowes for the same bowes}	iiijs.

Summa Paginae: xli. iijs.

[recto]

⁵⁴² He wrote to Sir Walter Mildmay from the Court on the 10th (BL, Egerton MS 2603, fo. 45).

xijth of June 1585

Paid to John Keyme the which he hath laid out
for your lordship's use for dyvers sorts of wynes
and for cariadg from vth of Januarye 1584 unto
the xijth of June 1585 as appeareth by his bille}   xliijs.

Paid to John Tracye the which he gave to the
French ambasodor's man for presenting chesses
and wyne at Leycester House}   ijs.

Paid for two messes of meate for your lordship's
servants for a fourthnight that is from the first
of June to the xiiijth of the same monethe}   lvjs. viijd.

Paid to Thomas the gardner of Wansteed for xlvij
potts of gillie flowers at xvjd. the pott the
same day}   lviijs.

Paid more to him for ysopp, thyme and earbes
the same daye}   xs.

Geven by your lordship's commandment to Mr
Townesend his mann for bringing of a Cli. to
your lordship the xijth of June 1585}   xxs.[543]

Geven by your lordship's commandment to Mr
Arundell's man for bringing a stagg's heade to
your lordship at Grenewiche the xiiijth of June}   xls.

Geven by your lordship's commandment to fishers
and foulleres of Windsore Forrest the xiiijth
of June 1585}   xs.

Summa Paginae: xjli. xixs. viijd.

[verso]
[*Hand C begins here*]

the xiiij of June [1585]

Gevin by your lordship's commandment to Savage
the keper the same day}   xs.

Payd by your lordship's commandment for a duck to
hunt the same day}   xijd.

Payd by your lordship's commandment to William
Ford* the warener at Wansted for a rabat haye the
same day}   xijs.

Gevin by your lordship's commandment to a man
of my Lord of Warickes for presenting a brach

[543] (Sir) Roger Townshend (1544–1590) of Raynham (Norf.), MP. Townshend had leased
the Robsart manors (Syderstone and Bircham Newton) from Leicester in 1579 (Brevis
Abstract, fo. 22). He owed Leicester £500 in 1589.

to your lordship the same day}   vjs. viijd.

Gevin by your lordship's commandment to a poore
man betwene Harrew and Totename the same day}   vjd.

Gevin by your lordship's commandment to Mr
Dockrey at his goyng from Tibboles to
Killingworth the same daye}   vli.

Gevin by your lordship's commandment to Thomas
the gardener of Wansted the same day}   xs.

Gevin by your lordship's commandment to my
Lord Treasorer's officers in his house at
Tibbols the same day, to the seller, butler,
pantrie, ewery, kytchen, wardrop}   iiijli. xs.[544]

Gevin by your lordship's commandment to a keper
of my Lord Treasorer's for bringing a bucke to
your lordship ther the same day}   xxs.

Payd by your lordship's commandment for on
cart from Grenewich to Tiboles to cary your
lordship's stoof the same daye}   ijs. viijd.

Gevin by your lordship's commandment to Mr
Wotten's man for caring a letter to his master
into Scotland the same day}   xs.[545]

Payd by your lordship's commandment to Steaven
Johnson of the wardrobe for dyverse necessaries
for your lordship as apereth by his byll the
same day}   iiili. iijs. xd.

Gevin by your lordship's commandment to Mearcer
my Lord of Warwickes man at his going into
Scotland the same day}   vli.

                Summa Paginae: xxjli. vjs. viijd.

[recto]

[544] According to Chambers, the Queen visited Theobalds c. 18 June, but the 14th-15th
seems more likely from the entries here and Walsingham's reference to her 'late repeire
to Theobaldes' in a letter to Edward Wotton of the 17th (*Hamilton Papers*, ii, 653).
Castelnau was also there, see BN, VCC 470, fo. 127, Henry III to Castelnau, 5/15 July.
Burghley later claimed that he first heard of the Queen's decision to extend the
prorogation of the parliament (which had been prorogued to 21 June) from Leicester at
Theobalds (PRO, SP12/180/76, to William Herle, 18 July).

[545] (Sir) Edward Wotton (1548–1628), of Boughton Malherbe, Kent, MP. Wotton
was ambassador in Scotland between May and October 1585, and Walsingham's
correspondence with him (printed in *Hamilton Papers*, ii, 643–705) is an extremely valuable
source for the events of the summer. Wotton was a pallbearer at Sidney's funeral and
attended Leicester's funeral. This letter has not survived but see n. 551 below.

the xvth of June [1585]

Payd by your lordship's commandment to Mr Grene
the which he gave to the sarvants of the house
at Edmonton wheare your lordship deyned the same day}   xxs.

Payd by your lordship's commandment for the
carges of your lordship's stouf from Tibeles to
Grenwich the same day}   iijs.

Payd by your lordship's commandment to Mr Thomas
Grene the coffermaker for a new chest leyned
with cotton for your lordship's rapers and for
meanding other trunkes as apperath by his byll
the same daye}   xlvjs. viijd.

Gevin by your lordship's commandment to Mr
Palmer at [h]is going into Scotland the same day
paye him at Leaster Hous}   xxli.⁵⁴⁶

Gevin by your lordship's commandment to Mr
Blunt the which he gave to a kepper's daughter
in Envill Chace the same day}   xs.

Gevin by your lordship's commandment to Mr
Blunt the which he gave to on Bull a kepper of
one of the walkes in the same chase and his
man the same day}   xvijs.

Gevin by your lordship's commandment to Mr
Blunt the which he gave to Pecoke the kepper
of the old parke at Envill and to his man the
same daye}   xvs.

Gevin by your lordship's commandment to a
poore woman at Tibells the same day}   xijd.

Delyvered by your lordship's commandment to
Mr Thomas Knolles he that delleth [sic]
by Wansted delyvered to him at Greneght the
same day}   vjli. xiijs. iiijd.

Gevin by your lordship's commandment to Thomas
the garner at Wansted the same daye}   vs.

Payd by your lordship's commandment iiij new
seastorens for Leaster House the same day payd
at Leaster Hous the some of as appereth
by the byll}   vjli. iiijs. viijd.

Payd by your lordship's commandment for a pare
of ores for your lordship from Leceaster House
to Starchamber the same day}   ijs.

Summa Paginae: xxxviijli. xvijs. viijd.ᵗ

⁵⁴⁶ See n. 551 below.

[verso]

the xvj daye of June [1585]

Payd by your lordship's commandment to Rychard
Warner for caring your lordship frome Grenewich
to Blackwall with his barge and iiij ores the same daye}   viijs.

Payd by your lordship's commandment to Rychard
Warner for caring your lordship from Grenewich
to to [*sic*] Blackwall and from
Ratlyfe to Leaster Hous the same day}   viijs.

Gevin by your lordship's commandment to Mr
Boyer's man for presenting chesses to your
lordship at Leaster Hous the same day}   ijs. vjd.[547]

Payd by your lordship's commandment to Roger
Gillions your lordship's bargeman for caringe
your lordship at iiij seaverall tymes as
appereth by his byll the same day payd
him at Leaster Hous}   xlviijs.

Payd by your lordship's commandment to Mr
Rychard Browne which he paid unto the Earl of
Oxford in part payment for his house and lands
by Wansted which your lordship bought of hym
payd him the same daye at Wansted}   <B>   lli.[548]

Gevin by your lordship's commandment to Daunyell
your lordship's futman when he went with letters
to my Lord Gray at Northampton the same daye}   vjs. viijd.[549]

Givin by your lordship's commandment to Mr
Docraye['s] man for bringing a buck from
Kyllingworth to your lordship to Leaster
Hous the same daye}   xxs.

Payd by your lordship's commandment to Roger
Gyllans your lordship's waterman for caring

---

[547] Probably Simon Bowyer (c.1550–1606), Gentleman Usher from 1569, MP. Although Bowyer is the hero of the much-repeated anecdote of Leicester's rebuff from Sir Robert Naunton's *Fragmenta Regalia*, Leicester had earlier referred to him as 'my frend Mr Bower' (LPL, MS 697, fo. 19, to Shrewsbury, 15 May 1569).

[548] The manor of Cranbrook, purchased to expand Wanstead Park, as Leicester noted in his 1587 will. The conveyance was dated 9 June, see Essex RO, D/DCw/T46/56, defeasance between Leicester and Israel Amyce, 6 July 1585.

[549] Arthur, 14th Lord Grey de Wilton (1536–93), former Lord Deputy of Ireland. 'Since my father's death you have been he that only I have depended on and followed', DP II, fo. 296, Grey to Leicester, n.d. [1588?]. He was considered as a possible alternative to Leicester as commander in the Netherlands (see Appendix II), and Leicester wanted him as his second-in-command, but debts to the Crown incurred during his Irish government prevented his appointment.

your lordship iij days betwene Lecester
Hous and Greynwich as appereth by his byll}   xxxvjs.
Payd by your lordship's commandment for ij
measse of meat for your lordship's servants for
a fortneyght that is from the xiiijth of June
unto the xxviijth of the same month}   lvjs. viijd.
Payd by your lordship's commandment to Pero the
French coke for his quarter's wages from Our Lady
Day to Midsomer 1585 the somme of the same daye}   vli.
Payd by your lordship's commandment to Mr Gren
which he gave to the kepper of Eltame Park the same day}   xs.
                Summa Paginae: lxiiijli. xvs. xd.

[recto]

                the xvij of June [1585]
Payd by your lordship's commandment to John
Keyme your lordship's searvant for xxvijth dossen
of stone bottells at iijs. iiijd. a dossen and
ij glase bottells covered with leather vjs.
viijd. as apereth by his byll payd
the same daye}   iiijli. xvjs. viijd.
Payd by your lordship's commandment to John
Robynson* your lordship's skynner at Leaster
Hous the same daye the some of}   xxli.
Payd by your lordship's commandment to Gilles
Homerston the which he gave to the gardener's
wyfe at Wansted the same daye}   ijs. vjd.
Payd by your lordship's commandment to Gilles
Homerston more the same day which he payd for
a lame which his hound kylled at Wansted the same day}   xijd.
Delivered by your lordship's commandment to Mr
Secretory which he sent to Mr Dr Ottymane* into
France the same day the some of}   xxxli.[550]
Gevin by your lordship's commandment to on[e] that
set a stole for your lordship to com into the
barge at Blackwall the same day}   iiijd.
Given by your lordship's commandment to a poore
man at Stratford the same day at your lordship's
goynge to Wansted}   vjd.

[550] On 5 June (see n. 539 above) Leicester promised to send Hotman the money he
had not received earlier by a safer means. Arthur Atye asked Hotman on 20 July if he
had received it yet (AMAE, CPH, II, fo. 89).

Payd by your lordship's commandment to Thomas
the gardener at Wansted for his quarter's wages
from Our Lady Daye to Midsomer 1585 paye
to hym at Wansted}   vli.
Gevin by your lordship to a smythe at Stratford
Lanton the same day}   vs.
Payd by your lordship's commandment to Rychard
Warner for caringe your lordship from Grenvich
to Blackwall in his barge with iiij owers and
for feching your lordship at Blackwall and caring
you to Grenvich the same day}   xvjs.
Gevin by your lordship's commandment to Mr Cave
the which he gave to a poore boy in the tiltyeard
the same day}   vjd.

                    Summa Paginae: lxjli. ijs. vjd.

[verso]

                    the xx of June [1585]
Payd by your lordship's commandment to John Par
the Quenes majesty's embrader for the quilting
of iij wastcotes for your lordship and for sylke
and workmanshep and for vj yeardes of flanell
that mad your lordship's wastcotes payd the
same day at Leaster Hous}   vijli. xviijs.
Payd by your lordship's commandment to Mr
Kechyen* for necessary things bought for your
lordship as handkyrches on dossen, on yard and
a halfe of cotworke at vs. a yeard, ij yeards
of nedellworke lace at iiijs. viijd. the yeard,
ij yeards and hall [sic] a quarter of nedellworke
lace at xxd. the yeard, v dossen of strings at
xijd. a dossen for making of your lordship's
bandes and setting to the shirtes at ijs. a
peces, iiij dossen of buttons at viijd. a
dossen, and for the making of the hankyrches,
and making and stiching at iijs. a pece for
your lordship's heus [sic] payd
at Leaster Hous the same daye}   iiijli. vs.
Gevin by your lordship's commandment to [a] man
of Mr Warkopes that he prefered to your lordship
the same daye}   xls.
Given by your lordship's commandment to Sir
Thomas Syssellis man for bringing chesses to

Grenweche to your lordship the same daye}   vs.
Payd by your lordship's commandment to John
Mansell the matlayer for laying mates at Wansted
by Mr Brownes commandment the same daye payd
at Wansted}   <a>   viijli. ixs. vjd.
Payd by your lordship's commandment to Mr
Blunt which he gave to one for caring horses
into Scotland the same daye payd at Wansted}   vjli. xiijs. iiijd.[551]
Payd by your lordship's commandment to Steven
Johnson of your lordship's wardrop that he
gave to a poore man at Seant Gorges Church
the same daye}   vjd.
Gevin by your lordship's commandment to a man
Mr Carleales for bringe faysants to your
lordship at Wansted the same daye}   vs.[552]
Payd by your lordship's commandment to Bedwell
of Wansted that he layd out to ij mowers, to
the brickemakers and to a poore woman at Wansted
the same daye}   iijs. iiijd.
          Summa Paginae: xxixli. xixs. viijd.

[recto]

                   the xxvjth of June [1585]
Gevin by your lordship's commandment to a poore
man betwene Stertford the Bowe and Stratford
Lanton at your lordship's coming to Leaster Hous}   xd.
Delyvered to your lordship's on handes at Wansted
which your lordship gave to Thomas the gardener
and to hys wyfe the same day}   xvs.
Gevin by your lordship's commandment to Warner

---

[551] As part of the diplomatic campaign to win him over, a stream of presents was sent to James VI in the summer of 1585, the grandest being a gift of horses conveyed by Robert Alexander (see n. 470 above). Although organised by Leicester, this gift was probably in in the Queen's name, for Alexander's expenses (£47 3s) were later paid by the Treasurer of the Chamber (BL, Harl. MS 1641, fo. 15). Alexander received a warrant on 12 May (PRO, SO3/1/18v), arrived in Edinburgh on 8 June and presented the horses on the 12th, see BL, Cotton MS Titus B VII, fo. 2, Alexander to Leicester, 13 June. Edward Wotton also wrote to Leicester on the 13th (BL, Cotton MS Caligula C IX, fo. 173), reporting Alexander's arrival and that James was looking forward to a gift of buckhounds promised by Leicester in a now-missing letter of the 3rd. This entry may be a reference to these horses, or to a later set. For other gifts, see the next page.

[552] Probably Christopher Carleill (1551?–93), Walsingham's stepson and lieutenant-general of the West Indies Voyage. See R. Lloyd, *Elizabethan Adventurer. A Life of Captain Christopher Carleill* (1974).

the watterman at Wansted the same day}   xs.
Payd by your lordship's commandment to Warner
the watterman for caringe your lordship from
Grenewich to Blackwall and backe agayne to
Grenewich the same daye}   xvjs.
Gevin by your lordship's commandment to my Lord
of Penbrokes page for presenting a halke to your
lordship at Grenewicht the same day}   xxs.
Gevin by your lordship's commandment to your
lordship's mariners at Wolledge the same day}   xls.
Gevin by your lordship's commandment to a poore
man betex the tow Stratfordes the same daye}   iiijd.
Gevin by your lordship's commandment to another
poore man at Stratford the same day}   iiijd.
Gevin by your lordship's commandment to Mr
Bowton that he gave to Savag the kepper when
your lordship keled a stage in his walke xs.
and to his mean the same day xijs., the holle some}   xxijs.
Gevin by your lordship's commandment to Mr
Dudley the page that he gave Dave the kepper
the same day}   xs.
Gevin by your lordship's commandment to John
your lordship's harpyer* at his goyng to my Lord
of Warick's hous the same daye}   xs.
Payd by your lordship's commandment to Warner
for caring your lordship from Grenewich to
Blackewall and from thens to Wolledg and backe
agayn as appereth by his byll}   xxvijs. iiijd.
                    Summa Paginae: viijli. xjs. xd.

[verso]

                    the xxixth of June [1585]
Payd by your lordship's commandment to Robart
Gwine your lordship's sarvant for a crosbowe
and all other necessaries to it to seand to the
Kynge of Scotts as it apereth by his byll the
same daye payd hym}   iijli. vijd.
Payd by your lordship's commandment to Fardenandoe
for his quarter's wages dewe for Mydsomer quarter
the same daye 1585 payd hym at Richmon}   ls.
Payd by your lordship's commandment to Mrs Gylliam
your lordship's laundres for her quarter's wages
dewe for mydsomer quarter the same daye 1585}   ls.

Gevin by your lordship's commandment to Mr Bouten
that he gave to a man that brought letters from
Mr Dockre from Kyllingworth to your lordship
the same daye}   vjs. viijd.
Gevin by your lordship's commandment to Mr Cave
which he gave to a man of Mr Fenton's for
presenting a halke to your lordship at Wansted
the same day}   xxs.[553]
Gevin by your lordship's commandment to Rychard
Pepper which he gave to a smyth at Stretford for
taking on[e] that stole venison the same daye}   vs.
Payd by your lordship's commandment to Mr Gren
which he gave to on[e] Thomas Harryson at Wansted
the same daye}   vli.
Gevin by your lordship's commandment to Gaskyng's
man the post master for bringe leatters from Mr
Secretery to Wansted to your lordship the same daye} vs.
Payd by your lordship's commandment for your
lordship's botheyre from Blackewall to Grenewich
the same day}   xijd.
Payd by your lordship's commandment for the hyre
of ij botes more for your lordship's men the same daye} xiiijd.
Payd by your lordship to Roger Gillans your
lordship's watterman for caring your lordship at
sundry tymes the first daye of June to the x
daye of July as apereth by his bill payd hym at
Leaster Hous the same day}   xxiiijs. iiijd.
              Summa Paginae: xvjli. iijs. ixd.

[recto]

              the frist [sic] day of July [1585]
Gevin by your lordship's commandment to the
post for bring leatters to your lordship to
Wansted the same day}   xijd.
Gevin by your lordship's commandment to Mr
Bramton which he gave Mr Kotes man for presenting
a hound to your lordship the same day at Wansted}   xxxs.
Gevin by your lordship's commandment between

[553] Probably (Sir) Geoffrey Fenton (1539–1603), Secretary of State in Ireland from 1580, who brought despatches from Ireland, see Bodl., MS Perrot 1, fo. 110, Perrot to Leicester, 10 June. Fenton had a long-standing association with Leicester and Warwick, and may have been Warwick's secretary in the 1570s.

Stratford and Blackewall to two poore folke the same daye}	iiijd.
Gevin by your lordship's commandment to Mr Goldinggeame which he gave to my Lord Stafford's man at Wanstead the same day}	xs.
Gevin by your lordship's commandment to Mrs Barates man for presenting preserved meates to your lordship at Wanstead the same day}	xs.
Gevin by your lordship's commandment to Ramsone the kepper at Wanstead the same day}	xs.
Gevin by your lordship's commandment to Ramsone['s] man the same daye more at Wanstead}	ijs. vjd.
Gevin by your lordship's commandment [to] Jacobes the glassmaker's man for presenting glasses to your lordship at Wanstead the same day}	vjs. viijd.
Payd by your lordship's commandment to Warner the watterman for caring your lordship with his barge ij days as apereth by his byll the same day}	xviijs.
Payd by your lordship's commandment that was geven in rewards at Leaster Hous to the Quenes offesers at hyr majesties dyning the same day as apereth by the byll payd to Rychard Browne your lordship's sarvante at Leaster Hous the same daye} <B>	vli. vs.[554]
Payd by your lordship's commandment for ij measses of meate for your lordship's servantes of the wardrope for a fornyght that is from the xxviij of June to the xj of July}	vs. viijd.
Delyvered by your lordship's commandment to Mr Sutton the seleaster to paye for wrytings for your lordship at Wansted the same day}	vli.

Summa Paginae: xvijli. xs. ijd.

[verso]

the iij daye of July [1585]
Gevin by your lordship's commandment to Mr Egworth

---

[554] There is no other evidence of the Queen's dining at Leicester House in June or July. It is curious that no reference is made to the arrival of the Dutch commissioners to negotiate the treaty of assistance. They arrived at Margate on 24 June, Gravesend on the 26th, had their first audience with the Queen at Greenwich on 29 June and their first meeting with the Privy Council on 1 July (see their Rapport, ARA, Eerste Afdeling, Staten Generaal 8299).

the preacher at Wansted the same day}   vjli. xiijs. iiijd.[555]
Payd by your lordship's commandment to William
Thomas for x yeards of rybband at xj*d*. the yeard
and for x yeardes of shexter riband at vj*d*. the
yeard to hange your lordship's Gorges the same day
payd at Leaster House the same daye}   xiiijs. ijd.
Gevin by your lordship's commandment to Gylles
Hommerstone the which he gave to Flower the
kepper of Eltame Parke the same daye}   vjs. viijd.
Payd by your lordship's commandment to Steaven
Johnson of your lordship's wardrope for hys
botheyr betwene Grenewich and Leaster Hous at
sundry tymes being sente ab[o]ut your lordship's
busynes and for a dossin of walkyng staves and
for a dossin yeardes of riband at v [*sic*]
the yeard as apereth by his byll}   xviijs. jd.
Payd by your lordship's commandment to Fardonando
which he payd to Poukes the tayler for makyng
Wat your lordship's boy ij doblates and ij pare
of hose and a cloke as apereth by his byll payd
the same daye}   vjli.
Payd by your lordship to Fardonando that he layd
out for Wat your lordship's boye for deyvers
necessaries as for shirtes and showes and other
things as apereth by his byll}   xxxs. iijd.
Gevin by your lordship's commandment to a poore
man betwene the tou Stratfordes the same daye at
your lordship's goyng to Wansted}   vjd.
Gevin by your lordship's commandment to Mr Harman's
man for bring a bucke to your lordship to Wansted
the same daye}   vjs. viijd.
Payd by your lordship's commandment to Couke the
habberdasher for vj sylke knet nightcaps for your
lordship the same day}   xls.
Payd by your lordship's commandment to Sheperd
the habberdasher for iiij pere of gloves for
your lordship the same day}   xijs.

         Summa Paginae: xixli. js. viijd.

---

[555] Edward Edgeworth (d.1595), a former chaplain. He was rector of St Anne and St
Agnes, Aldegate 1579–87, rector of Barking 1584–7, and then Bishop of Down and
Connor 1593–5. He may have been Irish by birth.

[recto]

the v day of July [1585]

Gevin by your lordship's commandment to Steven
Johnson that he gave to the pavyers at Algat in
London the same daye}   xijd.

Gevin by your lordship's commandment to Mr Gren
that he gave to the workemen at the glasse hous
in London the same daye}   xxs.

Gevin by your lordship's commandment to Mr Gren
the same daye that he gave to Javes man for bring
vj glasses to your lordship at Wansted the same day}   ijs.

Payd by your lordship's commandment to Steaven
of the wardrop that he payd for ij hunting horns
for your lordship and the baudrickes of grene
sylk and golde at xviijs. the pece the same daye}   xxxvjs.

Payd by your lordship's commandment to Robart
Gwine for iiij case of knyfes for your lordship
at xiijs. vjd. the case the same day}   liiijs.

Delyvered by your lordship's commandment to Mr
Rychard Lloyd at his going over the sease into
the Loe Countries the same daye}   vjli. xiijs. iiijd.[556]

Payd by your lordship's commandment for bothier
from Erythe to Wolledge for Mr. Dudley and
Mr Goldingame and Rafe More* the same daye}   ijs.

Payd by your lordship's commandment to William
Thomas the which he gave to the searvents' [sic]
clark and to the carpentor at Grenewich the same daye}   xs.

Payd by your lordship's commandment to John
Keme for ij newe hampers to cary your lordship's
drincke in and for his carges of caring wyne
and beare by water from London to Grenewich from
the xxijth of June to the xvij of July as apereth
by his byll the same daye}   xiiijs. ijd.

Payd by your lordship's commandment to Mr Grene
which he gave to the workemen in the glasse hous
the same daye}   xs.

---

[556] Lloyd was sent to appeal for the release of the admiral of Zeeland, Willem van
Bloys alias Treslong, who had been imprisoned in February for supposed negligence in
an attempt to relieve Antwerp. Presumably he carried Elizabeth's letter on the subject of
11 July (ARA, Eerste Afdeling, Regeringsarchieven, I-90B) with him, in which case he
could not have left before then. His interview with the Raad van State can be found in
the entries for 28–9 July/7–8 August in ARA, Eerste Afdeling, RvS 3 [Register van
Resoluties 1584–5], fos. 330–32v.

Payd by your lordship's commandment to Mr Grene
which he gave more the same daye to the carpentors
and mariners in the Quenes shep caled the
Triumpe at Wollege the same daye}   xxs.[557]
         Summa Paginae: xvli. ijs. vjd.

[verso]
[*Hand B resumes*]

         vjth of Julie 1585
Item geven by your lordship's commandment to
Edward Willperforce at his going to Northall}   xs.[558]
Paid to Roger Julian the master of your
lordship's bardge for carying your lordship
fyve daies by water as appeareth by his
bill from the xiijth of Julie till the xvjth
of the same moneth}   iijli. vjs.
Paid for your lordship's boathyer from Lyon Key
to Leycester House}   xijd.
Paid for your lordship's men theire boathyer
the same day}   xijd.
Delivered to Mr Blunt gentleman of your
lordship's horse by your lordship's commandment}   xli.
Paid to Gawene Smyth by your lordship's
commandment towards the making of a cotche the same daye}   xli.[559]
Paid to John Devyge Sir Thomas Henneage his
man for a piece of Orleans wyne by your
lordship's commandment}   xlviijs.
Paid to him more the same day remayning for
the Bargoine wyne}   ijs.
Paid for the fraight of the wyne and for the
man's paines}   xxxijs.
Geven by your lordship's commandment to the
Wardropp at Grenewiche}   xxs.
Geven more the same day to the servants}   vs.
         Summa Paginae: xxixli. xvs.

---

[557] The great ship *Triumph.*
[558] The Earl of Warwick's house at Northaw, Herts.
[559] Gawen or Gavin Smith, engineer, appointed trenchmaster in the Netherlands in 1586 (PRO, SP15/29/222, 338). BL, Harl. MS 286, fo. 147, is a letter from him to Leicester from Lübeck, 6 Sept. 1588. See also the references to him as a coach-maker below.

[recto]

vij Julij 1585

Paid to your lordship's yeomen ix of them for
their boathyer from Grenewich to Leycester
House and for theire suppers that night at
the mariadge of yonge Mr Heniage}   ixs. iijd.[560]

Paid by your lordship's commandment to Roger
Julian for caryng your lordship from Leycester
House to Grenewich the same daye}   xijs.

Paid for carying your lordship from Grenewich
to Putneye}   xviijs.

Paid for geven attendaunce at Putney by your
lordship's commandment}   xijs.

Geven by your lordship's commandment to the
keper of Grenewiche Parke}   xs.

Geven by your lordship's commandment to Cuttie
Musgrove at Grenewich the same daie}   iijli.

[Hand C resumes]

Geven by your lordship's commandment to on[e] of
your lordship's servants for goinge to Wansted
the same daye}   vjd.

Geven by your lordship's commandment to the
servants of Mr Allderses hous the same daye}   xxs.

Payd by your lordship's commandment the same
day for a saman takyn at Putney the same daye}   vjs. viijd.

Payd by your lordship's commandment to Mr
Blunt for the meat and standing of your
lordship's horsses ther willst the waytted
your lordship's coming at sundry tymes the vj
day and the xj day of July as apereth by his byll}   viiijs. iijd.

Summa Paginae: vijli. xvjs. viijd.

[verso]

the ix of July 1585

Payd by your lordship's commandment for my
lades horsses at London and your lordship's
own ther for ther meat and standing ther
the same daye}   viijs.

Gevin by your lordship's commandment to

---

[560] It is not clear who this was, for Sir Thomas Heneage's only child was a daughter,
and his younger brother Michael, MP, married in 1577.

Smulkyn your lordship's futman when he went to
overtake Mr Cary* with lettres of your lordship's
the same daye}   ijs. vjd.
Payd by your lordship's commandment to one
Maxley for presentinge to your lordship a
baye hobey from Mr Noris to your lordship which
Mr Blunt gave him as apereth by his byll}   xls.[561]
Payd by your lordship's commandment for the
carges of your lordship's stoufe carig from
Grenewich to Nunsuch which was x cartes the
same day}   xxijs. viijd.[562]
Payd by your lordship's commandment to your
lordship's yeomen which came with the cartes
from Grenewich to Nonsuch: Robert Pouvinton*,
John Gwyn*, Thomas Hall, Henry Millington,
Rychard Buck, Francis Johnson*, Robert Folys,
Mathew Wodword, Thomas Williams for ther carges
the same day payd them at Nonsuch}   xs.
Gevin by your lordship's commandment to Mr
Neytinggall* for a man that went to London
from Mr Laces the same day}   xs.[563]

---

[561] (Sir) John Norris (1547–97), son of Henry, Lord Norris (see n. 148 above). He had
been recalled from Ireland in May to command the troops to be sent to the Netherlands
(Bodl., MS St. Amand 8 [Norris Papers], fo. 67, Walsingham to Norris, 12 May). Leicester
later wrote in his Declaration (1587) following his quarrels with Norris in the Netherlands
'It is well known that the Erle hath alwaies ben a goode frende to Sir John Norreys his
howse and that he brought him uppe, he procured his first credytt in that country [the
Netherlands], he caused him to be sent for out of Ireland for that service' (BL, Add. MS
48116, fo. 77).

[562] The vagaries of Hand C create considerable difficulties in establishing the chronology
of Leicester's movements from this point on. During July the Court removed from
Greenwich to Nonsuch. According to Chambers this was between 20–24 July, and the
Queen also visited Barn Elmes (11 July) and John Lacy's house at Putney (c. 27–9 July).
At the same time the Council was also conducting the negotiations with the Dutch
commissioners, initially at Greenwich, but also in London, at Walsingham's house (8
July) and at Cecil House (18 July), see ARA, Eerste Afdeling, Staten Generaal 8299.
Leicester signed a Council circular for Drake's voyage on 11 July at Greenwich (PRO,
SP46/17/172), and sent a letter to the Countess of Shrewsbury from Greenwich on the
12th (SP12/180/53). He wrote to Archbishop Whitgift from Court on the 14th for Thomas
Cartwright (ITL, Petyt MS 538/52, fos. 19v–20), and Alexander Neville wrote to Whitgift
on the 19th on instructions from Leicester delivered at Court on the 18th (BL, Lansdowne
MS 45, fos. 98–100). Finally, Arthur Atye wrote to Hotman from the Court on the 20th,
Leicester 'being not himself at leisure' (AMAE, CPH, II, fo. 89). The implication from
the subsequent entries is that Leicester went to Nonsuch with his stuff c. 8–10 July and
then returned to London (and presumably Greenwich as well) and ultimately went back
to Nonsuch with the Court at some point after the 20th.

[563] John Lacy's at Putney, possibly John Lacy the mercer, see n. 246 above. It is difficult
not to associate this entry with the Queen's visit, see the previous note.

Payd by your lordship's commandment to Mr
Grise for xxiiij torkey skynes at ix*s*. the
pease for to cover a coch for your lordship
payd hym at Putney the sume of the same daye}   xli. xvis.
Paid by your lordship's commandment to Blakesbe
of Kyllingworth when he brought letters to your
lordship to Nonsuch from Kyllingworth the same day}   xs.
Gevin by your lordship's commandment to Gyllam me
Lord Lomles gardener for the bringing of redis rutes
and sedes to your lordship at Nonsuch the same day}   xxs.
Geven by your lordship's commandment to Vardenandou
which he gave to Frances Gall Mr Necados man
the same daye}   xs.[564]

Summa Paginae: "xvijli. ixs. ijd."
xvijli. vjs. ijd.

[recto]

the x of July 1585
Delyvered by your lordship's commandment to
Justis Young of London at Nonsuch the same daye}   vli.
Gevin by your lordship's commandment to on[e] of
your lordship's futmen when he went from Nonsuch
to Leaster House with leatters to Mr Atey the same day}   iiijd.
Payd by your lordship's commandment to Gylles
Hommerston for a lease for a hound for your
lordship the same daye}   xijd.
Payd by your lordship's commandment to Mr Hadin
when your lordship went to Wolleg which he payd
for oysters ther the same day}   xijd.
Gevin by your lordship's commandment to Colle
your lordship's sarvant at his goyng down from
Nonsuch to Lanley Park gevin him at Nonsuch
the same day}   xls.
Gevin by your lordship's commandment to Allyn
your lordship's man at his goyng to Lanley the
same day at Nonsuch}   xls.
Gevin by your lordship's commandment to the
kepper of Nonsuch Park the same daye at Nonsuch}   xxs.
Gevin by your lordship's commandment to Hary
Stringer which he gave to a poore blynd woman
the same daye at Nonsuch}   vjd.

[564] Presumably the Nicaches on p. 340 below. He cannot be otherwise identified.

Gevin by your lordship's commandment to the
poore mor the same daye at your lordship's
goyng from Nonsuch to London}   ijs.
Gevin by your lordship to Daniell your lordship's
futman the same daye that he gave to the poore
at your lordship's going to London}   vjd.[565]
Gevin by your lordship's commandment to on[e]
Meylt my Lord of Darbes man for presenting a
gyllt cop to your lordship at Battersey the
same day}   xls.
Payd by your lordship's commandment to Roger
Gillans your lordship's bargman for caryng your
lordship to Battersey and watting ther all day
and from Battersey to Leaster Hous the xiij and
xiiij of July and for caryng your lordship from
Blackfryers to Leaster Hous the same day as
apereth by his byll and gevin to the barg
the same time}   xljs.
              Summa Paginae: xiiijli. vjs. iiijd.

[verso]

                    the xx of July 1585
Payd by your lordship's commandment for ij measse
of meat for your lordship's sarvants for [*sic*] the
wardrop for a fornyght that is from the xj of
July to the xxv of the same month 1585}   <a>   lvjs. viijd.
Geven by your lordship's commandment at my
Lord of Darbes hous to the sarvantes that gave
your lordship drynck ther the same day}   vs.[566]
Geven by your lordship's commandment to Mr Ardyn
at his goyng downe into the contrey from Nonsoch
to Kyllingworth the same day}   iijli. vjs. viijd.
Paid by your lordship's commandment to Mr
Gylles Trasy which he gave to on[e] of the keppers
of Nonsuch Parke the same day your lordship
cylled a [*blank*] ther at Nonsuch}   xs.
Geven by your lordship's commandment to Humfrey
your lordship's futman at his goyng downe into the
contrey to Kyllingworth from Nonsuch the same daye}   xs.
Geven by your lordship's commandment to the kepper's

---

[565] Presumably c. 10 July, see n. 562.
[566] Derby House on Cannon Row, Westminster.

man of Nonsuch Parke the same daye}   vs.
Payd by your lordship's commandment to your
futmean for ther quarter's wages from Our Lady Day
last to Medsomer quarter 1585 for Daniell and
Smulkyn paye them at Nonsuch the same daye}   vli.
Geven by your lordship's commandment to Rychard
Pepper your lordship's futman the same daye at
Nonsuch at his goyng into Eyrland}   xls.
Payd by your lordship's commandment to Owin for
Mrs Roberts launder for hyr quarter's wages for
the last quarter from Our Lady Day to Medsomer
1585 paye at Nonsuch the same daye}   xs.
Geven by your lordship's commandment to on[e] of
my Lord Chambrlynes men for presentinge a pecoke
to your lordship at Nonsuch the same daye}   vs.[567]
Payd by your lordship's commandment to Robart
Pichfork which he payd for leamons for your
lordship at Nonsuch the same day}   iiijs.
Summa Paginae: xvli. xijs. iiijd.

[recto]

the xxix of July 1585
Payd by your lordship's commandment to Mr Browne
which he payd to the bricke maker at Wansted the
same daye above writen as apereth by his byll
payd at Wansted}   \<a\> \<B\>   xvjli. vijs. vjd.
Gevin by your lordship's commandment to Mr
Bramton's man for presenting foulle to your
lordship at Nonsuch the same day}   iijs. iiijd.
Gevin by your lordship's commandment to the
poore allmes hous at Croydon the same day att
your lordship's coming to Wansted}   xijd.
Gevin in reward to ij poor folke mor the same
daye by your lordship's commandment}   iiijd.
Payd by your lordship's commandment for a pare
of ouers for your lordship when your lordship

---

[567] On 4 July Howard of Effingham surrendered the lord chamberlaincy to Lord
Hunsdon (see n. 57 above) and on the 8th was appointed Lord Admiral. In March 1583
Bernardino de Mendoza reported that Leicester and Howard had reached an agreement
that when Lincoln died Leicester would succeed him as Lord Admiral and Howard
become Master of the Horse. In 1585 he claimed to have information that Leicester was
trying to prevent Howard succeeding Lincoln, see *CSPSp, 1580–6*, 452, 530. It is not clear
how much truth there in this.

went to Eris to sey the shepes ther the same day}	ijs.[568]
Gevin by your lordship's commandment to Thomas the gardener of Wansted for graveling the gardin at Wansted the same daye}	xijs.
Gevin by your lordship's commandment to a man that Mr Knolles brought to your lordship to Wansted the same daye}	vli.
Gevin by your lordship's commandment to Mr Sutton at his goyng into Warwickshere the same daye}	iijli. vjs. viijd.
Payde by your lordship's commandment to Mr John Robynson at Wansted the same daye}	xli.[569]
Gevin by your lordship's commandment to John Robarts* your lordship's futman for to by hym hose and dublat and cloke the same day at Nonsuch}	xls.
Gevin by your lordship's commandment to a futman that carid leatters from Nonsuch to Winworth the same day}	ijs.
Gevin by your lordship's commandment to [a] poore man that lay sycke betxt the tou Stratfords the same day}	iiijd.
Gevin by your lordship's commandment to another poore woman the same daye betext Startford and Wansted}	ijd.

Summa Paginae: xxxvijli. xvs. iiijd.ᵛ

[verso]

the xxx of July [1585]

Delyvered by your lordship's commandment to Mr Ftransses Knolles that he gave to your lordship's man Careles at Nonsuch the same daye}	vli.
Gevin by your lordship's commandment to the bayles man of Collcester for bringe oysters to Nonsuch to your lordship the same daye}	xs.
Delyvered by your lordship's commandment to Mr Bedwell the sume of xv pounds xvjs. to paye unto Gorge Ander for xxxvj thousand of slack [slates?]	

[568] Presumably Drake's ships. On 14 July Lord Talbot wrote to the Earl of Rutland that he was going to see Drake's ships at Woolwich, 'which sett forwards tomorrow' (Hist MSS Comm, *Rutland MSS*, i, 177). However, Drake did not leave until August, see Adams, 'Outbreak of the Elizabethan Naval War', p. 57. The reference to Francis Knollys, who commanded the *Galleon Leicester*, under 30 July is also evidence of the delay.

[569] A John Robinson served in the Netherlands 1586. He may have been one of the Drayton Basset Robinsons, see 'West Midlands', 48–9.

and the rest of the carges as doth apere
by his byll paye at Wansted the same day}   xvli. vjs.
Delyvered by your lordship's commandment to Mr
Thomas Dudley at Nonsuch to be gevin to Mr
Sparkes your lordship's selester at his goyng
into Somersetshere to the Queen's Aturney to
paye for his hors heyr and other carges as
doth apereth [*sic*] by his byll}   xli.
Payd by your lordship's commandment to Mr Blunt
which he payd for a cask to lay in provisition
for water and other provisition for the horses
and mares your lordship send into Barbery the same daye}   xls.[570]
Payd by your lordship's commandment to the
groome of the stabell and boy that kepe the
horsses in the shepe borde to furnysh the frayt
the same daye payd more}   iijli.
Payd by your lordship's commandment for x quarter
of outes at v*s.* iiij*d.* the quarter to lay into
shypbord for the horsses sent into Barbrey payd
the same daye as apereth by the byll}   liijs. iiijd.
Gevin by your lordship's commandment to [a]
futman that brought letters from Leaster Hous
to Nonsuch to your lordship the same daye}   xijd.
Gevin by your lordship's commandment to Mr Grene
which he gave to the poore when your lordship
was at Battersey the same daye}   ijs.
Gevin by your lordship's commandment to Syr
Thomas Secelles man for bringe foull to your
lordship to Nonsuch the same daye}   xs.
Payd by your lordship's commandment to Roger
Gyllans your lordship's waterman for hys
atandanse at Lambeth for your lordship the same daye}   ixs.
      Summa Paginae: "xxxixli. viijs. iiijd."
      xxxixli. xjs. iiijd.

[recto]

[570] Presumably a present for Muley Ahmed, King of Morocco. The letters patent for the charter of the Barbary Company were issued on 5 July (PRO, C66/1266/1–3), and the Company's agent, Henry Roberts, departed for Morocco on 14 August ('The Ambassage of Master Henry Roberts', in R. Hakluyt, *The Principal Navigations* (Glasgow, 1903–5), vi, 426). See also T.S. Willan, 'English Trade with Morocco', *Studies in Elizabethan Foreign Trade* (Manchester, 1959), pp. 225–6.

the frist of August 1585

Payd by your lordship's commandment to Mr Blunt
for horse heyre being sent by your lordship with
commission into Harfordshere to Syr Thomas
Heneges and to Mr Bramton the same daye}   vs.[571]

Payd by your lordship's commandment to Smulkyn,
Daunell and Rychard Pepper your lordship's futmean
for ther deners and suppers the same daye at Nonsuch}   iijs.

Payd by your lordship's commandment to Rychard
Warner waterman for caryng your lordship from
Grenewich to Blackwall the xxixth of July and
from the xxx of July to the first of August as
apereth by hys byll}   xxvijs. iiijd.

Paid by your lordship's commandment to Mr
Oxsenbrig your lordship's page which he gave
to the poore the same daye}   vjd.

Gevin by your lordship's commandment to a Skot
at Wansted Sir Phelep Sednes man the same daye
gevin hym at Wanstead}   xli.

Gevin by your lordship's commandment to John
Kelley your lordship's futman that he gave to
the hunse men of London when he went for houndes
to fech to Wansted to your lordship the same daye}   ijs.

Gevin by your lordship's commandment to my Lord
of Penbrock['s] page for presenting tow hauckes
to your lordship at Wansted the same day}   xxxs.

Gevin by your lordship's commandment to Edmondes*
the master of your lordship's shepes to the eating
of a buck the same day}   iijli.

Gevin by your lordship's commandment to the
huncemen sarvants at your lordship's goynge from
Wansted the same day}   xs.

Payd to Savege the kepper by your lordship's
commandment that he payd to Horsnall for hys halfe
yeare's wages dew at Medsomer last past 1585 the
same daye at Wansted payd him the sume of}   vjli.

Gevin by your lordship's commandment to Mr
Hellders my Lord Stranges man for caring off
leatters the same daye for your lordship}   xxs.[572]

---

[571] Leicester was appointed lord lieutenant of Hertfordshire and Essex on 3 July 1585.
Commissions for raising troops for the Netherlands were drafted on 19 July ((PRO,
SP12/180/80–5, see also BL, Add. MS 48084, f. 114).

[572] Ferdinando Stanley, Lord Strange (1559–94), later 5th Earl of Derby. The 'Letter
of Estate', one of the tracts derived from *Leicester's Commonwealth*, accused Leicester of

Gevin by your lordship's commandment to Thomas
Gouffe your lordship's gardener of Wansted the same daye}   xs.
Summa Paginae: xxiiijli. vijs. xd.

[verso]

the second of August 1585
Payd by your lordship's commandment to Mr Bedwell
and Lovell that they payd for the carig of your
lordship's tymber post and palles from Winsotch
to the Abby Mylles at Stratford payd them at
Wansted as apereth by ther byll the same daye}   vijli. xvs. ijd.
Payd by your lordship's commandment to Homfrey
your lordship's futtman that he gave to Mr
Lovell's man for breakyng open the hegges for
your lordship when your lordship came by Martin
Abey to Nonsuch the same daye}   ijs. vjd.
Gevin by your lordship's commandment to the poore
the same day at your lordship's coming to the Cort
at Nonsuch}   iiijd.[573]
Gevin by your lordship's commandment to Smulkyn
that he gave to the poore the same day more}   vjd.
Payd to Smylkyn for hys cargs goyng betext Nonsuch
and Wansted the same daye}   xijd.
Payd by your lordship's commandment to Smulkyn
which he gave at Booyebrige [sic] the same day}   ijs.
Payd by your lordship's commandment to John
Keyme your lordship's sarvant for caring of
bottells and both hyr and other necessary things
which he bought for your lordship's heuse as
apereth by his bill}   viijs. viijd.
Geven by your lordship's commandment to Mr
Docrell['s] man for bringe leatters to your
lordship to Nonsuch the same daye}   vs.
Geven by your lordship's commandment to John
Robarts your lordship's futman when he went

arranging his marriage to Alice, daughter of Sir John Spencer (see n. 599 below) in order
to disparage the ancient nobility. See D.C. Peck, ' "The Letter of Estate": An Elizabethan
Libel', *Notes and Queries*, new ser. xxviii (1981), 34.

[573] Sorting out the chronology is not easy here either. Leicester was at Court (i.e.
Nonsuch) on 28 July (when he wrote to John Maitland of Thirlestane, *Warrender Papers*,
i, 187–9) and presumably on 3 August (see n. 575 below). The entries suggest a certain
amount of coming and going between Nonsuch and Wanstead, either between the 20th
and 28th, or possibly between the 28th and 2 August.

to my Lord of Warweck's from Nonsuch the same daye}   xijd.
Geven by your lordship's commandment to Mr Cave
which he gave to my Lord Ambrell's man the same
day at Nonsuch}   xxs.
Gevin by your lordship's commandment to a futman
that went with leatters from Nonsuch to Wansted
the same daye}   xijd.
Payd to Mr Pollwhell* which he payd to my Lord
Lomles kepper for a skyne for your lordship
the same daye at Nonsuch}   xls.
Payd to Batty which he gave to on that cared
leatters to Wansted from Nonsuch the same day}   iijs.
                   Summa Paginae: xijli. ijd.

[recto]

                   the iij of August [1585]
Payd by your lordship's commandment for iij pare
of gloves for your lordship ij pare of short
gloves and on[e] pare of long payd the same daye
to Thomas Shepard}   xs.
Payd by your lordship's commandment for ij measse
of meat for your lordship's sarvants of the
wardrope for a fortneyght that is from the xxvth
of July to the viij of Agust 1585}   lvjs. viijd.
Payd by your lordship's commandment to Roger
Gyllans your lordship's waterman for caring your
lordship frome the Ould Sawne to Lambath the v
day of August and geving ateandanse at Lambath
the next daye being the vj day of Agust payd
the same daye}   xviijs.
Payd by your lordship's commandment to my Lord
Wellebes man for atanding iij days at Kynston
with hys coch payd to hym for hys horsmeat when
the States of Anwarp deyned with your lordship
at Nonsuch the same daye}   xxs.[574]
Payd by your lordship's commandment to Mr Blunt
which he payd for the hyre of xx hackenis for ij
days whylst the[y] attended on the States of the
Low Countrey at ther barge with your lordship

---

[574] Peregrine Bertie (1555–1601), Lord Willoughby d'Eresby, son of the Duchess of
Suffolk (n. 320 above). Willoughby had been appointed ambassador to the King of
Denmark at the end of June, but may not have left yet.

at Wanstead the same daye}   iiijli. ixs.[575]
Payd by your lordship's commandment for the meat
of iiij coch horses and ij other that stode in
the toune on nyght at Wanstead the same day}   vijs.
Payd by your lordship's commandment to Steaven
Johnson of your lordship's wardrop for a grose
and a halfe of black and grene sylke rebend
poyntes and rebend for your lordship's hose and
iij pare of black vellat spur leathers and black
thrid and brown thrid and sylk for your lordship
as apereth by his byll the same daye}   xliijs. vijd.
Gevin by your lordship's commandment to a poore
man that keppeth the torne betext London
[thys *deleted*] and Nonsuch the same daye}   vjd.
Gevin by your lordship to Mr Loveges man for
brekyng open the hegges for your lordship betext
London [thys *deleted*] and Nonsuch the same daye}   vs.
                Summa Paginae: xijli. ixs. ixd.

[verso]

                  the vj of August 1585
Gevin by your lordship's commandment at your
lordship's goyng to London from Nonsuch to the
corn cotter the same daye}   xs.
Payd by your lordship's commandment to Roger
Gyllans for caring of your lordship from Lambath
to Leaster House as apereth by hys byll the same daye}   ixs.
Payd by your lordship's commandment for ij dossen
of arows and for ij crosboys stryngs payd the same
day to Gylles Homerstone}   xjs.
Gevin by your lordship's commandment to Gylles
Homerstone the same day at hys goyng from Leaster
Hous to Greaves the same daye}   vs.
Gevin by your lordship's commandment to
Daunell your lordship's futman the same [*sic*]
at Leaster Hous}   xls.

[575] The chronology of these entries can be reconstructed in the following way. The
dining of the Dutch commissioners at Nonsuch presumably took place on 3 August, for
the treaty for the succour of Antwerp was signed on the 2nd, although the Provisional
Treaty of Assistance was not signed until the 10th. On the 4th Leicester went back to
London and Wanstead with the Dutch commissioners, then back to Nonsuch on the 5th
via the Old Swan (Old Swan Stairs near Fishmongers' Hall) and Lambeth, returning to
Leicester House on the 7th.

Gevin by your lordship's commandment to Stone my
Lord of Penbrockes man for presenting a pecok
at Leaster Hous for your lordship to sende to
Kyllingworth the same day}   xs.
Payd by your lordship's commandment [for] iij neyt
caps for your lordship the same day at Leaster House}   xviijs.
Payd by your lordship's commandment to John
Gressem for ij gyrdells of black vellet with
gyllt buckells for your lordship's skyne the
same day at Leaster Hous}   xijs.
Gevin by your lordship's commandment to John
your lordship's harper to by him doblat and hose
the same day at Leaster Hous}   xxs.
Paid by your lordship's commandment to Mr Blunt
that he payd to Martyn Decoster in part of
pament of your lordship's coch payd at Leaster
Hous the same daye}   xxli.
Gevin by your lordship's commandment to Dannell
your lordship's futman at hys [*sic*] doun to
Kyllingwort with leatters from Mr Hedyn's when your
lordship lay ther the same daye}   xs.[576]
                    Summa Paginae: xxvijli. vs.

[recto]

                    the ix of August 1585
Payd by your lordship's commandment to Homfrey
Hadlynton your lordship's futman which he gave
to the spittell hous at Heygat to labers in the
same heyway and to iij old women the same day as
apereth by hys byll}   ijs. ixd.[577]
Payd by your lordship's commandment for supper
for your lordship's men and sumter men William

---

[576] This is clearly out of sequence, Leicester was at Mr Heyden's on the 12th (see n. 580 below).

[577] The beginning of Leicester's journey to Kenilworth, which thanks the correspondence it generated is relatively easy to reconstruct. He left Leicester House on Wednesday 11 August for Northaw where he spent the night (PRO, SP12/181/145, to Walsingham, 11 Aug., see also *Hamilton Papers*, ii, 678). Walsingham was planning to join him. On 30 July Walsingham informed Wotton 'I am now going towardes the welles in Warwickshire, and shalbe absent from the courte a month or sixe weekes' (*Hamilton Papers*, ii, 664). When Leicester departed on the 11th he was expecting Walsingham to follow and wrote, 'God send you well to Warwyke water and that yt may do you as much good as I trust yt wyll do me', but Walsingham later decided the weather was 'unseasonable', see n. 585 below.

Fynch, Richard Asly, Rychard Connerbuck,
Johnson and Hall the same daye}   iijs.

Payd by your lordship the next daye for their
deners and supper as apereth by ther byll}   iijs.

Gevin by your lordship's commandment to the
gardener at North Hall the same daye when your
lordship lay ther}   vs.[578]

Gevin by your lordship's commandment to hym
that keppeth the chambers at North Hall the
same day}   xs.

Gevin by your lordship's commandment to Gawen
Smyth the coch maker the same day at Leaster Hous}   iijli.

Payd by your lordship's commandment to Humfrey
the futman the same daye at Leaster Hous}   ijs. vjd.

Geavin by your lordship's commandment to Syr
John Cottes man for bryng hys chyldren to my
Lord of Warweckes to your lordship the same daye}   xs.[579]

Gevin by your lordship's commandment to Syr
John Cottes kepper for brynge your lordship
thowutht [sic] the park the same daye}   vs.

Gevin by your lordship's commandment to a poore
woman the same day by the waye}   vjd.

Payd by your lordship's commandment to Mr Blunt
the same daye in prest}   xxli.

Summa Paginae: ^xxxvjli. js. ixd.^x

xxvli. xxjd.

---

[578] On the 12th he wrote to James VI (*Warrender Papers*, i, 197–8) and Walsingham (SP12/181/146) from Northaw. He informed James that he had 'obtained lycence of hir Majestie to vyssett some smale thingis of my owen in the countrey', but his letter to Walsingham was concerned mainly with the Bedford wardship, a matter that caused some dispute over the next few weeks. 28 July had seen the near-simultaneous deaths of both the 2nd Earl of Bedford (see n. 43 above) and his heir Lord Russell, making Russell's young son (b. 1572) the new 3rd Earl. His mother, a daughter of Sir John Foster, was dead, and the Earl of Warwick (who was married to the 2nd Earl's daughter Anne) claimed the wardship. When Leicester (who was an executor of Bedford's will, PRO, PROB11/69 [PCC 59 Windsor], fos. 350–51v) left Nonsuch he understood that the Queen had agreed that he and Warwick should have the wardship, and he wrote to Sir John Foster to that effect on 27 Aug. (see PRO, SP15/29/63, Foster to Leicester, 5 Sept.). Just before his departure from Leicester House he was visited by Lady Russell (the widow of one of Bedford's other sons), and her report of their conversation to Burghley later that day triggered Burghley's angry letter to Leicester of the 11th (BL, Lansdowne MS 102, fo. 230–v), see n. 585 below.

[579] Sir John Cutts (1545–1616), of Shenley Hall, Herts., MP. He had been knighted by Leicester in Essex in 1571. He may be the Mr Kotes referred to on p. 269 above.

[verso]

the xijth of August 1585

Payd by your lordship's commandment to Kaneth
Leavs* for your lordship's sarvants' suppers and
deners and loging at Barnat when your lordship
lay at North Hall which was the same daye as
apereth by hys byll}   xlviijs. vijd.

Payd by your lordship's commandment to Kaneth
Leavs for your lordship's sarvants' suppers at
Watford when your lordship lay at Mr Headynes
the same daye as apereth by hys byll}   xxixs.[580]

Payd by your lordship's commandment to Kaneth
Leavs for your lordship's and my lades one
deyat and your lordship's servants' dener at
Maydenhead the xiij of August as apereth by the
byll}   iiili. vjs. vijd.

Gevin by your lordship's commandment to iij
poore wemen at North hall that ware a wedeng
in the garden the same daye}   xijd.

Gevin by your lordship's commandment at Mr
Headyn's hous when your lordship lay ther to
the sarvants of the hous the same daye}   xxs.

Gevin by your lordship's commandment to Richard
Garner which he gave to a poore woman for lyting
a candell to your lordship when your lordship
came out of your barge at Leaster Hous the x day
of August}   xijd.

Payd to Mr Coke for a pare of gloves for your
lordship the same daye at Leaster Hous}   iijs.

Payd by your lordship's commandment for a case
for your lordship's spattakells the same daye}   vjd.

Payd by your lordship's commandment to Robart
Pichfork which he gave to a carter by the wayesyd
as your lordship went to Greaves the same daye}   xijd.

Gevin by your lordship's commandment to the geyd
that came with your lordship from Mr Hedyn's to
Maydenhed the same day}   vs.

Summa Paginae: viijli. xvs. viijd.

---

[580] The night of the 12th-13th, note the casual references to the Countess. The Queen's
discovery that she had accompanied him was one reason for her retraction of the offered
command of the Netherlands expedition at the end of the month, see Appendix II.

[recto]

the xiij of August 1585

Gevin by your lordship's commandment to a poore
man that carid letters to your sarvants Cheslecks*
at Blackwater the same day from Maydenhead the same daye}   xijd.
Gevin by your lordship's commandment to Nycolas
Harford tayler at his goyng downe in to the
contry to yonge Mr Dudley from Graves the same day}   ls.
Gevin by your lordship's commandment to a poore
man at Maydenhed the same daye}   vjd.
Gevin by your lordship's commandment to Mr Marster's
man for bring to your lordship feasants and partreges
the same daye to Graves}   vs.[581]
Payd by your lordship's commandment to Jhon
Robynson your lordship's skynner at Newellmes at
your lordship's goyng to Kyllingworth the same day}   xxli.
Payd by your lordship's commandment to Kaneth Leavs
for your lordship's men's charges at Henly uppon
Fryday supper the xiij of August and Satterdaye
dener and supper the xiiij daye and Sonday dener
the xv daye of August when your lordship lay at
Graves as apereth by ther byll}   viijli. xs. iiijd.
Payd by your lordship's commandment to Homfrey
your lordship's futman which he gave to the
poore betext North Hall and Watford the same day}   xvd.
Payd by your lordship's commandment to Humfrey
your lordship's futman mor[e] the same daye which
he gave to the poore between Watford and
Maydenhed the same day}   ixd.
Payd by your lordship's commandment to Edward
Willperfors which he gave to the poore at
Henley the same daye}   vjd.
Paid by your lordship's commandment to Edward
Willperfors which he gave to Nurse Blackewell
at Greaves the same day}   xs.
Geavin by your lordship's commandment to the
old kepper and hys son at Neweallme Parke
the same daye}   xviijs. viijd.

Summa Paginae: xxxijli. xviijs.

---

[581] He spent the 13–14th at Rotherfield Greys and the 14–15th at Ewelme.

[verso]

the xv of August 1585

Gevin by your lordship's commandment to the
sarvants at Newellme Parke when your lordship
lay ther: to the couke, and to the pantler, and
to the chamber, and to the sealler, and to the
butler and the maydes, to the groomes of the
stabell, the sume above written}   xxxvs. xd.

Payd by your lordship's commandment to my
fealow Meareday* for the holle charges of your
lordship and your lordship's sarvants at
Abington for Sundaye at neyght supper the xv
day and Monday at brea[k]fast the xvj day of
Agust as the byll apereth the same day payd
at Abbington}   viijli. xd.[582]

Gevin by your lordship's commandment to a
poore man that did cary letters from Newellmes
from your lordship to Justis Townesend the same day}   vs.[583]

Gevin by your lordship's commandment to the
sarvants of Mr Blak's hous at Newellmes when
your lordship deyned ther the same daye}   xs.

Gevin in reward to a poore man ther the same
day by your lordship's commandment when your
lordship deyned ther}   vjd.

Gevin in reward to the wayts that playd to your
lordship when your lordship supped at Abbington
the same daye}   xs.

Gevin by your lordship's commandment to Mr
Farslept* the xvj daye of August at Abbington
when your lordship sent hym post to the Cort
the same daye}   <a>   vjli. xiijs. iiijd.

Gevin in reward by your lordship's commandment
to the person of Abbington which he gave to the
poore of the toune when your lordship lay ther
the same daye}   xxs.

Gevin in reward to the sarvants of the hous at
Abbington when your lordship lay ther the same
day by your lordship's commandment}   xs.

---

[582] The 15th–16th, see n. 396 above for the Abingdon sources.

[583] Sir Henry Townshend (1537?–1621), puisne justice of the Chester circuit from 1578,
MP. The letter probably concerned the survey of the lordship of Denbigh in September
(PRO, LR2/235, part ii); Townshend was the chief commissioner.

Gevin in reward the same day to the poore that
wroght in the hous at Abbington when your lordship
lay there the same day}   vs.

Gevin in reward to iij syngerse that [*sic*] under
my lades wendow in the morning the same day}   ijs. vjd.

Gevin in reward to the ryngers of Abbington by
your lordship's commandment the same day}   xijd.

Summa Paginae: xixli. xiiijs.

[recto]

the xvj of August 1585

Payd by your lordship's commandment for iij sumter
mean and iij of your lordship's yeamen for ther
breckfast at Watford the xiij of August and for
ther deners at Maydenhead the same day as apereth
by ther byll}   viijs. vd.

Payd by your lordship's commandment for iij
sumter men and ij of your lordship's yeamen for
ther dener at Chalbury when the cam from
Abbington the same daye}   ijs. vjd.

Geavin in reward to the sarvants of Mr Bleckes
hous at Cornbere Park by your lordship's
commandment the xvij of Agust}   xxs.[584]

Geavin in reward to a purssevant that brought
leatters to your lordship to Cornbre Park the same day}   xs.[585]

Geavin in reward to a poore man the same day
that kepeth the deare in the forist the same daye}   xijd.

Geavin in reward to the poore that Houmfre
your lordship's futman gave the same daye}   ixd.

Geavin in reward to Mr Blunt which he gave to

---

[584] He travelled from Abingdon to Cornbury on the 16th and spent the night of the
16th–17th at Cornbury House. It would appear from this entry and one on p. 297 below
that Gabriel Blike (n. 433 above) was the keeper of Cornbury Park.

[585] These probably included Burghley's angry letter of the 11th (see n. 578 above) as
well as one from Walsingham cancelling his visit to Warwickshire. Leicester wrote to
both from Cornbury on the 17th. To Walsingham he regretted 'the season of the weather
serves no better for your coming, surely I am persuaded nothing in this world would
have done you more good, nor any man in England should be more welcome than
yourself' (BL, Harl. MS 285, fo. 131). To Burghley he dashed off three pages challenging
Lady Russell's story and denying any enmity. He mis-dated the letter (BL, Lansdowne
MS 45, fos. 79–81) 'from Cornbury Parke xv of August'. Given the chronology outlined
here it is difficult to see how Leicester could have reached Cornbury before the 16th,
and the letter to Walsingham suggests he used the 17th to catch up on his correspondence.
These were probably the letters carried to Court by Giles Tracy on the 18th.

a poore woman at Wodstock that fead the dear ther the same daye}	xs.
Geavin in reward by your lordship's commandment at Wodstock to my Lord Dudles musitions the same day}	xxs.
Geavin in reward by your lordship's commandment at Wodstock to the syngers of Wetney the same daye}	xxs.
Geavin in reward to Hary Lovell your lordship's man when he came downe into Oxfordshere to your lordship the same daye}	xs.
Geavin in reward by your lordship's commandment to a skolar of Oxford that wase Mr Robert Dudles boy the same daye}	xxs.
Geyvin by your lordship's commandment to Mr Gylles Trasey at hys reyding post from Wodstock to the Cort the xviij of August the same daye}	iijli.

Summa Paginae: ixli. ijs. viijd.

[verso]

the xvij of August 1585

Geyvin in reward that Mr John Trasey gav[e] by your lordship's commandment to a poore man that went to Mr Caryse to Graftone the same day}	vjs. viijd.
Geyvin in reward that Mr Poyllwhell gave by your lordship's commandment to the kepper that found the stage the same daye at Wodstock}	xs.
That your lordship lost at playe at Wodstock the same daye}	xls.
Geyvin in reward that Mr Poyllwhell gave by your lordship's commandment to Mr Wardes man for presenting a dad partreg to your lordship at Neweallmes the same daye}	vs.[586]
Geyvin in reward by your lordship's commandment which Richard Garner gave to an old man in the foryste the same day}	xijd.
Geyvin in reward which Hary Stevens* gave by your lordship's commandment to the kepper's man of Wodstock Park the same day}	ijs.
Geyvin by your lordship's commandment to a man that went to Mr Stafferton's from Wodstock to	

[586] Probably Richard Ward of Hurst, Berks., son of Richard Ward (1511– 78), Cofferer of the Household, MP. He served in the Netherlands in 1586.

Grafton with letters the same daye}   vs.[587]
Geyvin by your lordship's commandment to another
poore man the same daye that carid leters from
Wodstock to Kyllingworth the same daye}   vs.
Payd by your lordship's commandment to John
Robarts your lordship's futman which he layd
out for hys one expenses and gevin to the poore
at hys goyng to Kyllingworth with your lordship
the same day}   iijs. ijd.
Geyvin in reward which my fealow Pichfork gave
by your lordship's commandment to a poore man
at Abbington townd's end the same daye}   vjd.
Geyvin in reward to a pursevant that brought
letters to your lordship to Wodstock the same day}   xs.
              Summa Paginae: iiijli. viijs. iiijd.

[recto]

              the xixth of August 1585
Payd by your lordship's commandment to my fealow
Mearaday for your lordship's sarvants' holle carges
at Wodstock vj mealles and the bakyng of a red
deare when your lordship laye at Syr Hary Leays
at Wodstock the same day abov written as apereth
by hys byll the somme of}   xviijli. xxiijd.
Delyvered by your lordship's commandment to
Mr Blunt more in prest the same daye at Wodstock
when your lordship lay at Syr Hary Leays}   xxli.[588]
Payd by your lordship's commandment to Rychard
your lordship's spanell kepper for iij copell
on fortneyght and for v copell another forneyght
and for v copell and for a shepe to lead them
in payd the same daye at Wodstock}   xxs.
Geyvin in reward to Mr Docrell at Wodstock at
Sir Harry Leas by your lordship's commandment
the same day}   xls.
Geyven in reward more to Mr Docrell the same
day which he gave by your lordship's commandment

[587] Probably Thomas Stafferton or Staverton, who served in the Netherlands in 1586 and was a bearer of the body at Leicester's funeral. His office at Grafton is not clear.

[588] Leicester left Cornbury for Woodstock on either 17 or 18 August, and Woodstock for Hanwell probably on the 19th; it is not clear whether he spent two days at Cornbury or at Woodstock.

of [to] Sir Hary Leays servants of hys hous
at Wodstock when your lordship lay ther the same daye}   xls.
Geyvin in reward to iij keppers at Wodstock at
Sir Hare Leays: Henry Thornton, Thomas Panter,
John Bentley the same daye at Wodstock}   iijli.
Geyvin in reward to Mr Cave which he gave to
the poore at Wodstock at your lordship's coming
away the same day}   ijs.
Payd by your lordship's commandment to my fealo
Pichforke for a lock which he brought for your
lordship's wardrope dore at Wodstock the same day}   xvjd.
Geyvin in reward to a poore man betwene Sorend
and Kyllingworth as your lordship came over
the brige the same day to reyd tards Kyllingworth}   vjd.
Geyvin in reward the same daye to a geyd that
came with your lordship from Mr Copes to Killingworth
the same day by your lordship's commandment}   xs.[589]
Payd by your lordship's commandment to my fealow
Mearada for the carges of your lordship's sarvants
at Banbrey for ij meals Freyday supper and
Satterdaye dynner and for the carrige of a red
deare and iij Banbury cakes to Kyllingworth
as apereth by the byll the same daye payd the
summe of}   vli. vijs. viijd.

          Summa Paginae: ᵞlijli. iiijs. vd.ᵞ
               lijli. iijs. vd.

[verso]

             the xxjth of Agust 1585
Payd by your lordship's commandment to your
lordship's sarvant John Conawaye* which he payd
for the carges of your lordship's [servants]
that came with the wagen and for the heyr of
horsses that drew the wagen from Leaster Hous
to Kyllingworth with your lordship's plates
from the xij of Agust to the xv of the month
as apereth by hys byll payd the same daye

[589] (Sir) Anthony Cope (1550–1613) of Hanwell, Oxon., MP. Leicester presumably
stayed at Hanwell and his men in Banbury. This was probably the night of 19/20 August;
the final stage from Hanwell to Kenilworth appears to have been completed in one day,
probably the 20th. In the absence of any geographical references his route can only be
inferred, but the bridge was probably over the the Avon and 'Sorend' may have been
Bridgend at Warwick.

at Kellingworth}   iiijli. iijs. viijd.
Geyven in reward to Dampard* my lades futman
which he gave to the poore coming frome Syr
Hare Leas by your lordship's commandment the same day}   ijs.
Geyven in reward to on of my Lord of Essex's man
[*sic*] Treu for caring letters from Kyllingworth
to the Cort the same daye}   xxs.
Payd by your lordship's commandment for ij
eurenalls for your lordship the same daye
at Kyllingworth}   vijd.
Payd by your lordship's commandment for ij
measse of meat for your lordship's sarvants of
the wardrop for a forneyht that is from the
viij of August to the xxij day of the same
month 1585}   lvjs. viijd.
Geyven in reward to Mr Cartryght the precher
at Kyllingworth when your lordship laye ther
the same day by your lordship's commandment}   vli.[590]
Geyven in reward to the syngers of Coventry
by your lordship's commandment the same daye
at Kyllingworth when your lordship lay there}   xiijs. iiijd.[591]
Delyvered to your lordship's on handes which
your lordship gave to my Lord Lomles foull
at Kyllingworth the same day}   xxs.
Gevin in reward to Mr Cave which he gave to
Hary Walopes man for presenting to your
lordship a cast of hakes at Kyllingworth by
your lordship's commandment the same daye}   xs.[592]
Payd by your lordship's commandment to Steaven
Johnson for vij yeardes of wit cotton to leyn
your lordship's sleves of yor doublates the same daye}   vijs.
Gevin in reward to Mr Bramton which he gave to
the poore at Wodstock by your lordship's
commandment the same daye}   xijd.

---

[590] Thomas Cartwright (1535–1603) was appointed master of Leicester's Hospital at
Warwick at some point after December 1584, see 'West Midlands', 46, n. 227. Leicester's
attempt to persuade Whitgift to grant him a preaching licence (see his letter to Whitgift,
14 July, n. 562 above) probably followed his appointment.

[591] Three of Coventry's leading citizens also came out to see him and spent two days
at Kenilworth. As he normally did when visiting, Leicester sent the mayor and aldermen
a gift of four bucks, see Coventry RO, MS A.7b [Chamberlains' and Wardens' Accounts],
pp. 121–2, and 'West Midlands', 45, n. 203.

[592] Probably Henry Wallop (1568–1642), MP, then a student at Oxford. His father Sir
Henry Wallop (1531–99), Lord Justice of Ireland, MP, had connections of long standing
with Leicester.

Geyven in reward to Mr Feyn precher of Coventry
by your lordship's commandment at Kyllingworth
the same above written the some of}   vli.[593]
    Summa Paginae: xxli. xiiijs. iijd.

[recto]

    the xxiij of August 1585
Payd by your lordship's commandment to my fealow
Mearaday which he payd for Beacham['s] aparell and
xs. a money [sic] gevin hym to put in his purse
as apereth by hys byll payd the day above
written the some of}   iiijli. xiiijs. ixd.
Payd by your lordship's commandment to Ramsey
your lordship's man for hys loging at Wodstock
iij neyghts and on neyght at Colbrock and gevin
at Wetney to the poore as apereth by hys byll}   xviijd.
Geyven in reward to Mr Chamley* which he gave by
your lordship's commandment to Mr Leusses man
for presenting ij oyxsen and x shepe to your
lordship at Kyllingworth when your lordship
lay ther the same day}   xxs.[594]
Geyven in reward to Mr Cave which he gave to
one of my Lord of Darbes mean for presenting a
gyrvakyn to your lordship at Kyllingworth that
came from the Eylle of Man to your lordship
the same daye at Kyllingworth}   xxs.
Geyven in reward to Mr Blunt which he gave by
your lordship's commandment at Mr Copes hous
when your lordship lay ther to the sarvants of
the hous and to the groms of the stabell the same daye}   xxxs.
Geyvin in reward to Gramer your lordship's man
at Kyllingworth for carying a buck to the Cort
from Kyllingworth the xxvj day of August}   xxs.
Geyvin in reward to Mr Brownes man for bryng of

[593] Humphrey Fenn (1552–1631), rector of Holy Trinity, Coventry, suspended for non-subscription in 1584. Leicester appealed to Whitgift on his behalf as well as Cartwright's in July (see n. 562). He served as a chaplain in the Netherlands in 1586 (see pp. 352, 358, 363 below), and attended Leicester's funeral.
[594] Either Sir Thomas Lucy (see n. 321) or his son Thomas, who also attended Leicester's funeral.

letters to your lordship to Kyllingworth the same daye}   vs.[595]
Geyvin in reward to Mr Burgayn['s] man for
presenting to your lordship a sparowhack at
Kyllingworth the same day}   xs.[596]
Geyvin in reward to Mr Bramton which he gave
to a poore man at Kyllingworth the same daye}   vjs.
Geyven in reward to young Chissleck your
lordship's man at Kyllingworth the xxvij of August}   xxs.
Geyven in reward to Waller* your lordship's
kepper at Kyllingworth by your lordship's
commandment the same daye}   xxs.

            Summa Paginae: xijli. js. ixd.

[verso]

            the xxiiij of August 1585
Geyvin in reward to Adreyn your lordship's
gardener at Kyllingworth the same day}   xxs.
Geyvin in reward by your lordship's commandment
to Robyn my Lord Lomles foule at Kyllingworth
the same daye}   xs.
Geyvin in reward to Mr Cave which he gave by
your lordship's commandment to a poore man at
Kyllingworth that had hys hous burned gevin
hym the same daye}   ijs.
Geyvin in reward to Goch your lordship's
gardener of Wansted by your lordship's commandment

---

[595] It is probably this entry, rather than that under 27 August, that refers to the arrival of letters from both Walsingham and Burghley informing Leicester that the Queen wished to know whether he was willing to command the forces sent to the Low Countries, which had been forwarded by Richard Lloyd from Leicester House (see Appendix II). The letters themselves have not survived, but we do have Leicester's answers, both written from 'Mr Lee's' (Stoneleigh, see n. 597 below) on the 28th (PRO, SP12/181/222, to Walsingham; Hatfield MS 163, fo. 115-v, to Burghley, calendared in Hist MSS Comm. *Salisbury MSS*, iii, 108). They were probably sent with Pollwelle on the 29th. On the 27th Leicester wrote to Shrewsbury (Hist MSS Comm, *Bath MSS*, v, 57, mis- endorsed or calendared 17 Aug. 1586) informing him that the letters from Court had just arrived and that he would be forced to cancel an intended visit to him. He also related that he had injured his leg in a riding accident the previous Wednesday (he told Walsingham it was on Thursday) and could not ride, and thus was not able to 'make that spede to the Court which otherwyse I wold doe'. The recall had given him only a week at Kenilworth, not time enough to take the waters, and he observed to Walsingham, 'as for the water here no doubts the tyme having served yt wold have donn me much good'.

[596] Robert Burgoyne of Wroxall, Wars. Burgoyne contributed to a loan raised by Cartwright after 1588 to fight a lawsuit over the endowment of Leicester's Hospital, WCRO, CR1600/LH 118.

at Kyllingworth at hys being syck ther the same daye}   xxs.
Payd by your lordship's commandment for the iij
sumter men's breckfast and Rychard Buck and
Thomas Hall at Abbington and at Whetney and
for charges layd out at Kyllingworth as apereth
by ther byll}   iiijs. iiijd.
Payd by your lordship's commandment to Humfrey
your lordship's futman for hys supper and bead
on Tewsdaye the xviij of Agust when your
lordship came to Mr Bleckes the same daye}   viijd.
Geyvin in reward to Humfrey your lordship's
futman which he gave to the poore when your
lordship came from Wodstock to Banbrey the same daye}   vjd.
Delyvered by your lordship's commandment to
Mr Blunt more at Kyllingworth in prest the
xxvij day of August the some of 1585}   xxxli.
Gevin to a poore woman by your lordship's
commandment at Kyllingworth for doung of
necessary thyngs the same daye}   ijs.
Geyvin in reward to a man of my Lord of Darbes
by your lordship's commandment at Kyllingworth
the xxvii daye of August the some of}   iijli. vjs. viijd.
Geyvin in reward to Mr Breysses man for
presenting to your lordship troutes at
Kyllingworth the same day by your lordship's
commandment}   vs.
Payd by your lordship's commandment to my
fealow John Conaway for the caryge of your
lordship's plat up to London the same day from
Kyllingworth payd him in prest}   iijli. xixs. viijd.
                    Summa Paginae: xlli. xs. xd.

[recto]

                    the xxvij of August 1585
Geyvin in reward to on[e] Bagley a poore man at
Kyllingworth the same daye above wryten by your
lordship's commandment}   xijd.
Geyvin in reward to Mr Goldinggam which he
gave by your lordship's commandment to the
syngers of Brigmingam the same day at Kyllingworth
and to my Lord of Essext taber}   xls.
Payd by your lordship's commandment for the
carges of your lordship's sarvants John

Stringer*, Thomas Kyng and Morys Thomas* and for
iiij horses coming downe to Kyllingworth with
some of your lordship's plat the xj daye of
August as apereth by the byll the same daye}   xiiijs. vijd.
Payd by your lordship's commandment to my fealow
Mearada for the holle carges of your lordship's
sarvants at Coventry, Satterday supper the
xxviij of Agust and Sunday dener and supper
the xxix of August as apereth by hys byll}   vijli. ijs. viijd.
Geyven in reward to Wylliam the gonner* of
Kyllingworth by your lordship's commandment
the same daye}   xxs.
Geyven in reward to Mr Poyllwhell at Mr Lease
hous at hys ryding post to London when your
lordship lay ther the xxix day of August}   iijli.[597]
Geyven in reward to Dampard my lades futman
which he gave at Kyllingworth at your lordship's
coming awaye to the poore the same daye}   xijd.
Geyven in reward to Mr Leyse sarvants of hys
hous when your lordship lay ther the same daye}   xxs.
Geyven in reward to Mr Edward Blunt* which he
gave by your lordship's commandment to Mr Coples
man for bring letters to Kyllingworth by the
waye the same day}   xs.
Geyvin in reward to Evensud adales [sic] man
bring letters to your lordship at Stonley the same day}   vs.
Geyven in reward to Dampard my lades futman
which he gave to your lordship's on handes
which your lordship gave to the keppers of
Kyllingworth Parke the same day at Mr Lese hous}   xxs.
            Summa Paginae: xvjli. xiiijs. iijd.

[verso]

the xxix of August 1585
Geyvin in reward to John Munford* by your
lordship's commandment at Syr Jhon Haringten's
when your lordship lay ther the same day

[597] Sir Thomas Leigh of Stoneleigh, who hunted regularly at Kenilworth; his daughter
Alice married Sir Robert Dudley c. 1596. Leicester told Shrewsbury on the 27th he was
'removing this day away' from Kenilworth, he spent the 28th at Stoneleigh and probably
left on the 29th. It would appear that despite his injury the remove was planned before
the letters from London arrived.

above written}   xs.[598]

Geyvin in reward at Syr John Harington's to the
sarvants of hys hous when your lordship lay ther
the same day}   xls.

Payd by your lordship's commandment to Gylles
Homerstone your lordship's sarvant which he
payd for halfe a dossen of arows for your
lordship's crosbow the same daye}   ijs.

Geyvin in reward to Syr Hare Lease man for
presenting a marlen and a hagard to your
lordship when your lordship lay at Syr Jhon
Harington's the same daye}   xijs.

Geyvin in reward at Syr Jhon Spenser's hous
when your lordship lay ther the xxxj day of Agust}   xxxs.[599]

Geyvin in reward to the poore at the gat at
your lordship's goyng awaye the same daye by
your lordship's commandment}   vs.

Payd by your lordship's commandment to my fealow
Mearada that he payd for the charges of your
lordship's sarvants at Northhamton on Munday
supper the xxx daye of Agust for three skore
and xij parsones as apereth by hys byll}   iijli. xixs. iiijd.

Geyven in reward to John Robarts your lordship's
futman which he gave by your lordship's
commandment to the poore from the
xxj daye of Agust to the xxiij of the day
[*sic*] of the same month the same day}   ijs.

Geyvin in reward to Thomas Waler kepper of
Kyllingworth Park for bringe a stage to your
lordship at Grafton when your lordship lay
ther the fyrst day of September}   xs.[600]

Geyvin in reward to Mr Jhon Blunt's man for
bring ij spanells to your lordship at Grafton
the sam daye}   vs.[601]

[598] Combe Abbey, near Coventry (see n. 456 above), probably 29/30 August.

[599] Sir John Spencer (1524–89), of Althorp, Northants., MP. Spencer had an established association with Leicester, who had helped to arrange his daughters' marriages to Sir George Carew (see n. 100 above and PML, MS Rulers of England, II.2.28, Leicester to Spencer, 28 Dec. 1574) and, by repute, to Lord Strange (see n. 572 above). Leicester probably stayed at Althorp on 30/31 August.

[600] For Grafton, see Introduction, p. 26. He probably stayed at Grafton from 31 August to 2 September. He answered a letter from Walsingham, 'this Wensday in bedd to rest me' (PRO, SP12/182/1), see Appendix II.

[601] Probably the John Blount who was a tenant of the lordship of Warwick in 1576 (WCRO, CR1886 [Warwick Castle Deposit], Cupboard 4/8, survey of the lordship of Warwick, 1576, fo. 61).

Delyvered by your lordship's commandment to
Waller the kepper of Kyllingworth which he gave
to Mr Christover Docrell to cary to Kyllingworth
from Grafton the same [day]}   xls.
Geyvin in reward to Mr Hibbard's man for bring
ij spanells more the same day to Grafton to
your lordship}   vjs. viijd.[602]

          Summa Paginae: xijli. ijs.

[recto]

          the first daye of September 1585
Delyvered by your lordship's commandment to Mr
Blunt at Grafton when your lordship laye ther
the same daye above written in prest}   xli.
Geyvin in reward to on[e] that cared a buck from
Grafton to Mr Black's hous at Neweallmes the same daye}   vs.
Geyvin in reward to the kepper at Grafton by
your lordship's commandment for his feyse the same day}   vjs. viijd.
Delyvered by your lordship's commandment to
Battey at Grafton the same day for the bakyng
of red deare pasties for your lordship at Grafton}   xxs.
Geyvin in reward to the sarvants of Mr Cares
hous at Grafton when your lordship lay ther
the same day}   xxs.
Geyvin in reward the same daye by your lordship's
commandment to Eaton your lordship's godson Mr
Cares man at Grafton when your lordship lay ther}   xs.
Geyvin in reward to Torellton and hys fealou at
Grafton at Mr Caryses hous when your lordship lay
ther the ij daye of September by your lordship's
commandment}   iijli.
Geyvin in reward to on that cared leatters from
your lordship to my Lord North from Grafton the
same day by your lordship's commandment}   vs.[603]

[602] Ralph Hubaud, brother of Sir John Hubaud (d.1583), of Ipsley, Wars., MP, who in
the decade 1573–83 had been the central figure in Leicester's estate administration, see
'West Midlands', 41. Ralph Hubaud served in the Netherlands in 1586 and attended
Leicester's funeral.

[603] Roger, 2nd Lord North (1531–1600), MP. North was one of Leicester's closest
friends, a witness to his marriage in 1578, and an overseer of his 1582 will; he served in
the Netherlands in 1586–7. His absence from Leicester's funeral is curious, given that he
had attended Sidney's, but he wrote to Burghley lamenting 'the untimely death of that
noble lord' (BL, Lansdowne MS 57, fo. 117, printed in Wright, ii, 393).

Geyvin in reward to Mr Doctor James which he
gave by your lordship's commandment to a nurse
at Mr Farmarse hous when your lordship deyned
ther the same daye}   xxs.[604]
Geyvin in reward to a poore man by your lordship's
commandment coming from Mr Farmer's the same daye}   vjd.
Delyvered by your lordship's commandment to Mr
Blunt at Mr Harcotes at Leaconfeld when your
lordship lay ther the ij daye of September payd
hym ther more in prest}   xxli.[605]
Geyvin in reward at Mr Farmarse hous by your
lordship's commandment to on[e] of my Lord
Comton's men for presenting a cast of marlense
to your lordship ther the same day}   xs.
Geyven in reward to your lordship's taberyr
at Mr Harcotes hous when your lordship lay
ther the same day by your lordship's commandment}   xs.
Payd by your lordship's commandment to Kaneth
Leaus which he payd for the litell boy['s]
aparell that your lordship touke up by the
way payd at Mr Harcotes hous the same day}   xixs.
                    Summa Paginae: xxxixli. vjs. ijd.

[verso]

                    the ij day of September 1585
Payd by your lordship's commandment to my
fealow Mearadaye which he payd for the carges
of your lordship's sarvants at Stoney Stratford
from Tewdaye the xxxj of August to Freyday the
iij daye of September for lviij parsons as
apereth by hys byll payd the same daye above
written the some of}   xli. xiiijs. xd.
Payd by your lordship's commandment to my
fealow Ramsey for viij neyghts loging at
Kyllingworth and from thense tell he came to
London agayn as apereth by hys byll}   iiijs.
Geyvin in reward to the sarvants of Mr Harcotes
house by your lordship's commandment when your

---

[604] Easton Neston, see n. 513 above. His itinerary would appear to be Grafton to
Easton Neston on the 2nd, and then after dinner to Leaconfield.
[605] Michael Harcourt (d.c.1597), of Leckhampstead, Bucks., MP. He served in the
Netherlands in 1586.

lordship lay ther the same daye}   xxs.
Geyvin in reward to Mr Stafferton which he gave
to Mr Kyng the precher at Mr Harcotes hous by
your lordship's commandment the same daye}   xls.[606]
Payd by your lordship's commandment to my
fealou Mearaday wich he payd lordship's [*sic*] one
carges and your lordship's sarvants' at
Dunstabell when your lordship lay ther the iij
day of September}   vjli. xs. ijd.[607]
Geyvin in reward which my fealow Pychford gave
by your lordship's commandment to the poore at
Dunstabell the same daye when your lordship laye ther}   xxs.
Geyvin in reward which my fealow Pichford gave
by your lordship's commandment to the musitiones
at Dunstabell the same daye}   vs.
Geyvin in reward the same daye to the byll
ryngers at Dunstabell by your lordship's commandment}   vs.
Geyvin in reward the same day to taber [*sic*]
at Dunstabell that playd in the mornyng to
your lordship at your lordship's coming awaye
the same day}   vs.
Geyvin in reward the same daye to iiij wachmen
at Dunstabell that wach all neyght the same
daye by your lordship's commandment}   iiijs.
Geyvin in reward the same day which Mr Cave
gave by your lordship's commandment to Mr
Sherelles man for presenting a copple of
spannells to your lordship at Dunstabell the same day}   vs.[608]
            Summa Paginae: xxijli. xiijs. [ijd. *deleted*]

[recto]

                    the iij of September 1585
Geyvin in reward to Mr Oxsenbrig your lordship's
page which he gave to the poore by your lordship's
commandment betwene Mr Harcotes hous and
Dunstabell the same daye}   vjs. iijd.
Geyvin in reward which my fealow Pichford gave
by your lordship's commandment to the sarvants

[606] Andrew King of Towcester, see n. 405 above, and p. 327 below.
[607] His route would appear to be down Watling Street to St Albans, stopping at
Dunstable on the night of 3/4 September.
[608] Sir Thomas Shirley, see n. 512 above.

of the hous at Dunstabell when your lordship
lay ther the same day}   xs.

Geyvin in reward at Sant Albons when your
lordship deyned ther to the musitions the iiij
of September}   xs.[609]

Geyven in reward to the sargeant at Sant Albonse
the same day that brought weyne to your lordship
ther when your lordship deyned ther the same daye}   iijs. iiijd.

Geyvin in reward that Mr Jhon Trasy gave by
your lordship's commandment to a poore blynd
harper woman at Sant Albons the same day}   ijs. vjd.

Geyvin in reward to a poore woman the same
day by your lordship's commandment at your
lordship's comyng away at Sant Albonse town
end the same day}   vjd.

Geyvin in reward to my fealow Pichfork which
he gave to Mr Doctor James which Mr Doctor
James gave by your lordship's commandment to
Mr Benson at North hall the same daye}   xxs.

Geyvin in reward which my fealow Pitchfork
gave by your lordship's commandment to on[e] of
my Lord Gray's mean for presenting a buck at
North hall to your lordship the same day}   xs.

Geyvin in reward to Mr Goldingam which he
gave by your lordship's commandment to on[e]
that brought a buck from Grafton to North hall
to your lordship the same day}   vs.

Geyvin in reward to the sarvants of my Lord
of Warweck's hous when your lordship lay ther
the v day of September}   xls.

Payd by your lordship's commandment for ij
mease of meat for your lordship's sarvants
for the wardrope for a fortneyght that is from
the xxij of Agust to the v day of September 1585}   lvjs. viijd.

> Summa Paginae: viijli. iiijs. iijd.

---

[609] Leicester had been high steward of St Albans since 1579 (A.E. Gibbs, *The Corporation Records of St Albans* (St Albans, 1890), p. 13), and the stables of the former abbey were used as one of the outlying royal Stables (*King's Works*, iv, 240), see also p. 314 below. Having dined there he proceeded to Northaw where he stayed until 6 September. By the time he reached Northaw, the news had arrived that the Queen had had second thoughts about giving him and Warwick the Bedford wardship, see Warwick's angry letter to Walsingham, 31 Aug. (PRO, SP12/181/238). It is probable that Leicester's complaint to Walsingham about the Queen's taking 'every occasion by my marriage to withdraw any good from me' (see Appendix II) was also a reference to this.

[verso]

the v of Septeamber 1585

Geyven in reward the same day to Dampard my
lades futman which he gave by your lordship's
commandment to ij poore folke the same daye}   xijd.

Delyvered by your lordship's commandment to
Mr Blunt at my Lord of Warweck's hous more
in prest the same day}   xli.

Payd by your lordship's commandment to Mr
Goldingam which he payd to Mr Blacke for carges
of hys horsmeat and his man's comming from
Kyllingworth with your lordship to London as
apereth by hys byll payd at North Hall the same daye}   xxxs. vd.

Payd by your lordship's commandment to my
fealou Mearada which he payd for the carges of
your lordship's servants at Barnat Satterdaye
supper the iiij daye of Septeamber and Sunday
dener and supper the v day of the same month
as the byll apereth payd the same day the sum of}   vli. vijs.

Geyvin in reward to Essard your lordship's man
at Barnat when your lordship brack your fast
ther the vj day of September by your lordship's
commandment the same day}   iijli. vjs. viijd.

Geyvin in reward the same daye to Moleans*
your lordship's man at Barnat}   iijli. vjs. viijd.

Geyvin in reward to the musitions at Barnat
the same day}   iis. vjd.

Geyven in reward to Mr Poyllwhell which he
gave to lettell Thomas my Lord of Warweck's
man at Barnat by your lordship's commandment
the same daye}   xs.

Payd by your lordship's commandment for your
lordship's and my lades on breakfast and your
lordship's sarvants' at Barnat the vj daye of
Septeamber as apereth by the byll}   xxxjs.[610]

Geyvin in reward to Dampard my lades futman
which he gave by your lordship's commandment
to the poore coming up from Kyllingworth to
London as apereth by hys byll payd the same daye}   xxiiijs. iijd.

---

[610] He appears to have left Northaw early in the morning of the 6th, breakfasted at
Barnet, and reached Leicester House that evening. He spent the 7th there and went to
Nonsuch on the 8th.

Summa Pagina: xxvjli. xixs. vjd.

[recto]

the vj of Septeamber 1585
Payd by your lordship's commandment for iij
rame of wiht paper at vjs. the rame at Leaster
Hous the same daye}   xviijs.
Payd by your lordship's commandment for one
reame of cors wiht paper at iiijs. the rame
the same daye}   iiijs.
Payd by your lordship's commandment for ix
quere of fyne wight paper the same day}   vijs.
Payd by your lordship's commandment to Steaven
Johnson of the wardrop for iiij yeards of wit
cotton at xd. the yeard to leyne your lordship's
doublat sleves when your lordship lay at
Kyllingworth the same day}   iijs. iiijd.
Geyvin in reward to Movester the Franch
imbassater's man for presenting to your
lordship at Leaster Hous a glasse of oyll the
viij day of September}   xxxs.[611]
Geyvin in reward to on[e] of my Lord of Eassext['s]
man for bringe letters to your lordship to
Leaster Hous from the Cort the same day}   vs.
Geyvin in reward to Mr Jhon Heyne which he
gave by your lordship's commandment to Mr
Wotton's man for presenting a cast of torsseles
and a garvaken to your lordship at Leaster Hous the
same daye}   xxxs.[612]
Geyvin in reward to Robyn my Lord Lomlese foul
by your lordship's commandment at Nonsuch the same daye}   xxs.
Payd by your lordship's commandment to Mr Brock
which he payd for a hakyng bage trimmed with
gold for your lordship the same day}   xxxs.

---

[611] Castelnau was about to leave England. His passport from Elizabeth is dated 8
September, his replacement L'Aubépine had his initial audience on the 12th, and he
departed c. the 23rd (Bossy, *Bruno*, p. 58). BL, Cotton MS Galba C VIII, fo. 152, is an
undated letter to Leicester thanking him for various favours and wishing him well on his
appointment in the Netherlands; it can probably be dated the 7th, when Castelnau wrote
in a similar vein to Burghley (*CSPF, 1585–6*, 10–11). Leicester's servant Henry Slyfield*
went to France in his party, see AMAE, CPH, II, fo. 12, Atye to Hotman, 18 Sept.
[612] Wotton wrote to Leicester on the 4th (BL, Cotton MS Caligula C VIII, fo. 333),
but does not mention falcons.

Geyvin in reward to the poore at Putney by
your lordship's commandment at your lordship's
coming to the Cort the same day}   iiijd.[613]
Geyvin in reward to Mr John Hynd by your
lordship's commandment at Nonsuch at hys goyng
into the contrey from Nonsuch the ix daye of
September}   xls.
Geyvin in reward to Mrs Barrat's man for
brynge of iiij boxes of consarves of frut to
your lordship at Nonsuch the same day}   vs.
                    Summa Paginae: ixli. xijs. viijd.

[verso]

                    the vij of Septeamber 1585
Geyvin in reward to Hary Strynger which he
gave to on[e] of Syr Frances Cares men for
presenting a spanell to your lordship at
Nonsuch by your lordship's commandment the
same day gave him at Nonsuch}   xs.
Geyvin in reward which Hary Strynger gave to a
poore man at Nonsuch by your lordship's
commandment the same daye}   iiijd.
Geyvin in reward to the Duck of Bolynes man by
your lordship's commandment for presenting ij
hacks to your lordship at Nonsuch the same daye}   iijli.[614]
Geyvin in reward to my Lord of Essex's futman
at hys goyng to Plemworth from Nonsuch with
letters for your lordship the same day by your
lordship's commandment}   xxs.[615]

---

[613] On 12 September John Stanhope informed the Earl of Rutland that 'my Lord of
Leicester cam to Nonsuch on Wednesday [8 Sept.], went back on Saturdaye and is not
loked for here agayne these 4 or 5 dayes' (Hist MSS Comm, *Rutland MSS*, i, 179).

[614] William Robert de La Marck, Duke of Bouillon (d.1588). He had met Leicester
when he came to England in 1581 as a member of the French embassy to negotiate the
marriage treaty for the Duke of Anjou, and they had corresponded regularly since. His
agent François de Ceville had been in England since the autumn of 1584.

[615] Drake (who finally departed on 14 September) had been at Plymouth with his fleet
since the middle of August. Dom António arrived there from La Rochelle on the 7th.
More famously, Sir Philip Sidney was also there. According to Fulke Greville, Sidney
had offered to attend Dom António at Plymouth as a means of escaping to join Drake
and he was there for some time before Dom António arrived, see 'A Dedication to Sir
Philip Sidney', in J. Gouws (ed.), *The Prose Works of Fulke Greville, Lord Brooke* (Oxford,
1986), pp. 43–4. The contemporary reports of Sidney's departure are clearly at least a
good week later (Stanhope to Rutland, 12 Sept., see n. 613 above, and *CSPF, 1585–6*, 23–
4, Walsingham to Davison, 13 Sept.). Sidney's departure would appear to coincide with

Geyvin in reward to Mr Brock which he gave by
your lordship's commandment to on[e] that brought
troutes to your lordship to Nonsuch the same day} iijs. iiijd.

Payd by your lordship's commandment to Mr
Beneson of hys yearly fey payd him on[e] quarter's
wages at Nonsuch the ix daye of September} ls.

Geyvin in reward to Sir William Knowles's futman
for brynng letters to your lordship to Nonsuch
and carying letters from your lordship at
Nonsuch the same day} xs.

Payd by your lordship's commandment to John
Robarts your lordship's futman which he gave
to the poore betext Mr Harcotes hous and
Dunstabell and London as apereth by the byll} vs. iijd.

Payd by your lordship's commandment to Roger
Gyllanse for carying of your lordship frome
Leaster Hous to Putney the viiith daye of
September 1585} xiijs. iiijd.

Payd by your lordship's commandment to Roger
Gyllanse for carying of your lordship from
Barnellms to Chellse and then carying Mr Dyer
to Sant Marisoures at your lordship's commandment
the x daye of September as apereth by the byll} xvjs. viijd.[616]

Payd by your lordship's commandment to a poore
man for caring iiij peys of red deare to your
lordship to Nonsuch the same daye} ijs. vjd.

Geyvin in reward to Jhon Robarts your lordship's
futman when he went into Norhamptonsheare to Mr
Stafferton with letters for your lordship from
Nonsuch the same day} ijs. vjd.

Summa Paginae: ixli. xiijs. xjd.

[recto]

the x of Septeamber 1585
Gyvin in reward to vij poore folke betext
Nonsuch and Aldersbrocke when your lordship

---

the Queen's reconsideration of her offer of the Netherlands command to Leicester at the
end of August (see Appendix II). It is not impossible that this was the letter from a peer
of the realm offering Sidney employment in the Netherlands, to which Greville (p. 45)
refers.

[616] Edward Dyer, see n. 501 above. His destination may have been St Mary Overy
Stairs in Southwark.

went from Nonsuch the same day above written}   xiiijd.[617]

Geyvin in reward at Seant James the same daye
to sartayn Eyres poore folke}   xijd.

Geyvin in reward to William Jhonson* your
lordship's sallnor [sic] at Aldersbrock
when your lordship was ther the xij day of September}   xxs.

Geyvin in reward to Mr Huggens' man for presenting
to your lordship rose cakes and rose leaves
to your lordship betext the tou Stratfords and
Aldersbrock the same daye}   ijs. vjd.

Geyvin in reward to the spettell hous at
Mylend the same day by your lordship's commandment}   xijd.

Geyvin in reward to the tou warners at Wansted
the same daye that ware syck ther}   xxs.

Geyvin in reward to yonge Christopher Docrey
by your lordship's commandment for bring up a
hake to Nonsuch and at hys goyng downe again
the same daye}   xxxs.

Geyvin in reward to Mr Blunt which he gave to
the gromes of the stabell at my Lord of Bedfordes
by your lordship's commandment when your lordship
was ther the same daye}   xs.[618]

Geyvin in reward which my fealo Pich [sic]
gave by your lordship's commandment to Gorge
Gylles at Leaster House the xiij daye of September}   xxs.

Geyvin in reward to iij messengers that came
of the Quenes magistis by the waye to your
lordship betext Chanes and Ouxbrig the same daye}   xxs.

Geyvin in reward to [a] geyd that came with
your lordship from my Lord of Bedfordes with
your lordship to Oxbrig the same daye}   vs.

Geyvin in reward to Jhon Robarts your lordship's
futman which he gave to the poore betext London
and Chanes and bacagayn from Chanes to the Cort
to Nonsuch the same daye by your lordship's commandment}   ijs. ixd.

---

[617] It would appear that Leicester left Nonsuch on Saturday 11 September (see n. 613) and passed through London to Wanstead, where he spent the 12th.

[618] Leicester went to Chenies on 13 September to attend the Earl of Bedford's funeral on the 14th. The fate of the Bedford wardship had clearly been the subject of some discussion on his return to Court. Stanhope reported on the 12th (n. 613 above) 'whether he shall go to the funeraills of the Erle of Bedforde is in questyon upon poynts of havinge the wardes landes in ferme. Uppon promyse wherof, as yt is said, his Lordship undertoke the charge of the funerals; and sum staye beynge mad therof hath made the dowbt of the other'. From Chenies he returned to Nonsuch, where he remained until the 23rd.

Summa Paginae: vjli. xiijs. vd. [iiijd. *deleted*]

[verso]

the xij of Septeamber 1585
Geyvin in reward to my fealou Pichford which
he gave by your lordship's commandment to tow
poore mean in the Strand at London the same daye}   vjd.
Geyvin in reward to a poore woman the same day
by your lordship's commandment}   vjd.
Geyvin in reward to Ratless the kepper by your
lordship's commandment of Winworth for bringe
to your lordship a stage at Nonsuch the xiiij
daye of September}   xs.
Payd by your lordship's commandment to your
lordship's musitons for ther carges goyng with
your lordship's stouf with the carts to Kyllingworth
and back again as apereth by ther byll}   xxjs.
Delyvered by your lordship's commandment to Mr
Conaway x*li*. wich he delyvered to your lordship
in the Presents Chamber at Nonsuch wheare of
your lordship lost in playe the same tyme at
Nonsuch wich was the xv daye of Septeamber}   iijli. xs.
Geyvin in reward to a poore woman for presenting
a Holand chese to your lordship at Nonsuch the same daye} vs.
Payd by your lordship's commandment to the
sumter mean for hys goyng from Nonsuch to
Leaster Hous to feth a tru[n]ke and goyng from
Leaster Hous to Nonsuch agayn the same daye
for the meat of hym sealfe and hys horse the same tyme} xvjd.
Geyvin in reward to the locksmyth for presenting
a dobell kee at Nonsuch to your lordship
the same daye}   iijs. iiijd.
Geyvin in reward to Hary Strynger wich he gave
by your lordship's commandment to a poore woman
at Nonsuch the same daye}   vjd.
Geyvin in reward to my fealou Undrell at Nonsuch
at hyse goyng downe to Kyllingworth from Nonsuch
the same daye}   xls.
Geyvin in reward to Dampard my lades futman for
bring to your lordship to Nonsuch leatters the same daye} vs.
Summa Paginae: vijli. viijs.

[recto]

the xx of Septeamber 1585

Geyvin in reward to Mr Ardyn wich he gave by
your lordship's commandment to the kepper of
Nonsuch Park that brought to your lordship a
dog wich Mr Richtes had at Nonsuch the same daye} vs.

Your lordship lost at playe at Nonsuch the same daye} xxiiijs.

Geyvin by your lordship's commandment to my
Lord of Essext at Nonsuch the same daye which
was the xx daye of September} xxli.

Geyvin in reward to a kepper Sir Frances Cares
man that brought a dog to your lordship to
Nonsuch the same daye} xs.

Payd by your lordship's commandment to Mr
Sleyfeld* of his yearely feye at hys goyng over
into France halfe a yeare wages aforehand from
the xviij day of September 1585 to the xxv daye
of March next foloyng wich shall be Our Ladey
Daye next} vli.

Payd by your lordship's commandment for ij
mease of meat for your lordship's sarvants of
the wardrop for a fortneyght wich is from the
v daye to the xix day of Septeamber 1585} lvjs. viijd.

Geyvin in reward to Mrs Notes man for presynting
a pyge and a guse to your lordship at Nonsuch
the same daye} ijs. vjd.

Geyvin in reward to my fealow Robart Pichford
by your lordship's commandment at Nonsuch
the same daye} xs.

Geyvin in reward wich your lordship gave your
one sealfe to one of the Quenes falkners that
found your lordship's hake that Mr Hynd had
lost at Nonsuch the same daye} xs.

Geyvin in reward to Smulkyn your lordship's
futman for hys goyng to North Hall with leatters
from Nonsuch the same daye} xijd.

Geyvin in reward to on[e] that went to Barnat to
Bull and Moris the keppers of Envell Chase
the same daye from Nonsuch to tell them the[y]
should staye at Barnat for your lordship's
coming to North Hall the same daye} xviijd.[619]

[619] See Appendix II.

Summa Paginae: xxxjli. viijd.

[verso]

the xxj of Septeamber 1585
Geyvin in reward to Mr Ealmes at Nonsuch which
he gave by your lordship's commandment the xxij
daye of Septeamber to Mr Sherelles nurse and
medwyfe the some of}   xls.[620]
Payd by your lordship's commandment for your
lordship's musitones loging goyng downe to
Kyllingworth and back agayn to London: Willam
Burton*, Rychard Fealow*, James Warton* paid
the same daye}   xxijs.
Payd by your lordship's commandment to Turnnor*
your lordship's bruyer for hys carges goyng
downe to Kyllingworth and backe agayne from
Kyllingworth to Wansted for horse heyr and his one
expense as apereth by the byll payd the same daye}   xixs.
Payd by your lordship's commandment for ij
leynkes at Kyn[g]s[t]on when your lordship came
from Chanes the same daye}   viijd.
Geyvin in reward to Mr Fouler* by your lordship's
commandment at Nonsuch the same daye at hys
goinge into the contrey from Nonsuch the same
daye the some of}   <a>   vli.
Payd by your lordship's commandment to Jhon
Robarts your lordship's futman wich he gave to
the poore and hys one expenses by the waye betext
Nonsuch and London and betext London and Barnat
and Barnatt and Mr Butler's hous when your
lordship went to christen Mr Butler's chylld
the same daye}   vjs. xjd.[621]
Delyvered by your lordship's commandment to
Mr Blunt at Mr Butler's hous when your lordship
lay ther to christen hys chylld the same
daye wich was the xxij daye of Septeamber}   vli.
Geyvin in reward to the nurse at Mr Butler's
hous by your lordship's commandment the same daye}   xls.
Geyvin in reward to the mydwyfe at Mr Butler's

---

[620] Presumably either Robert or Anthony Shirley, for Thomas Shirley the younger
(MP) did not marry until 1591.
[621] See Appendix II.

hous the same daye by your lordship's
commandment when your lordship lay ther the same daye}   xls.
Geyvin in reward to the sarvants of Mr Butler's
hous by your lordship's commandment the same
daye when your lordship lay ther}   xls.

Summa Paginae: xxli. viijs. vijd.

[recto]

the xxij day of September 1585

Geyvin in reward to the ryngers at Wetshamsted
[*sic*] at your lordship's coming from Mr Butler's
hous the same daye}   iijs. iiijd.
Payd by your lordship's commandment to Mr
William Gorge which he payd for my lades carges
and your lordship's sarvants tell your lordship
came to Mr Butler's house which was iij days
before your lordship came and for the carges at
Sant Allbans the same day above written as
apereth by the bylls payd the some of}   vjli. ixs. xjd.
Payd by your lordship's commandment to Jhon
Robarts your lordship's futman wich he gave
to the poore at your lordship's coming from
Mr Butler's betext Mr Butler's and London as
apereth by hys bill}   iijs. jd.
Payd by your lordship's commandment to Robart
Gwen your lordship's sarvant for your lordship's
sarvants carges at Sant Allbons when your
lordship returned from Mr Butler's for supper
of Sattrday at neyght wich was the xxiij
of Septeamber}   xxjs. vjd.
Geyvin in reward to the sarvants at North Hall
at your lordship's coming from Mr Butler's
goyng to London your lordship sent bacagayn
to geve unto the sarvants at North Hall the
same day wich was the xxiij daye of Septeamber
the some of}   <a>   iiijli.
Geyvin in reward to on[e] that brought leatters
to your lordship by the waye wich came from
Kyllingworth the same daye}   vs.
Payd by your lordship's commandment to my fealo
William Pitchfork for a louking glase and xij
leamons for your lordship the same daye}   xs.
Payd by your lordship's commandment to Willam

Fynch and Rychard Connor, Jhon Robarts
sumtermean for fyching beare from Mr Campion's
for your lordship the xi of July to the xvj of
July to [the] iiij of August as apereth by ther
byll the same daye}   vs. iijd.[622]
Geyvin in reward to ij poore folke at Caryng
Crose the same daye by your lordship's
commandment the same daye}   vjd.
Payd by your lordship's commandment to Jhon
Keyme your lordship's sarvant for necassary
thynges that he bought for your lordship's
heuse as apereth by hys bill the same daye} xvs. viijd.
     Summa Paginae: xiijli. xiiijs. iijd.

[verso]

      the xxiij of Septeamber 1585
Payd by your lordship's commandment to Rychard
Warner for ataynding uppon your lordship at
Blackwall with hys barge the v day of Septeamber
as apereth by hys byll}   viijs.
Payd by your lordship's commandment to Roger
Gyllans your lordship's waterman for feyneng
of your lordship's barg and piching and for a
dossen pound of lead for your lordship's barge
the same day as apereth by the byll}   xvjs.
Geyvin in reward to on[e] that went to Mr Deyr's
to Wenchester Hous the same daye by your
lordship's commandment}   iiijd.
Payd by your lordship's commandment to Roger
Gyllans your lordship's waterman for carying
my lady to Barnard Castell and back agayn to
Leaster Hous the xxvj of Septeamber and for
carying your lordship from Leaster House to
Putney the xxvij of Septeamber and geving
atandans at your lordship's commandment at
Putney the xxix daye and for coming with your
lordship from Putney the second daye of October
as appeareth by the byll the same daye payd} iijli. iijs. iiijd.
Geyvin in reward to your lordship's tow
warners at Wansted by your lordship's

---

[622] Abraham Campion, brewer. He attended Leicester's funeral and claimed a debt of
£400 for beer supplied from his estate.

commandment the same daye}	xs.

Geyvin in reward to Buttell* your lordship's
feryr by your lordship's commandment for
setting on a show uppon on[e] of your lordship's
coch horsses betext Wansted and Stratford the same daye}   xijd.
Geyvin in reward to tou poore folkes at Mylend
at your lordship's commandment at your lordship's
coming to Leaster House the same daye}   vjd.
Geyvin in reward to the spettell hous at Mylend
the same daye by your lordship's commandment}   vjd.
Geyvin in reward to Jhon Robarts your lordship's
futman wich he gave by your lordship's
commandment betext Nonsuch and London and London
and Wansted the same daye as apereth by hys byll}   ijs. ixd.
Payd by your lordship's commandment for iij
yeardes and a halfe of black stoufe caled
boutey to make your lordship a doblat at xviijs.
the yeard payd at Leaster Hous to Mr Stone
the mearser the same daye}   iijli. iijs.

Summa Paginae: viijli. vs. vd.

[recto]

the xxiiij of Septeamber 1585
Geyvin in reward to Baxter [my lades *deleted*]
trumpetr by your lordship's commandment at
Leaster Hous the same daye above written}   xls.
Payd to Thomas Eygley* by your lordship's
commandment wich he payd for the makyng of a
seastorne and other thyngs wich he bought for
your lordship at Lester Hous the same daye}   <a>   xlixs.
Geyvin in reward to the man that brought hangs
[hinges?] to your lordship at Leaster Hous by your
lordship's commandment the same daye}   iijs.
Payd by your lordship's commandment for ryting
paper for your lordship at at [*sic*] Lester
Hous the same day}   iiijs. viijd.
Geyvin in reward to the musitons at Sant
Albons when your lordship went to survey the
Quenes great horses ther and your lordship
deyned ther the same daye}   xs.[623]
Geyvin in reward to [a] poor blynd woman by

[623] See Appendix II and, for the Stables at St Albans, n. 609.

your lordship's commandment at Sant Allbons
the same daye}   is.
Geyvin in reward to Jhon Comley* your lordship's
sarvant which he payd for your lordship's
horsemeat ther the same daye when your deyned ther}   vs.
Geyvin in reward to on[e] that went from your
lordship from Sant Allbons with leatters to my
Lord Graye the same daye}   is.
Geyvin in reward to the sargant that brought
wyne to your lordship at Sant Albons the same
daye your lordship deyned ther}   vs.
Geyvin in reward to the precher of Sant Albons
which he gave by your lordship's commandment to
the poore of the toune ther the same daye when
your lordship deyned ther wich was the xxv of
Septeamber}   xxs.
Geyvin in reward the same daye at your lordship's
coming away at the townd's end to the poore
ther by your lordship's commandment}   ijs.
Geyvin in reward which Mr Atey gave by your
lordship's commandment to the nurse and mydwyf
at North Hall when your lordship christened
my Lord of Combarlandes chylld ther the same
daye which was the xxvj of Septeamber}   vijli.[624]
Geyvin in reward to Codbard the purssuvant by
your lordship's commandment that brought leatters
to your lordship to North Hall the same day}   xs.
                    Summa Paginae: xiiijli. xs. viijd.

[verso]

                    the xxvj of Septeamber 1585
Payd by your lordship's commandment to Antoney
Leavse* your lordship's sarvant wich he payd
for the carges of your lordship's sarvants at
Barnat, supper on Satterday at neyght the frist
daye of October and dener a Sunday the second
of October as apereth by hys byll}   xxxvjs.
Payd by your lordship's commandment to Jhon
Comley your lordship's sarvant wich he payd
for the carges of your lordship's horsmeat
ther the same tyme}   xxijs.

---

[624] See Appendix II.

Geyvin in reward to Jhon Robarts your lordship's
futman wich he gave by your lordship's commandment
to the poore betext North Hall and London at
your lordship's coming from North Hall from the
chrissing of my Lord of Combarlandes chyld
the same daye}   iiijs. vjd.
Payd by your lordship's commandment for ij
mease of meat for your sarvants of the wardrop
for a fortneyght that is from the xix daye of
Septeamber to the iij daye of October}   lvjs. viijd.
Payd by your lordship's commandment to Thomas
Becket* at Leaster Hous your lordship's sarvant
the second daye of October the some of 1585}   lxli.
<quaere wherefore>^z
Geyvin in reward to Mr Sackford's man by your
lordship's commandment at Lester House the
same daye the som of}   iijli.[625]
Geyvin in reward to an Eyresman by your
lordship's commandment wich did present to
your lordship at Aldersbrocke premesettes and
other thynges the iij daye of October}   xvli.
Geyvin in reward to Mr Davis by your lordship's
commandment the same daye at Aldersbrock}   xls.
Geyvin in reward to Tyntell tan Dave [sic] the same
daye by your lordship's commandment at Aldersbrock}   xs.
Geyvin in reward to a pursevant that [came] to
your lordship from Setrey Wallsengam from
Nonsuch to Aldersbrock to your lordship the
same day}   vs.
Payd by your lordship's commandment to Mr
Doctor James for hys quarter's wages from
Medsomer to Myckellmas last past 1585 the
iiij day of October at Leaster House the same day}   xli.
                    Summa Paginae: lxxxxvjli. xiiijs. ijd.

[recto]

                    the iij of October 1585
Geyvin in reward to Turner your lordship's
bruyar by your lordship's commandment at
Wansted the same daye}   xxs.
Payd by your lordship's commandment to your

---

[625] Henry, see n. 443 above.

lordship's F[r]aynch couk hys quarter's wages
from Medsomer to Myckellmas last past 1585
at Aldersbrock the same daye}   vli.
Payd by your lordship's commandment on[e] ounce
of hard wax for your lordship the same daye at
Leaster House}   vjd.
Geyvin in reward to a poore blynd man betext
Alders[brook] and London the same daye}   iiijd.
Payd by your lordship's commandment to Mr Martyn
for a feyrshould for your lordship at Aldersbrock
the same day}   xiijs. iiijd.
Geyvin in reward to Mr Pecoke which he payd
by your lordship's commandment for the [shogers
deleted] soldiers' carges at Romford when your
lordship deyned ther the vj day of October 1585}   xxli.[626]
Payd by your lordship's commandment for your
lordship's oyne deyat and your lordship's on
sarvants at Romford the same daye}   vli.
Payd by your lordship's commandment to Mr
Blunt which he payd for your lordship's
horsmeat at Romford the same daye}   ixs.
Geyvin in reward to Mr Cave wich he gave to on[e]
of Mr Coukes men at Geddey Hall the same daye}   xs.[627]
Payd by your lordship's commandment to Mr
Bysbyge* which he payd to Nycolas Grenshew for
the bringe up of your lordship's teant from
Kyllingworth to London and caring downe a lod
bacagayn to Kyllingworth from Leaster Hous
the same day which was the viij of October 1585}   xxli.
Geyvin in reward to Mr Blunt which he gave to
Mr Butcot's man for bringe a gayllding to Leaster
Hous to your lordship the same daye by your
lordship's commandment}   xxs.
Geyvin in reward to Mr John Trasey and Mr Geylles
Trasey by your lordship's commandment at ther
goyng from Leaster Hous into the contrey the

---

[626] Robert Pecock, muster-master for Essex, who was originally appointed to command
the company raised in Essex for the Netherlands in the summer, but was replaced by
Robert Sidney (PRO, SP15/29/45). He nevertheless served in the Netherlands in 1586,
see p. 355, n. 700 below. October was relatively late for further recruiting of troops for
the Netherlands; this was probably the mustering of the Essex militia, which Leicester
was attending as lord lieutenant.

[627] Gidea Hall, home of (Sir) Anthony Cooke (1559–1604) the younger, MP, grandson
of Sir Anthony (n. 330 above).

viij of October 1585}   vjli. xiijs. iiijd.

Summa Paginae: lxli. vjs. vjd.

[verso]

the viij of October 1585

Payd by your lordship's commandment to Fardenando
your lordship's sarvant of his quarter wages
from Medsomer to Myckellmas 1585 at Rychmond
the same daye}   ls.[628]

Geyvin in reward to Fardenando wich he gave by
your lordship's commandment to Flent hir
magistis locksmeth for presenting a dobell key
to your lordship at Rychmond the same day}   vs.

Geyvin in rewarde to a poore woman the same
daye by your lordship's commandment at Rychmon
at the townesend}   iijd.

Geyvin in reward to yonge Mr Dudley at his
going doune into the contrey by your lordship's
commandment at Rychmon the same daye}   xls.

Payd by your lordship's commandment for floures
and boues for your lordship's chambars from the
second daye of May to Myckellmas last past the
same daye}   ixs. ijd.

Payd by your lordship's commandment to the
sumter man for feching of beare at Mr Campionse
for your lordship to Nonsuch for the carges
of hys one meat and hys horsses the xxiiij day
of Septeamber}   xvjd.

Payd by your lordship's commandment to the
sumter man for hys carges geving adtandance at
Wansted and at Leaster Hous iiij dayes uppon
your lordship and for caring your lordship's
thyngs to Nonsuch the viij daye of October}   ijs.

Payd by your lordship's commandment to my fealo
William wich he payd for the carige of your
lordship's steuf wich was xj cartes from Nonsuch
to Rychmon and gevin to the carters to drink
by the way the same daye}   xjs. vjd.

Payd by your lordship's commandment to one that

---

[628] The Court removed from Nonsuch to Richmond between 29 September and 1
October, probably while Leicester was at St Alban's and Northaw. The following entries
suggest that Leicester's belongings were moved to Richmond on 7 and 8 October.

mendid your lordship's cloth sekes the same daye}   iijs. viijd.
              Summa Paginae: vjli. ijs. xjd.

[recto]

              the ix of October 1585
Geyvin in reward to younge Christoper Docrell
for feting a hacke from Grenewich to cary to
Kyllingworth by your lordship's commandment
the same daye at Rychmon}   xxs.
Geyvin in reward to my fealou Willam wich he
gave by your lordship's commandment to on[e] that
brought a porklyng to Rychmon to your lordship
the same daye}   iijs. iiijd.
Payd by your lordship's commandment to Ducke*
your lordship's spannell kepper for the carges
of your lordship's spannellse for ij montes which
is from the xx daye of August to the xj daye of
October as apereth by hys byll for the kepping of
xxvjth coppell of spannells the same daye payd}   ljs. iiijd.
Payd by your lordship's commandment to Skot [the]
knytmarshalles man for Smulkin's charges when
he lay in the marshall's at your lordship's
commandment at Nonsuch payd hym at Rychmon
the same daye}   iijli.
Payd by your lordship's commandment for the
charges of your lordship's sarvants comying
with your lordship's stoufe from Nonsuch to
Richmon the vij of October: Robart Pottwinton,
John Grain, Thomas Hall, James the Baker,
Rychard Gardener, Robyn Folys, Thomas Bagnoll*
your lordship's sarvants for ther meat the vij
daye of October and the viij daye as apereth
by the byll}   xs.
Payd by your lordship's commandment to Roger
Gyllanse your lordship's bergman for carynge
of your lordship from Leaster [House] to
Barnellmes the ix of October, for geving
atandanse at Mortlacke at your lordship's
commandment and for caring your lordship
from Rychmon to Leaster Hous the xij day of

October as appereth by the byll}   liijs. iiijd.[629]
Payd by your lordship's commandment to yonge
Mr Robart Dudles man for necessary thynges wich
he bought for Mr Robert Dudly as apereth by hys
byll the same daye}   xxviijs. iiijd.
Geyvin to yong Mr Robart Dudles man the same
daye at Lester Hous at hys going to North Hall
from Leaster Hous the same daye}   xxs.

           Summa Paginae: xijli. vjs. iiijd.

[verso]

           the x of October 1585
Geyvin in reward to Mr Blunt which he gave by
your lordship's commandment to on[e] of Mr Walter
Rales men for presenting of x saddells to your
lordship at Lester Hous the same daye}   xls.
Payd by your lordship's commandment to Frances
Smyth merser for a hondred ells of sarnat at vs.
ijd. the ell and ix elles of whith taffety
sarnat at ixs. the ell for your lordship's
heuse the xiiij of Octobar 1585 payd him at
Leaster Hous the same daye the some of}   xxixli. xvijs. viijd.
<[taken _deleted_] delyvered to Polewhele>[aa]
Geyven in reward to Jhon Robarts your lordship's
futman which he gave by your lordship's
commandment to the poore the iij of October,
the vj daye and the viij daye of October}   ijs. ixd.
Geyvin in reward the same daye your lordship
went to Syr Seplep [_sic_] Butler's hous to the
poor by the waye the x of October}   ijs. jd.[630]
Geyvin in rewarde to Smulkyn your lordship's
futman when he went from Sir Phelep Buttler's
hous to Leaster Hous the same day}   vs.

---

[629] Assuming the date of 6 October for the muster at Romford is correct, it would
appear that Leicester was in London until 9 October, when he went to Richmond via
Barn Elms, and then returned to Leicester House on the 12th. Walsingham informed
Burghley on 12 October (BL, Harl. MS 6993, fo. 110) that Leicester wanted a Star
Chamber hearing postponed until Friday the 15th.

[630] The internal sequence is coherent: Leicester went to Sir Philip Butler's, spent the
night there and then returned to London via Hertford, Northaw and Barnet. The
difficulty lies in reconciling these dates with his return to Leicester House from Richmond
on 12 October. Given his request for the postponement of the Star Chamber hearing
until the 15th and the references to his return to Richmond from Leicester House on the
16th, the visit to Butler's probably took place on the 13th–14th.

Geyvin in reward to the sarvantes of Syr Felep Buttler's hous when your lordship lay ther the same daye}	xxs.
Geyvin in reward unto my Lord Chamberlynes musitions at Syr Phelep Butler's hous the same day by your lordship's commandment}	xxs.
Payd by your lordship's commandment for the charges at Wotton for your lordship's mean and horsses the same daye}	xxxiiijs. iiijd.
Geyvin in reward to the prisoners at Harford the same daye by your lordship's commandment}	vs.
Geyvin in reward to the poor at Harford the same daye by your lordship's commandment}	vjd.
Geyvin in reward to Mr Skores futman at North Hall the same daye by your lordship's commandment}	vs.[631]
Geyvin in reward to Mr Blunt which he gave by your lordship's commandment to my Lady of Comberlandes nurse at North Hall the same day}	xls.

Summa Paginae: xxxviijli. xijs. iiijd.

[recto]

the xj of October 1585

Geyven in reward to my Lord of Darbes man for wayting at the Star Chamber Stairs for your lordship the same daye}	iijs. iiijd.
Payd by your lordship's commandment for charges at Barnat for your lordship's hors meat and your lordship's sarvants the xvj daye of October}	xxvs.[632]
Payd by your lordship's commandment for charges at North Hall of your lordship's horsemeat the same daye}	xjs.
Geyvin to the poore in reward betext North Hall and London the same daye by your lordship's commandment}	xvjd.
Geyvin in reward to the madens at the meuse at Mr Poowell['s] when your lordship was mad you redy ther the same day}	ijs. vjd.
Geyvin in reward to Mr Blunt which he gave by	

[631] Sylvanus Scory (d. 1617), MP, son of John Scory, Bishop of Hereford. Scory had been in Leicester's service in the 1570s, he served in the Netherlands in 1586 and attended his funeral. He wrote to Leicester on 27 July asking for his assistance in the dispute over his father's estate (PRO, SP12/180/99).

[632] Probably the 14th, see n. 630 above.

your lordship's commandment to Mr Hongerfordes
man for presenting a baye horse to your lordship
at Leaster Hous the xv daye of October 1585}   xls.
Payd by your lordship's commandment to Hans
Carpion jeweller at Leaster Hous the xvj of
October for therty buttons of gold garnesshed
with deyamedes at xxxiijs. a pys for your
lordship payd hym at Leaster Hous in the year
1585 the some of}   xlixli. xs.
Geyvin in reward to Mr Cave which he gave by
your lordship's commandment to your lordship's
water men at your lordship's cominge to Rychmon
the same daye}   iijs. iiijd.[633]
Geyvin in reward to Steaven Jhonson your
lordship's sarvant wich he gave by your
lordship's commandment to a poore woman that
opened the gat at your lordship's coming to
Richmon the same daye}   xijd.
Geven in reward that that [sic] my fealou
Steven Jhonson gave by your lordship's commandment
to iij poore folke at Rychmon towndsend at your
lordship's coming to Richmon the same day}   ixd.
Geyvin in reward to Mr Farmar's man by your
lordship's commandment for hys staying her[e] at
the Cort for letters for your lordship which he
caryd downe into the contry from Rychmon the xx
of October}   xxs.
        Summa Paginae: liiijli. xviijs. iijd.

[verso]

        the xvij of October 1585
Payd by your lordship's commandment for ij mease
of meat for your lordship's sarvants of the
wardrop for a fornyght that is from the iij daye
of October to the xvij daye of the same month 1585}   lvjs. viijd.
Payd by your lordship's commandment to on[e]
Warl[t]er Jennell on[e] of the pages of the Preve
Chambar for Mrs Osemed of Grenewich for hyr
yearly feey payd at Myckellmas halfe yeare
wages dew at Myckellmas last past 1585 paye at
Richmon the xviij of October}   vli.

---

[633] Probably on the 16th, see the previous entries and n. 630.

Payd by your lordship's commandment to the Quenes
bargeman for carying your lordship frome the
Cort to Thessellworth to the Prynce of Portingall
and bacagayne to the Cort to Richmon the xvij
daye of October}   xs.[634]

Geyvin in reward to Smulkyn the futman which
he gave to the poore by your lordship's commandment
at Hosterley when your lordship went to
Thessellworth and bacagayn to the Cort the same
daye}   xijd.

Payd by your lordship's commandment to Mr
Browne which he payd to Mr Cave for a barbrey
hack for your lordship at Leaster Hous the
same daye the xvij day of October 1585} <B> vli.

Geyvin in reward to Mr Browne wich he gave by
your lordship's commandment to the armayer of
Grenewich at Leaster Hous the same daye} <B> xls.

Geyvin in reward to Mr Browne wich he gave by
your lordship's commandment to the workemen
which worast of the new sealer at Wansted the
same daye} <B>   xs.

Geyvin in reward to Mr Browne which he gave
by your lordship's commandment to Gyllames
wyfe the gardener of Wansted the same daye} <B> vs.

Payd by your lordship's commandment to Mathew
Wodward your lordship's sarvant for sartayn
thinges he laye out for your lordship's shep's [*sic*]
heus as apereth by hys byll the same daye} vs. xd.

    Summa Paginae: xvjli. viijs. vjd.

[recto]

    the xviij of October 1585
Geyvin in reward to Sulcot Deuk Cassemer's man
at hys going to hys master with leatters from
your lordship from Richmon the same daye above

---

[634] Dom António was then housed at Osterley, see Hist MSS Comm, *Rutland MSS*, i,
180, Stanhope to Rutland, 21 Sept., and *CSPF, 1585–6*, 47.

written by your lordship's commandment the some of}   vli.[635]

Geyvin in reward to [a] poore woman betext
Barnellmes and the Cort at your lordship's
coming to Rychmon the same daye by your
lordship's commandment}   iiijd.

Geyvin in reward to Mr Blunt which he gave to
Geaste* at Leaster Hous the same daye by your
lordship's commandment}   xxs.

Payd by your lordship's commandment to Gregory
Seton for sartayn books which he delyvered to
Humfer[y] Coll your lordship's sarvant, on[e] books
of martres at xls., a Callven on Jobe with
Pasalmes at iiijs., payd at Leaster Hous the
same daye the some of}   <a>   iiijli. iiijs.[636]
<some falce>bb

Payd by your lordship's commandment for both
heyr for your lordship's sarvants Rafe More,
Steaven Jhonson, Robart Pichford from Rychmon
to Leaster Hous the xxiij of October}   ijs.

Payd by your lordship's commandment for both
hyr for them more the same day from Leaster
Hous to Barnellms}   ijs.

Geyvin in reward to Mr Knolls wich he gave by
your lordship's commandment to [a] man of my
Lord of Darbes that he brought to your
lordship to Leaster Hous the xxiij of October}   iijli. vjs. viijd.

Payd by your lordship's commandment for xxiiij
yeards of whicht jane fustan at xijd. the
yeard for to make sewett bages for your
lordship's wardrop delyvered to my fealou
Willam Pichford at Leaster Hous the same daye}   xxiiijs.

Geyvin in reward to a pursevant by your
lordship's commandment that brought the great
Preve Salle from Mr Seatory Wallsinggames

---

[635] The Pfalzgraf Johann Casimir (1543–92), who had been a friend of Leicester's since
1577–8. They maintained a regular correspondence of which the largest surviving section
is to be found in the Kurpfälzische Bestände in the Bayerisches Geheimstaatsarchiv,
Munich (published in F. von Bezold (ed.) *Briefe des Pfalzgrafen Johann Casimir* (Munich,
1882–1903)). Nothing, however, survives from 1585, although there are drafts of letters
from Johann Casimir to Walsingham and Burghley of 11/21 October in BGSA, Kasten
Schwarz 16694, fos. 203–5.

[636] The 'book of martyrs' may be STC 11225, the 1583 edition of Foxe's *Actes and
Monuments*, and the 'Callven on Jobe', STC 4447, the edition of Calvin's *Sermons on Job*
published by Arthur Golding in 1584.

to Leaster Hous to your lordship the same daye}   xs.[637]
                    Summa Paginae: xvli. ixs.

[verso]

                    the xx of October 1585
Geyven in reward to a poore woman at your
lordship's coming to the Cort the same daye by
your lordship's commandment}   iijd.
Payd by your lordship's commandment to Mrs
Gyllam of hyr quarter's wages from Medsomer
quarter to Myckellmas 1585 at Rychmon the same daye}   ls.
Payd by your lordship's commandment to Gouf
your lordship's gardener of Wansted of hys
quarter's wages from Medsomer to Myckellmas
quarter 1585 the xxv of October}   vli.
Payd by your lordship's commandment to Ducke
your lordship's spannell kepper for the kepping
of iiij coppell of spannells from the xiij of
Septeamber to the xth of October the same daye}   xvijs. viijd.
Payd by your lordship's commandment to Jhon
Keyme your lordship's sarvant for iij botells
of sacke when your lordship was last at Sant
Allbons and for carying of beare from London
to Rychmon and for ij pond of corke the xv day
of October and a skyne for to caever your
lordship's bottells}   vjs.
Payd by your lordship's commandment to Roger
Gyllanse your lordship's waterman for carying
your lordship deyverse tymes as from the xv
daye of October to the xvj and the xix, the
xxth to the xxiiith of October as apereth
by hys byll}   vijli. vjs.
Payd by your lordship's commandment to Mr Blunt
wich he payd to Evans the bakyr of Stratford
Banford for horse bread wich he delyvered to
Wansted between Medsomer and Myckellmas last
past 1585 the some of}   ixli. xs.

[637] Since Elizabeth did not appoint a Lord Privy Seal, Walsingham, as Secretary of
State, had custody of the Privy Seal. A possible reason for sending it to Leicester is
discussed in Appendix II. He appears to have been at Court from 16 to 23 October
when he went to Leicester House. He wrote to the States-General from the Court on 23
October, and to Davison on the 25th, but without giving his address. Walsingham wrote
to him from the Court on the 26th, see Appendix II.

Geyven in reward to my Lord Welebes man for
presynting a pease caled a musket at Leaster
Hous to your lordship the same daye by your
lordship's commandment}   xxxs.[638]
Geyvin in reward to Mr Oxsenbrige [which he]
gave by your lordship's commandment to Gaste
at Leaster Hous the same daye}   xs.
    Summa Paginae: xxvijli. ixs. xjd.

[recto]

     the xxv of October 1585
Payd by your lordship's commandment to Gorge
Landall for a sellver trumpat for your lordship
at Leaster House the xxviij of October waying
xxiij ounces and a haulfe prysed at}   xijli.
Payd by your lordship's commandment for a
reallme of wit paper at Leaster Hous the same daye}   vjs. viijd
Payd by your lordship's commandment to Mr
Cetchen for xj elles of holand to mak your
lordship a wastcot at vjs. vjd. the ell, ij
dossen of hantowels at xxs. vjd. the dossen,
one dossen of hantowels at xiiijs. vjd.
the dossen as apereth by the byll payd at
Leaster Hous the same day}   vjli. vijs.
<yll entered ex[amine] this somme>[cc]
Payd by your lordship's commandment to
yonge Mr Robert Dudles man for hys horsemeat
goyng to North Hall and for the hyre of a
horse and hys meat at North Hall and for waiting
at London as apereth by hys byll}   xvs.
Payd by your lordship's commandment to Steaven
Jhonson of your lordship's wardrop wich he payd
for gylldinge of vj pare of spours for your
lordship at vs. the pare and iij pare of vellat
spurleathers at ijs. a pare the same daye}   xxxvjs.
Geyvin in reward wich Mr Blunt gave by your
lordship's commandment to Mr Roper's man for
presenting to your lordship a sorell bay
horse at Leaster Hous the same daye}   xxxs.

[638] Willoughby was then in Denmark and wrote to Leicester on 25 October (*CSPF*, *1585–6*, 120), proposing to join him in the Netherlands on the conclusion of his embassy. When he arrived in March 1586 he was appointed governor of Bergen-op-Zoom.

Geyvin in reward to Mother Ossomond of Grenewich
by your lordship's commandment at Leaster Hous
the same daye}   xls.
Geyvin in reward to Wednoll Twyste* the master
of your lordship's shepe at Leaster Hous the
same daye by your lordship's commandment}   xls.
Geyvin in reward wich Mr Blunt gave by your
lordship's commandment to Syr Rychardes Knyghtles
man for presenting a great graye horse to your
lordship at Leaster Hous the same daye wich was the
xxviij day of October 1585}   iijli.

        Summa Paginae: xxixli. xiiijs. viijd.

[verso]

        the xxvj of October 1585
Payd by your lordship's commandment to Nycolas
Grenshaw for bringe up of ij lod of armer of
your lordship's from Kyllingworth to Leaster
Hous the xxvij of October 1585}   viijli.
Payd by your lordship's commandment to Syr
Rychard Kneytly which he payd to Mr Kynge the
precher of hys yearly fee hallfe hys year wages
from Our Ladey Daye to Myckellmas last past in the
year 1585}   vli.
Payd to Matew Wodword your lordship's sarvant
by your lordship's commandment for hys bothheyre
when he went to Rychmon from Leaster Hous
to fech your lordship's lettell desk the same daye}   ijs.
Payd by your lordship's commandment to Smulkyn
your lordship's futman wich he gave to the
poore betx Leaster Hous and Richmon the
same daye}   xvd.
Payd by your lordship's commandment to my Lade
Lewn at Rychmon the xxix daye of October in
the year 1585 the some of}   xlli.[639]
Geyvin in reward to a poore woman that your
lordship came thoro hyr yeard at Barllms the
same daye by your lordship's commandment}   xijd.
Geyvin in reward that Smulkyn gave by your
lordship's commandment to the pore the same
daye at your lordship's goyng to London the

---

[639] Possibly Elizabeth, Lady Leighton, Sir Thomas's wife (see n. 527).

same daye}   xvd.
Geyvin in reward by your lordship's commandment
wich Mr Blunt gave to Mr Weston's man of
Essext for presenting to your lordship a graye
gyllding to your lordship at Leaster Hous the same daye}   xxxs.
Geyvin in reward wich Mr Flud gave by your
lordship's commandment to Mounser de Caroges's
man for presenting to your lordship a crosboy
and a dage at Leaster House to your lordship
the same daye}   ls.[640]
Payd by your lordship's commandment to the
sumterman for hys cargyes going to London and
from thense to North Hall and backagan
to the Cort for hys on meat and hys horse}   xijd.

                    Summa Paginae: lvijli. vjs. vjd.

[recto]

                    the xxviij of October 1585
Payd by your lordship's commandment for ij
measse of meate for your lordship's sarvants
of the wardrop for a fortneyght that is
from the xvij of October to the xxxj of the
same month 1585}   lvjs. viijd.
Payd by your lordship's commandment to Mr
Doctor James which he payd for a seallver
levray pott for your lordship waying xxxiiij
ounses at vijs. an ounce, wheareof ther was
receved of another sellver pott waying vj
ounces at vs. the ounce xxxs., wherof the rest
is the some of payd at Leaster House the xxxj of
October 1585}   xli. xs. iiijd.
Geyvin in reward to Mr Docrell's man by your
lordship's commandment for bryng to your
lordship cones to Rychmon the second daye of
November 1585}   iijs. iiijd.
Payd by your lordship's commandment to Mistris
Garner wich she payd and others to goodwyfe
Smeth for hemming and markyng of liij dossen

---

[640] Tanneguy le Veneur, Sieur de Carroges, Comte de Tillières. Leicester had met
him, like the Duke of Bouillon (see n. 614), when he took part in the embassy to England
in 1581. A single letter from him survives: Haarlem, Teylers Museum MS 2376, art. 7,
29 April 1582.

of napkyns and towells the same daye}   iijli. ijs.
                                                         [xijd. *deleted*]

Geyvin in reward to the poore that opened the
gat for your lordship at Barnellmes at your
lordship's goyng to Leaster House the same
daye by your lordship's commandment}   xijd.
Geyvin in reward to vj poore folke at your
lordship's goyng to Leaster Hous the same
daye by your lordship's commandment}   vijd.
Geyvin in reward to Syr Gorge Cary's man by
your lordship's commandment for presenting to
your lordship a boxt of routes at Leaster
House the iij daye of November 1585}   xs.[641]
Geyvin in reward by your lordship's commandment
to Mr Camellie he that teach[es] yonge Mr Dudley
at Leaster House the iiij daye of November 1585}   vli.
               Summa Paginae: xxijli. iijs. xjd.

[verso]

               the iiij of November 1585
Payd by your lordship's commandment to William
Edgeworth preacher of Wansted at Leaster House
the iij daye of November 1585 the somm of}   xxli.[642]
<exam[ine?]>[dd]
Payd by your lordship's commandment to Mr Payr
the Quenes imbradyr which he payd for a hondred
ells of sarnat for your lordship at vs. the
ell the v daye of November payd hym at Leaster
House the somm of}   xxvli.
Payd by your lordship's commandment to Mr Payr
mor the same day which he paye for carlat for
stomasters for your lordship the same daye at
Leaster House}   xxs.
Payd by your lordship's commandment to Thomas
Bedwell wich he payd to on[e] Ewre a carver at
Wansted uppon a pese a work which he doth for
your lordship at Wansted the v day of November

[641] Probably Sir George Carey (1547–1603), MP, Hunsdon's son and Captain of the
Isle of Wight, but possibly Sir George Carew (n. 100), whose surname was frequently
written Carey. It would appear from the chronology of the entries that Leicester went to
Richmond from Leicester House on 1 November and returned on the 3rd. He wrote to
the Earl of Huntingdon on 1 November (HEHL, HA 2379), but did not give his address.
[642] Possibly an error for Edward Edgeworth, see n. 555 above.

1585 about the condet}   \<a\>   xli.
Geyvin in reward to <u>Mr Grotrige*</u> at Leaster
House by your lordship's commandment the v of
November 1585 the summ of}   xli.
\<exam[ine?]\>ᵉᵉ
Payd by your lordship's commandment to Nycolas
Harford yong Mr Dudles man for hys quarter's
wages from Medsomer to Myckellmas last past
1585 the same daye}   xxvs.
Geyvin in reward to Mistres Croxsense man for
bring a cock[r?]ell to your lordship to Leaster
House the same daye}   vs.
Payd by your lordship's commandment to Edward
Willperforse wich he won of a wager which your
lordship lost coming from Leaster House to
Rychmon the vj of November}   xijd.
Geyvin in reward by your lordship's commandment
to [a] man [that] opened the gat at your
lordship's coming to Rychmon the same day}   vjd.[643]
          Summa Paginae: lxvijli. xjs. vjd. [xviijd. *deleted*]

[recto]

                    the vj daye of November 1585
Payd by your lordship's commandment to Roger
Gyllanes your lordship's bargeman for caring
of your lordship deyverse tymes as from the
xxiiij deye of October to [the] vj daye of
November as apereth by the byll 1585
the some of}   vjli. vjs. iiijd.
Geyvin in reward the same day by your
lordship's commandment to the bargemen}   iijs. iiijd.
Payd by your lordship's commandment to Gylles
Homerston your lordship's sarvant for horsemeat
and manes meat at Fullam when the[y] wayted
with your lordship's coch and horsses ther for
your lordship the viij daye of November}   vjs. ijd.
Payd by your lordship's commandment to on[e] that
brought your lordship's jeuell chest from London
to Rychmon the same daye}   xviijd.
Geyvin in reward to the poore by your lordship's

---

[643] It would appear that he went back to Richmond from Leicester House on 6
November.

commandment the same daye betwene Rychmon and
Leaster Hous the same day}   xijd.
Delyvered to your lordship's one handes at
Leaster House wich your lordship gave to Mr
Screven my Lord of Rutlandes man for presenting
a horse to your lordship at Leaster House
the viij day November 1585 the some of}   xli.[644]
Geyvin in reward to Doctors Doyles man by your
lordship's commandment at Leaster House the xj
of November for caryng of leatters for your
lordship into Flanderse}   xxs.[645]
Geyvin in reward to Christopher Seliock a
purssevant for bring leatters to Wansted to your
lordship the same day}   vs.
Geyvin in reward to on[e] that went to Beuley to
Mr Settles with leatters for your lordship
frome Leaster Hous the same daye by your
lordship's commandment}   xiijs. iiijd.
Geyvin in reward by your lordship's commandment
to Savege your lordship's kepper for bring a
heynd and a dog to the of [sic] of
Portinggallse the xj of November 1585}   xxs.
                Summa Paginae: xixli. xvjs. viijd.

[verso]

the xj of November 1585
Geyvin in reward to on[e] of my Lord of Bath['s] men
that caryd downe a quilt for a present gevin to

[644] Thomas Screven, many of whose letters to Rutland can be found in Hist MSS
Comm, *Rutland MSS*, i. The horse was probably the one Roger Manners was referring
to when he informed Rutland on 10 November, 'I told Lord Leicester that you have sent
him your best horse, which he accepted with many good words' (*ibid.*, 181). Leicester
appears to have returned to Leicester House on 8 November, gone to Richmond on the
9th, and returned again on the 10th. He wrote to the States-General from the Court on
the 9th (ARA, Eerste Afdeling, Regeringsarchieven I-92) and to Davison on the 10th
(PRO, SP84/5/50–1), but without giving his address.
[645] Dr Thomas Doyley, brother of Robert Doyley, MP. On 27 September Doyley was
about to depart for the Netherlands with letters from Leicester (*Leic. Corres.*, 6). On 14
October, either on his voyage over or his return, he was captured off Dunkirk by a
Spanish privateer and not freed until early November. This episode is narrated at length
in BL, Cotton MS Galba C VIII, fos. 184–6, 189, Doyley to Leicester, 12, 14, 23 Nov.
(the first and last are printed in Wright, ii, 266–71), and *CSPF, 1585–6*, 162–3. His servant
may have been carrying Leicester's letters of the 9th and 10th (see previous note) to the
Netherlands. In 1586 Doyley became a hostile critic of Leicester, possibly because he
was related to both Sir John Norris and Richard Huddleston (see n. 659 below).

him which he gave by your lordship's commandment
to the nurse and mydwyfe at the crysning of
the chyll the same daye above written at
Leaster House}   iijli.[646]

Geyvin by your lordship's commandment to
Smulkyn your lordship's futman which he gave
to the poore when your lordship deyned at
Doctor Loposes the same day}   xviijd.[647]

Gyven more to Smulkyn by your lordship's
commandment wich he gave to [the] poore betwene
Wansted and Leaster House the same daye}   ixd.

Payd by your lordship's commandment to Roger
Gyllans your lordship's bargeman [for] caryng
of your lordship deyverse tymes as from the
vj of November to the vij and viij and x daye
of November as apereth by the byll}   iijli. xijs.

Gyvin by your lordship's commandment to Mr
Cave which he gave to the poore at your
lordship's goyng from Doctors Lopose['s]
house to Wansted the same daye}   ijs.

Payd by your lordship's commandment to Sheperd
the mellener for ij pare of longe gloves for
your lordship at ixs. a pare the same daye}   xviijs.

Payd by your lordship's commandment to hym
for iij pare of gloves for your lordship more
at iijs. iiijd. the pare the same daye}   xs.

Payd by your lordship's commandment to my fealou
Ambrose* for necessary thynges wich he bought
for your lordship's heuse the same day}   xxiijs. vjd.

Payd by your lordship's commandment to Globe
your lordship's cutler for Mr Robart Dudley
for the gyllting of a raper and dagger for Mr
Robart Dudley and a velvat [s]cabard for the
raper and dagger and for ij gold handoles and
for a knyfe the same daye}   xixs. vjd.

---

[646] William Bourchier, 3rd Earl of Bath (1557?–1623). In 1601 Sir Thomas Cornwallis claimed that Leicester had arranged the annulment of Bath's first marriage to his (Cornwallis's) daughter (Hist MSS Comm, *Salisbury MSS*, xii, 223, to Sir Robert Cecil, 10 June 1601). Bath's second wife was Bedford's daughter Elizabeth.

[647] Dr Roderigo or Ruy Lopez, the Portuguese doctor and agent for Dom António executed in 1594. A correspondence with Leicester from 1580 survives and he had attended Dom António at Plymouth (BL, Harl. MS 1641, fo. 15v). His house may have been on the Wanstead estate, for the other entries on this page suggest that Leicester was on his way to Wanstead from Leicester House.

Summa Paginae: xli. vijs. iijd. [viijs. *deleted*]

[recto]

the xij of November 1585

Payd by your lordship's commandment for iiij
whit quellted nyghtcalps for your lordship at
iiij*s*. a pese the same daye}   xvjs.
Geyvin in reward to Mr Amys [h]is man for presenting
to your lordship a gyldin to your lordship at
Wansted the same daye [*sic*]}   xxs.[648]
Geyvin in reward to Robarts your lordship's futman
for caryng of leatters from Leaster House to the
Cort the same daye}   vjd.
Payd to a porter that brought rynwase rutes to
your lordship to Leaster House the same day by
your lordship's commandment}   iiijd.
Geyvin by your lordship's commandment to Robart
Addames* which Mr Browne ca[u]sed to be gevin at
Lester House the xiij of November}   xxs.
Payd by your lordship's commandment for ij
measse of meat for your lordship's sarvants
for a fornyght of the wardrop that is frome
the xxxj daye of October to the xiiij day of
November 1585}   lvjs. viijd.
Payd by your lordship's commandment to Sheperd
the mellener for perfermyng your lordship's
doblat and hose of leather the xiij of November 1585}   xxxs.
Payd by your lordship's commandment to Thomas
Eygley* wich he payd to Henry Pencost of Rychmon
for v hondred waight of match at iij*d*. a pound
the xvj of November 1585 at Leaster House the somme of}   vijli.
Payd by your lordship's commandment to Thomas
Bedwell wich he payd to your lordship's mat man
for lviij yeardes of mat and for laying of the
mat and caryge of it paye at Leaster House the
xvij of November as apereth by the byll}   iijli. xiiijs. vjd.
<Exam at what place>[ff]
Summa Paginae: xvijli. xviijs.

[648] Israel Amyce or Ames of Barking. He was involved in the purchase of Cranbrooke
in June, see n. 548 above.

[verso]

the xviij of November 1585
Payd by your lordship's commandment to Jhon
Ezard your lordship's sarvant ceuryng of Mr
Heigham which had a brokyn arame and Thomas
your honorse futman being hurt in the hepe
and for Perose leg being brokyn and for hyse
charges ateynding uppon your lordship at
deyvers tymes as apereth by hyse byll}   vli. vs. viijd.
Geyvin in reward to the Quenes majesties
playerse at Leaster House the xxth of November
1585 by your lordship's commandment the some of}   vli.[649]
Payd by your lordship's commandment to Kaneth
Leaus your lordship's sarvant which he payd
for ij torges for your lordship and wich he
gave by your lordship's commandment to on[e] that
mad cleane the stret when your lordship deyned
at Cossttomer Smethes the same daye}   iiijs. vjd.[650]
Payd by your lordship's commandment for iiij
yeardes and a halfe of sylke ryband for your
lordship's heuse at iijd. a yeard the same daye}   xiijd. ob.
Payd to Perou your lordship's Franch coke of
hys quarter's wages in prest the same daye by
your lordship's commandment}   ls.
Payd by your lordship's commandment to Mr
Powellwhell wich he payd for morynes neuleyned
for your lordship xxixth at vd. a pese and
borggonetts new leyned xiij the same daye}   xxjs. viijd.
Geyvin in reward to Mr Constabellse man at
Leaster House by your lordship's commandment
for caryng leatters downe into the contry
from your lordship from Leaster Hous the same daye} xxs.[651]
Payd by your lordship's commandment to Thomas
Bedwell wich he gave by your lordship's

[649] Although the previous entries suggest that Leicester was either at Leicester House or Wanstead between 10 and 20 November, he wrote to Shrewsbury from the Court on the 15th (Hist MSS Comm, *Bath MSS*, v, 63). On 18 November the Queen was at Whitehall on a brief visit from Richmond, and the London references after 15 November may be explained by his attendance on her there. Leicester wrote to Davison on the 18th (PRO, SP84/5/82–3), but did not give his address.

[650] See n. 205 above, presumably on the 20th.

[651] (Sir) Robert Constable of Flamborough (Yorks.) received livery in 1567 and was in Leicester's service in the early 1570s. The reference here may be to William Constable, who was in the Netherlands household in 1587.

commandment to Pryse of the Gard of Stratford
Lansone the same daye}   <a>^{gg} iijli.

Summa Paginae: xviijli. ijs. xjd. ob.

[recto]

the xx of November 1585
Gevyn to Mr Oxsenbryge wich he gave by your
lordship's commandment to the man's wyfe that
keppeth the orchard at Whithall the same daye}   vs.
Gevyn in reward wich Rychard Peper gave to the
poore by your lordship's commandment the same daye}   vjd.
Payd to Mr Barker which he gave by your
lordship's commandment to the nurse and mydwyfe
at the crysening of Syr Phelep Sednes chylld
the xxjth of November 1585}   vli.[652]
Payd to Batty your lordship's sarvant which he
payd to Wyllam Huckett for your lordship's diat
at the Cort the xxvjth of November 1585 for
xvij mont[h]es begenneng the fryst of Maye 1584
and endyng the last of September 1585 thes some
as douth apereth by hyse bylles}   xxijli. xiijs. jd.
Payd to Batty of hyse one bylles for charges
at the Cort for xvij montes begenneng the fryst
of Maye 1584 and ending the last daye of
September 1585 thys some the same daye by your
lordship's commandment}   vjli. xvs. ixd.
Payd by your lordship's commandment to Marten
de Coster for makyng your lordship's coch
xxvjth of November 1585 as apereth by the byll
the some of}   xxli. iiijs. vjd.
Your lordship lost in play at the Cort at
Rychmon the xxijth of November}   ijs.[653]
Payd by your lordship's commandment to Roger
Gyllans your lordship's waterman for carying
of your lordship deyverse tymes as from the
xijth of November to the xiij, xvth and xvj,
xvij and xviij, xix and xx daye of November as

---

[652] Sidney's daughter Elizabeth, who was christened on 15 November (R. Howell, *Sir Philip Sidney: The Shepherd Knight* (1968), p. 296), see also the reference to the Queen's christening present in BL, Harl. MS 1641, fo. 36. Sidney himself arrived in Flushing to take up his governorship on the 18th, see Appendix II.

[653] Assuming the date of this entry is correct, Leicester had returned to Court c. 21 November.

apereth by the byll the same day the some of 1585}   iiijli. xs.
Summa Paginae: lixli. xs. xd. [ixd. ob. *deleted*]

[verso]

the xxiiijth of November 1585
Payd by your lordship's commandment to Rychard
Warner ferreman at Grenewigh for the ferying
over of your lordship's horsses at sondrey
tymes at Grenewigh from the x daye of Desember
1584 to the xxth of October 1585 by the
commandment of Mr Blunt gentellman of your
lordship's horsses as apereth by the byll the
some of}   vli.
Gevyn in reward to my fealow Pichford wich he
gave by your lordship's commandment to one
that presented to your lordship at Rychmon
saddell clothes the same daye}   xxs.
Gevyn in reward to Dampard my lades futman by
your lordship's commandment for bryn[g]ing
leatters to your lordship to the Cort at Rychmon
from Leaster House the same daye}   vs.
Payd by your lordship's commandment for x horsses
ferying over the water at Putney the same daye}   xd.[654]
Gevyn in reward to the poor at Putney the same day
by your lordship's commandment}   vjd.
Gevyn in reward to a Skoch man of Syr Pheleps
Sednes by your lordship's commandment at [h]is
joing [*sic*] into [S]cotland from Leaster house
the xxvj of November}   xli.[655]
<note exam before>[hh]
Payd to Gylles Homerstone for a case for a
crosbo for your lordship and crosbo stryngs and
other thyngs for your lordship's heuse as
apereth by hyse byll}   vijs. viijd.
Payd by your lordship's commandment to Mr Bland
the Quenes skynner in Polles Chyrch yeard for
iiij leusardes skynes for your lordship's heuse

[654] This would appear to be 24 November. For Leicester's movements from this point
until his arrival in Flushing, see Appendix II.

[655] There are several earlier references to Sidney's Scottish servant, but his identity and
errand are unknown. James VI wrote to Leicester on 20 December in the belief that he
was still in England, but this does not appear to be an answer to a letter sent on this
occasion (BL, Cotton MS Caligula C IX, fo. 162; BL, Add. MS 23240, fo. 29, is a draft).

the xxvj of November 1585 the some of}   xxli.
      Summa Paginae: xxxvjli. xiiijs.

[recto]

        the xxvj of November 1585
Payd by your lordship's commandment to Cammelea
wich he payd for a hat for yong Mr Robart Dudley
the same daye}   ls.
Gevyn in reward to Mr Flud which he gave by your
lordship's commandment to Mr Watson's man the
same daye}   xxs.[656]
Gevyn in reward to Mr Flud wich he gave the
same [day] mor by your lordship's commandment
to my Lord of Penbrok's bargeman}   vjs. viijd.
Gevyn in reward to [a] man of my Lord of Darbes
that Mr Knolles brought to your lordship to
Leaster House the xxvijth of November 1585 by
your lordship's commandment the somme of}   xli.[657]
Payd by your lordship's commandment for iij
dreyfates and on[e] chest for the callerverse and
armery and for copper's worke and ij hondred
of nalles the same daye}   xxiijs.
Gevyn in reward wich yong Mr Baptiste gave by
your lordship's commandment to my Lord Norreses
man for pressenting of iij horsses to your
lordship at Leaster House the same daye}   xls.[658]
Gevyn in reward wich yong Mr Baptyste gave the
same daye mor by your lordship's commandment to
Mr Hurllstones man for presenting ij horsses to
your lordship at Leaster House}   xxxs.[659]
Payd by your lordship's commandment to Roger
Gyllans your lordship's bargeman for carying

[656] Probably Edward Watson (1549–1617) of Rockingham, Northants., MP. He served in the Netherlands in 1586.

[657] Possibly for the expenses of the 'fyfteen tall and stowt Lancashyre Laddes my countriemen presented to my Lord of Leycester by my Lord of Darby, to serve in the Low Countries as archers' (Hist MSS Comm, *Rutland MSS*, i, 184, T. Walmesley to Rutland, 2 Dec.). For the raising of these archers, see JRL, Leigh of Lyme Corres., folder 1, Derby to Sir Piers Leigh, 23 Oct. 1585. Leicester also tried to obtain archers from Shrewsbury, see his letter of 15 Nov., n. 649 above.

[658] Young Mr Baptist was probably Francis Castilion, see n. 414 above. For Lord Norris, see n. 148.

[659] Probably Richard Huddleston (c.1535–1589), MP, treasurer at war in the Netherlands 1585–7.

of your lordship and ateandyng of your lordship
deyverse tymes as from the xxj of November to the
xxijth, xxiijth, xxiiijth and the xxvth daye of
November 1585 as apereth by the byll}   iiijli. vijs.
Payd by your lordship's commandment for ij
measse of meat for your lordship's sarvants of
the wardrop for a fornyght that is from the
xiiij daye of November to the xxviij daye of
November 1585}   lvjs. viijs.

Summa Paginae: xxvli. xiijs. iiijd.

[verso]

the xxviij of November 1585

Gevyn in reward to Humfrey Adlynton your
lordship's futman which he gave by your lordship's
commandment to the poore at your lordship's
comyng from Rychmon the same daye}   xxijd.
Payd to my fealou Wyllam Pichford wich he payd
for ij elles iij quarters of taffetey for xxiiij
bages for your lordship's heuse and for lace
for them the same day}   xlijs. vjd.
Gevyn in reward by your lordship's commandment
to the tumbelerse that tumbled before your
lordship at Leaster Hous the xxvj of November
1585}   vjli. xiijs. iiijd.
Gevyn in reward to Mr Worley at the Cort at
Rychmon by your lordship's commandment the
xxviijth of November}   xls.
Gevyn in reward by your lordship's commandment
to a boy of my Lord Chamberlanse that brought
a pese of swettewood to your lordship to Leaster
House the xxix of November}   vs.
Gevyn in reward to the Quenese trumpeterse that
sownded before your lordship at Leaster House
the same daye by your lordship's commandment
the some of}   xli.
Payd by your lordship's commandment to Roger
Gyllans your lordship's waterman for caryng
your lordship from Leaster House to Barnellmes
the same daye}   xvs.
Gevyn in reward to the waterman the same day
by your lordship's commandment}   vs.
Gevyn in reward by your lordship's commandment

to Jacobe the armer of Grenewigh for bryng armer
to your lordship from Sir Chrystoper Hattonse
to Leaster House the xxix of November 1585}   vli.
        Summa Paginae: xxvijli. ijs. viijd.

[recto]

       the second of Desember 1585
Payd by your lordship's commandment to
Fardeynando your lordship's sarvant of his
quarter's wages from Mykellmas to Chris[t]mas
last past 1585}   ls.
Gevyn in reward to hym the same daye at Leaster
House by your lordship's commandment the some of}   ls.
Payd to my fealou Pichford which he payd by
your lordship's commandment for a case for a[n]
earthen pott for your lordship the same daye}   ijs. vjd.
Payd to Mr Grotrege by your lordship's commandment
at Leaster House the same daye for fyne oylles
for your lordship}   iiijli. xs.
Gevyn in reward to Mr Blunt gentelman of your
lordship's horse wich he gave by your lordship's
to on[e] Terrell Syr Christopher Hatton's man for
bryng ij armarse to yow from Syr Christopher
Hatton's to Leaster House to your
lordship the ij day of Desember 1585 the some of}   xxli.
Payd by your lordship's commandment the same
daye for seayllyng wax for your lordship}   iijs.
Payd to Mr Edward Blunt by your lordship's
commandment wich he gave to on[e] of Syr John
Pettrse men for presenting a horse to your
lordship at Leaster House the same daye}   xls.[660]
Payd to Mr Edward Blunt more the same daye wich
he gave by your lordship's commandment to Lackles
wyfe the Recorder full [sic] at Leaster [House]
for presenting poddings to yow at Leaster House
the same daye}   xs.
Paye by your lordship's commandment for ij quartes
of enke and halfe a peynt for your lordship's
heuse at viijd. the same daye}   iijs.

---

[660] Sir John Petre (1549–1613), MP, son of Sir William Petre (see n. 300 above). Leicester
stayed with him at Ingatestone Hall en route to Harwich, see pp. 343–4 and Appendix
II.

Payd by your lordship's commandment to Roger
Gyllans your lordship's barge[man] for ateanding
at Leaster House at your lordship commandment
the [*blank*] daye of December 1585}   ixs.
                Summa Paginae: xxxijli. xvijs. vjd.

[verso]

                the iij of December 1585
Payd by your lordship's commandment to Thomas
Sheppard mellener for a bage of fustan for your
lordship tremmed with sylk stryngs and sylk
tassells at [*blank*] and iij pare of glovese
for your lordship at iijs. a pare}   xixs.
Payd for a pare of ryting tabellse for your
lordship the same daye by your lordship's
commandment}   xijd.
Gevyn in reward wich Mr Dudley gave by your
lordship's commandment to Hobsones man of the
Toure for presenting tou horlbardes to your
lordship at Leaster House the same daye}   xs.
Payd to Cooke your lordship's haberdasser by
your lordship's commandment for large knyt sylk
neyghtcapes leyned with onshorne vellet for
your lordship at xijs. a pese and iij vellet
neyght capes at viijs. a pese and viij thike
sylk night capes at vijs. a pese, wich comes to}   vli. xvjs.
                Suma: vijli. vjs.
                [Suma Totalis} *deleted*]
Payd by your lordship's commandment to Edward
Willperforse which he cared to the cort to my
Ladey Layton the iij day of <u>December</u> 1585}   xlli.
<falce dated I think>[ii]
Payd by your lordship's commandment to Nicaches
for xij pare of vervelles at xijd. a pare and
ij pinse at xijd. a pyn the same daye}   xiiijs.
Payd by your lordship's commandment to Nycolase
Harford yong Mr Robart Dudles man for necessary
thynges which he hat[h] layd out for yong Mr
Robart Dudley as apereth by the byll the same daye}   iijli. xvijs.
<Exam how much this fellow hath rec>[ij]
                Summa Paginae: ljli. xvijs.

[recto]

the iiij of December 1585

Payd by your lordship's commandment for iiij
whyt selke neyght capes for your lordship at
iiijs. a pese}   xvjs.

Gevyn by your lordship's commandment to Mr
Willam Herell at Leaster House the same daye
above written the somm of}   xxxli.[661]

Gevyn by your lordship's commandment to Mr
Candyse at Leaster House the same daye more
the some of}   xxxli.

Payd by your lordship's commandment to your
lordship's playerse at ther goyng to the seaye
from Leaster House the same daye}   vjli.[662]

Gevyn by your lordship's commandment to Thomase
Leynt of Gloster that shold have playd uppon
the vergenollds at Leaster House the same daye}   iijli. vjs. viijd.

Gevyn by your lordship's commandment to Nycolase
Harford at Leaster House yong Mr Robart Dudles
man at your lordship's goyng awaye from Leaster
House the same daye}   xls.

Payd by your lordship's commandment to your
lordship's jewler for a chayne of gold for
your lordship at Leaster House as apereth by
the byll the iiij daye of December 1585
the some of}   lijli.
<with pomander>kk

Gevyn by your lordship's commandment to John
Robarts your lordship's futman which he gave
to the poor by your lordship's commandment
in London at your goyng to my lordes mares to
dener the same daye}   ijs.[663]

---

[661] See n. 493 above. The purpose of this payment is unclear. Herle later joined Leicester in the Netherlands (PRO, SP12/186/35, Herle to Walsingham, 29 Jan. 1586) and was employed on an embassy to the Count of East Friesland and Emden in the spring of 1586.

[662] Like many members of his 'train' (see Appendix II) the players preceded him to the Netherlands. For their tour, see MacLean, 'Leicester and the Evelyns', 490–1.

[663] Sir Wolstan Dixie, probably on 2 December. Dixie was the leading subscriber to the loan of £17,600 that Leicester raised from a consortium of London merchants by mortgaging the lordship of Denbigh, the indenture for which was signed on 2 December, see Appendix II. The extent to which he was dependent on the London merchant community explains why he was so keen to inform them of his successful reception in the Netherlands, see *Leic. Corres.*, 84–5, to the lord mayor and aldermen of London, 3 Feb. 1586.

Summa Paginae: Cxxiiijli. iiijs. viijd.[ll]

[verso]

the v of December 1585

Payd for vj pare of spactakells for your lordship at xij*d*. a pare}	vjs.
Gevin to Smetson* your lordship's coke to his wyfe of his quarter's wages Myckellmas to Cristmas by your lordship's commandment at [h]is going into Flanders the same day}	xls.
Gevin by your lordship's commandment to Perou your lordship's Fraynch coke at Leaster House the same daye}	iijli.
Payd for iij queare of fyne whit paper for your lordship the same daye}	js.
Gevin to my Lady Layton's man for bring[ing] a letter to Leaster House the same daye}	xs.
Payd by your lordship's commandment to Roger Gyllans your lordship's barg man for carring your lordship from Leaster Hous to my Lord Chambrlyn's and bacagan to Leaster Hous and to Ratlefe the same daye}	xijs.
Gevin in reward to the poste that broght leatters to your lordship from Mr Sectary's to Wansted to your lordship the vj of December 1585}	vs.[664]
Gevin in reward to Rychard Hodgs Mr Wincoll's man by your lordship's commandment for presenting horsses to your lordship at Wansted the same day} <quaere of Blount what became of the horses etc>[mm]	xli.[665]
Gevin in reward to Mr Treseur's futman for bring letters from the Cort to Wansted to your lordship the same daye by your lordship's commandment}	xs.[666]
Gevin in reward to a poore man by your lordship's commandment that dellys in a tree at Wansted that broght your lordship a coppell of capins the same daye}	xs.

Summa Paginae: xvijli. xiiijs.

---

[664] See Appendix II.
[665] Probably Isaac Wincoll, who served in the Netherlands.
[666] Sir Francis Knollys.

[recto]

the vj of December 1585

Gevin in reward to Robarts* the fysserman at Wansted the same daye}	xs.
Gevin in reward to Mr Warecopes boy for presenting wodcoks to your lordship at Wansted the same daye}	iijs. iiijd.
Gevin in reward to Ramsey your lordship's sarvant at Wansted the same daye}	vli.
Gevin to on[e] that went for your lordship's clock to Ratlefe from Leaster House the same daye}	xijd.
Gevin to Mr Thomas Dudley the wich he gave by your lordship's commandment to Mr Polewhell at Wansted the vij of Desember 1585 the some of}	xlli.
Gevin to Mister Doctor Holand at Wansted the same daye by your lordship's commandment the some of}	vli.[667]
Gevin in reward to the tou warners at Wansted the same daye by your lordship's commandment}	xxs.
Gevin to yong Mosgrave in reward that wayted on my Lord of Huntington at Wansted the same day by your lordship's commandment}	xs.
Payd to Goody Bocacket by your lordship's commandment at Wansted for wassing the same daye}	xijs.
Gevin to Mr Gylles Trasy by your lordship's commandment at Syr John Pettres at his ryding post to the Cort and bacagan to Harrig the viij of December}	iijli.[668]
Payd to Mr Rychard Browne at Syr Jhon Petter's at his goyng from Syr John Petter's to Harrige to mak provittione for your lordship the same daye}	xxli.

<exam the bills etc>[nn]

Summa Paginae: lxxvli. vs. iiijd.

[verso]

the viij of December 1585

Gevin by your lordship's commandment to a post that brought leatters to your lordship by the waye to Syr John Petter's}	ijs.
Gevin to Mr Grodregs by your lordship's commandment at Syr John Petter's the same daye	

[667] See n. 486 above.
[668] See n. 660 above and Appendix II.

the some of}   xxli.
Gevin to Mr Bulunt [*sic*] the wich
he gave to the stabells at Syr John Petter's by
your lordship's commandment}   xxs.
Gevin in reward to the offesers at Syr Jhon
Pettr's when your lordship lay ther the same daye}   xls.
Gevin in reward by your lordship's commandment
to Brownes wyfe of Che[l]msfordes the same daye}   xs.
Payd at Che[l]m[s]ford the same daye for feyre
and wyne when your lordship leyted to mak you redy}   vijs.
Payd by your lordship's commandment to Hary
Strynger wich he gave to Syr John Petter's
porter and to a man of Cholchester that carred
letters by nyght to Harrig the same day}   xs.
Gevin in reward to the offercs at Syr Thomas
Leucosses when your lordship lay ther the ix
of December 1585}   xls.[669]
Gevyn by your lordship's commandment to Mr
Semmell* wich he gave for the charges of Captyn
Twitty and xij of his company for ther charges
from Colchester to Flyssing as apereth by the
byll the some of}   vli. xiiijs. vjd.[670]
Payd by your lordship's commandment to Mr Blunt
gentellman of your lordship's horsses wich he
payd for the hyre of horsses from London to
Harrig for your lordship when your lordship
went into Flanders as apereth by his byll the
ix of December 1585}   xxvijli.
                    Summa Paginae: lixli. iijs. vjd.

[recto]

                    the x of December 1585
Gevyn in reward to Harry Strynger and Edward
Stoune the Quenes futmen at Harrig the same day}   xli.
Gevyn in reward to Mr Blunt gentellman of your
lordship's horsses wich he gave by your lordship's
commandment to a stranger at Harrig the same

---

[669] Leicester had knighted Lucas together with Sir John Cutts (n. 579) in 1571. See also Appendix II.

[670] William Twetty or Tutty, an officer of the garrison of Berwick since 1558, who had also served at Le Havre in 1562–3. In 1586 he was appointed acting governor of Bergen-op-Zoom, and then deputy to Willoughby after his appointment there.

daye the som of}   xli.
Gevyn in reward to Mr Dodson my Lord Admerrall's
man by your lordship's commandment at Harrig
the same daye}   iijli.
Gevyn in reward to Homfrey Coll your lordship's
sarvant by your lordship's commandment at Harrig
the same daye}   iijli.
Payd by your lordship's commandment to the
sumtermen for ther charges carring your lordship's
trunks from London to Harrig the same daye}   lis. ixd.
Gevyn by your lordship's commandment to the
watermen that brought your lordship from Harrig
into the shep in the pinnes the xj of December 1585}   xxxs.[671]
Payd to Mr Foskeu which he lent your lordship
in the shep wich your lordship lost in play
the same daye}   vs.[672]
Payd to a boye in the shep that did nesaris
things for your lordship in the shep the same daye}   xijd.
Payd to my fealou Robart Pichfork wich he payd
for the carig of your lordship's stoufe from
Harig to the shep the same daye}   iiijs.
Gevyn in reward at Flyssing when your lordship
lay ther the xiij of December to the Duch trompeters}   vli.[673]
Gevyn in reward the same daye at Flyssing to
[a] blynd Duch harper at your lordship's commandment}   xs.
                   Summa Paginae: xxxvjli. js. ixd.

[verso]

                   the xiij of December 1585
Payd for the carrig of your lordship's stoufe
from the brig at Flissing to your lordship's
loging and bacagan to the hoye when your
lordship went to Meddellborow the same daye}   vs.[674]
Payd by your lordship's commandment at Amserdam
for vj yeardese of blacke satten at xijs. a
yeard which your lordship gave the gentellwoman
of the house when your lordship lay ther the

[671] See Appendix II.
[672] Probably Francis Fortescue (c. 1563–1624), MP, son of Sir John (see n. 6), who served in the Netherlands.
[673] See Appendix II.
[674] See Appendix II.

xxj of March}   iijli. xijs.[675]

Geyven in reward the same daye by your lordship's
commandment to the sarvantes of the hous}   xxs.

Payd to Jhon Turcke* your lordship's servant
wich he gave by your lordship's commandment to
the bargemen at Amserdam that brought your
lordship into the shepe the same daye from your
lordship's loging}   xxs.

Gevin in reward to the skepper by your lordship's
commandment that brought your lordship from
Amserdam to [N]ardyn the same daye}   xxs.[676]

Gevin to him at Nardyn by your lordship's
commandment that mad an oracion to your
lordship ther the xxij of March}   xxs.

Gevin in reward to xvj poore folke the same
daye at Nardyn by your lordship's commandment}   xs.

Payd to Doctor James which he gave by your
lordship's commandment to iiij drommers at
Nardyn the same daye}   xls.

Payd to Doctor James which he gave more the
same daye by your lordship's commandment to a
[s?]coller at Nardyn when your lordship lay ther}   xs.

Payd to Houmfry your lordship's futman which
he gave to tow ospetalls betext Nardyn and
Utrick by your lordship's commandment the xxiij
of March}   xjs.

                    Summa Paginae: xjli. viijs.

[recto]

                    the xxiij of March 158[*tear*]

Gevin in reward by your lordship's commandment
to labring men that mendid the heyway betext
Nardyn and Utrick}   ijs.

Gevin to a poore old man by your lordship's
commandment the same daye by the waye}   vjd.

---

[675] This entry follows the preceding one directly. For the remainder of December and
January see the entries from the 1585–7 disbursement book. Leicester spent the whole of
February at the Hague. On 1 March he went to Leiden, then Haarlem (the 3rd) and
then Amsterdam (the 10th), where he remained until the 21st. As noted in the Introduction,
references to his movements are drawn from the journal of Dr John James (BL, Add.
MS 48014, fos. 149–64v), and the dates are those of the Julian calendar.

[676] Leicester went from Amsterdam to Naarden on 21 March and then to Utrecht on
the 22nd.

Payd to Mr Thomas Webbe wich he gave by your
lordship's commandment to the musitens of
Utrick the xxiiij of March}   xls.[677]
Payd to Robart Pichford your lordship's sarvant
wich he gave by your lordship's commandment to
the drommers at Utrick the xxiiij of March 1585}   xxxs.
Payd to John Borne* your lordship's sarvant
wich he payd for sledes to cary your lordship's
stoufe at Amserdam and Utrick the xxj and xxij
of March}   vjs. ijd.
Gevin to a poore man by your lordship's commandment
that caled lick birds to your lordship in your
lordship's chamber a[t] Utrick the xxv of March 1586}   vs.
Gevin to yong Mr Dudley by your lordship's
commandment at Utrick the xxvj of March}   ls.
Payd to Steven Jhonson your lordship's sarvant
wich he gave by your lordship's commandment to
ix Duch trumpeters that did soundid [sic] to
your lordship the same daye at Utrick}   iijli.
Gevin to Pero your lordship's Frances coke by
your lordship's commandment at Utrick the xxviij of March}   xls.
Payd to Mr Heanry Goodyer which he payd for vj
waggons for carige of your lordship's hollbard
gard from Leyden to Harlam the iij of March at
vjs. a waggon by your lordship's commandment}   xxxvjs.[678]
Payd to Mr Henry Goodyer wich he payd by your
lordship's commandment to the soulders of Mr
Brownes and Mr Treaseris Hollstones bands at
Nardyn the xxj of March}   vli.[679]

Summa Paginae: xviijli. ixs. vijd.

[verso]

[677] Thomas Webbe, clerk of the cheque to the Netherlands army in 1586 (PRO, SP15/29/222). Webbe was a member of the Netherlands household in 1587 and attended Leicester's funeral. He was a former servant of the Earl of Sussex, see BL, Cotton MS Titus B VII, fo. 79, John North to Leicester, 1 Dec. 1587.

[678] (Sir) Henry Goodere (1534–95), of Polesworth, Wars., MP, captain of Leicester's guard in 1586. Goodere attended both Sidney's and Leicester's funerals. For his earlier relations with Leicester, see 'West Midlands', 42–3, and 'House of Commons', 222ff.

[679] Hollestone is Richard Huddleston (see n. 659 above). Mr Browne is probably (Sir) William Browne (d. 1611), lieutenant of Robert Sidney's company and from 1597 his lieutenant-governor at Flushing, see M.V. Hay, *The Life of Robert Sidney, Earl of Leicester (1563–1626)* (Washington D.C., 1984), pp. 131–2.

the xxxj of March 1586

Payd to Mr Henry Goodyear wich he gave by your lordship's commandment to a blynd man that playd uppon the orgynes at Nardyn the same daye when your lordship was ther the xxj of March}	xs.
Payd to one John Gylles marchant of Anwarp for a pare of perfumed gloves for your lordship at Utrick the xxxj of March}	xls.
Geven to the corne cotter by your lordship's commandment at Utricke the same day}	xs.
Geven to Ramsey your lordship's sarvant at Utrick by your lordship's commandment the frist daye of Aprell}	vli.
Payd to Mr Gillpin which he gave by your lordship's commandment to one ymployed in searves at Utrick the second of Aprell the some of} <a>	xli.[680]
Geven to Thomas Symmell by your lordship's commandment at Utrick the second day of Aprell 1586}	iijli.
Gevin by your lordship's commandment to an ynggener at Utrick for bring[ing] plats to your lordship the xth of Aprell the some of}	xli.
Gevin by your lordship's commandment to on[e] Jhon Dudley Syr Thomas Sherly's man for bring[ing] letters to your lordship out of England and caring letters bacagan from your lordship into England the xiiij of Aprell at Utrick}	xls.[681]

Summa Paginae: xxxiijli.

[recto]

xxvjth of Maye 1586[682]

[680] Leicester remained at Utrecht between 22 March and 18 April, preparing for the investment of Nijmegen, see his letter to the Privy Council, 27 March (*Leic. Corres.*, 189. Curiously, he states here that he only spent four or five days at Amsterdam after the 10th). For George Gilpin, see n. 323 above; Leicester appointed him secretary to the Council of State (Raad van State) in March, see *CSPF, 1585–6*, 466, Gilpin to Burghley, 21 March.

[681] No official correspondence from Leicester for the period 7–11 April can be traced, nor does Dudley appear among the messengers paid by the Treasurer of the Chamber (BL, Harl. MS 1641); these were probably private letters. It might be noted that all his correspondence with his wife has disappeared.

[682] The gap in the account between 14 April and 26 May 1586 is unexplained. There are two entries surviving from the 1585–7 disbursement book for this period, see p. 374 below. On 18–20 April Leicester paid a brief visit to Amersfoort from Utrecht and then moved there on 2 May. On 7 May he left Amersfoort for Arnhem where 'the camp' (the field army) was assembled. On 11 May the camp advanced on Nijmegen and began the

Payd by your lordship's commandment to Mr William
Read sargant mayger in prest which he payd to
iiij corp[o]ralls of the feeld at Arnam the some of} <a>   xxli.[683]
Payd to Mr Webbe by your lordship's commandment
in prest at his goinge with Mr Candyse from Arnam
to Laydyn the xxvij of Maye 1586}   xli.
Payd to Mr William Leswood* by your lordship's
commandment for his charges goinge to Meddellborow
for your lordship's armar and comming bacagan
to Arnam as apereth by his byll the same daye}   xljs. iiijd.
Payd to Mr Heyden wich he gave by your lordship's
commandment to the shuldyears that came from
the enymyse the same daye at Arnam}   xxs.
Payd to him more the same tyme which he gave
by your lordship's commandment to the men that
came to gard the same shuldyrs}   vs.
Geven by your lordship's commandment to the
sargant mayger of Arnam for bringe viij shouldyears
to your lordship frome the enymyse at Grave
the same daye}   xls.
Geven to Mr Kellygray wich he gave by your
lordship's commandment to the viij shuldyrse
at Arnam the same tyme}   xxs.[684]
Payd by your lordship's commandment to Mr
Borgrave* master of the requestes for his
quarterwages of Medsomer quarter next coming
at Arnam the xxviijth of May 1586 the some of}   xxvli.
      Summa Paginae: lxjli. vjs. iiijd.

investment; this led to the capture of the sconce of Nijmegen on the 20th and the sconce
of Berkshof on the 25th.

[683] Sir William Reade (d. 1604), MP. Reade had been an officer of the Berwick garrison
since 1558 and may possibly have been an officer of the Calais garrison earlier. He served
in the 1560 Scottish campaign, at Le Havre in 1562–3, and was appointed sergeant-
major of the foot in 1586. Leicester's employment of such elderly officers as Reade and
Twetty (see n. 670 above) in senior positions became the object of derision on the part
of John Norris and his friends. According to Leicester (BL, Add. MS 48127, fos. 22v–3),
Norris called Reade 'K[ing] H[enry] the 8['s] man'.

[684] (Sir) Henry Killigrew (1528–1603), MP, who had been appointed one of the two
English members of the Council of State. Killigrew had been in the household of the
Duke of Northumberland and was one of Leicester's oldest followers, see 'Dudley
Clientèle', pp. 242, 245, 247, and A.C. Miller, *Sir Henry Killigrew: Elizabethan Soldier and
Diplomat* (Leicester, 1963). On 1 October 1588 he asked Walsingham for leave from the
Netherlands 'that I may yield him the last service and testimony of my devotion at his
funerals' (PRO, SP84/27/1). The Mr Killegrave given livery in 1567 was his brother
William (d. 1622), MP, who had also received livery in 1562 (DP Box V, fo. 154v).

[verso]

the xxviijth of Maye 1586
Payd by your lordship's commandment to William
Blaknall* in prest his holl pay that was dew
unto him from the xth of January to this daye
wich is the xxviij of May in foll payment of
his acounts as apereth by the byll at his going
into England from Arnam the xxviijth of May}　　　xiijli. js. iijd.
Geven by your lordship's commandment to old
William Williams* of your lordship's
cho[lere *deleted*] your lordship's sarvant at
Arnam the xxixth of Maye}　　　xs.
Geven by your lordship's commandment the same
day to on[e] Rychard Sawyear a poore man that had
a great cold at Arnam}　　　ijs.
Geven to on[e] John Graye a sargant by your
lordship's commandment at Arnam the xxixth of
May 1586 the som of}　　　vli.
Geven by your lordship's commandment to my Lord
North wich he gave to a man of Syr Skink's for
bring[ing]e word from Grave to your lordship at
Arnam the same daye}　　　lijs.[685]
Delyvered by your lordship's commandment to
Mr Meyell Darmar in prest at Arnam at his goinge
into England the xxixth of May 1586}　　<a>　　lli.[686]
Payd by your lordship's commandment to William
Massy* kepper of your lordship's gre[yho]unds
for ther meat on week twelve shellings the xxixth
of May at Arnam}　　　xijs.

[685] Sir Martin Schenk (d. 1589), who had commanded the forces of Archbishop
Truchsess (see n. 741 below) in the war for Cologne in 1583. He had been won over by
the Prince of Parma in 1584 and then by the Dutch in the summer of 1585. Schenk
controlled the rump of the territories of the archbishopric on the lower Rhine (see n.
696 below) and was given command of the local forces on the eastern frontier of the
United Provinces. Leicester knighted him on 23 April 1586. On 28 May Leicester
informed Elizabeth of Parma's investment of Grave (*CSPF, 1585–6*, 680). The town had
actually surrendered on that day, but this was not known until 30 May.

[686] Michael Dormer, who commanded a company of horse in 1586. He returned to
England to raise a further voluntary company in Oxfordshire, see *CSPF, 1586–7*, 1,
Leicester to Walsingham, 1 June 1586. A number of the following entries are to payments
for the expenses of officers sent to raise further companies in England in 1586, a scheme
of Leicester's to expand the English contingent. Leicester claimed that the States-General
had agreed to pay for them, an issue that was to cause great controversy later in the
year.

Payd by your lordship's commandment the same
daye to Conrod Duck kepper of your lordship's
hounds for thear meat one week fortene shellings}   xiiijs.
Payd to Mr Gorge Harvey* steward of your lordship's
house by your lordship's commandment in prest
for the charges of your lordship's house at Arnam
the xxx of Maye 1586}   xlli.
> Summa Paginae: Cxijli. xjs. iijd.ᵒᵒ

[recto]

> the xxxth of Maye 1586

Payd to Steaven Johnson of the wardrop your
lordship's sarvant by your lordship's commandment
for the heyre of a waggon from Arnam to Utrick
and bacagan from Utrick to Arnam to feth a
tronk of aparell and other thinges for your
lordship and for his o[w]ne charges and gevin to
the shuldyers that gardid him from Waggenar
to Arnam the same daye}   xls.
Geven to Mr Wake* which he gave by your lordship's
commandment to Thomas Kinge* on[e] of your lordship's
mussycions to by him aparell at Arnam the same day}   xls.
Geven to Robart Browene* by your lordship's
commandment on[e] of your lordship's mussyciones
at his going into England from Arnam the same daye}   xls.
Geven to old Roberts fyssrman by your lordship's
commandment the same daye at Arnam}   xs.
Paid to Mr Henry Goodyear wich he payd by your
lordship's commandment to the provest of Arnam
for the charges of xxvth presoners the same
daye at Arnam}   iijli.
Geven to Leause Mr Butler's man by your lordship's
commandment at Arnam the same daye}   xs.[687]
Payd to Mr George Brock by your lordship's
commandment wich he [paid] for on[e] hondred
shrits at ijs. vjd. a shrit comes to xijli. xs.,
on hondrd doblats of stronge canvas at iiijs.
xd. a pese comes to xxiiijli. iijs. iiijd.,
on[e] hondred pare of canvas hose at iiijs. jd.
a pare comes to xxli. viijs. iiijd., payd at
Arnam the xxx of Maye 1586 the som of}   lvijli. xxd.

---

[687] Philip Butler, see n. 430 above.

Delyvred by your lordship's commandment to my
Lord North wich[PP] he gave to Captayn Gronnat
wich he gave to the spyrates [*sic*] at Arnam
the xxxjth of Maye 1586}   vli.
                    Summa Paginae: lxxijli. xxd.

[verso]

                         the xxxj of Maye 1586
Geven by your lordship's commandment to Mr
Gorge clark of your lordship's checke wich he
gave to a shudger that lost his arme at Nemegam
skonce the same daye}   xs.[688]
Geven by your lordship's commandment to on[e]
William Moufe on[e] of my Lord of Essxt's men for
going over the water at Nemegam the same daye
at Arnam}   xxs.
Geven the same daye at Arnem to Leaus Mr Butler's
man by your lordship's commandment}   xs.
Payd to Mr Fen your lordship's preachear at
Arnam the same daye wiche he gave to the poore
by your lordship's commandment}   xls.[689]
Payd to Mr George Morton by your lordship's
commandment in prest at Arnam the xxxjth of Maye
at his going into England}   xxxli.[690]
Delyvered to Mr Grotreges by your lordship's
commandment the wich he gave to Mr Edward Yorke
the same day at Arnam}   xli.[691]
Geven by your lordship's commandment to iiij

[688] Probably on 20 May when the Nijmegen sconce was assaulted (see n. 682 above).

[689] Humphrey Fenn, see n. 593 above.

[690] George Morton (1540–?), MP. He carried letters to England (see *CSPF, 1586–7*, 48,
T. Doyley to Burghley, 24 June), but may have been sent to raise a voluntary company.
He served in the Netherlands again after 1589.

[691] Three sons of Sir John York (see n. 27 above) served in the Netherlands in 1586:
Edward, Edmund and the notorious Rowland. Edward commanded a company in the
original contingent sent over in the summer of 1585, but appears to have surrendered it
and returned to England by April 1586, possibly to raise a voluntary company. Edmund
had been in Leicester's service previously (see BL, Cotton MS Caligula E VII, fo. 138,
York to A. Atye, 7 Aug. [1579], and *CSPF, 1584–5*, 779, to Walsingham, 26 July 1584); he
held the office variously described as quartermaster-general or forage-master of the army
in 1586 (PRO, SP15/29/336; *CSPF, 1586–7*, 111), and attended Leicester's funeral. The
Edward York referred to here and below was probably Edmund, for the names were
commonly elided. Rowland was still in England (see *Leic. Corres.*, 305, Leicester to
Walsingham, 10 June) and did not reach the army until July.

of my Lords Stranges musicions at Arnam the
first daye of June 1586}   xxs.
Payd to Mr Henry Goodyear in prest at Arnam the
frist daye of June 1586 the som of}   \<a\>   xxli.
Payd to Mr Rychard Browne by your lordship's
commandment wich he gave to your lordship's
playears at Arnam at ther going to the Kinges
of Denmark's the same daye}   \<B\>   vli.[692]
Geven to Mr Gorge Brock by your lordship's
commandment wich he gave to a poore man betext
the camp at Nemegam and Arnam that dessyred a
paspo[r]t of your lordship the same daye}   vs.[693]
Geven by your lordship's commandment to Mr York
wich he gave to tow men that gave to your
lordship a stan[d]ard at the camp at Nemegam,
your lordship granted them a commission the same day}   xs.
                 Summa Paginae: lxxli. xvs.

[recto]

                    ij of June 1586
Gevin to Mr Heyam by your lordship's commandment
at his being lame at the camp at Nemegam at his
going from thens to Arnam the same daye}   xls.
Payd to Mr William Goodyeare wich he payd by
your lordship's commandment to the marshall for
the charges of the poore prisoners at the remove
of them from Utrick to Arnam the same daye}   iijli. xvs.[694]
Geven by your lordship's commandment to Smolkin
your lordship's futman the same daye at the
campe at his going to Syr Thomas Heneages to Dorte}   xs.[695]
Geven by your lordship's commandment to Docter
James wich he gave to on[e] that came to your

---

[692] For the players' tour in Denmark, see MacLean, 'Leicester and the Evelyns', 491–2. See also the introduction, p. 11, for the possible significance of this entry to the Halliwell-Phillipps' transcriptions.

[693] Leicester went to the camp from Arnhem on 1 June.

[694] Henry Goodere's brother, who was a bearer of the body at Leicester's funeral. The prisoners were probably soldiers who had taken part in the mutiny over pay at Utrecht in March, see *CSPF, 1585–6*, 495.

[695] This is the sole reference in these accounts to the mission of Sir Thomas Heneage (n. 409 above), who was sent by Elizabeth in February to demand that Leicester relinquish the governor-generalship. He remained in the Netherlands, attempting to arrange a compromise, until the beginning of June.

lordship from Skinckes Skonces the same daye}   xs.[696]

Geven by your lordship's commandment to a poore
fealow that gatherid bowes at the camp for your
lordship the same daye}   xijd.

Geven to Captayn Read sargant mayger by your
lordship's commandment which he gave to tow
gentellmen that came to your lordship at the
camp the iij of June 1586}   iiijli.

Delyverid to Thomas Jernegam* by your lordship's
commandment one of your lordship's clarkes
controller of your lordship's chetchen in prest
for your lordship's dyat at the camp and going
before from the camp to Telt and from Telt to
Bommell the iiij of June}   viijli.[697]

Geven by your lordship's commandment to on[e] Mouns
Grindefill's man at the campe the same daye}   vs.[698]

Geven by your lordship's commandment to Captayn
Borowes shuldyrs that waytted of your lordship
at your lordship's house at the camp the same daye}   xls.[699]

Geven to the sheppe your lordship cam in from
the campe to Telt the same daye}   xls.

Geven by your lordship's commandment to the man
of ware that mett your lordship by the waye and
garded your lordship to Telt the same day}   xxxs.

Summa Paginae: xxiiijli. xjs.

[verso]

the iiij of June 1586

Payd by your lordship's commandment [to] William
Marshall* your lordship's sarvant wich he payd
for the carige of your lordship's artelery and
blackbylls and pickes from Amserdam to Hacke [sic]
as apereth by the byll the same daye}   xxiijs. vjd.

Payd by your lordship's commandment for iij

[696] The Schenkenschanz or Schenk's Sconce, a fort built by Martin Schenk (n. 685) on the Rhine near Emmerich. Although technically within the Holy Roman Empire, it served effectively as the easternmost Dutch military outpost

[697] On 4 June, after the surrender of Grave was confirmed, Leicester broke up the camp and went first to Tiel (Tilt) and then to Bommel (the 5th), apparently in the belief that it was Parma's next target (*CSPF, 1586–7*, 2, to Elizabeth, 6 June).

[698] Arent van Groenevelt, governor of Sluys 1585–7.

[699] (Sir) John Borough (d. 1594), brother of Lord Burgh. He commanded a company in the Netherlands in 1585–6 and was appointed governor of Doesburg after its capture.

shepes that cam with your lordship's stoufe
and more from the camp to Telt the iiij of
June at xiij*s*. a shep}   xxxixs.
Payd the same day for iij shepes more that came
with your lordship's men and stoufe from the
campe to Telt at x*s*. a shep}   xxxs.
Delyvered by your lordship's commandment to
Captayn Pecoke in prest at Telt to paye to both
your lordship's gardes the iiij of June 1586}   \<a\>   xxli.[700]
Geven by your lordship's commandment to the
sarvants of the hous at Telt whear your
lordship laye the vth of June 1586}   xxs.
Geven by your lordship's commandment to Mr
Borgrave wich he gave to on[e] at Bommell the
same daye}   xxxs.
Geven by your lordship's commandment to the
sheppe that brought your lordship from Telt
to Bommell the same daye}   xxxs.
Payd to Steaven Johnson of your lordship's
wardrop wich he payd for the carrige of your
lordship's chambar stoufe and wardrop stoufe
from the watersyd at Telt to your lordship's
loging and for carring it bacagan in the
morning to the watersyd and from the water to
your loging at Bommell the vth of June 1586}   vijs. vjd.
Geven by your lordship's commandment to your
lordship's drommer and feyffer at Bommell the
same daye}   xls.
Geven by your lordship's commandment to John
your lordship's jeweler at Bommell the same daye}   xls.
Delyvered to Thomas Jernegam one of your
lordship's clarks comtrollers of your lordship's
chetchen in prest at Bommell the vjth of June 1586}   viijli.
            Summa Paginae: xljli.

[recto]

                    the vjth of June 1586
Delyvered to Mr Lewood gentellman of your
lordship's armar in prest wich he payd for
carige and other charges at Bommell the same day}   iijli.

---

[700] For Pecock see n. 626 above. Leicester's guard had two sections, one of shot
(musketeers) and one of halberdiers, see the 1587 household lists.

Geven by your lordship's commandment to Mr
Downell* on of your lordship's sectorys the
wich he gave to the ammarrallse sonn of Telt
the same daye}   xxxs.
Geven by your lordship's commandment to Mr
Downall wich he gave to the gounners of Bommell
that shot of the great ordynans at your lordship's
coming into the toun the same daye}   xs.
Payd to Mr Grotreges the wich he payd for serrapes
of vilats for your lordship at Bommell the same daye}   xxxs.
Payd by your lordship's commandment to Mr Famwayse
master of the great ordenans the wich he gave
to the marynars at Bommell the vij of June 1586}   xli.[701]
Geven by your lordship's commandment to on[e]
Chrells Francx at his going into England from
Bommell the same daye}   xli.[702]
Gevin by your lordship's commandment to Mr
Grotreges wich he gave to tow shuldyrs that came
to your lordship from the skonce at Nemegam to
Bommell to your lordship the same daye}   iijli.
Payd to Mounsr Asley that provydes the cariges
for your lordship by your lordship's commandment
for viij shepes that brought your lordship's
stoufe and men from the campe to Telt and from
Telt to Bommell the iiijth and vijth of June
as apereth by the byll}   ixli. xjs.[703]
Payd to William Massey kepper of your lordship's
gra[yho]unds for ther meat on[e] weeke twelve
shellings the vij of June}   xijs.
Payd the same day to Conrod Ducke kepper of
your lordship's hounds for ther meat on[e] week
fortene shellings}   xiiijs.
                    Summa Paginae: xxxixli. xvijs.

---

[701] Charles de Liévin, Sieur de Famars (d. 1592). Liévin had been in William of Orange's service since 1572 and had undertaken embassies to England in 1577 and 1578. Leicester appointed him master-general of the artillery on 24 March 1586 (ARA, Eerste Afdeling, RvS 1524 [Comissieboek van der Graaf van Leycester 1586–8], fo. 38).

[702] Charles Francx, described on p. 369 below as Charles, Mr Secretary's [Walsingham's] man. He brought Leicester's letter of 6 June to Walsingham, see Leic. Corres., 289, 300, and BL, Harl. MS 1641, fos. 25v-6. No reference to him can be found in C. Read, Mr. Secretary Walsingham and the Policy of Queen Elizabeth (Oxford, 1925).

[703] Aslyas on p. 358, presumably a Dutch carriage-master.

[verso]

the viijth of June 1586
Payd to Rychard Boocke your lordship's sarvant
the wich he layd out to the peyners [pioneers] by
your lordship's commandment at the camp at Nemegam
the xviij of Maye being Thursday ij*s*. and on
Fryday the xix day ij*s*., geven to the peyners
on Satterday the xx of Maye x*s*., geven the same
day to tow Duchmen for staying of your lordship's
coch x*d*.}   xvs.
Delyvred to Mr Leswood gentellman of your
lordship's armer by your lordship's commandment
fore pounds to geve unto iiij men that keppeth
your lordship's teant at Bommell the same daye}   iiijli.
Payd too Mr Leswood more the same daye wich he
payd for the sheppe that careth your lordship's
teant from Bommell to Utrick the same daye}   xxxs.
Geven by your lordship's commandment to Edward
Haward* your lordship's trompeter at Bommell
the same day}   xxxs.
Geven by your lordship's commandment to Charke*
your lordship's sarvant wich he gave to a poore
shuldyear at Bommell the same daye}   ijs.
Geven to Mr Edward Yorke which he gave by your
lordship's commandment to Captayn Williams'
drommer the same daye}   xs.[704]
Geven to the gentellwoman's man of the house
whear your lordship laye at Bommell by your
lordship's commandment for presenting strabres
to your lordship ther the same daye}   vs.
Geven to Kaneth Leause your lordship's sarvant
which he gave by your lordship's commandment to
the warders at Bommell the same daye}   xs.
Geven to the gentellwoman's kynswoman of the
house whear your lordship laye at Bommell the
ix June 1586 at your lordship's choming [*sic*] away}   iijli.
Geven to the sarvants of the house at Bommell
the same daye by your lordship's commandment}   xls.
Summa Paginae: xiiijli. ijs.

[704] Roger Williams was appointed sergeant-major of the horse in 1586.

[recto]

the ix of June 1586

Gevin to the Duch shuldyrs that cam into the
towne at Bommell at your lordship's coming
aweye wich came out of Friseland the same daye
the somm of}   xli.

Geven to on Roger Hasse by your lordship's
commandment leiftenaunt under Captan Barro
the same daye at Bommell}   iijli. vjs. viijd.[705]

Payd to William Williams wich he payd for
waggans to cary your lordship's stoufe from
the house to the wattersyd at Bommell the same daye}   xijd.

Payd to Mr Fen preacher by your lordship's
commandment the wich he gave to the poore the
xth of June 1586}   xls.

Payd to Mounser Aslyas wich he payd for tow
shepes for the Earell of Essex wich came with
himsealfe and stoufe from Bommell to Garkam
the ix of June 1586}   xxiiijs.

Payd to Mounser Aslyas wich he payd for vj sheps
by your lordship's commandment to cary your
lordship's stoufe and men from Bommell to Garkam
the ix of June 1586}   iijli. ijs.[706]

Payd by your lordship's commandment to the shepe
that brought your lordship from Bommell to
Garkam the same daye}   xxxs.

Gevin to tow byose [boys?] of the
same shepe by your lordship's commandment
wheare your lordship cam in the same daye}   vjs. viijd.

Geven to Mr Candyse wich he gave by your lordship's
commandment to the poore man's box at the
chirch at Garkam the x of June 1586}   xs.

Geven to Mr Teadder* wich he gave by your
lordship's commandment to a poore man the same
daye at Garkam}   xijd.

Geven to a poore man on[e] Rychard Squyeare at
Garkam at his going to Utricke to take fesseck
for his cold the same daye}   xs.

---

[705] Edward Barrow or Abarrow, who had previously served in Ireland. He had raised
a voluntary company in Hampshire and arrived at the camp in May (*CSPF, 1585–6*, 667).

[706] Leicester went to Gorinchem from Bommel on 9 June and then to Dordrecht on
the 13th.

Summa Paginae: xxiijli. xjs. iiijd.

[verso]

the x of June 1586
Delyvered to Goouge of your lordship's chek
wich he gave by your lordship's commandment
to on[e] Danell Turner of your lordship's gard
that leyeth secke at Bommell the same daye}   xls.
Delyvered to Thomas Jernegam on[e] of your lordship's
clarks controllers of your lordship's chetchen
by your lordship's commandment in prest at
Garkam the xij of June 1586}   xxli.
Geven to Monser Asleyas that provides the cariges
for your lordship at Garkam by your lordship's
commandment the same daye}   vli.
Geven to Rychard Garner on[e] of your lordship's
sarvants by your lordship's commandment at Garkam
the same daye}   xs.
Geven to on[e] Harry Wisant* your lordship's sarvant
for presenting of ofayells to your lordship at
Garkam the same daye by your lordship's commandment}   xs.
Geven to on[e] Jacob Kemp by your lordship's
commandment that shewed plats to your lordship
at Garkam the xij of June 1586}   iijli.
Payd to Mr Heydyn wich he gave by your lordship's
commandment to William Kemp your lordship's
sarvant which he payd for the meanding of an
anshant the same daye at Garkam}   xs.
Payd to Mr Haydyn which he gave to the shuldyars
at Garkam at your lordship's goinge away to
Dort the xiij of June 1586 by your lordship's
commandment}   xli.
Geven to the sarvants of the house at Garkam
by your lordship's commandment whar your
lordship laye the same daye}   xxs.
Gevin to Mr Haydyn wich he gave the same daye
more by your lordship's commandment at Garkam
to Count Neuares fotman}   xiijs.[707]

[707] Adolph von Solms, Count of Newenaar and Moeurs (d. 1589), stadtholder of Guelderland, Overijssel and Utrecht, president of the Council of Finance, June 1586. Although Newenaar was a prince of the Empire, he was related by marriage to the house of Nassau, and had supported Truchsess in the war for Cologne.

Payd for the carrige of your lordship's chamber stoufe and wardrop stoufe from the watersyd to your lordship's loging at Garkam the same day}	xxd.

Summa Paginae: xliijli. iiijs. viijd.

[recto]

the xiiij of June 1586

Geven to the wachmen by your lordship's commandment at Dorte at your lordship's coming the same day}	xxs.[708]
Payd to Mr Hayden wich he gave by your lordship's commandment at Dort to John your lordship's harper and to another that playd uppon the leutt before your lordship ther xs. a pese the same day}	xxs.
Payd to Mr Hayden more the same day wich he gave by your lordship's commandment to the porters at the gate}	xiijs.
Geven to the servants of the house at Dort whar your lordship laye by your lordship's commandment the same daye}	xxs.
Geven to the sheppe that brought your lordship from Dortt to Vianan by your lordship's commandment the same daye}	ls.
Gevin to the shouldyars of Dortt that gardid your lordship from Dortt to Vianan by your lordship's commandment the xiiij of June 1586 the som of}	vli.
Payd to one Coke my Lord of Warweck's man wich he gave by your lordship's commandment to tow poore men that healped to hall up your lordship's sheppe from Dortt to Vianan the same daye}	ijs.
Geven to Mr Hayden wich he gave by your lordship's commandment to the shuldyars of Vianan when your lordship came from Dortt to goye to Utrick the same daye}	xls.
Payd to tow skeppers on[e] that brought your lordship and another for your lordship's men from Vianan to Utrick the same day}	vjs. viijd.
Payd by your lordship's commandment for a skipper that brought Mr Grotreges and your lordship's garde from Vianan to Utrick the same daye}	xviijd.

[708] Leicester spent only the night of 13/14 June at Dordrecht, and then went to Vianen and Utrecht, where he remained until the 29th.

Payd to Mr Hayden wich he gave by your lordship's
commandment to a spettell house a lettell on
this syd Vianan at your lordship's coming to
Utrick the same daye}   ijs.
                    Summa Paginae: xiijli. xvs. ijd.

[verso]

                    the xiiij of June 1586 [*sic*]
Payd to Monser Aslyas which he payd by your
lordship's commandment for tow sheppes on[e] that
carid the governor of Grave and Mr William
Goodyear that gardid him and another that carrid
the captayns that ware prisoners and your
lordship's men that gardid them from Garkam to
Utrick the xiiij of June at xxij*s*. a shep}   xliiijs.[709]
Payd to Monser Asleyas the same daye which he
payd for tow shepps more, on[e] that carrid the
captan of the gard at xviij*s*. a shepe, another
that cared things partayning to the cetchen
and stabell at xx*s*. the shippe}   xxxviijs.
Payd to Mounser Asleyas by your lordship's
commandment wich he payd for tow sheppes that
carrid your lordship from Garkam to Dortt, on[e]
of them meat your lordship by the waye which
your lordship went into, on[e] ship more that
that [*sic*] carrid your lordship's gard from
Garkam to Dortt and so all thre to
Vianan bacagan on[e] of those ships at xxiij*s*.
the other tow at xviij*s*. a pese the xiiijth
of June 1586}   iijli.
Payd to Robart Pichford your lordship's sarvant
which he payd for the carrige of your lordship's
chamber stoufe and wardrop stoufe from Vianan
to Utrick the same daye}   viijs.
Geven to tow Borgollams [*sic*] by your lordship's
commandment that came from Nemegam skonces to
your lordship to Utrick the xv of June and
remaynes with your lordship to know your
lordship's pleasur}   iiijli.
Geven to [a] stranger of Dortt by your

---

[709] Lubbert Turk, Heer van Hemart, who had surrendered Grave on 28 May. He and
his officers were tried at Utrecht and executed on 18 June.

lordship's commandment that came to your
lordship from Dortt to Utrick the same
daye to tallk with your lordship}   vli.
                    Summa Paginae: xvjli. xs.

[recto]

                        the xvj of June 1586
Payd to Mr Appellyard by your lordship's
commandment in prest at his going into England
from Utrick the same daye}   vijli. xvs.[710]
Geven to him the same daye more by your lordship's
commandment at Utrick at his going to England}   xlvs.
Delyvered to Steven Johnson your lordship's
sarvant by your lordship's commandment foore
pounds xjs. to bey vellet to make your lordship
a pare of gaskin hose at Utrick the same daye}   iiijli. xjs.
Payd for wight waxe to seall up the lettell
leatters for your lordship at Utrick the same daye}   iiijd.
Payd by your lordship's commandment to iiij of
your lordship's sarvants, William Thomas, John
Borne, Allford Jhonson*, Nycholas Pynnocke* for
ther borde wagyes atendinge uppon your lordship's
wordrop stoufe and chambar stouf at Utrick from
the second of May tell the xiiij of June 1586 which
is xliiij days a pese}   xli.
Payd to William Massey kepper of your lordship's
gra[yho]unds for ther meat on[e] weeke tewell
shellings the same day wich is the xvj of June 1586}   xijs.
Payd to Conrod Ducke by your lordship's commandment
kepper of your lordship's hounds for ther meat
on week fortene shellings the same daye}   xiiijs.
Payd to John Conaway your lordship's sarvant
wich he payd for a cheare for your lordship
to sett in the shepp at Bommell when your
lordship went to Dortt the same daye}   ijs.
Payd to Robar[t] Gwyn* your lordship's sarvant
which he payd for the carrig of your lordship's
armar and pistalls from Vianan to Utricke the same daye}   ijs.
                Summa Paginae: xxvjli. js. iiijd.

[710] Henry Appleyard, son of John Appleyard*, who had been in Leicester's service in
the 1570s. He arrived in England with messages from Leicester on 21 June (BL, Harl.
MS 1641, fos. 27v, 35v).

[verso]

                    the xvij of June 1586
Payd to Mr Fen preacher by your lordship's
commandment wich he gave to the poore the
same daye}   xls.
Geven by your lordship's commandment to Mr
Meredith on[e] of the clarkes of your lordship's
ketchen at Utrick the xviij of June 1586}   vli.
Geven to Cuthbard Musgrave by your lordship's
commandment the same daye at Utrick}   xls.
Geven to Mr Heyam your lordship's sarvant at
Utrick the xix of June 1586}   xls.
Geven by your lordship's commandment to old
Robartes your lordship's fysserman at his beinge
sycke at Utrick the same day}   xs.
Payd to Nicolas Webber* your lordship's sarvant
by your lordship's commandment for his borde
wages from the last of Maye to the xiiijth of
June 1586 and for his bothehyre from Bure to
Bomell wich is tow shellings, his bord wages
is xij*d.* a day, the same daye}   xvs.
Payd to Thomas Eygley your lordship's sarvant
for his bord wages from [the] thrid of June to the
fortyne of the same at xij*d.* a daye the same daye}   xjs.
Payd to William Leswood gentellman of your
lordship's armer by your lordship's commandment
the wich he payd for the carrige of your lordship's
armer and tent and his o[w]ne dyat as apereth
by the byll the xxijth of June at Utrick 1586}   xxxjs. ixd.
Geven by your lordship's commandment to Rychard
Garner your lordship's sarvant and on[e] Antoney
Gates for presenting of larks to your lordship
at Utrick the xxijth of June Rychard Garner v*s.*
and Antoney Gates x*s.*}   xvs.
                    Summa Paginae: xvli. ijs. ixd.

[recto]

                    the xxijth of June 1586
Gevin to John Fox* on[e] of your lordship's gard
a mellor dilling at Stratford of the Boye by
your lordship's commandment at his going into
England from Utrick the same daye}   vli.

Payd by your lordship's commandment to one
Wooddosse* of your lordship's landers for the
charges of his removes from Utrick to Arnam
the xth of Maye and from Arnam back to Utrick
agane the frist of June and from Utrick to
Garkam the ix of June and from Vianan to Utrick
the xiij of June 1586}   xxs.
Payd by your lordship's commandment to Captayn
Wardes shuldyrs for watching at your lordship's
house tow nyghts ther the xxiiijth and xxvth of
June at Utrick geven to them the xxvijth
of June at Utrick}   vli.[711]
Payd to Mr Grotriges which he gave by your
lordship's commandment to the spettell house a
lettell a this syd Vianan the same daye}   xijd.
Payd to Robart Gwyn your lordship's sarvant
wich he payd for a black stafe teppid with
horne for your lordship at Utrick the same daye}   xijd.
Geven to Robart Gwyn your lordship's sarvant
at his going into England from Utrick the
xxviij of June 1586 by your lordship's commandment
the som of t[h]ree [pounds]}   iijli.
Geven by your lordship's commandment to Thomas
Turner* your lordship's gentellman porter at
his going into England from Utrick the xxixth
of June 1586}   iijli.

Summa Paginae: xvijli. ijs.

[verso]

the xxx of June 1586
Delyvered to my Lord North wich he gave by your
lordship's commandment to Mr Gorge North at
Utrick the same daye the som of three pounds
vjs. viijd.}   iijli. vjs. viijd.[712]
Geven by your lordship's commandment to on[e]
Frances Barti at Utrick the same daye}   iijli.
Payd to on[e] John Gylles by your lordship's
commandment for iiij pare of gloves for your
lordship at ijs. vjd. a pare at Utrick the same daye}   xs.qq

---

[711] John Ward, who may have served at Le Havre and in Ireland. His company was
raised in the summer of 1586, but disbanded in the autumn.
[712] Presumably one of Lord North's sons.

TEXTUAL NOTES

page

177   a. *Underlining and marginal correction in Leicester's hand.*

177   b. *Page damaged by damp.*

179   c. *Page damaged by damp.*

180   d. *Page damaged by damp.*

192   e-e. *Added later.*

203   f. *Deleted.*

207   g. *Underlining and marginal note in Leicester's hand.*

236   h. *Sum in different hand to the text.*

237   i. *Sum in different hand to the text.*

238   j. *Sum in different hand to the text.*

251   k. *Entered in a second hand.*

252   l. *Corrected to.*

253   m. *Corrected to.*

254   n. *Corrected to.*

257   o. *Sum in a different hand to the text.*

258   p. *Sum in a different hand to the text.*

259   q. *Initial sum deleted.*

259   r. *Leicester's hand.*

260   s. *Initial sum deleted.*

263   t. *Initial sum deleted.*

276   u-u. *Deleted.*

279   v. *Initial sum deleted.*

280   w-w. *Deleted.*

286   x-x. *Deleted.*

293   y-y. *Deleted.*

316   z. *Leicester's hand.*

320   aa. *Leicester's hand.*

324   bb. *Leicester's hand.*

326   cc. *Underlining and marginal note in Leicester's hand.*

329   dd. *Leicester's hand.*

330   ee. *Underlining and marginal note in Leicester's hand.*

333   ff. *Leicester's hand.*

335   gg. *Leicester's hand.*

336   hh. *Leicester's hand.*

340   ii. *Underlining and marginal note in Leicester's hand.*

340   jj. *Leicester's hand.*

341   kk. *Leicester's hand.*

342   ll. *Copied twice.*

342   mm. *Leicester's hand.*

343   nn. *Leicester's hand.*

351   oo. *Copied twice.*

352 pp. *Section deleted.*
364 qq. *Text ends in mid-page.*

D. DISBURSEMENT BOOK 1585-7
(THE STAUNTON MANUSCRIPT)[a]

Laied out the xith of December 1585
Delivered to Mr. Burburye wch he gave in
reward to the porters gunners & wachemen at
flushing by your l. commandment the sum of five
pounds   vli.[713]
To George Brooke yor l. servant which he gave
in reward to the poore of the church at flushinge
by your l. commandment twentye shillinges   xxs.
Paid to Mr. Grey the Shipmaster for the discharge
of all yor l. hoyes to the Burgomasters or
waterbalyfes of flushing by your l. commandment
twentye shillinges   xxs.[714]
More to George Brooke the same day wch he
gave in reward to the muzitions of the shipp
wch yor l. came in called the Amatist twentye
shillinges   xxs.[715]

The xiith of December
Delivered to Rafe Moore the same day wch he
payed to Edmund Carve yor l. servant being
borrowed of him & lost by yor l. in play on
shipborde as you came to flushing twentie shillinges   xxs.[716]

The xiiith of December
Paid to Lawrance Ramsey the xiijth of November [*sic*]
for his horse hyre from London to Harwitche as
appeareth by his byll vnder Mr. Blunte hands   xs.
Paied to foure of yor l. footemen the same day
for their dyet & lodginge at Harwch & there
suppers and lodginge at Mydlborowe the fyrst
night when yor l. lay at Flushing as appeareth
by their byll under mr. Blunte hand   [*blank*][717]

---

[713] Mr Burbury cannot be traced. These disbursements were made either on 10 December or on the morning of the 11th before Leicester departed from Flushing for Middelburg, see Appendix II.

[714] Probably Thomas Grey, one of the 'four masters of England', see Adams, 'New Light on the "Reformation" of John Hawkins', *E.H.R.*, cv (1990), 97, n. 3.

[715] For the name of the ship, see Appendix II.

[716] A transcriptional error for Edmund Carye.

[717] The 'first night' was 10 December.

To Robert Tyder the same day wch he gave in
reward by mr. Blunt commandmt from yor Ex. to
certen poore Duche men laborers wch workinge
stone out of a seller by the street craved of
yor Ex. as you ridd by to shewe yor selfe & see
the towne of myddelborow   [blank][718]
Delivered to yor l. three chaplens the xiiijth
of December vz to mr John Knewstub to mr
George Gyfford & mr Dudley Fenor at Myddlbrow
by yor l. commandmt the some of thertie pounds   xxxli.[719]
Geven to Owyn* yor l. Armorer of Kyllingworthe
the same day (xvth) by yor commandmt fortye
shillinge   xls.
Paied the xvth of December to Stevene Jonson
your l. servant for a gerdell and hangers of
gold silver & blacke silke made by yor Ex.
commandmt for a short sword wch was geven
yor l. by mr. Nycolas Sanders & for tow brushes
for yor l. wardrobe as appeareth by a byll
under his hand   lijs.[720]
Paied the same day (xvjth) to Doctor James by

[718] Leicester remained at Middelburg from 11 to 17 December.

[719] For Gifford, see n. 434 above. John Knewstub (1544–1624), rector of Cockfield
(Suff.), was the central figure in the Suffolk classis. No earlier direct connection to
Leicester is known, but in the dedication of his *Lectures upon Exodus XX* (STC 15043, 1578
edition) to the Countess of Warwick he referred to his 'dutie towards any of the
honourable house of Warwick, to the which I am in so many ways indebted'. Dudley
Fenner (d. 1589) was parson of Cranbrook (Kent), but had been suspended in the summer
of 1585. He had joined Thomas Cartwright in Antwerp in the late 1570s and was more
or less an open presbyterian. His christian name suggests some connection to the Dudleys
and he dedicated his 'Book of Religion' (BL, Harl. MS 6879) to Leicester and Warwick.
It is dated only 14 October, but the introduction by Cartwright refers to Fenner's recent
suspension, which suggests 1585. Leicester's choice of such a formidable group of
presbyterians as chaplains in the Netherlands has attracted attention, and it is the more
curious because they were not typical of his household chaplains (see Adams, 'A Godly
Peer? The Earl of Leicester and the Puritans', *History Today*, xl (January 1990), 18; it
should be noted that a line has been dropped in the list of chaplains in the text which
distorts their names). It may be that his choice was a political one (as is suggested in
Adams, 'The Protestant Cause: Religious Alliance with the West European Calvinist
Communities as a Political Issue in England, 1585–1630' (Unpub. Oxford University
D.Phil thesis, 1972), p. 67), but it should also be noted that Gifford, Fenner and Humphrey
Fenn (nn. 593, 689) had been recently suspended. They were thus free of pastoral
responsibility at home, and service abroad could be used to support a case for restoration.
Knewstub is the exception, but he appears to have returned to England after April 1586.

[720] Nicholas Saunders (d. 1605), MP. Leicester wrote a letter of recommendation for
him for a journey to Constantinople in 1584 (Bodl., MS Tanner 79, fo. 215, to William
Harbourne, 4 April 1584), and later recommended his appointment as ambassador there
(*CSPF, 1586–7*, 92, to Walsingham, 18 July 1586).

yor l. commandmt for a reame of paper eleven
shillings   xis.
Delivered the same day (xvijth) to mr Heigham
Captayne wch he gave in reward by yor Ex:
commandmt to nycolas Stase mayster of the barke
called the Grace of God wch caried yor l.
provision of beere wyne etc from London
to flushinge havinge suffered greate losse in
his passage by wether   [*blank*]⁷²¹
Paied the same day to charles mr Secretaries
man wch he gave in reward by yor commandmt to
a Ducheman that brought yor l. towe flowers of
waxe lyke unto nosegayes abord yor hoye at yor
l. firste enterance   xxs.⁷²²
Yor l. lost in play the same day (xxiijth) at
nighte in Counte morisses hoye at Doble hand Lodam   ls.⁷²³
To the mayster of my l. Embassadors hoye the
same day that carried yor l. alonge yor jorney
to Hollande havinge forsaken yor owne in the
way by reson of the unweetnes thereof by yor
l. commandmt twenty crownes   vli.⁷²⁴
Sente to yor l. the xviijth of December by mr
Flud yor l. secretarie to my l. Embassadors
hoye where yor l. played wth Sr William Russell
at Tantos by yor commandmt twentie pounds wch
money yor l. reservs still in yor owne purse for playe   xxli.⁷²⁵
Paied the same day (xxijth of December) at Dort for
three Flemish ells of blacke silke broad ryben
for your l. vse for a gerdell   iis. vid.⁷²⁶
Delivered to John wake your l. servante the

---

⁷²¹ At the same time as Leicester left Harwich, another convoy of ships carrying his
supplies and the remainder of his train had left London, see *Leic. Corres.*, 463.
⁷²² Charles Francx, see n. 702 above.
⁷²³ Leicester left Middelburg for Dordrecht on 17 December but his hoys and barges
were delayed by winds and fog and did not arrive until the 21st. On the 14th he informed
the Privy Council that Maurice of Nassau and the delegates from the States-General had
requested that he go to the Hague, see Appendix II.
⁷²⁴ Davison. It is not clear from the correspondence whether Davison was waiting for
Leicester at Flushing or came from Middelburg with Maurice of Nassau later on 10
December (see Appendix II).
⁷²⁵ Sir William Russell (1559?–1613), MP, later Lord Russell of Thornhaugh, the fourth
son of the 2nd Earl of Bedford and Warwick's brother-in-law. He had served in Ireland
and was appointed lieutenant of the horse in 1586. He succeeded Sidney as governor of
Flushing.
⁷²⁶ Leicester arrived at Dordrecht on 21 December and stayed until the 23rd when he
departed for Rotterdam.

same day at Dort wch he gave in reward by yor
Ex: commandmt to the Ducke hunters wch yor l.
wente to see for the straungenes of there
maner of takinge   xxs.
To mr. Gyfford yor l. chaplen wch he gave in
reward by your commandmt the same day to the
scolmasters at Dort that presented verses to yor l.   xls.
Geven in reward the same night by yor l.
commandmt to the mynister of Roterdam that
presented yor l. wth a booke   vli.

The xxvjth of December
To the orgen player of the churche of Delphe
the same day by yor l. commandmt   xxd.[727]

xxxth of December
To the saied Vnderhill the same day wch he
delivered yor l. to cast to a boy that slidd
uppon the ise under yor bed-chamber window at the Haghe   xiid.[728]
Paied to mr. Downhall yor l. Secretarie the
same day for tow cards brought by yor l.
commandmt on the whole world an other of Holland
Zealand Friseland & Gelderland   xiiis.
Geven in reward to yor l. players the same day
by yor l. commandment ten pounds   xli.[b]
Paied to Richard Gardner yor l. groome the same
day for tow fyreshovels & towe paire of tonge
for yor l. bed-chamber and wth drawinge chamber
at Delphe &c. as appereth by his byll   iiij[s?] iijd.

The first day of Januarie
Geven in rewarde the same day to the
corne-cutter by yor l. commandmt   xs.
Paied to Robart Falwell* Cole-bearer for an axe
to cleave wood for yor l. Chamber the same day
as appereth by his byll vnder mr George hand   ijs.[729]
Paied the same day at the Haghe for the furringe
of yor l. taffeta gowne wth fox foure pounds
ten shillings   iiijli. xs.

---

[727] On 24 December he left Rotterdam for Delft and stayed there until the 27th when he went to the Hague.

[728] He remained at the Hague until 3 January when he went to Leiden.

[729] George is a transcriptional error for (William) Gorge*.

To yor l. players that go backe into England
for ther charge by yor l. commandmt the same day   xls.[c]
Geven in reward by yor l. commandment to a
Ducheman Porter of the house that presented
yor l. with pyctoothe the same day   xs.
Yor l. gave William Kempe the player therten
shillings the same night (ij Jan) in yor
bedchamber out of the ten pounds which I gave
yor l. for play wth Count Moris & my lord of
Essex at doble hand Lodam with thertye shillings
yor l. saied was in exchange of a rose noble
wch was geven him by Count Hollocke yor l. lost
in playe the same night (the iiij) at Leiden in
yor bedchamber at the doble hand Lodam against
Count Moris & my l. of Essex & betting with
Sir William Russell[d]   xli.[730]
Paied to Robert Litchford yor l. servant the
same day for the washing of yor l. lynen at
Myddelborow Dort and Haghe & for the mending
of yor L. Clocke at Haghe and cariage of yor
bed trunke & chest with armor for yor owne
bodie from Haghe to London as appereth by a
byll under his hand   xxxjs.[731]
Geven more in reward the same day by your l.
commandment to William Kempe the player for
his charges into England   xxs.[e]
Yor l: loste in play wth my l. North Sr William
Russell & Mr Digbye the same night (iv Jan.) in
yor bed-chamber at single Lodam fortye shillings}   xls.[732]
To Richard Pepper yor l. footman wch he gave
in reward by yor l. command the same day (vth)
to Count Morices fawkener that presented yor l.
wth a cople of hearnes and a bitter in yor
coche as you ridd betweene Leiden and Haghe   xs.[733]

[730] Philip, Count of Hohenlohe-Langenberg (1550–1606), Hollock being the angli-cisation. Hohenlohe was connected to the house of Nassau by marriage and close to Maurice. In 1584 he had been appointed commander of the Dutch forces, and although Leicester recognised this by commissioning him lieutenant-general, he resented the English influence and a major antagonism developed later in 1586.

[731] Litchford is an error for Pitchford, and London for Leiden.

[732] (Sir) George Digby (1550–87), of Colshill, Wars., MP. Digby was an increasingly important figure in Leicester's following in the 1580s, see 'West Midlands', 42. He was to be a colonel in a proposed regimental reorganisation of the English contingent in 1586 (*CSPF, 1585–6*, 667, T. Doyley to Burghley, 24 May 1586).

[733] Herons and a bittern. Leicester returned to the Hague from Leiden on 5 January

Paied the same day at Leiden for six yards of
blacke satten at xijs the yard wch yor l. gave
to the gentle-woman that keeps the howse where
yor l. laye there by yor L. commandmt   iijli. xiis.
Paied to yor l. Goldsmythe in Haghe the vith
of Januarie 1585 for xij payre of agletts of
angell gold weighing one ounce three quarters
at three pounds the once as appereth by a bill
of his hand fyve shillings for the makinge of the
same agletts fiftene shillings   vili.
Paied the same day (vijth Jan.) for carnation
riben to xii paire of gold tags wch ware made
for yor l. at Haghe   vs. vid.
Paied the same day (ix Jan.) at Haghe by yor
l. commandmt to a merchant of myddleborow for
xiiij ounces of gold & silver lace wth a byase
worke in the myddest contayninge xxi yards at
viijs the ounce wch lace was laied uppon a
buffe gerkin the some fyve pounds twelve shillings   vli. xijs.
Paied the same day (xvj. Jan) at Leiden to
fredericke the Italian Inginer for a slead &
furniture brought at Amsterdam by yor l.
commandmt ten pounds   xli.[734]

The xxth of January

Paied the same day for a skryne of wicker for
yor l. bedchamber wthout a frame   iiijs.

xxith of January

To mr. Doctor James the xxith of January wch
he gave in reward at Leiden by yor l. commandmt
to mr. Dudley yor l. paige uppon his goinge
away with mr. Sidney forty shillings   xls.[735]
Paied to Humfrey Aldington yor Ex: footeman

and on the 7th began negotiations with the States-General over the governor-generalship; these continued until the 16th (17–26 January according to the Gregorian calendar), see the Dutch account of the negotiations, printed in H. Brugmans (ed.), *Correspondentie van Robert Dudley, Graaf van Leycester ... 1585–88* (Historich Genootschap, 3rd ser. lvi–viii, 1931), i, 31–62.

[734] Leicester returned to Leiden on 11 January, leaving the negotiations in the hands of Sidney and Davison, and remained there until the 20th. Fredericke was Frederigo Jenebelli, the engineer at Antwerp in 1584–5, who was employed by Leicester in the Netherlands in 1586–7 and then in England in 1588.

[735] Probably Robert, for Sir Philip did not return to Flushing until 11 February (CA, Vincent MS 216, p. 21).

for a bottle of new renishe wyne wch he was
commanded to fetche the xxiiij of January at
dinner tyme for yor Ex: to tast   ijs.
Paied the same day (xxx Jan) for the amendmt
of the small cheanes of that George wch yor l.
brake at yor lightinge of yor horse betwene
Leiden and Haghe   [*blank*][736]
Delivered to Lawrance Ramsay the laste of
January to bye the picture of a burgomaster
at Leiden wch was made by yor Ex: commandmt
ther foure pounds   ivli.
To mr Heiden the same day wch he gave in reward
by yor ex: commandmt to the three keepers of the
councell chamber dowers at the Haghe thertie shillings   xxxs.
Paied to Raffe Moore the same day for iiij
payre of spectacles at xijd the payre to yor Ex: vse   iiijs.

The therde of February

To mr Hynde the same day wch he gave in reward
by yor Ex: commandmt to the mayde in the Boores
house where yor Ex: lighte & went in as you ridd
a hawkinge at the pye   vs.
Paied by yor Ex: commandmt the vth of february
to mr. Wylliam Clerke Doctour of the Civill law
for the printing & bynding of rewle booke of the
mylitary lawes as appereth by his byll onder
his hand   iiijli. iiijs.[737]
Geven in reward the same day at the Haghe by
yor Ex: commandmt to mr. Edmond Carew at his
goinge over into England twentie pounds   xxli.[738]
More the xth of february to the saied Mr.
Carew uppon his request to yor Ex: as money
imprest thirtie pounds   xxxli.

---

[736] Leicester returned to the Hague from Leiden on 20 January and took the oath as
governor-general on the 25th.

[737] William Clarke (d. c.1587), MP, judge-martial in the Netherlands in 1586–7. This
entry suggests that Clarke, if not the author, was certainly the compiler of the *Lawes and
ordinances set downe by Robert, Earle of Leycester in the Lowe Countries* (STC 7288). It was printed
by Thomas Basson in Leiden, see his petition, BL, Cotton MS Titus B VII, fo. 96.

[738] Edmund Carey, to recruit a voluntary company, see Index of Servants. As noted
above, Leicester remained at the Hague throughout February.

4th March 1585–6[f]

Geven in reward the same day by your l. ex. [*sic*]
commandment to Wylson that playd at his goinge
into England with Sir Thomas Sherley, fortie shillinges.　　[739]

The xviijth of Aprill 1586 [g]

Geven in reward at Amersforde the xviijth of
Aprill by your Ex. commaundment to three Duchemen
that played before your Ex. in the halle after
supper thertie shillinges, & to a foole that
in the ende of the play came in laughinge with
a picture in his hand fyve shillinges, the some,　　xxxvs.[740]

6th May 1586[h]

To the saied Mr. Hynde which he gave in reward
by your Ex: commandment to William Kempe after
his leapinge into a ditche before your Ex: & the
Prince Elector as you went a walking at Amersford,
fyve shillinges　　vs.[741]

The Earl of Leicester was at Bath and Bristol in April, 1587.
MS Accounts at Longbridge[i]

TEXTUAL NOTES

page
367　　a. *The running text is the fragment published by Knowles. Entries found in
the Halliwell-Phillipps' scrapbooks are indicated in the textual notes by the
relevant references. Editorial intervention has been limited to the lowering of
superscriptions.*

370　　b. *Also entered in FSL, Wb 200, p. 71, under the date* 29 December
1585.

371　　c. *Also entered in FSL, Wb 200, p. 71, under the date* 1 January 1585–
6.

[739] This date must be wrong, for Shirley was at Court by Saturday, 5 March (*Leic. Corres.*, 160, to Leicester, 7 March). He had been sent to appease the Queen's anger over Leicester's acceptance of the governor-generalship, see also his further letters of 14 and 21 March (*ibid.*, 171–6, 180–3).

[740] This was during Leicester's visit to Amersfoort on 18–20 April, see n. 682 above.

[741] On this occasion Leicester was at Amersfoort en route from Utrecht to Arnhem (see n. 682). The Prince Elector was Gebhard Truchsess, the protestant Archbishop of Cologne, who had been driven into exile in the Netherlands following the war for Cologne in 1583.

page

371   d. *The section to* Count Hollocke *is also entered in FSL, Wb 160, p. 1. In this version* therten *is given as* therty *and* with thertye *as* wch thertye, *and the sum* xxxs. *is entered. It would appear that Knowles ran two entries together.*

371   e. *Entry from FSL, Wb 160, p. 1, under the date* 4 January 1585/6.

374   f. *Entry from FSL, Wb 200, p. 70.*

374   g. *Entry from Bald, 'Leicester's Men in the Low Countries'; I have been unable to trace the original.*

374   h. *Entry from FSL, Wb 160, p. 1.*

374   i. *Note from FSL, Wb 200, p. 78.*

APPENDIX I

Amy Dudley in 1559–60: the Identity of William Hyde.

The two Longleat accounts contain practically everything that is known about Amy Dudley in the eighteen months prior to her death. Canon Jackson very quickly appreciated their importance as sources and included what he considered to be a complete set of transcriptions of the relevant entries in his articles about her.[1] These have informed all subsequent accounts of her life and death and, as a result, Jackson's errors have now become deeply embedded in the literature on the subject. Apart from several relatively minor omissions or errors of transcription, he made three mistakes of importance: he thought that the references to Christchurch were to Christchurch in Hampshire; he failed to appreciate the effects of the categorisation in the Chancy account and thus considered each entry to be a record of a separate episode, when in fact they often relate to the same one; and he lent his authority to an earlier mis-identification of William Hyde.[2] The present edition of these accounts provides an obvious opportunity to re-examine the entries in context, but such are the effects of the revised identification of William Hyde advanced here that it alone justifies a re-examination of the whole vexed subject. However, owing to considerations of space, the discussion in this appendix will be limited to the entries in the accounts.[3]

Given the frequent delays in the making of payments, caution must be used in deducing a chronology from the entries, but the following reconstruction would appear to be reasonably accurate. The earliest entry relating to Amy Dudley is found at the beginning of the Chancy account and refers to a servant being sent to her in Lincolnshire.[4] Subsequent entries make it clear he was sent to arrange her journey out of Lincolnshire.[5] This had taken place relatively recently, either in November or early December 1558. Since the next references to her place her at Mr Hyde's at Christmas, it can be assumed that this had

[1] 'Amye Robsart', 84–5. The extracts are also found on pp. 422–3 of his later article 'Amye Robsart', *The Nineteenth Century*, xi (1882), 414–34. The later article is essentially a reprinting of the earlier, though with one or two significant additions.
[2] All can be found, for example, in the accounts of Amy Dudley in the three recent biographies of Leicester: A. Kendall, *Robert Dudley Earl of Leicester* (1980), pp. 24–4, D. Wilson, *Sweet Robin. A Biography of Robert Dudley, Earl of Leicester 1533–1588* (1981), pp. 92–5, and A. Haynes, *The White Bear. The Elizabethan Earl of Leicester* (1987), pp. 28–30.
[3] The circumstances of her death will not be discussed here.
[4] See p. 40 above.
[5] Pp. 41–2, 44–5 above.

been her destination.[6] She remained at Mr Hyde's during the early months of 1559 until Leicester himself paid her a visit. Three sets of entries relate to this visit, which took place on or after Easter (26 March) and before 8 April, when he is found gambling at Court.[7] It would appear to fit neatly into the famous parliamentary recess of 24 March–4 April. The entry to the four meals for his servants provides the only evidence for its duration – probably between two and four days.[8]

Roughly six weeks later she visited London. It is noted specifically that she was at Christchurch during Leicester's installation as a K.G. at Windsor (6 June), and it would appear that she left fairly soon thereafter, probably in mid-June when he took up residence at Greenwich with the rest of the Court.[9] When she arrived is less clear, but it was at some point in mid-May between his supper with Sir William Pickering (post 4 May) and the arrival of the French embassy (23 May), thus giving her about a month in or about London.[10] The entries give the impression that she went directly to Camberwell (her mother's family's home) and then to Christchurch. She obviously did a certain amount of shopping, but we cannot establish whether she spent any time at Kew, or even whether Leicester joined her at Christchurch.[11]

Thereafter the relevant entries diminish fairly dramatically. However, before discussing them the identity of Mr Hyde should be addressed, for it was with him that she spent the first months of 1559. For this a brief account of the origins of the accepted identification is necessary. The nineteenth-century fascination with the circumstances of Amy Dudley's death was inspired to a very large extent by Sir Walter Scott's novel *Kenilworth*, and in particular by the flagrant liberties he took with what were even in 1820 established historical facts.[12] In 1838 Thomas Wright included the one known letter by her in his selection of Elizabethan correspondence from the manuscript collections in the British Museum. It was written to John Flowerdew about business relating to the Robsart estate in Norfolk, dated only 7 August, and subscribed 'from Mr Heydes'. Wright included it, as he stated, not

[6] Pp. 41–2, 54 above.
[7] They are found under Foreign charges, p. 60, Diet, pp. 94–5 and Playing money, p. 99. The reference to 8 April is found in the next entry but one under Playing money.
[8] See p. 95.
[9] Pp. 64–5, 68, 71, 102–3.
[10] The first reference is found on p. 64.
[11] See pp. 71, 90–1. The entry on p. 68 suggests that she went back to Camberwell from Christchurch and departed from there, but it is difficult to be categorical.
[12] These were not errors of ignorance; Scott believed that as a writer of romances he was 'at liberty to commit anachronisms for the sake of effect' (J. Anderson, *Sir Walter Scott and History* (Edinburgh, 1981), p. 31, see also pp. 27–36 *passim*, and on *Kenilworth* itself, p. 80).

because of its historical importance but because it revealed 'another character from the Amy Robsart of Sir Walter Scott'.[13] The identification of Mr Hyde followed the discovery of what has since been the central source for any discussion of her death, the correspondence between Thomas Blount and Leicester of September 1560 in the Pepysian MSS.[14] This correspondence was noticed by Lord Braybrooke during the preparation of his edition of Pepys's diary in the 1830s, but it was not published until 1848.[15] Two years later the Berkshire antiquary A.D. Bartlett in his carefully-researched account of Cumnor Place noted that the Mrs Odingsell described by Blount as living at Cumnor in September 1560 was the sister of William Hyde the younger (c.1517–1567) of South Denchworth, Berks., and drew the understandable conclusion that he was the Hyde in question.[16]

Bartlett's identification was accepted by Jackson, and thereafter became the established one, despite the difficulty of finding any other connection between Hyde and Leicester.[17] It has remained largely unquestioned.[18] One reason for this has been its attraction to those writers who have wished to challenge the murder theories, for if Amy Dudley had been living at South Denchworth in 1559 then there was nothing necessarily sinister about her moving a few miles away to Cumnor. However, not only is there no direct evidence that she ever stayed at South Denchworth, but on the contrary it is clear that the Mr Hyde of her letter and the Chancy account was in fact William Hyde (d. 1580) of Throcking, Herts. The evidence for this identification is supplied in part by the Chancy account itself, but also by the

[13] Wright, i, 48–9. He criticises Scott's errors and anachronisms at some length. The original of the letter is Harl. MS 4712, fo. 275, a volume of papers of Norfolk origin collected by Peter Le Neve. It has been reprinted on numerous occasions since, most recently by Wilson, pp. 94–5.

[14] Pepys MS 2503 (Letters of State II), pp. 703–11.

[15] They were published simultaneously in Braybrooke's *Diary of Samuel Pepys F.R.S.* (4th ed., 1848), i, 381–8, and G.L. Craik, *The Romance of the Peerage* (1848)), i, 399–407. They have been reprinted in various forms since, but none of the various transcriptions are to be relied on (see n. 161 above).

[16] *An Historical and Descriptive Account of Cumnor Place, Berks.* (Oxford, 1850), pp. 34–5. This is the first work to identify Hyde that I know of. It is still one of considerable value. Bartlett, who later became the Berkshire county coroner, knew his local sources well, and Jackson consulted him about the possible survival of the verdict of the inquest into Amy Dudley's death ('Amye Robsart', 76).

[17] 'Amye Robsart', 63. By the time he wrote his later 'Amye Robsart' article, Jackson had discovered (see p. 421) that Hyde's father, the elder William Hyde, had purchased the manor of Kingston Lisle (Berks.) from Northumberland in the 1530s, but that is the extent of the connection.

[18] See Hasler *sub* Anthony Forster and William Hyde for good examples of the way in which the identification has influenced modern scholarship. There has been one sceptic, the author of the Cumnor and District Historical Society pamphlet *Amy Robsart and Cumnor Place*.

narrative of her death found in BL, Add. MS 48023. The latter states *inter alia* that Leicester 'left her first at Hydes house in Hertfordshire, where she saied she was poysoned and for that cause he desired she might no longer tary in his house, from thence she was conveyed to Verney's howse in Warwickshire, and so at length to Foster's house [i.e. Cumnor]'.[19] If the entries in the Chancy account relating to Leicester's visit to her at Hyde's at Easter 1559 are examined it will seen that they mention Ware, Waltham and Buntingford and nowhere in Berkshire.[20] With one exception, there are in fact no references to places or persons in Berkshire in connection with her in the Chancy account at all.[21]

What little we know about William Hyde of Throcking confirms this identification. He was a younger son of George Hyde of Throcking (d. 1553). His elder brother Leonard had predeceased their father, leaving a son also named William. The elder William Hyde was apparently living on the family estates after 1553 and became a Hertfordshire J.P. In 1561 he bought Throcking and the neighbouring manor of Sandon from his nephew under somewhat dubious circumstances and later rebuilt the house at Sandon, which was thereafter known as Hyde Hall. In his will (19 June 1580) he nominated Leicester 'my singular good lord' as overseer, and one of his daughters was (unusually for a girl) christened Dudley.[22]

Further discussion of Amy Dudley's residence at Throcking is dependent on the dating of her letter from 'Mr Heyde's'. It has been generally agreed that it was not from 1560, but it must be dated after the Robsart estate had been inherited by the Dudleys. What has attracted most attention, however, is her comment in the letter, 'Althowe I forgot to move my lorde therof before his departyng he being sore trubeled with wayty affars and I not beyng altogether in quyet for his soden departyng'. An apparently irresistable romantic desire to see in this evidence of his abandoning of her to pursue his ambitions at Court has led to an almost universal plumping for 1559.[23] However, it is impossible to reconcile this letter with the evidence of his and her movements in the summer of 1559 as given in the Chancy account.[24] 1558 has its attractions, partly because very little is known of their whereabouts in

[19] Fo. 353. This is not the place to discuss any of the other very interesting aspects of this account.

[20] See pp. 60, 94–5.

[21] The exception is the entry to Anthony Forster's servant discussed below.

[22] J.E. Cussans, *History of Hertfordshire: Hundred of Odsey* (1873), pp. 150–3, prints Hyde's will and a Hyde pedigree. See also V.C.H., *Hertfordshire*, iii, 274; iv, 112. It would appear from the entries on pp. 150–1 that Hyde was in Leicester's company in January 1560.

[23] Jackson, who appreciated that the letter could be dated as early as 1557, was almost explicit about this, see 'Amye Robsart', 61. Cf. Wilson, pp. 94–5.

[24] On 7 August 1559 Leicester was at Nonsuch with the court (see p. 78 above) and had not (apparently) seen his wife since June.

that year, but also because a letter of his to John Flowerdew (dated 22 July) survives in the same collection, and this from external evidence must date from 1558.[25] My own acceptance of 1558 as the date was, however, based on my belief that they did not inherit the Robsart estate until the winter of 1557–8. My more recent discovery of the evidence that the Robsart estate had descended to them in the early summer of 1557 has re-opened the question. A date of 1557 offers an immediate and obvious explanation for her unhappiness, for in early August he had just departed on the St Quentin expedition.[26]

Dating her letter to 1557 carries with it the implication that she resided at Throcking on and off for at least two years, from mid-1557 to mid-1559. For this there was a straight-forward reason: the house at Syderstone, the main Robsart manor, was uninhabitable.[27] As it was roughly mid-way between London and the Robsart estate, Throcking was not an inconvenient residence. It may have been intended initially as a temporary measure, for in the summer of 1558 Leicester was contemplating buying a house in Norfolk, 'if I am to live in that country'.[28] His own movements in 1557 and 1558 are not much clearer, but while he certainly used Christchurch as a London residence, he may well have spent part of the time at Hyde's with her.[29]

Placing Leicester and his wife in Throcking in 1557–8 is of immediate relevance to the no less debated question of Leicester's relations with Elizabeth prior to the accession. Throcking can by no stretch be considered adjacent to Hatfield, but it is not all that far away either, and his possible use of Hyde's house certainly strengthens the case for an association with Elizabeth during her residence at Hatfield in 1557 and 1558. Leicester is first noted as being in her company at the remove from the Charterhouse to the Tower on 28 November 1558, already acting as Master of the Horse. He is, however, mentioned in both of

---

[25] See n. 28 below. Her letter also refers to William Grice in connection with the business at hand in such a way that it must have been written in the period of his account rather than Chancy's.

[26] See 'Dudley Clientèle', p. 251, and Introduction, n. 52. The letter fits quite neatly into the chronology of the departure of the St Quentin expedition, but there is no space to discuss it here. The references to Grice pose no difficulty for he is found acting as an attorney for Leicester as early as March 1556 (BRL, HH MS 351614). The business referred to could have been handled easily by Leicester if he had departed from Hyde's to London; his leaving it to his wife to conclude makes more sense if he was intending to cross the Channel.

[27] 'Dudley Clientèle', p. 251.

[28] This is the subject of his letter to Flowerdew, Harl. MS 4712, fo. 273. It could not have been written in 1559 and in late July 1557 he was deeply involved in the preparations for the St Quentin expedition.

[29] The couple were probably together when they signed the documents for the conveyance of Hales Owen on 27 March 1558 (BRL, HH MSS 351493 and 390016). Conversely, Amy Dudley could have spent part of the time at Christchurch.

Cecil's initial memoranda on appointments of 17 and 18 November, in which he is nominated as Master of the Horse, and Elizabeth issued a warrant for the supply of cloth to him as Master of the Horse on 23 November, the day she travelled from Hadley to London via Barnet.[30]

Given the disappearance of the Grice account, it is particularly frustrating that the Chancy account does not begin even a month earlier and shed some light on Leicester's movements at the time of Elizabeth's accession. The only direct reference it makes to the events of November 1558 is the entry regarding the livery of his horses at Enfield.[31] Enfield was not on the Queen's route, but it was on the road from Throcking, and this may reflect some form of move from Throcking after the accession. Similarly the reference to the shipment of his tent from Hunsdon to London in March 1559 suggests, in the absence of any other reason for it being there, the possibility that it came from Throcking as well.[32]

After June 1559 Amy Dudley's movements become much more difficult to trace. The remaining entries of significance in the Chancy account refer to her being sent things by a servant of Sir Richard Verney's in September and then by a servant of Anthony Forster's in December.[33] They would appear to confirm the progression outlined in BL, Add. MS 48023, placing her at Compton Verney by September and Cumnor by December, which would imply that she spent the nine months or so prior to her death at Cumnor.[34] The Ellis account contains only a single reference to her before her death, and that is to her servant Huggenes buying or collecting clothes in London at an unspecified date.[35] Perhaps the most puzzling entry is that for her going into Suffolk.[36] Given its place in the Chauncy account it is difficult not to associate it with her departure from London in June 1559.[37] However, assuming she had moved to Compton Verney by September, it is odd to find no reference to her return from Suffolk, either to Hyde's or to

---

[30] See 'Feria Letter', n. 28, and 'Dudley Clientèle', p. 253. His presence on 28 November is noted in Machyn, 180, and the warrant of the 23rd is referred to in A. Kempe (ed.), *The Loseley Manuscripts* (1836), p. 65. The chronology of the Chancy account suggests that Amy Dudley was in Lincolnshire at the date of the accession, had she been sent there to keep her safely out of the way in case there was trouble?

[31] P. 41.

[32] P. 55.

[33] Pp. 92, 106.

[34] A letter from Verney to Leicester of 20 April 1560 survives (DP IV, fo. 10). It does not mention her, but apologises for the death of some of Leicester's hawks which were in the keeping of a cousin of Verney's in Warwickshire.

[35] P. 133.

[36] P. 102.

[37] Her reasons for going to Suffolk can only be guessed at. The Robsart estate had included the manor of Bulkham in Suffolk, but Leicester had sold it in 1557 (see 'Dudley Clientèle', p. 251).

London, and no expenses for what must have been a fairly major move to Warwickshire. On the other hand, the entry for the departure for Suffolk is found in a series of miscellaneous payments and may have been placed out of sequence. It may in fact refer to a trip made from Hyde's earlier in the year, and therefore when she left London in June it was for Warwickshire.

Compton Verney and Cumnor were definitely far more remote than Throcking, and there are no references to Leicester's visiting her or her coming to London thereafter. Indeed, there is no evidence that they ever saw each other again after June 1559. However, before seeing in this evidence of an estrangement or worse, two points should be borne in mind. Firstly, in November 1559 Leicester received his lieutenancy of Windsor Castle and during 1559–1560 he was seeking to buy land in Warwickshire.[38] If she had moved to a part of the country that was, geographically-speaking, presumably foreign to her, Warwickshire and Berkshire were by then counties of potentially greater interest to him than Hertfordshire. He was in fact at Windsor only thirty or so miles away when she died; was she expecting him to visit during the progress?[39]

Secondly, the nature of the accounts themselves is of importance when they are used as sources for this type of subject. As noted above the receipts from the Robsart estate do not appear in these accounts until Michaelmas 1560, three weeks after her death.[40] Nor do her basic expenses; the charges for her in the accounts are either for clothing or other extraordinary expenses. It is difficult to avoid the conclusion that the Robsart estate receipts were paid directly to her and that she financed her own immediate household out of them. This would apply both at Throcking and at Cumnor. On the other hand the despatching of servants to and from Throcking in early 1559 can be seen as a consequence of its proximity to London and to Leicester's own household. Once she had moved further away, this was no longer so easy and there was thus a more radical division of their two households. She certainly had 'her people' at Cumnor, who included both Mrs Picto and Huggenes.[41] Her letter to William Edney reveals that she had no difficulty in ordering dresses directly from him and having them

[38] For Windsor Castle see n. 299 above. For the Warwickshire negotiations see 'West Midlands', 31.

[39] His proposed visit to Huntingdon at Ashby de la Zouche in June (see n. 277 above) is worth noting in this context.

[40] See p. 13, n. 52 to the Introduction.

[41] In his initial report on her death of 11 September (Pepys MS 2503, p. 705), Thomas Blount referred to 'her people that waited upon her' and 'her sorte'. For Mrs Picto and Huggenes, see nn. 161, 262 above. The 1559 livery lists (p. 421) include hose delivered to 'thre of those that wayteth on my lady'.

sent by the Oxford carrier.[42] Edney made a number of dresses and
gowns for her, but his bill is a final account rendered after her death
and contains only one date (6 July presumably 1560), which makes it
impossible to establish precisely how far back it goes.[43] The fact that
no reference to Huggenes appears in Edney's bill suggests that she was
ordering from other tradesmen as well.[44] Items for her are also found
in John Guy's and James Crokeham's bills, but once again the period
they cover is not clear.[45] All that can be said is that her appearance
and non-appearance in the accounts, as with the Countess of Leicester
in the 1584–86 disbursement book, was largely the result of accounting
procedure, and cannot in itself be used as evidence of anything more
sinister.

[42] For the letter to Edney and his bill see n. 236 above.

[43] The bill is printed in Jackson 'Amye Robsart', 85–8. The dress mentioned in the
entry dated 6 July appears to be the one referred to in her letter of 24 August, and
presumably had been delivered by then. The various items are sub-divided into groups
of parcels, two delivered to Richard Ellis and two to William Grice. This may mean that
the bill goes back to the period of Grice's account.

[44] See n. 262 above.

[45] See pp. 173, 175 above.

APPENDIX II

Leicester's Departure for the Netherlands September–December 1585.

The period covered by the 1584–86 disbursement book includes one of the most important episodes of Leicester's life, his appointment as lieutenant-general of the English contingent in the Netherlands and his departure to take up his command in December 1585. This generated a considerable amount of correspondence, particularly in September and December 1585, but much of it is undated and the overall chronology unclear.[1] As a result, the existing accounts leave much to be desired.[2] However, the utility of the 1584–6 disbursement book as a corrective is vitiated to a considerable extent by the chronological vagaries of Hand C, which has the paradoxical effect of making the correspondence necessary to establish an accurate chronology for the book. The circumstances surrounding his appointment in September 1585 and his journey to Flushing in late November and December, in particular, demand an examination too detailed to be handled satisfactorily in the notes, although the discussion here, like that in Appendix I, is perforce restricted to subjects immediately relevant to the document.[3]

Throughout the discussions of possible English intervention in the Netherlands in 1584–85, Leicester's willingness to command any military force sent had been widely appreciated. He had nearly received a similar appointment in 1577–8, and it was no secret that the Dutch regarded him as the English nobleman most sympathetic to their cause. How far matters had proceeded during the treaty negotiations in July 1585 is not entirely clear, but it appears that no decision had been reached when he departed for Kenilworth on 11 August. What precipitated the issue was the confirmation of the surrender of Antwerp,

[1] The relevant correspondence is found mainly in BL, Harl. MS 285, Cotton MS Galba C VIII, and the various classes of the State Papers. These collections are a complex mixture of Leicester, Walsingham and Davison papers, see 'Leic. Pap. II', esp. 138. An initial reconstruction was attempted by John Bruce, the editor of *Leic. Corres.*, but this collection was compiled solely from the MSS in the British Museum.
[2] The fullest account is found in Read, *Walsingham*, iii, 112–31, but it contains some serious errors. Those in Strong and van Dorsten, *Leicester's Triumph*, pp. 23–31, C. Wilson, *Queen Elizabeth and the Revolt of the Netherlands* (2nd ed, the Hague, 1979), pp. 86–90, W.T. MacCaffrey, *Queen Elizabeth and the Making of Policy, 1572–1588* (Princeton, 1981), pp. 348–53, and F.G. Oosterhoff, *Leicester and the Netherlands 1586–1587* (Utrecht, 1988), pp. 45–9, are cursory.
[3] This is not the place for a discussion of Leicester's instructions or the wider political debate.

which reached England on 20 August.[4] On 22–3 August the Queen decided to increase her forces in the Netherlands and send an unnamed nobleman to command them, if the Dutch would deliver Flushing and the Brill for security.[5] William Davison was sent to the Netherlands on 25 August to offer these terms to the States-General and arrived in Flushing on 3 September.[6] It was at this point that Leicester was written to to ask if he was still willing to serve.[7] In the meantime, the further decision was taken, possibly on Davison's advice, to strengthen the proposal by drafting an amplified version of the 10 August treaty, which was to be signed reciprocally by the English Privy Council and the Dutch commissioners for the first treaty. This document became known variously as the Act of Amplification, the Amplification Treaty and simply the Contract. The English copy was ready by 4 September when Burghley signed it and sent it to Leicester to sign, but on the 12th Walsingham complained that he had not yet obtained all the Councillors' signatures.[8] The Dutch copy presented more difficulties because most of their commissioners had returned home and it was necessary to send it over to them for their signatures. It is not entirely clear what documents Davison had taken with him, but on 8 September he was instructed to await the despatch of a new text, and on the 13th Walsingham sent him the copy signed by the Dutch commissioners remaining in London for their colleagues' signatures.[9] The copy signed by the Privy Council was finally submitted to the Dutch commissioners on the 15th, but they then refused to accept it until they had heard

---

[4] The surrender was signed on 7/17 August and the Prince of Parma entered the city on the 17th/27th. The English receipt of the news is noted by Walsingham in a letter to Edward Wotton of 21 August, 'yesterdaye we had newse of the rendering of Antwarpe' (*Hamilton Papers.*, ii, 681).

[5] The initial stage is indicated by a request from Walsingham to Davison on 22 August to come immediately to Barn Elms for a meeting on the Netherlands (*CSPF, 1584–5*, 670). This letter also contains the quite useful piece of information that with the tide in his favour the journey from London to Barn Elms by river would only take Davison an hour.

[6] See Davison's instructions (25 Aug.), BL, Add. MS 48116, fo. 145, and Davison to Walsingham, 4 Sept., *CSPF, 1585–6*, 6. The purpose of his embassy is discussed in *Hamilton Papers*, ii, Walsingham to Wotton, 26 Aug., and Hist. MSS Comm, *Bath MSS*, v, 45, Lord Talbot to Shrewsbury, 26 Aug. (mis-calendared 1583). The intended function of the nobleman, a subject of great future controversy, cannot be discussed here.

[7] See n. 595. In his answers Leicester does not mention the dates of these letters (which included two from Walsingham), but the fact that Walsingham had apparently referred to Davison's departure suggests they were written on 25 September or possibly the 24th.

[8] *CSPF, 1584–5*, 682, Walsingham to Davison, 27 Aug.; BL, Add. MS 48127, fo. 91, Elizabeth to Davison, 3 Sept.; PRO, SP12/182/11, Burghley to Walsingham, 4 Sept.; *CSPF, 1585–6*, 5, 21, Dutch Commissioners to Walsingham, 2 Sept., Walsingham to Davison, 12 Sept.

[9] *CSPF, 1585–6*, 14, 23, Walsingham to Davison, 8, 13 Sept.

further from the Netherlands.[10] In the meantime, however, Davison had concluded an agreement with the States-General on 22–3 September which involved their ratification of a slightly different form of amplification of the 10 August treaty. A final form of this document was prepared on 25 September, but its despatch to England was delayed by weather and it did not reach the Court until 21 October.[11]

Throughout these negotiations the nobleman was not identified, although Leicester's name was widely circulated. Precisely when Leicester's letters of 28 August reached the Court is unclear, but he answered another (now missing) letter from Walsingham 'this Wensday in bedd to rest me', *i.e.* on 1 September at Grafton.[12] In the meantime he had also received a letter from the Queen, which he sent to Walsingham to 'kepe safe tyll I come', in which it appeared that she was considering appointing another nobleman on the ground 'that I shuld carye with me to great a trowpe', and also that 'she doth take every occasion by my mariage to withdraw any good from me'. This fits Walsingham's discouraged report to Davison on 5 September that Elizabeth was 'not disposed to use the service of the Earl of Leicester. There is great offence taken in the carrying down of his lady. I suppose the lot of the governor will light on the Lord Graye. I would to God the ability of his purse were answerable to his sufficiency otherwise'.[13] As is suggested in n. 615, it was probably this hesitation by the Queen, which threatened his own possible appointment at Flushing, that caused Sir Philip Sidney to leave for Plymouth.

After Leicester returned to Court on 8 September, the alternative of Lord Grey appears to have been abandoned, and on the 12th Walsingham informed Davison that the Queen was now postponing the appointment of Leicester until she had learned from him that the States-General would ratify the Amplification Treaty[14] This appears to have remained the position until Leicester returned from Bedford's funeral on the 15th. What tipped the balance seems to have been the argument that Leicester's appointment was the best means of persuading

[10] *Ibid.*, 26, 28, Commissioners to Walsingham, 16 Sept., Walsingham to Davison, 18 Sept.

[11] *Ibid.*, 35–42, Davison's reports to Walsingham, Burghley and Leicester, 24 Sept. The delay in the despatch of the Dutch act was first noted by J.L. Motley, *History of the United Netherlands* (1886 ed.), i, 320–1, but he was confused by the new style and old style dating, see Read, *Walsingham*, iii, 115. Copies of the Dutch act of ratification (dated 22 Sept./2 Oct.) can be found in both the PRO and ARA. The covering letters for its despatch to England are dated 25 Sept./5 Oct., see below. It is not clear whether Davison had received the copy of the English Amplification Treaty that Walsingham had sent him by 22 September.

[12] PRO, SP12/18/2/1.

[13] *CSPF, 1585–6*, 8. For Grey, see n. 549, and the Countess, n. 580.

[14] *Ibid.*, 21.

the Dutch to accept the Amplification Treaty, given the hesitation of the commissioners in London to accept it. It was thus on the 17th that she let it be known that Leicester would be appointed once the Dutch had ratified the treaty.[15] Having gone this far, her hand was forced on the 22nd when Jacob Valcke, the commissioner from Zeeland, received word from the States of Zeeland that they would accept the English occupation of Flushing.[16] She apparently gave Leicester a verbal agreement on the 23rd, which Walsingham confirmed on the following day. Leicester's description reveals the strong emotional aspect to Elizabeth's hesitations, 'hit pleased hir to sey to me yesterday that she was loth to give the sentence therof hirself, but wold send yt rather by some other'.[17]

At this stage further complexities intrude and it is simplest to begin with the fixed points. On Sunday 26 September Leicester signed and dated at Leicester House a number of circular letters drafted by his secretaries, requesting his friends and followers to prepare themselves to serve as the cavalry contingent in the expedition. Two of these letters have survived.[18] Later that day Walsingham relayed from Nonsuch an order from the Queen to Leicester to suspend his preparations until he spoke to her again, although he had no idea why.[19] Leicester received this letter at 1 o'clock in the morning of Monday the 27th and answered it immediately. In his letter he stated that upon the Queen's order to begin his preparations, he had 'despatched above ijC letters' between the night of Thursday the 23rd and 4 o'clock on the 26th, and that

---

[15] Arthur Atye informed Jean Hotman on 18 September that Elizabeth 'hath nowe even yesterday fully resolved to send my L. our master into the Low Countries' (AMAE, CPH, II, fo. 12). Walsingham told the Dutch commissioners on the 18th, see BL, Cotton MS Galba C VIII, fo. 205, Ortel to Leicester, 21 Sept., and their letter to the States-General, 18/28 Sept., ARA, Eerste Afdeling, Regeringsarchiven, I-92.

[16] See BL, Cotton MS Galba C VIII, fo. 146, Ortel and Paul Buys to Leicester, 22 Sept., 'Cest apres diner sont apportés a Monsieur Valck lettres des Estats de Zeelande'. Valcke himself wrote on the 23rd (ibid., fos. 148–9), 'Ayant le jour d'hier recu lettres d'avis'.

[17] PRO, SP12/182/67, to Walsingham [24 Sept.].

[18] One, NLW, MS 9015E (printed in 'North Wales', 147), was sent to John Wynn of Gwydir. A second, addressed to a Mr Burdett, has appeared in the catalogues of two manuscript dealers: John Wilson, Autograph Letters and Historical Documents Catalogue 63 (1988), item 112, and Roy Davids, Manuscripts, Literary Portraits and Association Items (n.d.), item 89. I am most grateful to Dr Henry Woudhuysen and Mr. A.J.A. Malkiewicz for bringing these catalogues to my attention. Burdett was either Robert Burdett (1558–1603) of Bramcote, Wars., MP, or John Burdett, who attended Leicester's funeral. Under the Amplification Treaty Elizabeth agreed to add 1,000 horse to the English contingent; see 'Puritan Crusade', pp. 17–22, 'North Wales', 137–9, for a further discussion of their recruiting. It is curious that the disbursement book contains no entries to the expenses of messengers, but the purchasing of substantial amounts of writing paper on his return from Kenilworth, see p. 305, may be relevant.

[19] Leic. Corres., 4–5.

most had already been delivered.[20] He had also gone to the Tower to prepare military equipment and had started to raise money.[21] Moreover, the Dutch commissioners had visited him at 9 o'clock in the morning of the 26th to urge him to leave as soon as possible, and they were returning in the morning of the 27th. In what was clearly a personal note enclosed to Walsingham himself he stated that he would avoid them by going to Wanstead to see some horses early in the morning and remain there until 3 o'clock in the afternoon. He also asked that Sidney be sent to join him.[22]

Around these dates several further less clearly-dated letters can be fitted. Leicester's letter to Walsingham dated only 'this Friday morning at Northall going to the christening of Mr Butlers child', contains the reference to the Queen's agreement 'yesterday' quoted above, and acknowledges receipt of a letter from Walsingham confirming it.[23] He goes on to state that he wanted from the Queen 'all things meet for her honour and the better accomplishment of her service there' and emphasises that Walsingham and the rest of the Council must support him in this. He concludes by noting his intention to return to London tomorrow 'to further my expedition', and in a postscript acknowledges 'so was hir gracious dealing with me yesterday such an assurance of hir great favor as yt ys encouragement suffycyant for me to pass all dangers that may happen with gretest comfort'. There is no doubt that the dating of this letter to 24 September by the PRO is correct, but it raises immediate queries about the chronology of the disbursement book. The book includes entries under 21 September to Leicester going from Nonsuch to London and from London to Barnet and then to Mr Butler's on the 22nd.[24] These dates are clearly wrong. His letters suggest that Leicester left the Court on the 23rd, began despatching his circular letters at Leicester House, and left for Barnet and Northaw either that evening or early in the morning of the 24th. He spent the day at Mr Butler's and the night probably at St Albans, and then returned to London on the 25th, when he may have gone directly to the Tower. More intriguing are the entries to the Countess and his servants waiting for him at Barnet and St Albans. John Stanhope's letter of Tuesday 21 September reported inconclusive discussions over Leicester's appoint-

[20] *Ibid.*, 5–7.

[21] On the raising of money see also PRO, SP12/182/108, Horatio Palavicino to Walsingham, 28 Sept. This was the initial stage of the loan raised in London discussed below and in n. 663.

[22] *Leic. Corres.*, 7–8. It is clear that Leicester expected that the Queen would see the letter and phrased it accordingly; the enclosure was intended for Walsingham's eyes only. This appears to have been a common practice, but while some other examples survive it is probable that most of the enclosures were destroyed on receipt.

[23] SP12/182/67, see n. 17 above.

[24] See pp. 311–2.

ment but also that he was going 'tomorrow' to christen Lady Garrett's child.[25] It would appear that his departure from the Court was delayed from Wednesday to Thursday and that the Countess and his servants had to wait for him.

Further to confuse matters the disbursement book records under 24 and 26 September a visit to St Albans to see the Queen's horses and then a visit to Northaw for the christening of Lady Cumberland's child, followed by the expenses of Leicester's servants at Barnet on Saturday and Sunday, 1 and 2 October.[26] Saturday and Sunday were in fact 2 and 3 October, but the more important question is how many visits were there to Northaw and St Albans? On 12 September Stanhope reported being sent by the Queen to Northaw to see Warwick 'who hath no use of his legs', his wife and her sister Lady Cumberland, who was expecting her delivery daily.[27] Given that neither Leicester on the 24th nor Stanhope on the 21st refer to Lady Cumberland's delivery, the probability is that there were in fact two visits, one on 24 September and the other at the end of the following week.

Within this framework we can fit several other letters. The first is one from Walsingham dated 27 September in *Leic. Corres.*, which is either a misreading or an error by Walsingham, for it is endorsed by Arthur Ayte 26 September.[28] Walsingham begins by noting Leicester's 'comfort' in the Queen's gracious dealing when she agreed to his employment in the Netherlands, then notes that the Council would support his requests and if any 'charges' were refused the Queen would be the one responsible. It also mentions that the Dutch commissioners wished Leicester to leave as soon as possible and that he hoped to see Leicester at Leicester House either the next day or the day after. This so obviously addresses the points raised in Leicester's letter of the 24th that it is clearly an answer to it, written on either the 25th or 26th and received by Leicester on the 26th.[29]

To this letter there is an undated answer.[30] In this Leicester states that he has no intention of increasing the Queen's charges, but that he would need sufficient and able men about him. He had given Sidney some notes for Walsingham 'this morning'. He then went on propose raising 500 or 600 of his own tenants, which he would discuss with

[25] Hist MSS Comm, *Rutland MSS*, i, 180. Catherine Butler was the widow of Lord Gerald Fitzgerald.

[26] See pp. 314–6, and, for the Stables at St Albans, n. 609.

[27] Hist MSS Comm, *Rutland MSS*, i, 178.

[28] *Leic. Corres.*, 8–10, the endorsement is taken from the original, BL, Harl. MS 285, fo. 133. For the significance of Atye's endorsements, see 'Leic. Pap. II', 131.

[29] By dating it 27 Sept., Bruce considered it an answer to Leicester's of the 27th, and assumed from it that the Queen had been won round in the meantime.

[30] *Leic. Corres.*, 10–12. Bruce correctly identified this as an answer to Walsingham's letter, but having mis-dated Walsingham's could only date it late September.

Walsingham when they met. This therefore should be dated to the 26th as well.[31] It is tempting to identify the undated page of notes in Leicester's hand in the State Papers as those referred to here, but they include the comment 'no man here doth believe' that the Queen will go through with her decision, which echoes passages in his letters to Walsingham and Burghley of 28 August. It is probably a private enclosure sent to Walsingham with his letter of 28 August.[32]

Perhaps the most curious letter of the series is the one to Walsingham dated simply 'this eveninge vij a clock'.[33] It was clearly written from the Court and refers to the Queen's unwillingness for him to go 'by reason of hir often decease taking hir of late & this last night worst of all, she used very pittyfull words to me of hir fear she shall not lyve & wold not have me from hir'. His answer was to 'lett hir know how farr I gonn in my preparacion' and in the end he inferred that she would let him go. He concluded by asking Walsingham (who was obviously not at Court) to 'send my wyfe word in the morning that I cannot come before Thursday to London'. The PRO have dated this 21 September, thus pre-dating the Queen's decision of the 23rd. It would also appear to account for his wife's waiting for him at Barnet on Friday the 24th. However, the reference to the extent of his preparations makes sense only for the period after the 26th. It was probably written on Tuesday the 28th, implying that Leicester came to court late on Monday the 27th, when the first late night emotional discussion took place, possibly by barge from London to Putney on the 27th.[34] Since it implies that Walsingham was in London it fits his announced intention on the 26th of going there, and in fact he wrote to Leicester on the 29th about Scottish and French affairs from London, intending to be at court 'tomorrow morning'.[35] Leicester was apparently still at Court on Thursday the 30th, when he signed a letter to Sir George Carey on

[31] Sidney had returned to Court on 21 September (Hist MSS Comm, *Rutland MSS*, i, 180), and the implication here is that he was at Leicester House on the 26th and sent to Walsingham then. He may have been with Leicester earlier in the weekend.

[32] PRO, SP84/3/205, calendared in *CSPF, 85–6*, 53, where Burghley is suggested as the recipient. The relevant passage in the letter to Walsingham reads, 'I doe find all sorts of men where I come so dauntyd with this conceatt as those who wold have runne to this servyce at the begining wyll slowly goe now yf they be entreated, for they will not beleave that hir Mat. wyll so deal in yt as they may hope ether of good assistance or such comfort as ys fitt for men that must goe hazard their lyves', and that in the letter to Burghley 'And men abroad begin now to doubt her persuasion in this case'. The reasons for considering that Walsingham was the recipient are not relevant here.

[33] PRO, SP12/182/41.

[34] For the barge journey, see p. 313.

[35] BL, Cotton MS Caligula C IX, fo. 180. There is no evidence of Walsingham being in London during the previous week. From the references cited above, he was at Court on the 18th and 23rd, and he wrote to Leicester from Barn Elms on the 21st, Bodl., MS Tanner 78, fo. 74.

musters on the Isle of Wight together with Hatton and Warwick, and must have departed on his second visit to St Albans immediately afterwards.[36]

After the end of September the internal correspondence diminishes and we have less detail about the events of October and November. One clear result of Leicester's discussions with the Queen during the week of 27 September was her agreement to his proposal to raise 500 men from his tenants, and letters patent commissioning him to do so were issued on 2 October.[37] However, his commission as lieutenant general was not issued until the 22nd, the explanation for which must be the delayed arrival on 21 October of the Dutch act of ratification of 22 September.[38] He wrote to the States General on the 23rd answering their letter of 25 September (which was probably sent with the act of ratification), and then to Davison on the 25th intimating that he hoped to arrive in the Netherlands by 10 November.[39] His letters to his followers of 26 September had instructed them to assemble at London on 15–16 October, and since no evidence of countermanding letters have survived, we must presume that they did so, and a muster was held of some 400 horsemen at Tothill Fields, Westminster, at some point in October or early November. Their arrival may explain the entry in the disbursement book to the despatch of the Privy Seal to Leicester House under 18 October, for he received £8000 pounds 'horsage' for them (at £20 a man and horse) and the seal may have been used for warrants to the Exchequer.[40]

The Queen reacted so angrily to the terms of the Dutch act of ratification when it arrived that Walsingham relayed his fears on 26 October that she would repudiate the whole agreement.[41] However, on 10 November Leicester informed Davison that 'the worst ys past here' and that he would be sending his horsemen directly into Holland as

---

[36] FSL, MS Xd 452 [Carey Papers], art. 6 (a copy). Given Warwick's health as reported by Stanhope earlier in the month, it is doubtful that he was at Court. Leicester probably took it to Northaw with him and obtained his signature there.

[37] PRO, C66/1255/43. For the raising of these tenants, see 'North Wales', 132–4.

[38] Also enrolled on roll 1255, memb. 43, which suggests that it might have been drafted at the same time as the earlier commission.

[39] ARA, Eerste Afdeling, Regeringsarchieven I-92 contains both the minute of the State-General's letter and Leicester's answer. The letter to Davison is calendared in *CSPF, 1585–6*, 118.

[40] The only reference to the Tothill Fields muster and the horsage that I have encountered is found in the discussion of Leicester's debts to the crown in BL, Lansdowne MS 61, fos. 206–7, Arthur Atye to Burghley, 9 Dec. 1589. Despite the numerous entries to the presenting of individual horses, nothing resembling an entry for the muster can be found in the disbursement book. However, it is possible that one of the lists of the horsemen mentioned in the Introduction, p. 23, may be the product of the muster.

[41] PRO, SP12/183/176, to Leicester, 26 Oct. See also Motley, i, 321–2, and Read, *Walsingham*, iii, 122–3.

he had been informed that there was not sufficient accommodation for them in Flushing and Middelburg.[42] Sidney himself left for Flushing on 9 November, and Leicester expected to follow him within a week, a theme he repeated during the next fortnight.[43] On 22–3 November 650 horse and 400 men were shipped into Holland and he in turn expected to depart from Harwich to Zeeland with only his household and the principal officers on 1 December.[44]

For Leicester's last fortnight in England the chronology of the disbursement book becomes particularly erratic and, while the sequence of his movements is clear, the dates of the entries are completely unreliable. Leicester's route to the Netherlands – Richmond, Leicester House, Wanstead, Ingatestone Hall (Sir John Petre's house), Chelmsford, Colchester (Sir Thomas Lucas's house), Harwich – poses no difficulties and with his departure from the Court the correspondence becomes more plentiful, but it too is frequently casual with dates and locations. However, there is an accurate account of the voyage from Harwich to Flushing in the detailed report by Stephen Borough, who commanded the shipping used for Leicester's transport, and this provides a starting point even if it means working backwards.[45]

According to Borough, Leicester left Colchester early in the morning of 8 December for Manningtree. There wherries were waiting for him and he was ferried to Harwich, which he reached at about 11 o'clock. It would therefore follow that he stayed at Sir Thomas Lucas's on the night of 7–8 December. His movements prior to 7 December are less straight-forward. He appears to have left Richmond on either 24 or 25 November for Leicester House, where on the 26th and 30th he signed the documents of incorporation for his hospital, although it is possible that he paid a brief visit to the Court on the 28th.[46] On 2 December (as suggested in n. 663) he dined with the Lord Mayor, and on 3rd he informed both Walsingham and Davison that he was leaving Leicester

---

[42] PRO, SP84/5/50–1, to Davison, 10 Nov. It is not clear how the Queen was mollified.

[43] On 6 November (*CSPF, 1585–6*, 146), Walsingham informed Davison that Leicester would leave at the same time as Sidney. On 15 November Leicester told Shrewsbury (Hist MSS Comm, *Bath MSS*, v, 63) he would leave within the next seven days. On the 18th he told Davison (PRO, SP84/5/82–3) 'within x days at furthest', and Roger Manners reported on the same day (Hist MSS Comm, *Rutland MSS*, i, 183) that he would leave a week from the next Friday.

[44] PRO, SP84/5/110–11, to Davison, 24 Nov.

[45] Printed in *Leic. Corres.*, 461–6, from BL, Harl. MS 6846, fos. 26–8, without omissions.

[46] The three founding documents for the hospital were signed at this time, the deed of incorporation on 21 November, the statutes on the 26th and the deed of endowment on the 30th (WCRO, CR1600/LH 1, 2,3). Leicester also wrote to the governor of Ostend from 'ma maison a Londres' on the 30th, PRO, SP77/1/92. For Leicester's visit to the Court on the 28th, see the reference to a reward at Richmond on p. 338.

House early the next morning, presumably for Wanstead.[47] On the 5th he wrote to Burghley apologising for not saying good-bye in person when he left the Court, but he had expected to see him in London later, and had only just learned that Burghley had been too ill to leave his bed.[48] On the same day he wrote to Walsingham, informing him that he was then on his way to Sir John Petre's, where he would spend the night.[49]

For all the pressure he was under to depart, Leicester had at this point a specific reason for delay. He had mortgaged the lordship of Denbigh to raise the loan of £17,600 from the London consortium, but Denbigh had already been mortgaged to the Queen for £15,000 in 1576, and at least £5,000 of the first mortgage was outstanding.[50] Therefore, although the agreement was concluded with the London consortium on 2 December, it had to be countersigned by the Queen, and Leicester refused to depart until she did so.[51] It was not until 7 December that he learned from Walsingham that she had finally signed 'the assurance', and he concluded his letter acknowledging this news 'haste towards Harwiche'.[52] It is probable that his letters of the 5th were written from Wanstead, and therefore he probably spent the nights of the 5th–6th and 6th–7th killing time at Ingatestone.

On reaching Harwich Leicester went immediately aboard his ship, which was anchored in the roads, and there he dined.[53] Here a further delay occurred. Borough had expected that Flushing would be

---

[47] PRO, SP84/5/152–3, 154–5, to Walsingham and Davison, 3 Dec. The letter to Davison is subscribed 'from London'. On the 2nd Roger Manners reported to the Earl of Rutland from the Savoy 'it is now certenly thought the Earle of Lecester setteth forwardes tomorrow. He hath taken leave of her Majestie' (Hist MSS Comm, *Rutland MSS*, i, 184). By implication, the leave-taking had occurred since his last letter to Rutland on 18 November.

[48] BL, Harl. MS 6993, fo. 119 (*Leic. Corres.*, 21–3), 'on my way to the sea side'. He had written to Burghley the previous day, giving no address, on a minor matter of business (BL, Lansdowne MS 45, fo. 84). According to Roger Manners (see the previous note) Burghley was suffering from an attack of gout.

[49] PRO, SP84/5/160–1, dated only 'this Sunday morning'.

[50] The history of the mortgages of Denbigh is a complex subject, see 'Leic. Pap. III'. The first mortgage was to be paid off in three instalments of £5,000. Leicester certainly paid off the first, and the last was outstanding at his death, but the position regarding the second is unclear.

[51] See n. 663 above. He sent the 'assurance' to Walsingham to present to the Queen on the 3rd (PRO, SP84/5/152–3). On the 5th he learned of her initial refusal to sign from Walsingham (PRO, SP84/5/160–1), and commented 'I lye this night at Sir John Peters & but for this doubt had I byn tomorrow at Harwich'. He clearly did not leave Wanstead until later in the day, for he answered another letter from Walsingham simply 'In all haste ready to horse' (PRO, SP84/5/162–3).

[52] *CSPF, 1585–6*, 201–2.

[53] In his letters from the ship (*Ibid.*, 205), he names it the *Amytyst*, as does the 1585–7 disbursement book, see p. 367. Borough calls it the *Amytie*.

Leicester's destination, but a week previously Leicester had been requested by the Dutch to go directly to the Brill.[54] However, Borough had not been informed, and he now told Leicester he would need further time to assemble sufficient pilots for the Brill for all the fleet. The following morning (9 December) he informed Leicester that it would be impossible to do so, and Leicester, with some irritation, agreed to go to Flushing.

The fleet finally left around 3 o'clock in the afternoon of the 9th, but it had an easy passage and by 8 o'clock the following morning was in sight of Ostend. Flushing was reached by noon and Leicester disembarked between 1 and 2 o'clock in the afternoon. Maurice of Nassau and a reception party from the States General were in fact waiting in Middelburg, but on news of his arrival they left immediately for Flushing where they arrived in the evening.[55] There they requested that Leicester make his way into Holland as soon as possible and leave immediately for Middelburg.[56] He left Flushing shortly after noon on the 11th and arrived at Middelburg some three hours later.[57]

---

[54] PRO, SP84/5/154–5, to Davison, 3 Dec. The request had come from Paul Buys.

[55] *CSPF, 1585–6*, 213–4, to the Council, 14 Dec. from Middelburg.

[56] They wished him to attend the meeting of the States-General at the Hague. This was probably the reason for the earlier request relayed by Buys to sail to the Brill.

[57] Borough's account concludes with Leicester's departure from Middelburg for Dordrecht on 17 December.

PART II

HOUSEHOLD LISTS

A. The Book of My Lords Servantts Wages
and Boord Wages, 1559–1561
(Longleat, Dudley Papers III, fos. 1–17)

A paper book bound into Dudley Papers III (a volume of miscellaneous papers assembled after Canon Jackson's sorting of the Longleat Papers).[a] It is the first item in the volume and the foliation is sequential throughout. There is a modern pencil note on fo. 1, 'E of Leycester. Book of Servants Bordwages Etc. 1 Eliz. 1558–9' [*sic*]'. Internal references (pp. 403, 417) reveal that it was compiled by Richard Ellis and the dates of his last payments coincide with those of his main account.

[fo. 1]

xixli. xviijs. vd. ob.

Note to charge Born of the stab[le] with ij metresses, ij bolsters and the furnyture delyverid to Curson for ther use.
Item j to the gardyner at Kewe.

[fo. iv]
The Booke of my lord's servantts wages and boord wages from the Mydsommer Anno Primo Elizabethae Reginae untyll Our Lady Day Anno Tercio Reginae Elizabethae.

[fo. 2]

William Hugganes, gentleman

Paid unto the same upon a bill for money by him laid owte as appeareth by a bill}   xxs.

William Chuncy

Paid to him uppon a bill}   xxxiijs. iiijd.

Mr Cary

Paid unto him uppon a bill}   viijs.
Item paid unto him uppon another bill}   ijs.
<Care bill>

William Beamount

[b]Paid unto him uppon a bill per pet[itionem] xj of June}   xxxviijs.
Item paid unto him the xiiijth of July anno secondo}   xls.[b]
Item paid unto him the xxj [iij *deleted*] of December for his
half yeres waigs ended at Christmas anno tercio}   xvli.

Item paid unto the same the xth of August by
Mr Thomas Blunt}   vijli. xs.
Item more paid unto him in prest at ij severall
tymes viz the [...] daie of June xxxviiis. and
the xiiijth day of July following xls.}   lxxviijs.
Item for his bedd at Grenewich by the space of xj weaks at
xijd. the weak}   xxjs.
<xxjth of December>
                    Summa Paginae} xxxiiijli. iiijd.

[fo. 2v]

Richard Hordeyne
Item paid unto him uppon accompt}   iiijli. xijs. vjd.

ᶜRichard Jinks
To him uppon a reckening}ᶜ

Robert Curson
Paid unto him uppon a bill for the rest due unto him
uppon a bill}   iiijli. ijs. iiijd.
Item to him uppon annother bill for the ferrary
of certayne my lord's horsees}   vjs.
Item to him for monney laid oute as appeareth by the
same bill xth of June}   ixs. iiijd.

Thomas Eaglamby
Paid to him uppon a bill of parceles}   viijs. vjd.
Item uppon one other bill}   ijs.
Item to him more uppon one other bill}   iijs. viijd.
Paid to him uppon one other bill}   ijs. ijd.
Item more to him uppon one other bill}   ijs. vjd.
Item to him by your lordship's commandment}   vjli. xiijs. iiijd.
and for charges xijs.   Suma vijli. vs. iiijd.
Item for his bedd at Grenewich by the space of xj weeks}   xjs.
                    Summa Paginae} xviijli.

[fo. 3]

Henry Gylmer
Paid him uppon a bill of charges at his retorne out
of Cambridgesheare when he tryed your lordship's greyhonds}   xls.
To him uppon one other bill}   vijs. viijd.
To him uppon other bill}   liiijs. xd.

Item paid to him uppon a bill with him remaining}   xs.

Thomas Eaton

Paid to him uppon one bill}   xxixs. iijd.
Item paid unto him uppon one other bill}   xxs. viijd.
Item paid unto him uppon one other bill}   iiijs.
Item paid to him uppon one other bill}   ixs.
Item paid unto him uppon one other bill the xxijth of
November anno tercio}   iiijs. vjd.

Elles Stampe

Paid to him uppon one bill}   xxiijs. iiijd.
Item to him uppon one other bill}   xiijs. iiijd.
Item for his bedd and William Bussheles}   vjs.
^dItem for his bedd at Kingston & other necessaries
by hym laid out}   xxxvjs. viijd.^d
          Summa Paginae} xjli. ijs. vjd.

[fo. 3v]

Mr Goore

Paid unto him uppon a bill for monney by him laid out}   iijs. xd.

Mr Cutteller

Paid unto him uppon a bill of parceles}   xxvjs.
For his bedd at Grenewiche for a xj weeks at xij*d.* the week}   xjs.

Mr Lye

Paid unto him uppon a bill for monney laid out by him
appeareth by the bill}   xijs. iiijd.
For his bedd at Grenewich by the spac of a xj weeks
at xij*d.* the week}   xjs.

Mr Petre Musicion

Paid unto him uppon [a bill *deleted*] sundry
billes for lute stringes as by the said bill appeareth}   xxxis. ijd.

Nicholas Gyrlington

Paid to him uppon a bill for monney by him laid furthe
to your lordship's use}   xviijs. ijd.
          Summa Paginae} vli. xijs. vjd.

[fo. 4]

Mr Newtreffeald
Paid to him uppon a bill for monney by him [dys]bursid in
reward by your lordship's commandment}

xxjs. ijd.

Mr Grisse
Paid unto him uppon a bill for monney by him laid oute
abought your lordship's affayres}

lviijs. viijd.

Edward Langham
Paid unto him uppon a bill for lodging and certayne
meales as by the bill appeareth in p[aymen]te thearof}

xjs. viijd.

Mr [Robert *deleted*] Thomas Darcye
Paid to him for [*sic*] dysbursid by your
lordship's commandment}

xijs. iiijd.

John Aspeley
Item to him uppon a bill}

ijs.

Summa Paginae} vli. vs. xd.

[fo. 4v]

John Marbray
[e] Item paid for the hier of ij horsses for him & his mane}

xxvs.

Item paid unto him uppon one bill for monney laid oute
at severall tymes as appeareth}

lxs.

Item to him uppon one other bill for monney by him laid
oute in riding charges to Hemmesby and for horse hier as
appeareth by his bill of parceles}

vjli. xvd.

Item for the hier of a horsse for him from London by the
[*sic*]}

xviijs.[e]

<vacat>

Mr Nicholson
Paid to him uppon a bill of xxxiiijs. x*d.*
due unto him for the carriage of hay}

xs.

Mr Yerwerth
Item paid to him for his chargies going to Kew abowte my
lord's busynes}

xs.

Mr Barneston

For his bedd at Grenewich at the progresse for the spac
of xj weks at xij*d.* the week sum}

xjs.

Mr Capell

For his bedd at Grenewich by the spac of xj weeks at xij*d.*
the week}

xjs.

Mr Hilliard

For his bedd at Grenewich by the spac of xj week at xij*d.*
the week}

xjs.

Summa Paginae} [xijli. viijs. iijd. *deleted*]

[fo. 5]

George Gyles

Item paid unto him uppon iiij severall billes of parceles
as appeareth by the same billes}

xxxvijs. jd.

ᶠItem paid unto him for one hole}ᶠ

Item paid unto him for hys wages for two yeares and a half
endid at [Mighelmas *deleted*] the Annunciation
of our Lady in the thirde yeare of the raigne of Quene
Elizabeth at iiij*li.* per annum. Whearof
he receaved of Wm Chuncy xxs. and the
residue being ix*li.* by me Richard Ellis}

ixli.

John Empson

Paid unto him for his wags as from the Annuntiacion of our
Lady anno primo regni Elizabethae predicto unto Mydsommer
anno secondo, beyng one yeare and a quarter at lxvj*s.*
xiij*d.* by yeare. Summa iiij*li.* iij*s.* iiij*d.*}

lxxxiijs. iiijd.

Item more paid unto him for his wages from mydsommer anno
predicto unto the Annuntiacion of Our Lady anno tertio dominae
Reginae being iij quarters of a yeare at iiij*li.* by year}

lxs.

Paid unto him uppon v severall billes of parcelles
as maye appeare}

vli. iijs. iijd. ob.

Summa Paginae} xxijli. xiijs. viijd. ob.

[fo. 5v]

William Wurtheley

ᵍPaid unto him the iiijth daye of Aprelle
in full payment of his bill due at the Annuciation of
Our Lady anno tercio}

xxiijs. vijd.ᵍ

Item paid unto him uppon a bill due at the Annunciation
of Our Lady Day for all his demands}   xxxvijs. vijd.

Henry Johannes

Item paid unto him for one yeare and iij quarters wags at
xl*s*. by yere endid at the Annunciation of Our
Lady anno tercio}   lxxs.
Item paid unto him for bordwages in the tyme of his sickness
by the space of xxij daies at x*d*. the daye as by
a by a [*sic*] appeareth}   xviijs. iiijd.
<Not[a?] bord wages>
Item for his bedd for the said xxij daies}   xviijd.
Item paid unto him for certayne parceles allowed unto him
uppon his billes}   xvjs. jd.

William Olyver

Paid unto him for his wages for one yeare iij quarters
ending at the feast of the Annuciation of Our Lady anno
tercio predicto at xl*s*. per annum}   lxxs.
Item paid unto him for his bedd from the first daye of January
anno secondo dominae Reginae unto the Annunciation of Our
Lady anno tercio being lxiiij weeks, wheareof he was allowed
at Grenewiche for xj weeks at viij*d*. the week and
the liij weeks residue at vj*d*. the week, suma}   xxxiijs. xd.
Item more paid unto him for certayne parceles allowed unto
him uppon his billes}   xxxijs.
          Summa Paginae} xiijli. xviijs. iiijd.

[fo. 6]

Thomas Davyes

Paid unto him for his wags for one yeare and a half endid
at Christmas anno tertio}   lxs.
Item paid unto him for his bedd from the first of January
anno secondo unto Christmas followinge beyng lj weeks
wheareof was allowed for a xj weeks at Grenewich
at viij*d*. the week and the xl weeks residewe at
vj*d*. the week, suma}   xxvijs. iiijd.
<per Yerweth per John Duddley xxs.>

Richard Glasior

Item paid unto him for his wags for one yeare and a half
endid the Annuntiacion of Our Lady anno predicto}   lxs.
Item paid uppon xij severall billes of parcels for monney

by him laid oute as appeareth}   ixli. xiiijs. iiijd. ob.

John Alleyne senior

Item for one hole yeares wags and iij quarters endid at
the Annutiacion of Our Lady anno tercio at xls. per annum}   lxxs.
Item paid to him uppon a bill of parcels}   ijs. iiijd.

John Alleyne junior

Item to him uppon a bill due at the Annuntiacion of Our
Lady anno tercio}   xxvjs. iiijd.

Summa Paginae} xxiiijli. xvijs. iiijd.

[fo. 6v]

Hewe Brystoo

Item paid unto him for one yeare iij quarters endid at
the Annuntiacion of Our Lady anno tercio regni Reginae
at xls. by yere}   lxxs.
Item paid unto him by the hands of John Marbury gentleman
the some of}   vjs. iiijd.

Thomas Braybrooke

Paid unto him for one yeare iij quarters wags endinge at
the Annuntiacion of our Lady anno predicto}   lxxs.
Item for his bedd at from [sic] the first of Maye following
which maketh xix wekes at vjd. the week}   ixs. vjd.
Item for his bedd at Grenewich by the space of xj
weeks at viijd. the week}   vijs. iiijd.
Item paid unto him uppon the rest of a bill of parceles
due in William Chancyes tyme}   vijs. viijd.
Item uppon one other bill of parceles}   iiijs. iiijd.

John Powell of the wardrobe

Paid unto him uppon a bill for bord wags and otherwyse
as appeareth by the same bill}   iiijli.
Item paid unto him uppon v billes of parceles by him laid
oute as appeareth by the said bils}   vjli. vs. xjd.
Item paid unto him the iiijth daie of Aprell uppon a bill
examined by Mr John Duddley}   vli.
Item more paid unto him at severall tymes uppon his
billes remayninge with him}   iiijli. vd.
Item paid unto him more by the hands of John
Marbury the some of}   viijs. viijd.

Summa Paginae} xxviijli. xs. viijd.

[fo. 7]

Fredericke Godfraye

Paid unto him for the [...] dewe of [...] for iij quarters
wages ended at Medsommer anno secondo Reginae at xl*s.*
per annum, soma}   xxxs.
Item more paid unto him uppon a bill of parceles}   viijs.
Item receaved more by him the iiijth of Aprell uppon
his bill at Somerset House}   xls.

Edward Robarts

Paid unto him for one quarters wags at xl*s.* per
annum endid at Christmas 1558}   xs.

Gyttones

Paid unto the same xiiijth of Marche for one quarter
wags due at Christmas anno secondo}   xs.

Heughe Johanes

Paid unto him for one hole yeares wags endid at Mydsommer
in the second yeare of the Quenes majesties raigne at
xl*s.* by yeare}   xls.
            Summa Paginae} vjli. xviijs.

[fo. 7v]

George Lewes Cooke

Paid unto him for one yeare iij quarters wags endid at
the Annuntiacion of Our Lady anno tercio reginae Elizabethae}   lxxs.
Item uppon his bills of parceles}   xixs. viijd.

William Hakesby Cooke

Paid unto him for one hole yeare and a halff for
his wags endid at the Annuntiacion of Our Lady anno predicto}   lxs.
Item paid unto him uppon iij severall bills for
monney by him laid out as more at lardge by the same
bills may appeare}   xxxijs. iiijd.
<per Yerwerth x*s.*>
Sum iiijli. xijs. iiijd.
Memorandum that he hath receaved at sondry payments
as doth appeare by the severall daies [*sic*]}   ixli. xijd.

Ph[ilip?]e Frennchman Cooke
Paid unto him by your lordship's commandment for his
service the some of}   [*blank*]
                    Summa Paginae} xviijli. iiijs.

[fo. 8]

Moryce Edwardes

Paid unto him for a rest of certayne billes due unto
him for borde wages and otherwise as appeareth by one
bill signed by Mr Dudley and others the some of}   lxvs. ijd.
Item paid unto him for his boordwags from the xijth
daie of November to the xxvth daye of Marche anno
secondo regni Reginae Elizabethae being Cxxxiij daies
at x*d*. the daye, summa}   vli. xs. xd.
Item paid unto him for his bed from the xxth daye
of January anno secondo dominae Reginae unto the xxviijth
daie of Aprell followinge being xiiij weeks}   vijs.
Item paid unto him for dyvers parcels laid oute by the
said Edwards as appeareth by billes therof}   ijs. viijd.
Item paid unto him the iiijth daie of Aprell anno tercio
regni Reginae uppon his bill sighned by Mr John Duddeleye
& others}   xlvjs. viijd.
Item paid unto him for his wages for one hole yeare and
iij quarters ended at the Annuntiacion of Our Lady last}   lxxs.
Sum}   xvli. ijs. iijd.
<not adhoc quae non>
Item more paid unto him at Kewe the xix daie of November
uppon his billes remayning with him}   xxs.
Item lennt to him January anno tercio Reginae}   vjs.
<there appeareth a not of twyce twenty shillings paid unto him more
deleted>

Henry Dobbynes Fawlconner

Item paid unto him uppon a Bill for his Bordwages horsemeat
and hawksmeat}   lxxs.
<uncleared note the daye & yere>

Henry Sherewood Fawlconner

Item paid unto the same the xxth daie of Aprell
anno secondo Reginae}   iiijli. xiiijs. ijd.

[fo. 8v]

John Awdwyne

Item for one yeare and iij quarters wages ended at the
feast of the Annunciation of our Lady anno tercio
dominae Reginae at liij*s*. iiij*d*. by yeare, summa}   iiijli. xiijs. iiijd.
Item for the rest of monney due unto him uppon a bill
sighned by Mr Blount and others the xxvijth of December
anno secondo}   xxxvjs. viijd.
Item more paid unto him uppon ij other bills aswell
for his board from Christmas anno secundo to the vijth
of May followinge as also for other chargs laid oute
by hym}   xxvjs. vijd.

Robart Holland

^hPaid unto him uppon ij severall Billes the one of
vij*s*. x*d*., one other of ix*s*. vj*d*., and the other of viij*li*. xvj*s*. x*d*. for all
his demands due at the Annuntiacion of Our Lady anno tercio Regine}
                                                   ixli. xiiijs. ijd.^h
Item paid unto him for one hole yeares wags due at
mid sommer anno secondo}   xls.
Item paid unto him uppon iij several billes as well
for iij quarters wags more endid at the Annuntiacion of
Our Lady anno tercio, as also for other demands as
appeareth by the said bills}   ixli. xiiijs. xd.
<per Yerwerth v*li*. xviij*s*.>
Item paid unto him for xj weeks bedd at Grenewich at
viij*d*. the week viij weeks}   vs. iiijd.

Henrye Fawlconner

Paid unto him in recompence of service by your lordship's
commandment}   lxvjs. viijd.
                    Summa Paginae} xxiijli. iijs. vd.

[fo. 9]

Marteyn Bott

Paid to him in full satisfacion of all his demands by a
bill}   lxs.

Rauffe Aldersaye

Paid unto him uppon his bill for bordwages from the
xxixth daie of July anno secondo regni Reginae unto

the last daie of Septembre followinge being ix weeks and
iij daies viz in dayes lxvj at viij*d*. the daie}   sum xliiijs.
Item more paid unto him for his boarde wags from the xxth
daie of October unto the xixth of Novembre which is xxix
daies at viij*d*. the daie, sume}   xixs. iiijd.
Paid unto him for his bedd from the first daie of January
anno secondo dominae Reginae unto the xxixth of July
followinge: which is xxx weeks wheareof xj weeks at
Greenwich allowed unto him after the rate of viij*d*.
the weeke and the residewe being xix weeks at vj*d*.
the week}   xvjs. xd.
Item for his bedd from the xxixth daie of July unto the
vj of October which maketh xj weeks at vj*d*. the week}   vs. vjd.
Item for his bedd from the first daye of January anno
tercio Reginae unto the vjth of Aprell being Our Lady
daie [*sic*] and maks xij weeks at vj*d*. the weeke, suma}   vjs.
Item paid unto him for his wags for one yeare and iij
quarters ending at Our Lady Day at xl*s*. by yeare
anno tercio Reginae}   lxxs.
Item paid unto him for dyvers chargs laid oute and allowed
unto him in his bills}   xvs. xd.
          Summa Paginae} xjli. xvijs. vjd.

[fo. 9v]

Gryffithe Lloyde

Paid unto him uppon his billes for bordwags from the
xxixth of July unto the xxiijth of September beyng lv
daies at iiij*d*. the daie xxxvij*s*. iiij*d*.
And for his bord wags from the xxth of October unto
the xxth daie [*sic*] being xxx daies at viij*d*.
the daie summa}   lvijs. iiijd.
<Memorandum that by Hylles byll he doth aske butt xxxv*s*.
for stadds [*sic*] boordwags for the time of the progress>
Item paid unto him for his bedd from the first daie
of January anno secondo Reginae unto the xxth of
October followinge and from the xxth of November
unto the xxvjth daye of March followinge which makes
in all lix weeks whearof xj weeks at Grenewich werr
allowed at xiij*d*. the weeke and the residewe being
xlviij weeks at vj*d*. the week, suma}   xxxjs. iiijd.
Item paid unto him for his wagies for one yeare and
iij quarters ending at our Lady Day at xl*s*. per annum, sum}   lxxs.
Item paid unto him for other charges laid oute and

allowed uppon his billes}   lxs. vjd.

Gryffithe Clune

Paid unto him for his bedd allowed from the first daye
of January anno secondo unto the xiiijth daye of May
followinge being xxtie weeks at vj*d*. the weeke}   xs.
Item for his bedd at Grenewich by the space of a xj
weeks at viij*d*. the week}   vijs. iiijd.
Item paid unto him for one hole yeare and iij quarters
wags ended at the Annuntiacion of Our Lady at xl*s*.
by yeare, sum}   lxxs.
<Memorandum alloc' quia non sol'>
Item paid unto him for monney laid oute uppon his billes}   vijs. viijd.
                        Summa Paginae} xiijli. iijs. ijd.

[fo. 10]

Edward Garlaund

Paid unto him uppon a bill of all demands unto the
Anuntiacion of Our Lady anno tercio reginae Elizabethae}   xxiiijs.
<per Yerwerth x*s*.>
Memorandum that he hath receavid xij*d*. more then his bill was.

Paule Vynton

Paid unto him the iiijth daie of Aprell anno tercio
Reginae uppon his bill due at the Anuntiacion
of Our Lady}   xxvjs. vjd.

Evan Johanes

Paid unto him the iiijth daie of Aprell anno superdicto
in full payment of his demands due at the anuntiacion
of Our Lady}   xxvjs. vjd.

Robert Dunkyn

Item paid unto him for one quarters wags ended at
Christmas 1559}   xs.
Paid unto him the iiijth daie of Aprell anno predicto
uppon his bill due at the Anuntiacion of Our Lady}   xxviijs. vjd.
                        Summa Paginae} vli. vs. vjd.

[fo. 10v]

William Devonsheere

Paid unto him the iiijth daie of Aprell anno tercio
regni Reginae uppon his bill for [*sic*] due
at the Annuntiacion of Our Lady}   xxvs. vjd.
<non alloc' quia non sol'>

John Heatherley

Paid unto him the iiijth daie of Aprell anno predicto
uppon his bill due at the Annuntiacion of our Lady}   xxijs.

John Forrest

Paid unto him uppon [ij severall *deleted*] billes
[the one of x*s*. and the other *deleted*] of
vj*li*. xiij*s*. iiij*d*. in full payment of his demands}   vjli. xiijs. iiijd.
                                                    [vijli. iiijs. iiijd. *deleted*]

Thomas Watson

Paid unto him uppon the iij severall bills for wags
and wurk done by him as appeareth by the said bill
examined before Thomas Blunt Esquier and others}   viijli. xvjs.
                    Summa Paginae} xvijli. xvijs. xd.

[fo. 11]

Thomas Forrest Huntesman

Paid unto him the xxiiijth daie of December anno
secondo Regine for the rest of a bill examined and
tryed by Mr John Dudley & others}   lxxvs. xd.
Item allowed unto him for his bordwags from the
xviijth daie of December anno predicto to the xxijth
daie of Novembre anno tercio dominae Reginae as by his
severall billes appereth}   xjli. xiijs.
Paid to him for his bedd [from the *deleted*] by the
space of lviij [*sic*] as appeareth by his
said severall billes more at lardge}   xxixs.
Item paid unto him for the keping of dyvers greyhounds,
howunds and spanielles as appeareth with the allowance
in his said billes}   ixli. xijs.
Item paid unto him for his wags for one yeare and iij
quarters endid at the Annuntiacion of Our Lady anno
tercio dominae Reginae}   lxxs.
<by my lord xl*s*. per the xx*s*.>
Item paid unto him uppon his bill of his demands
examined by Mr Dudley and others the iiijth daie of

Aprell anno predicto}   lxvjs. viijd.

John Ducke Huntesman
Paid unto him the viijth of February anno dominae
Reginae the some of}   xxs.
Item more paid unto him the xxijth of Januarye}   xxs.
Item more paid unto him the third daye of Aprell}   lxvjs. viijd.
                Summa Paginae} xxxviijli. xvs. ijd.

[fo. 11v]

Rauffe Fawlconner Huntesman
Item paid unto him at sondry tymes as by the particular
payments maye appeare}   xli.

Richard Fawlconner Huntesman
Item paid unto him uppon a bill for wags & bordwags
sighned by Mr Blunt}   iiijli. xiiijs. xd.

James Thompson Cator
Paid unto him for one half yeares wags endid at midsommer
anno secundo Reginae at xl*s*. per annum}   xxs.
<non alloc' quia non sol'>

Richard Flammocke
Paid unto him uppon ij severall bills the one sighned
by Mr Blunt}   xxxvijs. ijd.
<Memorandum M. Hoylles dothe ask allowance for Flammock's bord-
wags for tyme of the progresse butt xxiiij*li*.>
Item paid unto him the thirde daye of Aprell anno tercio
dominae Reginae}   [*blank*]
Item paid unto him the xxiijth of January 1560}   vs.
Item paid to him the xxiiijth of December}   xxvjs. xiijd.
Item paid unto him xvth of Novembre}   xs.
                Summa Paginae} xxli. xjs. iiijd.

[fo. 12]

William Woodman
Paid unto him uppon his bill of demand due at the
Annuntiacion of Our Lady Anno tercio reginae}   xxijs. vjd.

Archie Cragg Foteman

Paid unto him uppon a bill for his bedd from the first daie of January anno secundo Reginae unto the last daie of May followinge}	xs.
Item for his bead at Grenewich by the space of a xj weeks at viijd. the week}	vijs. iiijd.
Paid to him uppon his bills for dyvers chargs by him laid oute in the progras}	iiijli. xixs.
Item for one hole yeares wags and iij quarters endid at the Annuntiacion of Our Lady anno tercio}	lxxs.
Summa Paginae} xiijli. xvijs. ijd.[*sic*]	

John Garrett Foteman

Paid unto him uppon a bill signed by Mr Blunt}	xxviijs. iiijd.
Item paid unto him the iiijth daie of Aprell anno tercio Reginae Elizabethae uppon his bill signed by Mr John Duddley & others}	xxs.
Summa Paginae} xiijli. xvijs. ijd.	

[fo. 12v]

John Richards Trompeter

Paid unto him at Grenewich the xjth daie of June}	iiijli.
Item paid unto him the xxvijth daie of December}	xls.
Item receavid [of *deleted*] the vjth daie of Aprell}	xls.

Richard Evan Drompeplayor

Paid unto him uppon his allowance for one hole yeares wags and iij quarters endid at Christmas anno tercio dominae Reginae}	lxxs.
Item paid unto him for other allowances as appeareth by his bills}	xxxiiijs. viijd.

John Johnson Phiphe

Paid unto him at severall payments as maye appeare the some of}	[*blank*]
Paid unto him for his wags for one hole yeare and iij quarters endid at the Annuntiacion}	lxxs.
Item paid unto him for his bedd from the first daie of January anno secundo unto [*blank*]	
Item for his expences in the prograse and for his dynner one day in London}	xs. iiijd.
Summa Paginae} xviijli. vs.	

[fo. 13]

Frauncis Hedlein Ryder

ᶦPaid unto him at severall payments as may appeare
and confessed by the said Frauncis the some of}   xxvijli. vs. vjd.ᶦ
Paid unto the same Francis for ij yeares wags
endid at the Annuntiacion of Our Lady anno
tercio Regine at xxtie nobles by yeare, summa}   xiijli. vjs. viijd.
Item more paid unto him for his bordwags and
bedding due unto him from the xiiijth daye of
December anno secondo dominae Reginae unto the xxvth
daie of Marche as maye appeare by his particular
receipts the some of}   xiijli. xviijs. xd.
<and received at Ester vjli. xviijs. viijd.>
         Summa Paginae} xxvijli. vs. vd.

John Steaphinson Ferrar

Paid unto him for his wags for one hole yeare and a
half endid at the Annuntiacion of Our Lady anno tercio
dominae Reginae at iiijli. per annum}   vjli.
<Com' at this m' lxxiijs. iiijd.>
         Summa Paginae} xlixli. xvs. vjd.

[fo. 13v]

William Borne Grome of the Stable
Paid unto William Borne   [blank]

John Floyde grome of the Stable
Item   [blank]

[fo. 14]

Steaphin Rawson Grome of the Stable
Paid unto him for one hole yeares wages and a half endid
at the Annuntiacion of Our Lady anno tercio dominae Reginae}   lxs.

Patrick Hamlyn Grome of the Stable
Paid unto him for one hole yeare and a halff's wages endid
at the Annuntiacion of Our Lady anno tercio dominae Reginae
at xls. per annum}   lxs.
         Summa Paginae} vjli.

[fo. 14v]

      Robart Steaphinson Grome of the Stable
Paid unto him for iij quarters wages endid at the
Annuntiacion of Our Lady anno tercio dominae
Reginae, summa}   xxxs.

      Ph[ilip?]e Wattye Grome of the Chamber
Paid unto the same the xxviijth daie of July anno
secondo Reginae for one quarters wags endid at
midsommer next before}   xs.

      Roger Oswoold
Paid unto him for one yeares and iij quarters yeares
wages endid at the Annuntiacion of Our Lady anno tercio
Reginae}   lxxs.
Paid unto him uppon severall billes of parcels in monney
laid oute by him as appeareth in the said billes}   iiijli. xiijs. iiijd.
Paid unto him uppon one other bill sighned by Mr
Duddley and others the iiijth of Aprell anno tercio
dominae Reginae for parcels}   xs. xd.
Item for his bedd at Greenwich for a xj weeks at vj*d.*
the week, summa}   vs. vjd.
      Summa Paginae} xiijli. xs. vjd.

[fo. 15]

      Thomas Howlam Grome of the Chamber
Paid unto him for one hole yeares wags and a quarter
endid at the Annuntiacion of Our Lady anno tercio dominae
Reginae}   ls.
Item for his bed for the said tyme being lxiiij weeks
wheareof xj weeks at Grenewich was allowed after viij*d.*
[the week and the residewe being liij weeks at *deleted*]
Sum vijs. iiij*d.* allowed to John Thompett
[Trumpet?] in his reckening and the residewe being lij
weeks at vj*d.* the week, sum}   xxvjs. vjd.
Item paid unto him more uppon the delyvery of a French
crowne the second of Aprell to buy russhes}   iijs.
<Payd at Ester of this yeare but xiij*s.* iiij*d.* by Ellys>
Paid unto him for [*blank*]
      Summa Paginae} lxxixs. vjd.

[fo. 15v]

George Lovell Gardyner

Paid unto him uppon his demaund at ij severall payments}   iiijli.

Gwyllyam Horewood Gardyner

Paid unto him for one yeares wags and iij quarter endid
at the Annuntiacion of Our Lady anno tercio Reginae}   lxxs.
Item paid unto him for his borde wags by [the space of
deleted] from the first daye of July anno
primo Reginae unto the first daye of July anno secondo
dominae Reginae being CCClxv daies at viij*d*. the daie
which comethe to xij*li*. iij*s*. iiij*d*.}   xijli. iijs. iiijd.
Item paid unto him for one half yeres borde wages more
due at Christmas last past being after the rate of
viij*d*. the daie}   vjli. xxd.
Item for his bedd during the said tyme at vj*d*. the
week viz lxxviij weeks}   xxxixs.
Item [for *deleted*] paid unto him uppon dyvers
billes of parcels by him laid oute as doth appeare
by the particulars thearof}   vjli. iiijs.
Summa Paginae} xxxiijli. xviijs.

[fo. 16]

John Parterige Waterman

Paid unto him for one hole yeares wags and a half
due at Christmas [the Annuntiacion of Our Lady *deleted*]
anno tercio dominae Reginae at xl*s*. per annum}   lxs.
<Memorandum that his quarter[?] is paid in a bill of vj*li*. xiiij*s*.
iiij*d*.>
Item paid unto him uppon severall billes examined and
tryed by Mr Thomas Blunt and Mr Duddley as well for
chargs don uppon your lordship's barg by himself as also by
others and for necessaries for them as by the severall
billes of particulars more plainly maye appeare
the some of}   lvijli. vs. iiijd.
Summa} lxli. vs. iiijd.

Edward Wood Waterman

Paid unto him for a yeares wags endid at the
Annuntiacion of Our Lady anno tercio dominae Reginae}   [*blank*]

[fo. 16v]

Amye Wylton Launder

ʲPaid unto her for one half yeares wages endid
Paid unto her for a xj monethes wasshing the ewery from the
[*obscured*] daie of July anno secondo
at v*li*. vj*s*. viij*d*. by yeare which comethe to for the
same xj monethes}   iiijli. xvijs. ixd. ob.
Whearof was paid by William Chancy}   xxvjs. viijd.
And the residewe by me}   lxxjs. jd. ob.ʲ
Item paid unto her for wasshing the ewery for iij
quarters endid at Our Lady Daie 1561}   iiijli.
Item for wasshing the chamber iij quarters endid at .
Christmas anno tercio ᵏthe Annuntiacion of Our Lady
anno predictoᵏ}   lxs.
Item paid unto her for wasshing the ewery a xj monethes
at v*li*. vj*s*. viij*d*. per annum viz from the xxiiijth day
of July anno secondo regni Reginae unto the [*blank*] daie
of May next following which comethe to iiij*li*. xvij*s*.
ix*d*. *ob*. whearof was paid by William Chancy xxvj*s*. viij*d*.
and the rest by R.E.}   lxxjs. jd. ob.

Jane Langfford Launder

Paid unto her uppon a bill signed by Mr Duddley and
others for a rest due unto hir uppon the said bill
in William Chancyes tyme}   xlixs. xjd.
Item paid unto her for washing the chamber
for one half yeare endid at the Annuntiacion of
Our Lady anno secondo which was the half yeare
before Amye Wylton entrid, suma}   xls.
Item paid unto her for wasshing the chamber for one
quarter endid at the Annuntiacion anno tercio at
iiij*li*. per annum, suma}   xxs.

Mr Threasorers Launder

Paid unto her the iiijth of Aprell uppon her bill for
wasshing}   xjs. iiijd.
<non alloc' quia non sol'>
          Summa Paginae} xvjli. xiijs. iiijd. ob.

[fo. 17]

The Boyes of the Kytchen

ᴵItem for v yeards shepes russet at ijs. a yarde}	xs.
Item for iiij yards of walche playne lyning for the same hoos}	ijs. vjd.
Item for viiij yards of black fryse at xvjd. the yard}	xs. viijd.
Item for making of iiij paires of hoose}	[blank]ᴵ
Item for cloth lyning and making of cottes and hossen for them as appeareth by a bill of parceles, suma}	xxxijs.
Paid to Mighell Perry uppon a bill for lodging for the boyes of the kytchen}	viijs. ixd.

The Woodcarryer Row

Paid unto him for ij hole yeares [and iiij quarters *deleted*] wags endid at the Annuntiacion of Our Lady anno tercio dominae Reginae at xxvjs. viijd. the yeare}	liijs. iiijd.
Whearof iiij quarters was due in William Chancy's tyme	

Summa Paginae} iiijli. xiiijs. jd.

fo. 17v.
[*Signed*] Richard Ellis, Wyllyam Kynyat, Tho. Blunt.ᵐ

TEXTUAL NOTES

page

399   a. *For a further discussion of the composition of this volume, see 'Leic. Pap. III', 11.*

399   b-b. *deleted*

400   c-c. *deleted*

401   d-d. *deleted*

402   e-e. *deleted*

403   f-f. *deleted*

403   g-g. *deleted*

408   h-h. *deleted*

414   i-i. *deleted*

417   j-j. *deleted*

417   k-k. *deleted*

418   l-l. *deleted*

418   m. *This page also contains a number of scribbles and copies of these signatures, together with* Richard Hoverton. *It is not clear whether this is one of the original signatures or a later scribble.*

B. Bill for Livery [1559]
(Longleat, Dudley Papers Box V, fos. 280–3)

Endorsed (fo. 283v) 'Thomas Powell's bill for the bestowing of livery'.
Fos. 280–1 list those receiving coats, fos. 282–3 those receiving hose.
The endorsement may not apply to fos. 280–1, but both lists are in the
same hand. Undated, but probably for livery granted for the progress
of 1559. Whyttell (p. 420) was William Whittle, Leicester's tailor (see
p. 42, n. 22).

[fo. 280]
Jintylmen

William Hoggans	a cote
Arthur Heigham	a cote
Henry Knolles	a cote
Richard Beawe	a cote
Robard Darcey	a cote
Wyllyam Chauncey	a cote
Robert Curson	a cote
George Martyn	a cote
Edward Cary	a cote
[Antony Dering *deleted*]	
[Floide *deleted*]	
Dickenson	a cote
Wyllyam Saule	a cote
George Powlett	a cote
George Blunt	a cote
Edward Langham	a cote
John Aspley	a cote
Thomas Flowerdew	a cote
Rychard Stafford	a cote

Reseavyd for these same lyveryes syxe and fyftye yards and a halfe of
frost apon grene.

[fo. 281]
Yeomen

Thomas Braybrook	a cote
Robard Hollond	a cote
John Awdwyn	a cote
Edward Robards	a cote
James Cornyshe	a cote
George Coke	a cote
William Smyth	a cote

John Trompett	a cote
Thomas Davys	a cote
Brystow	a cote
Robert Donkyn	a cote
John Allyn	a cote
The drome	a cote
The fyffe	a cote
John Empson	a cote
George Gyles	a cote
Hendry Johns	a cote

Delyvered to the two fotemen fyve yards of cloth to make them clothes and the grome of the stable a cote.

Dylyveryd to Whyttell a yard and thre quarter of cloth for too make the pattyn of the fyrest cote and so it remayneth in his hands styll.

[fo. 282]

Jentylmen

Thomas Dudley	an ell of sarsenett
Henry Knolles	a payre of hose
Richard Beau	a payre of hose
Robard Darcy	a payre of hose
Robard Curson	a payre of hose
George Martin	a payre of hose
Edward Cary	a payre of hose
George Vaughan	a payre of hose
Antony Deryng	a payre of hose
Owyn Floid	a payre of hose
George Pawlytt	a payre of hose
George Blunt	a payre of hose
John Aspley	a payre of hose
John Wyllyams	a payre of hose
Eyton	a payre of hose
Pedro	an ell and a quarter of sarsnytt
Ellys	a payre of hose
Marshall	a payre of hose
Wyllyam Saule	a payre of hose
Hardyng	a payre of hose

Item resevyd of Mr Pope foure score and vij yards and thre quarters of cloth for the same hose.

[fo. 283]

Yeomen

Thomas Braybroke	a payre of hose
Davyd Powell	a payre of hose

Morys Edwards	a payre of hose
Robard Hollond	a payre of hose
John Awdyn	a payre of hose
Edward Robards	a payre of hose
Willyam Wyllett	a payre of hose
George Coke	a payre of hose
Richard Gyttings	a payre of hose
Hewe Jones	a payre of hose
John Trompett	a payre of hose
Thomas Davys	a payre of hose
Bristow	a payre of hose
Robard Donkyn	a payre of hose
Richard Glasyre	a payre of hose
John Empson	a payre of hose
George Gyles	a payre of hose
Henry Jones	a payre of hose
John Powlett	a payre of hose
Oswald	a payre of hose
The French butterman	a payre of hose
John Allyn	a payre of hose
The flute	a payre of hose
The drom	a payre of hose
Rayfe Hunt	a payre of hose
Foryst the dog-keeper	a payre of hose

Item delyvered to thre of those that wayteth on my lady thre payre of hose.

C. Bill for Livery, 1560
(Longleat, Dudley Papers Box V, fo. 17v)

Extract from fos. 17–23, bill of John Guy, haberdasher, from 21 September 1559 to 12 June 1562.

Caps delivered to my Lord Robert's servants, iiij April 1560 by Mr Ellyses appointment.

Richard the drome
Oswolde groom of the chamber
John Stevenson
John Flowde
Stephen Rawson
William Bourne
Patrick Hanlyn
George Gyles
John Trompet
Rauf Fawcon
Thomas Forest
Thomas Harloo
John Corson
Griffith Clunne
Griffith Fludd
William Hawksley
Richard Fl[ammoc]k
Hugh Johns
Johnson the fyfe

D. Bill for Badges [1567–8]
(Longleat, Dudley Papers Box V, fos. 270v-71)

Extract from fos. 269–72, endorsed 'Book of Edmund More between xxviij April anno nono [1567] and 2 March anno decimo [1568].' Fo. 270 contains the entry, 'Item for imbroderyng of vij^{xx} bagges sins the xxixth day of April 1567 unto this tyme at ij*s*. a pece one with another as may appere by a byll of names as they were delivered: xiiij*li*. x*s*.'

[fo. 270v]
Imprymis Jhons of my lord's chamber.
George Coringnew   g[en]t[leman]
Wylliam Dinshem   gt.
Wylliam Dennone   gt.
Jhon Northe   gt.
Roberte Persyville   gt.
Item delivered to Powell and for himselfe   gt.
one for Mr. Kennett   gt.
one for Mr. Robbster   gt.
Thomas Hunderhill   gt.   <Kyllyngworth>
Jhon Yerwerth   gt.
Jhon Holand   gt.
Water Reddyng   gt.
Thomas Butteler   gt.
Edward Sleggs   gt. of Cambs.
Lenard Hyd   gt.
George Hyd   gt.
Davey Tedder   y[eoman]
Mr. Salesbury   gt.
Edward Denne   gt.
Hewe Briscoe   gt.
Cornishe Remain   y
Hewe Floid   y
Robert Gwyne   y
Jhon Gwyne   y
Davey Floid   y
Leweys Richard   y
Olever Morys   y
Richard Berte   y
Jhon Jenkyns   y
Harry Yrrell   y
Jacobe Armorer   y
Wylliam Twyson   y

20

423

Jhon Griffin   y
Robert Holland   y
Rafe Alldersey   y
Jhon Kynge   y
Jhon Bosse   y
Robert Bett   y
Edward Wystone   y   40
Richard Combe grome
Thomas Bell ferriar
Edmund More   gt
Harry Cannoke   y
Thomas Newbye   y
Richard Evans drommer
Jhon Jhonson the fefte
Harry Weston   y
Bughton of one Forster
Richard Inglace
Nicholas Morys coke   gt.
Jhon Partryge   y
Edward Woode   y
Wylliam Kene   y
Jhon North   y
Nicholas Kydwell   y
Thomas Barlowe   y
Morgan Fittman   y
Morgan Harrye   y
Jhon Hardy   y   60
Morgan App Richard   y
Mr Foster [?]   gt
James Symon   y
Wylliam Christopher   gt.
Harry Rankyng   y

[fo. 271]
Mr Gorringe   gt.
One badge for the warden of Southwell
George Sydgewyck   y
Wylliam Woodmen   y
Jhon Twisse   y
Edward Spinser of the skoler
Thomas Raglan of the pantry
Morys Derby of the pantry
Gylbert Carlton   y
Gryffyn of the chamber

Lawrens Neghtibred   y
Roger Morell   y
Wyllyam Robinson   y
Bartyllemew Mokinmorbye   80
Roberte Gryffin   y
Jhon Hall   y
Mr Bull   gt.
Jhon Floid   y
Marten Borowe
Mr Mailer of Sense   gt.
Thomas Spinyers de lernotion   gt.
Christopher Preston   y
Jhon Mansfield   y
Robertt Floid usher   y
Jhon Littsome   y
Thomas Tompson upholster
Smart the sword bearer's son   gt.
My lord's cotteres   y
Thomas Appowell   gt.
Thomas Trenton   gt.
Delivered to Davy Floid
Delivered to Mr Bull x baygs of the Regged Staffe the x day of
September
Godfrey of the wardrope   9
Wylliam Olyver   y   Mr Kennett
Martyn Pope   Bussell
George Burlace
Thomas Bleckeborne
Delivered to Mr Steward the iiijth day of November xxix bagges which
is the whole sum of vij^{xx}
More byges delivered since the vth day of June as herafter may appere
by these names.
Item Hewe Andrewe   Mr Foster
[*obscured*] Chrystmas   Pervell
Mr Phylipp Sydney
James Bill farrer
Roberte Harryson   gt.
All these badges have byn delyvered to my lords use by Edmund More
[*signed*] per me Antho. Foster.

E. Bill for Livery Cloth [c.1567–8]
(Longleat, Dudley Papers Box V, fos. 285–6)

Extract from fos. 284–7v, bill of Richard Paramour, draper. Undated, but probably c. 1567–8. Fo. 287v contains the note, 'Memorandum that all these parcells of cloth abovesaid as well with names as without were delivered by Mr Anthony Forster's warrant'.

[fo. 285]
Cloth delivered by Richard Paramour to the use of the right honourable the Erle of Leicester.

Mr Robert Christmas
Mr Eglonbie
Mr Kylligrave
Mr Darcie
Mr Wulley
Mr Fyssher
Mr Eaton
Mr Stretch
Mr Bowes
Andro the page
Robyn Knolles
Mr Drake
Mr Barnabie
Mr Browton
Mr Higham
Mr Skydmore
Mr Gillman
Peter Techio
Mr Sowch
John Droytlyn
Hugh Brisco
Pearcevall
Richard Ellice
Richard Beawe
Humphrey Blunt
Mr Franklyn
Robert Constable
John Hare
Nicholas the cooke
George Rydeton
William Bussell
Thomas Duddeley

Mr Gorge
Mr Bryskett
Mr Braybrooke
Mr Fenner
Mr Sharpe
Mr Stepney
Mr Bowkley
Mr Kynwellmershe
Mr Earth
Mr Davers
Mr Beaumond
Mr Awdwyn
Mr Reading
Mr Shelton
Mr Vaws
Mr Bowlton
Richard Knolls
Mr Piggott
Mountaneo
Phillip de Corbie
James Holmes
Thomas Kellen
Henry Power
Arthur Robsert
William Chauncie
Richard Whitt
Baptist Vangencick
Cooke parfumier
John Marbery
John Jobson
Thomas Barker
Edward Jobson

Anthony Marten
Mr Bull
William Whittle
Mr Lanyson

Richard Spert
Mr Savage
George Barnestone
Henry Tyrrell
Mr Woodhouse

[fo. 285v]
Mr Strachie merchant
Mr Okeham
Mr Daye
Mr Girlington
Mr Denham
Mr Hallt
John Aburford
Mr Butteler
Mr George Blount
Mr Gilbert Blount
Mr Gower
Mr James Boies
Mr Coningsbie
Mr Thomas Miller
Mr Anthony Clerk
William Gwynne
Geffrey Holland
Mr Hide the younger
Mr Lyttleton
Bailye of Sowthwell
Mr Parker
George Whittney
Mr Curson
Mr Appleyard
My lord's clookbagge [cloak
badge?]
Sum: [blank]

George Giles
John Empson
William Wortley
Henry Johnes
Godfrey
Spillisbury
George Sedgewick
Henry Smyth
John Floid
Raufe Aldersley
Robert Holland
Henry Carnock
William Olyver
Paul Vynton
Devonshier
Morgan Harris
Robynson
William Middleman
Stoner
The trompetter
John Price
John Haull
Gilbert Carleton
Peter Burgerman
Conway
Diricke jerkynmaker
Maynard
Nicholas Purvaye
Powell
Kinge the brewer
William Walker
Richard Cooke
Steven Rawson
Robert Rayneford
John Sowche
Reignold Morrice

[fo. 286]

John Marten
Richard Marcer
James Samons
William Power
William Henne
Richard Partridge
Edward Woode
Rawfe Mowster
younge Glaseor
Dinstone Bray
Thomas Keys
Owen Lloid
John Duck
Thomas Forrest
Richard Evans
John Johnson
John Tomlynson
John Pypkyn
Thomas Bell
Thomas Reynolds
Peter Lucas
Marten Belle
Edward Wistowe
John Willson
Ledsham the skynner
George Symons
Henry Woode
John Westalle
Thomas Bowghton
William Bells
Albone the barvier [barber?]
John Twysse
John Hauke
William Brett
William Sowthen

Henry Swallow
Thomas Nurse
Thomas Glover
The tanner of Dartford
Bill of Towcetter
Rawfe Hunt
William Freckleton
William Wright
Jaques harnesmaker
The dwarfe
Bartilmewe Newsam
Thomas Carling
Sum: [*blank*]
William the grome
Hugh the grome
David the grome
Richard Englerer
Thomas Hurland
Henry Tyrrell
Henry Rankyn
Thomas Haslwoodde
Thomas Watson
The cuttler
John Garland
James Freshmans
Richard Cooke
Humphrey Malboune
Robert Swallowe
William Chandler
Humphrey Owen
Humphrey Woode ferd[..]
Thomas Collyer

F. A Note of the Number which are to attend your Lordship in your Journey into the Low Countries [1585]
(Longleat, Dudley Papers III, fo. 63)

Single page, undated, but undoubtedly autumn 1585. Endorsed 'The names of his lordship's attendants into the Lowe Countrys'.

A note of the number which are to attend your lordship in your jorney into the Low Countries:

Barons 2   theyr servants   10

Knights and gentlemen 20   theyr servants   40}   72

[Household?][a] Servants

1 a steward − servants 2	1 a harbinger
1 a secretarie − 1	1 a yeoman of the horse
1 a threasurer − 1	3 coatchmen
1 a gentleman of the horse − 1	8 gromes
1 a controwler − 1	1 a farriar
2 gentlemen ushers − 2	
4 gentlemen of the chamber − 2	The number of the gentlemen,
6 pages − 0	officers and yeomen: 75
4 grommes of the chamber − 0	The number of theyr servants: 24
10 gentlemen wayghters − 6	somma totalis: 99
2 devines − 2	
1 phesition − 1	Of those that are to goe with his
1 appotecary − 1	lordship of:
1 a chirurgion − 1	Lords ⎱
2 cornetts − 0	Knights ⎬ 72
6 trompetts − 0	Gentlemen ⎰
6 footmen six − 0	with theyr servants
4 cookes − 0	His lordship's owne retinue} 99
4 buttery, pantry [...][b]	
for the silver scullary	Of the lidg[er][c] his trayne} 30
1− a clarke of the kitchen & cator − 1	The [who]le[d] some is} 221

TEXTUAL NOTES

a. *Damaged by damp.*
b. *Tear in the page.*
c. *Presumably an abbreviation for* ambassador leger. *See above p. 369, n. 724.*
d. *Obscured*

G. The Names of your Excellency's Howsehould Servants, 21 July [1587] (British Library, Cotton MS Galba C VIII, fos. 98– 102)

Endorsed by Arthur Atye 'The names of your Excellency's howsehould servants with a coppye of the othe given them the 21th of Julye at Vluss[ing]'.[a] Undated but undoubtedly 1587. The text of the oath at the end is also in Atye's hand, but the list itself is not. The offices are given in the margin, but have been introduced into the text to eliminate the proliferation of brackets. The abbreviation iur[atus?] is obviously a reference to those who had taken the oath; it is possible that this is a copy of a formal household list used to record the oath-taking. Numbers on the right hand are probably an attempt to compute totals

[fo. 98]
The names of your Excellency's officers and servants this day attendant.
<Steward>
Mr Richard Browne   iur
<Secretaries>
Mr John Hynd   iur
Mr Atye   iur
Mr Lloyde   iur
Mr Downhall   iur
Mr Heydon junior   iur
Mr Ottamon   iur
Mr Junius   iur
Mr Adrian   iur
Mr Glover   iur
<Clerk Comptroller>
Thomas Ardern   iur
<Gentlemen Ushers>
Arthur Higham   iur
Mr Heydon Senior   iur
<Clarck of the Kichin>
William Cholmondley
Richard Wright of the Spycerie   iur[b]
Hugh Cholmondley   iur
John Traceye
William Poynts
William Hopton   iur
Symond Killegrewe

Edward Barker	iur
Francis Castilian	iur
George Brooke	iur
Henrie Jones	iur
Barnard Whetston	iur
Henrie Slyfield	iur
Hercules Loveden	iur
Roger Brereton	
William Waight	iur
Nicholas Huddie	
William Constable	
William Wood Mr of the Tents	iur
Lane	iur
Avelin	
Turvile	iur
Barker of Ipswich	iur
Feige	of this countrie[c]
Marnex	
Rafe Conisbie	
James junior	iur
<Pages>	
Adrian	
Reade	iur
[Thomas Webbe	iur *added*]
[Charles Harte	iur *added*] 41

[fo. 98v]
<The Chaplin>
Doctor Tompson
<Phisicions>

Doctor James	iur	
Doctor Hipocrates	iur	
<Surgions>		
Mr Goodwse		
John Isard	iur	
<Gentlemen Ryders>		
Thomas Storie	iur	enterteignment[d]
Robert Storie	iur	
John Digbie		
Robert Hunnyes		
<Trumpetters>		
Benedict Browne	enterteignment[e]	
John Jewkes		
Fowk Strange the Lord North's man		

Griffin Martin
<Drombes>
John Keynsey   iur   enterteignment[f]
John Vodett   iur
<Pantrie>
Owen Jones   iur
Thomas Perriman   iur
<Ewerye>
William Williams
Thomas Freeman   iur
<Celler>
Thomas Symmell
Edward Hamerton   iur
<Butterie>
Robert Daintie   iur
John Evans   iur
<Cookes in your Excellency's Kichen>
John Smithson
Piero Morowe   iur
Myles Rowlingson   iur
Paul Croxton   iur
<Cooks for the Livereis>
John Dickson
<Pastere>
Raulfe Battey   iur
John Rotche
<Larder>
Henrie Applebie   iur
Richard Moyle
William Broxall laborer   iur
<Baker>
John Evans
<Scaulding House>
John Bennett
<Purveyor>
William Warde
<Scullery>
Peter Daniell   iur
John Mason
Robert Holland   iur
Rafe Powell   iur   39

[fo. 99]
Thomas Tanner
<Porters>
Henrie Millington
<Woodyard>
William Freckington
<Turnbroches>
William Boyes
William Peter   iur
Robert Flower   iur
Thomas Molam   iur
<Labourers for both Kichins, Pasterie and Scullarie>
John May
[John Cornwell   iur *interlined by Atye*]
Christopher Walton
[William Bradshaw   iur *interlined by Atye*]
John Water
Thomas Troll
William Edward pasterie
Raulfe Powell
<Colbearer>
Robert Galloner   iur
<Keeper the 2 grew houndes and is for the picherhouse>
William Massie
Richard Spaniell keeper
<Groomes of the Chamber>
Raulfe More   iur
William Thomas
Robert Pitchford
John Bourne   iur
<Robes>
Stephan Johnson   iur
<Of the Bedds>
John Lloyd   iur
Nicholas Webber   iur
Nicholas Dymock
<Musiciones>
Thomas Cole
William Bainton
James Wharton
William Edgley
William Black
John the harper
Walter the boye

\<Groomes of the Utter Chamber\>
Richard Gardiner   iur
Thomas Bagnoll   iur
\<Harbingers\>
Anthony Lewes   iur   Bordwages[g]
Nicholas Lyons   iur
Roger Foster   iur
Henry Gryffyn   iur
William Williams   39

[fo. 99v]
\<Yeoman of the Horse\>
Thomas Baker
\<The Cotchman\>
Peter
\<Sadlers\>
Henry Crosse
William Sadler
\<Ferrior\>
Thomas Bottle
\<Purveyor\>
Thomas Waller
\<Garneter\>
Thomas Child
\<Armourers\>
Thomas Marshal   iur   Bordwages[h]
Thomas Owen   iur
\<Tentkeeper [s]\>
Thomas Grammer
Thomas Bryan   iur
Henrie Rutter   iur
William Clifton
Gabriel
\<Footmen\>
Conrad Ducke   iur
Henrie Daye   iur
John Evans   iur
Thomas Duffe   iur
Hugh the Irishman   iur   Omeloe
Humfrey Adlington   iur
Thomas Patten that was Gavin Smithes man
John Roberts
\<Groomes of the Stable\>
[Thomas Baker yeoman of the horse *deleted*]

Richard Gryme
John Thomas
John Conlie
Piers Aldersey   iur
George Bamefield
Joseph Glover
William Jordan
Price Davis
Richard Cooner
Thomas English
Thomas Berion
Rowland Morgan
Georg Dowson
Robert Gryme
John Storie
Robert Adams
John Hamond
William Hutton
Richard Davis
Richard Comlye
John Dennys
Thomas Howell
William Middleton
William Adams
Henrie Griffin
John Keyne

48

[fo. 100]
<Bardgmen ix of the Great Barge>
John Griffin master
John Howper
Hugh Jones
Richard Jones
John Larden
William Milborne
William Coyle
John Rogers
John Metcalf
<Of the Little Barge>

9

<The names of your Excellency's Guard>
John Conway   iur   ensigne bearer
Lyonell Blackie   iur   seriant
Rotherick Lewis   iur   marshall of the hall
Raulfe Hallsaye   yeoman ushers[i]

John Lacye	iur	
Thomas Gargrave	iur	
Nicholas Goodge		clarck of the check
Roger Andrewes		
Edmund Bradley	iur	
Steven Wood	iur	
Edmund Barrett	iur	
Robert Gwin		
Andrewe Speede	iur	
Evan Jones	iur	
Walter Long	iur	
William Courtney	iur	
[Arthur Hart *deleted*]		
Antonye Clarkson	iur	
John Masters		
Thomas Westcoll	iur	
Thomas Churchard	iur	
John Bourne	iur	
Michaell Austin	iur	
Evan Jones		
Thomas King	iur	brewer
John Gwin	iur	
[fo. 100v]		
Richard Ashton	iur	
William Acton	iur	
Raulfe Smith		
Thomas Sparge	iur	
John Edwardes	iur	
Francis Johnson	iur	
Rauf Richardson	iur	
William Sheldrake	iur	
John Carter	iur	
Richard Holney	iur	
William Morgan	iur	
John Roper		
John Smith	iur	
Sampson Austill		
Robert Buck	iur	
Thomas Topcliffe	iur	
John Peris	iur	
Gyles Cole	iur	
Richard Morgan	iur	
Humfrey Gryffin	iur	

Thomas Jackson	iur
Thomas Gill	iur
William Evans	iur
Bertram Andrewes	iur
Robert Beckett	iur
[Thomas Westcoll *deleted*]	
John Ticklin	iur
Richard Bremellcom	iur
William Barbar	iur
John Armin	iur

<The Names of the Musketiers>

Arthur Hart		sergeant
Henrie Hilling		
John Barton	iur	
John Kensis	iur	
John Huddleston	iur	
[Leonard Wilkinson *deleted*]		
John Harris		
Richard Trewman	iur	
John Sadler	iur	
[Joseph Bremington *deleted*]		
[Robert Jones *deleted*]		
Thomas Tailboies	iur	
[Thomas Browne *deleted*]		
Thomas Skarsmore	iur	
Thomas Davis	iur	
Robert Dyer	iur	
[Thomas Hutchins *deleted*]		
John Norris	iur	44

[fo. 101]

[John Richardson *deleted*]	
[John Collier *deleted*]	
[Roger Beaker *deleted*]	
[Richard Lawrence *deleted*]	
[Thomas Osborn *deleted*]	
Hugh Knowsley	iur
[John Warburton *deleted*]	
John Taylor	iur
John Sanders	iur
[Daniell Thompson *deleted*]	
John Drommer	iur
[Humfrey Massie *deleted*]	
William Massie	iur

[John Webbe *deleted*]
[Richard Webbe *deleted*]   15
[*The following names have been added in a different hand*]
William Taylor   iur
John Holmes   iur   267
Richard Borsey
James Delaber   iur
Henry Johnes   iur
Martin Green   iur
Henry Johnes   iur
Richard Etherton   iur
William Jenye   iur
Henry Gurnard   iur
John Spenser   iur
Phillip Lane   iur
John Downinge   iur
William Loch   iur
John Kelly   iur
John Johnson   iur
[John Sanders *deleted*]
Michell Harrington   iur
Harry Woods   iur
[Richard Trewman *deleted*]
John Partredg
William Bishop   iur
John Bayly   iur
[*The remaining names have been added by Arthur Atye*]
Henry Vaughan
Edmund Lorde   iur
Harry Robson   iur
William Maunsfelde drome   iur
Thomas Leave fiefe   iur

[fo. 102]
I A.B. do protest and sweare that I will allwayes beare fayth and true
allegiaunce to our soveraigne ladye Elizabeth Queen of England,
France, Irelande, Defender of the Faythe etc. I do also utterly renounce
all authoritye of the Bisshoppe of Rome in all causes ecclesiasticall or
civill in the realmes and territoryes of the Queen's Majestie of England
or within the Unyted Provinces of the Lowe Countryes. And I do
sweare to be true, faythfull and loyall to his Excellency, my Lord and
Master Robert, Erle of Leycester etc. And namely that I shall faithefullye
kepe secrett all suche things as secrettly by worde or wryting shalbe
from tyme to tyme by his Excellency or others in his name committed

to me, and shall not reveale the same to anye person but with the assent and good lyking of his Excellency, nor holde any intelligence by speache, wryting or message with any to the contrarye. And in case I shall hear or understande anythinge tending directly or indirectly to the hurt or prejudice of her Majesties person and dignitye, or of his Excellency or against the estate, service and weale of the United Provinces of these Lowe Countries, I shall fourthwith make the same knowen unto his Excellency. So healpe me God.

TEXTUAL NOTES

page

430 a. *Tear in the page.*

430 b. *No office given for the following (to* Pages), *presumably ordinary gentlemen of the household.*

431 c. *Against this and the following name.*

431 d. *Against this and the following name.*

431 e. *Against this name and the two following names.*

432 f. *Against this and the following name.*

434 g. *Against this and the following name.*

434 h. *Against this and the six following names.*

435 i. *Against this and the two following names*

H. Household Embarkation List, November 1587 (British Library, Cotton MS Galba D II, fos. 211–16)

No heading. Endorsed by Arthur Atye, 'The names of those of [...] footband by Charles Wednes[ter] November 1587'.[a] Text in a different hand. The date and the references to under-servants suggest that this was used as an embarkation list for the household on Leicester's final return from the Netherlands in December 1587. As with the previous list, offices listed in the margin have been introduced into the text.

[fo. 211]
<Offycers>[b]
Mr Francis Knolle
Mr Hollingworth   lieutenaunt
John Conwey   ensigne
Lionell Blackley   seriaunts[c]
Arthur Hart
John Lacie
Nicholas Goodge   cleark
John Vodett   drums[d]
John Kelse
John Harrys senior
<Gard of Holberds>   21[e]
John Gwyn
John Edwards
Ralf Richardson
John Carter
William Morgan
John Amice
Ralphe Smyth
John Borne senior
Michaell Awstine
Richard Arsshow
William Barber
Sampson Awstine
Anthonie Claxton
William Courtney
John Masters
Thomas Hole
Roger Arderne
Bartram Andrewes
Ralphe Hallsey

John Spurge
John Tykell [*added by Atye*]

[fo. 211v]
<Gard of Shott>
John Sadler
Hugh Knewsley
John Draynor
William Massey
John Spencer
Thomas Knowles
John Dennys als Smulkin
Malmaduk Baluwe
Thomas Starsmore
John Kyllie
Henry Jones
Martine Green
Richard Ederton
Henry Gornard
Phillip Lane
John Collman
John Downinge
John Barton
William Lock
John Saunders
Harbert Johnson
John Kynsley
John Harleston
Lewes Vaughan
William Byshopp
John Taylor
Michaell Harrington
Henry Wood
John Norrys
Henry Hillinge

[fo. 212]
Davie Kirberie
Robert Flower
Thomas Taylboyes
Georg Newman
William Jeames
Jeames Delaber
Edmund Lumner

[Piero Moerew *deleted*]
John Baylye
William Avenor
Richard Barzey
John Tailor junior
John Buach
Richard Trewman
William Mansfield
Thomas Leve
John Harrys   [47 *altered to*] 46
<Of the Bedchamber>
Ralf Moore
William Thomas
Robert Pitchford
John Bowne junior
Richard Pate Moores man
<Robes>
Steven Johnson
John Lloyd
Nicholas Webber
John Symmell Steven's man
<Bedds>
Alford Johnson
Nicholas Dymock

[fo. 212v]
<Musicions>
Thomas Cole
William Black
Walter Ridgwey
William Bull
John Harper
Michaell
<Pantrye>
Owen Jones
Thomas Perryman
Leonard Wilkinson his man
<Ewerye>
Thomas Freeman
William Williams
William Tailor his man
<Grooms of the Great Chamber>
Richard Gardiner
Thomas Bagnall

\<Buttrye\>
Robert Deintie
John Evans
Robert Leycester their man
\<Celler\>
Thomas Symmell
Edward Hammerton
Humfrey Massey   servants[f]
Thomas Fysher
\<Kytchin\>
John Smythson
[Piero *deleted*] Peter Moerew
Myles Rawlynson
Pawle Croxton
William West
Thomas Molam
William Boyes
John Clerk
Robert Bursis
John Moore
Robert Bayliff
Nicholas Pennington

[fo. 213]
\<Pastrie\>
Ralph Battye
John Roche
Leonard   servants[g]
William Edwards
\<Larder\>
Henry Applebye
Richard Moyle
William Bradshaw   servants[h]
William Brockson
\<Scaldinghowse\>
John Bennett
\<Spycery\>
Richard Wrighte
\<Skullerie\>
Peter Daniell
Robert [Ralph *deleted*] Holland
Ralph Powell   servants[i]
John Williams
\<Baker\>

Humfrey Evans
Hauskin
<Purveyor>
William Hunte
<Slaughterman>
Thomas Foster
<Porter>
Henry Millington
<Woodyard>
William Freckleton
Thomas Inglethorp his man
<Harbingers>
Anthonie Lewes
William Lyons
<Armorers>
Thomas Owen
Thomas Browne
Thomas Marshall

[fo. 213v]
<Tentkeepers>
Thomas Grammer
Thomas Bryan
Henry Rutter
Gabriell Lea
John Warberton
William Clyfton
<Of the Carryiage>
William Williams
<Colebearer>
Robert Falloes
Ellis Cethin Robert Gwyn's man
Henry Gryffin
John Keame
<Footmen>
Hughe Ambloye
Conrad Duck
John Roberts
Humfrey Adlington
Thomas Deff
Clement Prattent
Henry Dayes
Jennkin Jenkins
<Spaniell Keeper>

Richard Hussey
<Pycher Howse>
Morrys ap John Wyn
<Skinner>
Richard Robinson

[fo. 214]
<Mr Hyndes men>
Peter Springe
Abraham Masters
Peter Suger
<Mr Atyes men>
John Goodart
Alexander Whightak
John Pynsoone
Con Farn Yrish
Henry Nicholson
<Mr Brownes men>
Francis Norton
Arthur Putto
Edward Bradshaw
<The Auditor's men>
Francis Eyre
Edward Bryscoe
<Mr Lloyde>
Henry Harrys
Henry Lucas
<Mr Downhall>
Andrew Pallmer
Edward Hancocke
<Mr Glover>
Henry Udon
<Doctor James>
Phillip Wall
Richard Morrys
<Doctor Hippocrates>
Edward Richards
Thomas Hooper
<Mr Brooke>
Thomas Parker
Walter Gryffin
<Doctor Hollande>
Guy Betterton

[fo. 214v]
<Mr James>
Nicholas Field
William Ellys
Edward Bythell
Phillip David
Gyles de Marness
<Mr Whetstone>
Thomas
Jasper Lynes
<Mr Hughe Cholmleye>
Roger Mannering
Arthur Damport
Arthur Mannering
John Batty
William Sylver
<Mr Higham>
[Symond *deleted*]
<Mr Goodrouse>
William Wetheridge
William Goodrous
<Bargemen to the Great Barge>
Richard Fairwether
John Thomas
John Gryffin
John Rogers
John Kempe
William Modell
Robert Bryan
John Phillips
Charles Longe
Richard Williams
William Colinge
Robert Whighthorne

[fo. 215]
William Knebone
James Gare
Richard Jones
<Watermen to your Lesser Barge>
Richard Merick
Robert Dodinge
William Warner
Thomas Ides

William Ryse
Richard Highman
Walter Smellen
Lewes Williams
Robert Berry
<Mr Higham's man>
Symond Staremore
<Mr Heighdon's> 2

TEXTUAL NOTES

page

440 a. *Tears in the the page.*

440 b. *Despite the absence of a heading the list begins with the guard. Francis Knollys the younger would appear to have succeeded Sir Henry Goodere, the captain in 1586.*

440 c. *Against this name and the two following.*

440 d. *Against this name and the two following.*

440 e. *Corrected by Atye from 20.*

443 f. *Against this name and the following.*

443 g. *Against this name and the following.*

443 h. *Against this name and the following.*

443 i. *Against this name and the following.*

I. The Proceeding at the Earl of Leicester's Funeral
[10 October 1588]
(Bodleian Library, MS Ashmole 818, fo. 38)

The identities of several of the attendants have added in the margin and are indicated by angle brackets. The preceeding folio [fo. 37] gives the order of the proceeding without identifications.

The proceeding at the Earl of Leicester's funeral from Kenilworth to Warwick.
Conductors 2
The Poor 100
Servants in coats to the number of 40
Trumpets 2
Standard <Mr. Isley>
Gentlemen servants to the lords in cloaks 100
Trumpets 2
The guidon of Leicester bourne by Mr Griffin of Dingley
Windsor <Leicester> Herald
The horse of Leicester ledd by Mr Baptist
The Mayor of Coventry and his brethren
Gentlemen of the defunct in cloaks 100
The horse of the Lord Steward ledd by Mr [*blank*]
Esquires in gowns
Mr Auditor <Mr Wednester>
<Mr Downhall>
Mr Clerk Comptroller <Mr Besbedge>
Doctors of Physic
Knights
Chapleins
<Doctor Attaman and Mr Downhall [*sic*]>
Secretaries
Officers of the Household: Threasorer
                                        Steward
                                        Comptroller
Bishoppe
The great banner bourne by Sir Hugh Chomley, knight
Officers of Arms: Healme and crest
                     Sworde
                     Targe
                     Coat of arms
Gentleman huissher: Mr Thomas Ardern
The body bourne by:

Clement Fisher
William Goodyer
William Harman
John Wake
Thomas Stafferton
William Poynes
Supporters of the Pawle:
Sir John Poynes
Sir John Tracey
Sir Thomas Throckmorton
Bannerolles:
Mr John Jobson
Mr Edward Jobson
Mr Thomas Jobson

Mr Wright
Mr James Leighton
Mr John Flood of Yale
Mr Bold
Mr Kytchin
Mr Nicholas Poynes

Sir Charles Blount
Sir Philip Butler
Sir Thomas Gorges

Mr John Tracey
Mr John Dudley [*sic*]
Mr Edward Blount

Mr Garter with Mr William Heydon, gentleman huissher
The Chief Mourner:
The Earl of Essex
Sir Robert Sidney, assistant
Mr Nevell, trainbearer
The gentleman of the horse leading a spare of the defunct somewhat
of the left hand and a little behind.
The Earl of Huntingdon
The Earl of Lincoln
Sir John Harrington and Sir Thomas West, assistants
Lord Dudley
Lord Wentworth
Lord Rich
Lord Chandos
Sir William Knollys
Sir Francis Knollys
Yeomen Conductors 2
Yeomen in cloaks

J. Funeral of the Earl of Leicester, 10 October 1588 (College of Arms, Sir William Dethick's Book of Funeralls of the Nobility, 1586–1603, Volume I, fos. 108–v, 117–v, 119–124)

This 'book' is a compilation of the Heralds' official papers, those relating to Leicester's funeral being fos. 106–34. The section is headed (fo. 106), 'Funeral of the E of Leicester obijt 4 September', and endorsed (fo. 134v), '10 October 1588 at Warwick intoxerat ante uxoris ut fama vagatur'. Most of the items bound in this section are bills or memoranda and fo. 118–v (which contains notes on the Countess of Oxford's funeral) is a stray. Fo. 107 is a copy of the order of the proceeding without identities and therefore not printed here. The extracts printed are untitled, but fo. 108–v is obviously a list of principal attendants and mourners, and fos. 117–124 a list of those given mourning blacks, gowns for esquires and above and cloaks for the others. Ranks and and other categories are noted in the margins, these have been introduced into the text in bold. Otherwise the order follows that of the original. Other marginalia are indicated by angle brackets. The figures represent computations of the numbers involved.

[fo. 108]
Earls
The Erle of Huntingdon
The Erle of Essex
The Erle of Lincoln
Barons
Lord Rich
Lord Dudley
Lord Wentworth
Lord Chandos
Preacher
The Bishop of Sarum
Knights
Sir Robert Sidney
Sir William Knollis
Sir Francis Knollis
Sir Thomas West
Sir Charles Blunt
Sir Philip Butler
Sir Thomas Gorge
Officers of Household

Gentlemen Ushers
William Heydon
Thomas Arderne
Chaplains
Dr Holland
Dr Hinton
Phisicians
Dr Hipocrites
Dr James
[Knights]
Sir Henry Norris
Sir John Points
Sir John Tracey
Sir Thomas Throgmorton
Sir Fulke Greville
Sir Henry Poole
Sir Francis Hynde
Sir Edward Standley
Sir Ralph Egerton
Sir John Harrington

Mr Boughton
Mr Browne
Mr Gorge
Mr Nevile
Mr Wednister
Secretaries
Mr Atye
Mr Lloyde
Gentleman of the Horse
Mr Hynde

Sir Thomas Lucy
Sir Henry Goodere
Sir Walter Luson
Sir Hugh Cholmondley
   Esquiers
Mr Robert Knollis
Mr Edward Wotton
Mr John Wooton
Mr Edward Jobson
Mr John Jobson
Mr Henry Isley
Mr Thomas Dudley
Mr Quarles
Mr Poincts
Mr Harcortt
George Harvie

[fo. 108v]
John Wake
Mr Baynham
Mr Stafferton
Mr Fowler
John Tracye
Henry Besbeche
Gabryell Bleeke
Edward Blunt
William Harman
Mr Wilperforce
William Poynts
Mr Sutton
Doctor Stanhope
Mr Gooderows

[fo. 117]
The Earle of Essex
The Earle of Lyncoln
The Earl of [*blank*]
Barons
The Lord Rich
The Lord Dudley
The Lord Wentworth
The Lord Shandois
Preacher
The Byshop of Sarisbury

The Erle of Warwick
The Countess
The Lord Admiral
The Lord Chancellor
   Secretaries
   Mr Attye
   Mr Floide
  Chaplayns
   Doctor Holland
   Mr Cartwright

Knights
Sir Robert Sidney
Sir William Knowles
Sir Frances Knowles
Sir Thomas West
Sir Charles Blunt
Sir Philip Butler
Sir Thomas Shirley
Officers of Household
Mr Boughton
Mr Browne
Mr Gorge
Mr Garnett
Mr Wednister

Mr Fenn
Sir Henry Norris
Sir John Poynts
Sir John Tracye
Sir Thomas Throgmorton
Sir Fulke Greville
Sir Henry Poole
Sir Francis Hynde
Sir Edward Standley
Sir Ralph Egerton
Sir Thomas Gorge
Sir John Harrington
Sir Thomas Lucye
Sir Henry Goodyeer
Sir Walter Luson
Sir Hugh Cholmly

[fo. 117v]
Gownes
Esquiers
Mr Edward Wootton
Mr John Wootton
Mr Edward Jobson
Mr John Jobson
Mr Thomas Jobson
Mr Henry Isley
Mr Thomas Dudley
Mr Harcortt
Mr Quarles
Mr Poynes
Gentlemen Ushers
Mr William Heydon
Mr Arderne
Gentlemen
George Harvye
John Wake
Mr Baynham
Mr Stafferton
Mr Fowler
Mr John Tracye
Mr Besbiche
Mr Gabryell Bleeke
Mr Edward Blunt
Mr Wilperforce

Cloakes
Gentlemen in Cloaks
Mr Browne
Mr Atye
Mr Sandys
Robert Wrotte <not def>[a]
Edmund York
Francis Clare
Hugh Veure
John Claypoole
Rauf Hubaud
William Goodyer
William Wayts
Gregory Dunhall
Richard Glover
Francis Baptist
Henry Goldingham
Mr Eaton
Ralph Selby
Mr Glasyer
Captain Spenser
Lyeutenant Tanner
William Sprint
Richard Addams
William Colstone
Mr Slye

Mr William Poynes

Mr Harman

Mr Sutton

Mr Hinde

Apoticary

Pitchford the Apoticarie

Surgion

Goodrowse

Doctor Stanhope

Mr Robert Knollis

Gownes 69

Mr Osbourne

Barnard Whetstone

Alexander Morgan

Tucke

Ralph Colstone

Trentham

Symnell

Mr Bedwell

[fo. 119, *for fo. 118–v see introductory note*]

Cloakes

Leonard Chamberlain

Pitchfork the Apoticary <a gown>

Cooke the habberdasher

George Gyles

Christian per Mr Browne

Richard Williams

Robinson skinner

Thimbelthorpe

Edward Bradshaw

Thomas Dallicott

William Clarke vintner

Reginald Hollingworth

Spelman the jeweler

Ralph Halsye

Arthur Ludforde

Roger Andrew

Richard Cooke a purveyor

John Turveile

William Walker

Alfert Jonson

Robert the fisherman

William Blacknoll

Robert Pitchfork

Robert Tithe surgeon

Ralph More

Cloakes

John Conway

Toby Mathew

William Bird

Thomas King

Henry Cater

John Keyne

Fardinando

Richardson

John Stringer

Robert Dudley

Clement Prattin

Thomas Bottle

Pinnock

Thomas Underhill

Thomas Cole

Thomas Edgerley

John Binton

The Bayly of Knowsleye

Henry Barker

George Booth

Robert Teuder

The Bayly of Knole

Pawle Croxon

Robert Gwin

Geoffrey Whitney Mr Abdyes
man

[fo. 119v]

Cloakes

The Earl of Warwick 5 gentlemen

Cloakes

Sir Thomas Gorge 1 man

The Erle of Essex 6 gentlemen
<100>
The Lord Admiral 4 gentlemen
The Lord Dudley 2 gentlemen

The Lord Wentworth 2 gentlemen
The Lord Shandois 2 gentlemen
The Lord Rich 2 gentlemen
Sir Robert Sidney 1 gentleman
Sir Frances Knoles 1 gentleman

Sir Philip Butler 1 gentleman
<20>
Sir William Knowles 1 gentleman

cloakes to be disposed at Kenellworth

7 cloaks[b]
10 cloaks
9 cloaks

of the Stable

Christopher Aylworth
Peter the Cochman
Perce the Cochman
Joseph Glover per Hinde
246 cloaks

[fo. 120]

Gentlemen in Cloakes

Thomas Hones
Oxenbridge
Boyton
John Dudley
John Broune
Mr West <Pages>[c]
Adryan
Peter <40>
White
Martin Jonson
Thomas Webb
John Watts
Francis Stonard
Thomas Brunton
Ralph Hyde
Mr Gylman
Humphrey Blunt
Mr Goslett
Mr Slyfield
Mr John Heydin
Mr Denton
Mathew Holmes
Evan Loide
Bruerton
Latham
Penren
William Barradale

Gentlemen in Cloakes

Charles Chester <60>
William Hopton
John Challoner
Robert Forster
Addams Soman [*sic*]
Robert Hill
Robert Fulford
George Nowell
Dymmock
George Leycester
William Tatton
Walter Gylford
Edward Avelin
Edward Trayforde
John Warner
Thomas Ley
Davy Massye
Gerrard
Thomas Lynche
George Denham <40>
Thomas Parramore
George Bingham
James Digges
Robert Cotton
Stephen Thornhurste
Jerman Marram
Thomas Graye

[fo. 120v]

Cloakes

Mr Throckmorton
Robert Hutton
John Moore
John Reade
Charles Wright
George Kevitt
Thomas Kevitt
Thomas Hill <+ Warwick>
John Burdett
Eglonby
George Fearne
Robert Ley <100>
Lyons
Lambert
Edward Searle
Seale
George Roades
Richard Bull
John Fullar
John Andrews
Mychael Sariant
Arthur Longfield
Nicholas Beere
Barnes
Baldwin
Caroone

Cloakes

Symond Kyllegrewe
Brooke
Goulde
Townsend
Hobson
Mullins <20>
John Gwin
Francis Broughton
William Smithe
Thomas Wiseman
Henry Archer
Thomas Baker
John Barker
Captain Ley
Thomas Pitts
Alderman Citchen
George Tuberville
Silvan Scorye
Edward Pye
Geffrye Whitney
Richard Acton
Charles Acton
Mr Burgrave
Mr Thorp
William Battle
Walter Culpepper <40>
Hugh Hurlestone
Leonard Chamberland

[fo. 121]

John Kayne
John Taborer
Mark Crowe
Lawrence Granger
Humphrey Ashfield
Richard Grimshall
Thomas Hale
Richard Asheton
John Arm
Henry Daye
Robert Evans
Symond Yats

John Russell the gardener
William Baynton
Nicholas Hankin
Thomas Duffe
Robert Gryme
Jolyan the bargeman
Richard Gryne
Nycholas Bradley
John Kersy
John Evans
Robert Teddur
John Colgin

Richard Gardiner
Sampson Austin
Anthone Claxtone
William Morgan
John Lloide
William Barbour
Edward Hamton
William Massie
John Collier
Leonard Yate
Edward Bowman
Richard Bradshaw
James Godwin
Vennor
Anthony Boobye

Thomas Brynnion
John Gwin
Christopher Robinson
Lewis Harris
James Bradshoe
Thomas Walton
Richard Coomb
George Dawson
Robert Addams
Thomas Freeman
Robert Deyntye
Richard Glover turnebroch
Walter Edwards
Westreete
Henry Lane
La[wrence?] Chislett

[fo. 121v]
Thomas Haydon
Thomas Holte
Ratclef a keper
Chislet junior
Dry a keper
Rowden
Milton
Potter
Reginald Hawle
Henry Stevins keper
William Bennett
Wyddale
Humphrey Evans
Morrice
Ichers
Wagstaffe
William Yates
Adryan
Thomas Amis
Lawrence Cox
John Hale
Francis Phips
William Richmond
Richard Temple
Waller
Lyonell Blacklie

Richard Buck
Richard Pecock
John Nettleton
Ralph Turner
Richard Flower
Ralph Lewis
Michael Austin
Henry Millington
Richard Moyle
Robert Harryman
Robert Buck
Robert Settle[d]
Nicholas Boswell
Henry Lovell
Dowding
Merrick
Humphrey Watlos
John Wakelin
Manning the beedle
George Bamfield
Moore the cochmaker
Robert Labarrie sadler
John Booby

John Lacye
Thomas Lewis per Moore
Walter Ridgwaye

[fo. 122]
Gowens
Garter principal King of Arms
Clarencieux[e]
Windsor
York
Richmond
Lancaster
Segar
Chester
Cloaks
Powher the taylor
Abraham Campion brewer
Barnes the mercer
Mr Abdye the draper

[fo. 122v]

Edward Frank	Palliver
James Wherton	Embr[oider's] Prentise
Thomas Pennyman	William Bayne
Myles Rawlinson	Ryce Thomas
William Edgerley	Robert Messinger
Nicholas Pecover	John Moore
Humphrey Addington	James Mannox
Peter the cochman	Selman
Henry Stevins	Richard Peedee
Robert Birkett	The Foxtaker
William Williams	Tusk
Thomas Owin	Eggam
Thomas Vaughter	John Lowe per Moore
Nicholas Webber	
Thomas Goffe	Humerstone
John Raynal	John Crewe
Christopher Cocke[f]	William Cranmer
John Wootton	Thomas Bryan
Richard Broughton	William Ashe
William Bull	Humfry Dum
Mallis	William Lake
Edward Standishe	William Glasier
Richard Derrick	Thomas Griffen

Thomas Jenkinson   John Hancox
Richard Scragh   Richard Williams
John Gilbert   John Cox
William Wardinote
Thomas Payle
John Rich cornecutter
Owin Phillips

[fo. 123]
Mrs Garnett
Mrs Bridgett
Mrs Barker
Mrs Lettice
Mrs Atye
Mrs Wednister
Mrs Browne
Mrs Besbeche
Mrs Mawdlin
Mrs Cotton
Mrs Huggins

Alice the chambermayde
John Fullar^g
Elizabeth Jenkins
Margery
Ann Goffe
Mary the poore scullary at Leicester House
The dairy woman at Wansted
Smith's wief landerer at Court
Ann Crowe landerer at Kenelworthe

[fo. 124]
10 yeomen for the Earl of Essex   Mr Chomley
6 Lord Admiral
4 Lord of Lincoln
6 Lord Chancellor
10 yeoman Lord of Warwick [sic]
2 Lord Dudley
2 Lord Rich
2 Lord Chandois
2 Lord Wentworth   3 boyes of the kitchen

2 Sir Robert Sidney
2 Sir Thomas West

2 Sir Philip Buttlers
2 Sir William Knollis
2 Sir Francis Knowlis
2 Sir Charles Blunt
2 Sir Thomas Gorge

2 Mr Atye
2 Mr Arderne
2 Doctor James
1 Wilperforce
1 Mr Cartwright +
1 Mr Fenn +
1 Mr Glover
1 Dr Hipocrites +
1 Dr Holland
1 Clement Fisher
1 Henry Besbeche
1 Gregory Dunhall
2 Mr Wednester
2 Mr Boughton
1 Mr Bedwell
1 Mr Webbes man
4 Mr Browne
2 Mr Floide
2 Mr Gorge
1 Mr Harcortt
2 Mr Hinde

250

TEXTUAL NOTES

page
452 a. <Nota defunct[?]> *According to his biography in Hasler, Wrote died c. 25 September 1589.*
454 b. *Different sizes are given for each of the three groups of cloaks.*
454 c. *Against this name and the two following.*
456 d. per Mr Garnett *against this name and the following*
457 e. 5 yards in ther gowns *against the rest of the Heralds.*
457 f. keepers *against this name and the two following.*
458 g. Landerers at Leycester House *against this name and the three following.*

INDEX OF SERVANTS

Acone, James. No further evidence.

Acton, Mr. Either Richard or Charles Acton (probably of Elmsley Lovett, Worcs.), both of whom served in the Netherlands in 1586 and attended Leicester's funeral.

Adams, Robert. Funeral. Probably Robert Adams (d. 1595), Surveyor of the Works 1594–5, who was employed as a cartographer in the Netherlands. Robert Adams 'new made' the dial in the great garden at Whitehall in 1581–2, which suggests that he was the 'young Adams' who made the dial in the garden at Leicester House referred to on p. 179. He was probably described in this way to distinguish him from his father Clement, see *King's Works*, iii, 94–5. He was probably not the Adams of Wanstead referred to on p. 222.

Adlington, Humphrey, footman. Netherlands household 1587 (footman), funeral.

Adrian/Audrian/Awdrian, gardener at Kenilworth. Funeral. He is also referred to as a gardener at Kenilworth in DP II, fo. 220, W. Edmundes to Leicester, 10 Dec. 1580.

Aglionby, Thomas (d. c.1584), MP. BSW, livery 1567. William Glasier* married his sister. Aglionby was in Leicester's service by 1557 (see the reference to St Quentin on p. 71) and by 1578 held an office in his wardrobe (see DP II, fo. 183, Aglionby to Leicester, 30 July 1578). In 1581–2 he was associated with a plot in Malta, see A.P. Vella, *An Elizabethan-Ottoman Conspiracy* (Royal University of Malta Historical Studies, iii, 1972), 51–5. See also 'Dudley Clientèle', p. 245, and 'House of Commons', 228.

Aldersey, Ralph. BSW, badge and livery 1567 (yeoman).

Allen/Alleyne/Allin, John. BSW (senior and junior), livery 1559 (yeoman). One of them may have been the servant Allen referred to in October 1584 (p. 189).

Ambrose, see Waller.

Appleyard, John (c.1526–74), of Brakenash, Norf. Livery 1567. Appleyard was the son of Amy Dudley's mother by her first marriage and married to William Huggins'* sister Elizabeth. He was associated with Leicester by 1553, sheriff of Norfolk and Suffolk in 1559, and served under Warwick at Le Havre in 1562–3. He broke with Leicester in 1567 and participated in a rebellion for the Duke of Norfolk in 1570. His son Henry was also in Leicester's service, see n. 710.

Ardern, Thomas. Netherlands household 1587 (clerk comptroller), funeral (gentleman usher). Ardern was also in the Netherlands household in 1586, and may have been the compiler of the 1585–7 disbursement book, see the discussion on p. 16. His errand in France at the beginning of 1585 is discussed in n. 467.

Aspeley, John. BSW, livery 1559 (gentleman). A Michael Aspeley was in Northumberland's household in 1553.

Atye, (Sir) Arthur (d. 1604), MP. Netherlands household 1587 (secretary), funeral (secretary). See the discussion of his career in 'Leic. Pap. II', 132–5, where it is argued that Atye was Leicester's chief secretary from c. 1574. He was a deponent in the Sir Robert Dudley case, but his deposition, which might have clarified his period of service, has not survived.

Audwaine/Awdwyne, John. BSW, livery 1559 (yeoman), probably livery 1567 (Mr Awdwyne).

Bagnall, Thomas. Netherlands household 1587 (groom of the great or utter chamber).

Bakehouse. Probably George Backhouse, Netherlands guard 1586 (ordinary servant).

Barbor, Mr. Probably William Barbour, funeral.

Barker, Mr Edward. Lord of Denbigh funeral, served in the Netherlands in 1586, Netherlands household 1587. There were, however, two Edward Barkers associated with Leicester in the 1580s. One, Edward Barker of Little Ilford, was a leading tenant of Wanstead (GVE, fo. 11v, Brevis Abstract, fo. 79v). The other was the civil and ecclesiastical lawyer Edward Barker (d. 1602), of London, MP. Barker notarised the depositions made in 1582 by the witnesses to Leicester's marriage to the Countess in 1578, was a witness to the Countess's jointure in 1584, and notarised the copy of Leicester's 1587 will now Pepys MS 2503, pp. 406–19. It was with Leicester's backing that he was appointed registrar to the Court of Delegates in 1584–5 (see PRO, SP12/175/9, Doctors of the Court of Arches to Leicester, 11 Nov. 1584), and Walsingham described him as Leicester's servant when he acted as registrar at the trial of Mary, Queen of Scots, in 1586 (*CSPSc, 1586–8*, 93, Walsingham to Leicester, 15 Oct. 1586). He continued to provide legal counsel to the Countess of Leicester after 1588. It is probable that the Netherlands references are to Barker of Ilford, but one cannot be sure about the earlier ones.

Barker, Henry, cook. Funeral.

Barker, William, groom of the stable. No further evidence.

Batty, Ralph. Netherlands household 1587 (pastry). Batty was a deponent in the Sir Robert Dudley case. According to his deposition (DP Box VII, rots. 7–13) he was then aged 55, Sergeant of the Pastry and (thanks probably to his Household office) an esquire of West Ham. He had served in Leicester's pastry for seventeen years beginning in the year of the progress to Dover and in 1574–6 was sent to France for training. As is the case with many of these depositions the dates are not completely reliable, for the progress to Dover took place in 1573 and on 26 May 1577 Sir Amias Paulet wrote to Leicester (Bodl., MS Rawl. A 331, fo. 4) about his difficulties in trying to place Batty with a French nobleman.

Beacham. No further evidence.

Becket, Thomas. No further evidence.

Bedwell, Thomas. Lord of Denbigh funeral, funeral. He was possibly a leasee of the manor of Rudfen, Wars. (Brevis Abstract, fo. 75) and was owed £200 in 1589 for work done. Bedwell was a mathematician and engineer of some prominence (see M. Feingold, *The Mathematicians' Apprenticeship: Science, Universities and Society in England 1560–1640* (Cambridge, 1984), esp. pp. 77, 207), whom Leicester appointed colonel of the pioneers in the Netherlands in 1586 (PRO, SP15/29/340). I am most grateful to Dr Stephen Johnston for bringing his unpublished work on Bedwell to my attention.

Bennett, William. Funeral.

Bentall, Mr. No further evidence.

Besbeeche, Henry, (1534?–?). Funeral (clerk comptroller). Besbeeche was a deponent in the 1590 Chancery case over Kenilworth. According to his deposition, he entered Leicester's service c. 1570 and was initially keeper of Kenilworth Park; by 1587–88 he was ranger-general and keeper of the castle. Some items of his correspondence with Leicester in 1578–80 survive in the Dudley Papers. See 'West Midlands', 41–2, 71, for a further discussion.

Bewe/Beau, Richard. Livery 1559 (gentleman), livery 1567.

Bigot, James. Bigot was married to John Appleyard's* sister Anne. He was acting for Leicester in Norfolk by 1553 (GVE, fo. 22) and appears to have been steward of his Norfolk manors (Hemsby and the Robsart estate) in 1559–60.

Blacknoll/Blackwell, William. Funeral. A keeper and tenant of Drayton Bassett (see 'West Midlands', 72), and probably the William Blackwell of the Netherlands guard in 1586, identified as an old retainer.

Blacksley/Blackley, Lionel, of Kenilworth. Funeral. Sergeant of the Netherlands guard 1586–7.

Blount, (Sir) Christopher (ex. 1601), MP, Thomas Blount's* younger son. Blount was Leicester's master of the horse by 1584, lieutenant of his company of horse in the Netherlands in 1586–88, and possibly the most prominent catholic in his household. He married the Countess of Leicester in 1589 and later played a central role in Essex's Revolt.

Blount, (Sir) Edward (d. 1630) of Kidderminster, Worcs., MP, Thomas Blount's* heir and elder brother of Christopher*. Funeral (bannerol-bearer). By 1587 he was steward of Cleobury Mortimer (Salop.) and leased the iron works there, see 'West Midlands', 42. He may have served in the Netherlands in 1586.

Blount, George. Livery 1559 (gentleman), livery 1567. He was probably the only son of Sir George Blount of Kinlet (n. 55), who predeceased his father.

Blount, Thomas (d. 1568) of Kidderminster, Worcs., MP. Blount was a cousin of the Duchess of Northumberland and Northumberland's comptroller in 1553. He was in Leicester's service by October 1556, and from then until his death Leicester's principal administrative officer. He was probably the steward of Kenilworth between 1563 and 1568. See 'West Midlands', 40–1, for a more detailed discussion.

Boocke, see Buck

Boughton, Edward (1545–89) of Cawston, Wars., MP. Served in the Netherlands 1586, funeral (officer of household). Boughton was in Leicester's service by 1579 and by 1585 was his (and Warwick's) chief officer in the west Midlands. He may have become treasurer of Leicester's household by 1588. See 'West Midlands', 42.

Bourne, John. Senior, Netherlands guard of halberds 1587. Junior, Netherlands household 1587 (groom of the bedchamber).

Bourne/Bowrne/Burn, William. BSW (groom of the stable), livery 1560.

Brampton, Mr, of Herts. No further evidence.

Braybrooke, Thomas. BSW, livery 1559 (yeoman), probably livery 1567 (Mr Braybrooke).

Bristow/Briscoe, Hugh. BSW, livery 1559–60 (yeoman), badge and livery 1567 (gentleman). Bristow had previously been in Sir Andrew Dudley's service, he is referred to in the act of probate of Dudley's will (DP Box II, art. 3, see also n. 192), as *famulus eiusdem defuncti*. He was the messenger Leicester sent after Thomas Blount when he received the news of his wife's death.

Brooke, George (1558/9–1603), son of William, 10th Lord Cobham, executed for his involvement in the Bye Plot. Lord of Denbigh funeral, served in the Netherlands 1586, Netherlands household 1587, funeral. Other evidence confirms that Brooke was in Leicester's service by 1584, see Norfolk RO, Y/C19/4 [Great Yarmouth, Assembly Book D, 1579–86], fos. 78, 81.

Browne, Giles, falconer. No further evidence.

Browne, (Sir) Richard (1538–1604), MP. Lord of Denbigh funeral, victualler of the household in the Netherlands 1586, Netherlands household 1587 (steward), funeral (officer of household). Browne entered Leicester's service by 1566, and by the mid 1570s was the principal officer of Leicester's household. From 1576 he occupied a tenament in Leicester House (Longleat MS 2960), and in his 1582 will Leicester left him the keepership of Leicester House for life. See the biographical comments in 'Leic. Pap. I', 65–7, and p. 4 of the Introduction.

Browne, Robert, musician. No further evidence, but probably not the Robert Browne, messenger of the Chamber, who brought letters from Leicester in April and May 1586 (BL, Harl. MS 1641, fo. 23v).

Buck/Burck, Richard. Netherlands guard 1586 (ordinary servant), funeral.

Burgrave, Daniel. Daniel de Burchgrave, the former attorney-general of Flanders, whom Leicester employed as a master of requests and secretary in 1586–87 and also appointed an auditor to the Council of State (see Oosterhoff, *Leicester and the Netherlands*, p. 95). On Leicester's return from the Netherlands in 1587, Burchgrave went into exile in England. He was referred to as a secretary of Leicester's in March 1588 (Hist MSS Comm, *Report on the Manuscripts of Lord Montagu of Beaulieu* (1900), 19), and attended Leicester's funeral. Leicester left him a life interest in a house in Aldersbrook on the Wanstead estate in his 1587 will.

Burton, William, musician. No further evidence.

Butler, Anthony (1522–1570), of Rycote, Oxon., MP. Probably livery 1567. Butler, who was formerly a servant of Lord Williams of Thame, referred to his service to Leicester in his will. Leicester requested the wardship of his son Charles as favour to 'my old servant', see Hist MSS Comm, *Report on the Manuscripts of Mr A.G. Finch*, i (1913), 11, Leicester to Sir Thomas Heneage, 2 Sept. [1570]. He obtained it in 1571 (*CPR, 1569–72*, 376).

Buttell, farrier. No further evidence.

Bysbyge, see Besbeeche.

Careless. No further evidence.

Carey, (Sir) Edmund (1558–1637), MP, 6th son of Henry, Lord Hunsdon (n. 57). Carey was in Leicester's service by 1582, and was left an annuity of £20 in his 1582 will. References on pp. 291, 300 suggest he was the keeper of Grafton House in 1585. Carey accompanied Leicester to the Netherlands in December 1585. In February 1586 he returned to England to raise a voluntary company in East Anglia (see n. 738), which arrived in the summer.

Carey, Edward. Livery 1559 (gentleman). Probably (Sir) Edward Carey (d. 1618), MP, Groom of the Privy Chamber from 1562/3.

Cater, Henry. Funeral.

Cave, Mr. Probably Edward Cave, who served in the Netherlands in 1586.

Chamley, see Chumley

Chancie/Chancy/Chauncy, William. BSW, livery 1559 (gentleman), livery 1567. As noted in the Introduction (p. 12), Chancy ceased to act as Leicester's financial officer after December 1559; the nature of his later association with his household is unclear. It is tempting to identify him as the William Chancy, esq, who dedicated to Leicester, *The rooting out of the Romishe supremacie* (1580: STC 5103), and *The Conversion of a Gentleman long tym misled in Poperie* (1587: STC 5102). Although the dedications do not refer to his having been in Leicester's service, they do imply an acquaintance of some duration. The implication that Chancy had been a catholic until the late 1570s may explain why he retired from Leicester's household. It is also possible that he was the William Chancie (1511–85) of Edgecote, Northants., MP for Northamptonshire in the parliaments of March and September 1553, 1554, and 1555.

Charells the auditor, see Wednester.

Charke. No further evidence.

Chesleck. Probably La[wrence?] Chislett, funeral. 'Young Chissleck' (p. 296) was probably Chislet junior, funeral.

Chilmead/Chilesmeade, Ralph, groom of the stable. No further evidence.

Chumley/Cholmondley, Mr. There were three men of this name in Leicester's service in the 1580s. (Sir) Hugh Cholmondley (1552–1601) the younger, MP, served in the Netherlands in 1586, was a member of the Netherlands household in 1587, and bearer of the great banner at Leicester's funeral. The lawyer Jasper Chomley (c.1539–87), MP, was in Leicester's service by 1573 (see 'House of Commons', 229, n. 97). William Cholmondley was clerk of the kitchen in the Netherlands household in 1587.

Clunne, Griffith. BSW, livery 1560.

Cobham. It is clear from the references on pp. 41, 105, 154 (see n. 18) that Leicester had a servant named Cobham in 1559–60, although he does not appear in any of the household lists. He may have been the Thomas Brooke alias Cobham, a younger brother of the 10th Lord Cobham, who was in Leicester's service in 1571, see PRO, SP12/81/10, Lord Cobham to Burghley, 5 Sept. 1571. This Thomas Brooke should be distinguished from the more notorious Thomas Brooke alias Cobham (1533–78), MP, see D.B. McKean, 'A Memory of Honour': A Study of the House of Cobham of Kent in the reign of Elizabeth I' (Unpub. University of Birmingham PhD thesis, 1964), p. 367.

Cole, Humphrey. Cole is identified as one of the household staff of Kenilworth Castle in the 1583 inventory (CKS, U1475/E92). There is a reference to him acting for Anthony Dockwra* in 1582 in SBTRO, DR18 [Leigh of Stoneleigh Deposit]/1/488. See also 'West Midlands', 71.

Cole, Thomas. Funeral. Although his relationship to Humphrey Cole is unclear, Thomas Cole was also member of the household staff of Kenilworth and had the charge of the plate in the inventories of 1584–88 (DP, XI, XIII and Bodl. MS Malone 5).

Comley, John, see Conway.

Conway, John. Ensign of the Netherlands guard 1586–7, funeral. Conway was a deponent in the Sir Robert Dudley case, but his deposition has not survived. His relationship (if any) to Sir John Conway of Arrow (Wars.), who was captain of Ostend in 1587, is unclear.

Cooke/Coke, George. Livery 1559 (yeoman). Possibly the George the cook referred to on pp. 106, 147, and George Lewes, cook (BSW).

Cooke, William, see Hakesby.

Corncutter, see Rich, John.

Cornwall, Robert. No further evidence, but may be the Robert of Cornwall and the Cornish man referred to on pp. 69, 98.

Cragg/Craig, Archie, footman. BSW, livery 1560. There is also a reference to him in 1561 in DP Box V, fo. 116. His errand to France at the beginning of 1561 is discussed in n. 332.

Croxson/Croxton, Paul. Netherlands household 1587 (cook), funeral. In 1585 he was a kitchen boy, whom Leicester attempted to send to France for training, see n. 467. In n. 420 it is suggested that the Mrs Cruxstone referred to in the 1584–86 disbursement book may have been his mother; she may also have been the Alice Croxton of Wanstead who leased Stonehall from the Earl of Essex in 1594 (Longleat MS 749).

Curson, Robert. BSW, livery 1559 (gentleman), livery 1567. A servant of Curson's was arrested for robbery in December 1561 (PRO, SP12/20/82).

Cutteler, Mr. BSW.

Dampard, the Countess's footman. No further evidence.

Danyell, Peter. No further evidence.

Darcy, Robert. BSW (Thomas), livery 1559 (gentleman), livery 1567. Darcy was a son of Thomas, 1st Lord Darcy of Chiche (1508–58), who had been a friend of Northumberland's. On 11 July 1559 (DP I, fo. 25) Elizabeth, Lady Darcy, wrote to Leicester to thank him for taking her son into his service. The reference to Thomas Darcy in the BSW is probably an error.

Davers. The 'old Mr Davers' referred to on p. 219 was probably the Mr Davers given livery in 1567 and the Mr Davers who attempted to obtain the lease of the parsonage of Adderbury, Oxon., from New College, Oxford, in 1566 (see Pepys MS 2502, p. 627, Thomas White, warden of New College, to Leicester, 29 June 1566). He may have been Sir Richard Verney's cousin Davers, who had the keeping of some of Leicester's hawks in 1560 (DP IV, fo. 10, Verney to Leicester, 20 April 1560).

Davies, Thomas. BSW, livery 1559 (yeoman).

Dawlton/Dalton, Thomas, footman. No further evidence.

Day, Henry, fisherman. Funeral. Probably Harry the fisher referred to on p. 233.

Denys, John als Smulkin/Symwilkin, footman. Netherlands household 1587 (guard of shot).

Dennys, Mr. Probably (Sir) Thomas Denys (1559–1613), of Holcombe Burnell (Devon) MP. Denys served in the Netherlands in 1586 (retainer).

Dering, Anthony. Livery 1559 (gentleman), and possibly given livery in 1561 (DP Box V, fo. 116). He was a captain in the Irish garrison from 1566 to 1582, and referred to as 'your lordship's servant' (Wright, ii, 126, Sir Henry Wallop to Leicester, 26 Jan. 1581).

Dockwra, Anthony (d. 1586). Dockwra was keeper of the Chase at Kenilworth from 1571, and keeper or steward of the Castle c. 1580–86. See 'West Midlands', 41.

Dockwra/Dockrell, Christopher. He was Anthony Dockwra's youngest son, see Dockwra's will (7 Nov. 1586), PRO, PROB11/69 [PCC 59 Windsor]/461. He was therefore probably the 'young Docwraie' referred to on p. 186.

Downell, Daniel, footman. No further evidence.

Downhall/Downell, William. Served in the Netherlands 1586, referred to as a secretary on p. 356, Netherlands household 1587 (secretary), funeral. Downhall claimed in 1589 that Leicester owed him £100 for entertainment. There is also a reference to him in the Bristol chamberlains' accounts during Leicester's visit in April 1587 (Bristol RO, MS 04026(12) [Audit Book, 1587–92], p. 30), in which he is described as 'one of my lord's gentlemen of his horse'. In the 1590s he was a gentleman of the horse to Essex.

Drum, see Evans, Richard.

Duck, Conrad, hound-keeper 1585–6. Netherlands household 1587 (footman).

Dudley, Charles. Probably the Mr Dudley the page (p. 198), but his precise identity is unclear.

Dudley, John (1526–1580) of Stoke Newington, MP. A distant relation from the Yanwith (Cumberland) branch of the Dudleys and elder brother of Thomas*, Dudley had been a servant of Northumberland's and was one of Leicester's principal men of business. See 'Dudley Clientèle', p. 244ff, 'House of Commons', 225, 'West Midlands', 41, 43.

Dudley, Thomas (d. 1593), MP. Livery 1559 (gentleman), livery 1567, Lord of Denbigh's funeral (bearer of the great banner), Sidney funeral (pall-bearer), funeral. Brother of John, served Northumberland and the Duchess before entering Leicester's service. In 1571 he was described as his comptroller (*Black Book*, p. 36). He was possibly the most senior member of the household who did not take part in the Netherlands expedition. See 'Dudley Clientèle', p. 245ff, 'House of Commons', 225, 'West Midlands', 41, 43.

Dunkin, Robert. BSW.

Eaton/Eyton, Thomas. BSW, livery 1559 (gentleman), livery 1567, funeral (gentleman). Numerous references to deliveries to him as Leicester's clerk of the stable in 1560–6 can be found in the bills in DP Box V. He was probably the Thomas Eyton who was Surveyor of the Queen's Race [stud] between 1574 and 1589, see CUL, MS Gg.2.26 [a fragment of a Stables letter-book 1570–6], fo. 38v, and PRO, E101/107/33, the 1589 wage list for the Stables.

Edgerley, Thomas. Funeral. Edgerley was yeoman of the wardrobe at Leicester House by 1583 and a member of the household in the Netherlands in 1586, see the Leicester House inventories of 1583–4, DP VI-VII. On 31 May 1588 he and Alfred Johnson* succeeded Stephen Johnson as groom of the robes, see DP XIII.

Edmundes, Mr, master of sheep. Possibly William Edmundes, who was one of the officers at Kenilworth from 1576, see 'West Midlands', 73, n. 14.

Edwardes, Morys. BSW, livery 1559 (yeoman).

Eglamby/Eglinby, see Aglionby

Ellis/Ellice, Richard (d.c.1577). Livery 1559 (gentleman), livery 1567. Brother of Hugh Ellis (see n. 65), brother-in-law of John Marbury*, and a cousin of Sir Thomas Gresham (n. 97), Ellis succeeded Chancy as Leicester's financial officer in December 1559. Despite Leicester's displeasure with his account (see the Introduction, p. 14) Ellis was still a member of his household in 1566–7. In 1567 he received £50 from the Vintners' Company in 1567 for acting as an intermediary with Leicester (I owe this information to the kindness of Dr Ian Archer).

Empson, John. BSW, livery 1559 (yeoman), livery 1567.

Evans, Richard, drummer. BSW, livery 1559 (yeoman), badge and livery 1567.

Ezard/Isard, John, bonesetter. Netherlands household 1587.

Eygley, see Edgerley.

Falconer/Fawkner/Fawlconner, Richard. BSW (huntsman), livery 1560.

Falwell, Robert, coal-bearer. No further evidence.

Farslept, Mr. No further evidence.

Fealow, Richard, musician. No further evidence.

Fenner, Mr. A Mr Fenner also received livery in 1567. It is possible that this was the well-known sea captain Thomas Fenner (for a biographical note see M.F. Keeler (ed.), *Sir Francis Drake's West Indian Voyage 1585–86* (Hakluyt Society, second ser. cxlviii, 1981), 293). Fenner's letter to Leicester of 4 Feb. 1588 (BL, Cotton MS Otho E IX, fo. 164) suggests an established acquaintance.

Ferdinando, see Richardson, Ferdinando.

Fife, see Johnston, John.

Finch, William. No further evidence.

Flammock, Richard, acater. BSW (cator), livery 1560.

Flowerdew, Thomas. Livery 1559 (gentleman). His relationship to the Flowerdews of Hethersett, Norf., is unclear. Leicester had extensive connections with this family.

Fludd/Floyde, see Lloyd.

Ford, William, warrener at Wanstead. No further evidence.

Forrest, John. BSW.

Forrest, Thomas. BSW (huntsman), livery 1559 (the dog-keeper), livery 1567. He was probably the keeper and tenant of Kenilworth of that name, see 'West Midlands', 71, n. 11, and the servant whom Leicester assigned to send a gift of deer to the King of Sweden in 1579 (Kingston-upon-Hull RO, L23, Leicester to the mayor of Hull, 12 June 1579. I owe this reference to the kindness of Dr David Lamburn).

Forster, Anthony (c.1510–72) of Cumnor (Berks.), MP. Badge 1567. Forster had financial dealings with Leicester as early as 1557, but both his earlier Dudley connections and the precise office he held in Leicester's household in the early 1560s remain unclear. On 18 September 1564 he and William Grice* received a large grant of concealed lands (*CPR, 1563–6*, 62–7). By 1565–7 he was either steward of the household or an officer of the wardrobe, for practically all of the series of wardrobe warrants for those years in DP Box V (see n. 80 to the Introduction) were signed by him. See also 'Dudley Clientèle', 242–3, 251.

Fowler, Thomas. Funeral. Fowler was one of Leicester's more controversial servants. He was a Scot who had formerly been in the service of the Earl and Countess of Lennox, and entered Leicester's after the Countess's death in 1578. He may have been used as political agent in Scotland in early 1580s. He retired to Scotland after Leicester's death, amid accusations that he had embezzled the last instalments of the rent to the Crown for Leicester's farm of the customs on Sweet Wines, see *CSPSc, 1586–8*, 534, 552, and Hist MSS Comm, *Salisbury MSS*, xiv, 266.

Fox, John. Netherlands guard 1586 (old retainer).

Frenchman There were several Frenchmen in Leicester's household in both 1559–61 and 1585. In 1559–61 there was a French cook (BSW, Phe [Philippe?]) and a French gardener at Kew, see p. 102. John the

Frenchman (pp. 54, 69, 84, 170) may have been John the muleteer (p. 81). For the French cook in 1585, see Moerew, Pearowe. For the French gardener who Leicester sought to employ see nn. 401, 467; neither the accounts nor the related correspondence give his name.

Fulford, Robert. Funeral. Probably the servant Mr Fulford whom Leicester sent to the Netherlands with messages in June 1588, see *CSPF, Jan-June 1588*, 477, Sir William Russell to Leicester, 11 June 1588. A Roger Fulford and his brother served in the Netherlands in 1586.

Gardiner/Garner, Richard, groom. Netherlands household 1587 (groom of the great or utter chamber), funeral.

Garland. An Edward Garland is found in the BSW, and John Garland received livery in 1567. The reference on p. 221 is probably to the latter. There are also references to Garland as messenger of Leicester's in Ireland in 1581 in J.S. Brewer (ed.), *Calendar of Carew Papers*, ii (1868), 486, 492.

Garnet, William. Funeral (officer of household). Garnet, who had a chamber in Leicester House in 1588, appears regularly as a surveyor of the inventories of Leicester House and Wanstead in 1587-8 (see DP VI, VIII, IX, XI). His precise office is unclear, but a reference in DP VIII suggests that he may have been steward of the household at Wanstead.

Garrett, John, footman. BSW (footman). He may be the footman of that name in 1584 (see p. 192), who appears to have left Leicester's service in March 1585 (p. 234).

Gawen, the groom. No further evidence. Probably not Gawen Smith (n. 559).

Geaste/Gaste. No further evidence.

George the cook, see George Cooke

Giles, see Gyles.

Gilliam/Gillions/Jolyon, Roger, bargeman. Funeral (Jolyon the bargeman). His wife appears to have one of the laundresses of the household.

Gilliam, gardener. No further evidence, possibly Gwyllyam Horewood (BSW).

Gilmer, see Gylmer.

Gittones/Gyttings, Richard. BSW. He is probably not the same man as Lumley's servant referred to in 1584-5 (pp. 193, 247).

Glasier, William (1525-88), of Lea (Ches.), MP, brother-in-law of Thomas Aglionby*, and related to William Grice*. Glasier had financial dealings with Leicester as early as 1553 and was acting as his legal counsel in 1556. Thereafter he was one of his principal officers, steward of the lordship of Denbigh 1565-80, and vice-chamberlain of the county palatine of Chester, although he received this office in 1559, seven years before Leicester was appointed chamberlain (1566). His numerous offices in Chester made him a controversial local figure, and Leicester spent much time mediating between him and his enemies. See 'Dudley Clientèle', p. 244ff, and S. Adams, 'Office-holders of the Borough of Denbigh and Stewards of the Lordships of Denbighshire in the Reign of Elizabeth I', *Transactions of the Denbighshire Historical Society*, xxv (1976), 97–100.

Godfrey, Frederick. BSW, livery 1567. He was probably the Godfrey of the wardrobe to whom nine badges were delivered in 1567. There is a further reference to deliveries to him in February 1567 in DP Box V, fos. 422–3.

Goffe/Gouffe/Gough/Gousse/Goch, Thomas, gardener at Wanstead. Funeral. There is a reference to a hat given to him in the 1588 inventory of Leicester's robes, DP XIII, fo. 16.

Goldingham, Henry. Funeral. There are references to him in the account of the Kenilworth entertainment of 1575 (E.J. Furnivall (ed.), *Robert Laneham's Letter: Describing a part of the entertainment unto Queen Elizabeth at the Castle of Kenilworth in 1575* (1907), pp. 31, 71), and in 1578 (DP II, fo. 193, H. Besbeeche to Leicester, 23 Oct. 1578). A Christopher Goldingham served in the Netherlands in 1586.

Goodrouse, Mr, surgeon. Goodrouse was in the Netherlands household in both 1586 and 1587 (surgeon), he also attended Leicester's funeral. Leicester leased him a house in Woodgrange on the Wanstead estate, see his 1587 will.

Gorge/Gouge, William. Livery 1567, Lord of Denbigh funeral (standard-bearer), served in the Netherlands 1586, funeral (officer of household). As is the case with so many of Leicester's senior household officers, Gorge's precise office is unclear. He was described as Leicester's steward in 1571 (*Black Book*, p. 36) and variously as comptroller and (clerk?) 'of the cheque' in the Netherlands in 1586. He audited Richard Browne's provisioning account of 1585–6 (see n. 48 to the Introduction) and was employed by the Countess in 1588–9 to make the final survey of the contents of Kenilworth (see Bodl., MS Malone 5, and the Kenilworth Chancery case).

Gower, Mr. Livery 1567. Probably [Edmund] Goove (BSW), one of Leicester's servants arrested at King's Lynn in July 1553, see J.R. Dasent (ed.) *Acts of the Privy Council of England*, iv (1892), 305.

Grammer of Kenilworth, spaniel-keeper. There is a reference to him at Kenilworth in DP II, fo. 195, Henry Besbeeche to Leicester, 21 Nov. 1578. He may have been the tent-keeper Thomas Grammer in the Netherlands household in 1587.

Green, William, gentleman usher. Served in the Netherlands in 1586. Green was in Leicester's service before 1580, when he travelled in Italy, see his letter to Arthur Atye from Padua, 23 Sept. 1580, PRO,

SP12/142/82. Richard Madox dined at his table (presumably at Leicester House) in January 1582 (E.S. Donno (ed.), *An Elizabethan in 1582: the Diary of Richard Madox, Fellow of All Souls* (Hakluyt Society, second ser. cxlvii, 1976), 75. Green's politics are curious. He appears in the list of Leicester's agents c.1581–2 in the archives of the Inquisitor of Malta (Vella, *Elizabethan-Ottoman Conspiracy*, p. 85), but in 1584–6 he was recommended to Mary, Queen of Scots, by Thomas Morgan as a discreet catholic and a sympathetic member of Leicester's household (L. Hicks, *An Elizabethan Problem: some aspects of the careers of two exile adventurers* (1964), pp. 214–5). He may have become a Gentleman Pensioner by 1591 and later had some association with Essex.

Grice, William (d. 1593), of Great Yarmouth, MP, Clerk of the Stables by September 1564. BSW. Grice's father Gilbert, a bailiff of Yarmouth, had associations with Northumberland and supported Lady Jane in 1553. Grice was in Leicester's service by 1556, and was his financial officer for the period to December 1558. He undoubtedly owed his clerkship of the Stables to Leicester, but as a servant of the Crown was thereafter no longer a member of his household. Grice was related to William Glasier* and he and Anthony Forster* received a large grant of concealed lands in 1564. He was one of the most active parliamentarians among Leicester's followers. See also 'Dudley Clientèle', p. 244, and 'House of Commons', 221.

Griffen, Henry. Netherlands guard 1586 (ordinary servant, licensed to go to sea).

Griffen the undercook, see Lloyd.

Grotrege, Mr. No further evidence.

Gwyn, John. Livery 1567 (yeoman), Netherlands guard 1586 (ordinary servant), funeral.

Gwyn, Robert. Netherlands guard 1586 (ordinary servant), employed as a messenger in July 1586 (BL, Harl. MS 1641, fo. 28), funeral. Gwyn was a deponent in the Sir Robert Dudley case. According to his deposition (DP Box VII, rots. 21–8) he was then aged 69 and a Yeoman of the Guard. He had entered Leicester's service the day the 1st Earl of Pembroke was buried (1570) and served him for twenty years [*sic*] as a yeoman of the pantry. There are a few references to him in the Leicester House inventories (DP VI-VII). Assuming the date of his entry into Leicester's service is correct, he could not have been the yeoman servant given a badge in 1567.

Gyles, George. BSW, livery 1559 (yeoman), livery 1560, livery 1567. Presumably he was the man of that name referred to in September 1585 (p. 308) and who attended Leicester's funeral.

Gylmer, Henry. BSW.

Hadlington, see Adlington.

Hakesby, William, cook. BSW (cook), livery 1560. However, there is a reference to his leaving Leicester's service in September 1559 on p. 83.

Hale/Hall. At least three men of that surname attended Leicester's funeral. Reginald Hall is not found elsewhere. Thomas Hale was probably the yeoman servant Thomas Hall mentioned in 1584-5 (p. 275). John Hale was probably the John Hall who received a badge and livery in 1567 and a lease in Hill Wooton (Wars.) in 1578 (GVE, fo. 31).

Hance/Hanse/Vance. Leicester certainly had a servant of that name in 1559-60, see pp. 41, 44, 129, 151, but no further evidence is available.

Harlam/Howlam, Thomas. BSW (groom of the chamber), livery 1560.

Harman, William, of Hampton (Wars.). Served in the Netherlands 1586, funeral (bearer of the body), claimed a debt of £76 10s from Leicester's estate. In 1591 Harman was the keeper of Langley House and Park (Watney, *Cornbury*, p. 88); he was probably appointed by Leicester.

Harvey, George. Funeral. The reference on p. 351 to Harvey as 'steward of your lordship's house' in May 1586 suggests that it was he rather than Gabriel Harvey who audited the 1585-6 provisioning account (see n. 48 to the Introduction). That being the case it is odd that he is not identified as a household officer in the funeral list. Other references to Harvey are scarce, however. He was probably Leicester's servant George Harvey who was refused the reversion of the keepership of Ludgate Prison in 1566 (Corporation of London RO, Repertory 15, fo. 513. I owe this reference to the kindness of Dr Ian Archer). Whether he was the captain of that name in Ireland (1575-84) is unclear, but he was undoubtedly Sir George Carew's uncle Harvey, who was with Leicester in the Netherlands in the autumn of 1586 (LPL, MS 605, fo. 80, Leicester to Carew, 31 Aug. 1586), and possibly the servant Harvey for whom Leicester wrote to Shrewsbury on 1 August 1582 (Hist MSS Comm, *Bath MSS*, v, 38). What complicates further identification is both the still unresolved question of whether Gabriel Harvey was ever in Leicester's service and the fact that Leicester also had a servant named Robert Harvey (Hist MSS Comm, *Tenth Report: Appendix II (Gawdy MSS)* (1885), 57).

Haward, Edward, trumpeter. No further evidence.

Heigham/Higham, Arthur. Livery 1559 (gentleman), livery 1567, Netherlands household 1587 (gentleman usher). Heigham received an annuity of £10 in Leicester's 1582 will. In 1592 he asked Burghley to intercede in a dispute over the lease of a park in the lordship of Denbigh that Leicester had given him c. 1583 for his thirty-three

years of service (PRO, SP12/242/56, Heigham to Burghley, 23 May
1592). If this was his total period to 1588, he entered in 1555, but he
may have done so several years earlier. He served at Le Havre in
1562–3 and was appointed water-bailiff by Warwick ('Higham my
brother's man', PRO, SP70/47/140). The fact that he commanded
a company raised in Norfolk and Suffolk at Le Havre suggests that
he was one of the Suffolk Heighams, but his precise relationship to
that family is unclear (I am grateful to Dr Diarmaid MacCulloch for
his assistance on this point).
Hetherley, John. BSW.
Heybourne, see Richardson.
Heydon/Haydon, William. Heydon served in the Netherlands in
1586 and was employed as a messenger to England (BL, Harl. MS
1641, fo. 31v). He was probably the Mr Heydon snr, Netherlands
household 1587 (gentleman usher), funeral (gentleman usher). He
received a loan of £100 from King's Lynn for acting as an intermediary in a suit with Leicester in 1587 (Norfolk RO, KL/C7/7
[King's Lynn Hall Book, 1569–91], fo. 346), which suggests he was
one of the Norfolk Heydons. Mr Heydon jnr, Netherlands household
1587 (secretary), was probably Mr John Heydon, funeral, and presumably his son.
Hilliard, Richard. BSW. Possibly Richard Hilliard of Routh (Yorks.),
father of the MP Christopher Hilliard, see n. 324.
Hinde/Hynde, John. Served in the Netherlands in 1586, Netherlands
household 1587 (secretary), funeral (gentleman of the horse). Hinde
had chambers in both Leicester House and Wanstead in 1588. He
may have been related to the MP Sir Francis Hynde (1530–96), of
Madingley (Cambs.), who also attended Leicester's funeral.
Holland, Robert. BSW, livery 1559 (yeoman), badge and livery 1567
(yeoman). He is possibly the Robert Holland referred to on p. 195.
Homerstone, Giles. Netherlands guard 1586 (ordinary servant),
funeral.
Horden/Hordeyn, Richard, BSW. As noted in the Introduction
(p. 14), Horden was presumably clerk of the kitchen. The earliest
reference to him in the accounts is dated 10 November 1559 and the
last in the summer of 1560 (see pp. 106, 130), when he was apparently
replaced by Richard Jynkes*. He was one of the auditors of the
Chancy account and examined several bills in November 1559 (DP,
Box V, fos. 2,4, 26–7). Presumably he was in post earlier in 1559, but
the evidence is lacking.
Horsenall/Horsenaile/Horsemede, William. No further evidence.
Hotman [Dr Ottoman], Jean (1552–1636), Sieur de Villiers St Paul.
Netherlands 1586 (secretary), Netherlands household 1587 (secretary),

funeral. Hotman entered Leicester's service c. 1581, and may have been a secretary in 1582–3. At the end of 1583 he returned to France and entered the service of the King of Navarre, but he had rejoined Leicester in the Netherlands by January 1586. For this period of Hotman's life, see G.H.M. Posthumous Meyjes, *Jean Hotman's English Connection* (Mededelingen der Koninklijke Nederlandse Akademie van Wetenschappen, new series, liii, pt. 5, 1990). A considerable body of Leicester's papers is found among the extensive collection that Hotman left, which is now dispersed in several repositories in Paris and in the Teyler Museum in Haarlem; they will be discussed in the fourth and final part of the 'Leic. Pap.' series. Particularly valuable for this volume is the correspondence between Leicester and Hotman when the latter was in France in 1584–5. Most of this is to be found in the AMAE, CPH, but some items have strayed and, after passing through several manuscript sales and auctions, are presently in libraries in the USA.

Huggins/Hogan, William (1524–88), MP, Keeper of the gardens at Hampton Court from 1561. BSW, livery 1559. Huggins was the brother of the MP Thomas Hogan and the merchant Edward (see n. 11), and brother-in-law of John Appleyard*. He had been a servant of Northumberland's and possibly the Duchess (who owed him £15) as well. See 'Dudley Clientèle', p. 244ff.

Humphrey the footman, see Adlington.

Hunt, Ralph. Livery 1559 (yeoman), livery 1567. Possibly Ralph the huntsman referred to on p. 82.

Hussey, Richard, spaniel-keeper. No further evidence.

Hutton, Robert. Served in the Netherlands in 1586, funeral. Brother of John Hutton and in Leicester's service by 1562, see n. 294. There are several references to him as Leicester's comptroller in 1582–3, see DP II, fo. 224, A. Neville to Leicester, 23 July 1582, and NLW, Ruthin Lordship MS 71, a lease to Hutton of Moelwick Park (Denbs.), 18 Feb. 1583. He also audited two of the household inventories (DP VI-VII).

Hyde, Ralph. Funeral.

Jerningham, Thomas, clerk comptroller of the kitchen 1586. No further evidence.

John the Frenchman, see Frenchman.

John the harper. No further evidence.

John the muleteer, see Frenchman.

John Trumpet, see Richards.

Johns, Thomas, see Jones, Thomas.

Johnson, Alfred. Netherlands household 1587 (of the beds), funeral. In 1588 he was appointed groom of the robes jointly with Thomas Edgerley (DP XIII).

Johnson, Francis. Netherlands guard 1586 (ordinary servant).

Johnson, Stephen. He is referred to regularly in the 1584–5 disbursement book as a servant of the wardrobe, and was yeoman of the robes in the 1587 Netherlands household. He surrendered this office to Thomas Edgerley* and Alfred Johnson* on 31 May 1588 (DP XIII). He claimed a debt of £60 from Leicester's estate.

Johnson, William, sallnor [*sic*]. No further evidence.

Johnston, John, fife. BSW, livery 1559 (yeoman), badge and livery 1567.

Jones, Henry. BSW, livery 1559 (yeoman), livery 1567.

Jones, Hugh. BSW, livery 1559–60, badge 1567 (Jhons of my lord's chamber).

Jones alias Leicester, Owen. Netherlands household 1587 (pantry). Jones was a key witness in the Sir Robert Dudley case, for he was the only one of Leicester's former servants to testify that Leicester and Douglas Sheffield had married and that Leicester had acknowledged to him that Sir Robert was his legitimate son. According to his deposition (CKS, U1475/L2/2, fos. 1–7) he entered Leicester's service in the year before the Duke of Norfolk was executed [i.e. 1571] and 'sometimes attended in the Earl's chamber and was sometymes used as a footman'. He was also commanded to attend Sir Robert when he went to school at Offington. The Crown made major efforts to discredit his testimony, on the ground that he was prejudiced in favour of Sir Robert, and those former servants who were witnesses for the Crown were all asked whether Jones had been in Leicester's service at the time of Leicester's supposed marriage to Douglas Sheffield (1573), and whether he had been as much in Leicester's confidence as he claimed. The references to him in the 1584–5 disbursement book do, however, confirm that he was assigned to attend Sir Robert at Offington, see n. 499.

Jones, Thomas. No further evidence, but the reference on p. 90 to his purchasing a hood for Amy Dudley, suggests he might have been one of her servants.

Jyles, see Gyles.

Jynkes/Jenks/Yngle, Richard. BSW. Clerk of the kitchen from the summer of 1560, see the reference to his book [*i.e.* account] on p. 126.

Keame/Keane, John. Netherlands household 1587 (coal-bearer), funeral.

Kelly, John. Kelly was a deponent in the Sir Robert Dudley case. According to his deposition (DP, Box VII, rots. 29–36), he was then aged 60 and of Richmond. He had entered Leicester's service 'when the old Earl of Essex went first into Ireland' [presumably 1573] and served sixteen years [*sic*] as a footman until Leicester preferred him to the Queen's service (presumably as a footman) 'in the year after her majesty's progress to Norwich' [*i.e.* 1579]. He had been present at Wanstead when Leicester married the Countess in 1578.

Kemp, William. Despite the impression given by the references in the disbursement books there is no evidence that Kemp was ever in Leicester's service. Cf. the entry on Kemp in Bradbrook, *Common Player*.

King, the widow of Kenilworth (p. 199). Probably Anne King, who was a tenant of Kenilworth by 1581 (PRO, LR2/185/36v) and keeper of the napery at Kenilworth between 1583 and 1588, see 'West Midlands', 71.

King, Thomas. Netherlands guard 1586 (ordinary servant), 1587; probably Thomas King the brewer (pp. 178, 436).

King, Thomas, musician. No further evidence.

Kitchen, Mr. Two Kitchens are referred to in the funeral list, the Mr Kitchen who was a bearer of the body and Alderman Citchen. The latter was Robert Kitchen (1531?-1594), alderman and mayor of Bristol. He was a partner of Leicester's factor John Barker in the Spanish trade in the 1570s, and sub-leased the farm of the Sweet Wines customs of Bristol from Leicester in 1584 (GVE, fo. 42v). Leicester stayed with him when he visited Bristol in April 1587. The other Kitchen cannot as yet be identified. Alderman Kitchen is the subject of a typescript biographical note compiled by the staff of the Bristol RO; I am most grateful to them for supplying me with a copy.

Knowles, Mr. Livery 1559, hose supplied to 1566 (DP Box V, fo. 322). Either Henry Knollys the elder (1521–83), MP, brother of Sir Francis, or Henry Knollys the younger (1542–82), MP, Sir Francis's son, both of whom were in Leicester's service. The elder Henry Knollys was described as a follower of Leicester's by the French ambassador in 1568 (BN, fonds français 15971, fo. 143, La Forêt to Charles IX, 19 July 1568). The younger Henry Knollys was appointed an Esquire of the Body by 1567 (PRO, E179/69/82 [Household subsidy list 1567]), which would explain why he does not appear in Leicester's 1567 livery lists.

Knowles/Knollys, Richard (c.1548–1596), MP, son of Sir Francis. Livery 1567, and left an annuity of £20 in Leicester's 1582 will. Richard Knollys was present at his sister's marriage to Leicester in 1578, and was a trustee for her jointure in 1584. I was not aware of Richard Knollys's close association with Leicester when I wrote 'House of Commons'; I would now revise the conclusion I drew on p. 229 from his sitting for Wallingford in 1584.

Kynyat/Kennet, William (d. by 1574). Surveyor and auditor to Northumberland, auditor for the Court of Augmentations in the reign of Edward VI, auditor to Leicester and Warwick. See 'Dudley Clientèle', p. 244, n. 22, and 'West Midlands' 40–1, 71. Kynyat's marginalia can be found throughout the Chancy and Ellis accounts.

Lane, Henry, keeper at Wanstead. Netherlands household 1587, funeral.

Langham, Edward. BSW, livery 1559 (gentleman). Langham served in the Scottish campaign of 1560 (see DP I, fo. 1, Leicester to the sheriff of ?, 30 Dec. 1559), and was probably the officer of that name in the Irish garrison in 1566, who became constable of Carlow in 1568–9.

Langham, Thomas. No further evidence, possibly an error for Edward.

Ledsham/Lesham/Lesam, William, skinner. Livery 1567 (Ledsham the skinner). Possibly Leicester's man Ledsham, 'bailiff of the Duchy', whose negligance during an outbreak of plague in London in 1577 was the subject of a complaint from William Fleetwood to Burghley (Wright, ii, 66).

Leswood/Lewood, William, gentleman of your lordship's armour 1586. No further evidence.

Lewis, Anthony. No further evidence.

Lewis, Kenneth. No further evidence.

Lewis, Rutherick. Netherlands guard 1586 (ordinary servant), Netherlands household 1587 (marshall of the hall). Tenant of the lordship of Chirk, see Toby Mathew's* 1583–5 survey, PRO, LR2/238, fo. 103. Probably Lewis the yeoman usher referred to in December 1584 (p. 202). See also Introduction, p. 16 for the possible identification of Lewis as Hand C of the 1584–6 disbursement book.

Lloyd, Griffin/Griffith. BSW, livery 1560. Possibly Griffin the undercook, referred to on p. 49.

Lloyd, Richard (1545–?). Served in the Netherlands 1586, Netherlands household 1587 (secretary), funeral (secretary). Lloyd was secretary to Sir Amias Paulet and Sir Henry Cobham during their embassies in France in 1579–82, but he already had some association with Leicester, for he corresponded with Atye in 1579 (PRO, SP78/3/79) and Leicester in 1580 (BL, Cotton MS Caligula E VII, fos. 163, 169, 178). He is identified as Leicester's secretary in 1583 ('Leic. Pap. II', 134), and may have been the MP for Flint boroughs in 1584. His mission to the Netherlands in the summer of 1585 is discussed in n. 556.

Lovell, Henry. Funeral.

Marbury/Merbery/Mowbray, John. BSW, livery 1567. Marbury was a cousin of Sir Thomas Gresham and his sister was married to Richard Ellis. He was referred to as Leicester's secretary when he made a journey to France in the summer of 1561, see *CSPSp, 1558–*

67, 226. This was believed to be a political errand, but both Henry Killigrew (BL, Add. MS 35830, fo. 205, to Throckmorton, 28 Sept. 1561) and Leicester himself (see his letter to Throckmorton, 20 April 1562, referred to in n. 294) claimed that Marbury went without permission. He was probably Leicester's 'old servant' of that name serving in Ireland between 1579 and 1585, see *Carew Calendar*, ii, 270, N. Maltby to Leicester, 12 July 1580.

Marshall. Livery 1559 (gentleman). No further evidence, though possibly William Marshall

Marshall, William. Marshall had the charge of the ordnance at Kenilworth between 1583 and 1588 (see the Kenilworth Inventory, DP XI). He was probably the 'William the gunner' referred to on p. 298.

Martin, George. Livery 1559 (gentleman). He was possibly the George Martin who claimed to have served in Leicester's and Warwick's households for five years and was later involved in Spanish plots against William of Orange, see *CSPF, 1583–4*, 524–5. The identity of the Mr Martin referred to in March and April 1585 (see pp. 228, 243) is unclear.

Massey, William, greyhound-keeper. Funeral.

Mathew the groom, see Woodward.

Mathew, Toby. Netherlands guard 1586 (old retainer), funeral. In 1583–5 Mathew compiled the survey of the lordships of Denbigh and Chirk now PRO, LR2/238. His relationship (if any) to Tobias Mathew, the future Archbishop of York, is unclear.

Mearaday. There are frequent references to 'my fellow Mearaday' by Hand C in the latter of 1585, but no servant of that name can be identified. Mearaday is probably a transliteration of (Richard) Meredith*.,

Meredith, Richard, clerk of the kitchen, Netherlands 1586 (p. 363). Meredith was a deponent in the Sir Robert Dudley case. According to his deposition (DP Box VII, rots. 37–41), he was then aged 52 and Clerk of the Catrye [Accatry]. He had entered Leicester's service a little before the progress to Norfolk [*i.e.* 1577–8] and was clerk of his kitchen.

Merrick, Richard, waterman. Netherlands household 1587 (waterman to the lesser barge), funeral.

Millington, Henry. Netherlands household 1587 (porter), funeral.

Moerew, Pearowe [Pierre or Pierrot Moreau?]. Netherlands household 1587 (cook). He was the 'new French cook', hired in 1585, see n. 467.

Moleans. No further evidence, possibly a transliteration of Moreau.

More, Ralph. Netherlands household 1587 (groom of the chamber/bedchamber), funeral. More was a deponent in the Sir

Robert Dudley case. According to his deposition (DP Box VII, rots. 47–51), he was then aged 67 and a yeoman of St Albans. He had served Leicester for twenty years, and for fifteen of them waited in his chamber, but he could remember the date he began. He was present at Wanstead when Leicester married the Countess in 1578, and had the keeping of Leicester's 1587 will, which he surrendered to the Countess on the day Leicester died. More was left an annuity of £10 in Leicester's 1582 will; the chamberlain of Bristol, who termed him Leicester's chamberlain, gave him 10s 'to help me to speech of his lordship' in July 1584 (Bristol RO, MS 04026(11), p. 246); he is called Leicester's barber in 1585 in the *Black Book* (p. 358); and Coventry gave him 5s in 1588 (Coventry RO, MS A.7b., p. 175). He claimed a debt of £15 from Leicester's estate. See the Introduction p. 16 for the suggestion that he might be Hand A of the 1584–6 disbursement book.

More, Robert, coachmaker of Ipswich. Funeral (Moore the coachmaker).

Morrys, see Edwardes.

Munford, John. No further evidence.

Musgrave, Cuthbert/Cutty. Men of this name are found in both the 1559 (p. 64) and 1584–5 accounts (pp. 198, 214). It is possible that the Cutbert Musgrave of 1559 and old Cutty Musgrave of January 1585 were the same man. For Leicester's relations with the Musgraves in general, see n. 302. A Cuthbert Musgrave was in Northumberland's service.

Nettleton, John. Funeral.

Neville, Alexander (1544–1614), MP. Lord of Denbigh funeral, funeral (officer of household). A former servant of Archbishops Parker and Grindal, Neville entered Leicester's service at his own request in 1582–3 (DP II, fo. 224, Neville to Leicester, 23 July 1582). Precisely which household office he held is unclear but he had a chamber in Leicester House in 1588 and surveyed many of the household inventories between 1583 and 1588. In July 1585 Leicester used him as an intermediary with Archbishop Whitgift, see n. 562. His attachment to Leicester's household helps to explain why he edited the Cambridge eulogy for Sir Philip Sidney.

Nicholls, Edmund. No further evidence, but he may be the Nicolles of Southam, Wars., said to be a man of Leicester's in the *Black Book*, pp. 210, 215–6.

Nightingale, Mr. Probably Richard Nightingale, who until August 1583 had the charge of the wardrobe at Leicester House (DP VI, fo. IV). The clothing account for 1571–4 (DP XII) is basically his account.

Oswald, Roger. BSW, livery 1559 (yeoman), livery 1560 (groom of the chamber).

Owen. Possibly Humphrey Owen, livery 1567.

Owen, Thomas, armourer of Kenilworth. Netherlands household 1587 (armourer), funeral. Possibly a witness to the Countess of Leicester's jointure July 1584.

Oxenbridge, Mr, page. Funeral.

Partridge, John, waterman. BSW (waterman), badge 1567 (yeoman). A Richard Partridge received livery in 1567.

Pearowe, see Moerew.

Pepper, Richard, footman. No further evidence.

Pietro, musician. BSW.

Pinnock/Pyenock, Nicholas. Netherlands household 1587 (of the beds), funeral. Pinnock was given the charge of the wardrobe at Leicester House on 21 March 1588 (DP VI, fos. 3v, 43v).

Pitchford/fork, Robert. Netherlands household 1587 (groom of the chamber/of the bedchamber), funeral. Pitchford remained on the staff of Leicester House after 1588 and had the charge of the linen in Essex House (as it was then known) in 1599–1600, see FSL, MS Gb4 [A collection of inventories of the property of the Earl of Essex compiled by Michael Stanhope, 1601], art. 16, inventory of the linen at Essex House by Robert Pitchford, 21 July 1600.

Pitchford, William. No further evidence, possibly an error for Robert.

Pollwhell, Thomas. Lord of Denbigh funeral (Thomas Powle, ban-nerol-bearer), accompanied Leicester to the Netherlands in 1585, but returned in January 1586 to recruit a voluntary company (*CSPF, 1585–6*, 290). Possibly Thomas Appowell, livery 1567.

Povinton/Pottwinton, Robert. Possibly Robert Polewiston, Netherlands guard 1586 (old retainer).

Powell, David. Livery 1559 (yeoman).

Powell, John. BSW (of the wardrobe), badge (gentleman) and livery 1567. There are references to deliveries made to him in 1566–68 in DP Box V, fos. 263, 395.

Power, Mr. A William and a Henry Power received livery in 1567. On 16 June 1567 Leicester wrote to Cecil about the suit of a Mr Power, an old servant of the Queen, now serving under him (PRO, SP12/43/23v), but he may have been Robert Power, who was in Elizabeth's household in the reign of Henry VIII (BL, Cotton MS Vespasian C XIV, fo. 274), and a member of the Stables staff in 1559–76.

Ralph the huntsman, see Hunt.

Ramsay, Lawrence. No further evidence.

Ransome, keeper at Wanstead. No further evidence.

Ratless, keeper at Winworth. No further evidence.

Rich, John, corncutter. Funeral (John Rich corncutter).

Richard the cator, see Flammock.

Richard the spaniel-keeper, see Hussey.

Richards, John, trumpeter. BSW, livery 1559 (yeoman), livery 1560 (John Trompet).

Richardson alias Heybourne, Ferdinando. Funeral (cloak). In his 1582 will Leicester left Richardson 20 marks a year if he continued to serve his wife and son. Richardson was a deponent in the Sir Robert Dudley case. According to his deposition (DP Box V, rots. 14–20), he was then aged 45 and an esquire of Tottenham. He entered Leicester's service in 17 Elizabeth (1575) and served in his bedchamber until Leicester preferred him to the Queen's service as a Groom of the Privy Chamber (15 April 1587). Leicester supported a suit of his in 1588 (HEHL, EL 1364, Leicester to Thomas Egerton, 28 Feb. 1588). He should not be confused with Ferdinando Clarke (d. 1622), MP, a gentleman of Leicester's released from King's Bench prison by order of the House of Lords on 8 March 1585 (*Lords Journals*, ii, 93).

Ridgeway, Walter, your lordship's boy (p. 191). Funeral. Probably also the servant referred to simply as Walter or Wat.

Robert of Cornwall, see Cornwall.

Robert the trumpeter. No further evidence.

Roberts, Edward. BSW, livery 1559 (yeoman).

Roberts, John, footman. No further evidence.

Roberts, fisherman. No further evidence.

Robinson, John, skinner. Funeral (Robinson skinner). He claimed a debt £174 from Leicester's estate in 1589.

Robster, variant of Robsart

Robsart, Arthur. Livery 1567 (Mr Robster). Robsart was the illegitimate son of Sir John Robsart, and half-brother to Amy Dudley, whose funeral he attended at Leicester's invitation. He referred to 'my cheife frend gone the yerle of Lesseter' in a letter to Edmund Walpole, 19 June [1589?], FSL, MS Ld 505.

Row, wood-carrier. BSW.

Sandes/Sandys, Mr. Funeral. Sandys, who had a chamber in both Leicester House and Wanstead in 1588, is perhaps the most perplexing of Leicester's senior household servants of the 1580s, for neither the 1584–6 disbursement book nor the other known sources give his christian name. An Edmund Sandys witnessed a lease of the Countess's in 1580 (Longleat MS 3396), but interest focusses on two more prominent figures, Miles Sandys, brother of the Archbishop of York and MP for Abingdon in 1586, or his son Edwin, MP for Andover in 1586, because both sat for boroughs over which Leicester had some influence. See the discussion in 'House of Commons', 217–8, 220–1, 239.

Saule, William (d. 1563). Livery 1559 (gentleman). Saule was sent by Leicester to buy mules in France in 1561 (PRO, SP70/21/53, Throckmorton to Cecil, 22 Mar. 1561), and he was the Captain Saule 'your man', appointed lieutenant of the ordnance at Le Havre (PRO, SP70/49/87, Warwick to Leicester, 23 Jan. 1563), who was killed later in the siege. It is quite probable that he was the Captain Saule who had served at Calais during the siege of January 1558, and who had been badly burnt in attempting to lay the mine in the castle.

Semmell, see Symnell

Sermant, John. No further evidence.

Slyfield/Slyford, Henry. Netherlands household 1587, funeral. Probably the eldest son of Edward Slyfield (1522–90), of Slyfield Place (Surrey), MP. See n. 611 for his departure for France in September 1585 on a visit to learn the language.

Slyfield The Slifield mentioned in 1559 (see p. 48) was probably John, Yeoman of the Queen's Race [stud] by 1566–1570, see his account for 1566–8, PRO, E101/107/31.

Smetson, see Smithson.

Smith, William. Livery 1559 (yeoman), funeral, but may not be the same man. See also the reference (p. 180) to William Smith's wife, the laundress, in October 1584.

Smithson, John, cook. Netherlands household 1587 (cook).

Sparke, William. A lawyer (Lincoln's Inn) from Suffolk, Sparke was deputy-recorder of the lordship of Denbigh in 1580 (UCNW, Garthewin MS 2693, plea roll of the lordship 1580–1), and recorder by 1583 (PRO, LR2/270, rental of the lordship, 1583). He also acted as legal counsel for the Countess after 1588, see 'Leic. Pap. III', n. 125.

Speake/Spyke. No further evidence.

Sperte, Mr. Livery 1567 (Richard Sperte). He may also be Leicester's servant Sperte referred to as the captain of a ship in the fleet Henry Knollys the younger* commanded for Dom António in the autumn of 1581, see PRO, SP12/150/76, Edward Horsey to Walsingham, 13 Oct. 1581.

Stafford, Edmund. Served Netherlands 1586.

Stampe, Elles. BSW.

Stephen, see Johnson

Stevens, Henry. Funeral (two entries, one to a keeper).

Stringer, John. Funeral.

Sutton, Richard (d.1634), lawyer, MP. Sutton is referred to as Leicester's solicitor-general in 1581–3 (WCRO, CR 1886/2289, court roll of the manor of Knowle (Wars.), Oct. 1581, and NLW, Lleweni MS 369). In 1588 he was also steward of Balsall and Honiley (Wars.), see 'West Midlands', 72. He was granted the reversion of the common serjeantcy and under-sheriffwick of the City of London at Leicester's request in 1582, see Corporation of London RO, Repertory 20, fo. 298v, and Remembrancia I, fo. 185, Leicester to the lord mayor, 12 July 1582. In 1589 he owed Leicester's estate £49, and was then described as Warwick's solicitor. By 1600 he was an Auditor of the Exchequer.

Symmell/Symnell/Semmell, Thomas. Funeral. He witnessed a lease of the Countess in 1580 (Longleat MS 3396).

Symwilkin/Smulkin, see Denys, John.

Tavenor, Robert. Sub-tenant (by Michaelmas 1584) of Monkton (Kent) which Leicester leased from Christ Church, Canterbury (GVE, fo. 43).

Temple, Richard (b. 1549?) of Kenilworth. Funeral (cloak). Deponent in the 1590 Chancery case over Kenilworth.

Thomas, Morris. No further evidence.

Thomas, William. Netherlands household 1587 (groom of the chamber/of the bedchamber), charge of Leicester's jewels at court, 1588 (DP XI). Thomas was a deponent in the Sir Robert Dudley case. According to his deposition (DP Box V, rots. 42–6), he was then aged 60 and a gentleman of St Martin in the Fields. He entered Leicester's service a year or two after the Duke of Norfolk was beheaded (i.e. 1573–4) and served in his bedchamber till 1588. He should not be confused with William Thomas (1551–1586), of Caernarvon, MP, one of Leicester's leading followers in north Wales, who was killed at Zutphen in 1586 (see 'North Wales', 133–5).

Thompson, James, cator [acater]. BSW (cator).

Tracy, Giles. Son of Sir John Tracy (d. 1591), of Toddington (Glos.), MP, and brother of John*. Bannerol-bearer, Lord of Denbigh funeral, served in the Netherlands in 1586.

Tracy, (Sir) John (c.1561–1648) the younger, MP. Lord of Denbigh funeral (bannerol-bearer), commanded a company in the Netherlands 1586, Netherlands household 1587, funeral (bannerol-bearer). Equerry of the Stables by 1589, see PRO, E101/107/33.

Tudor/Teddar/Tyder, Robert. Lieutenant, Netherlands guard 1586, funeral. Keeper of Whitley Park (Windsor) by 1583, see Surrey RO, More-Molyneux of Loseley MSS, Correspondence V, fos. 105–6, Leicester to Sir William More, 8, 19 Dec. 1583. Tudor was the servant whom *Leicester's Comonwealth* claimed Leicester had suborned to kill the Duke of Anjou's agent Jehan Simier in 1579, see D.C. Peck (ed.) *Leicester's Commonwealth: The Copy of a Letter written by a Master of Art of Cambridge (1584)* (Athens, Ohio, 1985), p. 92

Turk, John. No further evidence.

Turner, Thomas, gentleman porter. Served Netherlands 1586.

Turner the brewer. Possibly Ralph, who attended Leicester's funeral and claimed a debt of £8 from Leicester's estate.

Twyste, Wednoll, 'Master of your lordship's shepe' [presumably sheep rather than ship]. No further evidence.

Underhill/Underell, Thomas (1545–1591). Badge (of Kyllingworth) 1567, served in the Netherlands 1586, funeral. Underhill was the son of Hugh Underhill, Keeper of the Wardrobe at Greenwich Palace (n. 471), and keeper of the wardrobe at Kenilworth from c. 1567. He was a deponent in the 1590 Chancery case over Kenilworth and is referred to extensively in the Kenilworth inventories. See 'West Midlands', 41, 71, and Morrison, *Underhills of Warwickshire*, pp. 66–8, 79–85.

Vance, see Hance

Wagstaff, Ralph. Funeral. Wagstaff was on the staff of Kenilworth by 1580, see *Black Book*, p. 306, and the references to his bed in the Kenilworth inventories of 1581 and 1583 (Evelyn MS 263, fo. 35, and CKS, U1475/E92, fo. 33).

Wake, John (d. 1621), of Salcey Forest, Northants. Served Netherlands 1586, funeral (bearer of the body). Wake was a keeper of the Forest of Grafton, see his letters to Leicester of 8 Nov. 1571 (BL, Add. MS 32091, fo. 254) and 3 Mar. 1572 (DP II, fo. 64). He was active in Northamptonshire puritanism and possibly the brother of the minister Arthur Wake, see Shiels, *Puritans in the Diocese of Peterborough*, 45, 106, 113–4.

Waller, Ambrose. Funeral. Although he appears to have died before 1604, Waller is referred to frequently in the depositions in the Sir Robert Dudley case. On the basis of these, he was clearly in Leicester's service by 1573, and was undoubtedly the 'Ambrose of my lord's chamber' referred to in the *Black Book* c.1576, see pp. 216–7. Leicester left him an annuity of £10 his 1582 will.

Waller, Thomas, keeper of Kenilworth Park 1585.

Warton, James, musician. No further evidence.

Wat your lordship's boy, see Ridgeway, Walter.

Watson, Thomas, armourer. BSW, livery 1567.

Watty, Philip. BSW (groom of the stable).

Webber, Nicholas. Netherlands household 1587 (yeoman of the beds in the July list, but of the robes in the November list), funeral. Webber was a member of the wardrobe staff at Wanstead by 1582 (Evelyn MS 264, unfoliated), and given the whole charge of the wardrobe at Wanstead on 1 April 1588 (DP IX, fos. 1v, 21v; DP XI, fo. 105).

Wednester, Charles (d. 1597), MP. Netherlands household 1587 (auditor), funeral (officer of household/auditor). Wednester may have been in Leicester's service as early as 1566, but is regularly referred as his auditor from 1583 (see e.g. NLW, Lleweni MS 369, commission for survey of the lordship of Denbigh, 5 Oct. 1583). In 1590 he was Essex's auditor-general (Longleat MS 1462), and by 1594 an Auditor of the Prests. See 'West Midlands', 43 and 71, n. 7.

Wigges, Mr. Presumably Thomas Wigges, who wrote to Leicester on 6 and 14 Feb. 1588 concerning the fitting out of the *Galleon Leicester* (copies from an unknown source in Pepys MS 2878, pp. 494–8, 501–4).

Wilberforce/Wilperforce, Edward. Funeral. Possibly the Edward Wilperforce of Drayton Bassett, who died in June 1621 (Stebbing Shaw, *The History and Antiquities of Staffordshire* (1790–1801, reprinted 1976), ii, 10).

William the gunner, see Marshall.

Williams, Edward. Possibly the Surveyor of the Stables 1576–89 (see PRO, E351/3340 [account of reparations to the Stables, 1574–7], and E101/107/33 [wage list 1589]).

Williams, Griffin. No further evidence.

Williams, William. Funeral. The old William Williams referred to on pp. 350, 358 may not be the same man.

Wisant, Harry. No further evidence.

Wood, Edward. BSW (waterman), badge and livery 1567.

Wooddouse, launderer. No further evidence.

Woodhouse, George. Probably the Mr Woodhouse who received livery in 1567, and the George Woodhouse found in the list of Leicester's servants arrested at King's Lynn in July 1553 (*Acts of the Privy Council*, iv, 305). He was the third son of Sir Roger Woodhouse of Kimberley, Norf.

Woodman, William, cator [acater]. BSW, badge 1567.

Woodward, Matthew. Keeper of the wardrobe at Leicester House, July 1587–March 1588 (DP VI, fos. iv, 3v), and probably the Matthew the groom referred to in April 1585 (p. 244).

Wortley/Wortheley, William. BSW, livery 1567. May be the same man mentioned in 1584–5 on p. 207.

Wrote, Robert (1544–89, but see note a to text II: J) of Bungay (Suff.), MP. Funeral. Wrote (who has been confused with the better-known MP Robert Wroth, see n. 508) was acting as legal counsel for Leicester by 1582 (WCRO, CR1600/LH125) and was steward of Wanstead in 1585–8 (Essex RO, D/DCw/M5 [Wanstead court rolls 1585–8]). Wrote was active in Suffolk puritan politics, see D. MacCulloch, *Suffolk under the Tudors* (Oxford, 1986), esp. pp. 213–4.

Yerwerth/Earth, John (d. 1587) of Chester, MP. BSW, badge 1567. Like William Glasier*, with whom he enjoyed a long if not always amicable association, Yerwerth combined Leicester's service with extensive local office-holding in Chester (he was clerk of the pentice from the 1550s). He was working for Leicester by the summer of 1559 (see his survey of Watton, n. 125), payments by him are entered in the BSW, and frequent references to him either as a receipient of goods or an auditor are found in bills of 1559–61 (DP Box V, fos. 11–2, 29, 35–7 et seq.). Leicester appointed him receiver of the lordship of Denbigh c. 1564, and from 1579 he is referred to as Leicester's receiver-general (see e.g. UCNW, Gwynsaney MS 741), though it is not clear whether this office applied to the lordship of Denbigh alone, Leicester's Welsh estates as a whole, or all his lands. See 'Dudley Clientèle', 244, 'House of Commons', 225, and 'West Midlands', 43 and 71, n. 6

Yngle, see Jynkes, Richard.

GLOSSARY

baite	bait: hasty meal or refreshment
boutey	boutel or bouter [?]: a fine cloth
brayche	brach: bitch-hound
brett	bret or birt: brill or turbot
codynock	codiniac: quince marmalade
cumphett/cumsett	comfit: sweatmeat preserved in sugar
cupers	cypers: cloth of gold
di/dy	dimidium: one half
drencher	apparatus for drenching a horse or other beast
dreyfate	dryfat or dry vat: large vessal to hold dry things
fett	fetch
girkin	jerkin
hedstall	part of a bridle that fits round the head
heromies	herons [?]
joyle	jowl: head and shoulders of a large fish
leonett	larneret or leonard: falcon
leusard	lusard: lynx
loddom	loddam or loadum: card game, early version of hearts
luer	lure used to recall hawks
lyan	line: leash
marchpayne	marzipan
marlyne	merlin: falcon
moyle	mule
moryne	morion
netherstocks	stockings
patrell	peytral: armour to protect the breast of a horse
peppering	to wash a hawk in pepper and water solution
pewett	pewit: lapwing
philbud	filbert
porpontyne	porcupine
premesett	primrose [?]
rinlet	runlet: vessel for drink
round	section of a fish analogous to a round of beef
run	enclosure for hounds
rynwase rutes	rhubarb [?]
sesterne	cistern: for cooling wine bottles
sevel	shewel: 'scarecrow' for dear
shovel	shoveller [?]: shovel duck
sparver	canopy or frame for a bed

standish	ink and pen stand
stocks	stockings
stonebow	crossbow or catapult
stoned horse	stallion
stropp leathers	straps
sucket	succade: preserved fruit
tantos	tanto: counter used in gaming
tapnet	basket of rushes in which figs were imported
vyrkin	firkin
wardon	warden: baking pear
woodlace	woodlice [?]

GENERAL INDEX

All persons found in the household lists as well as those mentioned in the accounts are included here, with the exceptions of underservants and the bargemen in the two 1587 lists (Documents II: G and H). * denotes an entry in the Index of Servants. Wives are entered under their most relevant married name, with their maiden names in parentheses. Occupations or offices supplied in the texts or notes are not repeated except to distinguish persons of the same name or to identify those referred to solely by a christian or surname. Christian names or other information relevant to the identities of persons entered only by their surnames in the household lists are supplied, where known, in square brackets. The spelling of names is that found in the notes, with some standardisation and modernisation. Places in the Cities of London and Westminster (the latter including the liberty of the duchy of Lancaster between the Strand and the Thames), the borough of Southwark and offices and departments of the Court and Household are gathered under those headings. The entry for Leicester himself is necessarily a selective one.

Abdye, Mr, 453, 457
Abergavenny, Lord, see Neville
Abingdon (Berks.), 189, 216–8, 252, 289–
    90, 292, 297
Aburford, John, 427
Acone, James*, 145, 172
Acton, Mr*, 200
    Charles*, 455
    Richard*, 455
    William, 436
Adams, of Wanstead, 222
    Robert*, 179, 333, 435, 456
    William, 435, 452
Adlington, Humphrey*, 187, 192, 194, 214,
    234, 248, 253, 277, 282, 285–6, 288,
    290, 297, 338, 346, 372, 434, 444, 457
Adrian, gardener*, 193, 197–8, 215, 296,
    456
    page, 431, 454
Adrian, Mr, secretary, 430
Aglionby, [Edward?], 455
    Thomas*, 42–3, 45, 47, 50, 63, 71, 102,
    151, 400, 426
Ailly, François de, Vidame of Amiens, 123,
    138
Albone, barber, 428
Aldersbrook (Essex), 307–8, 316–7, 465
Aldersey, Piers, 435
    Ralph*, 55, 60, 74, 145, 408, 424, 427
    Thomas, 113, 118; house 194, 274
Aldersham (Ildersham), Mr, 44, 99
Alexander, Sir Robert, 222, 267
Alford, Roger, 115, 117, 120
Alice, chambermaid, 458
Allen, crossbow-maker, 70

John*, 76, 103, 135, 189, 235, 276, 405,
    420–1
    Thomas, skinner, 87–8, 123
Allycock, Henry, 121
Almery, butcher, 124
Althorp (Northants.), 299
Amersfoort, 348, 374
Amiens, Vidame of, see Ailly
Amsterdam, 10, 345–8, 354
Amyce (Ames), Israel, 264, 333
    John, 440
    Thomas, 456
Anders, George, slater, 250, 279
Andrew, page, 426
Andrew, Hugh, 425
Andrews, Bertram, 437, 440
    John, 455
    Roger, 436, 453
Anjou, Francois, Duke of, xiii, 485
    negotiations concerning, 34, 306, 328
Anthonio, John, tailor, 43, 87, 89–91, 121
Anthony, fiddler, 153
Anthony, Derek, goldsmith, 90–1, 132–3
António, Dom, 256, 306, 323, 331–2, 484
Antwerp, xiii, 58, 139, 283, 372, 385–6; post
    of, 158
ap Powell, Thomas, 425
ap Richard, Morgan, 424
Appleby, Henry, 432, 443
Appleyard, Henry, 362, 461
    John*, 13, 40, 47, 122, 169, 427
Aquila, Bishop of, see La Quadra
Archer, Henry, 455
Ardern, Thomas*, 16, 179, 216, 220, 257,
    277, 310, 430, 448, 450, 452, 459

491

Argill, Thomas, matter, 132
Armin (Arm), John, 437, 455
Arnhem, 348–53, 364
Arran, Earl of, *see* Hamilton
Arthur, goldsmith, 127
Arundel, Earl of, *see* Fitzalan, Howard
Mr, 167–8; Mrs, 155, *see also* London: Arundel's
John, 213, 261
Ashby de la Zouche (Leics.), 141
Ashe, William, 457
Ashfield, Humphrey, 187, 455
  John, 187, 214, 216
Ashton (Arsshow), Richard, 436, 440, 455
Asly, Richard, 286
Aslyas, Monsr, 356, 358–9, 361
Aspeley, John*, 59, 70, 402, 419–20
Astley, Katherine, 43
Atye, (Sir) Arthur*, 12, 177, 202, 212, 251, 265, 275–6, 315, 388, 390, 430, 440, 445, 451–2, 459
  Mrs [Judith], 458
Audley, Arthur, gilder, 126
Audley, Thomas, Lord, 43
Audwine, John*, 74, 83, 107, 160, 408, 419, 421, 426
Austin, Michael, 436, 440, 456
  Sampson, 436, 440, 456
Avelin, Edward, 431, 454
Aylesbury (Bucks.), 214
Aylesworth, Richard, 39, 123
Aylmer, John, Bishop of London, 210
Aylworth, Christopher, 454

Babbington, Philip, 211
Bacon, Mr, of Kew, 153
  Sir Nicholas, 71, 114
Bagley, 297
Bagnall, Sir Nicholas, 55
  Sir Ralph, 55, 99
  Thomas*, 319, 434, 442
Bagnoll, grocer, 132
Bailiff, Robert, 443
Baily, John, 438, 442
Bainton, William, musician, 433
Bakehouse, George*, 206
Baker, Thomas, 434, 455
Bald, R.C., 7
Baldwin [William], 455
Ballet, goldsmith, 91
Baluwe, Marmaduke, 441

Bamfield, George, 435, 456
Banbury (Oxon.), 293, 297
Banyster, [Henry?], merchant, 110
Barbary, 280
Barbary Company, *see* London
Barbour, William*, 120, 157, 437, 440, 456
Barker, of Ipswich, 431
  Edward*, 220, 227, 242, 335, 431; Mrs, 458
  Francis, shepster, 60, 99, 119, 129; Mrs, 87, 258
  Henry*, 184, 453
  John, 455
  Thomas, 426
  William*, 74–5
Barley, Mr, 154
Barlow, Thomas, 424
Barn Elms (Surrey), 26, 179, 247–8, 275, 307, 319–20, 324, 327, 329, 338, 386, *see also* Walsingham
Barnaby, Mr [John], 426
Barnes, 455
  of Waltham Forest, 151–2, 155, 158, 160
  Richard, mercer, 125, 457
Barneston, George, 403, 427
Barnet (Herts.), 287, 304, 310–1, 315, 320–1, 382, 389
Barradale, William, 454
Barrett, Edmund, 436
  Lettice (Mrs Lettice), 28, 205, 270, 306, 458
Barrow, Capt Edward, 358
Bartie, Francis, 40, 125, 364
Bartlett, page, 257
  A.D., 379
Barton, John, 437, 441
Bashe, Edward, 153–4, 166, 241
Basing (Hants.), 143
Bath, 7, 10, 374
  Earl of, *see* Bourchier
Battersea (Surrey), 277, 280
Battle, William, 455
Batty, Ralph*, 237–8, 240, 247, 252, 283, 300, 335, 432, 443
Baxter, trumpeter, 314
Bayne, William, 457
Baynham, Mr [William], 451–2
Baynton, William, 455
Beacham*, 181, 295
Beale, Robert, 35
Beane, Augustine, 127–8

Beaumont, William, 104, 399, 426
Becket, Robert, 437
  Thomas*, 316
Bedford, Earl of, *see* Russell
Bedford wardship, *see* Russell, Edward, 3rd
  Earl of Bedford
Bedwell, Thomas*, 177, 184, 222, 227, 237–
  8, 244, 259, 267, 279, 282, 329, 333–
  4, 453, 459
Beere, Nicholas, 455
Bell, Thomas, farrier, 424, 428
Belle, Martin, 428
Bellenden, Sir Lewis, 228, 231
Bellingham, Mr, 191
Bells, William, 428
Benbolt, 105
Benington (Herts.), 26, 246–7
Benison, Barnabas, 194, 210, 234, 303, 307
Bennett, John, 432, 443
  William*, 192, 456
Bentall, Mr*, 209, 231
Bergen-op-Zoom, 326, 344
Berion, Thomas, 435
Berkeley, Sir Maurice, 150
Berkeley law suit, 153, 245
Berkshire, 48, 380, 383
Berte, Richard, 423
Bertie, Katherine (Willoughby), Duchess of
  Suffolk, 44, 157; household, 30
  Peregrine, Lord Willoughby d'Eresby,
  283, 326, 344
Berwick, 72, 152, 161, 344, 349
Besbeeche, Henry*, 317, 448, 451–2, 459;
  Mrs, 458
Best, 144
  haberdasher, 147
Bett, Robert, 424
Beverley (Yorks.), 100
Bewe, Richard*, 47, 50, 58, 134, 419–20,
  426
Beynton, Mr [Andrew?], 63
Bigot, James*, 116, 157
Bill, James, farrier, 425
  of Towcester, 428
Bingham, George, 454
Binton, John, 453
Birch, 199
Bircham Newton (Norf.), 13, *see also*
  Robsart estate
Bird, William, 453
Birkett, Robert, 457
Birmingham Reference Library fire (1879),
  1, 4, 7

Bishop, William, 438, 441
Black, 187
  Mr, of Ewelme, 289, 300, 304
  William, musician, 433, 442
blackamore, the, 178
Blackbourne, Thomas, 425
Blacknoll/well, 'mother', of Rotherfield
  Greys, 211–2, 218; 'nurse', 288
  William*, 350, 453
Blacksley, Lionel*, 232, 276, 435, 440, 456
Blackwall (Middx.), 171, 208, 220–1, 232,
  234, 240–3, 245, 250, 252, 256–7, 259,
  264–6, 268–70, 281, 313
Blackwater (Hants.), 288
Bland, Adam, Queen's skinner, 126, 336
Blike, Gabriel, 204, 209, 235, 257, 290, 297,
  451–2
Blount, Mr, of Windsor, 206
  Sir Charles (8th Lord Mountjoy), 449–
  50, 452
  Sir Christopher*, 179, 186–7, 193, 195–
  7, 200–1, 203, 211, 213, 218–20, 222,
  225–6, 235–6, 247, 252, 254, 258, 263,
  267, 273–5, 283, 285–6, 290, 292, 297,
  300–1, 304, 308, 311, 317, 321, 324–8,
  336, 339, 342, 344, 367–8
  Sir Edward*, 298, 339, 449, 451–2
  Sir George, 50, 53, 102
  George*, 50, 77, 82–3, 105, 419–20, 427
  Gilbert, 427
  Humphrey, 426, 454
  John, of Warwick, 299
  Thomas*, 13, 29, 39–41, 50, 54, 57, 69–
  70, 74, 88, 92, 97, 102, 114, 124, 126,
  130–2, 148, 379, 400, 408, 411, 413,
  416, 418
  Thomas, customer, 110, 115, 120
Bocacket, goodwife ('goody'), 343
Boddy, William, 128
Bold, Mr [Richard], 449
Bommel, 354–9, 362–3
Bond of Association (1584), 187
Booby, Anthony, 456
  John, 456
Booth, George, 453
Bordeaux, 123
Borough, Sir John, 354
  Stephen, 393–5
Borowe, Martin, 425
Borsey, Richard, 438, 442
Bosse, John, 424
Bostock, Lancelot, 189
Boswell, Nicholas, 456

Bott, Martin, 408
Bottle, Thomas, 434, 453
Boughton, Edward*, 28, 216, 241, 268–9,
  451–2, 459
  Thomas, 428
Bouillon, Duke of, *see* La Marck
Bourchier, William, 3rd Earl of Bath, 331–2
Bourne, John*, 347, 362, 433, 436, 440
  (snr), 442 (jnr), 454
  Peter, milliner, 132
  William*, 74–5, 107, 399, 414, 422
Bowes, 91
  Sir Jerome, 195, 199
  Mr [Ralph], 426
Bowkley, Mr [Bulkeley, Sir Richard], 426
Bowlton, Mr, 426
Bowman, Edward, 456
Bowyer, Mr, master of the children, Chapel
  Royal, 162
  Simon, 264
Boyes, James, 427
  William, 433, 443
Boyton, 454
Bradley, Edmund, 436
  Nicholas, 455
Bradshaw, Edward, 453
  James, 456
  Lawrence, 43
  Richard, 456
  William, 433
Braithwait, Richard, 28
Brampton, Mr*, 188, 203, 269, 278, 281,
  294, 296
Brandon, scrivener, 138–9
  Robert, 47, 50, 224
Bray, Dinstone, 428
Braybrooke, Thomas*, 56, 74, 77, 82, 172,
  405, 419–20, 426
Brentford (Middx.), 67, 95, 191, 197
Brereton, Roger, 431, 454
Brett, William, 428
Bricknell, 49, 61
Bridges, Mr, 53
  tailor, 76
  Edward, 2nd Lord Chandos, 180
  Gyles, 3rd Lord Chandos, 187, 211, 215,
    220, 449–51, 454, 458
  William, 195
Brightman, Mr, 126
Brill, the (Brielle), 386, 395
Bristol, 7, 10, 374, 478
Bristow, Hugh*, 75, 77, 83, 107, 154, 405,
  420–1, 423, 426

Brooke, George*, 183, 195, 215, 219, 245,
  251, 305, 307, 351, 353, 367, 431, 445,
  455
  William, 10th Lord Cobham, 157; house,
    see Cobham Hall
Broughton, Mr, 426
  Francis, 455
  Richard, 457
Browne, old, of Wanstead, 225, 233, 239
  Benedict, trumpeter, 431
  Giles, falconer*, 227
  Sir Richard*, 4, 12, 16–19, 25, 28, 221,
    239, 250, 254, 258–9, 264, 267, 270,
    278, 295, 323, 333, 343, 353, 430, 445,
    451–3, 459; Mrs, 458
  Robert, musician*, 351
  Thomas, armourer, 444
  Sir William, 347
Broxall, William, 432
Brüner, Caspar, Baron, 122
Bruern Abbey (Oxon.), 213–4
Brunton, Thomas, 454
Brussels, cutler of, 128
Bryan, Thomas [of Kenilworth], 434, 444,
  457
Brynnion, Thomas, 456
Bryse, Mr, 189, 216, 254, 297
Bryskett, Mr [Ludowick?], 426
Buck, Richard*, 211, 251, 275, 297, 357, 456
  Robert, 436, 456
Buckhurst, Lord, *see* Sackville
Buckinghamshire, 242
Buckley, Richard, butcher, 126
Bull, keeper of Enfield Chase, 263, 310
  Mr [Richard], 257, 425, 455
  William, musician, 442, 457
Buntingford (Herts.), 95, 380
Burbury, Mr, 367
Burchgrave (Burgrave), Daniel de*, 349,
  355, 455
Burckhard, Lord Hunsdon's physician, 56,
  58
Burdett, John, 388, 455
Burford (Oxon.), 189
Burgerman, Peter, 427
Burgess, Isaac, 139
Burghley, Lord, *see* Cecil
Burghley House (Northants.), 27
Burgoyne, Robert, 296
Burlace, George, 425
Bursis, Robert, 443
Burton, carpet-cleaner, 207
  William*, 311

Bushy Park (Middx.), keeper of, 80
Bussell, William, 425–6
Butcot, Mr, 317
Butler, Anthony*, 47, 125–6, 158, 427
    Catherine (Knollys), Lady Garrett, 203, 390
    Sir Philip, 203, 223, 311–2, 320–1, 351, 389, 449–50, 452, 454, 459; house, see Watton Woodhall
    Sylvestra, 42
    Thomas [of Warwick], 423
Butter, Richard, 124
Buttell, Mr, 217
    farrier*, 314
Buxton (Derbys.), 179, 245
Buys, Paul, 395
Byrde, William, 46, 50, 52, 109, 113, 118, 124, 134, 142, 147, 160, 165, 169, 171, 241

Calais, 66, 95, 349, 484
Camberwell (Surrey), 64, 68, 102, 378
Cambridgeshire, 400
Campion, Abraham, 313, 318, 457
Canellae, Mr, 188, 329, 337
Cannock, Henry, 424
Canterbury, 251
Capell, Mr, 403
Carcano, Christopher, 76, 86, 89, 103, 119, 144, 147
Careless*, 205, 232, 236, 279
Carew, Sir Francis, 192, 306, 310
    Sir George, 66, 299, 329
    Lady [Margaret], 157
    Sir Peter, 66
    Sir Peter, the younger, 66
Carey, Edmund*, 26, 51, 275, 291, 300, 367, 373; see also Grafton
    Edward*, 40, 53, 67–8, 72, 74, 81, 101, 132, 138, 166, 169–71, 399, 419–20
    Sir George, 329, 391
    Henry, 1st Lord Hunsdon, 51, 125, 152–3, 157, 166–7, 278, 321, 338, 342; physician, see Burckhard
    Robert, 51, 166–7
Carleill, Christopher, 267
Carleton, Mr, 203
    Gilbert, 424, 427
Carling, Thomas, 428
Caroges, Tanneguy le Veneur, Sieur de, 328
Caroone, 455

Carter, Francis, 121
    John, 436, 440
    Reynold, 121
Cartwright, Thomas, 294, 296, 368, 451, 459
Case, John, 230
Castelnau, Michel de, Sieur de Mauvissière, 33–4, 182, 226, 244, 246, 256, 261–2, 305
Castiglioni, Giovanni Baptista (Mr Baptist), 196, 207, 223, 226, 252
Castilion, Sir Francis (young Mr Baptist), 196, 337, 431, 448, 452
Cateau-Cambrésis, treaty of, 66
Cater, Henry*, 206, 208, 453
Cave, Sir Ambrose, 43, 65, 172
    Edward*, 237, 247, 252, 266, 269, 283, 293–6, 302, 322–3, 332
Cavendish, Richard, 234, 341, 349, 358
Cecil, Sir Thomas, 217–8, 220–1, 266–7, 280
    William, Lord Burghley, 12, 60, 138, 141, 157, 161, 166, 187, 224, 227–9, 255, 262, 286, 290, 296, 386, 391, 394; papers, 2, 19; household, 30, 262; houses, see Burghley House, Theobalds, Westminster: Cecil House, Wimbledon
Ceville, François de, 306
Challoner, John, 454
Chamberlain, Leonard, 453, 455
    Sir Thomas, 166
Champernown, Sir Arthur, 244
Chancery, cases:
    Dudley vs Hugh Ellis (1559), 54, 58, 71, 148
    Dudley vs Lyttelton (1560), 114, 118, 132
    Kenilworth case (1590), 3, 29, 463, 486
Chancy, William*, 12, 14, 17–20, 25, 27, 39, 71–2, 99, 105–10, 118–119, 124, 128, 131, 134, 399, 403, 405, 417, 419, 426
Chandler, William, 428
Chapman, John, 113, 118
Charke*, 357
Charlbury (Oxon.), 290
Charles, Archduke of Styria, 122
Chawood, 78
Cheake, Margaret (Hill), Lady, 59, 88
Chelmsford (Essex), 344, 393
Chelsea (Middx.), 57, 202, 307; gardener of, 156, 158, 167
Chelsham, William, 77, 87, 98, 109, 123, 134

Chenies (Bucks.), 308, 311
Chesleck, Lawrence*, 258, 288, 456
    young, 258, 296, 456
Chester, 179, 471–2, 487; post of, 247
Chester, Sir William, 144, 165–6
Chetwoode, Richard, 159
Chichester, 255
Child, waterman, 172–3
    Thomas, 434
Chilmead, Ralph*, 238
Chirk, lordship of (Denbs.), 479–80
Chiswick (Middx.), 85
Choldmondley*, see also Chumley
    Sir Hugh, 430, 446, 448, 451–2
    William, 430
Christ Church, Oxford, see Oxford University
Christian, 453
Christmas, Robert, 17–8, 425–6
Christopher, William, 252, 424
Chumley, Mr*, 295, 458, see also Cholmondley
Churchyard, Thomas, 436
Clare, Sir Francis, 452
Clarentius, Mrs, see Tonge, Susan
Clarke, Lady [of the Privy Chamber], 44, 91
    Anthony, 427
    Ferdinando, 483
    John, 443
    Dr William, 373
    William, vintner, 453
Clarkson (Claxton), Anthony, 436, 440, 456
Claypoole, John, 452
Cleobury Mortimer (Salop.), 464
Clifford, Henry, 2nd Earl of Cumberland, 73
    George, 3rd Earl of Cumberland, 213, 217–8, 258
    Margaret (Russell), Countess of Cumberland, 321, 390
    Robert (1585–89), 315–6
Clifton, William, 434, 444
Clinton, Lord, see Fiennes
    Thomas, see Fiennes
Clunne, Griffith*, 56, 62, 152, 410, 422
Cobham, Lord, see Brooke
Cobham, Mr*, 41, 57, 105, 154
    Sir Henry, 479
Cobham Hall (Kent), 76, 100, 105
Cocke, Christopher, 457
Colbrooke see Colnbrook

Colchester (Essex), 100–1, 257, 279, 344, 393
    see also Lucas, Sir Thomas
Cole, Gyles, 436
    Humphrey*, 187, 239, 251, 276, 324, 345
    Thomas*, 453
    Thomas, musician, 433, 442
Colgin, John, 455
Collier, John, 456
    Thomas, 428
Collman, John, 441
Colnbrook (Bucks.), 186, 190, 211–3, 295; hospital, 224
Colshill (Wars.), 246
Colstone, Ralph, 453
    William, 452
Combe Abbey (Wars.), 298–9
Comlye, Richard 435
Compton, Henry, 1st Lord, 217, 301
Comptroller, Mr, see Rogers, Sir Edward
Coningsby, Mr, 427
    Ralph, 431
Connerbuck (Cooner), Richard, 286, 313, 435
Constable, Sir Robert, 334, 426
    William, 334, 431
Conway, 427
    John*, 293, 297, 309, 315, 362, 435, 440, 453
Coo, Mrs, 161
Cooke, haberdasher, 180, 242–3, 271, 287, 340, 453
    Sir Anthony, 160
    Sir Anthony the younger, 317; house, see Gidea Hall
    George [Lewis]*, 56, 68–9, 74, 79, 106, 147, 406, 419, 421
    Henry, 69
    Richard, 69, 427–8
    Richard, purveyor, 453
    Robert, herald, 126
    Thomas, perfumier of St Martins, 62, 65, 69–70, 102, 107, 119, 426
    William*, see Hakesby
Coombe, Richard, 424, 456
Cooper, Mr, 152
Cope, Sir Anthony, 293, 295
Copley, Mr, 298
Copt Hall (Essex), 237–8
Cordell, Sir William, 42, 45, 64
Coringnew, George, 423
Cornbury House (Oxon.), 188, 290

Corson, John, 422
Cornwall, Robert*, 69, 98
  John, 433
Cornwallis, Sir Thomas, 168, 332
  Thomas, 168
Cornyshe, James, 419
Corpreo (Carpion), Hans, 210, 322
Cotton, Lady, 69
  Mr, 46
  Mr, of the Wardrobe, 204
  Mrs, 458
  Robert, 454
The Court and the Royal Household, 4,
  28, 32, 58, 205
  New Year's gifts to: (1560), 149–50; (1561),
    162–3; (1585), 207
  Chapel Royal, 156, see also Bowyer,
    Hunnis
  Guard, the, (Swan of), 156; (Pryce of),
    335, see also St Loe, Sir William
  Jewel House, 208
  Knight-Marshal, 319
  Presence Chamber, 309
  Privy Chamber, 155, 169, 257
    page of (Walter Jennell), 190, 322
  Privy Kitchens (Greenwich), 158
  Queen's bargeman (Ralph Smith), 171,
    323
    falconers, 310
    footmen, 231
    glazier, 98
    locksmith (Flint), 318
    musician (Jeronomye), 220
    trumpeters, 338
    watermen, 200, 203, 229
  Sergeant-Painter, 59
  Stables, personnel, 160, 469, 473, 482,
    484–5
Courtney, William, 436, 440
Coventry, 6, 294, 298
Cowdry, Mr, 119
  Katherine, shepster, 53
Cox, John, 458
  Lawrence, 456
Cragg, Archie*, 59, 61–2, 66, 75–6, 80, 82,
  140, 146, 152, 158–9, 161, 171–2, 413
Craik, Alexander, 154
Cranbrook (Essex), 236, 264
Cranmer, William, 457
Crewe, John, 457
Crokeham, James, 43, 45, 62, 102, 122; bill,
  174–5, 384
Crompton, William, 114

Crosse, Henry, 434
Crowe, Ann, laundress, 458
  Mark, 455
Croxson, Paul*, 199, 220, 235, 432, 443, 453
  Mrs, 198–9, 207, 330
Croydon (Surrey), 78–9, 231; court at
  (1585), 246–8, 250; almshouse, 278
Culpepper, Walter, 455
Culverwell, Nicholas, see London: Staplers'
  Company
Cumberland, Earl of, see Clifford
Cumnor (Berks.), 379–80, 382–3
Cunningham, Alexander, 5th Earl of Glen-
  cairn, 146
Cure, carver, 226
  Thomas, 121
  William, 121, 172
Curson, Robert*, 48, 57, 67, 78, 81, 128,
  400, 419–20, 427
Curward, William, 131
Cutteler, Mr*, 151, 160, 401
Cutts, Sir John, 269, 286, 344
Cyall, German, 88

Dacre, Lady, see Fiennes
Dainty, Robert, 432, 443, 456
Dallicott, Thomas, 453
Dalton, Thomas*, 184, 216, 219, 250
Dampard*, 294, 298, 304, 309, 336
Damsell, Sir William, 85
Dane, Mrs, 147
Dannet, Thomas, 35, 66
Danyell, Peter*, 257, 432, 443
Darcy, Robert*, 81, 84, 137, 402 (Thomas),
  419–20, 426
Dartford (Kent), 75; tanner of, 428
Dave (keeper), 268, 316
Davers, Mr*, 219, 426
Davies, Thomas*, 69, 71, 74, 76, 82, 85,
  138, 145, 158, 404, 420–1
Davis, Mr, 316
  Price, 435
  Richard, 435
  Thomas, 437
Davison, William, 179, 207, 229, 244, 334,
  369, 372, 386–7, 392–3, 429
Dawe, William, 119
Dawson, George, 435, 456
Day, Mr, 427
  Henry*, 225–6, 233, 246, 434, 444, 455
de Vere, Edward, 17th Earl of Oxford, 236,
  264; house, 236
  John, 16th Earl of Oxford, 100

Decoster, Martin, 285, 335
Dedick (Earl of Pembroke's hosier), 88, 129, 135–6, 139
Delaber, James, 438, 441
Delabere, John, 188, 212, 216
Delft, 370
Denbigh, 179
    lordship of, 246, 289, 341, 394, 471, 474, 476, 480, 484, 486–8
    lord of, see Dudley, Robert
Denham, George, 454
    William, goldsmith, 90, 121, 157
    William, 423, 427
Denmark, King of (Frederick II), 283
    players to, 353
Dennone, William, 423
Denny, Edward, 423
Denton, Mr, 454
Denys, John (Symwilkin)*, 181, 183, 185, 187–8, 192, 212–3, 215, 226, 238, 250, 275, 278, 281–2, 310, 319, 327, 332, 353, 435, 441
    Sir Maurice, 95
    Sir Thomas*, 234, 247
Deptford (Kent), 138, 154, 164, 238, 252–4; Sayes Court, 4, 17–8
Derby, Earl of, see Stanley
Derby, Moris, 424
Dering, Anthony*, 98, 129, 167, 174–5, 419–20
Derrick, Richard, 457
Detersall, 66
Dethick, Sir Gilbert, 125
Devereux, Robert, 2nd Earl of Essex, 236, 310, 358, 371, 449–51, 454, 458
    papers, 1–2; servants, 294, 297, 305–6, 352
    Robert, 3rd Earl of Essex, 3
    Walter, Viscount Hereford, 1st Earl of Essex, 161, 182
    Walter (d. 1591), 190
Devonshire, 180
Devonshire, William, 411, 427
Dewes, goldsmith, 117, 126
Dickenson [Edward], 419
Dickson, John, 432
Digby, Sir George, 246, 371
    John, 431
Digges, James, 454
Diricke, jerkin-maker, 427
Dixie, Sir Wolstan, 341, 393
Dixson, Francis, 130
Dobbynes, Henry, 407

Dockwra, Anthony*, xiii, 29, 178, 214–5, 232, 241, 255, 262, 264, 269, 282, 292, 328
    Christopher*, 186, 204, 213, 300, 308, 319
Doesburg, 354
Dorchester (Oxon.), 186, 217
Dordrecht, 353, 358–62, 369–71
Dormer, Michael, 350
Dorsten, J.A. van, 22–3
Doughty, Thomas (bit-maker), 123
Douglas, James, 4th Earl of Morton, 146
Dowding, Robert, 256, 456
Downell, Daniel*, 208, 211–2, 215, 224, 251, 257, 264, 277–8, 281, 284–5
Downhall, William*, 356, 370, 430, 445, 448
Downing, John, 438, 441
Doyley, Dr Thomas, 331
Drake, Sir Francis, 190, 192, 228, 306, see also West Indies Voyage
    Richard, 192, 213, 215, 221, 426
Draynor, John, 441
Drayton Bassett (Staffs.), 3, 279, 463, 487
Droytlyn, John, 426
Dry, keeper, 456
Dublin, 100, 117
Duck, Conrad*, 319, 325, 351, 356, 362, 434, 444
    John, huntsman, 412, 428
Duckett, Sir Lionel, 139
Dudley, Lord, see Sutton
    Alice (Leigh, 1st wife of Sir Robert Dudley), 298
    Ambrose, Earl of Warwick, xiii, 24, 43, 60, 63, 78, 80, 105, 114, 122, 136, 146, 164, 192, 214, 245, 269, 303–4, 390, 392, 451, 453, 458
        servants, 60 (Mr Blount), 225 (Edward Roberts), 226, 254, 261, 304 (Little Thomas), 262 (Mercer), 360 (Coke)
        houses, see Holborn, Northaw
    Amy (Robsart), 3, 8–9, 13, 25, 31, 40, 42, 44, 49, 54–5, 60–5, 68, 71, 87, 90–2, 94, 102–3, 106, 122, 125, 133, 173, 175, 377–84, 421
        death of, 35, 90, 141; funeral, xiii, 42, 84, 125, 132, 143, 159
    Sir Andrew, 73, 107; house see Westminster: Tothill Street
    Anne (Russell), Countess of Warwick, 286, 368, 390
    Anne (Seymour), Countess of Warwick, 41, 67, 188

Anne (Windsor, 1st wife of Edmund Dudley), 160
Charles* (page, young Mr), 198–9, 225, 268, 318, 347, 372
Elizabeth (Grey, 2nd wife of Edmund Dudley, wife of Arthur Plantagenet, Viscount Lisle), 50
Lord Henry, xiii, 40, 43, 61
Joan, Duchess of Northumberland, xiii, 40, 42–4, 50, 69–70, 102, 109, 114, 128, 157, 165, 179, 188, 231
John, Duke of Northumberland, 25, 44, 50, 54–5, 68, 70, 73, 154, 156, 349, 379; household, xiii
John, Earl of Warwick (d. 1554), 41, 67
John*, 29, 42, 100, 108, 115, 123, 151, 156, 405, 407, 411, 413, 415–7
John, 454
Katherine, 44
Katherine (d. 1620), see Hastings
Lettice (Knollys), Countess of Leicester, xiii–iv, 3, 17, 26, 28–9, 161, 182, 197, 201, 209, 259, 274, 287, 290, 304, 312–3, 348, 384, 387, 389–91, 451, 478, 481; footman, see Dampard
Margaret (Audley, later Duchess of Norfolk), 40, 43
Mary, see Sidney
Robert, Earl of Leicester:
    personal and biographical:
        in 1553, 42, see also King's Lynn
        restitution (1558), 52
        earliest letter by (1558), 381
        and accession, 381–2
        illness (1559), 69
        marriage, Elizabeth and, 303
        journey, summer 1584, 179, 182, 245
        journey to Langley (1584), 186–91, 196–7
        journey to Oxford (1585), 211–8
        journey to Kenilworth (1585), 284–304, 317, 385
        appointment to the Netherlands, 296, 307, 385, 387
        recruiting for the Netherlands, 388–92
        loan from London, 341, 389, 394
        journey to Flushing (1585), 344–5, 367, 385, 393–5
        Laws and Ordinances, 373
        oath of loyalty to (1587), 438–9
        funeral, 24, 28, 349, 448–50

grants to (1558), 25, 42; (1559), 151; (1560), 73–4, 116, 151, 157; (1561), 15; (1566), 18; (1571), 26
        farm of customs on Sweet Wines, 249
    offices:
        chancellor of Oxford University, 165
        Chief Justice in Eyre, 203
        Constable of Windsor, 151, 383
        deputy Earl Marshal, 180
        lord lieutenant of Warwickshire and Worcestershire (1559–60), 43, 114, 172
        lord lieutenant of Hertfordshire and Essex (1585), 281, 317
        Master of the Horse, 46, 110, 117, 231, 381–2, see also Court: Stables
    possessions:
        armour, 47, 80–1, 103–4, 137–8
        barge, 51, 53, 57, 59, 134, 313
        bear, 144
        books, 152, 324
        books dedicated or presented to, 230, 259, 368, 466
        clock, 343, 371
        coach, 228, 273, 276, 285, 335
        desk, 327
        houses, see Benington, Grafton, Kenilworth, Kew, Langley, Wanstead, Westminster: Leicester House
        Galleon Leicester, see ships
        Georges, 89, 105, 271, 373
        jewel chest, 330
        maps, 256, 370
        musical instruments, 58–9, 70, 97, 136, 140
        papers of, xiv, 1, 3; wills, xiii–xiv, 28–9
        pedigrees, 61, 73, 126
        pictures purchased, 373
        portraits, see Segar, Sir William
        privy coat, 151
        spectacles, 287, 342, 373
    servants:
        household, 19–30
        chaplains, 31, 368: see also Craik, Alexander; Edgeworth, Edward; Fenn, Humphrey; Fenner, Dudley; Gifford, George; Holland, Thomas; James, William; Knewstub, John; Underhill, John; Willoughby, Thomas

servants—*cont.*
　chaplains—*cont.*
　　guard (Netherlands), xiv, 22–4, 355, 361
　　musicians, 178, 259, 309, 311, *see also* Pietro
　　mariners, 256, 268
　Robert, Lord of Denbigh (1581–4), xiii, 50, 179, 183, 226
　Sir Robert, xiv, 3, 29, 186, 188–9, 216, 231, 236, 238, 245, 256, 288, 320, 332, 337, 340
　　servants, 238, 260, 291, 326, *see also* Harford, Nicholas
　　schoolmaster, *see* Canallae
　Robert, 453
　Thomas*, 28, 100, 103–4, 115, 124, 128, 131, 151, 155–6, 155–6, 161, 167, 170–2, 179, 184, 194–5, 198, 201, 210, 221, 249, 272, 280, 340, 343, 420, 426, 449, 451–2
Dudley Plot (1555–6), 42, 59
Duffe, Thomas, 334, 434, 444, 455
Dum, Humphrey, 457
Dunhall, Gregory, 452, 459
Dunkin, Robert*, 72, 74, 76, 82, 105, 410, 420–1
Dunkirk, privateers, 331
Dunstable (Beds.), 302–3, 307
Dutton Park (Ches.), 257
dwarf, the, 428
Dyer, Sir Edward, 31, 236–7, 307, 313
　Robert, 437
Dymock, 454, *see also* Pinnock

Easton Neston (Northants.), 301
Eaton, Thomas*, 103–4, 131, 401, 420, 426, 452
Edgerley, Thomas*, 314, 333, 363, 453
　William, musician, 433, 457
Edgeworth, Edward, 270–1
　William, 329
Edmonton (Middx.), 263
Edmund, footman, 46, 54, 56, 75
　apothecary, 137
Edmundes, William*, 281
Edney, William, 122, 383–4
Edward, William, 433
Edwardes, John, 436, 440
　Morys*, 47–58, 60–1, 65, 67, 69, 71, 74, 102, 407, 421
　Walter, 456

Effingham, Lord of, *see* Howard
Egerton, Sir Ralf, 159, 450, 452
　Thomas, mercer, 115, 120
　Sir Thomas, solicitor-general, 177
Elizabeth I:
　New Year's gifts (1559), 45 (1585), 210
　coronation, 46–8, 108–9
　(1559), 57, 61, 63, 72, 75–6, 78, 80, 92, 94, 117
　(1560), 138, 140–3, 145, 152, 154, 158, 164
　(1584), 185, 194, 203
　(1585), 224, 227, 235, 238, 244, 262, 267, 270, 275, 286, 303, 307–8, 334, 350, 374, 381–2, 386–92, 394
Ellis, Hugh, 54, 58, 71, 148
　Richard*, 13–4, 18–20, 25, 54, 65, 96, 107, 109–10, 113, 117–8, 134, 167, 384, 399, 403, 417–8, 420, 422, 426
　Richard, glover, 140
Ellyot, John, 120
Elmes, Mr [William Helmes?], 311
Elspyt, Anthony, 126
Eltham Palace (Kent), 61, 63, 100, 105
　banquet at (1559), 78–9, 95–6
　banquet at (1560), 145–6, 172
Eltham Park, 158; keeper, 265, 271 (Flower)
Elverston, *see* Helffenstein
embroiderer's apprentice, 457
Empson, John*, 62–3, 69, 75–7, 89, 102, 117, 124, 135–6, 145–6, 403, 420–1, 427
　in the Strand, 227
Enfield (Middx.), 41, 382
　Chase, 263; keeper, 310, *see also* Bull, Pecock
Englefield, Sir Francis, 151
Englerer, Richard, 428
English, Thomas, 435
Eric XIV, King of Sweden, 78, 141–2
Erith (Kent), 272, 279
Eryth, Edith, 235
Essex, lieutenancy of (1585), 281, 317
　Earl of, *see* Devereux
Essex House, 482, *see also* Leicester House
Etherton, Richard, 438
Evans, Humphrey, 444, 456
　John, 455
　John, buttery, 432, 443
　John, baker, 432
　John, footman, 434
　Richard*, drummer, 76–7, 160, 413, 420–2, 424, 428
　Robert, 455
　William, 437

Evelyn, John, 1, 4, 16–8
Everard, goldsmith, 89, 102, 124, 160
Ewelme (Oxon.), 217, 288–9
Ezard, John*, 218, 304, 334, 431

Falconer (Fawkner), Henry, 56, 81, 408
  John, 53, 84
  Ralph, huntsman, 412, see also Hunt,
    Ralph
  Richard*, huntsman, 147, 412
Falwell, Robert*, 370, 444
Farmer, Sir George, 243, 301, 322; house,
  see Easton Neston
Farnham (Hants.), 142
Farnham, John, 250, 256
Farslept, Mr*, 289
Fealow, Richard*, 311
Fearne, George, 455
Featherstone, Leonard, 202
Feige, 431
Fenn, Humphrey, 295, 352, 358, 363, 368,
  452, 459
Fenner*, 217
  Mr, 426
  Dudley, 368
Fenton, Sir Geoffrey, 269
Feria, Count of, see Figueroa
Ferdynando (1560), 144
Fermer, Mr, 167
Fettiplace, Bridget (Mrs Bridget), 28, 458
Fiennes, Anne (Sackville), Lady Dacre 'of
  the South', 249
  Edward, Lord Clinton, 1st Earl of
    Lincoln, 22, 40, 80, 99, 117, 123, 153–
    4, 161, 171, 206, 208
    death and funeral, 220, 224; house, see
    West Horsley
  Elizabeth (Fitzgerald), Countess of
    Lincoln, 92, 220
  Henry, 2nd Earl of Lincoln, 449–51,
    458
  Richard, Lord Saye and Sele, 215
  Thomas (Clinton), 3rd Earl of Lincoln,
    188, 190, 213
Figueroa, Gomez Suarez de, Count of
  Feria, 32, 63
  Jane (Dormer), Countess of Feria, 42
Finch, William*, 286, 312–3
Finland, John, Duke of (John III of
  Sweden), 100, 106, 133, 163–4, 170
Fisher, Clement, 426, 449, 459
Fittman, Morgan, 424

Fitzalan, Henry, 12th Earl of Arundel, 46,
  78, 84–5, 141, 154, 181, 183
  houses, see Westminster: Arundel House,
  Nonsuch
Flammock, Richard*, 21, 122, 130, 412, 422
Flanders, 66, 185, 257, 331, 342, 344, see
  also Netherlands
Fletcher, John, stopper at Whitehall tennis
  court, 138, 156, 159
Flower, Richard, 456
  Robert, 433, 441
Flowerdew, John, 378, 381
  Thomas*, 62, 70, 74, 78, 81, 419
Flushing, 9–11, 345, 367, 369, 393–5
Foix, Gaston de, Marquis de Trans, 84,
  164
Folys, Robert, 275, 319
Ford, William*, 261
Forman, yeoman purveyor, 130
Forrest, Mr, 90
  John*, 41, 46, 48–9, 56, 75, 82–4, 411
  Thomas*, 107, 137–8, 140, 143, 411, 421–
    2, 428
Forster, Anthony*, 39, 66, 106, 120, 125,
  380, 382, 425–6
  Robert, 454
Fortescue, Dudley, 39, 47
  Francis, 345
  Henry, 39, 41, 47, 59, 93, 130
  Sir John, 39, 109
Foster, Sir John, 286
  Roger, 434
  Thomas, 444
Fowler, John, 99
  Thomas*, 311, 451–2
Fox(e), John*, 363
  John, hosier, 130
foxtaker, the, 457
Francis, milliner, 132
Francx, Charles, 356, 369
Frank, Edward, 457
  Hans, 86, 90, 117, 142
Franklin, Mr, 426
Frecklington, William, 428, 433, 444
Freeman, Thomas, 432, 442, 456
French, Mr, of Windsor, 224
French butterman, 421
Freshmans, James, 428
Friesland, 358
Fryce, Rowland, 122
Fulford, Robert*, 229, 454
Fulham (Middx.), 247–8, 330
Fuller, John, 455, 458

Gabbed, John, 126
Galloner, Robert, 433
gardener, French (1559)*, 102
　French (1584–5)*, 191, 220, 225–6, 239–40
Gardiner, Richard*, 183, 205, 223, 242,
　257, 287, 291, 319, 359, 363, 370, 434,
　442, 456; Mistress Garner, 328
　Thomas, 25
Garland*, Edward, 221, 410
　John, 428
Garnet, William*, 28, 452; Mrs, 458
Garrett, John*, 177, 192, 253, 413
Garter, Order of the, 62, 65, 67–8, 140,
　166, see also Windsor
Gaskyn, postmaster, 269
Gates, Anthony, 363
Gawen, groom*, 183, 191, 194
Geaste*, 324, 326
Gemini, Thomas, 66, 138
Gentili, Alberico, 212
George, sweeper, 206
Gerrard, 454
Gidea Hall (Essex), 317
Gifford, Sir George, 181, 228
　George, 204, 368, 370
Gilbert, goldsmith, 127
Gilbert, John, 458
Gill, Thomas, 437
Gilliam, Roger*, 182, 185, 194, 199, 201–2,
　205, 209–10, 219, 221–2, 224–6, 228,
　231–2, 235, 239, 243, 245, 251, 254–6,
　258–60, 264, 269, 273–4, 277, 280,
　283–4, 307, 313, 319, 325, 330, 332,
　335, 337–40, 342, 455
Gilliam's wife*, laundress, 184, 207, 209,
　248, 268, 325
Gillingham, (Kent), 76
Gilpin, George, 139, 158, 348
Girlington, Nicholas, 401, 427
Gittones, Richard*, 153, 406, 421
Glaser, butler, 105
Glasier, [John]. 452
　Richard, 404, 421; young, 428
　William*, 54, 56–8, 64, 71, 73, 105, 147
Glencairn, Earl of, see Cunningham
Globe, cutler, 244, 332
Gloucester, Dean of [William Jennings], 67
Glover, Joseph, 435, 454
　Richard, secretary, 430, 445, 452, 459
　Richard, turnbroch [turnspit], 456
　Thomas, 428
Godfrey, Frederick*, 144, 406, 425, 427
Godwin, James, 456

Goffe, Ann, wife of Thomas, laundress,
　265, 267, 323, 458
　Thomas*, 248, 261–3, 266–7, 282, 296,
　325, 457
Goldingham, Henry*, 210, 270, 272, 297,
　303–4, 452
Goodere, Sir Henry, xiv, 347–8, 351, 353,
　451–2
　William, 353, 361, 449, 452
Goodge, Nicholas, 436, 440
Goodrich, Richard, 59
Goodrouse*, 182, 431, 446, 451, 453
Goodyneir, 177
Gorge, Sir Thomas, 449–50, 452–3, 459
　William*, 12, 28, 197, 312, 352, 359, 370,
　426, 451–2, 459
Gorinchem, 358–61, 364
Gorringe, Mr, 424
Goslett, Mr [William], 454
Gosling, Robert, 98, 121
Goulde, 455
Gower (Goore), Mr* [Edmund], 40, 42,
　44, 47, 61, 401, 427
Grafton (Northants.), 26, 232, 291–2, 299–
　300, 303, 387
Grain, John, 319
Grainger, Lawrence, 455
Grammer, Thomas*, 201, 205, 208, 295,
　434, 444
Grave, 349–50, 354; governor of, 361
Gray, Patrick (Master of), 6th Lord, 207
Graye, John, 350
　Thomas, 454
Great Newton (Norf.), 13
Green, John, coffermaker, 102, 122
　Martin, 438, 441
　Robert, 259
　Thomas, coffermaker, 263
　William*, 182, 202, 218, 223–4, 228–9,
　246, 250, 253, 257, 263, 265, 269, 272–
　3, 280
Greenwich (Kent), 63
　ferryman of, 133, see also Warner,
　Richard
Greenwich Palace, 26–7, 40
　(1559), 59, 70–5, 77, 85, 96, 400–1, 403–
　5, 408–10, 413
　(1560–1), 117, 129, 138, 141–2, 145, 159–
　60, 164, 171–2
　(1584–5), 177, 180, 203, 205–11, 219–20,
　222, 227–9, 231, 233–5, 237–8, 240–3,
　245–6, 248–54, 256–60, 263–9, 271–5,
　281, 319

armoury, 47, 50, 53, 64, 81–2, 104, 137–
8, 151, 153; *see also* Jacob
orchard keeper, 234
Privy Kitchen at, 158
tournament at, *see* tournaments
Grenado, Bernardine, 155
Sir Jacques, 155
Grenshaw, Nicholas, 317, 327
Gresham, John, mercer, 115
the younger, 285
Sir Thomas, 40, 65, 73, 77, 110, 139, 158,
165, 479
Gresley, Mr, 234
Greville, Sir Fulke, 168–9, 450, 452
Sir Fulke, the younger, 306–7
Grey, Arthur, 14th Lord Grey de Wilton,
264, 303, 315, 387
Thomas, naval officer, 367
of Wisbech, 232
Grice, William*, 17, 19, 39, 42, 45, 47, 49,
68, 86, 121, 153–4, 276, 381–2, 384,
402
Griffin, of the chamber, 424
Henry*, 198, 211, 434, 435
Humfrey, 436
John, 424
John, bargemaster, 435
Mr [Richard?], of Dingley, 448
Robert, 425
Thomas, 457
Grimshall, Richard, 455
Groenveldt, Arent van, 354
Gronnat, Capt, 352
Grotrege, Mr*, 330, 339, 343, 352, 356,
360, 364
Gryme, Richard, 435, 455
Robert, 435, 455
Gryse, Jacques de, 34
Guildford (Surrey), 80–1
Gunter, Philip, 115, 119
Gurnard, Henry 438, 441
Guy, John, 88, 98, 110, 121; bills, 13, 173–
4, 384, 422
Gwyllam, *see* Tyan
Gwyn, John*, 275, 423, 436, 440, 455–6
Robert*, 183, 224, 258, 260, 268,
273, 312, 362, 364, 423, 436, 444,
453
William, 427
Gyles, George*, 20, 45–7, 51, 54, 56, 75–6,
87, 138, 168, 308, 403, 420–2, 427,
453
Gylford, Walter, 454

Gylles, John (merchant of Antwerp), 348,
364
Gylman, Mr, 426, 454
Gylmer, Henry*, 157–8, 167, 400

Haarlem, 346–7
Hackney (Middx.), 251
Hague, the, 23, 346, 370–3
Hakesby, William*, 53, 71, 74, 83, 101, 147,
406, 422
Hales, John, 131; wife, 95, 102, 153
Hales Owen (Worcs.), xiii, 69–70, 102, 114,
118, 128, 381
Hall (Hale)*, John, 425, 427, 456
Reginald, 456
Thomas, 182, 275, 287, 295, 319, 455
Halle, George, armourer, 131
Halliwell-Phillipps, Henrietta, 6
J.O., 5–8, 10–11, 35–6
Hallt, Mr, 427
Halsey, Ralph, 435, 440, 453
Ham (Surrey), 238
Hamerton (Hamton), Edward, 432, 443,
456
Hamilton, James, 3rd Earl of Arran, 146
Hamlyn, Patrick, 107, 414, 422
Hammersmith (Middx.), 181; hospital, 218
Hampden, Mr, 61
Hampton Court Palace (Middx.), 27
(1559–60), 35, 80–3, 96, 143–5, 174
(1584), 181, 183, 185–6, 191, 194, 196–7
gardener of, 160
Hampton Court Park, keepers of, 80, 179,
185
Hampton ferry, 192
Hampton-in-Arden (Wars.), 202
Hance*, 41, 44, 67–9, 97, 151
hosier, 91, 107, 129
Hancox, John, 458
Handforth, Richard, 126
Hankin, Nicholas, 455
Hanwell (Oxon.), 292–3
Harcourt, Michael, 301–2, 307, 451–2, 459
Harding, 420
Hardy, John, 424
Hare, John, 426
Harford, Nicholas, 288, 330, 340–1
Harington, John, of Stepney, 46, 69, 99,
113
Sir John, 214, 225, 298–9, 449–50, 452;
house, *see* Combe Abbey
Michael, 438, 441

Harlam, Thomas*, 137, 144–6, 148, 171–2, 415, 422
Harman, William*, 187, 449, 451, 453
Harriman, Robert, 456
Harris, John, senior, 437, 440
  John, 442
  Lewis, 456
  Morgan, 424
  Thomas, shoemaker, 178, 208, 257
Harrison, John, goldsmith, 127
  Robert, 425
  Mr [Thomas?], 236
  Thomas, 269
Harrow (Middx.), 262
Hart, Arthur, 437, 440
  Charles, 431
  (Sir) Percival, 77
Harvey, Gabriel, 12, 474
  George*, 12, 28, 351, 451–2
  William, 125
Harwich, 343–5, 367, 369, 393–5
Haslewood, Thomas, 428
Hastings, Edward, Lord Hastings of Loughborough, 43, 159
  Francis, 2nd Earl of Huntingdon, 156; funeral, 141
  Henry, 3rd Earl of Huntingdon, 19, 43–4, 120, 138, 141, 156, 159, 162, 168, 329, 343, 383, 449–50
    household, 30; servant (Musgrave), 343
  Katherine (Dudley), Countess of Huntingdon, 43–4, 69, 114, 120, 182
Hatfield (Herts.), 44, 381
Hatton, Sir Christopher, 24, 186, 258, 451, 458
  papers, 2; armour, 339; servants, 252–3
Hauk, John, 428
Haward, Edward*, 357
Haynes, William, 132
Hedlein, Francis, 414
Heigham, Arthur*, 55, 80–2, 105, 125, 166, 254, 334, 353, 363, 369, 419, 426, 430, 446
Helffenstein, George, Count, 122, 135, 155, 164–5
Hemsby (Norf.), 54, 116, 148, 157, 402
Heneage, young Mr, 274
  Sir Thomas, 2, 195, 238, 274, 281
    mission in Netherlands, 353
    house, see Copt Hall
    servants, 237, see also Vic, John de
Henley on Thames (Oxon.), 186, 190, 217, 288

Henne, William, 428
Henry III, King of France, 244, 250
Henry, King of Navarre, 244, 476
heralds, 67, 110, 125, 150, 152, 159, 163, 457 see also Cooke, Robert; Dethick, Sir Gilbert; Harvey, William; Segar, Sir William
Herbert, Henry, 2nd Earl of Pembroke, 212, 240–1
  servants, 268, 281, 285, 337
  Mary (Sidney), Countess of Pembroke, 240
  William, 1st Earl of Pembroke, 22, 52, 61–2, 69–70, 138, 146, 165, 168; hosier, see Dedick
    houses, see London: Baynard's Castle, Wilton
Herdson, Mr, 226
Hereford, Viscount, see Devereux
Herle, William, 232–3, 341
Hertford, 320–1; gaol, 162
Hertford, Earl of, see Seymour
Hertfordshire, 383; lord lieutenancy of (1585), 281
Hetherley, John*, 169, 411
Hewet, Sir William, 133, 151–2, 157, 161, 164–5
Heyden, Mr, 285, 287; house, see Watford
Heydon*, John, 430, 454
  Thomas, 456
  William*, 255, 258, 276, 349, 359–61, 373, 430, 447, 449–50, 452
Highgate, hospital, 285
Hill, Mary (shepster), 129
  Robert [of Shilton, Devon], 454
  Thomas [of Honiley, Wars.], 455
Hilliard, Christopher, 158
  Richard*, 20, 172, 403
Hilling, Henry, 437, 441
Hilton, Thomas, 192
Hinton, Mr [Dr William], 450
Hipocrates, Dr, 431, 445, 450, 459
Hobson [James?], 455
Hodgkynes, Charles, 125
Hohenlohe-Langenberg, Philip, Count of, 371
Holborn (Middx.), 142, 164
Holborne, William, 87, 122, 138–9, 142, 146–7, 158; Mrs, 89, 91
Holcroft, Thomas, 157
Hole, Thomas, 440
Holland, province, of, 369, 392–3, 395

Holland, Geoffrey, 427
  John, 423
  Robert*, 44, 46, 48–9, 56, 71, 74, 76, 82,
    139, 195, 408, 419, 421, 424, 427
  Robert, of the scullery, 432, 443
  Dr Thomas, 229, 234, 343, 445, 450–1,
    459
Hollingworth, Reginald, 440, 453
Holloway, Thomas, 53, 123
Holme, Thomas, scrivener, 147
Holmes, James, 426
  John, 438
  Matthew, 454
  Thomas (Hones), searcher, 249, 454
Holney, Richard, 436
Holstein-Gottorp, Adolph, Count of, 140,
    156, 167–8
Holte, Thomas, 456
Homerstone, Giles*, 190, 219, 233, 240, 249,
    265, 271, 276, 284, 299, 330, 336, 457
Hood, William, 126
Hopton, William, 430, 454
Horden, Richard*, 14, 96, 106, 108, 130–1,
    136, 157, 400
Horewood, mercer, 123
  Gwyllyam, gardener, 416
Horsenall, William*, 237, 281
hostages, French (1559–60), 66, 75, 77, 95,
    104, 135 see also Ailly, Foix, Lux-
    embourg
Hotman, Jean*, 191, 198, 220, 258, 265,
    430, 448
Howard, Charles, 2nd Lord Howard of
    Effingham, 24, 58, 184, 190, 198, 278,
    283, 451, 454, 458
  servants, 191, 345
  barge, 229, 234, 237–8, 249
  Sir George, 169
  Philip, Earl of Arundel, 181
  Thomas, 4th Duke of Norfolk, 22, 40,
    43, 64, 72, 99, 181, 461
  Thomas, Lord Howard de Walden, 213,
    217
  William, 1st Lord Howard of Effingham,
    72, 168
Howell, Dr, 43
  Thomas, 435
Hubaud, Sir John, 300
  Ralph, 300, 452
Huckett, William, 335
Huddleston (Hurleston), 92
  John, 437, 441
  Richard, 331, 337, 347

Huddy, Nicholas, 431
Huggins (Hogan), Lady Amy's man, 102,
    133, 383–4
  Edward, 40, 109
  Mrs [Elizabeth], 458
  William*, 40, 55, 57–8, 60, 64–5,
    67–8, 72, 79, 84, 93, 95, 99–100,
    107, 128, 130, 156, 166–7, 308, 399,
    419
Hull (Yorks.), 100
Humphrey, Lawrence, 212
Hungate, Thomas, 117
Hungerford, Mr, 322
Hunnis, Robert, 431
  William, 235
Hunsdon (Herts.), 55, 382
Hunsdon, Lord, see Carey
Hunt, Ralph*, 75, 81–2, 84, 107, 421–2,
    428
  William, 444
Huntingdon, Earl of, see Hastings
Hurland, Thomas, 428
Hussey, Richard*, 183, 191, 232, 292, 433,
    445
Hutton, John, 150–1, 225
  Robert*, 151, 455
  William, 435
Hyde, George, 423, 427 (Mr Hyde the
    younger)
  Leonard, 423
  Ralph*, 251, 454
  William, of South Denchworth, Berks.,
    379
  William, of Throcking, Herts., 41–2, 45,
    48–9, 60, 65, 95, 99, 102, 115, 122,
    150, 156, 377–80
Hynde, Sir Francis, 450, 452
  John*, 202, 305–6, 310, 373–4, 430, 445,
    451, 453–4, 459

Ichers, 456
Ildersham, see Aldersham
Ilford (Essex), 239
Imperial ambassador, 146, see also Helf-
    fenstein
Ingatestone Hall (Essex), 343–4, 393–4
Ireland, 250–1, 254, 275, 278; garrison of,
    468, 479–80
Irish, James, 198
Isleworth (Middx.), 68, 323
Isley, Henry, 448, 451, 452
Islington (Middx.), 136

Jackson, Canon J.E., 3, 8, 13, 36, 39, 113, 122, 377, 379, 399
 Thomas, 437
Jacob, armourer of Greenwich, 323, 339, 423
 goldsmith, 127
 master of the glasshouse, 221, 270, 272
Jacques, harness-maker, 428
James VI, King of Scotland, 207, 228, 267–8, 286, 336
James the baker, 319
James, junior, 431
 Mr, 446
 Dr John, 218, 301, 303, 316, 328, 346, 353, 368, 372, 431, 445, 450, 459; diary (1586), 32, 346
 Dr William, 212
 William, 441
Jasper, instrument-maker, 184
 joiner, 125
Jelp, instrument-maker, 226
Jenebelli, Frederigo, 372
Jenkins, 95
 Elizabeth, laundress, 458
 Jenkin, 444
 John, 423
Jenkinson, Thomas, 458
Jenye, William, 438
Jerningham, Sir Henry, 53–4
 Thomas*, 354–5, 359
Jewkes, John, trumpeter, 431
Jobson, Edward, 50, 426, 449, 451
 Lady Elizabeth, 50
 Sir Francis, 50, 136
 John, 50, 426, 449, 451
 Thomas, 50, 449
Johann Casimir, Pfalzgraf, 323–4
John, the Frenchman*, 54, 69, 84, 170
 harper*, 268, 285, 360, 433, 442
 jeweler, 355
 muleteer*, 81
 stopper, see Fletcher, John
Johnson, Alfred*, 362, 442, 453
 Francis*, 275, 286, 436
 Herbert, 441
 John, 438
 Martin, 454
 Stephen*, 15, 178, 181, 187, 193–4, 200–1, 203, 206, 208–9, 223, 231, 237–8, 243, 248–9, 251, 255, 262, 267, 271–2, 284, 294, 305, 322, 324, 326, 347, 351, 355, 362, 368, 433, 442
 William*, 308

Johnston, John, fifer*, 76–7, 160, 413, 421–2, 424, 428
Jones, Evan, 410, 436
 Henry*, 47, 56, 77, 82, 93–4, 135, 144, 154, 156, 404, 420–1, 427
 [Sir] Henry, 431
 Henry, 438, 441
 Hugh*, of the chamber, 21, 41, 45–6, 52, 57, 61–2, 64, 68, 71, 74, 92, 94, 106, 406, 421–2, 423
 Owen*, 194, 199, 201, 209, 236, 245, 256, 278, 432, 442
 Randal, 72
 Robert, Sir Nicholas Throckmorton's secretary, 145–6
 Thomas*, 41, 49, 55, 62, 68, 87, 90
Jordan, William, 435
Junius, Mr [Johan, de Jonghe], 430
Jynkes, Richard*, 14, 130–1, 137, 140, 172–3, 400, 424 (Inglace)
 William, 142

Keame/Keane, John*, 178, 211, 221, 225, 249, 261, 265, 272, 282, 313, 325, 435, 444, 453, 455
Kellen, Thomas, 426
Kelly, John*, 200, 257, 281
 John, Netherlands guard, 438, 441
Kelsey/Keynsley, John, drummer, 432, 437, 440–1. 455 (Kersey)
Kemp, William*, player, 7, 249, 371, 374
 William, 359
Kempe, Mr, 63
Kempton Park (Middx.), 183
Kene, William, 424
Kenilworth, castle and lordship, 3, 5, 26, 28–9, 124, 178–9, 181, 198, 215, 239, 241, 255, 262, 269, 276–7, 285, 288, 300–1, 304–5, 309, 311–2, 317, 319, 327, 463, 466–8, 472, 478, 480, 486
 'game book', xiii
 Leicester's visit to (1585), 292–8
Kenningham, 66
Kent, 178, 202
Kettle, William, 141
Kettlewood, goldsmith, 127
Kevitt, George, 455
 Thomas [of Balsall, Wars.], 455
Kew (Surrey), Leicester's house at, 25, 27, 42, 44, 48–9, 59, 60, 64, 67–70, 74–5, 79–80, 82–3, 95–8, 105, 130–1, 140, 143–6, 153, 159, 173

banquet at (1560), 108, 141–2
gardener of, *see* Lovell, George
grant of (1558), 42, 73
Kew ferry, 95
Keys, Thomas, 67
  Thomas, servant, 428
Kidwell, Nicholas, 424
Killigrew, Sir Henry, 14, 21, 349
  Simon, 430, 455
  William, 349, 426
King, Andrew, 193, 244, 302, 327
  Anne*, 25, 199
  John, 424
  Thomas*, brewer, 178, 207, 233, 298, 427, 436, 453
  Thomas*, musician, 351
King's Lynn (Norf.), 13, 42, 472, 475, 487
King's Newnham (Wars.), well at, 201, 285, 296
Kingston-upon-Thames (Surrey), 83–4, 173, 186, 190, 283, 311, 401
Kinwelmersh, Mr [Francis], 426
Kirberie, David, 441
Kitchen, Mr*, 266, 326, 449
  Robert, alderman of Bristol, 455
Kitssen, Jeanneken, 242
Knewstub, John, 368
Knightley, Sir Richard, 193, 243, 327
Knightsbridge (Middx.), 180, 248; hospital, 185, 218, 247
Knolles, Thomas, of Wanstead, 263
Knollys, Catherine, *see* Butler
  Dorothy (Bray), Lady Chandos, 180–1
  Dudley Warwick, 49
  Elizabeth, *see* Leighton
  Sir Francis, the elder, 49, 231, 342
  house, *see* Rotherfield Greys
  Sir Francis, the younger, 206, 279, 440, 449–50, 452, 454, 459
  Henry*, the elder, 49, 155, 171, 419–20
  Henry, the younger, 484
  Lettice, *see* Dudley
  Richard*, 179, 197, 324, 337, 426
  Robert, 426, 451, 453
  Sir William, 180, 307, 449–50, 452, 454, 459
Knowle (Wars.), guildbook of, 6; bailiff of, 453
Knowles, E.H., 5, 10–11, 15, 35–6
  Thomas, Netherlands guard, 441
Knowsley (Lancs.), bailiff of, 453
Knowsley, Hugh, 437, 441

Knyvet, Sir Henry, 58, 68, 88
  Thomas, 185, 196
Kynyat, William*, 13–4, 77, 108, 110, 123, 148, 176, 418, 423, 425

La Marchk, William Robertde, Duke of Bouillon, 306
La Quadra, Alvaro de, Bishop of Aquila, 32, 68, 74, 78, 80, 84, 135, 141, 154
Labarrie, Robert, 456
Lacy, John, mercer, 125; house, 275, *see also* Putney
  John, 436, 440, 457
Lake, William, 457
Lambert, 455
Lambeth, 59–60, 85, 193, 246, 280, 283–4
  ferryman of, 133
  Paris Garden Stairs, 210, 228–9, 253–4
  Palace, Elizabeth visits, 141, 235, 238
  conference at (1584), 31, 202
Landall, George, 326
Lane, keeper of Windsor Forest, 246, 250
  Henry*, 178, 431, 456
  Philip, 438, 441
Langford, Jane, laundress, 417
Langham, Edward*, 68, 74, 77–8, 402, 419
  Thomas*, 155
Langley (Oxon.), 26, 67, 186–8, 193, 196–7, 214, 235, 474; Park, 276
Latham, 454
Laurens, player, 63
L'Aubépine, Guillaume de, Baron de Châteauneuf, 33–4, 305
Le Havre, garrison of (1562–3), 72, 95, 165, 250, 344, 349, 364, 461, 475, 484
Lea, Gabriel, 434, 444
Leak, Sir Francis, 198, 250
Leave, Thomas, 438, 442
Leckhampstead (Bucks.), 301
Ledsham, William*, 63, 103, 110, 121, 428
Lee, Sir Henry, 84, 186, 213–5, 237, 292–4, 299, *see also* Woodstock
  Capt [John], 455
Lees [Great Leigh and Little Leigh, Essex?], 183
Leicester, 182
Leicester, George, 454
  Earl of, *see* Dudley
Leicester House, *see* Westminster
Leicester's Commonwealth, 244, 281
Leicester's Hospital, *see* Warwick
Leiden, 346–7, 349, 371–3

Leigh, Sir John, 58
 Sir Piers, 197, 337
 Sir Thomas, 296, 298, 454
Leighton, Lady Elizabeth (Knollys), 250, 256, 327, 342
 James, 449
 Sir Thomas, 250
 Thomas, the younger, 254
Lennox, Earl of, see Stewart
Leonard the Frenchman, 104
Leonard, William, 119
Leswood, William*, 349, 355, 357, 363
Lewis, 44; wife, 49
 crossbow-maker, 51, 147
 Anthony*, 315, 434, 444
 George, see Cooke, George
 Kenneath*, 287–8, 301, 334, 357
 Ralph, 456
 Richard, 423
 Rutherick*, 16, 187, 189, 196, 202, 230, 233, 239, 435
 Thomas, 457
Ley, Robert, 455
Leynt, Thomas, 341
Leyton (Essex), 177
Lichfield, Thomas, 44
Liéven, Charles de, Sieur de Famars, 356
Lincoln, Earl of, see Fiennes
Lincolnshire, 40, 44, 377
Lisle, Viscount, see Plantagenet, Arthur
Littsome, John, 425
liveries, 74, 419, 422, 426
 Great Statute of (1504), 22
Lloyd, David, 423, 425
 Evan, 454
 Griffith*, 49, 56, 62, 74, 80, 172, 409, 422
 Hugh, 423
 John (Little John), groom of the stables, 107, 414, 422, 425, 427
 John, yeoman of beds, 433, 442, 456
 [Sir] John of Yale (Denbs.), 449
 Owen, 419–20, 428
 Richard*, 15, 179, 226, 230, 233, 239–41, 251, 272, 296, 328, 337, 369, 430, 445, 451, 459
 Robert, 425
Lock, William, 438, 441
Lockeye, Rauffe, 141
Lodge, Sir Thomas, 122
London, City of:
 Corporation:
  Lord Mayors:
   1559–60, see Hewet, Sir William

   1560–1, see Chester, Sir William
   1585–6, see Dixie, Sir Wolstan
  Lord Mayor's banquet (1560), 144, 165
  under-sheriffwick, 484–5
 livery companies:
  Ironmongers' Company, barge, 256
  Vintners' Company, 469
  Mercers' Company, feast (1560), 159, 165
  Shearmens' Company, 123–4
 trading companies
  Barbary Company, 249, 280
  Merchant Adventurers, see Gilpin George
  Russia Company, 249
  Staplers' Company, 115–6, 118, 134
 Aldgate, 272
 Arundel's (tavern), 59
 Baynard's Castle, 313
 The Beare Inn, 163–4
 Blackfriars, 230
 Bosom's (Blossom's) Inn, 144
 Bridewell, 240
 Christchurch (Duke Place), 25, 43, 46, 52, 61, 63, 68, 94, 377–8, 381
 Fleet Street, 200
 Ludgate prison, 474
 Lyon Quay, 140, 256, 273
 Old Swan Inn, 69
 Old Swan Stairs, 283–4
 The Poultry, 142
 St George's, Buttolph Lane, 267
 St Katherine's Stairs, 77
 St Paul's Cathedral, 171
  churchyard, 165, 336
  Paul's Cross, 166
 Smithfield, 77
 The Steelyard, 92; Maiden Head Inn, 144
 Three Cranes Wharf, 154, 243
 The Tower, 25, 45–6, 164, 166, 381, 389
  lieutenant of, see Warner, Sir Edward
  Hobson of, 340
  Mint, 154
 Tower Hill, 207–9, 231
 Tower Street, Salutation of Our Lady Inn, 164
 Tower Wharf, 66, 72
Long, papist from Oxford, 202
 Walter, 436
Long Itchington (Wars.), 202

Longfield, Arthur, 455
Longleat House (Wilts.), 1–3, 8, 18, 122
Lonison, John, 45, 88, 94, 119, 124, 427
Lopez, Dr Roderigo, 332
Lord, Edmund, 438
Lord Admiral (1559–85), see Fiennes,
    Edward
    (1585–6), see Howard, Charles
    Chamberlain (1559–61), see Howard,
    William
    (1584–85), see Howard, Charles
    (1585), see Carey, Henry
    Chancellor (1588), see Hatton, Sir Christopher
    Deputy of Ireland (1559–61), see Radcliffe, Thomas
    (1584–5), see Perrot, Sir John,
    see also Grey, Arthur
    Keeper (1559–61), see Bacon, Sir Nicholas
    President of the Council in the Marches,
    see Sidney, Sir Henry
Lorraine, Christina, Duchess of, 155
Lovedon, Hercules, 431
Lovege, Mr, 284
Lovell, Mr [Gregory, Cofferer of the
    Household], 282
    George, gardener of Kew, 146, 399,
    416
    Henry*, 178, 229, 242, 291, 456
Lucas, skinner, 89
Lucas, Peter, 428
    Sir Thomas, 344
Luck, fool, 183, 245
Lucy, Sir Thomas, 157, 295, 451–2
    Thomas, the younger, 295
Ludford, Arthur, 453
Lumley, John, 6th Lord, 159
    servants, 155, 236, 247, 276, 283; fool
    (Robin), 183, 294, 296, 305
Lumner, Edmund, 441
Luson (Leveson), Sir Walter, 451–2
Luxembourg, Louis de, Count of Rouci,
    164
Lye, Mr, 401
    Sir Percival, 159
Lylly, Henry, 123
Lynch, Thomas, 454
Lyons, 455
    Nicholas, 434
    William, 444
Lyttelton, Mr [Francis?], 427
    Sir John, 114, 118, 132

Maclean, S.-B., 4, 10
Macwilliam, Henry, 59, 210
    Henry, the younger, 59, 210
Maddy, 45, 95, 130
Madox, Richard, 472
Maidenhead (Berks.), 287–8, 290
Maidstone (Kent), 177
Mailer, Mr, 425
Maitland, John, laird of Thirlestane, 282
    William, laird of Lethington, 146–7,
    165
Malboune, Humphrey, 428
Maldon (Essex), 191, 204
Mallis, 457
Malone, Edmund, 7
Malta, 461, 473
Man, Isle of, 295
Manners, Edward, 3rd Earl of Rutland,
    331
    Henry, 2nd Earl of Rutland, 68
    Roger, 331, 393–4
Manning, beadle, 456
Manningtree (Essex), 393
Mannox, James, 457
Mansell, John, 267
Mansfield, Henry, 161
    John, 425
    William, 438, 442
Marbury, John*, 14, 21, 65, 116, 135, 167,
    402, 405, 426
    William, 115–6, 120
Margery, laundress, 458
Maria, John, cutler, 121
Markham, Jerome, 454
    Thomas, 255
Marnex, 431
Marshall, Mr*, 44, 155, 420
    Thomas (armourer), 434, 444
    William*, 298, 354
Marsters, Mr, 288
Martin, Mr*, 228, 243, 317
    Anthony, 427
    George*, 77–9, 419–20
    Griffin, trumpeter, 432
    John, 428
    Sir Richard, 249, 251–2
Mary, Queen of Scots, 12, 180, 207, 462,
    473
    scullery-maid, 458
Maryano, Angelo, 79, 126
Mason, Lady Elizabeth (Isley), 165, 179
    Sir John, 165
    John, of the scullery, 432

Massey, David, 454
  William*, 350, 356, 362, 433, 437, 441, 456
Masters, John, 436, 440
Mathew, Mr, Scottish preacher, 200
  Toby*, 204, 228, 453
Maurice, Count of Nassau, 369, 371, 395
Mauvissière, see Castelnau
Mawdlin, Mrs, 458
May, John, 433
Maynard, hosier, 18, 42, 129, 140, 160, 427
Mendoza, Don Bernardino de, 33, 278
Mercer, Richard, 428
Meredith, Richard*, 15, 199, 289, 292-3, 298-9, 301-2, 304, 363
Merrick, Richard*, 185, 201-2, 246, 446, 456
Mertes, Kate, 25
Messinger, Robert, 457
Michael, musician, 442
Middelburg, xiv, 9, 345, 349, 367-9, 371, 395
Middleton, William, 427 (Middleman), 435
Mildmay, Sir Walter, 260
Mile End Green (Middx.), 230; hospital, 232-3, 245, 255, 258, 308, 314
Miller, Thomas, 427
Millington, Henry*, 224, 275, 433, 444, 456
Milton, 456
Minster Lovell (Oxon.), 214
Mokinmorbye, Bartholomew, 425
Molam, Thomas, 433, 443
Mompesson, Richard, 250
Monday, James, 124, 148; Mrs, 141, 232
Mordaunt, Lewis, 3rd Lord, 199
More, Edmund, embroiderer, bill, 423-5
  Edmund, 424
  John, 443, 455, 457
  Ralph*, 16, 272, 324, 367, 373, 433, 442, 453
  Robert*, 201, 228, 260, 456
Moreau, Pierre*, 220, 234, 241, 252, 265, 317, 334, 342, 347, 432, 443
Morell, Roger, 425
Morgan, Alexander, 453
  Richard, 436
  Rowland, 435
  William, 436, 440, 456
Morrice (Morys), 456
  Nicholas (cook), 424, 426
  Oliver, 423
  Reginald, 427
Mortlake (Surrey), 193, 319

Morton, Earl of, see Douglas
Morton, George, 352
Mott, Humphrey, 132
Mountaneo, 426
Mowster, Ralph, 428
Moyle, Richard, 432, 443, 456
Mullins, 455
Munford, John*, 298
Muscovy, 249, see also Bowes, Sir Jerome, London: Russia Company
Musgrave, Cuthbert/Cutty*, 64, 77 (Cuthbert of the stables), 198, 214, 274, 363
  Sir Simon, 100, 151

Naarden, 346-8
Necado/Nicaches, Mr, 276, 340
Netherlands, the, United Provinces of
  Council of State (Raad van State), 272, 348-9
  States-General, 34, 369, 386-7, 395
  English policy towards (1584-5), 183, 229, 385
  embassy to England (1585), 34, 270, 275, 283-4, 287, 386-90 see also Nonsuch, treaties of; Ortel, Joachim; Valcke, Jacob
  mission of Richard Lloyd to (1585), 272
Nettlebed (Oxon.), 192
Nettleton, John*, 211, 456
Neville, Alexander*, 28, 195, 230, 235, 240, 449, 451
  George, 5th Lord Abergavenny, 22
  Henry, 6th Lord Abergavenny, 198
  Henry, 5th Earl of Westmorland, 60, 155
  Sir Henry, 199
Nevison, Dr, 147
Newby, Thomas, 424
Newington, see Stoke Newington
Newman, George, 441
Newsom, Bartholomew, 428
Newtrefield, Mr [Netterville, Richard?], 402
Neyle, Paul, 132
Nicholls, Edmund*, 74
Nicholson, Mr, of Kew, 75, 402
  Thomas, mercer, 119
Nightibred, Lawrens, 425
Nightingale, Richard*, 275
Nijmegen, 348-9, 352; camp before, 353, 357
  sconce of, 349, 352, 356, 361

Noailles, Gilles, de, Abbé de l'Isle, 32–4, 66, 69, 72, 80, 135, 164
Nonsuch, treaties of (1585), 284, 386–7, 392
   see also Netherlands, embassy to England (1585)
Nonsuch Palace (Surrey):
   (1559–60), 78–9, 82, 159
   (1584–5), 180, 183, 192, 194, 236, 275–84, 305–11, 314, 316, 318, 380, 388–9
   gardener, 193, 247
   keeper of wardrobe at (Gittones), 193, 247
   see also Fitzalan, Lumley
Nonsuch Park, 193, 276–8, 310
Norfolk, 48, 54, 56–7, 378, 381
   Duke of, *see* Howard
Norris, Henry, Lord, 84, 337
   Sir Henry, the younger, 450, 452
   Sir John, 275, 331, 349
   John, 437, 441
   Margery, Lady, 84, 132
North, George, 364
   John, 423
   John, yeoman, 424
   Roger, 2nd Lord, 300, 350, 352, 364, 371
   household, 30; servant (Fulk Strange), 431
Northampton, 264, 299
Northampton, Marquess of, *see* Parr
Northamptonshire, 307, 486
Northaw/Northall (Herts.), 268, 273, 285–8, 303–4, 310, 312, 315–6, 320–1, 326, 328, 389–90
Northumberland, Duke and Duchess of, *see* Dudley
   Earl of, *see* Percy
Norton, Thomas, 35
Notes, Mrs, 247, 310
Nowell, Alexander, 172
   George, 454
Nurse, Thomas, 428

Oatlands Palace (Surrey), 81, 141, 180–1
Offington (Sussex), 188, 231, 236, 238, *see also* West, Sir Thomas
Offley, Hugh, 165
Okeham, Mr, 427
Oliver, William, 404, 425, 427
O'Meloe, Hugh (Ambloye), 434, 444
Onslow, Richard, 167
Ortel, Joachim, 34, 229, 259

Osbourne, Mr, 453
Ostend, 180, 395
Osterley (Middx.), 323
Osunis, Mr, 96
   Mrs (Osemed), 85, 190 (mother), 206, 237, 322, 327
Oswald, Roger*, 46–7, 56, 70, 172, 415, 421–2
Otford (Kent), 76–8
Owen, Humphrey*, 78, 81, 174, 428
   Thomas*, 368, 434, 444, 457
Oxenbridge, Mr*, 192, 281, 302, 326, 335, 454
Oxford, City of, 143, 186, 194, 212–3, 216–7; carrier of, 384 *see also* Dudley, Amy, funeral
Oxford, Earl of, *see* de Vere
Oxford University, 165, 186, 188, 212–3, 291 *see also* Dudley, Robert: chancellor of Oxford University
   Press, 230
   Christ Church, 1, 4, 17, 212
   New College, 467
Oxfordshire, 218–9, 291

Paget, Henry, 2nd Lord, 141
   Thomas, 3rd Lord, 26
Paget Place, *see* Westminster: Leicester House
Palavicino, Sir Horatio, 184–5, 389
Palliver, 457
Palmer, Andrew, goldsmith, 40
   Mr, 263
   Simon, goldsmith, 40; Mrs, 40, 72, 106
Paramour, Richard, draper, bill of, 426
   Thomas, 454
Parker, Mr [John?], 427
   Matthew, Archbishop of Canterbury, 138
Parliament:
   (1559), 48, 55
   (1584), 183, 191, 222, 227, 262; proxies for, 197–9
Parliament House, 200–1, 203, 228, 246
Parr, John, Queen's embroiderer, 199, 266, 329
   William, Marquess of Northampton, 59, 91, 158, 169
Parry, Sir Thomas, 138; servants, 45, 49, 53, 57, 120, 161, 417
   Dr William, 228

Partridge, goldsmith, 127
  John*, 52–3, 59–60, 63–6, 70, 75, 81, 139, 154, 159, 416, 424, 438
  Richard, 428
Paulet, Sir Amyas, 258, 463, 479
  George, 419–20
  John, 421
  William, Marquess of Winchester, 59
Payle, Thomas, 458
Peckesall, Mr, 68
Pecock, keeper of Enfield Old Park, 263
  Richard, mercer, 118
  Richard, 456
  Capt Robert, 317, 355
Pecover, Nicholas, 457
Peedee, Richard, 457
Pembroke, Earl of, see Herbert
Pennington, Nicholas, 443
Pennyman (Penyston), Thomas, 432, 442, 457
Penren [Penrhyn, William]. 454
Pepper, Richard*, 180, 185, 189–90, 193, 209, 213, 217, 220, 224, 234, 237, 254, 269, 278, 281, 335, 371
Pepys, Samuel, 18
Perce (coachman), 454
Percival, Robert, 423, 426
Percy, Henry, 8th Earl of Northumberland, 104
  Henry, 9th Earl of Northumberland, 19
  Thomas, 7th Earl of Northumberland, 165; household, 30
Peris, John, 436
Perkins, mother, 221
Perne, Christopher, 100, 124
Perrot, Dorothy (Devereux), 181, 226, 245
  Sir John, 209
  Sir Thomas, 181, 226
Pervel, 425
Peter, coachman, 434, 454, 457
  page, 454
Peter, William, 433
Petre, Sir John, 151, 339, 343–4; house, see Ingatestone Hall
  Sir William, 2, 19, 30, 141, 151
Philipe, French cook, 1559–60*, 138, 407, 426 (de Corbie)
Phillips, Owen, 458
Phillit, Henry, 234
Philpot, Thomas, 50
Phips, Francis, 456
Pickering, Sir William, 46, 63, 65, 72, 378
Pickman, John, 137

Picto, Mrs, 25, 90, 102, 383
Pietro, musician*, 131, 401, 420, 426 (Peter Techio)
Piggot, Mr, 426
Pilkington, James, Bishop of Durham, 166
Pinnock, Nicholas*, 362, 433 (Dymock), 442 (Dymock), 453
Pipkin, John, 428
Pitchford, apothecary, 453
  Robert*, 15, 180, 190, 195, 208, 233, 243, 249, 251, 256, 278, 287, 292–3, 302–3, 308–10, 324, 336, 345, 347, 361, 371, 433, 442, 453
  William*, 15, 312, 318–9, 324, 338–9
Pitts, Thomas, 455
Plantagenet, Arthur, Viscount Lisle, 50
Platt, of Iremonger Lane, 39, 50, 102
players:
  Leicester's, 7–8, 11, 56, 68, 248, 255, 341, 353, 371
  Queen's, 243, 334
  see also Laurens, Kemp, Tarlton
Plymouth, 306
Pollwhell, Thomas*, 283, 291, 296, 298, 304, 320 334, 343
Poole, Sir Giles, 153
  Sir Henry, 153, 216, 259, 450, 452
Pope, vintner, 40
  Francis, draper, 25, 43, 98, 121, 420
  Martin, 425
Popeley, Henry, 131
Portsmouth, 141, 143, 183, 191, 217, 249
Potter [John], 456
Poukes, tailor, 271
Povinton, Robert*, 275, 319
Powell, fool, 231
  David*, 56, 74, 144, 420
  John (of the wardrobe)*, 41, 48, 56, 63, 66–8, 71, 74, 76, 86, 96, 405, 423, 427
  Ralf, 432, 433
  Mr [Stephen?], 321
Powell's daughter, 152, 156–8
Power, Mr*, 158
  Henry, 426
  William, 428
Powher, tailor, 457
Poynter, Richard, 120
Poyntz, Sir John, 449–50, 452
  Sir Nicholas, 83
  Nicholas, 449, 451–2
  William, 430, 449, 451, 453
Prattin, Clement, 444, 453
Prelly, Joyce, 70

Preston, Christopher, 425
Price, John, 427
Privy Council, 52, 183, 187, 228–9, 348, 386, 389; registers, 30–1
Privy Seal, 73, 126, 128, 156–7, 324–5, 392
progresses, royal:
  (1559), 75–80, 413
  (1560), 141–3, 145
  (1573), 463
  (1575), 472
  (1578), 477
  (1584), 180
Pryncell, Gregory, 133
Purvey, Nicholas, 51, 427
Putney (Surrey), 182, 193–4, 274, 276, 306–7, 313, 336, 391 see also Aldersey, Thomas; Lacy, John
Putney Park, 194
Pye, Edward, 455
Pyerson, Thomas, 113

Quarles, James, 241, 248, 451–2

Radcliffe, Frances (Sidney), Countess of Sussex, 142
  Sir Humphrey, 145
  Thomas, 3rd Earl of Sussex, 22, 55, 99–100, 104, 117, 137, 141, 143, 153, 170, 203, 347
Raglan, Thomas, 424
Ralegh, Sir Walter, 210, 245, 320; black-amore, 178, 210
Ramsey, Lawrence*, 239, 295, 301, 343, 348, 367, 373
Rankin, Henry, 424, 428
Ransome (keeper)*, 252, 270
Ratclef (Ratless), keeper*, 309, 456
Ratcliff (Middx.), 178, 204, 251, 256, 264, 342–3
Rawlinson, Miles, 432, 443, 457
Rawson, Stephen, 107, 414, 422, 427
Raynal, John, 457
Rayneford, Robert, 427
Reade, Mr, of Abingdon, 189, 216–7
  capper, 51, 86
  page, 431
  John, 455
  Sir William, 349, 354
Reading, Walter, 423, 426
Reignold, tailor, 90
Remain, Cornish, 423

Requests, Court of, cases:
  Philpot vs Dudley, 50
  Dudley vs Earl of Cumberland, 73
retainers, xiv, 22
Revett, Sir Thomas, 40, 113–4, 118, 147, 171
Reynolds, Thomas, 428
Rich, Mr, 310
  John, corncutter*, 227, 233, 348, 458
  Richard, 1st Lord, 151–4
  Robert, 2nd Lord, 26, 166, 169
  Robert, 3rd Lord, 166, 449–51, 454, 458
Richards, John*, 76–8, 138, 141–2, 160, 413, 415, 420–2, 427
Richardson, Ferdinando*, 184, 190, 206, 209, 226, 246, 248, 268, 271, 276, 318, 339, 453
  Ralph, 436, 440
Richmond, Mr, 167
  William, 456
Richmond Palace (Surrey), 26
  (1560), 141, 159
  (1584), 180
  (1585), 268, 318–20, 322–5, 327–8, 330–1, 334–6, 338, 393
  garden-keeper (Lovell), 161
Ridgeway, Walter*, 181, 191, 271, 433, 442, 457
Roades, George, 455
Robert, trumpeter, 228
Roberts, fisherman*, 343, 351, 363, 453
  Mrs, laundress, 278
  Edward*, 45, 56, 71, 74–5, 82, 86, 99, 406, 421
  John*, 279, 282, 292, 299, 307–8, 311–4, 316, 320, 333, 434
Robinson, Christopher, 456
  John, skinner*, 265, 288, 453
  John, 279
  Peter, coffer-maker, 124
  Richard, poulterer, 131
  Richard, 445
  William, 425, 427
Robotham, bookbinder, 152
  Robert, 119
Robsart, Amy, see Dudley
  Arthur*, 47, 423, 426
  Lady Elizabeth, 13, 64
Robsart estate, 13, 42, 261, 378, 380–3 see also Syderstone, Bircham Newton, Great Bircham
Robson, Henry, 438
Roche, John, 432, 443

Rochester (Kent), 75–6
Rodd, Thomas, 4
Rogers, Sir Edward, 100, 168
Romford (Essex), 317, 320
Roper, Mr, 326
  John, 436
Rotherfield Greys (Oxon.), 180, 185–6, 189–90, 192, 197, 211–2, 217–8, 223, 284, 287–8
Rotterdam, 369–70
Row*, wood-carrier, 418
Rowden, 456
Rowe, Sir Thomas, 115
Rowley, Stephen, 123
Rudfen (Wars.), 463
Russell, Anne, see Dudley
  Lady Elizabeth (Cooke), 286
  Elizabeth, see Bourchier
  Edward, 3rd Earl of Bedford, wardship of, 286, 303, 308
  Francis, 2nd Earl of Bedford, 46, 146, 155, 179
    death and funeral, 286, 308, 387; surgeon (Marwood), 179
    houses, see Westminster: Bedford House, Chenies
  John, gardener, 455
  Margaret, see Clifford
  Sir William, 369, 371
Rutland, Earls of, see Manners
Rutter, Henry, 434, 444
Rydeton, George, 426

Sackville, Thomas, Lord Buckhurst, 254
Sadler, John, 437, 441
  William, 434
St Albans (Herts.), 302–3, 312, 314–5, 325, 389–90; Stables at, 303, 314
St Bees (Cumb.), 5
St James's Palace, 26, 52–3, 55, 94, 194, 196–8, 202–3, 205–6, 208, 308
St James's Park, 58, 61, 68, 72, 94, 194 keepers, 185, 202, 247, 258
St Michael, order of, 5
St Quentin (campaign 1557), 40, 61, 68, 71, 75, 105, 160, 165, 381
St Loe, Sir William, 155
Salesbury, Mr, 423
Salisbury, Bishop of [John Piers], 450–1
Samons, James, 428
Sandys, Mr*, 15, 28, 179, 185, 189, 191–2, 194, 196–200, 452

Sariant, Michael, 455
Saule, William*, 53, 59, 64–5, 80, 147, 419–20
Saunders, John, 437, 441
  Nicholas, 368
Savage, Mr, 427
  keeper, 200, 238, 245, 252, 261, 268, 281, 331
  John, mat-maker, 204
Sawyer, Richard, 350, 358
Schenk, Sir Martin, 350
Schenkenschanz, 354
Scory, Sylvanus, 321, 455
Scotland, (intervention in, 1560), 140–1, 349, 479
  (1585), 262–3, 267, 336, see also James VI
  embassies from:
    (1560), 146, 165
    (1584), see Gray, Patrick
    (1585), see Bellenden, Lewis
  embassies to, see Davison, William; Wotton, Sir Edward
Scott, Mr, of Camberwell, 64, 102–3
  Sir Walter, 378–9
Scoward, Mr, 245
Scragh, Richard, 458
Screven, Thomas, 331
Scroop, Henry, 9th Lord Scroop of Bolton, 103
Seale, 455
  Thomas, 195
Searle, Edward, 455
Seckford, Henry, 209–10, 316
Sedgewick, George, 424, 427
Sedgrave, William, 137
Segar, Sir William, 177, 255
Selby, Ralph, 452
Selman, 457
Sermant, John*, 48, 56, 62
Seton, Gregory, 324
Settle, Mr, 331
  Robert, 456
Seurre, Michel de, 33, 143, 164
Seymour, Edward, Duke of Somerset, 34, 152
  Edward, Earl of Hertford, 1, 100
  Frances, Duchess of Somerset, 3
Sharpe, Mr, 426
Shaw, Robert, 108, 122
Sheffield, Douglas (Howard), Lady, 135, 184, 188, 233
Sheldon, William, 114, 118, 134, 138, 141, 153

Sheldrake, William, 436
Shelton, Mr, 426
Sheppard, Thomas, 195, 225, 233, 271, 283, 332–3, 340
Sherman, Thomas, 201
Sherwood, Henry, falconer, 407
ships:
   Amythyst/Amity, 367, 394
   Elizabeth Jonas, 72
   Galleon Leicestr, 238, 252–3, 279, 487
   Grace of God, 369
   Triumph, 273
Shirley, Mr, 311
   Sir Thomas, 242, 302, 374, 452; servant, 348
Shrewsbury, 179
Shrewsbury, Earl of, *see* Talbot
Sidney, Elizabeth (b. 1560), 142
   Elizabeth (b. 1585), 335
   Sir Henry, 1, 2, 55, 85, 101, 113, 117, 136, 142, 165–8, 244
   Lady Mary (Dudley), 44, 55, 57, 123, 139, 142, 165
   Mary, Countess of Pembroke, *see* Herbert
   Sir Philip, xiv, 173, 181, 207, 212, 244, 255, 306–7, 335, 369, 372, 389–91, 393, 425, 481
   Scottish servant, 281, 336
   Sir Robert, 173, 317, 347, 372, 449–50, 452, 454
Signet warrants, 62
Simon, George, 428
   James, 424
Singleton, Thomas, 101–2, 128
Skarsmore, Thomas, 437, 441
Skydmore, Mr [Scudamore, Sir John?]. 426
Sleggs, Edward, 423
Slead, mercer, 125
Sluys, 256, 354
Slye, Mr, 452
Slyfield, Henry*, 305, 310, 431, 454
   John*, 48, 51, 53, 57–8, 99
Smart, sword-bearer's [Ralph Smart, of the City of London] son, 425
Smith, fletcher, 128
   Mrs, silkwoman, 120
   Ambrose, mercer, 87–9, 123, 177
   David, embroiderer, 45, 102, 106, 120, 127–8, 171
   Francis, mercer, 320
   Gawen, 273, 286; servant, 434
   Henry, 427

John, 436
Ralph, Queen's bargeman, 171
Ralph, 436, 440
William*, 81, 93, 419, 455; wife, laundress, 180, 458
Smithson, John*, 342, 432, 443
Smythe, Thomas, customer, 114–5, 119, 334
Sola, Ferdinando, 128
Solms, Adolph von, Count of Newenaar and Moeurs, 359
Somerset, 280
Somerset, Duke of, *see* Seymour
Sonett, John, 128
Southam (Wars.), 481
Southampton, 143, 249
Southwark, borough of, 54, 56
   Old Kent Road, 221; hospital, 209, 253–4
   St Mary Overy Stairs, 307
   tennis court in, 133
   White Lion (gaol), 254
   Winchester House, 179–80, 313
Southwell (Notts.), warden of, 424, 427
Sowthen, William, 428
Spain, factor in, 18
Sparge, Thomas, 436
Sparke, William*, 249–50, 280
Speake*, 238–9
Speede, Andrew, 436
Spelman, jeweler, 453
Spenser, Capt [James]. 452
   Edward, scullery, 424
   Sir John, 282, 299
   John, 438, 441
Sperte, Richard*, 75, 427
Spillisbury, 427
Spinola, Benedict, 41, 53, 161
Spinyers, Thomas, 425
Sprint, William, 452
Spurge, John, 441
Stafferton, Thomas, 291–2, 302, 307, 449, 451–2
Stafford, Lady Dorothy, 233
   Edmund*, 198
   Edward, 13th Lord, 197, 270
   Sir Edward, 229, 233
   Richard, 419
Staffordshire, 234
Stampe, Elles*, 140, 401
   Sir James, 62, 157
Standish, Edward, 457
Stanhope, Dr, 451, 453
   John, 306, 308, 389–90
   Sir Thomas, 185, 191

Stanley, Alice (Spenser), Countess of Derby, 282, 299
Edward, 3rd Earl of Derby, 49, 51, 54, 56, 59, 93
Sir Edward, 450, 452
Ferdinando, Lord Strange, 5th Earl of Derby, 281; musicians, 352–3
Henry, 4th Earl of Derby, 220, 229, 232, 235, 242, 258–9, 277, 295, 297, 321, 324, 337; household, 30; house, see Westminster: Derby House
Margaret (Clifford), Lady Strange, 73
Thomas (Mint master), 115
Sir William, 155
Star Chamber, see Westminster, Palace of
Court of, case (1585), 320
Sir Robert Dudley case, xiv, 84, 135, 250, 462, 467, 473, 477, 483, 485–6
Starkey, Henry, 133
Staunton, Joseph, 4–6
William, 4–7, 17
Stedman, John, 133
Stephenson, John, farrier, 414, 422
Robert, 415
Stepney (Middx.), 178–9
Stepney, Mr, 426
Stevens, Henry*, 291, 457
Henry, keeper, 456
Steward, Mr, 425
Stewart, Margaret (Douglas), Countess of Lennox, 80
Matthew, Earl of Lennox, 58–9
Stock, James, 106, 119
Stoke Newington (Middx.), hospital, 243
Stokes, William, 156, 168
Stonard, Francis, 454
Stone, Mr, mercer, 314
Edward, Queen's footman, 211, 344
Stoneleigh (Wars.), 296, 298
Stoner, Mr, 427
Stony Stratford (Bucks.), 301
Storie, John, 435
Robert, 431
Thomas, 431
Strachie, Mr, 427
Strange, Mr [Roger?], 70
Stratford Bamford (Essex), 325
Stratford Langthorne (Essex), 258, 265–9, 271, 308, 314, 335
abbey mills, 282
Stratford-le-Bow (Middx.), 50, 258, 267–71, 308, 363; almshouse, 226

Stratford-upon-Avon (Wars.), 6
Streat/Stretch, Mr, 81, 426
Stringer, Henry, Queen's footman, 182, 211, 231, 276, 306, 309, 344
John*, 298, 453
Strong, Sir Roy, 22–3
Stuckley, Thomas, 165
Sturman, 144
Suffolk, 102, 382–3, 487
Suffolk, Duchess of, see Bertie
Sussex, Earl of, see Radcliffe
Sutton, Edward, 4th Lord Dudley, 151; musicians, 186, 291
Edward, 5th Lord Dudley, 449–51, 454, 458
Elizabeth, 230
Katherine (Bridges), Lady Dudley, 151
Richard*, 191, 270, 279, 451, 453
Sutton Place (Surrey), 141
Swallow, Henry, 428
Robert, 428
Sweden, embassy from, 78, see also Finland, Duke of; Eric XIV
Syderstone (Norf.), 13, 116, 381
Symmell, Thomas*, 344, 348, 443, 453
Syon House (Middx.), 182, 186

Tailboys, Thomas, 437, 441
Taillor, Rauffe, 133
Talbot, Elizabeth (Hardwick), Countess of Shrewsbury, 240
George, 6th Earl of Shrewsbury, 22, 180, 240, 246, 296, 334, 337
Gilbert, Lord Talbot, 7th Earl of Shrewsbury, 253, 255, 279
Tamworth, John, 46, 52, 61, 99, 113, 137, 156, 169
Tanner, Lieut, 452
Thomas, 433
Tarlton, Richard, 253, 300
Tattershall, Richard, 120
Tatton, William, 454
Tavernor, Robert*, 202, 206, 240
Taylor, John, 437, 441–2
William, 438
Tempest, Roger, hosier, 106, 129
William, hosier, 129
Temple, Richard*, 257, 456
tennis, match with Sussex (1560), 153
courts, see Southwark, Whitehall, Westminster

Theobalds (Middx.), 60, 238; Queen's visit
    (1585), 262–3
Thimblethorpe, 453
Thomas, John, 435
    Morris*, 298
    Ryce, 457
    William*, 203, 223, 231, 235, 271–2, 362,
        433, 442
Thompson, Dr, 431
    James*, 41, 56, 74, 82, 101, 106, 130, 412
Thorneton, 188
Thornhurst, Stephen, 454
Thorp, Mr, 455
Throcking (Herts.), 379–81, 383
Throckmorton, Mr [Job?], 455
    Lady Anne, 64, 151
    Sir Nicholas, 64, 145, 160–1
    Sir Thomas, 449–50, 452
Thynne, Thomas, 1st Viscount Weymouth,
    3
Tiel, 354–6
Tipping, George, 215
Titbache, John, 132
Tithe, Robert, 453
Tomlinson, John, 428
Tompson, Thomas, 425
Tonge, Susan (Mrs Clarentius), 42, 57
Tookey, George, 114
Topcliffe, Richard, 219
    Thomas, 436
Tottenham (Middx.), 262
tournaments:
    1559 (Coronation), 47
    1559 (Greenwich), 72
    1559 (West Horsley), 80
    1559 (Whitehall), 104
    1560 (Whitehall), 137, 153
    1584 (Whitehall), 196, 203
Towcester (Northants.), 193
Townsend, 455
Townshend, Sir Henry, 289
    Sir Roger, 261
Tracy, Giles*, 182, 187, 226, 244, 255, 277,
    290–1, 317, 343
    Sir John (the elder), 449–50, 452
    (Sir) John (the younger)*, 214, 261, 291,
        303, 317, 430, 449, 451–2
Trans, Marquis de, see Foix
Trappes, 230
Trayford, Edward, 454
Treasurer (of the Household), Mr, see Parry,
    Sir Thomas
Trencher, Mr, 201

Trentham, Jane, 239
    Thomas, 239, 425 (Trenton)
Tresham, Sir Thomas, 191–2
Treslong, Admiral (Willem van Blois), 272
Troll, Thomas, 433
Truchsess, Gebhard, Archbishop of
    Cologne, 350, 359, 374
Trueman, Richard, 437, 442
Tuberville/Turville, George, 455
    John, 431, 453
Tudor, David, 423
    Robert*, 358, 368, 453, 455
Turk, John*, 346, 453 (Tucke)
Turner, Daniel, 359
    Ralph*, 311, 316, 456
    Thomas*, 364
Tusk, 457
Twetty, William, 344, 349
Twickenham (Middx.), 184–5
Twisse, John, 424, 428
Twyson, William, 423
Twyste, Wednoll*, 327
Tyan, Gwyllam, 89, 124
Tykell, John, 437, 441
Tyler, Randall, 152
Tyrrell, Henry, 423, 427–8

Underhill, Edward, 99
    Hugh, 222
    Dr John, 202
    Thomas*, 99, 178, 205, 309, 370, 423, 453
Underwood, 78; wife, 96
Unton, Sir Edward, 41, 67, 213
    Sir Henry, 41, 213–6, 219, see also Bruern
        Abbey
Upcott, William, 4–5, 9–10, 15–6
Utrecht, 346–8, 351, 353, 357–8, 360–4, 374;
    mutiny at, 353
Uxbridge (Middx.), 308

Valcke, Jacques, 388
Vance, see Hance
Vane, Peter, 155
Vangencick, Baptist, 426
Varnham, John, gardener of Westminster,
    223
Vasa, Gustavus, King of Sweden, 78
Vaughan, Cuthbert, 72, 161
    George, 420
    Henry, 438
    Lewes, 441

Vaughter, Thomas, 457
Vaws [Vaux?], Mr, 426
Vendra, 235
Vennor, 456
Verney, Sir Richard, 92, 380, 382–3
Veure [Vere?], Hugh, 452
Vianen, 360–2, 364
Vic, John de, 237, 273
Vodett, John, drummer, 432, 440, 455 (John taborer)
Vynton, Paul, 410, 427

Waggenar (Wageningen), 351
Wagstaff, Ralph*, 225, 456
Waight (Wayts), William, 431, 452
Wake, John*, 351, 369–70, 449, 451–2
Wakelin, John, 456
Waldegrave, Sir Edward, 108–9
Wales, 230, 254
Walgrave, John, 152, 166
Walker, Richard, Dean of Chester, 128
  William, 427, 453
Waller, Ambrose*, 15, 209, 219, 238, 332
  Thomas*, 296, 299–300, 434, 456
Wallop, Henry, 294
Walsingham, Sir Francis, 179, 187, 197, 207, 227–9, 262, 265, 269, 285, 290, 296, 299, 303, 316, 324–5, 342, 386–94
  papers, 2; house, see Barn Elms
  servants, 250, see also Francx, Charles
Waltham (Cross, Herts.), 61, 94–5, 380
  Forest, 137, 147, 168, see also Barnes
  court (justice seat), 203, 242–3
Walton, Christopher, 433
  John, silkman, 120
  Thomas, 456
Wanton (apothecary), 135
Wanstead House (Essex), 26–7, 100
  (1584), 177–9, 182, 196, 200, 204–5
  (1585), 207–8, 221–3, 225–7, 229–30, 232–42, 244, 248, 250, 252, 254–5, 257–9, 264–8, 270–2, 274, 278–84, 308, 311, 313–4, 316, 318, 323, 325, 329, 331–3, 342–3, 389, 472
  bailiff of, 233
  conduit, 329–30
  garden, 178, 227
  gardener, 233, 238–40, see also Goffe, Thomas; gardener, French
  gardener's wife, 177, see also Goffe, Ann
  keepers, 479

warreners, 239, 256, 308, 313, 343; see also Ford, William
  works at, 238, 244, 250, 258–9, 323, see also Cranbrook, Aldersbrook
Wanstead Heath, 208
Warberton, John, 444
Warcop, Thomas, 100, 151, 221, 266, 343
Ward, skinner, 70
  Capt John, 364
  Richard, 291
  William, 432
Wardinote, William, 458
Ware (Herts.), 60, 94–5, 380
  Park, 76
Warensby, William, 110
Warley, John, 109, 134
  Margaret, 109
Warneford, Mr, 214
Warner, Sir Edward, 92
  John, 454
  Richard, ferryman at Greenwich, 208, 220, 229, 232, 238, 243, 248–52, 256–9, 264, 266–8, 270, 281, 313, 336
Warton, James*, 311, 433
Warwick, 6, 256, 260, 293; Leicester's Hospital, 6, 230, 294, 296, 393
  Earl and Countess of, see Dudley
Warwickshire, 195, 206, 279, 383
  lieutenancy (1559–60), 43, see also Cave, Sir Ambrose
  water, see King's Newnham
Washington, Thomas (shepster), 129
Watford (Herts.), 287–8, 290
Water, John, 433
Watling Street, 302
Watlos, Humphrey, 456
Watson, Edward, 337
  Thomas*, 131, 411, 428
Watton (Yorks.), 13, 73, 77, 117, 128, 135
Watton Woodhall (Herts.), 311–2, 320–1
Watts, John, 454
Watty, Philip*, 140–1, 145–6, 157, 415
Weale, George, 183
Webbe, Thomas, 347, 349, 431, 454, 459
Webber, Nicholas*, 363, 433, 442, 457
Wednester, Charles*, 28, 244, 258–9, 445, 448, 451–2, 459; Mrs, 458
Wentworth, Thomas, 2nd Lord, 157
  Henry, 3rd Lord, 449–51, 454, 458
West, Mr, page, 454
  Sir Thomas, (11th Lord De La Warre), 231, 236, 247, 449–50, 452, 458
  William, 443

West Hampstead (Middx.), 312
West Horsley (Surrey), 40, 80–1
West Indies Voyage (1585–6), 190, 206, 228, 253, 267, 275, 279, 306
Westalle, John, 428
Westcoll, Thomas, 436
Westminster, City of, 60, 92–3, 171, 202, 247
  Arundel House/Place, 84–5, 200
  Bedford House, 182
  Cannon Row, 170
  Cecil House, 228–9
  Charing Cross, 196, 313; joiner at, 98
  Covent Garden, 58
  Derby House, Cannon Row, 277
  Durham House, 25
  Hawnce's house, 135
  Ivy Bridge Lane, 182
  Leicester House, 3, 17, 26–7
    (1584), 177, 179–84, 191–3, 196, 198, 200, 202–7
    (1585), 208–11, 213, 216, 218, 221, 223–4, 227–8, 230, 233–4, 237, 243, 245–9, 251, 253–8, 260–1, 263–7, 269–71, 276–7, 280, 284–5, 293, 296, 305, 308–9, 313–4, 316–20, 322–34, 336–43, 388–90, 392–3
    Elizabeth visits (1585), 270
    inventories, 178
    garden, 179, 256 (Leicester garden)
    pictures in, 181
    laundresses at, 458
  Savoy, 77
  Somerset House, 41–3, 83, 92, 96, 222–3, 227, 231, 406
  Strand, the, 230, 309
  tennis court, 67, see also Whitehall
  Tothill Fields, 223; muster at, 392
  Tothill Street (Sir Andrew Dudley's house), 25, 136–7
Westminster, Palace of, 41, 45, 52, 84–5, 117
  gatehouse, 234; keeper, 184, 219
  Star Chamber, 196, 251, 263; stairs, 321
Westmorland, Earl of, see Neville
Weston, Mr, of Essex, 328
  Andrew, 124, 148
  Henry, 424
  Richard, 252
Westreete, 456
Westwood, Mr, 153
Wherton, James, 457
Whetell, Richard, 125

Whetston, Bernard, 431, 446, 453
Whight, John, 120
  Richard, of the Privy Bakehouse, 129
White, 454
  gardener, 227
  tailor, 90
Whitehall, Palace of
  (1558–60), 41, 46, 54, 64, 71, 80, 83, 85, 104, 117, 137, 139, 145–6, 170
  (1584–5), 177, 179, 185, 196, 249, 259
  garden, 157; gardener, 200
  keeper (Bright), 248
  orchard-keeper, 335
  tennis-court, 70, 74, 154–7; keeper, 133
  tiltyard, 196, 203, 266
  see also Westminster: Hawnce's house
Whitehead, Mr, 51
Whitgift, John, Archbishop of Canterbury, 275, 294–5 see also Lambeth Palace
Whitney, Geoffrey, 455
  George, 427
Whitt, Richard, 426
Whittle, William, 18, 42, 52, 61, 66, 72, 88, 121, 129, 134, 138, 150, 154, 159, 419–20, 427
Wigges, Thomas*, 198
Wilkenson, Mrs, 122
Willett, William, 421
William, fool, 236
Williams, Edward*, 145
  Griffen*, 257
  John, 420
  Richard, 453, 458
  Sir Roger, 244, 357
  Thomas, 275
  William*, old, 350, 358, 457
    ewery, 432, 442
    harbinger, 434, 444
Williamson, Sir Joseph, 17
Willoughby, Lord, see Bertie
  Thomas, 70
Wilperforce, Edward*, 178, 207, 214, 217, 219, 273, 288, 330, 340, 451–2, 459
Wilson, player, 374
  John, 428
Wilton, Amy, 417
Wilton House (Wilts.), 188
Wimbledon (Surrey), 26, 60, 96
Winchester (Hants.), 143
Winchester, Marquess of, see Paulet
Wincoll, Isaac, 342
Windsor (Berks.), 63, 206
Windsor, Edward, 3rd Lord, 160, 164, 168

Windsor Castle, 27, 52, 80, 141, 143, 155, 197, 199
  garter installation at (1559), 66–8, 378
  funeral of Lincoln at (1585), 224
  Little Park, 68
  see also Dudley, Robert: Constable of Windsor
Windsor Forest, 151, 246, 261; keeper (Dowger), 224
Winsotch/Winworth (Winslow, Bucks.?), 279, 282, 309
Wisant, Harry*, 359
Wiston, Edward, 424, 428
Witney (Oxon.), 187–9, 191, 197, 214–6, 219, 295, 297; singers of, 291
Wolley, Sir John, 236, 255, 426
Wood, Edward*, 77, 79, 104, 416, 424, 428
  Henry, 428, 438, 441
  Humphrey, 428
  Steven, 436
  William, 431
Wooddouse*, 364
Woodhouse, George*, 150, 161, 427
  Sir William, 161
Woodman, William*, 130, 412, 424
Woodstock (Oxon.), Palace of, 84, 186–8, 190, 213, 291–2, 294, 297 *see also* Lee, Sir Henry
Woodstock Park, 186, 291
Woodward, Mathew*, 197, 211, 223, 244, 259, 323, 327
Woolwich (Kent), 47, 72, 252–4, 268, 272–3, 276, 279
Wootton, John, 457
Worcestershire, 54, 102, 240
  lieutenancy of (1559–60), 114
Worley, Mr, 338
Wortley, William*, 207, 231, 403, 427
Wotton (Surrey), 4
Wotton, Sir Edward, 262, 267, 305, 451–2
  John, 451–2

Wotton-under-Edge (Gloucs.), 245
Wray, Sir Christopher, 246
Wright, Mr, 449
  Charles, 455
  Richard, 430, 443
  Robert, baker, 129
  Thomas, 378
  William, 428
Wrote*, Robert, 240, 252, 452
Wroth, Sir Robert, 240, 487
Wyatt's Rebellion (1554), 46, 59, 72, 92
Wychwood, Forest of (Oxon.), 188, 190
Wyddale, 456
Wyn, Moris ap John, 445

Yates, 189
  Leonard, 456
  Simon, 455
  William, 215, 456

Yaxley, Francis, 78, 80
Yerwerth, John*, 164, 169, 402, 406, 408, 423, 426
Yetswert, Nichasius, 155–6
York, Edmund, 352, 357, 452
  Edward, 352
  Sir John, 42–3, 84, 115, 148, 158, 172, 352
  Rowland, 352
Young, Justice, 276
  Mr, 152, 159
  Mrs, 44
  Roger, upholsterer, 124
  Thomas, Archbishop of York, 192

Zinzan, Alexander, 222
Zouche, young Mr, 162, 426
  Sir John, 56, 67
  John, 427